FOURTH EDITION

Computers
in Your Future
Future

FOURTH EDITION

Computers
in Your
Future

Bryan Pfaffenberger
University of Virginia

Prentice
Hall

Upper Saddle River, New Jersey

Library of Congress Cataloging-in-Publication Data

Pfaffenberger, Bryan
  Computers in your future / Bryan Pfaffenberger.—4th ed.
    p. cm.
  Includes index.
  ISBN 0-13-089815-5
  1. Computers. I. Title.
  QA76.5 .P3982 2002
  004—dc21   00-053057

Acquisitions Editor: Lucinda Gatch
Editor-in-Chief: Mickey Cox
Managing Editor: Monica Stipanov
Assistant Editor: Jennifer Cappello
Editorial Assistant: Mary Toepfer
Senior Development Editor: Rebecca Johnson
Media Project Manager: Cathleen Profitko
Senior Marketing Manager: Sharon Turkovich
Marketing Assistant: Jason Smith
Production Manager: Gail Steier de Acevedo
Production Editors: Lynne Breitfeller, April Montana, and Kelly Warsak
Permissions Coordinator: Suzanne Grappi
Associate Director, Manufacturing: Vincent Scelta
Manufacturing Buyer: Natacha St. Hill Moore
Creative Director: Pat Smythe
Art Director: Cheryl Asherman
Interior and Cover Design: Amanda Kavanagh
Interior Illustration: Precision Graphics
Composition: Carlisle Communications
Full-Service Project Management: Carlisle Publishers Services
Printer/Binder: World Color/Quebecor

Credits and acknowledgments borrowed from other sources and reproduced, with permission, in this textbook appear on page C-1.

Microsoft Excel, Solver, and Windows are registered trademarks of Microsoft Corporation in the U.S.A. and other countries. Screen shots and icons reprinted with permission from the Microsoft Corporation. This book is not sponsored or endorsed by or affiliated with Microsoft Corporation.

Selected screen shots supplied courtesy of Prentice-Hall, Inc.

10 9 8 7 6 5 4 3 2 1
ISBN 0-13-089815-5

To Suzanne, Michael, and Julia,
for their love, patience,
understanding, and inspiration

ARE YOU HUNGRY FOR A BETTER COMPUTER CONCEPTS TEXT?

You've made suggestions, and we've listened.

▶ You want the fourth edition of *Computers in Your Future* to be more current and streamlined than the third edition—but without forcing changes in the way you're teaching the course.

▶ You want a concepts book with great learning tools that hold your students' interest and reinforce critical material—but without causing them to lose focus.

▶ You want a text-specific, interactive Web site that enhances your students' learning ability—as long as they are lead intuitively to key information that is concise, intelligent, and clearly laid out.

SO YOU WANT TO HAVE YOUR CAKE AND EAT IT TOO?

Well, open up (the book that is), because at Prentice Hall we're serving *Computers in Your Future*, 4th Edition!

With a clean new design, revised content, and updated coverage, this text is ready for the challenge of teaching even your most diversified class—without sacrificing quality, integrity, or taste. A new recipe for success—*Computers in Your Future*, 4th ed., is low in fat, high in flavor, and with all the right ingredients for computer novices and naturals alike.

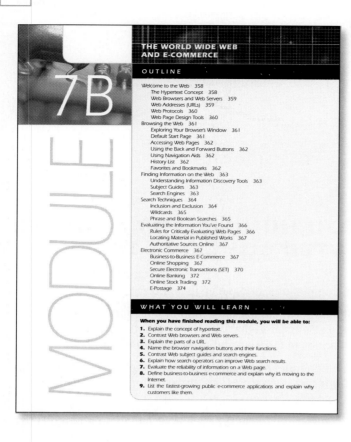

The fourth edition is streamlined and shortened (*low in fat!*)

▶ **A streamlined book with contents keyed to the order in which you present material.** For example, former Module 3B (Programming Languages) now appears within Chapter 8, Creating Information Systems. Chapters 7 and 8 (the Internet and the World Wide Web) in the third edition have been combined into one chapter (Chapter 7) in the fourth edition.

▶ **A shorter book that omits modules you couldn't cover before due to time constraints.** The best of the critically praised coverage of computer impacts in the third edition (formerly Chapter 11) now appears in optional **IMPACTS** boxes within each chapter. This feature deepens and broadens each chapter's coverage—but without adding to overall length.

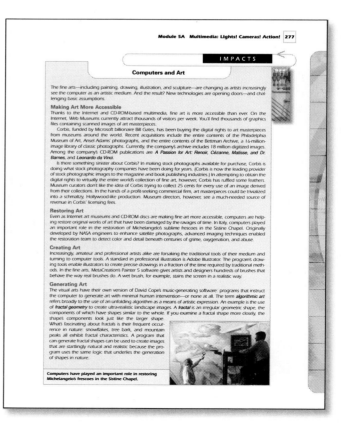

Module 5A   Multimedia: Lights! Cameras! Action!   277

IMPACTS

Computers and Art

The fine arts—including painting, drawing, illustration, and sculpture—are changing as artists increasingly see the computer as an artistic medium. And the result? New technologies are opening doors—and challenging basic assumptions.

Making Art More Accessible
Thanks to the Internet and CD-ROM-based multimedia, fine art is more accessible than ever. On the Internet, Web Museums currently attract thousands of visitors per week. You'll find thousands of graphics files containing scanned images of art masterpieces.

Corbis, funded by Microsoft billionaire Bill Gates, has been buying the digital rights to art masterpieces from museums around the world. Recent acquisitions include the entire contents of the Philadelphia Museum of Art, Ansel Adams' photographs, and the contents of the Bettman Archive, a 16-million-image library of classic photographs. Currently, the company's archive includes 18 million digitized images. Among the company's CD-ROM publications are *A Passion for Art: Renoir, Cézanne, Matisse, and Dr. Barnes*, and *Leonardo da Vinci*.

Is there something sinister about Corbis? In making stock photographs available for purchase, Corbis is doing what stock photography companies have been doing for years. (Corbis is now the leading provider of stock photographic images to the magazine and book publishing industries.) In attempting to obtain the digital rights to virtually the entire world's collection of fine art, however, Corbis has ruffled some feathers. Museum curators don't like the idea of Corbis trying to collect 25 cents for every use of an image derived from their collections. In the hands of a profit-seeking commercial firm, art masterpieces could be trivialized into a schmaltzy, Hollywood-like production. Museum directors, however, see a much-needed source of revenue in Corbis' licensing fees.

Restoring Art
Even as Internet art museums and CD-ROM discs are making fine art more accessible, computers are helping restore original works of art that have been damaged by the ravages of time. In Italy, computers played an important role in the restoration of Michelangelo's sublime frescoes in the Sistine Chapel. Originally developed by NASA engineers to enhance satellite photographs, advanced imaging techniques enabled the restoration team to detect color and detail beneath centuries of grime, oxygenation, and abuse.

Creating Art
Increasingly, amateur and professional artists alike are forsaking the traditional tools of their medium and turning to computer tools. A standard in professional illustration is Adobe Illustrator. The program's drawing tools enable illustrators to create precise drawings in a fraction of the time required by traditional methods. In the fine arts, MetaCreation's Painter 5 software gives artists and designers hundreds of brushes that behave the way real brushes do. A wet brush, for example, stains the screen in a realistic way.

Generating Art
The visual arts have their own version of David Cope's music-generating software: programs that instruct the computer to generate art with minimal human intervention—or none at all. The term *algorithmic art* refers broadly to the use of an unfolding algorithm as a means of artistic expression. An example is the use of *fractal geometry* to create ultra-realistic landscape images. A *fractal* is an irregular geometric shape, the components of which have shapes similar to the whole. If you examine a fractal shape more closely, the shape's components look just like the larger shape.

What's fascinating about fractals is their frequent occurrence in nature: snowflakes, tree bark, and mountain peaks all exhibit fractal characteristics. A program that can generate fractal shapes can be used to create images that are startlingly natural and realistic because the program uses the same logic that underlies the generation of shapes in nature.

Computers have played an important role in restoring Michelangelo's frescoes in the Sistine Chapel.

The fourth edition is packed with ingredients to engage your students (*high in flavor!*)

► **A new electronic commerce Web case, E-COMMERCE IN ACTION, appears at the end of every chapter!** Readers learn about PFSWeb, Inc., a company based in Plano, Texas, that helps e-commerce companies keep up with the online buying and selling marketplace. Each case includes a Web-based research task and motivates students to think critically about electronic commerce issues and strategies.

► **The Web publishing chapter (Module 7D) now features "what-you-see-is-what-you-get" (WYSIWYG) software—with an emphasis on Microsoft Front Page and Front Page Express.** You don't have time to teach HTML—and with today's WYSIWYG software, there's less need to do so.

► **New SPOTLIGHT boxes highlight innovative thinking in each module subject area.** For example, the Module 1A **SPOTLIGHT** features composer David Cole, whose EMI software processes musical motifs characteristic of classical composers. The result? "New" compositions by composers who have been dead for a century or more—and new controversies concerning computer applications.

Module 1A Becoming Fluent with Computers and the Internet **9**

SPOTLIGHT — ROLL OVER, BEETHOVEN

In the spring of 1997, an orchestra in Santa Cruz, California performed Mozart's 42nd symphony—a remarkable event, considering that Mozart only wrote 41 symphonies. Concert-goers agreed that the symphony indeed sounded Mozartean, even if it wasn't the equal of the composer's greatest works. But where did the score come from? Mozart, after all, had been dead for more than 200 years, and there's no evidence of a freshly-discovered symphony that had somehow evaded discovery.

Mozart didn't write the symphony that was performed that afternoon. In fact, nobody wrote it. It was created by a computer program, called Experiments in Musical Intelligence (EMI), authored by Santa Cruz-based composer and music theory professor David Cope.

Cope started developing EMI to help him overcome the composer's equivalent of writer's block. He wanted to write a program that could analyze his own style as a composer; originally, Cope intended to use the program as a source of insight and inspiration.

Listening to EMI's output, Cope soon realized that he had developed a powerful new algorithm—a step-by-step procedure—for analyzing a composer's style. By analyzing all of a composer's works, EMI can isolate what Cope calls the composer's "signature": the distinctive, melodic patterns that a composer tends to use repeatedly. These patterns are like a signature on a letter or a bank check in that they uniquely identify the person who wrote it. When music-literate people hear these melodic patterns in a composition that they don't recognize, these patterns—the composer's signature—tip them off. They say, "Oh, that's Beethoven."

EMI doesn't use any intelligence when it analyzes a composer's works. Actually, it uses nothing more than the computer's simple, built-in capabilities, such as adding up and comparing numbers. But it does

these tasks very quickly, so that before long the composer's distinctive melodic patterns begin to emerge.

Intrigued, Cope gave EMI the works of long-dead classical composers such as Bach and Chopin, just to see what would happen. The results astonished Cope. EMI's better compositions sounded like they really were written by the likes of Bach, Chopin, and Scott Joplin. And the best of them not only sounded like they had been written by these composers, they were beautiful works, capable of engaging listeners and drawing them into the joy of beautiful music. If a computer can produce those kinds of results, what does this say about the meaning of human creativity? Is the genius of Bach, Mozart, and Beethoven nothing more than the repetitive use of a few, idiosyncratic melodies?

Initially, Cope wouldn't let anyone but a few close friends listen to EMI's creations, fearing that the musical world would be deeply threatened by his discovery. Cope's friends persuaded him to let others in on EMI's achievements.

EMI's first concert was held at the University of Illinois in 1987. Cope explained how EMI worked, and turned the stage over to EMI. When the composition finished playing, the audience didn't budge—no clapping, no laughter, nothing. Cope feared that they'd hated the piece. But then it came out. One member of the audience told Cope that they'd sat there like stones because they were thunderstruck by the composition's quality and beauty. And anyway, would a computer appreciate a round of applause?

Cope introduced EMI to a broader public by means of a 1994 CD, titled *Bach by Design*, but that's when the backlash started. After all, the great composers—the likes of Bach, Beethoven, and Mozart—are considered to be among the greatest of all human geniuses. Is what they accomplished really so simple that it could be captured and imitated by a computer program? At an EMI performance in Germany, an enraged member of the audience shouted "Music is dead!" and tried to punch Cope in the nose.

Since then, a more balanced view has emerged, one that Cope himself endorses. EMI can imitate Bach, but Bach is better. Even at its best, EMI's compositions always sounded like one of the composer's lesser works. And Bach, after all, did something that EMI can't do: he created a new musical style that we instantly recognize and associate with one of the greatest composers of all ages. No computer's done that . . . yet.

Imagine being able to listen to completely "new" works from long-dead composers such as Bach and Chopin. Thanks to computer technology, you can!

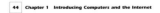

44　Chapter 1 Introducing Computers and the Internet

MOVERS & SHAKERS

Amazing Grace

The computer's history isn't an all-male story. Among the many women who have made significant contributions to the computer's development, Admiral Grace Murray Hopper (1906–1992) stands like a giant. She is admired for her considerable technical accomplishments and, perhaps most of all, for her insight, wisdom, and leadership.

Admiral Grace Hopper, the first woman to receive a doctorate in mathematics from Yale University, joined the U.S. Naval Reserve in 1943 and was assigned to Howard Aiken's Mark I computer project at Harvard University. Subsequently, Hopper joined the team that created UNIVAC, the first commercial computer system.

While working with the UNIVAC team in 1952, Hopper invented the first language translator (also called compiler), which for the first time freed programmers from the drudgery of writing computer programs in 1s and 0s. In 1955, Hopper led the development effort that created COBOL, the first high-level programming language that enabled programmers to use familiar English words to describe computer operations. COBOL is still the world's most widely-used programming language.

During her long career, Hopper lectured widely. Her favorite audience was young people, especially in the age group of 17–21. Hopper believed that young people were receptive to the idea of change—a good thing, in Hopper's view, because older people tended to fall into the trap of believing that change isn't possible. Hopper ought to know: experts at first refused to examine her compiler, claiming no such thing was possible. In her retirement speech, Admiral Hopper looked not to the past, but to the future: "Our young people are the future," she said. "We must give them the positive leadership they're looking for."

Hopper's observations inspired generations of computer science students, and seem particularly wise today. Going against the "bigger-must-be-better" philosophy of computer design, Hopper insisted that "we shouldn't be trying for bigger computers, but for more systems of computers." Subsequent years would see the demise of major supercomputer firms as networked computers surpassed the big machines' performance. Hopper also warned that computer systems needed to boil information down to just what's useful, instead of flooding people with more information than they can handle. And once the key information is obtained, Hopper insisted, the job isn't finished. "A human must turn information into intelligence or knowledge. We've tended to forget that no computer will ever ask a new question."

The recipient of more than 40 honorary doctorates from colleges and universities, Hopper received the U.S. Navy's Distinguished Service Medal in a retirement ceremony aboard the U.S.S. Constitution. In recognition of Admiral Hopper's accomplishments, President George Bush awarded her the 1991 National Medal of Technology, the nation's highest honor for technological leadership. Hopper died in 1992 and was buried in Arlington National Cemetery with full military honors.

Admiral Grace Hopper originated COBOL, which is still the world's most widely used programming language.

A FIFTH GENERATION?

If there is a fifth generation, it has been slow in coming. After all, the last one began in 1975. For years, experts have forecast that the trademark of the next generation will be **artificial intelligence (AI)**, in which computers exhibit some of the characteristics of human intelligence. But progress towards that goal has been disappointing.

Technologically, we're still in the fourth generation, in which engineers are pushing to see how many transistors they can pack on a chip. This effort alone will bring some of the trappings of AI, such as a computer's capability to recognize and transcribe human speech. Although fourth-generation tech-

► **New! MOVERS & SHAKERS boxes showcase the people who created computing—and are redefining it.** These biographies bring computing to life. They also show that computing attracts an increasingly diverse group of people. Featured portraits include Greg Lowney (Microsoft), Parry Aftab (Cyberangels), Linus Torvalds (Linux creator), and T.V. Raman (IBM programmer and developer of Emacspeak).

▶ **New! CURRENTS boxes examine issues in computing as well as cutting-edge computer technology.** Students learn about what's going to change the face of computing by the time they become professionals. **CURRENTS** boxes include Chapter 1, The U.S. Software Industry and Software Quality: Another Detroit in the Making?; Chapter 6, Universal Service: The End of an Era?; Chapter 8, Telemedicine; Chapter 9, Spies in the Sky; and Chapter 10, Is There an Acute Shortage of IT Workers—or just Rampant Age Discrimination?

---

138 Chapter 2 Exploring Computer Hardware: What's in the Box?

CURRENTS

Which Computer Would You Like to Wear Today?

Anyone who has grown up in the age of electronics knows that every electronic device keeps shrinking. Radios that took up space in the corner now fit on a wristwatch. Televisions have followed suit, and can now easily fit into your shirt pocket. Telephones will keep getting smaller and lighter, until you can conceal a cell phone just about anywhere.

Computers are no different. In their early days, computers took up entire rooms. Now you can fit just as much computing power into the palm of your hand. Why stop there? If you can make computers even smaller and more powerful, you can wear them like clothing or jewelry.

Those days are now here. Powerful computers are being designed into rings, stuffed in brooches, and concealed in eyeglasses. Computers are even being placed inside prosthetics that replace amputated arms or legs.

The effects of these wearable computers have not fully hit society yet but are poised to do so in the next few years. Business people will be able to augment their memory with a wearable computer that keeps track of their contacts and recalls information without visible prompting. Journalists can record what goes on around them and annotate the information as necessary to accomplish their jobs.

Imagine how wearable computers can affect the lives of maintenance workers. A computer on the belt could easily be connected to a display monitor concealed in an ordinary pair of eyeglasses. As the worker looks at the inside of some equipment being fixed, the computer pops up a schematic for the equipment. The schematic, shown on the inside of the eyeglass lens, can be positioned over the real layout for the equipment. The result is the ability to quickly pinpoint the name, purpose, and condition of each component in the equipment.

This blending of virtual reality with the real world, known as **augmented reality**, is not science fiction. It's already underway in some large corporations. Taken to another level, the schematics shown in the worker's field of vision can be interfaced with motion and position sensors so that when the worker moves his or her head, the schematics projected by the computer change to reflect whatever is being looked at.

New uses for augmented reality are being discovered all the time. For instance, agents for the U.S. Customs Service are using special wearable computers that utilize voice-recognition software and full-color monitors. The agents, looking for stolen vehicles, use the computers to recall the license number of any vehicle in the United States. This happens as the agent strolls through a parking lot or along a lane of traffic.

The biggest drawbacks in wearable computers at the present time are twofold: batteries and communications. Batteries, which must be used to power wearable computers, are still large and bulky for any extended use of the electronics. The classic tradeoff is to either limit the usable life of the electronics (without recharging) or wear a large battery pack on the belt or in a backpack.

Wearable computers are often configured as a collection of small components, and communications between those components can be a problem. For instance, when a belt-worn computer needs to communicate with a head-mounted monitor, the natural way is through a cable running between the two. Although this may make electrical sense, it may not be acceptable in some surroundings and for some uses. Some cutting-edge wearable computers are now using wireless components, but this adds to power consumption and potentially shortens battery life.

The potential uses for wearable computers are unlimited. As components continue to shrink, capabilities continue to expand, and technology rushes to meet imagination, each of us may add a computer to our wardrobe.

A wearable computer.

variety of technologies, including **tactile displays** that stimulate the skin to generate a sensation of contact. Stimulation techniques include vibration, pressure, and temperature changes. When used in virtual reality environments, these technologies enhance the sense of "being there" and physically interacting with displayed virtual objects.

Module 6A Telecommunications: Exchanging Data via the Telephone System 307

CURRENTS

Universal Service: The End of an Era?

It's called **universal service**—and thanks to the rise of Internet telephony, it may very well be coming to an end. An outgrowth of Depression-era New Deal legislation, universal service has long been a cornerstone of U.S. telecommunications policy. In the telecommunications industry, universal service assures that people in all parts of the country have equal access to "reasonably-priced" telephone services.

There's just one problem: it's much more expensive to provide telephone service in lightly-populated rural areas, where wires must be strung dozens or hundreds of miles just to serve a few houses. To pay for local phone service, long-distance companies collect surcharges from their customers, and kick back most of these surcharges to local telephone companies in the form of **access fees**. In turn, the local telephone companies use these fees—more than $25 billion per year—to hold down the cost of residential telephone services.

But all that's changing. Thanks to the U.S. Telecommunications Act of 1996, competitive access providers (CAPs) can sell direct access to the long-distance market without paying access fees—and that's one of the reasons Internet telephony is booming. Internet telephony service providers (ITSPs) such as Net2Phone don't pay access fees. According to conventional long-distance providers, that isn't fair. Long-distance, regional, and local telephone companies want the U.S. Congress to hit ITSPs with access fee charges—or abandon the idea of universal service altogether.

The 1996 Telecommunications Act does give telephone companies a break. The legislation calls for gradual reductions in access fees until they're completely eliminated. But it doesn't let consumers off the hook. Universal service must still be paid for somehow, so the Telecommunications Act extended the concept of universal service to digital-based services such as the Internet. For now, consumers are taking the hit, as you'll discover if you examine your next phone bill: there's a welter of incomprehensibly-named taxes, such as the Presubscribed Interexchange Carrier Charge, the Federal Access Charge, state-imposed Universal Service charges, and—chances are—several more. The various taxes and fees can add up to 60% to the cost of your monthly phone bill.

At least there's one tax you won't be paying any more. In 2000, the U.S. Congress voted to terminate the Federal Excise Tax on telephone service—a tax that was initially created in 1898 to pay for the Spanish-American War.

Internet Faxing

If the Internet isn't perfect for voice calls, it has none of those shortcomings for faxes. Faxes don't have to be delivered in real time, like voice does, so slight service delays don't cause a problem. But faxing through the PSTN is expensive, particularly for international calls. With annual worldwide fax volume nearing the 400 billion page mark in 1998, it's clear that many organizations could save a great deal of money by routing faxes over the Internet.

How does Internet faxing work? You'll need an Internet connection and an account with an Internet fax service provider. From a fax machine or computer, you can send the fax through the Internet to the fax service provider, which then automatically routes the fax through the Internet to a local telephone near your fax's destination. The service isn't free, but it's 25- to 50-percent cheaper than sending the fax through the phone system.

New subject coverage puts this book ahead of the pack

▶ **The fourth edition emphasizes computer fluency.** It's one thing to be computer literate, but it's quite another to be computer fluent. Computer literate people are skilled computer and Internet users; computer fluent people are able to navigate the digital world easily. Their knowledge of the underlying concepts and principles of computers and the Internet gives them a tremendous advantage. The more computer fluent people work with computer technology, the deeper and richer their understanding grows. They also understand enough about computing to recognize the technology's risks as well as its benefits.

Computers are all around us, and they're changing our lives—and sometimes in ways that aren't always pleasant. Many people find computers to be confusing, even impenetrable. More and more people use them every day, but without having the slightest idea how they work—which isn't a comfortable sensation. What's more, trying to get a handle on the world of computing is like trying to change a tire on a moving truck. Each day seems to bring news of some new type of computer, or a new way to apply the computer to jobs people previously did without the computer's assistance. We're pelted with advertising that tries to persuade us to buy the latest computer gizmo, but we don't understand what the gizmo is for, let alone why it's supposed to be so great. And then there's the Internet, which sometimes strikes even the experts as unfathomably too complex.

When you're lost and confused, as many people feel when they confront the world of computing, it's smart to look for a map. That's just what you'll find in this module. It introduces the world of computing, piece by piece, in small, manageable chunks. You'll begin by understanding what computers are and

In more ways than most people can imagine, computers play key roles in our lives.

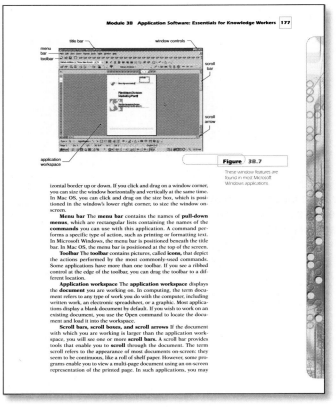

Figure 3B.7

These window features are found in most Microsoft Windows applications.

izontal border up or down. If you click and drag on a window corner, you can size the window horizontally and vertically at the same time. In Mac OS, you can click and drag on the size box, which is positioned in the window's lower right corner, to size the window on-screen.

Menu bar The **menu bar** contains the names of **pull-down menus**, which are rectangular lists containing the names of the **commands** you can use with this application. A command performs a specific type of action, such as printing or formatting text. In Microsoft Windows, the menu bar is positioned beneath the title bar. In Mac OS, the menu bar is positioned at the top of the screen.

Toolbar The **toolbar** contains pictures, called **icons**, that depict the actions performed by the most commonly-used commands. Some applications have more than one toolbar. If you see a ribbed control at the edge of the toolbar, you can drag the toolbar to a different location.

Application workspace The **application workspace** displays the **document** you are working on. In computing, the term document refers to any type of work you do with the computer, including written work, an electronic spreadsheet, or a graphic. Most applications display a blank document by default. If you wish to work on an existing document, you use the Open command to locate the document and load it into the workspace.

Scroll bars, scroll boxes, and scroll arrows If the document with which you are working is larger than the application workspace, you will see one or more **scroll bars**. A scroll bar provides tools that enable you to **scroll** through the document. The term scroll refers to the appearance of most documents on-screen: they seem to be continuous, like a roll of shelf paper. However, some programs enable you to view a multi-page document using an on-screen representation of the printed page. In such applications, you may

Module 3A System Software: Keeping the Computer Running Smoothly 153

Recently, a number of GUI interfaces have been developed for UNIX, improving the usability picture (see Figure 3A.8).

UNIX's greatest success lies in **client/server computing,** a type of computer usage that is widely found in corporations today. In client/server computing, programs are broken into two parts, called the *client* program and the *server* program. The client program handles interaction with the user and is installed on users' desktop systems. The server program runs on a high-powered, centralized minicomputer that everyone on the network can access (if they have the appropriate security clearance). Examples of such programs include massive databases that track all of a company's financial data. UNIX-based client/server systems have enough sheer number-crunching capabilities to replace much more expensive mainframe systems, and they are very popular in corporations.

Xerox PARC and the First GUI

While UNIX was defining how operating systems should manage computer resources, work at Xerox Corporation's Palo Alto Research Center (PARC) established how an OS should look. In the mid- to late-1970s, PARC researchers originated every aspect of the now-familiar GUI interface, including the idea of the screen as a "desktop," icons, on-screen fonts, windows, and pull-down windows. Although Xerox released a GUI-based computer (called the Star) in 1981, the company was never able to capitalize on its researchers' innovations.

MS-DOS

MS-DOS (or DOS for short) is an operating system for Intel-based PCs that uses a command-line user interface. Developed for the original IBM PC in 1981, MS-DOS was marketed by IBM in a virtually-identical version, called PC-DOS. Like every operating system discussed in this module, MS-DOS shows the influence of UNIX. DOS commands for managing and navigating directories, for example, are almost identical to those in UNIX.

Because DOS was developed for early 16-bit Intel microprocessors, it can't take full advantage of the advanced capabilities of Intel's 32-bit microprocessors (beginning with the 80386). For example, DOS runs in the Intel processors' *real mode,* in which the operating system cannot prevent applications from invading each others' memory space (which causes crashes). In addition, DOS can work with only 640KB of RAM at a time. Although some users still run DOS to take advantage of applications that aren't available for other operating systems, its use is declining.

Mac OS

Just as MS-DOS brought key UNIX ideas to personal computing, **Mac OS** introduced the graphical user interface to the world. Closely modeled on the system developed at Xerox PARC, the original Macintosh operating system was released in 1984. It consisted of the operating system (called System) and a separate shell (called the Finder). By the late-1980s, the Mac's operating system was the most technologically-advanced in personal computing, but Apple Computer was unable to capitalize on its lead and the Mac OS (as it came to be

Figure 3A.8

UNIX's greatest success lies in client/server computing, a type of computer usage that is widely found in corporations today. Recently, a number of GUI interfaces have been developed for UNIX, improving the usability picture.

► **Cutting-edge topics.** Some examples: 3D hardware, new microprocessors, new operating systems (including Windows 2000 and Mac OS X), open source software (including open source development and open source software licenses), information warfare, antitrust issues, digital copyrights, software patents, and women and minorities in computing.

► **New or significantly updated chapters and modules.** These include Module 1B (emphasizes recent history and the rise of the Internet), Chapter 4 (illustrates application software concepts from the best-selling office suites), Module 7B (extensive coverage of electronic commerce and the World Wide Web), Module 7C (illustrates email concepts with Microsoft Outlook and Outlook Express), and Chapter 9 (expanded coverage of privacy, security, and intellectual property issues).

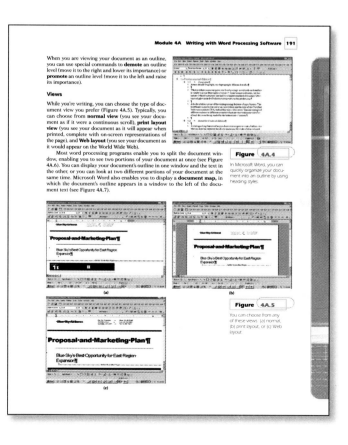

Module 4A Writing with Word Processing Software 191

When you are viewing your document as an outline, you can use special commands to **demote** an outline level (move it to the right and lower its importance) or **promote** an outline level (move it to the left and raise its importance).

Views

While you're writing, you can choose the type of document view you prefer (Figure 4A.5). Typically, you can choose from **normal view** (you see your document as if it were a continuous scroll), **print layout view** (you see your document as it will appear when printed, complete with on-screen representations of the page), and **Web layout** (you see your document as it would appear on the World Wide Web).

Most word processing programs enable you to split the document window, enabling you to see two portions of your document at once (see Figure 4A.6). You can display your document's outline in one window and the text in the other, or you can look at two different portions of your document at the same time. Microsoft Word also enables you to display a **document map,** in which the document's outline appears in a window to the left of the document text (see Figure 4A.7).

Figure 4A.4

In Microsoft Word, you can quickly organize your document into an outline by using heading styles.

Figure 4A.5

You can choose from any of these views: (a) normal, (b) print layout, or (c) Web layout

SUPPLEMENTS

The icing on the cake!

Instructor's Manual

The comprehensive *Instructor's Manual* includes additional material on how to use the text in conjunction with the Web site to help you understand the key concepts and exercises in the text.

Test Manager

The Prentice Hall Test Manager allows faculty to organize and choose test material by providing true/false, multiple-choice, fill-in, and essay questions.

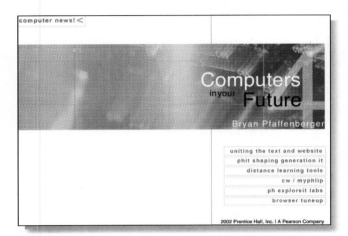

Instructor's Resource CD-ROM

One convenient disk contains all of the instructor resources needed for the text, including the IM, Test Manager, and PowerPoint slides.

Companion Web site/my PHLIP site (*www.prenhall.com/pfaffenberger*)

A complete online Web site includes chapter-specific and interactive quizzes; Web exercises that expand on the book's Spotlights, Currents, Impacts, and Movers and Shakers features; and video cases. Professors can use the site to communicate online with the class and download instructor's resource materials.

WebCT and Blackboard Content

The custom-built distance learning course features all new interactive lectures, exercises, sample quizzes, and tests.

Video

Through our partnership with *The Computer Chronicles* television series, we have developed a CIS Volume II Video compilation that features real-life computer stories and problems, and how technology is changing.

Twelve Labs!

Explore IT Labs

Prentice Hall's Explore Generation IT Labs illustrate, via interactivity, key computer concepts not easily covered in a lecture. These twelve labs bring challenging topics in computer concepts to life and assess students knowledge via a Quiz section, that can be emailed, saved to a floppy, or printed. The labs can be delivered via the web or on CDRom for added flexibility. The labs are as follows: Building a Web Page; Internet and WWW; E-Commerce; Introduction to Computer Programming; Application Software; Operating Systems; Multimedia; Building a Network; Buying a Computer; Hardware; Directories, Folders, and Files; and Binary Representation.

Acknowledgments

We are grateful for the assistance from the following reviewers of the fourth edition: Beverly Amer, Northern Arizona University; Dennis Anderson, Pace University; Bob Bretz, Western Kentucky University; Joseph DeLibero, Arizona State University; Mark DuBois, Illinois Central College; Said Fares, Valdosta State University; Nancy Grant, Community College of Allegheny County; Carolyn Hardy, Northwest Missouri State University; Michelle Hulett, Southwest Missouri State University; Emilio Laca, University of California at Davis; Kuber Maharjan, Purdue University; Karen Norwood, McLennan Community College; Anthony J. Nowakowski, Buffalo State College; Chuck Riden, Arizona State University; John Ross, Fox Valley Technical College; Ray Smith, Salt Lake City Community College; Steve Smith, El Paso Community College; Lynn Wermers, North Shore Community College; and Linda Woolard, Southern Illinois University.

We are also grateful for the assistance from the following reviewers of the third edition: William H. Allen, University of Central Florida; Dr. William Cornette, Southwest Missouri State University; Allen Dooley, Pasadena City College; Patricia Dreven, Community College of Southern Nevada; Susan Fry, Boise State University; Seth Hock, Columbus State College; Eric Jacobson, Peninsula College; Sann Lavallee, New Hampshire Technical College of Laconia; Anthony J. Nowakowski, Buffalo State College; Nancy Strickland, El Paso Community College; and Debbie Wenger, Blue Ridge Community College.

Special thanks go to Becky Johnson at Prentice Hall and Larry Goldberg at Carlisle Publishers Services, who made extraordinary contributions to this project. This book couldn't possibly have reached your hands in a timely way without their outstanding, beyond-the-call-of-duty contributions. I would like to add that I received the same contribution from everyone with whom I worked at Prentice Hall, including acquisitions editor Lucinda Gatch, managing editor Monica Stipanov, production editors Lynne Breitfeller, April Montana, and Kelly Warsak, and the designer Cheryl Asherman. I would like to express my deepest appreciation to everyone at Prentice Hall, which I've come to appreciate: it's a truly extraordinary company staffed with some equally extraordinary people.

Bryan Pfaffenberger

CONTENTS AT A GLANCE

Chapter 8   **Creating Information Systems**   **420**

Module 8A   **Introducing Information Systems**   **422**

Module 8B   **Systems Analysis and Design**   **439**

Module 8C **Programming Languages
and Program Development** **453**

FOURTH EDITION

Computers
in Your Future
Future

1

CHAPTER

Introducing Computers and the Internet

Think about what you did today. How many activities can you name that involve a computer or a computer network in at least one way? Did you:

- *Watch the morning news on TV? Studios use computerized graphics and a state-of-the-art, computer-controlled lighting system.*

- *Read the weather report in the newspaper? Weather agencies use computer networks and sophisticated, satellite-linked computer forecasting systems.*

- *Eat your breakfast? Trucks brought it to your hometown with the assistance of nationwide computer networks, and you bought it with a computerized scanner at the supermarket.*

- *Start your car? A computer-controlled ignition system gets you going. Were there traffic lights on the way to school? A computer-based system regulates lights for maximum traffic flow.*

Increasingly, it's hard to find an activity that doesn't involve computers, often in ways we're not aware of. Computers are playing an increasingly direct and noticeable role in our personal lives, as well.

- *Personal computers help families educate kids, manage finances, obtain needed information, keep in touch with distant friends and family, and track family history.*

- *Thanks to the explosive growth of e-commerce (online shopping), people are doing much more of their purchasing while they're online.*

- *At schools and colleges, personal computers help students get in contact with instructors, perform research, write papers, and make presentations.*

- *At work, personal computer skills are all but essential for career success. Studies consistently show that workers with computer and Internet skills make more money and have more satisfying careers.*

You'll be wise to learn as much about computers as you can. This chapter introduces the computer and the Internet (Module 1A), and tells the fascinating story of how these technologies were created (Module 1B).

M O D U L E S

1A

MODULE

BECOMING FLUENT WITH COMPUTERS AND THE INTERNET

WHAT YOU'LL LEARN . . . .

When you have finished reading this module, you will be able to:

1. Distinguish between computer literacy and computer fluency, and explain why both are needed.
2. Define the word *computer* and name the four basic operations in the information processing cycle.
3. Give an example of the information processing cycle in action.
4. Explain why responsible computer usage always involves ethical considerations.
5. Provide examples of hardware devices that handle input, processing, output, and storage tasks.
6. Explain the difference between system software and application software.
7. Define the Internet and explain the rapid acceptance and growth of electronic commerce.
8. List the most popular Internet services.

In more ways than most people can imagine, computers play key roles in our lives.

Computers are all around us, and they're changing our lives—and sometimes in ways that aren't always pleasant. Many people find computers to be confusing, even impenetrable. More and more people use them every day, but without having the slightest idea how they work—which isn't a comfortable sensation. What's more, trying to get a handle on the world of computing is like trying to change a tire on a moving truck. Each day seems to bring news of some new type of computer, or a new way to apply the computer to jobs people previously did without the computer's assistance. We're pelted with advertising that tries to persuade us to buy the latest computer gizmo, but we don't understand what the gizmo is for, let alone why it's supposed to be so great. And then there's the Internet, which sometimes strikes even the experts as unfathomably too complex.

When you're lost and confused, as many people feel when they confront the world of computing, it's smart to look for a map. That's just what you'll find in this module. It introduces the world of computing, piece by piece, in small, manageable chunks. You'll begin by understanding what computers are and how they work—concepts that, incredible as it might seem, are actually quite easy to understand. You'll then learn how to parcel out the various aspects of computing in an orderly way, including hardware (the computer's physical components) and software (the programs that tell the computer what to do). Next, you'll examine computer networks, and you'll learn how to fit the Internet into the picture. That's a lot to cover, but this module doesn't go into a lot of detail. Subsequent chapters return to each of these topics, and go much deeper.

THE NEED FOR COMPUTER FLUENCY

As you've just learned, this module gives you an overall map of computing, and serves as an introduction to the rest of this book. Before you unfold the map and get started, though, you'll find it helpful to consider what the map is for. What's your destination? Where are you headed? And what's the best way to get there?

Let's start with some reassurance. You don't need to become an expert in computing. Perhaps you'll decide to go on in your study of computing, but for now, your goal is to learn just enough about computing so that you can use computers effectively, both while you're at school and later, on the job. So just what, exactly, should you learn?

Educators agree that today's students need **computer literacy.** This term's meaning emphasizes skills—in particular, knowledge of how to use a personal computer, a personal computer operating system (such as Microsoft Windows), office suite applications, and Internet basics (including finding information on the Web and using e-mail).

Computer literacy will help you do well in college and, later, it will help you achieve your career goals. But computer literacy alone is not sufficient. The skills you learn now may be obsolete in just a few years. Computer technology changes very rapidly. Just a few years ago, the Internet was all but unknown to the general public. Today, it is a household word.

The rapid pace of computing's change leaves many people feeling uncomfortable, helpless, and confused, even though they use a computer every day. When training focuses on skills alone, people learn which button to press with a certain word processing program, but they lack the deeper knowledge that would enable them to move to a new word processing program rapidly—or even to a new version of the same program. They have not learned the deeper, underlying concepts and principles that would enable them to cope with rapid change (see Figure 1A.1).

An example should help to illustrate what's wrong with the type of computer literacy instruction that focuses on skills alone. Suppose you are traveling in a foreign country, but you do not know the language. You have a phrase book that enables you to ask questions such as "May I please have my check?" and "Which way to the restroom?" Later, you board a train, but you begin to suspect that you got on the wrong one and it's going to the wrong place. You turn to the phrase book for help, but you can't find the phrase you need.

If you knew just a little about the language's grammar, the type of knowledge you could easily gain in a semester of language study, you could figure out how to ask whether this train is really headed for Paris.

This book teaches the underlying concepts and principles of computing. These concepts and principles are like the grammar of a language in some ways. Once you understand them, you will have a much better appreciation of what computers and the Internet can do—and what they cannot do. You

Figure 1A.1

Computer training that focuses only on skills leaves many people feeling lost and confused when they are asked to learn to use a new program.

will be able to apply computer technology to your studies, and subsequently to your career, much more effectively. In the future, you won't be blindsided by rapid technological changes. You will understand where the changes came from, what they mean, and how you can adapt to them.

The term **computer fluency** describes the knowledge possessed by people who are able to navigate the digital world successfully. Computer-fluent people are also computer-literate, meaning they are skilled computer and Internet users. But their knowledge of the underlying concepts and principles of computers and the Internet gives them a tremendous advantage. The more they work with computer technology, the deeper and richer their understanding grows. Instead of being threatened by new technologies, they are excited about them and eager to try them out. As their confidence and knowledge grow, they become more and more adept in their use of computing technology. They are better citizens, too, because they understand enough about computing to recognize the technology's risks as well as the benefits.

WHAT IS A COMPUTER, ANYWAY?

To grasp the need for computer fluency, just ponder this fact: every day, millions upon millions of people use a computer, but few are able to define the term "computer" in an acceptable way. (If you're skeptical, try conducting an informal survey, and see how many people can come up with anything close to the correct definition.) Without an understanding of even this most basic concept, computer users cannot begin to grasp the nature of computing and its potential to transform our lives.

Understanding the Computer: Basic Definitions

A **computer** is a machine that, under a program's direction and control, performs four basic operations: input, processing, output, and storage (see Figure 1A.2). A **program** is a list of instructions that tells the computer how to perform these four simple operations in order to accomplish a task.

Input

In the first operation, called **input,** the computer accepts data that has been represented in a way the computer can use. Here, the term **data** refers to unorganized raw materials, which can be made up of words, numbers, images, or sounds (or a combination of these).

Processing

In the second operation, called **processing,** the computer performs arithmetic or comparison (logical) operations on the represented data.

These operations are really very simple. In fact, much of what a processor does boils down to adding two numbers or comparing them to see which is larger. What makes computers so amazing is that they can perform these simple operations at very high speeds. The most brilliant human mathematicians

Destinations

Like to learn more about the computer fluency concept? Being Fluent with Information Technology, an influential report authored by the U.S. National Research Council is available online at **http://bob.nap. edu/html/beingfluent.**

Figure   1A.2

Under a program's direction and control, a computer performs four basic operations: input, processing, output, and storage.

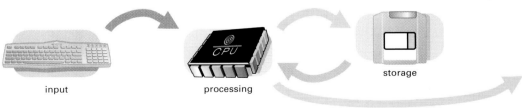

input   processing   storage   output

can perform only a few dozen of these operations per second, while an inexpensive computer can perform millions of them in a second. The computer's speed gives it amazing capabilities. For example, a transcontinental computer network used for research purposes is capable of moving the equivalent of all the information stored in the Library of Congress from Washington to San Francisco in the space of a few minutes.

Another factor in the computer's success is the reliability of its processing operations. Even the least expensive personal computers can perform several million operations per second, and can do so for years without making an error caused by the computer's physical components. (Almost all "computer errors" are actually caused by flaws in computer programs or mistakes in the data people supply to computers.)

Output

In the third operation, called **output,** the computer can show the results of the processing operation in a way that people can understand. The processed data becomes **information.** This term refers to data that has been organized in a way that people can use.

Storage

In the fourth operation, **storage,** the computer saves the results so that they can be used again later. Computers can store enormous amounts of information. Even an inexpensive desktop computer can store and provide quick access to a 32-volume encyclopedia, the entire collected works of William Shakespeare, a world atlas, an unabridged dictionary, and much more.

Together, these four operations are called the **information processing cycle.** Input, processing, output, storage—that's what computers do.

What Computers Can't Do (Yet)

Computers can transform data into information. But they can't ride bicycles, fall in love, or write poems about the moonlight—unless, that is, somebody figures out how to write a program that mimics these complex human activities by means of simple, repetitive processing actions organized into a step-by-step procedure, called an **algorithm.**

The term algorithm refers to the overall, step-by-step procedure used to solve a problem. Recipes contain an algorithm for cooking delicious dishes. Long division is an algorithm for dividing numbers that are too big to divide in your head. These examples suggest the important point about

Figure **1A.3**

A recipe is a common algorithm many of us use everyday. It provides the cook with a step-by-step procedure for creating a delicious meal.

A Recipe for Red Velvet Cake	
1/2 c. shortening	1. Cream shortening & sugar; add eggs.
1 1/2 c. sugar	2. Make paste of cocoa & food coloring,
2 eggs	add to creamed mixture and mix well.
2 Tbls. cocoa	3. Add salt and vanilla to buttermilk.
2 oz. red food coloring	4. Alternately add buttermilk and flour
1 tsp. vanilla	into shortening mixture, mixing well.
1 tsp. salt	5. Mix baking soda to vinegar and fold
1 c. buttermilk	gently into batter. Do not beat. Makes
2 1/2 c. sifted cake flour	3 layers. Bake at 350 degrees F for
1 1/2 tsp. baking soda	20-30 minutes.
1 Tbls. vinegar	

SPOTLIGHT

ROLL OVER, BEETHOVEN

▶In the spring of 1997, an orchestra in Santa Cruz, California performed Mozart's 42nd symphony—a remarkable event, considering that Mozart only wrote 41 symphonies. Concert-goers agreed that the symphony indeed sounded Mozartean, even if it wasn't the equal of the composer's greatest works. But where did the score come from? Mozart, after all, had been dead for more than 200 years, and there's no evidence of a freshly-discovered symphony that had somehow evaded discovery.

Mozart didn't write the symphony that was performed that afternoon. In fact, nobody wrote it. It was created by a computer program, called Experiments in Musical Intelligence (EMI), authored by Santa Cruz-based composer and music theory professor David Cope.

Cope started developing EMI to help him overcome the composer's equivalent of writer's block. He wanted to write a program that could analyze his own style as a composer; originally, Cope intended to use the program as a source of insight and inspiration.

Listening to EMI's output, Cope soon realized that he had developed a powerful new algorithm—a step-by-step procedure—for analyzing a composer's style. By analyzing all of a composer's works, EMI can isolate what Cope calls the composer's "signature": the distinctive, melodic patterns that a composer tends to use repeatedly. These patterns are like a signature on a letter or a bank check in that they uniquely identify the person who wrote it. When music-literate people hear these melodic patterns in a composition that they don't recognize, these patterns—the composer's signature—tip them off. They say, "Oh, that's Beethoven."

EMI doesn't use any intelligence when it analyzes a composer's works. Actually, it uses nothing more than the computer's simple, built-in capabilities, such as adding up and comparing numbers. But it does

these tasks very quickly, so that before long the composer's distinctive melodic patterns begin to emerge.

Intrigued, Cope gave EMI the works of long-dead classical composers such as Bach and Chopin, just to see what would happen. The results astonished Cope. EMI's better compositions sounded like they really were written by the likes of Bach, Chopin, and Scott Joplin. And the best of them not only sounded like they had been written by these composers, they were beautiful works, capable of engaging listeners and drawing them into the joy of beautiful music. If a computer can produce those kinds of results, what does this say about the meaning of human creativity? Is the genius of Bach, Mozart, and Beethoven nothing more than the repetitive use of a few, idiosyncratic melodies?

Initially, Cope wouldn't let anyone but a few close friends listen to EMI's creations, fearing that the musical world would be deeply threatened by his discovery. Cope's friends persuaded him to let others in on EMI's achievements.

EMI's first concert was held at the University of Illinois in 1987. Cope explained how EMI worked, and turned the stage over to EMI. When the composition finished playing, the audience didn't budge—no clapping, no laughter, nothing. Cope feared that they'd hated the piece. But then it came out. One member of the audience told Cope that they'd sat there like stones because they were thunderstruck by the composition's quality and beauty. And anyway, would a computer appreciate a round of applause?

Cope introduced EMI to a broader public by means of a 1994 CD, titled **Bach by Design**, but that's when the backlash started. After all, the great composers—the likes of Bach, Beethoven, and Mozart—are considered to be among the greatest of all human geniuses. Is what they accomplished really so simple that it could be captured and imitated by a computer program? At an EMI performance in Germany, an enraged member of the audience shouted "Music is dead!" and tried to punch Cope in the nose.

Since then, a more balanced view has emerged, one that Cope himself endorses: EMI can imitate Bach, but Bach is better. Even at its best, EMI's compositions always sounded like one of the composer's lesser works. And Bach, after all, did something that EMI can't do: he created a new musical style that we instantly recognize and associate with one of the greatest composers of all ages. No computer's done that . . . yet.

Imagine being able to listen to completely "new" works from long-dead composers such as Bach and Chopin. Thanks to computer technology, you can!

algorithms: By detailing the exact step-by-step procedure to follow, they enable people—and machines—to solve problems without requiring a lot of intelligence or skill.

Some computer scientists believe that there are algorithms out there for doing just about anything, including writing good poems about moonlight, but they just haven't been discovered yet. For example, experts once thought that decades would pass before computers could transcribe human speech accurately. Thanks to the discovery of powerful new algorithms, speech recognition is a reality right now. In fact, you can equip a personal computer to transcribe your speech with an accuracy of 95 percent or more—which is better than most people's typing accuracy.

What all this means is simple: Don't put your money down on a statement such as "A computer could *never* compose music like Mozart's or Beethoven's." All it takes is for someone to come up with the necessary algorithm.

The Information Processing Cycle in Action: Batch vs. Interactive Processing

In the early days of computing, the four basic operations—input, processing, output, and storage—had to be conducted in a rigid, lockstep sequence, called **batch processing.** You made an appointment to use the computer, fed the data into the computer, the computer processed that data, and out came the results. If the results proved that there was something wrong with the program, you had to wait until your next appointment to run the program again. Needless to say, using the computer in those days was very frustrating.

Today's computers use **interactive processing,** in which you initiate several information processing cycles in a single session. If something goes wrong, you see the problem right away, and you can launch a new information processing cycle to get better results.

Here's an example that shows how interactive processing works:

Input   You've just finished writing your college paper. It's loaded with misspellings, so you run your word processing program's spell-checking utility. Here, your entire document is the input.

Processing   A spell-checking utility makes use of the computer's ability to perform very simple operations, but at very high speeds. To check your document's spelling, a word processing program uses a simple but reasonably effective algorithm. Here's how it works: The program begins by constructing a list of all the words in your document. Then it compares these words, one by one, to a huge list of correctly spelled words. (If you tried to do this manually, it would take you many hours.) If you've used a word that isn't in the dictionary, the program puts the word into a list of suspect words.

Output   The result of the processing operation is an organized list of apparent misspellings. The word "apparent" is important here because the program doesn't actually *know* whether the word is misspelled. It is able to tell only that these words aren't in its massive, built-in dictionary. But many correctly-spelled words, such as proper nouns (the names of people and places) aren't likely to be found in this dictionary. For this reason, the program won't make any changes without asking you to confirm them.

Be aware that the computer isn't really "checking spelling" when it performs this operation. The computer can't check your spelling because it does not possess the intelligence to do so. The computer can only perform simple tasks and repeat them at high speeds. All it can do is tell you which of the words you've used aren't in the dictionary. Ultimately, only you can decide whether a given word is misspelled!

Storage   Once you've corrected the spelling in your document, you save the completed document to disk.

In sum, computers transform some kind of raw material (here, a document full of misspellings) into a more polished product (a document that is free from misspellings). They do so by performing very simple operations over and over, and at very high speeds.

So What?

Earlier, you learned that computer-fluent people are more adept with computers, and better able to adapt to rapid change, than people who do not understand the basic concepts and principles of computing. So here's the test: if that's true, what's to be learned from the earlier definition of computing? Actually, just about everything you'll learn in the rest of this book flows from this definition, but here are three points that everyone should understand.

Don't Let Hardware Scare You

There's no reason to be frightened of computer hardware. Many people feel threatened by computers because they fear that computers are too intelligent. But computers have no intelligence at all. The processing operations they do are almost ridiculously simple. The average insect is a genius compared to a computer.

The computer's saving grace is that it performs these simple operations quickly and reliably. So there is nothing scary about computer hardware. Without a program to tell it what to do, the computer is no more frightening— or useful—than a lump of clay.

What's disturbing about computers isn't the computers themselves, but what people might *do* with them—which leads to the next point.

Techtalk

cyberphobia
An exaggerated fear of computing that leads people to avoid computers. People experiencing cyberphobia may suffer physical symptoms, such as nausea, when confronted with a computer.

Do Take Ethics Seriously—Very Seriously

Responsible computing requires that you understand the limitations and risks of using the computer, as well as the potential that computer misuse could subject others to harm.

Take spell-checking as an example. As you've just learned, word processing programs employ a spell-checking algorithm that actually doesn't check spelling. To use a spell-checker responsibly, you must realize that it doesn't really check spelling. All it can do is highlight words that aren't in its dictionary. It is *your* responsibility to identify which of these words are spelled incorrectly. What's more, spell-checkers can't detect certain types of spelling errors at all, such as homonym errors. In a homonym error, a correctly-spelled word is used in the wrong place. For example, suppose you begin a letter with "Deer Professor So-and-So." You should have typed "Dear," but the spell-checker won't catch your mistake. The moral of the story: *You must always do a final, manual proofreading of anything you write with the computer.*

Is there really an ethical issue here? Just consider what might happen if you get tired of confirming the spelling mistakes, and let the computer do all the rest of the replacements without your intervention. You're behind schedule, so you skip the proofreading, or do it too quickly. The result could mean that you'll be in some serious hot water, and you could even cause severe embarrassment to your organization. Skeptical? Read on:

In Britain, 48,000 posters promoting literacy had to be discarded after it was discovered that a spelling mistake slipped through the computerized spell-check. The posters urged young people to learn about writing "though their own work." (The posters should have read "through their own work.") In Parliament, the Government's opponents called for an investigation to determine whether the Ministry of Education possessed personnel with the appropriate level of competence.

A memo distributed to every employee of a major corporation ordered them to report to the cafeteria for their "annual peyote." The spell-checker substituted *peyote*, a hallucinogenic drug, for the correct word, *payout*.

Resume writers everywhere have discovered the perils of letting spell-checkers work on proper nouns without intervention. A St. Louis newspaper printed an article in which a municipality named "Des Pere" was given as "Despair," thanks to a spell-checker's substitution. The residents of Des Pere were *not* amused. Curious, a reporter tried a number of celebrities' names, and came up with the following list of substitutions that a popular word processing program would perform, if allowed to operate unaided: Pariah Cares (Mariah Carey), Value Killer (Val Kilmer), Christian Slayer (Christian Slater), and Whiny Pooch (Winnie the Pooh).

Recognize the Risks of Using Flawed Software

Computer hardware is amazingly reliable, as you've just learned. But software's another matter.

All programs contain errors, and here's why: computers can perform only a limited series of simple actions, which makes constructing a computer program that accomplishes something meaningful similar to trying to build a house out of toothpicks. Many programs contain millions of lines of programming code (see Table 1A.1). In general, each line of a program tells the computer to perform an action, such as adding two numbers or comparing them.

You'll learn more about programs in Module 8C. For now, here's the main point. With so many lines of code, errors inevitably occur—and they are impossible to eradicate completely. On average, commercial programs contain between fourteen to seventeen errors for every thousand lines of code. The best software, such as the avionics software for NASA's space shuttle, only contains about one error for every thousand lines of code, but achieving such a low error rate with traditional methods is very expensive. And the more lines of code you add, the more complex the program becomes—and the harder it is to eradicate the errors.

Techtalk

bug
An error or defect in an electrical or electronic system, synonymous with **glitch.** The term derives from the Old English **bugge** ("anything that terrifies"), and was used in Shakespeare's day: "Sir, spare your threats: The bugge which you would fright me with [is the one that] I seek."

Table (1A.1)

To Do Interesting Things, Programs Need to Be Big— and They're Getting Bigger	
Program	**Lines of Programming Code**
ATM machine	90,000
Air traffic control	900,000
Microsoft Office 97	10 million
Microsoft Windows 98	18 million
Microsoft Windows 2000	27 million (estimated)
Internal Revenue Service (IRS)	100 million (all programs)

The fact that every computer program contains errors means that *all* computer use entails a certain level of risk. A bug might leap out at you when you least expect it, and cause your computer to freeze up. You may be forced to restart the computer, and you'll lose the unsaved work that was present in your computer's memory.

The foregoing explains why it's very, very unwise to put off writing that paper until the night before your assignment is due. Picture yourself at four o'clock in the morning, just putting the finishing touches on a brilliant English paper, and zap! A bug rears its head, and your computer goes into the electronic equivalent of catatonia. Did you save your work to the disk drive? If not, you've lost everything. If this hasn't happened to you already, rest assured that it will. (Tip: Always use your word processing program's Autosave feature, which records your work at a specified interval—say, every five minutes—so that you'll lose, at the most, only five minutes of work.)

Bugs in a word processing program may not rise to the life-threatening level, but computers are increasingly being used in **mission-critical systems** and **safety-critical systems.** Mission-critical systems are essential to an organization's viability, such as a company's computerized cash-register system. If the system goes down, the organization can't function—and the result is a fiasco, often a very expensive fiasco (see Table 1A.2). A safety-critical system is one on which human lives depend, such as the air traffic control system or the computerized signaling systems used for high-speed commuter trains. When these systems fail, human lives are at stake. Don't worry too much about getting on a plane or train, though, because safety-critical systems are designed to much higher quality standards. In addition, safety-critical systems have all sorts of backup systems that kick in if the main computer goes down.

A software error caused the European Space Agency's $3 billion missile to spiral out of control.

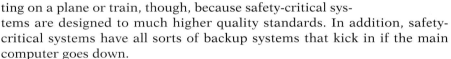

Bitten by the Bug (Famous Software Fiascos)	Table 1A.2

A computer in Paris charged 41,000 parking ticket offenders with a series of much more serious crimes, including prostitution, drug dealing, extortion, and murder.

A bug in a British bank's payment order system mistakenly transferred $2 billion to the bank's customers within the space of one hour.

Due to a software glitch, a Japanese bank overvalued certain investments, leading to a loss of $83 million.

In Los Angeles County, pension fund managers used a bug-ridden model to forecast the fund's performance. As a result, they put too little money into the fund, leading to a $1.2 billion shortfall.

A department store chain's new computerized cash-register system failed the day after Thanksgiving, which is the busiest shopping day in the U.S. each year. The firm lost 20 percent of its normal holiday revenues.

After two software vendors failed to coordinate on a software change, the resulting glitch brought down the U.S. Air Force's new, $39-million Unmanned Aerial Vehicle (UAV).

A software glitch caused the Mars Polar Lander to switch off its braking engines too early, leading to the loss of the $139 million spacecraft and further delays in our understanding of our nearest planetary neighbor.

IMPACTS

Automated Highway Systems: The Right Road?

You're cruising down the freeway at 120 mph. It's foggy, and the driver of the vehicle in the next lane over has apparently fallen asleep. But you're not concerned. In fact, you're not even watching the road. Instead, you're watching TV. Sound crazy? Actually, you're quite safe. You're driving a computer-equipped smart car on the next century's Automated Highway System (AHS), which—according to its proponents—will eliminate 1.2 million crashes per year, save thousands of lives, and save $150 billion in annual economic losses due to car crashes. Gains such as these are worth the estimated $40 billion investment of public funds that will be required to develop the needed technologies, proponents say.

AHS sounds great, but the system has attracted its share of critics. Some warn of the dangers involved in placing a complex, computer-based system in a human environment that's imperfectly understood. For example, they point to the use of computers in today's cars, specifically in antilock bracking systems (ABS), which employ on-board computers to prevent tires from locking up in a panic stop. Since you can't steer when locked-up tires are skidding, the on-board computer senses when a wheel locks up and adjusts the brake pressure so that you get maximum braking effect without locking the wheels. The result? Faster stops without the loss of steering.

You'd think antilock brakes would make cars much safer. But that's not what the Insurance Institute for Highway Safety (IIHS) discovered. After analyzing crash statistics, IIHS found that occupants of cars equipped with antilock brakes were *more* likely to be in fatal crashes, not less. What's the problem? The human factor. When you slam on the brakes with an antilock system, the pedal pulsates. Apparently, drivers wrongly think the pulsations indicate that something is wrong with the brakes, and they either pump the brake pedal or release it entirely, resulting in longer braking distances (and more fatalities).

Of course, the whole point of AHS is to take vehicles out of human control, but that doesn't mean people aren't involved. The automated highway's "smart cars" will require much more maintenance to make sure they're working correctly. Will people make sure that this maintenance is performed regularly? And what about system failures? As you've learned, all computer programs contain programming errors. How would a car's occupants react if the vehicle's guidance and collision avoidance systems froze up while the car is hurtling down the road at 125 mph?

Other AHS critics argue that the proposed investment of taxpayer funds—$40 billion—won't pay off in the way that AHS proponents envision. According to AHS critics, AHS is typical of the American transportation pattern: too much investment in smog-producing automobiles and too little in low-pollution alternatives, such as bicycle paths and light rail systems. The U.S. is taking a different road than Europe, where the average person makes 40 to 50 percent of trips by walking or biking and another 10 percent using public transit. In the U.S., 97 percent of trips are made by car, while only 3 percent involve other transportation.

Could AHS actually make traffic worse in the long run? AHS is designed to relieve congestion by moving more vehicles down existing roads in a tight, platoon-like formation. In this sense, AHS is like adding more lanes to a freeway. But adding more freeway lanes solves traffic problems only temporarily. As transportation officials in crowded urban areas have learned to their dismay, if you build more road capacity, more people drive—and they take longer trips. If AHS brings a massive expansion of road capacity, traffic will soon increase to fill this capacity, and we'll be right back to the same problem we have now: too much congestion.

Still, AHS has its advantages, as even its critics concede. Efforts to develop AHS will create dozens of safety-enhancing spinoff technologies, such as collision avoidance systems. And much can be said for taking the control away from impaired or aggressive drivers. Fully-automated vehicle control systems would eliminate "road rage," which is increasing at an alarming rate. Incidents of aggressive driving have increased by 51 percent since 1991, and nearly 90 percent of motorists have experienced an aggressive driving incident within the past year. According to a U.S. Department of Transportation estimate, as many as two-thirds of the 250,000 traffic fatalities that have occurred since 1990 may have been caused by violent, aggressive drivers.

1. Printer
Produces output on paper
or transparencies

2. Network connection
Enables the computer to
communicate with other
nearby computers in a local
area network

3. Subwoofer
Adds deep bass to the
computer's audio output

4. Modem
Communicates with other
computers and the Internet
through the telephone system

5. Microphone
Accepts voice input that can
be translated into text or used
to control the computer

6. Speaker
Plays the computer's
audio output

7. Mouse
A pointing device that moves an
on-screen pointer, enabling the
user to select items and choose
options

8. Monitor
A television-like display that
shows you what the computer
is doing

9. Keyboard
The most common means of
getting data into the computer
as well as controlling computer
operations

10. Floppy disk drive
Accepts magnetically coated 3.5" disks,
which allow the computer to read data
from other computers, or write data for
backup or exchange

11. CD-ROM or DVD-ROM
Accepts CD-ROM or DVD-ROM discs,
which can store large amounts of data.
Most software publishers provide their
programs on CD-ROM discs.

12. System unit
Contains the computer system's
processing and storage components,
including the motherboard
(the computer's main circuitry),
memory, and the hard disk drive (the
most important storage device)

Figure   1A.4

Components of a typical
computer system.

Computer professionals are working hard to develop more reliable software. In Chapter 8, you'll learn how businesses approach the critical task of developing a new information system—a task that could make or break the company.

Computer Systems

You'll often hear the term **computer system,** which is normally shortened to *system* (as in "Sorry, our system is down."). This term is more inclusive than *computer*. A computer system is a collection of related components that have all been designed to work together smoothly (see Figure 1A.4). It includes the following:

Hardware   The physical components of the computer, including the computer itself and matched peripherals.

Software   The programs that run on the computer.

You'll get a quick introduction to hardware and software later in this module. Chapter 2 goes into hardware in more detail, while Chapters 3 and 4 examine software more closely.

INTRODUCING HARDWARE: THE COMPUTER'S PHYSICAL COMPONENTS

As you'll surely agree after looking at a computer retail company's mail order or online catalog, computer systems have lots of parts—keyboards, mice, speakers, and more. But catalogs are organized to make money; therefore, the high-profit items come first. In this section, you'll see how the various

Destinations

One of the most promising uses of the computer lies in online education, the use of the Internet as a teaching medium. Try it yourself—and learn more about PCs—at free-ed.net's Introduction to PCs, a free online course located at **http://www. free-ed.net/fr02/lfc./ course.%200212_02/.**

components of the computer system are designed to implement the four stages of the information processing cycle: input, processing, output, and storage (refer to Figure 1A.1). Let's start with input.

Input: Getting Data into the Computer

Input devices enable users to get data into the computer for processing. In interactive processing, input devices are also used to give commands to the computer and to respond to the computer's messages. A **command** is a type of input in which the user tells the program what to do. In response, most programs usually provide some sort of **confirmation,** a message that indicates that the command was carried out. If the command fails, you'll see an **error message.** The best error messages explain what went wrong and suggest strategies for overcoming the error, but not all programs are this helpful.

Explore IT Lab

Hardware

By far the most widely-used input device is the **keyboard,** which resembles an electric typewriter's keyboard in that it enables users to input characters. A **character** is one of a standard set (called a **character set**) of letters, numbers, and punctuation marks. However, computer keyboards also include special keys that enable users to give commands to programs. For example, the keyboard's **arrow keys** are used to move the **cursor** around on the screen. The cursor, also called the *insertion point,* shows where text will appear when you start typing.

Most computers are also equipped with a type of **pointing device** that enables the user to move an on-screen **pointer,** which usually looks like an arrow. By moving the pointer to certain areas on-screen and clicking one of the mouse's buttons, you can issue commands. A **mouse** is a type of pointing device that's designed to roll around on the desktop, next to the keyboard. As you move the mouse with your hand, the pointer moves in tandem. Some programs transform the mouse into an input device. When you're running a painting or drawing program, a mouse can be used to input lines, shapes, colors, and textures.

Increasingly, computers are equipped with **microphones.** In a computer equipped with **speech-recognition** software, which transcribes spoken words into on-screen text, you can enter data as if you were typing. You can also control the computer by giving spoken commands.

Many additional devices provide alternative ways of getting data into the computer, including scanners, digital cameras, video capture boards, and more. You'll learn about these devices in Module 2C.

Processing: Transforming Data into Information

The computer's processing circuitry, called the **central processing unit (CPU),** is located within the system's case. This case, called the **system unit,** contains many additional components as well, including storage devices and connectors for input and output devices.

Most of today's computers use a miniaturized CPU called a **microprocessor** (or just *processor* for short). A microprocessor is a complex electronic circuit fabricated on a wafer, or **chip,** of silicon. The achievement of microprocessor technology is responsible, in large measure, for the computer revolution. On a single, postage-stamp-sized flake of silicon, today's microprocessors offer CPU circuitry for a few hundred dollars that's far more advanced than computers of just twenty years ago—computers that cost millions of dollars. Microprocessor technology enables manufacturers to create millions of copies of this complex circuitry, as if they were printing a book. Module 1B tells the fascinating story of how this technology was achieved.

The microprocessor is one of several chips on the computer's main circuit board, also known as a **motherboard.** Among the other chips are those that provide the computer's **memory.** Like a clocksmith of old, the CPU needs an orderly, accessible workbench—a place where the smith can find the tools and parts that are needed, and find them quickly. That's the job performed by the computer's memory. The chips that make up the memory store program instructions (the tools) and data (the parts) so that the CPU can access them quickly.

As you'll learn in Module 2A, a typical computer includes several different types of memory, but the most important of these is **random-access memory (RAM),** also called RAM memory. The computer's RAM stores the programs and data you're working with. To work with programs successfully, you'll need to make sure that your computer has enough RAM. The capacity of RAM is measured in **megabytes (MB).** A megabyte is roughly one million characters. That sounds like a lot, but most of today's programs require at least 16 MB of RAM—and that's a bare-bones minimum.

Also found on the motherboard are **expansion slots.** An expansion slot is a receptacle that's designed to accept a plug-in **expansion card,** which is also called an expansion board, adapter board, or adapter. (This is one of several areas you'll run into where the terminology isn't very well standardized.) Expansion cards are used to connect the computer with various **peripherals.** A peripheral is an input or output device that's housed outside the system unit, such as a monitor or printer. Some peripherals connect to built-in connectors on the back of the computer's case. Module 2A explores the system unit's contents in more detail.

Output: Displaying the Information

Output devices show the results of processing operations. You'll learn more about output devices in Module 2B; for now, here's an overview.

The **monitor** shows the results of processing operations on the screen. Most monitors are **cathode ray tube (CRT)** devices. Also used in televisions, CRTs form an image by projecting a tightly-focused light beam on a matrix of light-sensitive materials. Although the best computer monitors can produce a brilliant, detailed, and colorful display, CRTs are expensive and heavy. They consume a great deal of electrical power and produce heat as an unwanted byproduct. Increasingly popular are **LCD displays** (also called **flat-panel displays),** which use low-power, liquid crystal diodes (LCDs) to generate the display. Used primarily in portable computers, flat-panel displays are increasingly popular as an alternative to CRTs on the desktop.

Speakers enable you to hear the results of sound processing, including music and synthesized speech. They also reproduce the signals that programs provide to confirm successful commands or alert the user that an error has occurred.

The **printer** generates output on paper. Printers fall into two general categories, **impact printers** and **non-impact printers.** An impact printer forms an image on paper by physically striking an ink-saturated ribbon, while non-impact printers use various other technologies to transfer the image to the page. Most printers in use with today's computer systems are non-impact printers, including **inkjet printers** and **laser printers.** Inkjet printers form an image by spraying tiny droplets of ink on the page, while laser printers use a laser beam to transfer patterns to a rotating drum. The drum then uses a heat process to fuse tiny particles (called toner) to the page in a way that duplicates the laser-generated patterns.

Storage: Holding Programs and Data for Future Use

In the best of all possible worlds, computers would be equipped with enormous amounts of RAM, and storage devices wouldn't be needed. Perhaps this day is coming, but it isn't here yet. RAM is very fast, but it's also very

Destinations

The Intel Museum's How Chips Are Made provides a nicely illustrated overview of the chip fabrication process. It's located at **http://www.intel. com/education/chips/ introduction.htm.**

expensive. Most computers are equipped with enough RAM to hold the programs and data that the computer will work with, but no more. There must be additional space to keep programs and data that aren't in use at the moment. What's more, RAM is *volatile*. This term means that the memory's contents will disappear—"evaporate" into thin air—if the power is switched off. (Tip: If you're working with the computer and you hear thunder, save your work! Thunderstorms create power outages—and when the power's gone, so are the memory's contents.)

Storage devices are used to hold all of the programs and data that the computer system uses. Typically, storage devices are much slower than RAM memory, but they also have much more storage capacity. As you'll learn in Module 2B, there are lots of different types of storage media, a term that is used collectively to describe all types of storage devices. (The term *media* is plural; the singular form is *medium.*) The two basic types are **magnetic storage media,** which store data on disks or tape encoded with magnetically-sensitive material, and **optical storage media,** which store data in the form of microscopic pits that are etched into the surface of a disc. Storage devices are also distinguished by whether they can "record" data or just "play" it. In computing, the process of recording data is called **writing,** while the playback process is called **reading.** A device that can read and write is called a **read/write** device, while a device that can read (but not write) is called a **read-only** device.

Most computers are equipped with both types of storage media. Magnetic media include the **floppy disk drive** and the **hard disk drive.** Both are read/write devices.

Floppy disk drives are a removable medium. They are designed to work with **floppy disks,** which can be inserted into the drive and withdrawn when no longer needed. Because they are a removable medium, floppy disk drives provide a convenient way to move data from one computer to another, but standard floppy disk drives are woefully short on storage space (1.44 MB). Because of this fact, many computers are equipped with **Zip drives,** which are designed to work with **Zip disks.** A Zip disk can store up to 200 MB of data.

The computer's hard disk provides the lion's share of storage. Most hard disks are non-removable media. They typically include two or more disks that are enclosed within a permanently sealed case, which is mounted inside the system unit. Major advances in magnetic media technology are leading to ever-increasing hard disk capacities. Many new computers come equipped with hard disks capable of storing 15 **gigabytes (GB)** of programs and data. A gigabyte is roughly equivalent to one *billion* characters.

Because software publishers typically use optical media to distribute their products, almost all computers are equipped with a **CD-ROM drive.** A CD-ROM drive is a read-only, optical storage medium. The drive reads the data encoded on the CD-ROM by using a laser to detect tiny pits etched into the CD-ROM's plastic surface. A CD-ROM closely resembles an audio CD, except that it contains computer-readable data rather than sound. Most CD-ROM drives can also read audio CDs, however. Increasingly, computers are equipped with **DVD-ROM drives.** DVD-ROM drives are designed to work with DVD-ROM discs, which can store much more information than a CD-ROM.

Communications Devices

Much of what computers do involves moving data around within the computer, and at very high speeds. This same capability can be used to move data *between* computers as well. To move data between computers, **communications devices** are necessary. Communications devices enable computers to connect

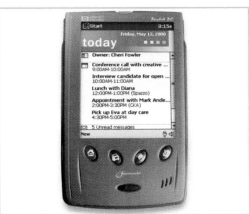

Figure 1A.5

Computers for individuals.

to **computer networks.** A computer network links two or more computers by means of some type of physical connection, called a **network medium.**

You'll learn more about computer networks in Modules 6A and 6B. For now, take note of components that you'll need to access the Internet.

Many computers are equipped with a **modem,** which enables the computer to access other computers and the Internet by means of a telephone line. Other computers use a **network interface card (NIC)** to hook up to a **local area network (LAN).** A local area network is a group of computers situated within a limited geographic area (a building or several buildings situated next to each other). The computers are connected by special, high-speed cables.

Types of Computers

Computers come in all sizes, from large to small. It's convenient to divide them into two categories: computers for individuals (see Figure 1A.5) and computers for organizations (see Figure 1A.6).

Computers for Individuals

Professional workstations provide powerful tools for engineers, architects, circuit designers, financial analysts, and other professionals who need exceptionally powerful processing and output capabilities. They are the most expensive type of computers made for individuals.

Chances are you've used a **personal computer** already. A personal computer is designed to meet an individual's computing needs. (As you'll see, larger computers are designed to meet an organization's computing needs.) Also called **microcomputers,** personal computers have steadily dropped in

Figure 1A.6

Computers for organizations.

price, even as they have become more powerful and more useful. The two most commonly used types of PCs are Apple Computer's Macintosh systems and the more numerous **IBM-compatible** personal computers made by many manufacturers. These machines are called "IBM compatible" because the first of them was made by IBM.

Desktop computers are personal computers designed for an individual's use. They run programs designed to help individuals accomplish their work more productively. Increasingly, they're also used to gain access to the resources of computer networks, such as the Internet.

Network computers (NCs) provide much of a PC's functionality at a lower price. Because they get their software from a computer network, they don't need disk drives. In the consumer market, NCs such as WebTV enable consumers to use their televisions to connect to the Internet.

Notebook computers are small enough to fit in a briefcase. Many of them are as powerful as desktop PCs and include nearly all of a PC's components, such as stereo sound, CD-ROM drive, and a modem. People also speak of **laptop computers,** which are portable computers that are a bit too large to fit into a briefcase, but few are being made now that notebooks have become so powerful.

Subnotebooks are notebook computers that omit some components (such as a CD-ROM drive) to cut down on weight and size. Some of them weigh less than three pounds.

Personal digital assistants (PDAs), also called **handhelds,** pack much of a notebook's power into a much lighter package. Most include built-in software for appointments, scheduling, and electronic mail, and **pen computers** accept handwritten input.

Computers for Organizations

Supercomputers are ultra-fast computers designed to process huge amounts of scientific data and then display the underlying patterns that have been discovered. An IBM supercomputer built for the Department of Energy can execute 3 trillion program instructions per second and is equipped with 2.5 terabytes of memory. The price tag for the computer is $95 million.

Mainframes are huge, multiuser systems designed to handle gigantic processing jobs in large corporations or government agencies, such as handling an airline's reservations. Some mainframes are designed to be used by tens of thousands of people. People connect with mainframes using **terminals** (remote keyboard and display units) as well as personal computers. Mainframes are usually stored in special, secure rooms that have a controlled climate. They generally cost several hundred thousand to several million dollars.

Minicomputers are **multiuser** systems that can handle the computing needs of a smaller corporation or organization. They enable dozens, hundreds, or even thousands of people to use them simultaneously by means of remote terminals or personal computers. Minicomputers range in cost from $10,000 to several hundred thousand dollars.

Servers aren't designed to be used directly. They make programs and data available for people hooked up to a **computer network,** a collection of computers connected together so that they can exchange data. To use servers, employees run desktop programs called **clients,** which know how to contact the server and obtain the needed information. This use of desktop clients and centralized servers is called **client/server** computing. It plays an important role in today's businesses. Servers range in cost from $5,000 to $150,000.

INTRODUCING SOFTWARE: TELLING THE COMPUTER WHAT TO DO

In a computer system, **software** includes all the programs that give the computer's hardware its step-by-step marching orders. Without software to tell it what to do, the computer is completely useless, unless you think a very expensive paperweight is a useful item.

Creating Software

Trained experts called **programmers** create computer programs by writing these instructions in a **programming language,** a special-purpose language that enables them to describe step-by-step processes. Most programming languages are designed to make things easy for the human programmer, rather than the computer. Before a program can be used, the **source code**—

n source ...ware

Almost all commercial software is distributed as compiled object code, which hides the programmer's instructions. Most of these programs come with licenses that prohibit users from analyzing the object code in order to see how the program was written. Increasingly, software vendors are experimenting with open source software (OSS), in which the source code is made available to the program's users. Program users are invited to scrutinize the source code for errors and to share their discoveries with the software's publisher. Experience shows that this approach is often a very effective measure against software defects.

Explore IT Lab

Operating Systems

the program instructions as they are actually written by the programmer—must be translated into **object code,** which the computer can read. Most object code is created by programs called **compilers,** which read the source code and generate the object code as output.

Using Software

Most computer programs are not a single, monolithic entity; instead, they consist of hundreds or even thousands of distinct units, called files, that must be properly installed on the computer's hard disk. A **file** is a basic unit of storage in a computer system. Every file has a name, and is stored along with a variety of attributes. An **attribute** is a setting that provides information such as the file's date of creation, its size, and the date of its last modification. Because most programs consist of so many files, they are sometimes called packages. A **package** is a set of program files, as well as associated data and configuration files, that are all designed to work together.

In order to use a compiled program, you must transfer the program to the computer's memory. This process, called **loading,** enables the program to **execute** (carry out the instructions that it contains).

Types of Software

You'll find it helpful to divide programs into two categories: system software and application software. **System software** includes all the programs that help the computer function properly. **Application software** consists of all the programs you can use to perform a task, such as writing a research paper or browsing the World Wide Web.

SYSTEM SOFTWARE

System software falls into two general categories: the operating system and system utilities.

Operating System (OS)

The most important type of system software is the computer's **operating system (OS).** The operating system is designed to work with a specific type of hardware, such as a PC or a Macintosh. Its most important role lies in coordinating the various functions of the computer's hardware. The operating system also provides support for running application software. Before you can use the computer, the operating system must be loaded into memory. This may take a minute or two.

Most operating systems come with a built-in **user interface.** The user interface provides the means by which users and programs can communicate with each other.

Early computers offered only a primitive user interface, called a **command-line interface.** In this type of interface, users must interact with the computer by typing instructions at the keyboard, one line at a time. To give the command correctly, it's necessary to follow complicated rules, called **syntax,** that specify just how the command must be typed.

Computers would not have become a mass-market item without the development of the **graphical user interface** (**GUI,** pronounced "gooey"). In a graphical user interface, users interact with the computer by choosing items from menus and using a pointing device to click on-screen pictures, called **icons,** which represent various computer resources and commands.

System Utilities

System software also includes a variety of **utility programs,** which are used to keep the computer system running smoothly. An example of a utility program is

CURRENTS

The U.S. Software Industry and Software Quality: Another Detroit in the Making?

Flash back to the 1950s, and take a look at the average new car produced by one of Detroit's "Big Three" automakers (GM, Ford, and Chrysler). You'd see lots of cool features—big, gutsy V-8 engines, flashy chrome bumpers, and (in 1957, anyway) fins that made the cars look like low-flying rockets. If you owned one of these monsters, though, you'd discover another, less appealing characteristic: shoddiness. The cars were riddled with defects and needed frequent repairs.

When challenged to defend their low-quality products, the automakers complained that the cost of building quality cars was simply too high. It could be done, but you'd pay much more for that shiny new Chevy. Consumers were content with the low-quality/low-price tradeoff, the automakers believed. After all, consumers were buying the cars.

You probably know the rest of the story. For years, U.S. industrial quality guru W. Edwards Deming was trying to convince Detroit that it's possible to make high-quality products, and what's more, that it's not much more expensive to do so, as long as you design the quality into the product at the beginning of production instead of trying to fix the problems at the end. But Deming's words fell on deaf ears—except in Japan.

Japanese carmakers took Deming's teachings to heart, and they started making some exceptionally fine automobiles—and what's more, they were cheap. The result? Japanese automakers grabbed nearly a third of the U.S. market and most of the international market. As a result, thanks to mounting Japanese automobile exports and the collapse of the U.S. auto industry overseas, the U.S. was plunged into the ranks of the world's debtor nations.

Today's commercial software packages have much in common with shoddy U.S. automobiles of the 1950s and 1960s, according to the software industry's critics.

The U.S. software industry regularly turns out programs with as many as a dozen or more flaws per thousand lines of code. (Now you know why your computer crashes so much.) To be sure, it's possible to create much better software—but the conventional wisdom says that it's too expensive to do so. Near-flawless code, such as the space shuttles' navionics software can cost up to 10 times as much as ordinary software. Is the extra expense justified for a program that isn't safety-critical, such as a word processing program?

According to growing numbers of experts in the field of software engineering, software quality doesn't have to cost more—and in fact, it winds up costing less, just as Deming claimed with respect to auto manufacturing.

Inspired by Deming's writings, software development expert Watts Humphrey—developed a version of Deming's work for the software industry.

What's Humphrey saying? It's simple: software companies *can* make high-quality products, and what's more, doing so isn't expensive. Humphrey's work has evolved into the Capability Maturity Model (CMM), which shows software developers how to build quality in from the get-go. It also provides a way to rank a company's commitment to quality. At Level 1, companies aren't doing much of anything about quality. At Level 5, they're up to the Toyota level, building quality consciousness into everything they do, and constantly refining and improving their processes.

Who's listening to Humphrey? At this writing, only 19 software companies are certified at Level 5—and 13 of them are in India. That's right, India. If you think that India's a backward country that couldn't possibly compete in the high-tech sweepstakes, you'd better think again, because Indian software companies are putting out some of the best software in the world.

When asked whether Indian software firms pose a threat to their near-stranglehold on the consumer software market, U.S. software executives laugh. They point out that these silly foreign companies don't know anything about style or marketing—there's no way they could make it in the U.S. market. Now where have we heard *that* before?

Windows 2000 provides a graphical user interface.

Explore IT Lab

Applications Software

an **antivirus** program, which checks your system for computer viruses. A **computer virus** is rogue programming code, devised by a prankster, that attaches itself to the programs in your computer. If you give an "infected" program to other people and they run the program on their computers, the virus will spread.

APPLICATION SOFTWARE

Application software (also called applications) includes all the programs that enable the user to apply the computer in a useful way.

Packaged vs. Custom Software

In the world of application software, a basic distinction is made between **off-the-shelf software** (also called shrink-wrapped software or packaged software) and **custom software.**

As the name implies, custom software is developed by programmers to meet the specific needs of an organization, such as a company or university. Custom software is expensive, but sometimes an organization's needs are so specialized that no alternative exists.

Off-the-shelf software, in contrast, is aimed at a mass market that includes home as well as business users. Although off-the-shelf software can be customized in certain limited ways, it is designed to be immediately useful in a wide variety of contexts. The payoff comes with the price: off-the-shelf software is much cheaper than custom software.

Office Applications

Office applications are the best selling packaged software products. Whether sold individually or in an **office suite** (a package containing all of these programs), they typically include the following:

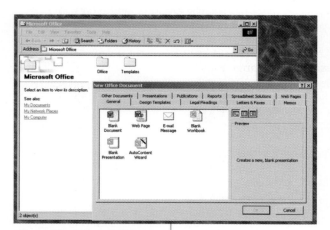

Microsoft Office 2000 is a popular office suite containing a word processing program, a database program, a spreadsheet program, and a presentation graphics program.

Word processing programs enable users to create, edit, and print written work. They also offer commands that enable users to format their documents so that they have an attractive appearance on-screen and when printed. Although some people still prefer to use other writing tools, nearly all professional authors have embraced word processing software.

Spreadsheet programs present users with a grid of rows and columns, the computer equivalent of an accountant's worksheet. By embedding formulas within the cells, users can create "live" worksheets in which changing one of the values forces the entire spreadsheet to recalculate. Spreadsheets are indispensable tools for anyone who works with numbers.

Presentation graphics programs enable users to create transparencies, slides, and handouts for oral presentations.

Database programs give users tools to store data in an organized form, as well as to retrieve this data in such a way that it can be meaningfully summarized and displayed.

THE INTERNET

The **Internet** is a globe-spanning computer network.

Since 1988, the Internet has been doubling in size every year. Currently, the network links hundreds of millions of users worldwide. It is creating a pool of shared resources that exceeds anything previously seen in human history. For example, according to growth rate estimates published in the respected journals *Science* and *Nature,* there are currently several billion pages of information available on the Internet—and roughly four to five million more are added each day. According to the Internet Society, a professional organization devoted to advancing Internet technology, the Internet is on track to exceed the size of the global telephone network in 2006.

Most users connect to the Internet by means of a dial-up connection, which requires a modem and telephone line. The connection is provided by an **Internet service provider (ISP).** Some ISPs are local, mom-and-pop operations. Others are national or even international in scope. Among the largest ISPs are America Online and The Microsoft Network (MSN).

To use the Internet, you take advantages of **Internet services.** An Internet service is a set of standards and software that make a specific type of resource available to Internet users, such as Web pages, files, or electronic mail. Two types of software are required: a server and a client. Client software enables users to request a specific resource from the server. Server software accepts these requests and sends the resource to the client.

Following are the most popular Internet services:

Electronic mail (also called e-mail) enables Internet users to send and receive messages via the network. Transmission isn't instantaneous, but it rarely exceeds five minutes. E-mail is fast becoming indispensable for individuals as well as businesses, and it is well on its way to replacing the postal system as the medium of choice for interpersonal written communication. To use Internet e-mail, you need an e-mail address and an e-mail account. These are usually provided by your Internet service provider (ISP). You also need an e-mail client program.

World Wide Web (also called Web or WWW) enables Internet users to access billions of Web pages worldwide. To use the Web, you need a client called **Web browser.** Web browsers provide tools for accessing Web sites, searching the Web, and bookmarking your favorite Web sites.

File Transfer Protocol (FTP) enables Internet users to exchange files via the Internet. Web browsers can act as FTP clients.

Buddy lists such as AOL's Instant Messenger let you know when a friend or business associate is **online** (connected to the Internet). You can then contact this person and exchange messages.

Electronic commerce (also called e-commerce) makes use of the Internet to provide goods and services to the public and other businesses. Web-based retail sites, called *e-tailers,* sell books, CDs, clothes, toys, and much more. Most successful are *click-and-brick* e-commerce sites, which offer the convenience of solving customer service issues and returns at a local conventional store. The ups and downs of famous e-tailers such as Amazon.com make splashy news stories, but the bulk of e-commerce involves **business-to-business (b2b)** exchanges, which link corporations with suppliers, research labs, and industrial customers. E-commerce isn't about to replace older methods of buying and selling, but it's growing. In 2000, e-commerce accounted for two percent of the U.S. gross national product—but this figure is expected to more than double by 2002. You'll learn more about e-commerce in Module 7B.

The Internet is a network that spans the entire globe.

Explore IT Lab

Internet and WWW

Destinations

Keep up with the latest e-commerce developments on 2Dnet's e-commerce news page **(http://www.2dnet.com/enterprise/e-business).**

Explore IT Lab

E-Commerce

TAKEAWAY POINTS

- Computer literacy refers to the skills needed to use a personal computer, a personal computer operating system, office suite applications, and Internet services, such as the Web and e-mail. Computer fluency refers to the conceptual knowledge possessed by computer-literate people who are able to increase their knowledge of computing, move to new computer technologies with ease, and grasp the risks as well as the benefits of computing.

- A computer is a machine that performs the following four operations under a program's guidance: input, processing, output, and storage. These four operations are called the information processing cycle.

- In batch processing, the four basic computer operations are performed in a rigid sequence: input, processing, output, and storage. In interactive processing, the user can initiate and repeat information processing cycles without exiting the computer.

- Spell-checking a word processing document exemplifies the information processing cycle. The input consists of the original document, which contains spelling mistakes. In processing, the computer detects and flags spelling errors by checking every word in the document against a massive spelling dictionary. Output consists of a list of apparently misspelled words. User interaction is required to confirm whether the apparent misspelling needs to be corrected. In storage, the user saves the corrected document for future re-use.

- In a typical desktop PC, a keyboard and a mouse provide input capabilities, while the processing is done by the microprocessor (CPU) and RAM (random-access memory). You see the results on a monitor, and you typically use a hard disk for long-term storage.

- System software refers to the programs that help the computer to function properly, such as the computer's operating system and system utilities. Application programs enable users to perform useful tasks.

- The Internet is a network of networks that combines the advantages of LANs (a community of resource-sharing computers) and WANs (the ability to transfer data over continental and intercontinental distances). The more the Internet grows, the richer its resources become.

- Popular Internet services include electronic mail, the World Wide Web, FTP file transfer, and buddy lists.

MODULE REVIEW

KEY TERMS AND CONCEPTS

algorithm	computer literacy	gigabytes (GB)
antivirus	computer network	graphical user interface (GUI)
application software	computer system	hard disk drive
arrow keys	computer virus	hardware
attribute	confirmation	IBM-compatible
batch processing	cursor	icons
business-to-business (b2b)	custom software	impact printers
cathode ray tube (CRT)	data	information
CD-ROM drive	database programs	information processing cycle
central processing unit (CPU)	desktop computers	inkjet printers
character	DVD-ROM drives	input
character set	electronic commerce	input devices
chip	(e-commerce)	interactive processing
clients	electronic mail (e-mail)	Internet
client/server	error message	Internet client
command	execute	Internet service provider (ISP)
command-line interface	expansion card	Internet services
communications device	expansion slots	keyboard
compilers	file	laser printers
computer	file transfer protocol (FTP)	laptop computers
computer networks	floppy disks	LCD displays or flat-panel
computer fluency	floppy disk drive	displays

loading	online	resource
local area network (LAN)	operating system (OS)	safety-critical systems
magnetic storage media	optical storage media	servers
mainframes	output	software
megabytes (MB)	output devices	source code
memory	package	speakers
microcomputers	pen computers	speech recognition
microphones	peripherals	spreadsheet programs
microprocessor	personal computer	storage
minicomputers	personal digital assistants (PDAs)	storage devices
mission-critical systems	or handheld computers	subnotebooks
modem	pointer	supercomputers
monitor	pointing device	syntax
motherboard	printer	system software
mouse	presentation graphics program	system unit
multiuser	processing	terminals
network interface card (NIC)	professional workstations	user interface
network computers (NCs)	program	utility programs
network medium	programmers	Web browsers
non-impact printers	programming language	Web sites
notebook computers	public data networks (PDN)	word processing programs
object code	random-access memory (RAM)	World Wide Web (WWW)
off-the-shelf software	reading	writing
office application	read-only	Zip disks
office suite	read/write	Zip drives

TRUE/FALSE

Indicate whether the following statements are true or false.

1. Computer fluency describes the knowledge possessed by people who are skilled computer and Internet users and whose interest and understanding of computers expands the more they work with computer technology.

2. A computer performs four basic operations: input, processing, output, and storage.

3. A computer program is a hardware device that tells a computer what to do.

4. An algorithm is a step-by-step procedure used to solve a problem.

5. Today's computers use batch processing, in which several information processing cycles are initiated in a single session.

6. A computer system is a collection of dissimilar components that have been designed to work with minimal problems.

7. IBM-compatible personal computers are made by many different manufacturers.

8. A modem is used to store information used in computer programs.

9. The most important piece of system software in a computer system is productivity software.

10. Internet technology creates a community of computers and enables resource-sharing.

MATCHING

Match each key term from the left column to the most accurate definition in the right column.

_____ 1. computer

_____ 2. program

_____ 3. processing

_____ 4. hardware

_____ 5. software

a. the most important type of system software

b. the operation that describes the computer performing arithmetic or comparison operations

c. enables a computer to access other computers and the Internet via a telephone line

_____ 6. personal computer

_____ 7. modem

_____ 8. server

_____ 9. operating system

_____ 10. electronic mail

d. enables Internet users to send and receive messages

e. a machine that performs input, processing, output, and storage operations

f. a list of instructions that describes how to perform input, processing, output, and storage operations to accomplish a task.

g. makes programs and data available for people hooked up to a computer network

h. includes all the programs that give the computer its instructions

i. the computer's physical components

j. a computer that meets a person's computing needs

MULTIPLE CHOICE

Circle the letter of the correct choice for each of the following.

1. What term best describes a person who can "successfully navigate the digital world"?
   a. computer consultant
   b. programmer
   c. computer illiterate
   d. computer fluent

2. What are the four basic operations performed by a computer?
   a. processing, communication, storage, data creation
   b. input, output, storage, communication
   c. storage, processing, input, output
   d. input, printing, storage, retrieval

3. A computer system consists of which of the following:
   a. hardware and communications devices
   b. hardware and software
   c. application software and system software
   d. communications devices and application software

4. Which of the following is a common input device?
   a. keyboard
   b. printer
   c. disk drive
   d. monitor

5. Which of the following is not a type of output device?
   a. monitor
   b. speakers
   c. disk drive
   d. printer

6. Which of the following is not a type of storage device?
   a. floppy drive
   b. CD-ROM
   c. network medium
   d. Zip disk

7. Which of the following are computers for individuals?
   a. supercomputers
   b. professional workstations
   c. minicomputers
   d. mainframes

8. Which of the following is not considered application software?
   a. operating system software
   b. project management software
   c. word processing software
   d. presentation graphics software

9. Which of the following characterizes local area networks?
   a. often use high-speed fiber optic cables and satellites
   b. create point-to-point connections between widely separated computers
   c. a network capable of spanning the globe
   d. limited in geographic scope, thereby creating a community of computers

10. Which two types of software are required to use Internet resources?
    a. WWW and FTP
    b. client and server software
    c. LAN and WAN network software
    d. FTP and client software

FILL-IN

In the blank provided, write the correct answer for each of the following.

1. A(n) _____ is a machine that performs four basic operations, namely, _____ , _____ , _____ , and _____ .

2. A(n) _____ refers to the overall, step-by-step procedure used to solve a problem.

3. Today's computers use _____ processing in which several information processing cycles are initiated in a single session.

4. A computer _____ is a collection of related components designed to work together smoothly.

5. Most computers use a miniaturized CPU called a(n) _____ .

6. A computer _____ links two or more computers by means of a physical connection called a(n) _____ .

7. Professional _____ are powerful tools for professionals who need potent processing and output capabilities.

8. A type of notebook computer that is actually smaller than a notebook computer is called a(n) _____ .

9. A(n) _____ is anything available to the computer including hardware, software, or data that increases the computer's value to users.

10. The _____ enables Internet users to access billions of Web pages worldwide.

SHORT ANSWER

On a separate sheet of paper, answer the following questions.

1. Define computer literacy and computer fluency. Why does computer literacy need to be supplemented with computer fluency?

2. How are mission-critical and safety-critical systems essential to an organization's survival?

3. Describe, in detail, the information processing cycle. Provide examples of each phase of the cycle.

4. Why is it important to take ethics seriously when using computers? How can computers cause harm to others?

5. What types of computers are designed for individuals? What specific uses can you think of for each type?

6. What types of computers are designed for use in organizations? How do these differ from computers designed for individual use?

7. What's the difference between hardware and software?

8. What's the difference between system software and application software?

9. What is a computer network? What is a local area network?

10. What are three or more popular services that the Internet provides users? Describe each one in detail.

1B

MODULE

HISTORY OF COMPUTERS AND THE INTERNET

WHAT YOU'LL LEARN . . .

After reading this module, you will be able to:

1. Define the term "electronics" and describe some early electronic devices that helped launch the computer industry.

2. Discuss the role that the stored-program concept played in launching the commercial computer industry.

3. List the four generations of computer technology.

4. Identify the key innovations that characterize each generation.

5. Explain how networking technology and the Internet has changed our world.

6. Discuss the lessons that can be learned from studying the computer's history.

What would the world be like if the British had lost to Napoleon in the bat-tle of Waterloo, or if the Japanese had won World War II? In *The Difference Engine,* authors William Gibson and Bruce Sterling ask a similar question: What would have happened if nineteenth-century inventor Charles Babbage had succeeded in creating the world's first automatic computer? (Babbage had the right idea, but the technology of his time wasn't up to the task.) Here is Gibson and Sterling's answer: with the aid of powerful computers, Britain becomes the world's first technological superpower. Its first foreign adven-ture is to intervene in the American Civil War on the side of the U.S. South, which splits the United States into four feuding republics. By the mid-1800s, the world is trying to cope with the multiple afflictions of the twentieth cen-tury: credit cards, armored tanks, and fast-food restaurants.

Alternative histories are fun, but history is serious business. Ideally, we would like to *learn* from the past. Not only do historians urge us to study his-tory, but computer industry executives also say that knowledge of the com-puter's history gives them an enormous advantage. In its successes and fail-ures, the computer industry has learned many important lessons, and indus-try executives take these to heart.

Although the history of analog computers is interesting in its own right, this module examines the chain of events that led to today's digital comput-ers. You'll begin by looking at the computing equivalent of ancient history, including the first mechanical calculators and their huge, electromechanical offshoots that were created at the beginning of World War II. Next, you'll examine the technology—electronics—that made today's computers possi-ble, beginning with what is generally regarded to be the first successful elec-tronic computer, the ENIAC of the late 1940s. You'll then examine the sub-sequent history of electronic digital computers, divided into four "genera-tions" of distinctive—and improving—technology. The module concludes by examining the history of the Internet and the rise of electronic commerce.

STEPS TOWARD MODERN COMPUTING

Today's electronic computers are recent inventions, stemming from work that began during World War II. Yet the most basic idea of computing—the notion of representing data in a physical object of some kind, and getting a result by manipulating the object in some way—is very old. In fact, it may be as old as humanity itself. Throughout the ancient world, people used devices such as notched bones, knotted twine, and the abacus to represent data and perform various sorts of calculations (see Figure 1B.1).

First Steps: Calculators

During the sixteenth and seventeenth centuries, European mathematicians developed a series of calculators that used clockwork mechanisms and cranks (see Figure 1B.1). As the ancestors of today's electromechanical adding machines, these devices weren't computers in the modern sense. A **calculator** is a machine that can perform arithmetic functions with num-bers, including addition, subtraction, multiplication, and division.

The Technological Edge: Electronics

Today's computers are **automatic,** in that they can perform most tasks with-out the need for human intervention. They require a type of technology that was unimaginable in the nineteenth century. As Figure 1B.1 shows, nine-teenth-century inventor Charles Babbage came up with the first design for a

Steps Toward Modern Computing: A Timeline

quipa (15th and 16th centuries) At the height of their empire, the Incas used complex chains of knotted twine to represent a variety of data, including tribute payments, lists of arms and troops, and notable dates in the kingdom's chronicles.

abacus (4000 years ago to 1975) Used by merchants throughout the ancient world. Beads represent figures (data); by moving the beads according to rules, the user can add, subtract, multiply, or divide. The abacus remained in use until a worldwide deluge of cheap pocket calculators put the abacus out of work, after being used for thousands of years.

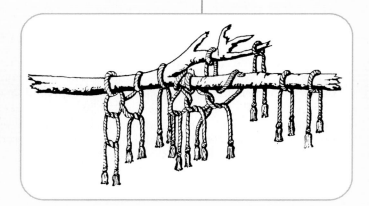

Jacquard's loom (1804) French weaver Joseph-Marie Jacquard creates an automatic, programmable weaving machine that creates fabrics with richly detailed patterns. It is controlled by means of punched cards.

Pascal's calculator (1642) French mathematician and philosopher Blaise Pascal, the son of an accountant, invents an adding machine to relieve the tedium of adding up long columns of tax figures.

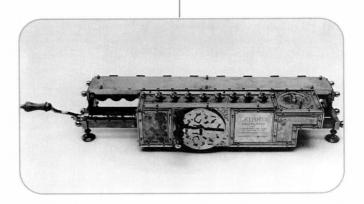

Leibniz's calculator (1674) German philosopher Gottfried Leibniz invents the first mechanical calculator capable of multiplication.

Hollerith's tabulating machine (1890) Created to tally the results of the U.S. Census, this machine uses punched cards as a data input mechanism. The successor to Hollerith's company is International Business Machines (IBM).

Babbage's difference engine (1822) English mathematician and scientist Charles Babbage designs a complex, clockwork calculator capable of solving equations and printing the results. Despite repeated attempts, Babbage was never able to get the device to work.

Mark I (1943) In a partnership with Harvard University, IBM creates a huge, programmable electronic calculator that used electromechanical relays as switching devices.

Zuse's Z1 (1938) German inventor Konrad Zuse creates a programmable electronic calculator. An improved version, the Z3 of 1941, was the world's first calculator capable of automatic operation.

recognizably-modern computer. It would have used a clockwork mechanism, but the technology of his day could not create the various gears needed with the precision that would have been required to get the device to work.

The technology that enables today's computer industry is called electronics. In brief, **electronics** is concerned with the behavior and effects of electrons as they pass through devices that can restrict their flow in various ways. The earliest electronic device, the **vacuum tube,** is a glass tube, emptied of air, in the flow of electrons that can be controlled in various ways. Created by Thomas Edison in the 1880s, vacuum tubes can be used for amplification, which is why they powered early radios and TVs, or switching, their role in computers. In fact, vacuum tubes powered all electronic devices (including stereo gear as well as computers) until the advent of **solid-state devices.** Also referred to as a **semiconductor,** a solid-state device acts like a vacuum tube, but it is a "sandwich" of differing materials that are combined to restrict or control the flow of electrical current in the desired way.

Putting It All Together: The ENIAC

With the advent of vacuum tubes, the technology finally existed to create the first truly modern computer—and the demands of warfare created both the funding and the motivation.

In World War II, the American military needed a faster method to calculate shell missile trajectories. The military asked Dr. John Mauchly (1907–1980) at the University of Pennsylvania to develop a machine for this purpose. Mauchly worked with a graduate student, J. Presper Eckert (1919–1995), to build the device. Although commissioned by the military for use in the war, the ENIAC was not completed until 1946, after the war had ended (see Figure 1B.2).

Although it was used mainly to solve challenging math problems, **ENIAC** was a true programmable digital computer rather than an electronic calculator. One thousand times faster than any existing calculator, the ENIAC gripped the public's imagination after newspaper reports described it as an "Electronic Brain." The ENIAC took only 30 seconds to compute trajectories that would have required 40 hours of hand calculations.

The Stored-Program Concept

ENIAC had its share of problems. It was frustrating to use because it wouldn't run for more than a few minutes without blowing a tube, which caused the system to stop working. Worse, every time a new problem had to be solved, the staff had to enter the new instructions the hard way: by rewiring the entire machine. The solution was the stored-program concept, an idea that occurred to just about everyone working with electronic computers after World War II.

With the **stored-program concept,** the computer program, as well as data, is stored in the computer's memory. One key advantage of this technique is that the computer can easily go back to a previous instruction and repeat it.

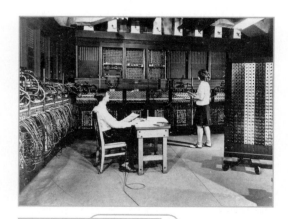

Figure 1B.2

Using 17,480 vacuum tubes, ENIAC was a true programmable digital computer that was one thousand times faster than any existing calculator.

Most of the interesting tasks that today's computers perform stem from repeating certain actions over and over. But the most important advantage is convenience. You don't have to rewire the computer to get it to do something different. Without the stored-program concept, computers would have remained tied to specific jobs, such as cranking out ballistics tables. All computers that have been sold commercially have used the stored-program concept.

The Generations of Computer Development				Table 1B.1
Generation	**Years**	**Circuitry**	**Characterized by**
First	1950s	Vacuum tubes	Difficult to program; used only machine language
Second	Early 1960s	Transistors	Easier to program (high-level languages); could work with business tabulating machines; cheaper
Third	Mid-1960s to 1970s	Integrated circuits	Timesharing, minicomputer (SSI, MSI, LSI)
Fourth	Mid-1970s to Present	VLSI and the Microprocessor	Personal computer; graphical user; user interface; LANs; Internet

THE COMPUTER'S FAMILY TREE

The PC that's sitting on your desk is, in many respects, a direct descendent of ENIAC-inspired research, including the stored-program concept. Of course, your computer is thousands of times faster and thousands of times less expensive than its room-filling, electricity-guzzling predecessors. When we're talking about a PC, the "computer" is the microprocessor chip, which is about the size of a postage stamp and consumes less energy than one of the desk lamps in ENIAC's operating room. How was this amazing transformation achieved?

Today's computers weren't achieved in a gradual, evolutionary process, but rather by a series of technological leaps, each of which was made possible by major new developments in both hardware and software. To describe the stage-by-stage development of modern computing, computer scientists and historians speak of computer generations. Each generation is characterized by a certain level of technological development. Some treatments of this subject assign precise dates to each generation, but this practice overstates the clarity of the boundary between one generation and the next. Table 1B.1 introduces the four generations of computing technology. In subsequent sections, you'll learn about each in more detail.

The First Generation (1950s)

Until 1951, electronic computers were the exclusive possessions of scientists, engineers, and the military. No one had tried to create an electronic digital computer for business. And it wasn't much fun for Eckert and Mauchly, the first to try. When the University of Pennsylvania learned of their plans to transform ENIAC into a commercial product, University officials stated that the university owned the duo's patent. Eckert and Mauchly resigned to form their own company, the Eckert-Mauchly Computer Company, and landed a government grant to develop their machine. They underestimated the amount of effort involved, however, and would not have delivered the computer if they hadn't been bailed out by Remington Rand, a maker of electric shavers. With Rand's financial assistance, Eckert and Mauchly delivered the first UNIVAC to the U.S. Census Bureau in 1951 (see Figure 1B.3).

Figure 1B.3

Eckert and Mauchly delivered the first UNIVAC to the U.S. Census Bureau in 1951. UNIVAC gained fame when it correctly predicted the winner of the 1952 U.S. presidential election, Dwight Eisenhower.

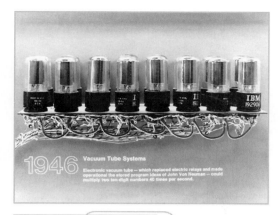

Figure 1B.4

The first generation of computers used vacuum tubes. Vacuum tubes failed frequently, so first-generation computers did not work most of the time.

Figure 1B.5

IBM's first commercial computer, the 701, wasn't popular because it didn't work with IBM's own punched-card equipment.

Destinations

Explore the history of computing visually at The History of Computing, an outstanding Web presentation created by the Institute of Electrical and Electronic Engineers (IEEE).

UNIVAC gained fame when it correctly predicted the winner of the 1952 U.S. presidential election, Dwight Eisenhower. Since then, computers have been used to predict the winners in every presidential election.

From today's perspective, first-generation computers are almost laughably primitive. For input, punched cards were used, although UNIVAC could also accept input on magnetic tape. Power-hungry vacuum tubes provided the memory (see Figure 1B.4). The problem with vacuum tubes was that they failed frequently, so first-generation computers were down (not working) much of the time.

For all the limitations of first-generation technology, UNIVAC was a much more modern machine than ENIAC. Because it used fewer vacuum tubes than ENIAC, it was far more reliable. It employed the stored-program concept, provided a supervisory typewriter for controlling the computer, and used magnetic tapes for unlimited storage. Because the stored-program feature enabled users to run different programs, UNIVAC is considered to be the first successful **general-purpose computer.** A general-purpose computer can be used for scientific or business purposes, depending on how it is programmed.

Although the stored-program concept made first-generation computers easier to use, they had to be programmed in **machine language,** which is composed of the numbers 0 and 1 because electronic computers use the binary numbering system, which contains only 0 and 1. People often find binary numbers difficult to read. Moreover, each type of computer has a unique machine language, which is designed to communicate directly with the processor's **instruction set,** the list of operations it is designed to carry out. Because machine language was difficult to work with, only a few specialists understood how to program these early computers.

Realizing that Rand's new computers posed a threat to its core business, IBM reacted quickly. In 1953, the company announced its first commercial computer, the IBM 701, but it wasn't popular because it didn't work with IBM's own punched-card equipment (see Figure 1B.5). The 701 was quickly followed by the highly-successful (and more user-friendly) IBM 650, which interfaced with the most widely-used punched-card technology in the world. Thanks to IBM's aggressive sales staff, IBM sold over a thousand 650s in the first year of the computer's availability.

The Second Generation (Early 1960s)

First-generation computers were notoriously unreliable, largely because the vacuum tubes kept burning out. To keep the ENIAC running, for example, students with grocery carts full of tubes were on hand to change the dozens that would fail during an average session. But a 1947 Bell Laboratories invention, the **transistor,** changed the way computers were built, leading to the second generation of computer technology. A transistor is a small electronic device that, like vacuum tubes, can be used to control the flow of electricity in an electronic circuit, but at a tiny fraction of the weight, power consumption, and heat output of vacuum tubes. Because second-generation computers were created with transistors instead of vacuum tubes, these computers were faster, smaller, and more reliable than first-generation computers (see Figure 1B.6).

Second-generation computers looked much more like the computers we use today. Although they still used punched cards for input, they had printers, tape storage, and disk storage. In contrast to the first-generation computer's reliance on cumbersome machine language, the second generation saw the development of the first **high-level programming languages,** which are much easier for people to understand and work with than machine languages. A high-level programming language enables the programmer to write program instructions using English-sounding commands and Arabic numbers. Also, unlike assembly language, a high-level language is not machine-specific. This makes it possible to use the same program on computers produced by different manufacturers. The two programming languages introduced during the second generation, Common Business-Oriented Language (COBOL) and Formula Translator (FORTRAN), remain among the most widely-used programming languages even today. COBOL is preferred by businesses, and FORTRAN is used by scientists and engineers.

Figure 1B.6

The transistor heralded the second generation of computers.

A leading second-generation computer was IBM's fully transistorized 1401, which brought the mainframe computer to an increasing number of businesses. (A mainframe computer is a large, expensive computer designed to meet all of an organization's computing needs.) The company shipped more than 12,000 of these computers. A sibling, the 1620, was developed for scientific computing and became the computer of choice for university research labs.

In business computing, an important 1959 development was General Electric Corporation's **Electronic Recording Machine Accounting (ERMA),** the first technology that could read special characters. Banks needed this system to handle the growing deluge of checks. Because ERMA digitizes checking account information, it has helped to lay the foundation for electronic commerce (e-commerce).

In 1963, an important development was the **American Standard Code for Information Interchange (ASCII),** a character set that enables computers to exchange information and the first computer industry standard. Although ASCII didn't have much of an impact for 15 years, it would later help to demonstrate the importance of standardization to industry executives.

In 1964, IBM announced a new line of computers called System/360 that changed the way people thought about computers. An entire line of **compatible computers** (computers that could use the same programs and peripherals), System/360 eliminated the distinction between computers designed primarily for business and those designed primarily for science. The computer's instruction set was big enough to encompass both uses.

The Third Generation (Mid-1960s to Mid-1970s)

It's possible to separate the first and second computer generations on neat, clean technological grounds: the transition from the vacuum tube to the transistor. The transition to the third generation isn't quite so clear-cut because many key innovations were involved.

One key innovation was **timesharing.** Early second-generation computers were frustrating to use because they could run only one job at a time. Users had to give their punched cards to computer operators, who would run their program and then give the results back to the user (see Figure 1B.7). This technique,

Figure 1B.7

Early second-generation computers were frustrating to use because they could run only one job at a time. Users had to give their punched cards to computer operators, who would run their program and then give the results back to the user.

Figure 1B.8

Integrated chips are shown here with first-generation vacuum tubes and second-generation transistors.

Figure 1B.9

DEC's first commercially-available minicomputer, the PDP-8, did not require the attention of a full-time computer operator.

called **batch processing,** was time-consuming and inefficient. In timesharing, however, the computer is designed so that it can be used by many people simultaneously. They access the computer remotely by means of **terminals,** control devices equipped with a video display and keyboard. In a properly-designed timesharing system, users have the illusion that no one else is using the computer.

In the third generation, the key technological event was the development of computers based on the **integrated circuit (IC),** which incorporated many transistors and electronic circuits on a single wafer or chip of silicon (see Figure 1B.8). Invented by Jack St. Clair Kirby and Robert Noyce in 1958, integrated circuits promised to cut the cost of computer production significantly because ICs could duplicate the functions of transistors at a tiny fraction of a transistor's cost. The earliest ICs, using a technology now called **small-scale integration (SSI),** could pack up to 10 to 20 transistors on a chip. By the late 1960s, engineers had achieved **medium-scale integration (MSI),** which placed between 20 and 200 transistors on a chip. In the early 1970s, **large-scale integration (LSI)** was achieved, in which a single chip could hold up to 5,000 transistors.

Integrated circuit technology unleashed a period of innovation in the computer industry that is without parallel in history. By the second generation, scientists knew that more powerful computers could be created by building more complex circuits. But because these circuits had to be wired by hand, these computers were too complex and expensive to build. With integrated circuits, new and innovative designs became possible for the first time.

With ICs on the scene, it was possible to create smaller, inexpensive computers that more organizations could afford to buy. Mainframe computer manufacturers such as IBM, however, did not perceive that this market existed. In the first of two key events that demonstrated the inability of large companies to see new markets, the mainframe computer manufacturers left the market for smaller computers open to new, innovative firms. The first of these was Digital Electronic Corporation (DEC), which launched the minicomputer industry. (A minicomputer is smaller than a mainframe and is designed to meet the computing needs of a small- to mid-sized organization or a department within a larger organization.)

DEC's pioneering minicomputers used integrated circuits to cut down costs. Capable of fitting in the corner of a room, the PDP-8 (a 1965 model) did not require the attention of a full-time computer operator (see Figure 1B.9). In addition, users could access the computer from different locations in the same building by means of timesharing. This minicomputer's price tag was about one-fourth the cost of a traditional mainframe. For the first time, medium-sized companies (as well as smaller colleges and universities) could afford computers.

By 1969, so many different programming languages were in use that IBM decided to unbundle its systems and sell software and hardware separately. Before that time, computer manufacturers received software that was "bundled" (provided) with the purchased hardware. Now buyers could obtain software from sources other than the hardware manufacturer, if they wished. This freedom launched the software industry.

The minicomputer industry strongly promoted standards, chiefly as a means of distinguishing their business practices from mainframe manufacturers. In the mainframe industry, it was a common practice to create a **proprietary architecture** (also called a **closed architecture**) for connecting computer devices. In a proprietary architecture, the company uses a secret technique to define how the various computer components connect. Translation? If you want a printer, you have to get it from the same company that sold you the computer. In contrast, most minicomputer companies stressed **open architecture.** In open architecture designs, the various components connect according to non-proprietary, published standards. Examples of such standards are the RS-232c and Centronics standards for connecting devices such as printers.

Figure   1B.10

The Intel 4004, the world's first microprocessor.

The Fourth Generation (1975 to the Present)

As the integrated circuit revolution developed, engineers learned how to build increasingly more complex circuits on a single chip of silicon. With **very-large-scale integration (VLSI)** technology, they could place the equivalent of more than 5,000 transistors on a single chip—enough for a processing unit. Inevitably, it would occur to someone to try to create a chip that contained the core processing circuits of a computer.

In the early 1970s, an Intel Corporation engineer, Dr. Ted Hoff, was given the task of designing an integrated circuit to power a digital watch. Previously, these circuits had to be redesigned every time a new model of the watch appeared. Hoff decided that he could avoid costly redesigns by creating a tiny computer on a chip. The result was the Intel 4004, the world's first **microprocessor** (see Figure 1B.10). A microprocessor chip holds the entire control unit and arithmetic-logic unit of a computer. Compared to today's microprocessors, the 4004 was a simple device (it had 2,200 transistors). The 4004 was soon followed by the 8080, and the first microcomputers—computers that used microprocessors for their central processing unit (CPU)—soon appeared. (The central processing unit processes data.)

Repeating the pattern in which established companies did not see a market for smaller and less expensive computers, the large computer companies considered the microcomputer nothing but a toy. They left the market to a host of startup companies. The first of these was MITS, an Arizona-based company that marketed a microcomputer kit. This microcomputer, called the Altair, used Intel's 8080 chip.

In the mid-1970s, computer hobbyists assembled microcomputers from kits or from secondhand parts purchased from electronics suppliers. However, two young entrepreneurs, Steve Jobs and Steve Wozniak, dreamed of creating an "appliance computer." They wanted a microcomputer so simple that you could take it out of the box, plug it in, and use it, just as you would use a toaster oven. Jobs and Wozniak set up shop in a garage after selling a Volkswagen for $1,300 to raise the needed capital. They founded Apple Computer, Inc., in April 1977. Its first product, the Apple I, was a processor board intended for hobbyists, but the experience the company gained in building the Apple I led to the Apple II computer system (see Figure 1B.11).

Destinations

Learn more about the people who created the personal computer industry at "Triumph of the Nerds," a Public Broadcasting System (PBS) Web site created as a companion for the PBS documentary with the same title **(http://www. pbs.org/nerds).**

Figure   1B.11

The Apple I was intended for hobbyists, but the experience Apple gained in building it led to the highly-successful Apple II.

Figure 1B.12

The first IBM PC was released in 1981. Intel provided the microprocessor chip and Microsoft Corporation provided the operating system.

Techtalk

look and feel
The on-screen visual ("look") and user experience ("feel") aspects of a computer program. Some software publishers claim that a program's "look and feel" are copy-rightable, but courts have had a tough time distinguishing between truly original features and those that are in wide-spread usage (and there-fore not subject to copy-right protection). In 1988, Apple Computer sued Microsoft Corporation, alleging that Microsoft Windows infringed on the "look and feel" of the Macintosh interface. After six years of litigation, a Federal court ruled in Microsoft's favor.

The Apple II was a huge success. With a keyboard, monitor, floppy disk drive, and operating system, the Apple II was a complete microcomputer system, based on the Motorola 6502 microprocessor. Apple Computer, Inc. soon became one of the leading forces in the microcomputer market, making millionaires out of Jobs, Wozniak, and other early investors. The introduction of the first electronic spreadsheet software, VisiCalc, in 1979 helped convince the world that these little microcomputers were more than toys. Still, the Apple II found its greatest market in schools and homes, rather than in businesses.

In 1980, IBM decided that the microcomputer market was too promising to ignore and contracted with Microsoft Corporation to write an operating system for a new microcomputer based on the Intel 8080. (An *operating system* is a program that integrates and controls the computer's internal functions.) The IBM Personal Computer (PC), with a microprocessor chip made by Intel Corporation and a Microsoft operating system called MS-DOS, was released in 1981 (see Figure 1B.12). Based on the lessons learned in the minicomputer market, IBM adopted an open architecture model for the PC (only a small portion of the computer's built-in startup code was copyrighted). IBM expressly invited third-party suppliers to create accessory devices for the IBM PC, and the company did not challenge competitors who created **IBM-compatible** computers (also called **clones**), which could run any software developed for the IBM PC. The result was a flourishing market, to which many hardware and software companies made major commitments.

IBM's share of the PC market soon declined. The decline was partly due to stiff competition from clone makers, but it was also due to IBM management's insistence on viewing the PC as something of a toy, used chiefly as a means of introducing buyers to IBM's larger computer systems. Ironically, thanks to IBM's reputation among businesses, the IBM PC helped to establish the idea that a PC *wasn't* just a toy or an educational computer, but could play an important role in a business.

The Apple II and IBM PC created the personal computer industry, but they also introduced a division that continues to this day. Because software must be tailored to a given processor's instruction set, software written for one type of machine cannot be directly run on another type. Apple chose Motorola processors for its line of computers, while IBM chose Intel. Today's PCs use advanced Intel microprocessors; the Apple II's successor, the Macintosh, uses PowerPC chips provided by Motorola.

Why were the Apple II and IBM PC so successful? Part of the reason was attributable to the lessons taught by the minicomputer industry. Computer buyers don't like it when manufacturers use proprietary protocols in an attempt to force them to buy the same brand's accessories. Both the Apple II and IBM PC were open architecture systems that enabled users to buy printers, monitors, and other accessories made by third-party companies. Although an open-architecture strategy loses some business initially, in the end it benefits a company because it promotes the growth of an entire industry focused around a given company's computer system. As more software and accessories become available, the number of users grows—and so do the profits.

The first microcomputers weren't easy to use. To operate them, users had to cope with the computer's **command-line user interface.** (A **user interface** is the means provided to enable users to control the computer.)

In a command-line interface, you must type commands to perform such actions as formatting a disk or starting a program. Although the Apple II and IBM PC were popular, computers would have to become easier to use if they were to become a common fixture in homes and offices. That's why the **graphical user interface (GUI)** was such an important innovation.

The first GUI was developed at Xerox Corporation's Palo Alto Research Center (PARC) in the 1970s. In a graphical user interface, users interact with programs that run in their own sizeable windows. Using a mouse (also developed at PARC), they choose program options by clicking symbols (called icons) that represent program functions. Within the program's workspace, users see their document just as it would appear when printed on a graphics-capable printer. To print these documents, PARC scientists also developed the laser printer.

It's difficult to underestimate the contribution that PARC scientists made to computing. Just about every key technology that we use today, including Ethernet local area networks (see Module 6B), stems from PARC research. But Xerox Corporation never succeeded in capitalizing on PARC technology, repeating a theme that you've seen throughout this module: big companies sometimes have difficulty perceiving important new markets.

The potential of PARC technology wasn't lost on a late-1970s visitor, Apple Computer's Steve Jobs. Grasping instantly what the PARC technology could mean, the brilliant young entrepreneur returned to Apple and bet the company's future on a new, PARC-influenced computer called the Macintosh. In 1984, Apple Computer released the first Macintosh, which offered all the key PARC innovations, including on-screen fonts, icons, windows, mouse control, and pull-down menus (see Figure 1B.13). Apple Computer retained its technological leadership in this area until Microsoft released an improved version of Microsoft Windows in the early 1990s. Windows is designed to run on IBM-compatible computers, which are far more numerous and generally less expensive than Macintoshes. Also showing the influence of PARC innovations, Windows is now the most widely-used computer user interface program in the world (see Figure 1B.14).

Although fourth-generation hardware has improved at a dizzying pace, the same cannot be said for software. Throughout the fourth generation, programmers have continued to use high-level programming languages. In fact, COBOL, which dates to the dawn of the second generation, is still the most widely-used programming language in the world. High-level programming languages are inefficient, time-consuming, and prone to error. In short, software (not hardware) has slowed the development of the computer industry—at least, until very recently. You will learn about several improvements to computer programming languages, such as object-oriented (OO) programming, a method of dividing programs into reusable components, in Module 8C.

Figure   1B.13

Apple Computer's Macintosh was the first commercial personal computer to offer a PARC-influenced graphical user interface.

Figure   1B.14

Microsoft Windows 2000 includes the latest version of the world's most popular user interface.

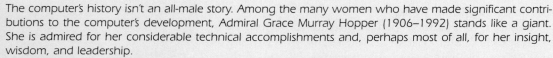

MOVERS & SHAKERS

Amazing Grace

The computer's history isn't an all-male story. Among the many women who have made significant contributions to the computer's development, Admiral Grace Murray Hopper (1906–1992) stands like a giant. She is admired for her considerable technical accomplishments and, perhaps most of all, for her insight, wisdom, and leadership.

Admiral Grace Hopper, the first woman to receive a doctorate in mathematics from Yale University, joined the U.S. Naval Reserve in 1943 and was assigned to Howard Aiken's Mark I computer project at Harvard University. Subsequently, Hopper joined the team that created UNIVAC, the first commercial computer system.

While working with the UNIVAC team in 1952, Hopper invented the first language translator (also called compiler), which for the first time freed programmers from the drudgery of writing computer programs in 1s and 0s. In 1955, Hopper led the development effort that created COBOL, the first high-level programming language that enabled programmers to use familiar English words to describe computer operations. COBOL is still the world's most widely-used programming language.

During her long career, Hopper lectured widely. Her favorite audience was young people, especially in the age group of 17–21. Hopper believed that young people were receptive to the idea of change—a good thing, in Hopper's view, because older people tended to fall into the trap of believing that change isn't possible. Hopper ought to know: experts at first refused to examine her compiler, claiming no such thing was possible. In her retirement speech, Admiral Hopper looked not to the past, but to the future. "Our young people are the future," she said. "We must give them the positive leadership they're looking for."

Hopper's observations inspired generations of computer science students, and seem particularly wise today. Going against the "bigger-must-be-better" philosophy of computer design, Hopper insisted that "we shouldn't be trying for bigger computers, but for more systems of computers." Subsequent years would see the demise of major supercomputer firms as networked computers surpassed the big machines' performance. Hopper also warned that computer systems needed to boil information down to just what's useful, instead of flooding people with more information than they can handle. And once the key information is obtained, Hopper insisted, the job isn't finished. "A human must turn information into intelligence or knowledge. We've tended to forget that no computer will ever ask a new question."

The recipient of more than 40 honorary doctorates from colleges and universities, Hopper received the U.S. Navy's Distinguished Service Medal in a retirement ceremony aboard the U.S.S. Constitution. In recognition of Admiral Hopper's accomplishments, President George Bush awarded her the 1991 National Medal of Technology, the nation's highest honor for technological leadership. Hopper died in 1992 and was buried in Arlington National Cemetery with full military honors.

Admiral Grace Hopper originated COBOL, which is still the world's most widely used programming language.

A FIFTH GENERATION?

If there is a fifth generation, it has been slow in coming. After all, the last one began in 1975. For years, experts have forecast that the trademark of the next generation will be **artificial intelligence (AI),** in which computers exhibit some of the characteristics of human intelligence. But progress towards that goal has been disappointing.

Technologically, we're still in the fourth generation, in which engineers are pushing to see how many transistors they can pack on a chip. This effort alone will bring some of the trappings of AI, such as a computer's capability to recognize and transcribe human speech. Although fourth-generation technology will inevitably run into physical barriers, engineers do not expect to encounter these for many years (perhaps decades).

What appears to truly differentiate the late 1990s from previous years is the rocket-like ascent of computer networking, both at the LAN and WAN levels. Many new homes now include local area networks (LANs) to link the family's several computers and provide all of them with Internet access. At the WAN level, the Internet's meteoric growth is creating a massive public computer network of global proportions, and it has already penetrated close to 50 percent of U.S. households. You'll learn more about the growth and development of the Internet in Module 7A.

Another third-generation innovation was the development of standards for computer networking. Since the late 1960s, the U.S. Advanced Research Projects Agency (ARPA) had supported a project to develop a **wide area network (WAN),** a computer network capable of spanning continents. Headed by Vincent Cerf, this project created a test network, called the ARPANET, that connected several universities that had Defense Department research contracts. The outcome of this project, the Internet, would later rock the world. Interestingly, the ARPANET proved a point that's been seen throughout the history of computing: innovators often cannot guess how people will use the systems they create. ARPANET was designed to enable scientists to access distant supercomputers. Most users, however, viewed it as a communications medium. They developed real-time chatting, electronic mail, and newsgroups. The Internet continues to play an important social role for users.

In 1973, ARPANET fully implemented the **Internet protocols** (also called **TCP/IP**), the standards that enable the Internet to work. Coincidentally, in the same year, Bob Metcalfe and other researchers at Xerox Corporation's Palo Alto Research Center (PARC) developed the standards for a **local area network (LAN),** a direct-cable network that could tie in all computers in a building. Called Ethernet, these standards are now the most widely-used in the world.

THE INTERNET REVOLUTION

As you've learned in this chapter, wartime needs played a crucial role in the computer's development. The same is true of computer networking. In this case, the impetus was the Soviet Union's 1957 launch of the first artificial satellite, Sputnik, during the Cold War. Perceiving a need to play catch-up with Soviet science, the U.S. Congress established the Advanced Research Projects Agency (ARPA). Equipped with generous funds and a mandate to explore cutting-edge science and technology, ARPA was to play a key role in the Internet's development. (You'll learn more about the Internet and its underlying technology in Module 7A; this section recounts the Internet's historical development.)

As Cold War tensions mounted, U.S. military officials became concerned about the survival of its command and control system in the event of a nuclear war. Computer networks were increasingly seen as the command and control system of the future, but the then-existing computer networks were based on a highly-centralized design. A direct hit to the network's central facility would knock out the entire network. A 1962 Rand Corporation study identified a new and unproven networking technology, called packet-switching, as the best bet for creating a decentralized network, one that could keep functioning even if portions of it were knocked out by an enemy hit.

In brief, a **packet-switching network** works by dividing messages up into small-sized units called **packets.** Each packet contains a unit of data as well as information about its origin, its destination, and the procedure to be followed to reassemble the message. While en route, the packets can travel more than one path to reach their destination. If some do not arrive, the receiving computer requests a re-transmission until it has received all of the packets.

In 1968, ARPA awarded a contract to Bolt, Beranak, and Newman (BBN), a technology consulting firm, to build a **testbed** network called ARPANET. In engineering, a testbed is a small-scale version of a product that is developed in order to test its capabilities. Originally, the ARPANET connected only four computers, which were located in California and Utah.

The network grew slowly at first, from an estimated 20 users in 1968 to millions of users today. In the beginning, no one dreamed that the network would one day span the globe. Still, the Internet surprised its creators right away. Originally, the ARPANET's designers thought the network would be used to give researchers remote access to high-powered computers. Instead, ARPANET users figured out how to use the network for communication. The first e-mail program was created in 1972, and was quickly followed by a set of topically-focused mailing lists. (A **mailing list** is an e-mail application in which every member of the list receives a copy of every message sent to the list.) Even though the ARPANET linked researchers at top universities and defense installations, the mailing list topics included many less-than-serious ones, including discussions of science fiction novels, romance and dating, and Star Trek.

The original ARPANET used a set of packet-switching standards that were closely tied to the network's physical medium. In 1973, work began on TCP/IP, a set of standards for packet switching that would enable data to be transferred over virtually any type of physical medium, including cable of all kinds, radio signals, and satellite transmissions. In 1983, every **host** on the ARPANET was required to convert to the TCP/IP standards. In ARPANET terms, a host is a computer that is fully connected to the Internet. (Since many Internet hosts are multi-user machines, the number of people actually using the Internet at a given time is many times larger than the number of hosts.)

By the mid-1970s, local area networks (LANs) were flourishing, and the ARPANET research team realized that the TCP/IP standards had an important strength: they could be used to connect networks as well as hosts. For this reason, Vincent Cert and Bob Kahn, the developers of the TCP/IP standards, began to refer to TCP/IP networks as *internets,* networks capable of linking networks.

Because the ARPANET was fast becoming indispensable for university researchers, the U.S. National Science Foundation (NSF) created a civilian version of ARPANET, called CSNET, in 1981. In 1984, this network was renamed NSFNET. NSF's contribution included construction and maintenance of the network's **backbone,** the long-distance transmission lines that transfer data over interstate and continental distances. Because NSFNET was publicly supported, commercial use of the network was forbidden, but it linked growing numbers of colleges and universities. Meanwhile, the military portion of the ARPANET was separated from the growing public network, and in 1990 the original ARPANET long-distance lines were taken out of service.

In the early 1990s, the term *Internet* was increasingly used to describe the growing network that relied on the NSFNET backbone—and increasingly, regional extensions of the network were being constructed by for-profit firms. In 1995, NSF announced that it would withdraw support for the Internet's backbone network. Commercial providers stepped in to take up the slack, and the restrictions on the Internet's commercial use were finally withdrawn completely.

What has happened since is the most important technological story of the twentieth century. From its origins as a Cold War concept for keeping the military in operation in the event of a nuclear war, the Internet has emerged as an unparalleled public medium for communication and commerce—and

SPOTLIGHT

COMPUTERS AND ELECTIONS: PICKING THE WINNER

▶On the eve of the 1952 U.S. presidential election, the polls suggested a tight race between Republican hopeful Dwight D. Eisenhower and his Democratic challenger, Adlai Stevenson. On the night of the election, the CBS television network featured a new guest commentator: a UNIVAC computer, which was asked to predict the outcome of the election based on the patterns seen in early returns from the East Coast. At 9 PM Eastern Standard Time, with only 7 percent of the votes tallied, UNIVAC forecasted an Eisenhower landslide. Eisenhower would win 43 states and 438 electoral votes, but Stevenson would win only 5 states and a meager 93 votes. But CBS did not report UNIVAC's prediction. Because most of the polls had called for a close race, the UNIVAC programmers feared they had made a programming error. Instead, they added fudge factors to the program in an attempt to make the results seem more like the close race that the polls were predicting. With the fudge factors added, UNIVAC called the election a toss-up, and that's what CBS viewers heard at 10 PM that evening.

But UNIVAC's program was right. Eisenhower indeed won the election by almost exactly the landslide that UNIVAC had originally predicted: the final tally was 442 electoral votes for Eisenhower, and 89 for Stevenson. "The trouble with machines," CBS commentator Edward R. Murrow later reflected, "is people."

All too often, the trouble with computers is software, too. In a 1981 provincial election in Quebec, Canada, a computer-based election eve forecast gave the nod to the all-but-written-off Union Nationale (UN), a small splinter party that no one thought had the slightest chance of winning the

election. Asked to explain the UN's meteoric rise, television commentators came up with a slew of on-the-spot analyses that accounted for the party's sudden popularity. One of them concluded that the experts were wrong to write off the Union Nationale; "the people have spoken," he declared. But there was only one little problem. A software glitch had scrambled the results, leading to a wildly inaccurate prediction. In reality, the Union Nationale was trounced, just as the polls predicted.

As long as the software functions correctly, computers can indeed forecast election results with great accuracy—too great, according to some critics. On the night of the 1980 U.S. presidential election, computer predictions showed incumbent President Jimmy Carter headed for defeat against challenger Ronald Reagan, and the networks declared Reagan the winner. However, they did so before the polls closed on the West Coast, leading some Democrats from the western states to charge that the prediction harmed their chances in state and local elections; with Carter headed for defeat, they argued, Democrats stayed home instead of voting. Carter didn't help matters much by conceding defeat—again, before the West Coast polls closed.

Did computers affect the outcome of the 1980 election? Experts are still divided. Some point out that West Coast Republicans were just as likely as Democrats to skip voting: after all, Reagan had already won. Still, the major networks decided to hold off on releasing the computer projections until the last West Coast polling stations close, and that's their policy to this day.

it's changing our world. For example, growing numbers of people use the Internet to **telecommute** to work. In telecommuting, employees work at home, and stay in touch by means of computer-based communications. The Internet is proving indispensable in every conceivable professional field. For example, physicians use the Internet to stay in touch with colleagues around the world, and learn of life-saving new therapies. The growing role of **electronic commerce,** or **e-commerce,** is even changing the way we shop. In e-commerce, people use the Internet to view and order goods and services online.

The Internet has grown and changed in ways that its designers could not anticipate. But what about its effectiveness in its anticipated use: a military situation? In the Gulf War, the U.S. and its allies had a very difficult time knocking out Saddam Hussein's command and control system. After the war's conclusion, military officials learned the reason: Iraq's military was using a TCP/IP-based network—and the network passed its wartime test with flying colors.

LESSONS LEARNED

What's to be learned from the computer's history? Perhaps the most important lesson is an appreciation of the two forces that are currently driving massive changes in our society:

- **Moore's Law** Computers double in power roughly every two years, but cost only half as much.

- **Metcalfe's Law** A network's social and economic value increases steeply as more people connect to it.

These two laws explain why we're witnessing the distribution throughout society of incredibly inexpensive but powerful computing devices, and why the Internet is growing at such an impressive rate. At the same time that computers are rapidly becoming more powerful and less expensive, the rise of global networking is making them more valuable. The combination of these two forces is driving major changes in every facet of our lives.

TAKEAWAY POINTS

- The technology that enables today's computer industry is called electronics. Electronics is concerned with the behavior and effects of electrons as they pass through devices that can restrict their flow in various ways. The vacuum tube was the earliest electronic device.
- The first successful large-scale electronic digital computer, the ENIAC, laid the foundation for the modern computer industry.
- The stored-program concept fostered the computer industry's growth because it enabled customers to change the computer's function easily by running a different program.
- First-generation computers used vacuum tubes and had to be programmed in difficult-to-use machine languages.
- Second-generation computers introduced transistors and high-level programming languages, such as COBOL and FORTRAN.

- Third-generation computers introduced integrated circuits, which cut costs and launched the minicomputer industry. Key innovations included timesharing, wide area networks, and local area networks.
- Fourth-generation computers use microprocessors. Key innovations include personal computers, the graphical user interface, and the growth of massive computer networks.
- An unparalleled public medium for communication and commerce, the Internet has created a massive public computer network of global proportions. It has already penetrated close to 50 percent of U.S. households.
- As computers become more powerful and less expensive, the rise of global networking is making them more valuable. The combination of these two forces is driving major changes in every facet of our lives.

MODULE REVIEW

KEY TERMS AND CONCEPTS

American Standard Code for Information Interchange (ASCII)
artificial intelligence (AI)
automatic
backbone
batch processing
calculator
command-line user interface
compatible computers
electronic commerce or e-commerce
electronics
Electronic Recording Machine Accounting (ERMA)
ENIAC
general-purpose computer
graphical user interface (GUI)

high-level programming languages
host
IBM compatibles, or clones
instruction set
integrated circuit (IC)
Internet protocols, or TCP/IP
large-scale integration (LSI)
local area network (LAN)
machine language
mailing list
medium-scale integration (MSI)
Metcalfe's Law
microprocessor
Moore's Law
open architecture
packet-switching network

packets
proprietary architecture, or closed architecture
semiconductor
small-scale integration (SSI)
solid-state devices
stored-program concept
telecommute
terminals
testbed
timesharing
transistor
user interface
vacuum tubes
very-large-scale integration (VLSI)
wide area network (WAN)

TRUE/FALSE

Indicate whether the following statements are true or false.

1. Today's electronic computers are recent inventions, stemming from work that began during the Korean War.

2. Electronics is the technology that enables today's computer industry.

3. One key advantage of the stored-program concept is that the computer can easily return to a previous instruction and repeat it.

4. Although the stored-program concept made first-generation computers easier to use, they

had to be programmed in machine language, which is composed of the numbers 0 and 1.

5. Power-hungry transistors provided the memory for first-generation computers.

6. A high-level programming language enables programmers to write program instructions using Arabic-sounding commands and Roman numerals.

7. The key event in the third generation was the development of computers based on integrated circuits.

8. The first graphical user interface was developed at Apple Computer.

9. A third-generation innovation was the development of standards for computer networking.

10. The Advanced Research Projects Agency (ARPA), established by the U.S. Congress during the Cold War, played a key role in the Internet's development.

MATCHING

Match each key term from the left column to the most accurate definition in the right column.

_____ 1. calculator

_____ 2. vacuum tube

_____ 3. transistor

_____ 4. stored-program concept

_____ 5. instruction set

_____ 6. timesharing

_____ 7. integrated circuit

_____ 8. microprocessor

_____ 9. Internet protocols

_____ 10. backbone

a. the list of operations a processor is designed to carry out

b. a small, second-generation electronic device that can control the flow of electricity in an electronic circuit

c. a device that contains the entire control unit and arithmetic logic unit of a computer

d. a machine that can perform arithmetic functions

e. the standards that enable the Internet to work

f. a device that incorporates many transistors and electronic circuits on a single chip of silicon

g. the earliest electronic device that powered all electronic devices until the advent of solid-state devices

h. long-distance transmission lines that transfer data over interstate and continental distances

i. enables many people to use a computer simultaneously

j. the idea that the program and data should be stored in memory

MULTIPLE CHOICE

Circle the letter of the correct choice for each of the following.

1. Which of the following was considered the first true programmable digital computer?
   a. UNIVAC
   b. ERMA
   c. ENIAC
   d. Apple II

2. All computers that have been sold commercially have used which of the following?
   a. terminals
   b. transistors
   c. the stored-program concept
   d. vacuum tubes

3. What characterizes first-generation computers?
   a. vacuum tubes and punched cards
   b. magnetic tape and transistors
   c. minicomputers
   d. high-level programming languages

4. What kind of computer can be used for scientific or business purposes?
   a. timesharing computer
   b. general-purpose computer
   c. ENIAC
   d. abacus

5. Which of the following does not apply to high-level programming languages?
   a. They are easier to understand than machine languages.
   b. They are not machine-specific.
   c. They use English-sounding commands.
   d. They are composed entirely of the numbers 0 and 1.

6. What invention enabled developers to create microcomputers?
   a. integrated circuits
   b. transistor
   c. vacuum tube
   d. magnetic disk

7. What are Steve Jobs and Steve Wozniak known for?
   a. the first IBM-compatible computer
   b. UNIVAC
   c. the first Apple computer
   d. the stored-program concept

8. Which of the following is not true of computers as we progress from one generation to the next?
   a. computer size decreases
   b. computer cost decreases
   c. speed of processing increases
   d. memory and storage capacities decrease

9. Which technology describes people using the Internet to view and order goods and services online?
   a. electronic exchange
   b. home shopping network
   c. electronic commerce
   d. telecommuting

10. Which law states that a network's social and economic value increases steeply as more people connect to it?
   a. Moore's Law
   b. Metcalfe's Law
   c. Job's Law
   d. Mauchly's Law

FILL-IN

In the blank provided, write the correct answer for each of the following.

1. Also called a(n) _____ , a solid-state device acts like a vacuum tube, but it is a "sandwich" of differing materials that combine to restrict or control the flow of electrical current in the desired way.

2. With the _____ , the computer program, as well as data, is stored in the computer's memory.

3. UNIVAC is considered to be the first successful _____ .

4. _____ is composed entirely of the numbers 0 and 1.

5. Second-generation computers used _____ instead of vacuum tubes and were faster, smaller, and more reliable.

6. COBOL and FORTRAN are examples of _____ programming languages.

7. The _____ is a character set enabling computers to exchange information.

8. In a(n) _____ architecture, a company uses a secret technique to define how the various computer components connect.

9. With _____ technology, engineers could place the equivalent of more than 5,000 transistors on a single chip.

10. A(n) _____ network works by dividing messages up into small units called _____ .

SHORT ANSWER

On a separate sheet of paper, answer the following questions.

1. Explain why ENIAC is considered the first true programmable digital computer. What kinds of problems did it have?

2. Explain the stored-program concept. How did this concept radically affect the design of computers we use today?

3. What major hardware technology characterized each of the four generations of computers?

4. What are the differences between a command-line interface and a user interface? Which one is easier to use and why?

5. How does a machine language differ from a high-level programming language?

6. What were the various transistor capacities for small-scale, medium-scale, large-scale, and very-large-scale integration?

7. Explain the differences between an open architecture and a proprietary, or closed, architecture.

8. What differentiates the last 10 years of computing technology from the last 60?

9. How did the Cold War contribute to the growth of the Internet revolution?

10. In what ways has the Internet changed the way we work and live?

PFSweb, Inc.

Have you ever purchased music, books, or clothes over the Web? Congratulations! You've participated in e-commerce! "E" what?? E-commerce. The "e" stands for electronic, and "commerce" means business. Doing business online, rather than in a "bricks-and-mortar" store, is what e-commerce is all about. It's taking the traditional buyer-seller relationship and moving it into cyberspace.

Lots of companies are getting into the dance, with hopes that their online stores will generate profits. It's easy for a company to put up a pretty marketing Web site in cyberspace to build their brands and promote their products. But moving it to the next level where customers can actually make purchases is a much trickier dance step. Behind the scenes, the site needs a way to process customer payments, check for fraudulent credit card usage, and get the merchandise shipped from the warehouse without missing a beat. It also needs a way for customers to ask questions—where's the order, how do I return something, and so on.

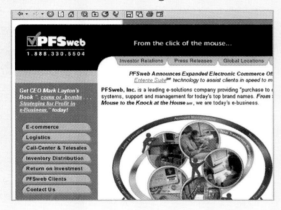

There's a company you've probably never heard of in Plano, Texas that helps e-commerce companies keep in step with the online buying and selling marketplace. It's called PFSWeb, Inc. The company's job is to orchestrate all the pieces that comprise an e-commerce site so that buying or selling is simple and seamless. Mark Layton, president of the company, has helped hundreds of growing e-commerce companies with their online stores by running all the "behind the scenes" tasks. The company can design Web sites, prepare online catalogs, process payments, check for fraud, calculate taxes, ship merchandise, and more for any size e-commerce site. Pretty much the same activities any physical business must manage if it's going to make money. The only difference is that online, all steps in buying are automated. The people at PFSweb have done their job if the buyer can't tell where the marketing Web site ends and the business transaction side begins. In fact, Mark's company has a saying that pretty much says it all: "From the Click of the Mouse, to the Knock at the House." They'll deliver. Now there's a reason to dance!

What do you think? Describe a recent online purchase you've made. Why did you buy online? Were the buying instructions clear? How did you pay for your purchase? Did the actual merchandise meet your expectations? Why? If you had problems or needed to make a return, how easy was it to take care of it?

WebLink Go to **www.prenhall.com/pfaffenberger** to see the video of Mark Layton and explore the Web.

E-COMMERCE IN ACTION

CHAPTER 2

Exploring Computer Hardware: What's in the Box?

Ever wonder how computers actually work? You probably decided that the topic is way too technical. And it is, if you're talking about the technical details. But the overall concepts aren't at all difficult to understand—and what's more, you need to understand them if your goals include computer fluency. A computer-fluent person knows enough about computer hardware to select the appropriate system for a task, and to do so intelligently. To do so, you'll need to know more about the range of technical options that are available for central processing functions, storage, input, and output.

This chapter takes the case off the computer, and walks you through a guided tour of those mysterious-looking innards. As you'll discover, the basic concepts you've already learned (from Module 1A) will help you solve these mysteries to the point that you'll be able to identify the function of just about every one of the computer's components, even the strange-looking internal ones. What's more, you'll gain useful knowledge about the range of technical options available for processors, memory, storage devices, input devices, and output devices—and the next time you pick up a thick catalog of computer components, you'll feel right at home.

M O D U L E S

Inside the System Unit   56

Storing Data: Electronic Filing Cabinets   88

Input and Output: Data In, Information Out   112

MODULE 2A

INSIDE THE SYSTEM UNIT

OUTLINE

WHAT YOU WILL LEARN . . .

When you have finished reading this module, you will be able to:

1. Explain and illustrate the difference between hardware and software.

2. Describe the terminology that's used to describe how much data computers can transfer or store.

3. Describe the various physical connectors on the exterior of the system unit and explain their use.

4. List the components found inside the system unit and explain their use.

5. List the components found on the computer's motherboard, and explain the role they play in the computer's systems functioning.

6. Discuss (in general terms) how a computer's central processing unit (CPU) processes data.

7. Explain the characteristics that determine a microprocessor's performance.

8. List the various types of memory found in a computer system and explain the purpose of each.

9. Explain the purpose of the computer's expansion bus and list the types of expansion buses in common use.

10. Differentiate analog and digital methods of representing data, and explain the advantages and disadvantages of each.

For most users, what's inside the system unit—the big box that contains the processing circuitry and storage devices—is a mystery. Yet a little knowledge of what's inside that box is essential for computer literacy. You should know enough about the system unit's components to make intelligent selections when buying a computer (see Module 10A). And sooner or later, if you own a computer, you'll unscrew the cover to add accessories. How about adding a 3-D sound card, which enables you to listen to three-dimensional surround sound while playing a state-of-the-art computer game? In addition, you may need to make decisions about which computer to choose for given application. To do so wisely, you'll need to understand the fundamentals of computer hardware.

You don't have to be a computer genius to enhance or upgrade your computer, but you do need to know the essentials about what's inside the case.

This module begins your exploration of the world of computer hardware by going from the known to the unknown. You'll start by examining the hardware that's visible on the outside of the computer's case, also called the system unit. Next, you'll take a look under the hood to see what's inside. You'll examine the essential components on the computer's motherboard, its main circuit board, including the most important components of all: the microprocessor (the computer's processing unit) and the memory (the circuits that retain information so that the computer can work with it). Module 2B turns to an examination of storage devices, including disk drives, while Modules 2B and 2C complete your hardware exploration by surveying the world of input and output devices, such as keyboards, mice, and printers.

HARDWARE VS. SOFTWARE

A computer includes both hardware and software. What's the difference between the two? Here's the simplest answer: If you can touch it, it's **hardware.** This term refers to the computer system's physical components. In contrast, you can't touch software. The term **software** refers to the instructions that tell the computer what to do.

An ordinary, printed book illustrates the hardware vs. software distinction. You can touch the pages, cover, and stitching. These are like hardware in a computer system. However, you can't touch the concepts and ideas on the page. These are like software in a computer system. Just as a book isn't very enlightening if it doesn't contain meaningful words, a computer's hardware requires well-written software in order to do something useful.

MACS AND PCS

As you learned in Chapter 1, many different types of computers exist, from tiny handheld computers (such as personal digital assistants) to giant, room-filling mainframe computers. But the world of computing you'll encounter consists almost exclusively of desktop and notebook computers that conform to one of two major standards:

- **IBM-Compatible Personal Computer (PCs)** By far the most numerous, these computers descended directly from the original IBM Personal Computer, first marketed in 1981. The first IBM-compatible PCs, also called **clones,** were created by IBM's competitors, who emphasized that these computers were compatible with the IBM PC. What they meant was that these computers could run all or most of the software developed for IBM PCs. Today, the term **PC** generally

Destinations

Here's the ultimate Web guide to personal computer hardware: PC Guide (**http://www.pcguide. com**). Author Charles Kozierok presents a free, detailed survey of PC system components, including special sections on system care, system enhancement, and troubleshooting. If you're looking to upgrade your system or understand what a particular component does, this site is a great place to start.

Explore IT Lab

Hardware

Although today's PCs and Macs are very much alike, PCs still outsell Macs by a wide margin.

refers to IBM PCs and IBM PC-compatible computers. PCs are powered by processors manufactured by Intel Corporation and other firms that make Intel-compatible processors, such as Advanced Micro Devices (AMD).

- **Apple Macintosh** The Macintosh (called Mac for short) first appeared in 1984, and was the first computer to offer a built-in graphical user interface. A **graphical user interface (GUI)** enables the user to interact with the computer by means of a mouse, on-screen pictures (called **icons**), menus, dialog boxes, and other easy-to-use features. Today's **Power Macintosh** features **PowerPC** processors created by Motorola.

Although PCs and Macs come from differing heritages, they currently resemble each other very closely. PCs now have a graphical user interface, thanks to Microsoft Windows. Macs have incorporated many features made popular by PCs, such as the use of internal expansion slots for easy, inexpensive system upgrades. Still, PCs outsell Macs by a wide margin. Macs account for only 3 percent of annual computer sales worldwide. But these are overall figures. Macs continue to lead in the educational market, traditionally an Apple stronghold, with more than 30 percent of the market in early 2000. Because you will see many Macs as well as PCs while you're at school, this module covers both types of hardware.

DESCRIBING HARDWARE PERFORMANCE

As you've learned, computers perform four basic functions: inputting and representing data, processing this data, displaying the results using output devices, and storing the results for subsequent use. When we're talking about hardware, the following questions frequently come up: how much data? And how fast?

To understand the capabilities of computer hardware, you need to learn some of the terminology that's used to describe how much data computers can transfer or store. Accordingly, this section presents the terminology that is used to describe hardware capabilities.

Bits and Bytes

A basic distinction differentiates *bits* from *bytes:*

- **Bit** A **bit** (short for *binary digit*) is the basic unit of information in a computer. A bit is either a 1 or a 0, the only two options available in the computer's binary numbering system. Bits are the point of reference for measuring the **data transfer rate** (the number of bits transmitted per second) of communication devices, such as modems.

- **Byte** A **byte**—consisting of eight bits—is adequate to store the essential numbers (0–9), the basic letters of the alphabet in English and European languages, and the most common punctuation symbols. For this reason, humans can use the byte as a meaningful baseline for understanding just how much information a computer is storing. For example, a typical college essay contains 250 words per page, and each word contains (on average) 5.5 characters. The page contains about 1,375 characters. In other words, you need about 1,375 bytes of storage for one page of a college paper.

Destinations

Tom's Hardware Guide **(http://www.tomshardware.com)** is a cool place to keep up with the latest PC hardware. For the latest Mac hardware, it's hard to beat Apple's Hardware page **(http://www.apple.com/hardware)**, which covers the newest and hottest Macintosh technologies.

Term equivalent	Abbreviation	Approximate amount	Exact amount	Text
Kilobyte	KB or K	1 thousand bytes	1,024 bytes	
Megabyte	MB or M	1 million bytes	1,048,576 bytes	
Gigabyte	GB or G	1 billion bytes	1,043,741,824 bytes	
Terabyte	TB or T	1 trillion bytes	1,099,511,627,776 bytes	

Figure 2A.1

Terms that describe units of data.

Thousands, Millions, and More

As you've just learned, bits (a 1 or a 0) are commonly used for measuring the data transfer rates of computer communication devices, while bytes are commonly used to measure data storage. But computers fling millions of bits around, and they can store millions of bytes of data. For this reason, terms such as *kilobyte, megabyte, gigabyte,* and *terabyte* are used to describe larger units of data. See Figure 2A.1 for the definition of these terms. Because computer data is stored using binary numbers, a *kilobyte* is not exactly one thousand; nor is a *megabyte* exactly one million. However, the exact amount is close enough that you can think in these rounded, approximate terms (such as one thousand, one million, or one billion) for most purposes.

To describe rapid data transfer rates, terms such as **kilobits per second** (abbreviated **Kbps**), **megabits per second (Mbps),** and **gigabits per second (Gbps)** are used. These rates correspond (roughly) to one thousand, one million, and one billion bits per second. Remember that these terms refer to bits per second, not bytes per second. A modem that can transfer 53 Kbps (about 53,000 bits per second) is transferring only about 8,000 bytes per second, or about 5 pages of text.

INTRODUCING THE SYSTEM UNIT

Now that you've learned the basic concepts and terms you'll need, let's take a look at the system unit. The **system unit** is a box-like case that houses the computer's main hardware components. In desktop computing systems, the system unit generally doesn't contain the keyboard, mouse, monitor, or printer (an exception is the iMac's system unit, which includes the monitor). Notebook computers include all or almost all components within the system unit.

What is the system unit for? It's more than a box. The ideal system unit provides a sturdy frame for mounting internal components, protects these components from physical damage, and keeps them cool. Cool components are happy components; they last longer, and they are less likely to fail. A good case also provides room for system upgrades, such as additional disk drives. Cases come in a variety of styles (see Figure 2A.2). They also vary in their *form factor*. A form factor is a specification for mounting internal components, such as the motherboard.

The following sections explore the system unit of a typical desktop computer, beginning with what's visible from the outside. Next, you'll pop off the

Techtalk

ATX form factor
Refers to the form factor of today's standard PC case. The previous design, called the **AT case,** didn't handle ventilation very well. It drew air in from anywhere, and expelled it by means of a fan mounted on the case's back cover. The result? Dust, dirt, and grime were drawn into the case, coating the components with a nice layer of greasy fuzz, which insulated them from the cooling fan. The ATX case solves this problem. It reverses the fan and adds a filter—which means that clean air is drawn into the case. If you're using a PC with an ATX case, be sure to keep the cover tightly sealed so the fan can do its work.

A notebook computer's system unit contains everything but the printer. A desktop computer's system unit usually doesn't contain the keyboard, mouse, or monitor. An exception is the iMac, in which the monitor is included within the system unit's case.

cover and take a look at what's inside. Later in this module, you'll explore the most important of these internal components, the processor (CPU) and the memory, in more detail.

WHAT'S ON THE OUTSIDE OF THE BOX?

You'll find the following on the outside of a typical desktop computer's system unit: the power switch; receptacles for plugging in keyboards, mice, monitors, and more; and a front panel with various buttons and lights. The following sections examine the system unit components that you can see on the outside of the case.

Power Switch

Usually, the power switch is located in the rear of the computer so you can't hit it by accident. Computers don't handle power losses well. For example, a power outage caused by a service interruption could scramble the data on your hard drive. You should always shut off your computer by following an orderly shutdown procedure. In Microsoft Windows, for example, you click Start and choose Shut Down. In the Macintosh operating system (Mac OS), you click Special and choose Shut Down. If you're using Unix or Linux, you shouldn't shut down the system at all. That's a job for the system administrator.

Connectors

The connectors you'll find on the outside of the case enables you to connect peripherals, such as a printer, a keyboard, or a mouse. A **connector** is a physical receptacle that is designed for a specific type of plug, which fits into the connector (and is sometimes secured by thumbscrews). The plug, in turn, is connected to a cable, which is designed to connect to a peripheral device. Connectors are described as **male** (external pins) or **female** (receptacles for external pins). A **peripheral device** (or just *peripheral* for short) is a device that isn't absolutely essential for the computer's ability to function in the most minimal sense. A computer can function without a printer, for example, but it can't function without memory.

Some of these connectors are found on the back of **expansion cards,** which are plug-in adapters that are pressed into the computer's **expansion slots.** (See "Input/Output (I/O) Buses" later in this chapter for a discussion of expansion cards and expansion slots.) Others are directly mounted on the case's exterior.

Connectors are designed to work with plugs that can be securely fastened to the connector. Usually, this is done by means of screws that are mounted on the plug.

In general, you shouldn't connect anything to a computer while it's running. Some of the newer peripheral connection technologies, such as USB, allow **hot swapping** (connection and disconnection while the computer is running), but it's best to play it safe. If you plug in or unplug most connectors while the computer is running, you will probably cause the computer to crash and you will lose any unsaved work in the computer's memory. To make sure that a cable doesn't come loose accidentally, make sure the plug is securely fastened to the connector.

Figure 2A.3 summarizes the connectors you may find on the computer's case. Most of these connectors are on the back of the case, but sometimes you'll find one or more of them on the front.

People often call these connectors *ports*, but this usage is not necessarily accurate. A **port** is an electronically-defined pathway, called an **interface,** for getting information into and out of the computer. In order to function, a port must be linked to a specific receptacle. This is done by the computer system's startup and configuration software. In the following, the term *port* is used as if it were synonymous with *connector,* in line with everyday usage, but it's important to keep the distinction in mind.

The following briefly discusses the types of connectors found on the exterior of a typical computer system's case.

Serial Port

A **serial port** creates an interface in which data flows in a series of pulses, one after another. Because serial ports do not transmit data rapidly, they are used for devices that do not require fast data transfer rates. One device that uses a serial port is called a *modem,* which is discussed in Module 6A. A modem enables your computer to connect to the telephone line, which does not permit fast data transfer rates.

On IBM-compatible personal computers (PCs), there are four serial ports. They are named COM1, COM2, COM3, and COM4. However, a PC may have only one or two physical connectors for serial devices. In addition, some *expansion boards,* the plug-in adapters to be discussed later in this chapter, contain serial ports that connect directly to the computer's internal wiring.

As you can see from this discussion, it's important to remember that a physical connector isn't the same thing as a port. The port is the interface, not the connector. A given serial port can be linked to a given serial connector, or to an expansion board.

Serial ports conform to one of two international standards. The **RS-232 standard** is commonly used on PCs. The faster **RS-422 standard** is used on Macintoshes. On the exterior of a PC's case, male 9-pin (DB-9) connectors provide access to serial ports, although older PCs may use 25-pin (DB-25) male connectors. Macs provide serial port access by means of a round, 8-pin (DIN-8) female connector.

Parallel Port

A **parallel port** has eight wires. The difference between a serial port and a parallel port is similar to the difference between a one-lane road and a freeway. Unlike a serial port, which can transfer only one unit of information (a *bit*) at a

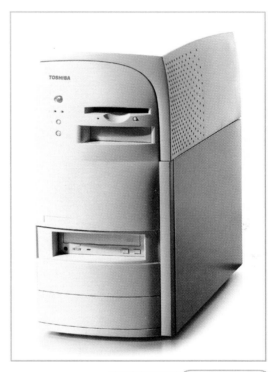

Figure 2A.2

Desktop cases are inconvenient due to their large footprint (the amount of space they take up on a desk's surface). Mini-tower and tower designs offer a smaller footprint, but the smaller ones may provide only limited room for system expansion.

Figure 2A.3

Most of these ports are on the back of the computer's case, but some of them may be in the front.

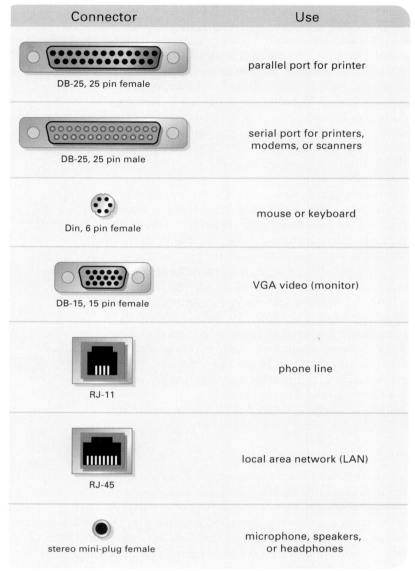

Connector	Use
DB-25, 25 pin female	parallel port for printer
DB-25, 25 pin male	serial port for printers, modems, or scanners
Din, 6 pin female	mouse or keyboard
DB-15, 15 pin female	VGA video (monitor)
RJ-11	phone line
RJ-45	local area network (LAN)
stereo mini-plug female	microphone, speakers, or headphones

Destinations

Beyond Logic (http://www.beyondlogic.com) is crammed with information about PC interfaces, including serial and parallel ports. If you're having trouble getting a serial or parallel device to work, this page offers helpful tips and troubleshooting strategies.

time, parallel ports can transfer eight bits of information simultaneously. As you may have already concluded, parallel ports are much faster than serial ports. They are used for printers, which require high-speed connections. Parallel ports are sometimes called *Centronics ports* (or *Centronics interfaces*) after the printer company, named Centronics, that first defined the parallel interface.

On PCs, access to the parallel port is provided by means of a 25-pin (DB-25) female connector. Older PCs use *Amphenol* connectors, which have distinctive wire clamps on either end of the plug. Macs use a 6-pin (mini-DIN) connector for this purpose.

The newest parallel ports, called **enhanced parallel port (EPP)** and **extended capabilities port (ECP),** offer higher speeds than the traditional. In addition, they enable two-way communication between the printer and computer. If the printer encounters an error, it can send back a detailed message explaining what went wrong and how to fix it.

PS/2 Port

Most of today's PCs hook up mice using a PS/2 port. Named after the early IBM personal computer that introduced it, the **PS/2 port** (also called a *mouse port*) is a type of serial port, but it is electronically differentiated from the serial ports mentioned previously (COM1, COM2, COM3, and COM4). Before the PS/2 port was introduced, mice used one of these standard serial ports. With a PS/2 port available, a mouse with a 6-pin PS/2 connector can use the PS/2 port, leaving the serial ports free for other uses. PS/2 connectors (also called mini-DIN connectors) are round, female connectors. On today's PCs, the PS/2 connector looks exactly the same as the connector used for the keyboard. If these connectors are not labeled, which is often the case, it is easy to plug the keyboard and mouse into the wrong connectors. Although this error will probably not damage the computer, it will prevent it from starting and operating correctly.

On Macintoshes, keyboards and mice connect by means of the *Apple Desktop Bus (ADB)*, which can connect more than one device in a daisy-chain-like series. The ADB connector is a round, female, 4-pin connector.

SCSI Port

Short for Small Computer System Interface, **SCSI** is a type of parallel interface that is found on all Macintosh computers, and increasingly on PCs. Unlike a standard Centronics parallel port, a SCSI port enables users to connect up to eight SCSI-compatible devices, such as printers, scanners, and digital cameras, in a daisy-chain series. The most recent SCSI standard, called SCSI-2, can transfer data at very fast rates.

External connectors for SCSI peripherals vary. Some SCSI adapters have 50- or 68-pin connectors with a click-in locking mechanism for the plug, while others use a standard 50-pin (D50) connector.

Some high-end systems use a SCSI-2 connection, made internally, to hook up the computer's hard disk. (A *high-end system* is a computer priced higher than systems with a typical configuration.) These hard disks offer the best performance.

Universal Serial Bus (USB) Port

Like a SCSI port, a **universal serial bus (USB) port** can connect more than one device at a time—up to 127 of them. In addition, it's possible to connect and disconnect devices without shutting down your computer. This capability is called *hot swapping*. It is a great convenience when you're using devices that you often want to disconnect, such as a digital camera.

An additional advantage of USB is its built-in **Plug and Play (PnP)** support. With Plug and Play, the computer automatically detects the brand, model, and characteristics of the device when you plug it in, and configures the system accordingly.

1394 Port (FireWire)

Closely resembling the universal serial bus (USB) design, the **FireWire port** offers a high-speed connection for dozens of peripheral devices (up to 63 of them). On non-Apple systems, this port is called a **1394 port** after the international standard (IEEE 1394) that defines this port. Like USB, FireWire enables hot swapping and Plug and Play. However, it is more expensive than USB, and is used only for certain high-speed peripherals, such as digital video cameras, that need greater *throughput* (data-transfer capacity) than USB provides.

IrDA Port

Some keyboards, mice, and printers are designed to communicate using an **IrDA port.** (IrDA is an abbreviation of the Infrared Data Association, which created the IrDA standard.) IrDA ports use infrared signals. This method is also used by television remote controls. No physical connection is required, but the transmitter must be in the direct line of sight with the receiver, a transparent panel mounted on the computer's surface.

Monitor Connector

Most computers use a **video adapter** (also called a **video card**) to generate the output that is displayed on the computer's screen. On the back of the adapter, you'll find a standard **VGA connector,** a 15-pin male connector that is designed to work with standard monitor cables.

Some computers have the video circuitry built into the motherboard. This type of video circuitry is called **on-board video.** On such systems, the video connector is found on the back of the case.

Additional Ports and Connectors

You may find the following additional ports and connectors on the exterior of a computer's case or one of the computer's expansion cards:

- **Telephone connector**   Provided with modems, this connector (called RJ-11) is a standard modular telephone jack that will work with an ordinary telephone cord.

- **Network connector**   Provided with networking adapters, this connector (called RJ-45) looks like a standard telephone jack, but it's bigger.

- **PC card slots**   On notebook computers, one or more PC Card slots are provided for plugging in PC Cards. A **PC Card** is a credit-card-sized adapter that provides notebook users with modems, networking, and additional functions. Like USB devices, PC Cards can be inserted or removed while the computer is running.

- **Sound card connectors**   PCs equipped with a **sound card** (an adapter that provides stereo sound and sound synthesis), as well as Macs with built-in sound, offer two or more sound connectors. These connectors, also called *jacks*, accept the same stereo mini-plug used by portable CD players. Most sound cards provide four connectors: Mic (microphone input), Line In (accepts output from other audio devices), Line Out (sends output to other audio devices), and Speaker (sends output to external speakers).

- **TV/sound capture board connectors**   If the computer is equipped with TV and video capabilities, you will see additional connectors that look like those found on a television monitor. These include a connector for a coaxial cable, which can be connected to a video camera or cable TV system.

Front Panel

On most computers, you'll find a *reset switch* (which enables you to restart your computer in the event of a failure), a *drive activity light* (a light that tells when your hard disk is accessing data), and a *power-on light* (a light that tells you whether the power is on). You may also find a *keylock* that enables you to prevent others from operating the machine. Do not press the reset switch unless you are certain that your computer is no longer operating. If you have any unsaved work, you will lose it.

Inside the System Unit

Let's have a look inside the case—but please, don't open up one of your school's computers! If you'd like to peek inside your own desktop computer's case, bear in mind that the computer's components are sensitive to static electricity. If you touch certain components while you're charged with static, you could destroy them! Always disconnect the power cord before

Techtalk

PCMCIA
Short for *Personal Computer Memory Card International Association,* PCMCIA refers to the input/output (I/O) bus design that this organization invented. Developed for notebook computers, PCMCIA provides one or more slots for credit-card-sized adapters, such as modems and networking cards. Originally, these cards were called PCMCIA cards—but just try pronouncing that phrase! Today, PCMCIA cards are simply called PC Cards.

removing a computer's case, and discharge static electricity by touching something that's well grounded, such as a water faucet. If it's one of those dry days when you're getting shocked every time you touch a door knob, don't mess with your computer's innards.

Once you've got the cover off (see Figure 2A.4), you'll see the following components:

- **Motherboard** (also called *main board*)   The **motherboard** is a large *printed circuit board (PCB)*, a flat piece of plastic or fiberglass that contains thousands of electrical circuits. These circuits are etched into the board's surface. They connect numerous plug-in receptacles, which accommodate the computer's most important components (such as the microprocessor). In the next section, you'll take a closer look at the motherboard.

- **Power supply**   A computer's **power supply** transforms the alternating current (AC) available from standard wall outlets into the direct current (DC) needed for the computer's operation. It also steps the voltage down to the low voltage required by the motherboard. Power supplies are rated according to their peak output in watts. A 250 watt power supply is adequate for most desktop systems, but 300 watts provides a margin of safety if you plan to add many additional components.

- **Cooling fan**   The computer's components can be damaged if heat accumulates within the system unit. Fans are used to keep the system unit cool. Often, the fan is part of the power supply. Some systems include *auxiliary fans*. An auxiliary fan provides additional cooling for high-powered systems.

- **Speaker**   The computer's internal speaker isn't designed for high-fidelity reproduction. It's useful only for the beeps you hear when the computer encounters an error. To produce good sound from a PC, you need to upgrade the system with sound components (including a sound card and speakers). Macintoshes come with built-in stereo sound.

- **Drive bays**   These are designed to accommodate the computer's disk drives, such as the hard disk drive, floppy disk drive, and CD-ROM or DVD-ROM drive. **External drive bays** mount drives so that they are accessible from the outside (a necessity if you need to insert and remove disks from the drive). **Internal drive bays** do not enable outside access. They are used for hard disks, in which the disk is permanently contained within the drive's case. Bays also vary by their size. Some bays are designed to accommodate 5.25-inch drives, while others are designed for 3.5-inch drives.

Figure   2A.4

Inside the system unit, you'll find the motherboard, power supply, cooling fan, speaker, internal drive bays, and external drive bays.

WHAT'S ON THE MOTHERBOARD?

As you've just learned, the motherboard provides both the physical and the electrical setting for the computer's most important components. Most of these components are integrated circuits. An **integrated circuit (IC),** also called a *chip*, can emulate thousands or millions of transistors. A **transistor** is an electronic switching device. Much of what a computer does boils down to using these switches to route data in different ways, according to the software's instructions. Housed in black plastic boxes, most chips are designed so that their pins fit into specially-designed receptacles on the

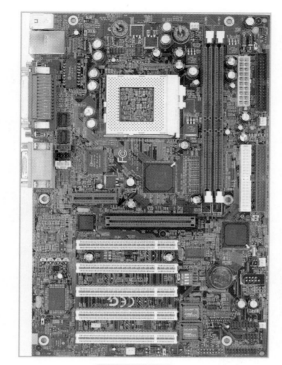

Figure 2A.5

A typical PC motherboard.

motherboard's surface. However, some chips may be soldered directly to the motherboard.

So what do these chips do? Take a look at a typical PC motherboard (see Figure 2A.5). The following section examines the most important components that you'll see on the motherboard.

System Clock

Within the computer, events happen at a pace controlled by a tiny electronic "drummer," called the **system clock.** This component is an electronic circuit that generates pulses at a rapid rate, measured in millions of cycles per second (MHz). A given processor's clock rate is called its **clock speed,** and a single beat of the clock is called a **clock tick.** Note that the system clock doesn't have anything to do with keeping the time and date (in most computers, there's another circuit that handles this job); the system clock synchronizes the computer's internal activities.

The Microprocessor

A **microprocessor** contains almost all of a computer's **central processing unit (CPU)** on a single chip, one that's smaller than the average postage stamp. The CPU interprets the instructions given to it by software, and carries out these instructions by processing data and controlling the rest of the computer's components. No other single element of a computer determines its overall performance as much as the CPU.

In the following section, you'll learn more about microprocessors, including the essentials of how they work. Although microprocessors are complex devices, the underlying ideas are easy to understand. Any computer-literate person should understand these ideas, because they help to explain what computers can do (and what they cannot do). In addition, you need to know enough about microprocessors to understand the capabilities and limitations of a given computer system.

Processor Slots and Sockets

An integrated circuit (IC) of fabulous complexity, a microprocessor is designed to plug into a motherboard in much the same way that other ICs do. However, motherboard designers have created special slots and sockets to accommodate microprocessors. Part of the reason is simply that microprocessors are larger and have more pins than most other chips. In addition, microprocessors also generate so much heat that they could destroy themselves or other system components. The microprocessor is generally covered by a **heat sink,** which drains heat away from the chip. To accomplish this, the heat sink may contain a small auxiliary cooling fan. The latest, high-end microprocessors include their own built-in refrigeration systems, which are needed to keep these speedy processors cool.

Older PCs use a **processor socket** to provide the microprocessor the electrical connections it needs. On older PC motherboards, the socket is positioned on the motherboard itself. To enable easy insertion of the processor, these receptacles offer **zero insertion force (ZIF),** in which a lever is used to tighten the pins in place. Today's PC motherboards provide a slot for a **daughterboard,** a small circuit board that contains the microprocessor and additional components (see Figure 2A.6).

Instruction Set

Every processor can perform a fixed set of operations, such as getting a character from the computer's memory or comparing two numbers to see which is larger. Each of these operations has its own unique number, called an **instruction.** A processor's list of instructions is called an **instruction set.** Different processors have different instruction sets. That's the reason a program must be developed with a particular processor in mind.

Control Unit

CPUs contain two subcomponents, the **control unit** and the **arithmetic-logic unit (ALU).** The control unit coordinates and controls all the other parts of the computer system. Under the direction of a program, the control unit manages four basic operations (see Figure 2A.7):

■ **Fetch**   Getting the next program instruction from the computer's memory.

■ **Decode**   Figuring out what the program is telling the computer to do.

■ **Execute**   Performing the requested action, such as adding two numbers or deciding whether one of them is larger.

■ **Write-back**   Writing the results to an internal register (a temporary storage location) or to memory.

This four-step process is called a **machine cycle,** or a **processing cycle,** and consists of two phases: the **instruction cycle** (fetch and decode) and the **execution cycle** (execute and write-back). Today's microprocessors can go through this entire four-step process millions of times per second. Typically, a machine cycle requires more than one tick of the system clock. Some instructions take many clock ticks to execute.

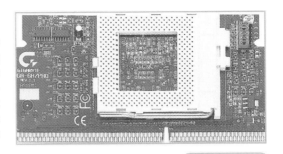

Figure 2A.6

Today's microprocessors are mounted on daughterboards, such as this Single Edge Contact (SEC) package. The SEC package fits into a specially-designed slot on the motherboard's surface.

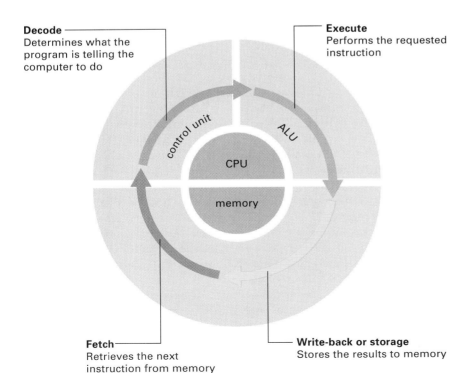

Decode
Determines what the program is telling the computer to do

Execute
Performs the requested instruction

Fetch
Retrieves the next instruction from memory

Write-back or storage
Stores the results to memory

Figure 2A.7

The control unit manages four basic operations.

Arithmetic-Logic Unit (ALU)

The arithmetic-logic unit (ALU), as its name implies, can perform arithmetic or logical operations. **Arithmetic operations** include the usual grade school calculations, including addition, subtraction, multiplication, and division. **Logical operations** involve comparing two data items to see which one is larger or smaller.

Registers

Some operations require the control unit to store data temporarily. **Registers** are temporary storage locations in the CPU that are designed for this purpose.

Compatibility

Because each processor has a unique instruction set—the list of all the instructions that a given CPU can execute—programs devised for one computer will not run on another (with two exceptions, discussed shortly). Programs must be written using instructions recognized by that CPU. For example, a program written for the Apple Macintosh will not run on an IBM PC. A program that can run on a given computer is **compatible** with that computer's processor. Alternatively, it's said that a given program is a **native application** for a given CPU design.

Microprocessor manufacturers must carefully consider compatibility when introducing new models. In particular, manufacturers must decide whether to make the new chip downwardly compatible with previous models. A **downwardly compatible** chip can run the programs designed to run with earlier chips. To introduce a microprocessor that is not downwardly compatible with previous models is risky. People may not buy a computer that cannot run the programs they already own. Manufacturers learned this lesson with early mainframe computers.

Data Bus Width and Word Size

What determines a given microprocessor's performance? The first element is its data bus width, which is measured in bits (8, 16, 32, or 64). The **data bus,** a highway of parallel wires, connects the internal components of the microprocessor. The bus is a pathway for the electronic impulses that form bytes. The more lanes this highway has, the faster data can travel.

The width of a CPU's data bus partly determines the maximum number of bits the CPU can process at once (its **word size**). Data bus width also affects the CPU's overall speed, because a CPU with a 32-bit data bus can shuffle data around twice as fast as a CPU with a 16-bit data bus. But other factors play a role in determining a CPU's word size, such as the width of internal *registers* (temporary storage locations for intermediate processing steps). The terms *8-bit CPU, 16-bit CPU, 32-bit CPU,* and *64-bit CPU* are used to sum up the maximum number of bits a given CPU can handle at a time. A Pentium III is a 32-bit CPU, despite the fact that it has a 64-bit data bus. Overall, a Pentium III can handle only 32 bits at a time, but certain internal operations can involve transfers of 64-bit chunks.

A CPU's word size is important because it determines which operating systems the CPU can use. An Intel 8088 is limited to 8-bit operating systems, which—like CPUs with 8-bit word lengths—can work with only 8 bits at a time. Table 2A.1 lists the word length requirements of past, current, and future operating systems.

Word Length Requirements of Popular Operating Systems for Intel Processors	
Operating System	**Required Word Length**
CP/M	8
MS-DOS	8
Windows 3.1	16
Windows 95/98/NT/2000	32
Linux	32
64-bit Linux	64

Table   2A.1

Today's personal computer market is dominated by 32-bit CPUs and 32-bit operating systems. However, 64-bit CPUs and 64-bit operating systems are currently in use in high-end, high-capacity server systems. Intel's 64-bit Itanium processor, introduced in late 2000, brings 64-bit computing to the personal computer market for the first time. 64-bit versions of popular operating systems, such as Linux and Microsoft Windows, are under development.

Destinations

Get the latest info on new processors at Future Technology's CPU site (**http://cpusite. examedia.al/**).

Operations per Cycle

The number of operations per clock tick (one pulse of the system clock) also affects performance. You might think that a CPU can't perform more than one instruction per clock tick, but thanks to new technologies, that's not true. Any CPU that can execute more than one instruction per clock cycle is referred to as *superscalar,* and its design is called a **superscalar architecture.** Today's fastest CPUs, such as the Pentium II, use superscalar architectures. One of the design tricks that makes superscalar architectures possible is called **pipelining,** a processing technique that feeds a new instruction into the CPU at every step of the processing cycle so that four or more instructions are worked on simultaneously (see Figure 2A.8).

Pipelining resembles an auto assembly line, in which more than one car is being worked on at once. Before the first instruction is finished, the next

Machine cycle (without pipelining)

fetch	decode	execute	store
			instruction 1

Machine cycle (with pipelining)

fetch	decode	execute	store
			instruction 1
		instruction 2	
	instruction 3		
instruction 4			

Figure   2A.8

Pipelining.

Figure 2A.9

Parallel processing computers have many processors running simultaneously.

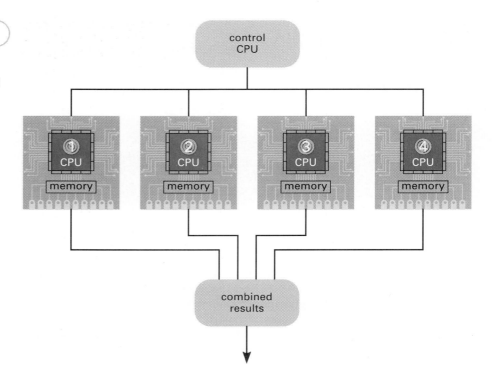

one is started. But what if the CPU needs the results of a completed instruction to process the next one? This problem is called *data dependency*. It can cause a *pipeline stall*, in which the assembly line is held up until the results are known. To cope with this problem, advanced CPUs use techniques called *speculative execution*, in which the processor executes and temporarily stores the next instruction anyway in case it proves useful, and *branch prediction*, in which the processor tries to predict what will likely happen (with a surprisingly high degree of accuracy).

Another way to improve CPU performance doesn't involve making CPUs faster. It involves using more than one of them at the same time. A **parallel processing** computer has many processors running simultaneously, in parallel (see Figure 2A.9). Parallel processing computers come in different sizes and designs.

CISC and RISC

Another aspect of microprocessor design that you should be aware of is the distinction between CISC and RISC. Each has advantages and disadvantages.

CISC stands for **complex instruction set computer (CISC).** A CISC chip, such as the Motorola 68040 or the Intel Pentium, provides programmers with many instructions, and the processing circuitry includes many special-purpose circuits that carry out these instructions at high speeds. Because the chip provides so many processing tools, CISC designs make the programmer's job easier. CISC chips, however, are complex and expensive to produce, and they run hot because they consume so much current.

RISC stands for **reduced instruction set computer (RISC).** A RISC chip offers a bare-bones instruction set. For this reason, RISC chips are less complex, less expensive to produce, and more efficient in power usage. The drawback of the RISC design is that the computer must combine or repeat operations to complete many processing operations. (For example, you can eliminate multiplication circuitry by repeated addition.) RISC chips also place extra demands on programmers, who must consider how to get com-

SPOTLIGHT

THE MAKING OF A MICROPROCESSOR

▶It seems like every time you turn around, some chip manufacturer is bringing out a new version of a CPU. Gordon Moore, one of the founders of Intel, coined a now-famous law that states the number of circuits on a CPU doubles every 18 to 24 months. Moore's Law has certainly proven true in the past 25 years.

The modern CPU is indeed a marvel. So, how are these marvels of modern electronics developed and brought to market? A modern CPU starts its life in a research lab, where engineers use complex software to help design the integrated circuits that make up the microprocessor. Research can take several years to get to the point where the manufacturer can begin to contemplate production. During that time, extensive testing is performed to make sure that the circuits envisioned for the chip are as foolproof as possible. The circuits are also improved so that they can be reduced in size as much as possible. (This is how the latest CPUs can cram over seven million circuits into an area about as large as your thumbnail.)

The building blocks of a CPU are composed of silicon. The pattern for the circuits is printed on the surface of large silicon wafers measuring about eight inches in diameter. The wafers are then exposed to different photosensitive chemical compounds that etch the circuits into the silicon.

The electronic pathways, or traces, are quite small. Very-large-scale integration (VLSI) and ultra-large-scale integration (ULSI) techniques have allowed chipmakers to create traces that are about .35 microns in width. (A millimeter contains 1,000 microns; an inch contains approximately 25,400 microns.) Many chipmakers are starting to produce chips using .25 micron traces, and widths of .18 and .13 microns are envisioned for the future.

Because chipmakers are working with materials at an extremely-high precision, any impurity in the silicon wafer or the etching process can ruin a CPU. This is understandable when a speck of pollen can be 10 microns in diameter, which is approximately 30 or 40 times the size of the surface traces on the silicon wafer. To help ensure purity, CPUs are manufactured in labs that are the cleanest places on earth. Dust, pollen, smoke, and other impurities are removed from the air. Workers must perform their jobs in special suits that stop them from polluting the environment through the normal shedding of hair and skin cells, not to mention impurities in the air they exhale. The huge demand for purity, compactness, and complexity means that CPU development is an expensive business. The current cost for building a plant to produce 40,000 chips per month is close to two billion dollars.

When the imprinting and etching process is complete, the silicon wafers are sliced up into properly-sized CPU chips. Testing is then performed to ensure that all the circuits are functioning as expected. If any malfunction is detected, the chip is destroyed. It is not unusual, particularly when developing a new CPU, for the chip yield from a large silicon wafer to be small. Because the manufacturing process is expensive, a low yield means that the cost of the final CPUs can be high. As the manufacturing process is perfected and yield is increased, the cost of the CPUs often goes down.

As new technology is developed and the demands we place on that technology increase, the Herculean task faced by chipmakers will only continue to increase. We hope manufacturers will be able to meet the challenge and produce more electronic marvels.

The modern CPU is a marvel of electronic technology.

Table 2A.2

The Continuing Evolution of Intel Microprocessors				
Year	Chip	Word Size	Clock Speed	Transistors
1971	4004	4 bits	740 KHz	2,300
1974	8080	8 bits	2 MHz	6,000
1979	8088	8 bits	Up to 8 MHz	29,000
1982	80286	16 bits	Up to 12 MHz	134,000
1985	80386	32 bits	Up to 33 MHz	275,000
1989	Intel 486	32 bits	Up to 100 MHz	1.6 million
1993	Pentium (original)	32 bits	Up to 200 MHz	3.3 million
1995	Pentium Pro	32 bits	200 MHz and higher	5.5 million
1997	Pentium MMX	32 bits	233 MHz and higher	4.5 million
1998	Pentium II	32 bits	233 MHz and higher	7.5 million
1998	Xeon	32 bits	400 MHz and higher	7.5 million
1998	Celeron	32 bits	400 MHz and higher	7.5 million– 19 million
2000	Pentium III	32 bits	450 MHz and higher	9.5 million– 28.1 million
2000	Pentium 4	32 bits	1.4 GHz and higher	34 million
2000	Itanium	64 bits	800 MHz and higher	25 million

plex results by combining simple instructions. But careful tests show that this design results in faster processing than the CISC chips.

Even so, the distinction between CISC and RISC is becoming less meaningful. The earliest CISC processors included what were then advanced design features, such as superscalar architecture, pipelining, and branch prediction. But RISC processors now include these, and their performance has improved. In the meantime, RISC manufacturers are finding that they must include some CISC design components to ensure compatibility. Today, the leading CISC processor (Motorola PowerPC) and RISC processor (Intel Pentium II) are virtually indistinguishable in terms of instruction set size.

Math Coprocessors

For applications requiring intensive computation, such as spreadsheets, system performance can be enhanced by including a **floating-point unit (FPU),** also called a **math coprocessor.** An FPU enables computers to perform floating-point (math) operations more quickly. Until recently, math coprocessors were separate chips that could be added to a computer system as an option. Increasingly, math coprocessing circuitry is included in the microprocessor design.

Popular Microprocessors

The most commonly-used microprocessors are those in IBM PC compatibles and Macintoshes. In general, the chips powering PCs are made by Intel Corporation, although Advanced Micro Devices (AMD), Cyrix Corporation, and other firms make Intel-compatible chips. Table 2A.2 shows how Intel microprocessors have improved since the days of the first PC.

The IBM PC, introduced in 1981, used the Intel 8088, a 16-bit processor running initially at 4.77 MHz. A major limitation of this processor was its maximum memory size of 1MB. Another major limitation was that programs could directly access the computer's memory. If you tried to run more than one program at a time, one of the programs might overwrite the other one's portion of memory, causing a crash.

To deal with this problem, Intel introduced the 80286, which had two modes. The first mode, called *real mode*, emulated the 8088. The second mode, called *protected mode*, introduced two major technical improvements. In protected mode, programs could use up to a gigabyte of RAM. Also, the processor gave programs a certain section of memory and prevented other programs from trying to use this section. This allocation reduced the number of system failures when users tried to run more than one program. The 80286 was followed by the 80386, also called the 386, Intel's first 32-bit microprocessor.

The IBM PC's operating system, MS-DOS, runs in real mode and cannot take advantage of the benefits of protected mode. The reason for the popularity of Microsoft Windows lies in its capability to switch the 80386 and later processors into protected mode, enabling users to make full use of more than 640KB of memory and providing protection for **multitasking,** in which the processor runs more than one program at once by switching among them. You'll learn more about Windows in Module 3A.

By the time the 80486 came along, several manufacturers had created clones of Intel processors, and a court ruled that Intel could not protect the 80×86 nomenclature. So the 80486 came to be called the Intel 486. In 1993, Intel released the first Pentium microprocessors, which used a 64-bit data bus. Pentium is derived from the Latin word for five. (This chip would have been called the 80586 if Intel had stuck to the old numbering system.) The Pentium chip was followed by the Pentium Pro, an advanced Pentium design intended for use in servers and engineering workstations. In 1997, the **Pentium MMX** was introduced, containing a new set of 57 multimedia instructions. These instructions enabled Pentium MMX-based systems to run games and multimedia applications more quickly (see Figure 2A.10).

The year 1998 saw the first of a series of Pentium II processors, which incorporated the Pentium Pro's advanced design as well as MMX graphics and the games circuitry of earlier chips. A low-priced version of the Pentium II, called Celeron, reduced costs by cutting down on the amount of secondary cache. An advanced version of the Pentium II, the Xeon, was designed for professional applications. In 1999, Intel released the Pentium III (shown in Figure 2A.11), an upgraded version of the Pentium II with clock speeds of up to 1000 MHz (1 gigahertz). However, Intel's main competitor, Advanced Micro Devices (AMD), beat Intel to the 1-gigahertz mark with the company's Athlon processor (see Figure 2A.12).

Providing the CPU for Macintoshes over the years are chips made by Motorola Corporation. They fall into two processor families: the 68000 series (68000 to 68040) and the PowerPC family. PowerPC microprocessors are RISC chips that run earlier Macintosh software by emulating the earlier

Techtalk

overclock
To configure a computer system so that it runs a processor faster than it is designed to run. Some processors can run faster than the manufacturer's rated clock speed. However, overclocking can make your system unstable. At the extreme, it could destroy the processor, leaving your computer useless.

Figure 2A.10

The Pentium MMX.

Figure 2A.11

The Pentium III. In 2000, Intel released the Pentium 4.

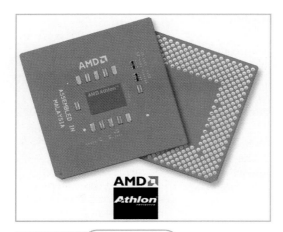

Figure 2A.12

Advanced Micro Devices (AMD) beat Intel to the market with the first 1 gigahertz processor.

Destinations

Want the latest info on the hottest and fastest processors? Take a look at the aptly-named Chip Geek **(http://www.ugeek.com/ procspec/procmain.thm)**. You'll find the latest news on new, super-fast processors, including performance comparisons, reviews, and tips on putting together the ultimate high-speed system.

processor's characteristics. Table 2A.3 shows how these processors have improved since the first ones appeared in 1979. Note that Apple Computer gives its own name to the PowerPC chips: Motorola's 750 is the same thing as Apple's G3, while Motorola's 7400 becomes the G4 in Apple's marketing.

Benchmarks

As the previous discussion suggests, two 200-MHz processors made by different manufacturers may turn out to perform very differently, depending on variations in bus width and architecture. To provide some basis for comparison, **benchmarks** have been developed. A benchmark is a test that puts a processor through a series of operations to provide a basis for comparison. The idea sounds good, but a variety of benchmarks are available, and some do a better job than others of measuring the real-world conditions that a processor is likely to encounter. Another problem is that benchmarks don't only test the CPU, but may react to other system components.

Among the available benchmarks, those supplied by the Standard Performance Evaluation Corporation (SPEC) are respected in the industry. The SPEC95 benchmark consists of two tests: an integer test (which tests the CPU's performance when dealing with character data) and a floating-point test (which tests the CPU's mathematical performance).

Which is faster, the Motorola G3 processor that powers many Macintoshes or the Pentium II found in comparable PCs? At a given clock speed, the G3—a RISC processor—performs somewhat better on the SPEC95 benchmarks. (The 266-MHz G3 scores 12.4 to the comparably-clocked Pentium II's 10.8, and the spread is similar on the floating-point tests.) To get a PC that performs as well as a G3-powered Macintosh, you will need a higher clock speed.

Although benchmark tests provide information about processor performance, they may fail to describe a computer system's overall performance accurately. Real-world benchmark tests measure a system's overall performance in running complex applications.

Table 2A.3

The Continuing Evolution of Motorola Microprocessors				
Year	Chip	Bus Width	Clock Speed	Transistors
1979	68000	16 bits	8 MHz	68,000
1984	68020	32 bits	16 MHz	136,000
1986	68030	32 bits	Up to 40 MHz	272,000
1988	68040	32 bits	Up to 40 MHz	888,000
1993	PowerPC 601	64 bits	Up to 120 MHz	2.8 million
1994	PowerPC 603	64 bits	Up to 160 MHz	1.6 million
1995	PowerPC 603e	64 bits	Up to 300 MHz	2.6 million
1995	PowerPC 604e	64 bits	Up to 300 MHz	3.6 million
1998	PowerPC 750 (G3)	64 bits	200 MHz and higher	6.35 million
2000	PowerPC 7400 (G4)	64 bits	400 MHz and higher	10.5 million

Memory

Another important motherboard component is the computer's **memory,** a general term for any device that enables the computer to retain information. As you will see in this section, the computer's motherboard contains several different types of memory, each optimized for its intended use.

Volatile vs. Nonvolatile Memory

Every computer has several types of memory. They fall into two categories, **volatile memory** and **nonvolatile memory.** In volatile memory, the memory's contents are erased when the computer's power is switched off. This is obviously a disadvantage. However, volatile memory technologies provide much higher data transfer rates. Nonvolatile memory, in contrast, retains information even when the power is switched off.

ROM (Read-Only Memory)

If everything in random-access memory (RAM) is erased when the power is turned off, how does the computer start again? The answer is **read-only memory (ROM).** The instructions to start the computer are stored in read-only memory chips, which are nonvolatile. (They don't lose their contents when the power is switched off.) To allow ROM upgrades, most computers use **flash memory,** also called **flash BIOS.** The use of flash memory enables the ROM to be upgraded. If the computer manufacturer finds an error in the ROM code, he can obtain an upgrade disk that writes the revised code to the flash memory circuit.

In PCs, ROM is used to store the computer's **basic input/output system (BIOS).** When you start your computer (also called **booting** your computer), BIOS executes a **boot sequence.** In the boot sequence, the BIOS conducts various **power-on self-tests (POST),** including memory tests; configuring and starting the video circuitry, configuring the system's hardware, and locating the disk drive containing the **boot sector.** The boot sector contains the computer's **operating system (OS),** the software that controls the computer's basic functions. Similar software performs the same functions on Macintosh systems.

PCs enable users to access a **setup program** during the boot sequence. Typically, you start the setup program by pressing the Del key, although some computers use different keys for this purpose. The setup program enables you to configure your system settings, including the type and number of disk drives attached to the system, the number of physical connectors available for serial ports, and the location of the disk drive containing the boot sector. You should not attempt to change any of these settings; if you choose the wrong setting, your computer may not work.

CMOS

The settings you choose in the BIOS setup program are stored in a special type of memory referred to as the **complementary metal-oxide semiconductor (CMOS).** CMOS is a special type of memory used to store essential startup configuration options, such as the amount of memory that has been installed in the computer. CMOS chips also track the time and date. Unlike ROM, CMOS is volatile. Although it requires battery power, CMOS has the advantage of drawing very little power, meaning the battery should last for years. A common cause of system errors in older computers is a failed battery. If you see a dead battery warning when you start the computer, or if your system suddenly loses the correct time and date, take your computer to a technician. On Macintoshes, this type of memory is called *parameter RAM*.

Destinations

Need help comparing microprocessor performance? Take a look at the Processor Buyer's Guide at **http://www.buybuddy. com.** You'll find up-to-date information on the latest processors, as well as tips on how to compare them meaningfully.

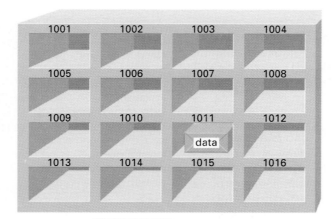

1001	1002	1003	1004
1005	1006	1007	1008
1009	1010	1011	1012
1013	1014	1015	1016

Figure 2A.13

In random-access memory, each memory location has an address, just like a post office box. Using this address, called a memory address, the processor can store and retrieve data by going directly to a single location in memory.

 Destinations

Want to know more about RAM? Kingston Technology's Ultimate Memory Guide **(http://www.kingston. com/tools/umb/default. asp)** thoroughly explains how memory works, what memory technologies are available, and how to select the best RAM chips for your computer system.

 Techtalk

PC 100 SDRAM

A type of SDRAM that is capable of keeping up with the latest and fastest motherboards, which have bus speeds of 100 MHz.

RAM (Random-Access Memory)

The large memory modules housed on the computer's motherboard contain the computer's **random-access memory (RAM).** A volatile memory technology, RAM stores information temporarily so that it's directly and speedily available to the microprocessor. This information includes software as well as the data to be processed by the software. RAM is designed for fast operation because the processor acts directly on the information stored in RAM.

Why is it called *random-access* memory? The term *random-access* doesn't imply that the memory stores data randomly! A better term would be *direct-access*. In random-access memory, each memory location has an address, just like a post office box. Using this address, called a **memory address,** the processor can store and retrieve data by going directly to a single location in memory (see Figure 2A.13).

Of the various types of RAM available, today's computers use a type of RAM called **dynamic RAM** (also called **DRAM**). DRAM (pronounced "dee-RAM") must be energized constantly or it loses its contents. Most new computers contain a faster, improved type of DRAM called **synchronous DRAM** (also called **SDRAM**). SDRAM's operations are very fast because they are synchronized to the pulses of the computer's system clock.

DRAM and SDRAM are typically packaged in two different types of modules, **single inline memory modules (SIMM)** and **dual inline memory modules (DIMM).** SIMMs pack memory chips into modules with 30- or 72-pin connectors. Some SIMMs have connectors on both edges, but they are the same. SIMMs are available in 1MB, 4MB, 16MB, and 32MB versions. DIMMs have 168-pin connectors, which are different on each edge of the package. DIMMs are newer and are available in larger sizes (8MB, 16 MB, 32 MB, and 64 MB), reflecting the heftier memory demands of today's computers.

How much RAM does a computer need? In general, the more memory, the better. For today's Microsoft Windows, Linux, and Macintosh applications, 16MB of RAM is a practical working minimum, but the computer will not run well with so little memory. That's because all these operating systems use **virtual memory.** In virtual memory, the computer can use the hard disk as an extension of RAM. It does this when RAM gets full (which can easily happen if you run two or more programs at once). As you have just learned, disk drives are much slower than RAM. When virtual memory kicks in, the computer slows down to a frustratingly slow pace. To avoid using virtual memory, you're better off with 32MB of RAM, and increasingly, systems are sold with 64MB or even 128MB of RAM.

Cache Memory

RAM is fast, but it isn't fast enough to support the processing speeds of today's super-fast microprocessors, such as the Motorola G3 or Pentium II. To enable these microprocessors to function at maximum speed, computer designers use **cache memory.** (The term cache is pronounced "cash.") Cache memory is much faster than RAM, but it's also more expensive. Although generally no larger than 512KB, cache memory greatly improves the computer system's overall performance. The processor can use the cache to store frequently-accessed program instructions and data.

Two types of cache memory are available. The first type, called **primary cache,** is included in the microprocessor chip. The second type,

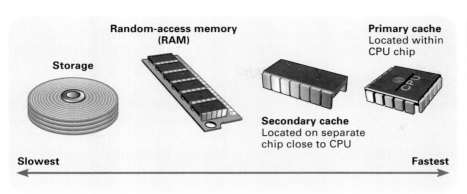

Storage — Random-access memory (RAM) — Secondary cache Located on separate chip close to CPU — Primary cache Located within CPU chip

Slowest ← → Fastest

Figure 2A.14

Primary cache is included in the microprocessor chip. Secondary cache is included on a separate printed circuit board. By keeping the secondary cache as close as possible to the processor, performance improves.

called **secondary cache,** or **level 2 (L2) cache,** is included on a separate printed circuit board. To improve secondary cache performance, the latest microprocessors are provided in plastic modules that contain a special type of secondary cache, called *backside cache.* By keeping the secondary cache as close as possible to the processor, performance improves (see Figure 2A.14).

Chipset

The **chipset** is a collection of chips that are designed to work together (that's why they're called a "set"). They provide the switching circuitry that the microprocessor needs in order to move data to and from the rest of the computer. One of the jobs handled by the chipset involves linking the microprocessor to the computer's input/output (I/O) buses.

Input/Output (I/O) Buses

An **input/output (I/O) bus** extends the computer's internal data pathways beyond the boundaries of the microprocessor, so that the microprocessor can communicate with input and output devices. Typically, an I/O bus contains **expansion slots,** which are designed to accommodate **expansion cards** (also called *expansion boards, adapter cards,* or *adapters*). An expansion card is a printed circuit board that's designed to fit into an expansion bus's receptacles.

Today's PCs and Macs use the **Personal Computer Interface (PCI) bus,** which supports the Plug and Play (PnP) system. With PnP, the computer detects a new card and configures the system automatically. Many motherboards still contain an **Industry Standard Architecture (ISA)** bus, and make one or two ISA slots available. The **Accelerated Graphics Port (AGP)** is a bus designed for video adapters.

HOW COMPUTERS REPRESENT DATA

Whether we're talking about PCs or Macs or any other type of computer in widespread use today, we're talking about a *digital computer.* To understand computer hardware, you'll need to understand the basic concepts of digital computing—and that means you'll need to know the essentials of how computers represent data.

Why is this topic important? As you've already learned in Module 1A, computers are devices that accept input, process that input according to a program's instructions, generate output showing the results of the processing, and store the output for future use. In order to work with data, some means must be used to represent the data inside the computer. Computers can't do anything without represented data to work with. In the next section, you'll learn that the technique used to represent data within the computer—by means of *digits*—explains a very great deal about both the strengths and the limitations of modern computers.

Digital vs. Analog Representation

Explore IT Lab

Binary Representation

Digital computers represent data by means of an easily-identified symbol of some kind (called a *digit*), one that can't be confused with any other. In electronic computers, digits can be represented in only two possible ways: a high-power circuit and a low-power circuit. The computer's components can tell the difference between them with an infinitesimal chance of error. To be sure, people are always talking about computer "glitches," such as the $1 million gas bill that was delivered to a very surprised customer. But such errors are almost always attributable to mistakes in the underlying programming, not the computer's hardware.

Computers can do more than just represent data without error. They can also process this data at amazing speeds. Almost any computer available today can perform millions of mathematical operations per second. In this respect, computers outstrip human capabilities by a very wide margin. Working unaided, even a gifted mathematician can perform, at best, only a few dozen mathematical operations per second.

Not all computers use digital representation. **Analog** computers use a continuously variable scale, like the mercury in a thermometer, to measure an ongoing process. (The term *analog* suggests the mode of representation that's used. Analog computers work with a continuously variable model, or analogy, of whatever they're measuring.) Analog computers are used in scientific labs and commercial devices, such as computerized gas pumps that are automatically linked to point-of-sale terminals.

A good way to sum up this discussion is to say the following: digital computers count, while analog computers measure. The human brain can do both, albeit more slowly, but it can perform additional operations that today's computers can only emulate, and very imperfectly. One such capability is *pattern recognition*, the ability that enables you to pick a friend's face out of a crowd, or to tell the difference between an apology sincerely delivered and one that sounds contrived. Computers can be programmed to emulate this and other capabilities of human intelligence, but progress in this area (called *artificial intelligence*) has been slow. Part of the reason is that scientists still do not fully understand how the human brain works.

Numbering Systems

Every numbering system has a *base* (also called *radix*). For example, the decimal numbers you use every day have a base of 10. Different numbering systems use other bases. You are already familiar with this concept because, once again, you use it every day. You keep track of time using a numbering system with a base of 60! Historians have proven that this numbering system dates all the way back to ancient Babylonia.

What's the difference between numbering systems with varying bases? The answer lies in what happens when you count up to the maximum number that the numbering system allows. In base 10 numbers (decimals), you can count from 0 to 9, and then you have to carry over to the next column (tens). In base 60 numbers, you can count from 0 to 59 minutes, and then you have to carry over to the next column (hours). In other words, these numbering systems are positional. When you look at the decimal number 840, for example, you know what the numbers mean from their position (8 = 800, 4 = 40, and 0 = 0). A number's position is called its *place value*.

Representing Numbers

Because computers represent information using only two possible states, they're ideally suited to **binary numbers.** With binary numbers, you must carry over to the next column when you reach the equivalent of decimal 2. Binary numbers are difficult for people to read and use but perfectly suited to the two-state world of computer circuits. In binary numbers, 0 refers to a low-power (off) circuit, and 1 refers to a high-power (on) circuit. When used to represent a computer circuit in this way, a binary number is called a binary digit, or bit for short. A bit is the smallest unit of information that a computer can work with (see Figure 2A.15).

In decimal numbers, each place value is a power of ten (10, 100, 1000, and so on). In binary numbers, each place value is a power of 2 (2, 4, 8, 16, and so on).

Binary numbers are difficult to work with because so many digits are required to represent even a small number. (In binary, for example, decimal 14 is 1110.) Also, it's tedious to translate binary numbers into their decimal equivalents. For these reasons, programmers like to translate binary numbers into **hexadecimal numbers** (called hex for short), a numbering system with a base of 16. These numbers use the symbols 0 through 9 and A through F to make a total of 16 symbols. It's easy to translate binary numbers into the much more readable hexadecimal ones. For example, a commonly-used code for the letter K, 01001011, quickly translates to 4B (see Table 2A.4).

Binary digit	0	1
Bit	○	●
Status	On	Off

Figure   2A.15

A binary number is called a binary digit, or bit for short. A bit is the smallest unit of information that a computer can work with.

Counting with Binary, Decimal, and Hexadecimal Numbers

Table   2A.4

Decimal Number	Binary Number	Hexadecimal Number
0	0	0
1	1	1
2	10	2
3	11	3
4	100	4
5	101	5
6	110	6
7	111	7
8	1000	8
9	1001	9
10	1010	A
11	1011	B
12	1100	C
13	1101	D
14	1110	E
15	1111	F

Representing Very Large and Very Small Numbers

Although character codes are useful for representing textual data and whole numbers (0 through 9), they are not useful for numbers that have fractional points, such as 1.25. To represent and process numbers with fractions, as well as extremely large numbers, computers use **floating-point notation.** The term floating point suggests how this notation system works: no fixed number of digits are before or after the decimal point, so the computer can work with very large, as well as very small, numbers. Floating-point notation requires special processing circuitry, which is generally provided in a separate unit called the **floating-point unit (FPU).** Almost a standard in the circuitry of today's microprocessors, the FPU on older computers was sometimes a separate chip, called a **math coprocessor.**

Representing Characters

Computers would be impossible to use if they just spat out binary numbers at us. Fortunately, thanks to character code, it doesn't. A **character code** can translate between the numerical world of the computer, and the letters, numbers, and symbols we're accustomed to using.

ASCII and EBCDIC

The most widely-used character code is the **American Standard Code for Information Interchange (ASCII),** which is used on minicomputers, personal computers, and computers designed to make information available on the Internet. IBM mainframe computers and some other systems use a different code, called **Extended Binary Coded Decimal Interchange Code (EBCDIC,** pronounced "ebb-see-dic").

Originally, ASCII and EBCDIC used a total of seven bits to represent **characters** (letters, numbers, and punctuation marks). Seven bits allows the computer to encode a total of 128 characters, which is enough for the numbers 0–9, uppercase and lowercase letters A–Z, and a few punctuation symbols. This 128-bit code is only suitable, however, for English-speaking users. Looking for a wider market for their personal computers, both IBM and Apple expanded the amount of space reserved for the character code to 8 bits, equivalent to one byte (see Table 2A.5). However, these **extended character sets** (characters added to the standard 7-bit set) are not standardized; the Macintosh and PC versions differ. This explains why you may encounter some character representation errors if you try to open a Macintosh document on an IBM PC. (There's less of a problem going the other way because the Macintosh comes with translation software that automatically translates IBM PC characters.) You may see errors if the document contains special characters such as foreign language characters or special punctuation marks.

Unicode

Although ASCII and EBCDIC contain some foreign language symbols, both are clearly insufficient in a global computer market. **Unicode** solves this problem for most languages by expanding the number of available bits to 16. Because 16 bits is enough to code more than 65,000 characters, Unicode can represent many, if not most, of the world's languages. At this writing, nearly 40,000 characters have been encoded. Some languages are not represented because more research is needed to determine how best to encode their scripts. Examples of as-yet-unsupported languages are Cherokee, Mongolian, and Sinhala (the most-widely spoken language on the island nation of Sri Lanka).

ASCII and EBCDIC Character Codes

Character	ASCII Representation	EBCDIC Representation
0	00110000	11110000
1	00110001	11110001
2	00110010	11110010
3	00110011	11110011
4	00110100	11110100
5	00110101	11110101
6	00110110	11110110
7	00110111	11110111
8	00111000	11111000
9	00111001	11111001
A	01000001	11000001
B	01000010	11000010
C	01000011	11000011
D	01000100	11000100
E	01000101	11000101
F	01000110	11000110
G	01000111	11000111
H	01001000	11001000
I	01001001	11001001
J	01001010	11010001
K	01001011	11010010
L	01001100	11010011
M	01001101	11010100
N	01001110	11010101
O	01001111	11010110
P	01010000	11010111
Q	01010001	11011000
R	01010010	11011001
S	01010011	11100010
T	01010100	11100011
U	01010101	11100100
V	01010101	11100101
W	01010101	11100110
X	01011001	11100111
Y	01011001	11101000
Z	01011010	11101001

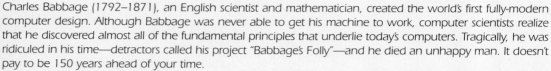

MOVERS & SHAKERS

Babbage's Folly

Charles Babbage (1792–1871), an English scientist and mathematician, created the world's first fully-modern computer design. Although Babbage was never able to get his machine to work, computer scientists realize that he discovered almost all of the fundamental principles that underlie today's computers. Tragically, he was ridiculed in his time—detractors called his project "Babbage's Folly"—and he died an unhappy man. It doesn't pay to be 150 years ahead of your time.

Babbage studied mathematics at Cambridge University, and from an early age took an interest in using machines to calculate and print mathematical tables. This isn't surprising, if you realize that Babbage and his colleagues spent long hours calculating artillery trajectories and navigation data for the British military and naval forces. After a particularly grueling afternoon of cranking out such tables, Babbage is said to have remarked, "I wish these calculations had been executed by steam."

With the help of a grant from the British government, Babbage began working on a steam-powered machine, which he called the Difference Engine. Made from clockwork gears, the machine would calculate mathematical tables and print the results. Unfortunately, the technology of Babbage's day just couldn't produce the thousands of necessary gears with the required precision.

After spending ten years trying to create the Difference Engine without success, Babbage abandoned his plans in favor of a far more ambitious project, called the Analytical Engine. This device would have been a full-fledged modern computer with a recognizable IPOS (input, processing, output, and storage) cycle and would have used Jacquard's punched cards for input.

Babbage worked on his plans for years with Augusta Ada Byron, the Countess of Lovelace. She was the daughter of the famed poet Lord Byron. Augusta Ada (1815–1842), a brilliant mathematician, contributed greatly to Babbage's plans. Ada played a key role in formulating the notion of programming the Analytical Engine to perform different functions. She is therefore considered to have been one of the world's first computer scientists. A programming language called Ada is named in her honor.

The end of Babbage's story isn't a happy one. He depleted much of his fortune trying to build the Analytical Engine, which he was never able to complete. The British government lost interest and withdrew funding. He became a cranky old recluse and was best known in his latter days for his ill-tempered campaign against London street musicians. He died in 1871, without knowing that his ideas would lay the foundation for some of humanity's greatest technological achievements.

In 1991, London's Science Museum constructed a Difference Engine at a cost of nearly $1 million, raised by donations. Ten feet wide and six feet tall, the machine included 4,000 parts. It worked perfectly, returning results to 31 digits of accuracy (better than most electronic calculators).

What would the world be like if Babbage had succeeded in creating a programmable digital computer a century ahead of its time? *The Difference Engine*, a novel by noted science fiction authors William Gibson and Bruce Sterling, asks precisely this question, and begins with the premise that Babbage succeeded rather than failed. With the aid of powerful computers, Britain becomes the world's first technological superpower. Its first foreign adventure is to intervene in the American Civil War on the side of the U.S. South, which splits the U.S. into four feuding republics. By the late-1800s, the world is trying to cope with the multiple afflictions of the twentieth century: credit cards, armored tanks, and fast-food restaurants.

In 1991, the London Science Museum built the Difference Engine using Babbage's plans, as shown in this woodcut. It works perfectly.

Parity

No matter which coding system is used to represent characters in the computer's memory, the code must be stored correctly in order to avoid errors. To check each character on-the-fly, computers are designed to add an additional bit to each character code. This extra bit, called a **parity bit,** is generated by an automatic operation that adds all the bits in the character's code. It records a 0 or a 1 to make the total number of bits odd **(odd parity)** or even **(even parity).** If one of the bits in the code has been changed due to a storage error, the computer generates a **parity error.** Some systems stop processing data if a parity error occurs because the error may indicate a component failure that could scramble all the data. Most personal computers, however, are configured so that **parity checking** (the procedure followed to check for parity errors) is turned off. Although parity errors are rare, they do sometimes occur. But they rarely cause problems serious enough to warrant shutting down the computer, which could cause users to lose hours of work.

TAKEAWAY POINTS

- The term *hardware* refers to the physical components of the computer, the ones you can see and touch. The term *software* refers to the programming that tells the computer what to do.

- The basic unit of information in a computer is the bit, a single-digit binary number (either 1 or 0). An eight-bit sequence of numbers, called a byte, is sufficient to represent the basic letters, numbers, and punctuation marks in most European languages. For this reason, the term *byte* is synonymous with *character* (a letter or number). Larger units of data are described by the terms *kilobyte* (K or KB, approximately one thousand bytes), *megabyte* (M or MB, approximately one million bytes), *gigabyte* (G or GB, approximately one billion bytes), and *terabyte* (T or TB, approximately one trillion bytes). Data transfer rates are measured in bits per second (bps). Common terms to describe data transfer rates include Kbps (approximately one thousand bits per second), Mbps (approximately one million bits per second), and Gbps (approximately one billion bits per second).

- To use a computer system, you need to know how to hook up the computer's external components to the connectors on the outside of the case. Almost all computers have serial ports (for mice, external modems, and some printers), parallel ports (mainly for printers), a PS/2 port (for PS/2 mice), and a video port. Some computers also have a SCSI port (for SCSI devices such as scanners), a USB port (for USB peripherals, including USB digital cameras and USB printers), a 1394 (FireWire) port (for FireWire peripherals), an IrDA port (for infrared keyboards and mice), input and output jacks for microphones and speakers, a telephone connector, or a network connector.

- The computer's motherboard contains numerous receptacles for a variety of chips, including the system clock (generates pulses to synchronize the computer's activities), the microprocessor (the CPU), memory modules, ROM (flash BIOS) chips, and the chipset (chips that help the processor move data around). Also provided are slots, which give expansion cards access to the computer's input/output (I/O) bus.

- A computer's central processing unit (CPU) contains two components, called the control unit and the arithmetic-logic unit (ALU). The control unit follows a program's instructions, and manages four basic operations: fetch (get the next program instruction from memory), decode (figure out what to do), execute (issue commands that carry out the requested action), and write-back (record the results of the operation in memory). Each completed four-step cycle is called a machine cycle.

- Factors that affect a microprocessor's performance include the data bus width (how many bits it can process at once), and the number of operations the chip can execute per clock cycle. Also important is the speed and amount of cache memory.

- A computer's memory includes several different components, each of which uses a memory technology appropriate to its purpose. Read-only memory (ROM) uses a type of nonvolatile memory, called flash memory, that can be altered should an upgrade be required. The computer's configuration settings are stored in CMOS, a volatile memory that is powered by its own, on-board battery. The computer's main memory, random-access memory (RAM), uses high-speed but volatile dynamic RAM chips, which require power in order to operate correctly. Included within the microprocessor is a small amount of primary cache memory, which operates at very high speeds and keeps frequently-accessed data available to the processor. Processor performance is greatly enhanced through the use of secondary cache memory, which is usually provided on a separate set of chips kept in close proximity to the microprocessor.

- Most of today's popular computers contain expansion buses, which enable users to upgrade the system by adding expansion cards (plug-in adapter boards). The expansion bus provides access to the computer's input-output (I/O) bus. Most well-equipped computers come with a sound card and video adapter. Sometimes these capabilities are included in the computer's motherboard, so the connectors are found on the exterior of the case rather than the back of an expansion card.

- Analog computers measure, while digital computers count. Analog computers provide a quick, rough-and-ready measurement of a fluctuating quantity. Digital computers can perform calculations and move data with a very low probability of error.

MODULE REVIEW

KEY TERMS AND CONCEPTS

1394 port
Accelerated Graphics Port (AGP)
American Standard Code for
    Information Interchange
    (ASCII)
analog
arithmetic-logic unit (ALU)
arithmetic operations
basic input/output system
    (BIOS)
benchmarks
binary numbers
bit
boot sector
boot sequence
booting
byte
cache memory
central processing unit (CPU)
character code
characters
chipset
clock speed
clock tick
clones
compatible
complementary metal-oxide
    semiconductor (CMOS)
complex instruction set
    computer (CISC)
connector
control unit
data bus
data transfer rate
daughterboard
decode
digital
downwardly compatible
dual inline memory module
    (DIMM)
dynamic random-access
    memory (DRAM)
enhanced parallel port (EPP)
even parity
execute
execution cycle
expansion card
expansion slots
Extended Binary Coded
    Decimal Interchange Code
    (EBCDIC)

extended capabilities port
    (ECP)
extended character sets
external drive bays
fetch
FireWire port
flash memory, or flash BIOS
floating-point notation
floating-point unit (FPU)
gigabits per second (Gbps)
graphical user interface (GUI)
hardware
heat sink
hexadecimal numbers
hot swapping
icons
Industry Standard Architecture
    (ISA) bus
input/output (I/O) bus
instruction
instruction cycle
instruction set
interface
integrated circuit (IC)
internal drive bays
IrDA port
kilobits per second (Kbps)
logical operations
machine cycle, or processing
    cycle
math coprocessor
megabits per second (Mbps)
memory
memory address
microprocessor
motherboard
multitasking
native application
nonvolatile memory
odd parity
on-board video
operating system (OS)
parallel port
parallel processing
parity bit
parity checking
parity error
PC

PC Card
Pentium MMX
peripheral device
Personal Computer Interface
    (PCI) bus
pipelining
Plug and Play (PNP)
port
power-on self-tests (POST)
Power Macintosh
PowerPC
power supply
primary cache
processor socket
PS/2 port
random-access memory (RAM)
read-only memory (ROM)
reduced instruction set
    computer (RISC)
registers
ROM BIOS (Basic
    Input/Output System)
RS-232 standard
RS-422 standard
SCSI
secondary cache, or level 2 (L2)
    cache
serial port
setup program
single inline memory modules
    (SIMM)
software
sound card
superscalar architecture
synchronous DRAM (SDRAM)
system clock
system unit
transistor
Unicode
universal serial bus (USB) port
VGA connector
video adapter
video card
virtual memory
volatile memory
word size
write-back
zero insertion force (ZIF)

TRUE/FALSE

Indicate whether the following statements are true or false.

1. The system unit houses the computer's main hardware components.

2. Peripheral devices are necessary for a computer to function.

3. Serial ports transmit data rapidly and are used for devices that require fast data transfer rates.

4. A processor's clock rate is called its clock tick and the single beat of the clock is called its clock speed.

5. The control unit and the arithmetic-logic unit are located on the data bus.

6. In volatile memory, the memory's contents are erased when the power is switched off.

7. To enable ROM upgrades, most computers use flash memory.

8. CMOS memory stores essential startup configuration options and it is volatile.

9. Random-access memory stores information permanently.

10. All computers use digital representation.

MATCHING

Match each key term from the left column to the most accurate definition in the right column.

_____ 1. Parallel port

_____ 2. USB port

_____ 3. expansion card

_____ 4. data bus

_____ 5. parallel processing

_____ 6. CISC chip

_____ 7. setup program

_____ 8. cache memory

_____ 9. character code

_____ 10. parity bit

a. describes a computer that has many processors running at the same time

b. a code that translates the numerical words of the computer and the letters, numbers, and symbols we're accustomed to using

c. a program that enables users to configure their system settings

d. an extra bit that adds all the bits in a character's code

e. a port that can connect more than one device at a time

f. a printed circuit board designed to fit into an expansion bus's receptacles

g. a port used for peripherals that require high-speed connections

h. provides programmers with many instructions, and the circuitry that includes special-purpose circuits that carry out the instructions at high speed

i. a highway of parallel wires that connects the microprocessor's internal components

j. additional memory that is used to improve the computer system's overall performance

MULTIPLE CHOICE

Circle the letter of the correct choice for each of the following.

1. Which of the following is not typically located outside the system unit?
   a. ports
   b. power switch
   c. console
   d. motherboard

2. Which of the following describes the processing cycle of a CPU's control unit?
   a. gather, parse, do, store
   b. fetch, decode, execute, write-back
   c. examine, decode, fetch, execute
   d. fetch, parse, execute, write

3. A CPU that will run the same software that ran on older CPUs is said to be what?
   a. software compatible
   b. outmoded
   c. defective
   d. downwardly compatible

4. Which of the following is not a variation of the Intel Pentium CPU?
   a. PowerPC
   b. Pentium II
   c. Xeon
   d. Celeron

5. Which of the following is not a type of memory?
   a. RAM
   b. ALU
   c. cache
   d. ROM

6. CMOS is a special type of memory used for what purpose?
   a. to store startup configuration options for a computer
   b. to store frequently-used programs
   c. to improve video display performance
   d. to hold the computer's BIOS

7. What is the name given to an electronic circuit that carries data from one computer component to another?
   a. trace
   b. data lead
   c. bus
   d. chip

8. What term refers to a digit's position in a number?
   a. base
   b. place value
   c. binary
   d. bit

9. Which numbering system is preferred by programmers for use in computers?
   a. hexadecimal
   b. binary
   c. octal
   d. decimal

10. Which of the following is not a code set used in computers?
    a. ASCII
    b. Unicode
    c. FPU
    d. EBCDIC

FILL-IN

In the blank provided, write the correct answer for each of the following.

1. Bits are the point of reference for measuring the _____ of communication devices.

2. A(n) _____ is a physical receptacle designed for a specific type of plug.

3. With _____, the computer automatically detects the brand, model, and characteristics of the device when you plug it in and configures the system accordingly.

4. A(n) _____ can emulate thousands or millions of transistors.

5. The _____ contains almost all of a computer's central processing unit on a single chip.

6. The machine cycle consists of two phases: the _____ and the _____.

7. A CPU that can execute more than one instruction per clock cycle is called _____ and its design is called a(n) _____ .

8. A(n) _____ chip offers a "bare bones" instruction set and is less complex and less expensive to produce than a CISC chip.

9. A test that puts a processor through a series of operations to provide a basis for comparison is called a(n) _____.

10. The most widely-used character code is the _____.

SHORT ANSWER

On a separate sheet of paper, answer the following questions.

1. Why do you think PCs outsell Macs?

2. Describe the components of a computer system that can be found in and outside the system unit.

3. What's the difference between a serial port and a parallel port? What are the advantages of a universal serial bus (USB) port?

4. What is the system clock and how does it work?

5. What are the two components that make up a CPU? How do they work together?

6. What elements affect the performance of a computer system?

7. Discuss the distinction between CISC and RISC computer chips.

8. Describe the different types of memory used in a typical computer system.

9. What are buses used for? What types of buses are in a computer system?

10. Describe how numbers are stored and manipulated in a computer system.

2B

MODULE

OUTLINE

WHAT YOU WILL LEARN . . .

When you have finished reading this module, you will be able to:

1. Distinguish between memory and storage.

2. Discuss how storage media are categorized.

3. List the two ways to measure a storage device's performance.

4. Explain how data is stored on hard disks and floppy disks.

5. List the characteristics of hard drives that affect their performance.

6. Explain the uses of removable disks.

7. List and compare the various optical storage media available for personal computers.

Storage (also called *mass storage* and *auxiliary storage*) refers collectively to all the various media on which a computer system can store software and data. Storage devices provide nonvolatile (permanent) storage for programs and data. In this module, you'll learn why storage is necessary. You'll also take a look at the storage devices you're likely to find on today's personal computers and on computers at work.

MEMORY VS. STORAGE

To understand the distinction between memory and storage, think of the last time you worked at your desk. In your file drawer, you store all your personal items and papers, such as your checking account statements. The file drawer is good for long-term storage. When you decide to work on one or more of these items, you take it out of storage and put it on your desk. The desktop is a good place to keep the items you're working with; they're close at hand, and available for use right away.

Computers work the same way. Storage devices are like file drawers in that they hold programs and data. In fact, programs and data are stored in units called **files.** In turn, the files are stored in digital envelopes called **directories** on PCs and **folders** on Macintoshes. When you want to work with the contents of a file, the computer transfers the file to the computer's **memory,** a temporary workplace (like the top of your desk).

WHY IS STORAGE NECESSARY?

Why don't computers just use memory to hold all those files? Here are some solid reasons:

- Storage retains data when the current is switched off. The computer's random-access memory (RAM) is *volatile*. When you switch off the computer's power, all the information in RAM is irretrievably lost. Storage devices are *nonvolatile*. They do not lose data when the power goes off. Without some way to store data and software permanently, a computer system would be much less useful.

- Storage is cheaper than memory. RAM is designed to operate very quickly so that it can keep up with the computer's CPU. For this reason, RAM is expensive—much more expensive than storage (see Table 2B.1). Most computers are equipped with just enough RAM to accommodate all the programs a user wants to run. RAM doesn't have enough room to store a whole library of software, including programs that are important even though you use them infrequently.

Techtalk

storage media
In a computer system, the devices that can store software and data, even when the computer is turned off. **Media** is plural; the singular is **medium.**

Explore IT Lab

Directories, Folders, and Files

Memory vs. Storage			
	Device	**Access Speed**	**Cost per MB**
MEMORY	Cache Memory	Fastest	Highest
	RAM	Fast	High
STORAGE	Hard Disk	Medium	Medium
	CD-ROM disc	Slow	Low
	Backup tape	Very slow	Lowest

Table   2B.1

Table 2B.2

Measuring Storage		
Term	Abbreviation	Bytes (approximate)
kilobyte	K or KB	one thousand
megabyte	M or MB	one million
gigabyte	G or GB	one billion
terabyte	T or TB	one trillion

Various storage devices.

- Storage devices do not transfer data as rapidly as memory (see Table 2B.2), but they are much less expensive. A computer system's storage devices typically hold much more data and software than the computer's memory. Today, you can buy a storage device capable of storing 26 gigabytes (GB) of software and data for about the same amount you'll pay for 128 megabytes (MB) of RAM. (See Table 2B.2 for a reminder concerning the meaning of these and other essential ways of measuring a storage device's capacity.)

- Storage devices play an essential role in system start-up operations. When you start your computer, the BIOS (Basic Input/Output System), discussed in Module 2A, reads essential programs into the computer's RAM memory, including one that begins loading essential system software from the computer's hard disk.

- Storage devices also play an input role when you start an application. The computer's operating system transfers the software from the computer's hard disk to the computer's memory, where it's available for use. If you use the application to work on a document that you previously stored on disk, the storage system functions as an input device again as it reads your document from the disk.

- Storage devices are needed for output, too. When you've finished working, you use the computer's storage system as an output device in an operation called **saving.** When you save your document, the computer transfers your work from the computer's memory to a read/write storage device, such as a hard or floppy disk. If you forget to save your work, it will be lost when you switch off the computer's power. Remember, the computer's RAM memory is volatile!

- Storage devices are increasing in capacity to the point that they can hold an entire library's worth of information. Organizations are increasingly turning to computer storage systems to store all of their information, not just computer software and data. The reason? Storing information on paper is just too expensive. Hard disks can store the same information for about $10 per gigabyte that would cost $10,000 to store on paper.

For all these reasons, demand for increased storage capacity is soaring. According to one estimate, the need for digital storage is increasing 60 percent each year, and the pace shows no signs of slowing down.

TYPES OF STORAGE DEVICES

Storage media are categorized in various ways, including the type of operations they can perform (reading or read/write), the method used to access the information they contain (sequential or random-access), the technology they use (magnetic, optical, or a combination of these), and where they're located in the storage hierarchy. The following sections explain these points.

Read/Write Media vs. Read-Only Media

Most storage devices are **read/write media.** They enable the computer to perform writing (output) operations as well as reading (input) operations.

Some storage devices are **read-only,** which means they cannot perform writing operations. CD-ROM drives are read-only devices; CD-R drives are read/write media.

Sequential vs. Random-Access Storage

Storage devices are categorized according to the way they get to the requested data. In a **sequential storage device,** such as a tape backup unit, the computer has to go through a fixed sequence of stored items to get to the one that's needed. (This is like a cassette tape, which forces you to fast forward or rewind to get to the song you want.) Sequential storage devices are slow but inexpensive (see Figure 2B.1a).

A **random-access storage device** can go directly to the requested data without having to go through a sequence. For example, a disk drive is a storage device that has a read/write head capable of moving across the surface of the disk. By moving across the disk, the read/write head can get to the requested data's location quickly. Random-access storage devices are faster but more expensive (see Figure 2B.1b).

Storage Technologies: Magnetic and Optical

Two storage technologies are in widespread use: magnetic storage and optical storage. Most storage devices use one or the other; occasionally, they are combined.

Magnetic storage media use disks or tapes that are coated with tiny, magnetically-sensitive materials. In all magnetic storage devices, the basic principle is the same: an electromagnet, called a **read/write head,** records information by transforming electrical impulses into a varying magnetic field. As the magnetic materials pass beneath the read/write head, this varying field forces the particles to rearrange themselves in a meaningful pattern. This operation is called **writing.** In **reading,** the read/write head senses the recorded pattern, and transforms this pattern into electrical impulses. The two most common types of magnetic media are magnetic tapes, which are sequential storage devices, and magnetic disks, which are random-access devices. Popular magnetic disk devices include floppy disks, hard disks, and removable disks, all of which are examined later in this module.

Just how much computer data can be stored in magnetic media? Scientists still aren't sure. In laboratories, storage densities of 35 gigabits per square inch have been achieved.

Optical storage media use tightly-focused laser beams to read microscopic patterns of data encoded on the surface of plastic discs (see Figure 2B.2). Tiny, microscopic indentations, called **pits,** absorb the laser's light in certain areas. The drive's light-sensing device receives no light from these areas, so it sends a signal to the computer corresponding to a 0 in the computer's binary numbering system. Flat, reflective areas, called **land,** bounce the light back to a light-sensing device, which sends a signal equivalent to a 1.

(a)

(b)

Figure 2B.1

(a) A tape backup unit is a sequential storage device. The computer has to go through a fixed sequence of stored items to get to the one that's needed. (b) A disk drive is a random-access storage device. The computer can access the requested data without having to go through a sequence.

  Destinations

Looking for the latest news and information concerning storage media? **SearchStorage. com (http://www.search storage.com)** offers a wealth of information about storage technologies, including product reviews, background information, storage-related software, on-line discussions, and troubleshooting tips.

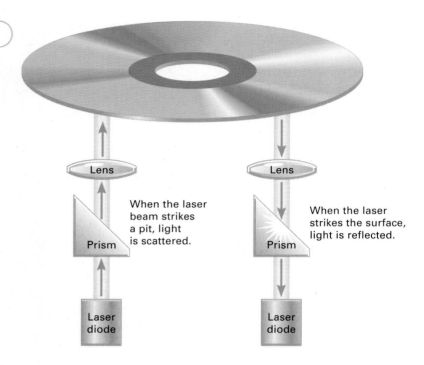

Figure **2B.2**

In optical media, a tightly-focused laser beam reads data encoded on the disc's surface. Some optical devices can write data as well as read.

Techtalk

disk or disc?

If the subject is magnetic media, the correct spelling is **disk.** However, some people prefer to use **disc** for optical media.

CD-ROM discs and CD-ROM drives are read/only media. However, several types of optical read/write media are available, including one-time-recordable CD-ROM (CD-R) discs, rewritable CD-ROM (CD-RW), and DVD-ROM.

How much data can an optical medium store? Scientists believe that the physics of light limit optical media to a maximum of 5 gigabits of storage per square inch. However, new optical technologies break this barrier by using discs with more than one layer (see "Storage Horizons," later in this chapter).

Some storage devices combine the two basic technologies. **Magneto-optical (MO) drives** combine the two basic storage technologies. In the coming years, MO discs no larger than today's CD-ROMs will contain up to 100 GB of storage.

THE STORAGE HIERARCHY

Storage devices fit into one of three locations in the **storage hierarchy.** Consisting of three levels, the storage hierarchy differentiates storage devices according to the availability of the data they contain. The three levels are as follows:

■ **Online storage**   Also called *primary storage*, this is the most important component of the storage hierarchy. It consists of the storage devices that are actively available to the computer system and do not require any action on the part of the user. The computer's hard disk is a personal computer's online storage system.

■ **Near-online storage**   Also called *secondary storage*, this portion of the storage hierarchy consists of storage that isn't directly available. However, it can be made available easily by some simple actions on the user's part, such as inserting a disk. Examples of near-online storage devices for personal computers are floppy disks and CD-ROMs.

■ **Offline storage**   Also called *tertiary storage* or *archival storage*, this portion of the storage hierarchy consists of storage that is not readily available. Offline storage devices, such as magnetic tapes, are used for infrequently-accessed data that needs to be kept for archival purposes. Some personal computers are equipped with tape drives, which can be used for archival storage.

Capacity of Storage Devices

A storage device's capacity is measured in bytes (a unit of data composed of eight bits). Capacities range from the floppy disk's 1.44MB to huge, room-filling arrays of storage devices capable of storing a dozen or more terabytes of data. To provide this much storage with print-based media, you'd need to cut down several million trees.

People have varying storage needs. PC and Macintosh users want to store items such as their e-mail, word processing documents, graphics and music files. A 2GB or 4GB disk may be needed to hold these items plus software. A scientist working with laboratory data may need 50GB of storage, while a huge corporation may need several terabytes of storage to hold all the information it works with.

Speed of Storage Devices (Access Time)

A storage device's most important performance characteristic—the speed with which it retrieves the desired data—is measured by its **access time,** the amount of time it takes for the device to begin reading the data. For disk drives, the access time includes the **seek time,** the time it takes the read/write head to locate the data before reading begins.

The speed of storage devices varies considerably, but all storage devices are significantly slower than RAM memory (see Table 2B.3). RAM's speed is measured in **nanoseconds** (billionths of a second, abbreviated **ns**); a storage device's speed is measured in **milliseconds** (thousandths of a seconds, abbreviated **ms**).

One type of storage device offers the speed of memory with the high capacity of a storage device. **Solid state disks (SDD)** are designed to trick the computer into thinking that they are an ordinary hard disk. However, they contain dynamic RAM or flash memory chips. Onboard batteries make sure the data remains secure when the power is switched off. They can store up to 8GB of data. SDD drives are much more expensive than hard disks, but they are also much faster.

(a)

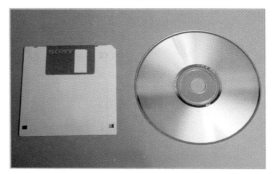

(b)

Figure   2B.3

(a) A hard disk is an example of an online storage system. (b) Floppy disks and optical discs are near-online storage devices.

Table   2B.3

Access Times: Memory vs. Storage	
Device	**Typical Access Time**
Static RAM (SRAM)	5–15 nanoseconds
Dynamic RAM (DRAM)	50–70 nanoseconds
Solid state disk (SDD)	0.1 millisecond
Hard disk drive	6–12 milliseconds
CD-ROM drive	80–800 milliseconds

Figure 2B.4

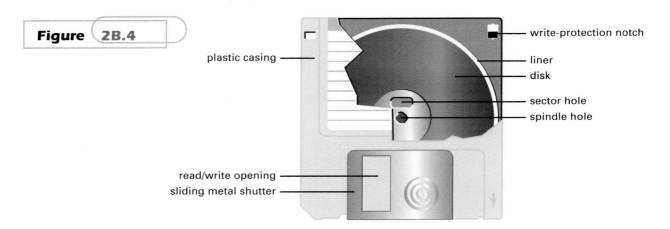

write-protection notch

plastic casing

liner

disk

sector hole

spindle hole

read/write opening

sliding metal shutter

Table 2B.4

3.5-inch Floppy Disk Storage Capacities		
	Double Density	**High Density**
PC	720KB	1.44MB
Macintosh	800KB	1.2MB

FLOPPY DISKS AND FLOPPY DISK DRIVES

A **floppy disk** (also called **diskette**) is a circular plastic disk coated with a magnetically-sensitive film, the same material that's on a cassette tape. Designed to work with a **floppy disk drive,** floppies have long provided personal computer users with convenient, near-online storage. However, as computer programs (and users' data files) have grown significantly in size, floppies are becoming less useful. Their capacity is so small that they cannot accommodate some of the larger files people create. Still, almost every personal computer includes a floppy disk drive.

What Does "Floppy" Mean?

Introduced by IBM in the 1970s, the first floppy disks were packaged in eight-inch flexible packages. That's where the term "floppy" came from. Most of today's floppy disks are packaged in 3.5-inch hard plastic cases (see Figure 2B.4). Even though the package is no longer flexible, the term "floppy" is still used.

Storage Capacities of Floppy Disks

Compared to other storage media, floppy disks provide little room for storing data (see Table 2B.4). The storage capacity of a floppy disk is determined by the density of the magnetic material on the disk's surface. **Double-density (DD)** floppy disks offer up to 800K of storage, while **high-density (HD)** floppy disks offer up to 1.44MB of data.

Why do people put up with a storage medium that offers so little storage capacity? One reason is that floppy disks are **portable** media, which means that you can remove a floppy disk from one computer and insert it into another. Accordingly, 3.5-inch disks are designed to keep your data safe. A sliding metal shutter protects the disk from fingerprints, dust, and dirt. Another reason for the floppy disk's popularity is that it's universal. Almost every computer has a floppy disk drive. Floppy disks enable a computer user to exchange data with almost any other computer user.

Techtalk

network effect
This term is used by economists to describe the rewards consumers get when they purchase a popular product rather than a less-popular one, even if the less-popular product offers superior technology. In computer markets, network effects are powerful due to compatibility issues. If you choose a popular product (such as a 3.5-inch floppy disk drive), you can exchange data with more people.

Don't expose disks to magnetic fields.

Don't touch the surface of the disk. Fingerprints can contaminate the disk and cause errors.

To avoid contamination, don't eat or drink around disks.

Don't smoke and use disks at the same time!

To avoid condensation, keep disks away from humidity.

Don't expose disks to excessive temperatures.

Taking care of disks.

Protecting Your Data

Floppy disks contain a **write-protect tab** (also called a write-protect notch) that you can open to protect data from being overwritten or deleted. The write-protect tab enables you to turn any floppy disk into a read-only disk. If you store an important document on a floppy disk, be sure to set the write-protect tab so that you don't erase the document accidentally. If you have difficulty writing data to a floppy disk, make sure the write-protect tab is set to read/write (see Figure 2B.5).

Floppy Disk Drives

Floppy disks are designed to work with floppy disk drives. In desktop computer systems, this drive is installed in one of the system unit's drive bays. In notebook computers, the drive is often provided by means of an external unit that plugs into the system's case (see Figure 2B.6).

In PCs running Microsoft Windows, the first floppy drive is called Drive A (this drive is called fd0 in PCs running Linux). The second drive, if there is one, is called Drive B (Windows) or fd1 (Linux). Macintoshes usually have just one floppy drive, if any (the iMac dispenses with floppy drives entirely).

How Floppy Drives Work

To use a floppy disk, you insert it into the drive. With 3.5-inch disks, you can insert the disk in only one way: the sliding metal shutter must face the drive door (see Figure 2B.7). When the computer needs to read data from

notch open means you cannot write on the disk

write-protected

not write-protected

notch closed means you can write on the disk

Figure 2B.5

To set the write-protect tab on a 3.5-inch floppy, move it into the locked position.

(a)

(b)

Figure 2B.6

(a) A floppy disk drive and
(b) an external floppy drive.

Figure 2B.7

You can insert a 3.5-inch floppy in only one way. Make sure the sliding metal shutter faces the drive door.

the disk, the **head actuator** moves the read/write head over the surface of the disk. The head actuator is a mechanism that moves the read/write head to the area that contains the desired data. When the read/write head is in the correct position, it begins reading the data into the computer's memory.

How does the read/write head know where to look for data? To answer this question, you need to know a little about how stored data is organized on a floppy disk (and on other magnetic disks as well). Like an old-style vinyl LP, floppy disks contain circular bands called **tracks.** Each track is divided into pie-shaped wedges called **sectors.** Two or more sectors combine to form a **cluster** (see Figure 2B.8).

To keep track of just where specific files are located, the computer's operating system records a table of information on the disk. This table contains the name of each file and the file's exact location on the disk. On Microsoft Windows systems, this table is called the **file allocation table** or **FAT** (see Figure 2B.9).

Sometimes disks develop a defect that prevents the computer from reading or writing data to one or more sectors of the disk. These damaged areas are called **bad sectors.** If you see an on-screen message indicating that a floppy disk has a bad sector, try to copy the data off the disk, if possible. Don't use it to store new data.

To store data as compactly as possible, the file might be stored in a **fragmented** form, which means that it is split up into pieces and stored in whatever disk sectors happen to be available. Although it's disconcerting to think that a valuable document might be split up and stored here and there on the disk, it's actually quite safe. However, repeated write operations may result in excessive fragmentation. As the percentage of fragmented files reaches ten percent, the drive's access time declines in a noticeable way. It declines because the read/write head must travel back and forth across the disk's surface to retrieve the various parts of the file.

To remove a floppy disk from a PC disk drive, press the eject button. While the read/write head is reading or writing data, the drive illuminates the **activity light.** Do not remove the disk while this light is on. On a Macintosh, you'll need to drag the floppy disk icon to the Trash. (Alternatively, select the disk drive icon, click Special on the menu bar, and choose Eject.)

Formatting: Preparing Disks for Use

Before a magnetic disk can be used for storage, it must be prepared using a process called **formatting.** This process is necessary because different types of computers store data in different ways. For this reason, PCs cannot read Macintosh floppies unless the PC is running special software. Most Macintoshes are equipped with software that enables them to read PC floppies.

In the formatting process, the disk drive's read/write head lays down the magnetic patterns of tracks and sectors on the disk's surface. This pattern enables the disk drive to store data in an organized manner.

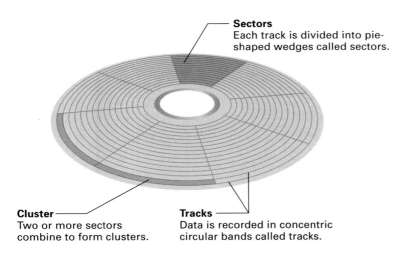

Sectors
Each track is divided into pie-shaped wedges called sectors.

Cluster
Two or more sectors combine to form clusters.

Tracks
Data is recorded in concentric circular bands called tracks.

Figure   2B.8

Floppy disks contain circular bands called tracks, which are divided into sectors. Two or more sectors combine to form a cluster.

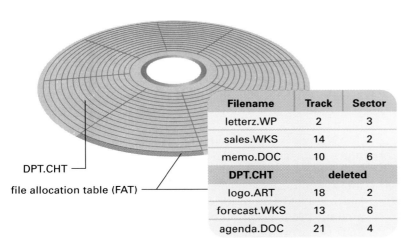

DPT.CHT

file allocation table (FAT)

Filename	Track	Sector
letterz.WP	2	3
sales.WKS	14	2
memo.DOC	10	6
DPT.CHT	**deleted**	
logo.ART	18	2
forecast.WKS	13	6
agenda.DOC	21	4

Figure   2B.9

The FAT keeps vital records that show exactly where a given file is stored.

You can format floppy disks yourself, using the formatting utility supplied with the computer's operating system (see Figure 2B.10). However, you will seldom need to do so. Most of the floppy disks sold today are **preformatted,** which means that they are already formatted for the Windows or Macintosh formats. (If you're buying floppies, make sure you purchase the correct format for your computer.)

Be aware that formatting destroys all the data that has been recorded on a disk. You should never format a disk that contains valuable data. In addition, you should never format the computer's hard disk, unless you have just purchased a new hard disk and are following the installation instructions.

Beyond the Floppy: High-Capacity Disks and Drives

Floppy disks do not offer enough storage for today's computer users. For this reason, several companies offer alternatives with much higher storage capacities. These higher-capacity disk drives fall into two categories: those that are *downwardly compatible* with previous floppy disks, and those that are not. (When a device is downwardly-compatible, it can work with previous versions of the technology.)

Two downwardly-compatible disk drive technologies are available. Developed by Imation, **SuperDisk** is a storage device that uses 120MB SuperDisks. Sony's **High FD (HiFD)** uses 200MB floppy disks. Both drives

Techtalk

slack space
This term refers to space that is wasted when a disk's cluster size is too large. In older versions of Microsoft Windows, large hard disks required clusters of 32KB or more. However, each cluster can store only one file. If the file is smaller than the cluster, the remaining space is slack space, which cannot be used. More recent versions of Windows fix this problem by using an updated file system called FAT 32.

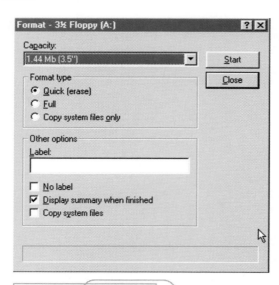

can read standard, 3.5-inch floppies. However, neither of these drives has gained widespread acceptance.

More widely-accepted is Iomega's **Zip drive,** which is not downwardly compatible with floppy disks. Capable of storing up to 100MB of data, Zip drives come in internal versions (mounted in one of the system unit's drive bays) as well as external versions, which can be used with notebook computers (see Figure 2B.11).

HARD DISKS

On almost all computers, the **hard disk** is by far the most important online storage medium. A hard disk is a high-capacity, high-speed storage device that usually consists of several fixed, rapidly-rotating disks called **platters** (see Figure 2B.12). Most hard disks are **fixed disks,** which use platters that are sealed within the mechanism's case.

Figure 2B.10

You can use this Windows utility to format a floppy disk, but most floppy disks sold today are preformatted.

Why Are Hard Disks Needed?

In the early days of personal computing, hard disks were optional. Programs were small enough to fit on floppy disks, and users rarely created files that exceeded a floppy disk's capacity. But those days are gone. Today's computer systems require a hard disk—preferably, one with at least several gigabytes of storage.

Why does an ordinary PC or Macintosh user need so much storage? Today's operating systems (such as Microsoft Windows or Mac OS) may require 250MB of storage or more. Applications can easily eat up another 750MB of disk space. To leave room for data, you'll need roughly twice the amount taken up by software. According to this guideline, 2GB is a working minimum—and you'll be wise to double this figure to provide room for additional software. As computer users ruefully observe, there is no such thing as enough storage space. As you keep on adding more software and data, you'll soon exhaust the available space. Most PCs come with at least 6GB of storage capacity, and many come with 10GB or more. Increasingly commonplace are systems with 20GB of storage.

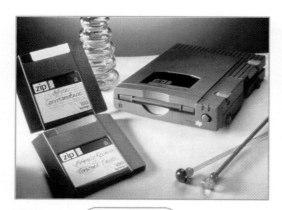

Figure 2B.11

Iomega's Zip drive and 100MB Zip disks offer an easy-to-use personal storage solution designed to make it easier for consumers to move, protect, share, and back up information on their computers.

How Hard Disks Work

A hard disk works like a floppy disk. Magnetic read/write heads move across the surface of a disk coated with magnetically-sensitive material. But that's where the resemblance ends. A hard disk contains two or more vertically-stacked platters, each with two read/write heads (one for each side of the disk). The disk spins much faster than a floppy disk. The platters spin so rapidly that the read/write head floats on a thin cushion of air, at a distance three hundred times less than the width of a human hair.

To protect the platter's surface, hard disks are enclosed in a sealed container. If the read/write head were to encounter an obstacle, such as dust or smoke, the head would bounce on the disk surface, causing serious damage (see Figure 2B.13). Hard disks can absorb minor jostling without suffering damage, but a major jolt—such as one caused by dropping the computer while the drive is running—could cause a **head crash** to occur. Head crashes are one of the causes of bad sectors—areas of the disk that have become damaged and can no longer hold data reliably.

Like floppy disks, hard disks must be formatted before use. The formatting process creates tracks and sectors, like those of a floppy disk. Because most hard disks have two or more platters, it is possible to define an additional storage area called a **cylinder.** A cylinder is a location made up of the same track location on all the platters (see Figure 2B.14). If the platters contain 1,200 tracks, the hard disk will have 1,200 cylinders. In a six-platter drive in which data is recorded on both platter surfaces, each cylinder contains 12 tracks.

Hard disks can be divided into **partitions.** A partition is a section of a disk set aside as if it were a physically-separate disk. Sometimes partitions are used to enable computers to work with more than one operating system. For example, Linux users often create one partition for Linux, and another for Microsoft Windows. In this way, they can work with programs developed for both operating systems.

Figure 2B.12

Hard disks contain several rapidly-rotating platters, each with its own read/write head.

Factors Affecting Hard Disk Performance

A hard disk's performance is determined by two factors: positioning performance and transfer performance.

Positioning performance refers to how quickly the drive can position the read/write head so that it can begin transferring data. This aspect of a drive's performance is measured by the drive's seek time, the amount of time required to move the read/write head to the required position. Constant advances in head actuator technology are continually driving seek times down.

Transfer performance refers to the drive's ability to transfer data from the drive as quickly as possible. To improve transfer performance, engineers use ever-increasing **spindle speeds.** Spindle speed refers to the speed, measured in revolutions per minute (rpm), at which the platters rotate. Many hard disks spin at a spindle speed of 7,200 rpm, and high-end drives operate at speeds as high as 15,000 rpm. Higher spindle speeds reduce the time that is wasted after the read/write head moves to the correct track. The read/write head must wait until the spinning disk brings the desired data around to the head's location. The amount of time wasted in this way is called **latency.** In a slow drive (3,600 rpm), latency can be as high as 17 milliseconds. In a fast drive (10,000 rpm), latency typically averages only 3 milliseconds.

Hard Disk Interfaces

To communicate with the CPU, hard disks require a **hard disk controller.** A hard disk controller provides an interface between the CPU and the hard disk's electronics. The controller may be located on the computer's motherboard, on an expansion card, or within the hard disk.

The most widely-used interface for PCs is called **Integrated Drive Electronics (IDE),** also called **ATA** (short for **AT attachment**) or **IDE/ATA.**

Techtalk

mean time between failure (MTBF)
An estimate, provided by a hard disk's manufacturer, of how many hard disk drives of the same brand and model would need to be in operation for one of them to fail per hour. For example, an MTBF of 500,000 hours means that one half million of these drives would need to be in operation for the drives to hit the one-per-hour failure rate. This number does **not** mean that the drive will last 500,000 hours (57 years). Most hard disk drives have an estimated service life of five years. The MTBF tells you only how likely it is that the drive will fail during its service life. The lower the number, the better, but don't expect to get 57 years of service out of a hard disk.

Figure 2B.13

The read/write head "floats" just above the disk, at a distance three hundred times less than the width of a human hair. If the read/write head encounters an obstacle, such as dust or a smoke particle, a head crash will occur.

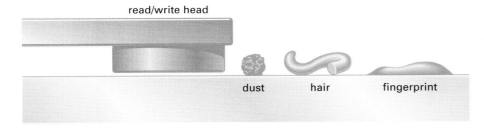

read/write head

dust   hair   fingerprint

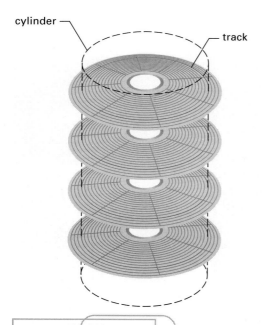

cylinder

track

Figure **2B.14**

All the tracks of the same number on a hard disk's platters are grouped as a cylinder.

IDE drives incorporate the controller within the drive unit. The original IDE/ATA specification has been updated several times, generally by drive manufacturers, who have used a profusion of names to describe the newer standards. The current standard IDE/ATA interface for **entry-level drives** (drives found on the least expensive computers) is called **Fast IDE, Fast ATA,** or **ATA-2.** This type of interface enables users to connect up to four IDE-compatible drives, including CD-ROM drives, to the motherboard, and transfers data at a rate of 16 megabits per second (Mbps). The newest version of the IDE/ATA standard, called **Ultra DMA/66** or **ATA-5,** transfers data at speeds of up to 66 MHz. Most IDE/ATA drives are downwardly compatible with earlier standards, so they will work with motherboards that do not support the latest standards.

A standard feature on Macintoshes, and available for PCs, is the **Small Computer System Interface (SCSI)** interface. SCSI has many advantages. Up to seven SCSI-compatible devices, including hard disks, scanners, CD-ROM drives, and other peripherals can be "daisy-chained" to a single SCSI connector. In addition, the newest SCSI standard, called **Ultra3 SCSI** or **Ultra160 SCSI,** supports data transfer rates of up to 160 Mbps, more than twice as fast as Ultra DMA/66. However, the fastest SCSI hard disk controllers are expensive and add considerably to the cost of the computer's storage system. The fastest SCSI controllers and drives are found only in high-end systems, which are the most expensive systems in a manufacturer's product line.

Disk Caches: Improving a Hard Disk's Performance

To improve hard disk performance, most computers have a type of cache memory called **disk cache** (see Figure 2B.15). A disk cache is a type of RAM (random-access memory) that is used to store the program instructions and data you are working with. When the CPU needs to get information in the drive, it looks in the disk cache first. If it does not find the information it needs, it retrieves the information from the hard disk. Because RAM chips are much faster than the disk, the use of a disk cache dramatically improves hard disk performance. On Macintosh computers, the disk cache is part of the computer's main memory (RAM). On PCs, the disk cache is part of the hard disk.

Figure **2B.15**

Disk cache, a type of RAM, dramatically improves hard disk performance. When the CPU needs to get information in the drive, it looks in the disk cache first.

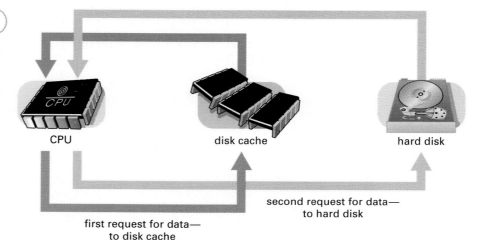

CPU

disk cache

hard disk

second request for data— to hard disk

first request for data— to disk cache

Hard Disk Longevity

Hard disks can and do fail. Many continue operating flawlessly for as long as five years (or even longer), but sometimes they fail sooner. When they do, all the data on the drive may be destroyed. Responsible computer use requires regular backup procedures to ensure that hard disk failures do not lead to costly losses. Backup software is discussed in Module 3A.

RAID

A device that groups two or more hard disks that contain exactly the same data is called **RAID,** which is short for **redundant array of inexpensive disks** (see Figure 2B.16). The key word in this phrase is *redundant,* which means "extra copy." No matter how many disks a RAID device contains, the computer "thinks" it's dealing with just one drive. Should one of the drives fail, there's no interruption of service. All the drives contain an exact copy of all the data, so one of the other drives kicks in and delivers the requested data. RAID devices offer a high degree of **fault tolerance;** that is, they keep working even if one or more components should fail. For this reason, RAID devices are widely-used wherever a service interruption could prove costly, hazardous, or inconvenient to customers. Most of the major Web sites use RAID devices to ensure the constant availability of their Web pages. Most personal computer users don't need RAID devices, as long as they back up their data regularly.

To duplicate the data, two techniques are used, called **striping** (RAID Level 0) and **mirroring/duplexing.** In striping, each disk in the RAID device contains a portion of the hard disk's data (see Figure 2B.17). Striping improves access time, but it is not a true RAID technique because it cannot guarantee that the data will survive a drive failure. In mirroring/duplexing, also called **RAID Level 1,** each hard disk is paired with at least one additional disk that contains an exact copy of its data (see Figure 2B.18). Mirroring is the most fault-tolerant approach, but it is also the slowest in terms of access time. The latest RAID standards (such as RAID Level 10) combine striping with mirroring/duplexing to ensure fault tolerance as well as fast data access (see Figure 2B.19).

Removable Hard Disks

Most hard disks are fixed disks, a type of hard disk that has non-removable platters. **Removable hard disks** enclose the platters within a cartridge, which can be inserted into the drive and removed, much like a floppy disk. Removable hard disks are a near-online storage medium. A computer system equipped with dozens of removable cartridges will have a near-online storage system that is many times larger than the hard disk's capacity.

Although removable hard disks aren't as fast and can't store as much data as one-piece hard disks, they are convenient additions to a personal computer system. Removable hard disks are very useful for **data archiving** (keeping long-term copies of important files) and **data backup** (performing regular backup operations that ensure full system recovery after a total system failure). The cartridges can be exchanged with other computer users, as long as they have the same type of drive. Removable hard drives have security benefits, too. If you are working with sensitive data, you can remove the cartridge at the end of a working session and keep it under lock and key.

Figure 2B.16

In a RAID device, all the drives contain an exact copy of all the data. If one of the drives fails, one of the other drives kicks in and delivers the requested data.

Destinations

For an excellent Web-based tutorial on the many varieties of RAID, see RAID Technology **(http://www.acnc.com/raid.html),** developed by Advanced Computer & Network Corporation.

RAID 0

Figure 2B.17

Striping (RAID Level 0) apportions the data over several disks. Access time is excellent, but this technique is not fault-tolerant.

RAID 1

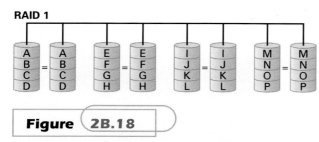

Figure 2B.18

In mirroring/duplexing (RAID Level 1), each disk is paired with a backup disk that contains an exact copy of the data. Fault tolerance is excellent, but access speed suffers.

RAID 10

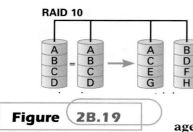

Figure 2B.19

The latest RAID standards (such as RAID Level 10) combine striping with mirroring/duplexing to ensure fault tolerance as well as fast data access.

Figure 2B.20

Iomega's Jaz drive can store up to 2GB of data in removable cartridges.

An example of a removable drive is Iomega's popular Jaz drive, which can store up to 2GB (see Figure 2B.20). Most removable drives are used for **backup** purposes. In a backup, users make a copy of their data so that they will not lose this data should the fixed disk fail. Because fixed disks are faster than removable disks, most users prefer to rely on fixed disks as their main storage medium.

MAGNETIC TAPE: STILL USEFUL

Magnetic tapes were once the most commonly-used storage medium. You've probably seen film clips of 1960s-era "electronic brains," with big banks of whirling reel-to-reel tapes. The earliest personal computers came with cassette tape drives. Although tapes store data sequentially, making access times slow, they are still useful for storing very large amounts of data that don't need to be accessed frequently.

Quarter-inch cartridge (QIC) tape drives work with cartridges that can store up to 10GB of data, enough to back up most PC hard disks with just one cartridge (see Figure 2B.21). Although QIC tape drives have the lowest data transfer rates among today's tape backup technologies, they are inexpensive. **Digital audio tape (DAT)** drives offer better data transfer rates and higher storage capacity. The most popular DAT format is called **DDS (digital data storage),** which stores up to 40GB on a cartridge. **Digital linear tape (DLT)** drives are more expensive than QIC or DAT drives, but they transfer data much more rapidly and offer cartridge capacities of up to 100GB. The latest tape drive technology, **advanced intelligent tape (AIT),** offers cartridge capacities of up to 100GB.

In corporate information systems, mass storage systems store hundreds or even thousands of high-capacity tape cartridges in a carousel-like system.

CD-ROM DISCS AND DRIVES

The most popular and least expensive type of optical disc standard is **CD-ROM** (see Figure 2B.22), short for compact disc-read only memory. As the ROM part of the name indicates, this near-online storage medium is strictly read-only; CD-ROM drives cannot write data to optical disks.

Because most software is distributed by means of CD-ROM discs, CD-ROM drives are standard and necessary equipment for today's personal computers. CD-ROM discs are capable of storing up to 650MB of data, the equivalent of more than four hundred floppy disks. These discs provide the ideal medium for distributing operating systems, large applications, office suites, and multimedia products involving thousands of large graphics or audio files.

CD-ROM disc drives vary in speed, which is measured in the unit's **data transfer rate** (the number of bits transferred per second). The original CD-ROM format transferred data at a maximum rate of only 150,000 bits per second, a very slow speed in comparison to hard disks (or even floppy disks). Faster CD-ROM drives improve the transfer rates by spinning the disc faster. The speed of such drives is claimed to be a multiple of the original 150,000 bits per second standard; a 2X (double-speed) drive, for example, can transfer data at 300,000 bits per second. The latest drives can transfer as much as 7.8 million bits per second (Mbps), within the range of slower hard disks.

Most CD-ROM drives can play audio CDs. However, you may not hear the sound unless the drive's audio output is connected to the computer's sound card. You will also need a program that can control the drive and play the tracks you want to hear.

Most CD-ROM drives can also work with Kodak **PhotoCDs.** Developed by photography giant Kodak, this format makes use of **multisession CDs.** Unlike **single-session CDs,** the type of CD used to distribute software, PhotoCDs can accept more than one "burn" (recording session). When you have your film developed, you can get a PhotoCD that contains digitized images of the prints. The next time you shoot a roll, you can take the same PhotoCD back and have more prints added.

Some CD-ROM drives can accommodate more than one disc. CD-ROM "jukeboxes," containing as many as 256 CD-ROM drives, make large amounts of software or data available to network users.

Figure   2B.21

Quarter-inch cartridge (QIC) tape drives work with cartridges that can store up to 10GB of data.

CD-R and CD-RW Discs and Recorders

Read/write CD technologies, called CD-R and CD-RW, are now available. Declining prices have placed these devices within the budget of many computer owners. For this reason, CD-R and CD-RW discs are fast emerging as a popular, cost-effective alternative medium for archival and storage purposes.

CD-R drives can read standard CD-ROM discs. They can also write data to **CD-R discs,** which have a coating of temperature-sensitive dye, greenish-gold in color. When the laser hits this dye, it changes the color and alters the dye's reflective properties. Although the writing technique differs from that used to create CD-ROM discs, standard CD-ROM drives can read the data from CD-R discs.

CD-R is a "write-once" technology. After you've saved data to the disc, you can't erase it or write over it. An advantage of CD-R discs is that they aren't expensive; in quantities of 20 or more, they're often available for less than $1 per disc.

CD-RW drives provide full read/write capabilities using erasable **CD-RW discs,** which are more expensive than CD-R discs. CD-RW drives can also write to less expensive CD-R discs, giving users the best of both worlds.

Figure   2B.22

The CD-ROM is the most popular and least expensive optical disc. CD-ROM drives are standard and necessary equipment for today's personal computers.

DVD-ROM Discs and Drives

The newest optical disc format, digital video disc (DVD), also called digital versatile disk (DVD), is capable of storing an entire digitized movie. DVD discs are designed to work with DVD video players and televisions, and have proven very popular with movie-watching consumers.

The computer version of DVD, called **DVD-ROM,** has not proven as popular. One reason is that most computers are still equipped with CD-ROM drives, and few users see a reason to upgrade (unless they want to watch DVD movies on their computers). Another reason involves competing standards. Until recently, several competing DVD-ROM standards were being pushed by product manufacturers, leading consumers to worry that they might be stuck with a worthless drive if the manufacturer's favored format lost out.

Do not

Do not expose the disc to excessive heat or sunlight.

Do not touch the underside of the disc.

Do not write on the label side of the disc.

Do not eat, smoke, or drink near a disc.

Do not stack discs.

Do

Do store the disc in a jewel box when not in use.

Do hold a disc by its edges.

Do's and don'ts of handling discs.

Figure 2B.23

A DVD-ROM drive and DVD-ROM disc. DVD discs are designed to work with DVD video players and televisions and are popular with movie-watching consumers.

Still, DVD has much to offer. DVD-ROM discs can store up to 17GB of data, and DVD-ROM drives can transfer data at high speeds (up to 12 Mbps, comparable to the data transfer rates of hard drives). In addition, DVD-ROM drives are downwardly compatible with CD-ROM. This means that DVD-ROM drives can read CD-ROM discs as well as DVD-ROM discs (see Figure 2B.23).

A read/write version, called **DVD-RAM** (digital video disc-RAM), enables computer users to create DVD-ROM discs containing up to nearly five gigabytes of data. As with DVD-ROM, a profusion of incompatible formats has made consumers reluctant to embrace DVD-RAM, but this technology—like DVD-ROM—is expected to take off once clear standards emerge.

More Optical Storage Technologies

Although other optical storage technologies exist, they have not proven popular due to a lack of standards. As a result, discs must be read by the same brand and type of drive that created them. Similar to CD-R, **write once, read many (WORM)** systems use recordable 12-inch optical discs that can store up to 15GB. Also used for large-scale data archiving are **magneto-optical**

SPOTLIGHT   DECAYING DATA

▶ Many people believe that computers are a great boon to society because once information is stored on the computer, paper records are then no longer necessary. After all, after data is digitized, it's available forever, right?

Recent studies, however, have concluded that the data you store in your computer may not be as safe as you think. As we rush further and further into the computer age, much of the world's data is either decaying or becoming obsolete.

How can data decay? Any data is only as reliable as the medium on which it is stored. Perhaps the least reliable storage medium is the RAM in your computer system. When the power goes off, anything stored in memory is lost forever. Diskettes run a close second in lack of reliability. Many "old school" computer users have war stories of data that was corrupted or lost because it was on a floppy disk that became damaged or accidentally erased.

Diskettes aren't the only physical medium that suffers from reliability problems. Much of the world's data is stored on some sort of magnetic tape. Despite the fact that these tapes hold quite a bit of information, they are also very susceptible to environmental influences. Tapes can physically break down from exposure to air, heat, and humidity. As they deteriorate, the information stored on them becomes unrecoverable.

Problems with data recovery from deteriorating media have led to the loss of quite a bit of priceless data. For instance, some researchers believe that up to 20 percent of the data generated during NASA's 1976 Viking mission to Mars is no longer accessible due to deteriorated tapes. Computerized data archives at other government agencies and at large corporations are experiencing similar problems.

The data decay problem even reaches to relatively new storage devices. For instance, CD-ROM drives were once heralded as a permanent storage medium. Findings by different laboratories have shown that CD-ROMs can deteriorate in as few as five years, depending on how they are stored.

Decay is not the only problem. A bigger problem with stored data is outright obsolescence. If you have been using computers for any length of time, you know that programs and equipment change rapidly. Every year or so, a new version of an old software program is brought to the market. Frequently, the program changes the way it stores information on disk. Over time, some older programs are no longer available on computer systems. In addition, new computer systems are brought into an organization to replace older systems, and the new systems don't use the same technology as the old.

The upshot is that if the programs or equipment used to create data are gone, and the data files have not been updated or transferred to a new format, the data becomes essentially worthless. A simple example of this problem can easily be seen in many organizations. At one time, a lot of data was stored on 5 1/2-inch floppy disks. New computer systems gradually replaced the old systems, and the new systems had only 3.5-inch drives. The old data is no longer accessible.

With more and more of the world's data being either converted to digital formats or created that way in the first place, the longevity of the data is bound to become a bigger and bigger issue. Government, business, and educators are going to have to test their data periodically and review their storage methods to make sure that their information is still accessible. The problem (and subsequent solutions) may lead to a new category of computer career for those specializing in data storage and recovery.

(MO) discs, erasable discs that combine the magnetic principles used on tape and disk with new optical technology.

STORAGE HORIZONS

In response to the explosive demand for more storage capacity, designers are creating storage devices that store more data and retrieve this data more quickly. Exemplifying these trends are FMD-ROM discs and storage area networks.

IMPACTS

Computers in Science

Is Science Going Too Far?

Computers are helping science make impressive gains, but some people worry about the consequences of a scientific enterprise that accepts no limits on its work. For example, with the aid of computers and fast-breaking biological discoveries, scientists could unintentionally create a ravenous, uncontrollable bacterium—an artificially-created "gray goo"—that could pose a genuine threat to the survival of life on our planet. Such fears have long been voiced by environmentalists and other critics of science, but some scientists and engineers are joining them. Sun Microsystems co-founder Bill Joy, a leader of the team that developed the Internet, puts the point this way: "There are certain technologies that are so terrible that you must say no. We have to stop some research. It's one strike and you're out." If Joy is right, some hard questions follow. How do we decide whether we've gone too far?

Others believe the problem doesn't lie with science so much as the inability of human societies to prepare themselves for scientific advances. For example, the Human Genome Project has already unveiled the genetic basis of many human diseases, but little thought has been given to the impact of this knowledge on peoples' lives. In the U.S., health insurance is predicated on not having a preexisting condition. If health insurance companies say that having a high genetic risk is the same as having a preexisting condition, people could lose their health insurance and find themselves facing huge bills for medical treatment. Sound unlikely? It's already happened. In the early 1970s, for example, some insurers denied coverage or hiked rates for African Americans who carried the gene for sickle cell anemia. Although these people were not ill, and may never have gotten ill, they still had to pay higher insurance rates (or do without health insurance) simply because of their genes.

What about employers? Routinely, employers screen applicants by consulting databases containing records of criminal arrests, drug offenses, worker's compensation claims, and much more. If database vendors start collecting genetic information about people, employers are likely to use this information to exclude employees who have high genetic risks for disease, such as alcoholism. Such employees could cost the company a lot of money in lost work, increased health insurance costs, and absenteeism. Information developed by the Human Genome Project could create a new class of people who are unemployable because they *might* develop a disease in the future.

Privacy is a problem, too. What will happen if an enterprising database vendor decides to obtain a copy of your genetic code and place this information in a database so that anyone can search it for a fee? Currently, no law would prohibit anyone from doing so. Like so many other innovations set in motion by computing, the Human Genome Project will increase the demand for laws that prevent intrusion into a citizen's deeply personal affairs. What could be more personal than your genes?

And what about the ownership of basic genetic information? Concerns about the misuse of human genetic information are growing now that for-profit companies are entering the sequencing game. A U.S.-based company called Celera Genomics has been giving the Human Genome Project a run for its money—and in early 2000, Celera announced that it had finished a complete sequence of the human genome. Celera's stockholders expect a return on their investment. The company plans to make money by selling subscriptions to its huge databases of genomic information, which will prove invaluable to scientific and medical researchers. But how will Celera protect this information? Will the company seek to obtain copyrights or patents on the information that underlies living organisms?

International security experts are concerned about a new wave of biological terrorism as scientists come closer to synthesizing living viruses and bacteria in the laboratory. For example, researchers at the Institute for Genomic Research, located in Rockville, MD, are trying to identify the minimum number of genes an organism needs to survive. If they succeed, they believe they will be able to synthesize viruses and bacteria in the laboratory. Before long, anyone with a $1,000 personal computer and a $10,000 gene sequencer can start creating their own viruses and bacteria—including deadly viruses and bacteria. Perhaps the "gray goo" scenario is not as far-fetched as it initially sounds.

FMD-ROM

A single optical disk, scientists believe, can store no more than about 5 giga-bits per square inch. But why not create transparent disks with more than one layer? Here's the idea: each layer contains data, but it is transparent enough to allow a laser beam to shine through. The laser beam focuses on only one layer at a time. If this sounds futuristic, take a look at a DVD-ROM disc. It contains two layers—which is why DVD-ROM stores so much more data than its single-layer predecessor, CD-ROM.

Why not create more than two layers? In research laboratories, efforts to create more than two layers failed because the layers created too much reflect-ed light, which caused errors in reading the data. However, a new technology called **FMD-ROM** (short for **florescent multilayer disc-read only memory**) solves this problem. In a FMD-ROM drive, each layer is coated with a flores-cent substance. When the laser beam strikes this layer, the light that is bounced back is also florescent. This type of light can pass undisturbed through the disc's many layers, so the errors are eliminated. Research indi-cates that FMD-ROM discs of up to 100 layers are possible. While no larger than today's CD-ROM, such discs could each contain up to 1 terabyte of data.

Storage Area Networks (SAN)

In large organizations, storage is generally provided by devices (such as RAID drives and CD-ROM jukeboxes) that are attached to servers. A **server** is a high-powered computer that makes resources available to all network users. But this approach creates a bottleneck. Users must be able to locate and gain access to the server that contains the appropriate storage. If the server is not available, the storage isn't available, either. One solution to this problem is called a **storage area network (SAN).** A storage area network links high-capacity storage devices to all of the organization's servers. In this way, any of the storage devices are accessible from any of the servers.

TAKEAWAY POINTS

- Memory uses costly, high-speed components to make software and data available for the CPU's use. Memory needs to be large enough to hold the software and data that are currently in use. RAM memory is volatile and does not retain information when the computer is switched off. In contrast, storage is slower and less costly, but it offers far greater capacity. Storage devices are nonvolatile; they retain information even when the current is switched off. Storage devices play important input and output roles, too. When you start your computer or launch an application, storage devices function as input devices as they transfer information into memory. When you've created valuable documents with your application, storage devices play an important output role by saving your work.

- Storage media are categorized by the type of operations they can perform (read-only or read/write), the type of data access they provide (sequential or random-access), the type of technology they use (magnetic or optical), and their location in the storage hierarchy (online, near-online, or offline).

- A storage device's performance is measured in terms of its capacity (in bytes), as well as its access speed, the time that elapses before the device begins transferring the requested data.

- Floppy disks are portable and provide a convenient way to exchange files with other computer users. However, their storage capacity is so small that they are close to obsolete.

- Floppy disks store data in circular bands called tracks. Each track is divided into pie-shaped wedges called sectors. The sectors are combined into clusters, which provide the basic unit for data storage. To access data on the drive, the drive's actuator moves the read/write head to the track that contains the desired data.

- Hard disks store data in much the same way floppies do, except the hard disk contains multiple platters. Because hard disks offer so much storage space, it is sometimes convenient to divide them into sections, called partitions, which appear to the operating system as if they were separate disks.

- A hard disk's performance is measured by its positioning performance (how quickly the drive can position the read/write head so that it begins transferring data) and its transfer performance (how quickly the drive sends the information once the head has reached the correct position). Positioning performance is expressed by the drive's seek time, while transfer performance is affected by the drive's spindle speed.

- The two leading hard disk interfaces are descended from the original IDE and SCSI specifications. IDE drives are cheaper and more widely-available. SCSI drives are faster and offer greater storage capacity, but they require an expensive interface card.

- Removable disks are useful for data archiving and data backup purposes.

- CD-ROM discs and drives are standard equipment in today's computer systems, largely because most software is now distributed on CD-ROM discs. CD-ROM is a read-only technology. CD-R drives can record once on inexpensive CD-R discs; CD-RW drives can write repeatedly to erasable CD-RW discs, which are more expensive. Read-only DVD-ROM discs offer much more storage capacity, and DVD-ROM drives are downwardly compatible with CD-ROM discs. A read/write version, DVD-RAM, has been slow to catch on due to standardization squabbles.

MODULE REVIEW

KEY TERMS AND CONCEPTS

access time	CD-R drives	digital data storage (DDS)
activity light	CD-RW discs	digital linear tape (DLT)
advanced intelligent tape (AIT)	CD-RW drives	DVD-RAM
ATA (AT attachment)	CD-ROM	DVD-ROM
ATA-2	cylinder	directories
backup	data archiving	disk cache
bad sectors	data backup	double-density (DD)
cluster	data transfer rate	entry-level drives
CD-R discs	digital audio tape (DAT)	Fast ATA

Fast IDE
fault tolerance
file allocation table (FAT)
files
fixed disks
floppy disk (diskette)
floppy disk drive
FMD-ROM (Florescent
   Multilayer Disc-Read Only
   Memory)
folders
formatting
fragmented
hard disk
hard disk controller
head actuator
head crash
high-density (HD)
High FD (HiFD)
IDE/ATA
Integrated Drive Electronics
   (IDE)
land
latency
magnetic storage media
magneto-optical (MO) discs

magneto-optical (MO) drives
memory
milliseconds (ms)
mirroring/duplexing
multisession CDs
nanoseconds (ns)
near-online storage
offline storage
online storage
optical storage media
partitions
PhotoCDs
pits
platters
portable
positioning performance
preformatted
quarter-inch cartridge (QIC)
RAID (redundant array of
   inexpensive disks)
RAID Level 1
random-access storage device
reading
read-only
read/write head

read/write media
removable hard disks
saving
sectors
seek time
sequential storage device
server
single-session CDs
Small Computer System
   Interface (SCSI)
solid state disks (SDD)
spindle speeds
storage
storage area network (SAN)
storage hierarchy
striping
SuperDisk
tracks
transfer performance
Ultra3 SCSI or Ultra160 SCSI
Ultra DMA/66 or ATA-5
write once, read many (WORM)
write-protect tab
writing
Zip drive

TRUE/FALSE

Indicate whether the following statements are true or false.

1. Storage devices provide nonvolatile storage for programs and data.

2. A tape backup unit is an example of a random-access storage device.

3. A CD-ROM is classified as offline storage in the storage hierarchy.

4. The amount of time it takes for a storage device to begin reading data is called access time.

5. A floppy disk is a portable media device.

6. Before you can use a disk, it must be formatted.

7. Disk cache is a type of memory that improves a floppy disk's performance.

8. The most popular and least expensive optical disc standard is now DVD-ROM.

9. CD-RW is a "write-once" technology which means that after you've saved data to the disc, you can't erase or write over it.

10. Storage area networks link high capacity storage devices to all of an organization's servers.

MATCHING

Match each key term from the left column to the most accurate definition in the right column.

_____ 1. storage

_____ 2. memory

_____ 3. read/write head

_____ 4. sequential storage

_____ 5. optical storage

_____ 6. near-online storage

_____ 7. seek time

_____ 8. track

_____ 9. hard disk

_____ 10. RAID

a. a device that groups two or more hard disks that contain exactly the same data

b. storage that isn't directly available

c. a circular band on a disk

d. all the various media on which a computer system can store software and data

e. a high-capacity, high-speed, online storage device

f. characterized by a computer going through a fixed sequence of stored items to locate the one that's needed

g. media that use tightly-focused laser beams to read microscopic patterns of data encoded on a disk's surface

h. a temporary storage location

i. an electromagnet that records information by transforming electrical impulses into a varying magnetic field

j. the time it takes the read/write head to locate data before reading begins

MULTIPLE CHOICE

Circle the letter of the correct choice for each of the following.

1. What is the name for a storage device that allows you to record and retrieve data?
   a. input/output device
   b. read-only device
   c. read/write device
   d. digital output device

2. Which of the following storage devices do not use magnetic-sensitive materials for recording information?
   a. CD-ROM drive
   b. tape drive
   c. hard disk drive
   d. floppy disk drive

3. The storage hierarchy consists of the following three levels:
   a. offline storage, random-access storage, online storage.
   b. online storage, near-online storage, offline storage.
   c. online storage, offline storage, read/write storage.
   d. online storage, near-online storage, optical storage.

4. Which of the following is an important factor in storage performance?
   a. latency
   b. portability
   c. access time
   d. high-density

5. Which of the following enables you to turn any floppy disk into a read-only disk?
   a. head actuator
   b. write-protect tab
   c. sector
   d. read/write head

6. Which of the following is not an important factor in hard disk performance?
   a. transfer performance
   b. disk cache
   c. positioning performance
   d. cable type

7. Which of the following is not associated with RAID technology?
   a. A group of more than two hard disks containing different data.
   b. They offer a high degree of fault tolerance.
   c. Most major Web sites use RAID technology.
   d. RAID is widely-used wherever a service interruption would prove costly or inconvenient.

8. Removable hard disks are what kind of storage medium?
   a. offline storage
   b. online storage
   c. near-online storage
   d. sequential storage

9. Which device is now considered standard and necessary equipment for modern personal computers?
   a. floppy drive
   b. CD-ROM drive
   c. DVD-ROM drive
   d. CD-R drive

10. Which of the following is not true about a CD-R drive?
   a. It allows you to record information on a special disc.
   b. It can read standard CD-ROMs.
   c. It can write to a disc only once.
   d. It is still a very expensive medium for archival and storage purposes.

FILL-IN

In the blank provided, write the correct answer for each of the following.

1. A tape backup unit is one example of a(n) _____ storage device.

2. MO is an acronym for _____ , a type of optical storage device.

3. _____ storage is the most important component of the hierarchy.

4. Floppy disks are an example of _____ media, which means you can remove a floppy disk from one computer and insert it into another.

5. Floppy disks contain a(n) _____ that you can open to protect data from being overwritten or deleted.

6. Each track on a disk is divided into wedges called _____ , which in turn group together to form _____ .

7. Damaged areas on a disk are called _____ .

8. _____ refers to how quickly the hard disk drive can position the read/write head so that it can transfer data.

9. To communicate with the CPU, hard disks require a(n) _____ , which provides an interface between the CPU and the hard disk's electronics.

10. CD-ROM disc drives vary in speed, which is measured in the unit's _____ rate.

SHORT ANSWER

On a separate sheet of paper, answer the following questions.

1. How is a magnetic disk prepared to store information? What happens during the preparation process?

2. Discuss the purpose of partitions, clusters, and sectors in a disk drive.

3. What factors affect disk drive performance?

4. What different types of hard drive interfaces are available for small computer systems?

5. What makes a Zip drive a convenient peripheral for a computer system?

6. Discuss how the technology used in optical storage media differs from that used in conventional disk drives.

7. What are the differences between DVD-ROM and CD-ROM?

8. Why are DVD-ROM drives not as popular as CD-ROM drives yet?

9. What benefits are possible with FDM-ROM technology?

10. What problem does a storage area network solve?

2C

MODULE

WHAT YOU WILL LEARN . . .

When you have finished reading this module, you will be able to:

1. List the four types of input and explain the purpose of each.
2. List the characteristics of a computer keyboard that differ from typewriter keyboards.
3. Explain the purpose of the special keys on the computer's keyboard.
4. Describe the benefits and drawbacks of speech recognition as an alternative to keyboard use.
5. List the most frequently used pointing devices, and explain why users sometimes prefer alternatives to the mouse.
6. Describe the different mouse types.
7. List devices that are used to get sound, video, and images into the computer.
8. Identify the two major types of output and give examples of each.
9. Explain how the characteristics of the computer's video adapter determine the overall quality of the image displayed on the monitor.
10. List the various types of monitors, and indicate the advantages and disadvantages of each.
11. Explain how to judge a monitor's quality.
12. Identify the two major types of printers, and indicate the advantages and disadvantages of each.

The heart of the computer is the CPU, experts say. But that's not the part of the computer that users experience. When you're using the computer, what commands your attention are the input and output devices you're using—typically, a keyboard, a mouse, and a monitor. Input devices enable you to transform information into a digital representation that the computer can process. Output devices transform processed digital information into forms that make sense to humans.

This module explores the world of input and output devices. You're about to begin a journey into the senses, both the computer's artificial senses and your natural ones. The computer's input devices can be compared to human senses in that they enable the computer to see, hear, and even detect odors. The computer's output devices put our senses into contact with processed data, engaging our eyes, our ears, and even our sense of touch.

Explore IT Lab

Hardware

UNDERSTANDING INPUT: NOT JUST DATA ENTRY

The term **input** refers to data, software, or instructions that you enter into the computer's memory. There are four types of input:

- **Software** Storage devices function as input devices when they are used to transfer software from storage media to the computer's memory. If you're sitting down at the computer to write a college essay, you will begin by launching your word processing application. This causes your computer to transfer the word processing program from your computer's hard disk to its memory.

- **Data** The term **data** refers to unorganized (or relatively unorganized) words, numbers, images, or sounds that the computer can transform into something more useful. The first draft of a college essay is an example of a collection of data—in this case, words—that will need some organization. After all, very few writers produce polished work from the get-go!

- **Commands** A **command** tells the program what to do. To revise and polish your essay, you'll use several of the word processing program's commands. You'll delete unnecessary words, move sentences and paragraphs around, sort tables into alphabetical order, number pages, and check spelling. In other words, you use commands to tell the computer how to process the data that you have typed into the computer.

- **Responses** Sometimes programs ask you to decide what to do. For example, if you quit your word processing application without saving your essay, you will be asked whether you want to abandon the file or save it on a disk.

INPUT DEVICES: THE COMPUTER'S "SENSES"

Input devices are hardware components that enable you to get programs, data, commands, and responses into the computer's memory.

You're probably familiar with computer keyboards and mice, the two most-commonly used input devices. What you may not realize is how many ways the computer can "sense" the world around it. Increasingly, computers have "eyes" and "ears," and even a way to detect odors.

Figure **2C.1**

The keyboard.

The following sections explore the world of input devices, beginning with the most common ones: keyboards and pointing devices (such as mice and trackballs). Next, you'll learn about additional input devices you may encounter. The module concludes by examining how automated input systems are used in business.

Introducing Keyboards

Unfortunately for those of us who hate to type, the **keyboard** is still the best way to get data into the computer.

When you press one of the keys, the keyboard sends a digital impulse to the computer. Generally, this impulse travels through a cable that is connected to the computer's keyboard connector. Some computers are equipped with an infrared port that enables them to use a **wireless keyboard.** These keyboards work on the same principle as a TV remote control device.

When the computer receives the impulse from the keyboard, it displays a **character** on-screen. A character is a letter, number, punctuation mark, or symbol (such as $ or #). The character appears at the onscreen location of the **cursor,** which shows where text will appear when you type. The cursor (also called the **insertion point**) may be a blinking vertical line, a blinking underscore, or a highlighted box.

Using a Computer Keyboard

A standard computer keyboard looks and works much like an electric typewriter keyboard (see Figure 2C.1). For example, to enter a capital letter, you hold down the Shift key and type the letter. Like an electric typewriter, the computer keyboard also has an **autorepeat** function. If you hold a key down, it begins entering multiple copies of the character.

Despite the resemblance, computer keyboards differ from typewriter keyboards in several important ways. On the computer keyboard, some keys work differently than they do on a typewriter. On a typewriter, you press Enter to start a new line. When you are writing with a computer, you press Enter only when you want to start a new paragraph. (The software automatically determines when it's time to start a new line.)

Another way in which computer keyboards differ from typewriter keyboards concerns the way in which certain keys work differently at times. When you are typing text with a word processing program, for example, the Tab key works like a typewriter's Tab key: it indents the text. On a computer keyboard, the Tab key works differently when you are displaying a dialog box, a type of window that appears when a program needs information from you. In a dialog box, the Tab key moves the cursor to the next available area. If you hold down the Shift key and press Tab, the cursor moves to the previous area. These keys work the same way when you are filling out a form on a Web page.

The most striking difference between a typewriter and a computer keyboard lies in the number of keys. Computer keyboards typically have many more keys than a typewriter does.

Desktop PCs typically come equipped with an **enhanced keyboard,** which has 101 keys (see Table 2C.1). (The Macintosh equivalent, called the **extended keyboard,** uses almost exactly the same key layout.) Notebook computers have fewer keys. However, you can hold down a special function key that enables you to duplicate the functions of the additional keys on the enhanced keyboard. To use a desktop or notebook computer successfully, you need to learn what these extra keys do.

Special Keys on the PC Enhanced Keyboard		Table 2C.1

Key Name	Typical Function
Alt	Enters a command (used with another key, as in the following example: Alt + X).
Backspace	Deletes the character to the left of the cursor.
Caps Lock	Toggles caps lock mode on or off.
Ctrl	Enters a command (used with another key, as in the following example: Ctrl + C).
Delete	Deletes the character to the right of the cursor.
Down arrow	Moves the cursor down.
End	Moves the cursor to the end of the current line.
Enter	Starts a new paragraph.
Esc	Cancels the current operation or closes a dialog box.
F1	Displays on-screen help.
F10	Activates the menu.
Home	Moves the cursor to the beginning of the current line.
Insert	Toggles between insert and overwrite mode, if these modes are available in the program you are using.
Left arrow	Moves the cursor left.
Num Lock	Toggles the numeric keypad's num lock mode, in which the keypad enters numbers.
Page Down	Moves down one screenful or one page.
Page Up	Moves up one screenful or one page.
Pause/Break	Suspends a program. This key is not used by most applications.
Popup menu key	Displays the popup menu for the current context (Windows only).
Print Screen	Captures the screen image to a graphics file, or prints the current screen on the printer.
Right arrow	Moves the cursor right.
Scroll Lock	This key is not used by most applications.
Shift	Types a capital letter.
Tab	Indents one tab stop or moves to the next entry area.
Up arrow	Moves the cursor up.
Windows key	Displays the Start menu in Microsoft Windows.

Cursor-Movement Keys

As you've learned, the cursor (also called insertion point) shows where your text will appear when you start typing. If you don't want to type where the cursor is located, you should use **cursor-movement keys** (also called **arrow keys**) to move the cursor around. Although programs implement the Home and End keys in different ways, they can also be used to move the cursor.

Numeric Keypad

Most keyboards have a **numeric keypad.** Trained operators can use this keypad to enter numerical data quickly.

Toggle Keys

The numeric keypad has two modes: a number-entry mode and a cursor-movement mode. To switch this mode on and off, press the Num Lock key.

The **Num Lock** key is a **toggle key.** This type of key is named after a type of electrical switch that has only two positions (on and off).

The **Caps Lock** key also functions as a toggle key. It switches the Caps Lock mode on and off. When the Caps Lock mode is engaged, you do not have to press the Shift key to enter capital letters. To turn the Caps Lock mode off, just touch the key again.

The keyboard uses **status indicators** to show whether a toggle key's function is turned on or off. If the function is on, the indicator lights up.

Function Keys

Above the letters and numbers on the keyboard, you'll find **function keys** (labeled F1 through F10 or F12). Programs can give these keys different functions, although F1 is almost always used to provide help to the user.

You'll also notice a key called **Esc,** which is short for Escape. The Esc key's function also depends on which program you're using, but it is generally used to interrupt or cancel an operation.

Modifier Keys

Some keys have no effect unless you hold them down and press a second key. They are called **modifier keys** because they modify the meaning of the next key you press. You'll use modifier keys in **keyboard shortcuts,** which provide a keyboard shortcut to menu commands.

On PCs, the modifier keys you use are called the Alt and Ctrl. On Macintosh, the modifier keys are called Ctrl, Command (indicated with the symbol ?), and Option.

In most program manuals, instructions for holding down keys list the keys to press, separated by plus signs, as in the following examples:

```
Alt+P       Hold down Alt and press P or p
Ctrl+Y      Hold down Ctrl and press Y or y
+E          Hold down Command and press E or e (Macintosh
            only)
```

In most cases, it doesn't matter whether you type an uppercase letter (such as P, Y, or E in the previous examples) or a lowercase letter (p, y, or e); Alt + P and Alt + p do the same thing.

Sometimes you need to hold down more than one special key to give the command. Here are some examples:

```
Shift + Ctrl + B        Hold down Shift and Ctrl, and
                        press B or b
Ctrl + Alt + Home       Hold down the Ctrl and Alt keys,
                        and press Home
Command + Option + G    Hold down the Command and Option
                        keys, and press G (Macintosh only)
```

Sometimes you need to type more than one letter while you're holding down the special key. Here's an example:

```
Ctrl + N, 1     Hold down Ctrl, press N or n, then release
                these keys, and press 1.
```

Standard Keyboard Shortcuts

PC Shortcut	Mac Shortcut	Purpose
Ctrl + A	+A	Select all available items
Ctrl + B	+B	Bold
Ctrl + C	+C	Copy text from clipboard
Ctrl + F	+F	Find text
Ctrl + I	+I	Italic
Ctrl + J	+J	Justify text
Ctrl + N	+N	Create a new document
Ctrl + O	+O	Open an existing document
Ctrl + P	+P	Print
Ctrl + Q	+Q	Quit
Ctrl + S	+S	Save
Ctrl + U	+U	Underline
Ctrl + V	+V	Paste
Ctrl + X	+X	Cut

See Table 2C.2 for a list of standard keyboard shortcuts. Although these short-cuts aren't actually standardized by any independent standards body, they are widely used in Windows, Macintosh, and Linux (GNOME/KDE) applications.

Windows Keys

On keyboards specially-designed for use with Microsoft Windows, you'll find two additional keys. The key with a window icon opens the Windows Start menu. The one with a box containing an arrow does the same thing as click-ing the right mouse button.

Alternative Keyboards

Unlike typewriter keyboards, computer keyboards are fully programmable. Most use the standard **QWERTY keyboard** layout, which is named after the first five letters at the upper left of the letter area (Figure 2C.2). However, some typists prefer the Dvorak keyboard layout. A Dvorak keyboard places the most-frequently used keys under the strongest fingers, which is claimed to reduce wasted finger motion and awkward keystrokes. Some people firmly believe that a long string of scientific studies proves that the Dvorak keyboard is clear-ly superior, and that it has not been adopted because people are so used to the inferior QWERTY layout. However, scholars have recently shown that such claims fall into the category of urban myth. It is simply not true: scientific studies haven't proved the Dvorak keyboard's superiority. On the contrary, these studies prove that it is not worth learning Dvorak if you already know QWERTY. At best, with the Dvorak layout, you might type a little faster.

Entering International Characters

If you are studying a foreign language, you may need to write an assign-ment in French, Spanish, or German. To do so, you will need to type **dia-critical marks** that are not found in English. These diacritical marks

Techtalk

urban myth
An urban myth is a false or inaccurate story about city life (and often, about technology) that is unin-tentionally perpetuated by people (often highly-educated people). Such tales often have a mea-sure of truth to them that lends credibility. An exam-ple is the oft-told story that GM suffered huge sales losses in Mexico when the company intro-duced a new Chevrolet named Nova. In Spanish, **no va** means "It doesn't go." However, the name did not hurt the Nova's sales. It sold very well in Mexico. For more infor-mation on urban myths, visit **http://www. urbanlegends.com**.

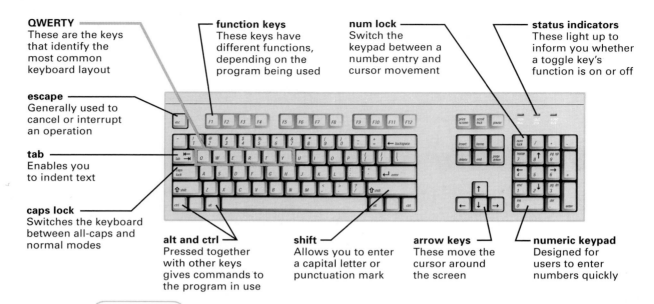

QWERTY
These are the keys that identify the most common keyboard layout

function keys
These keys have different functions, depending on the program being used

num lock
Switch the keypad between a number entry and cursor movement

status indicators
These light up to inform you whether a toggle key's function is on or off

escape
Generally used to cancel or interrupt an operation

tab
Enables you to indent text

caps lock
Switches the keyboard between all-caps and normal modes

alt and ctrl
Pressed together with other keys gives commands to the program in use

shift
Allows you to enter a capital letter or punctuation mark

arrow keys
These move the cursor around the screen

numeric keypad
Designed for users to enter numbers quickly

Figure 2C.2

The QWERTY keyboard is named after the first five letters at the upper left of the letter area.

include accent marks, tildes, and umlauts. To enter diacritical marks, **dead keys** are used.

A dead key is a type of keyboard shortcut that adds a diacritical mark to the next letter you type. To use a dead key, press and release the dead key shortcut. Nothing should appear on-screen. You won't see a character until you press one of the letters on the keyboard, which then appears with the appropriate diacritical mark.

Macintosh dead key shortcuts make use of the Option key, as in the following example:

```
Option + `, a
```

To use this shortcut, hold down the Option key and press the acute accent key (`). Then release both keys and press a. The result is an "a" with an acute accent (à).

Macintosh users should note that many international characters are entered with direct keyboard shortcuts rather than dead keys. To see which keyboard shortcut to use for these characters, click the Apple menu, choose Key Caps, and press the Option key.

Windows dead key shortcuts make use of the Ctrl key, as in the following example:

```
Ctrl + `, a      à
```

To use this shortcut, hold down the Ctrl key and press the acute accent key (`). Then release both keys and press a. The result is an "a" with an acute accent (à).

If you're writing in Spanish, note that you can enter Spanish punctuation using Alt + Ctrl + Shift + ? (for ¿) and Alt + Ctrl + Shift + ! (for ¡).

Table 2C.3 lists the dead keys you can use on Macintosh and Windows systems.

Health Risks of Keyboard Use

Be aware that prolonged keyboard use can cause **cumulative trauma disorder (CTD)**, also called **repetitive strain injury (RSI).** This type of injury involves damage to sensitive nerve tissue due to motions repeated thousands of times daily. Sometimes these injuries are so serious that they require surgery. To help prevent these problems, **ergonomic keyboards** are avail-

Inserting International Characters

Table 2C.3

Mac OS Dead Key	Microsoft Windows Dead Key	Letter to Press	Example of Result
Option + ` (acute accent)	Ctrl + ` (acute accent)	any vowel	à
Option + e	Ctrl + ' (apostrophe)	any vowel	á
Option + ^ (caret)	Ctrl + Shift + ^ (caret)	any vowel	â
Option + n	Ctrl + Shift + ~ (tilde)	a, n, o, A, N, O	ñ
Option + u	Ctrl + Shift + : (colon)	any vowel	ä
	Ctrl + Shift + @	a or A	å, Å
	Ctrl + Shift + &	a or A	æ, Æ
	Ctrl + Shift + &	o or O	œ, Œ
	Ctrl + Shift + &	s	β
	Ctrl + , (comma)	c or C	ç, Ç
	Ctrl + ' (apostrophe)	d or D	∂, D
	Ctrl + /,	o or O	ø, Ø

able. Ergonomic keyboards such as the Microsoft Natural Keyboard (see Figure 2C.3) keep the wrists straight, reducing (but not eliminating) the chance of an injury. For more information on typing-related injuries, see Module 10B.

Speech Recognition

Keyboards are unpleasant, difficult, and risky to use. Many experts believe that computing will not come into its own until computers learn to understand and respond to human speech. Thanks to recent advances in **speech recognition,** this day may be close at hand (see Figure 2C.4).

Also called **voice recognition,** speech recognition is a type of input in which the computer recognizes spoken words. Depending on the context, the word may be interpreted as part of a command (such as "Open Microsoft Word") or as data input. If the word is interpreted as data, it appears within a document as if you had typed it at the keyboard. Speech recognition requires special software as well as a microphone.

To understand speech recognition, it is important to grasp that speech recognition doesn't require the computer to understand the *meaning* of human speech. When you speak the words "I don't like you" into a speech recognition system, it does not suffer from hurt feelings. Instead, it scrutinizes the sounds it detects and tries to match them with the sound patterns of the words that it knows. If all goes well, you see the words "I don't like you" on-screen. Efforts to endow computers with the intelligence to understand the meaning of speech are part of the field of artificial intelligence, discussed in Module 10D.

Although far from perfect, today's speech recognition software is much better than its predecessors. In the past, speech recognition systems used **discrete speech recognition.** In discrete speech recognition systems, you must speak

Figure 2C.3

Ergonomic keyboards like this one can help prevent cumulative trauma disorder (CTD).

Destinations

For the latest on speech recognition technology, including reviews of the latest software, visit 21st Century Eloquence (**http://www.voice recognition.com**).

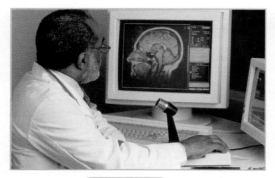

Figure 2C.4

Speech recognition technology enables users to use spoken words to command the computer and enter textual data.

each word separately, as in this example: "Please. Record. This. Sentence." If you didn't pause between words, the software would make a mistake. Today's **continuous speech recognition** software enables users to speak without pausing between words. Still, even the best of today's programs make many mistakes. An error rate of 5 percent is considered excellent. In addition, most speech recognition programs perform well only after users go through a lengthy training process, in which the software learns to adjust to the speaker's idiosyncratic speech patterns.

Will speech recognition replace the keyboard? Most writers dislike speech recognition systems. Speaking and writing differ, so it's a challenge to learn how to "write" by speaking. (Readers expect written text to be more organized than a speech.) Also, writers are accustomed to typing. Perhaps a new generation of writers will grow up with speech recognition systems rather than keyboards, so they won't have to go through an adjustment to write with such systems.

Speech recognition may not be the choice of future Hemingways, but it's already widely used in business. When you dial 411 to get someone's telephone number in most areas of the U.S., speech recognition systems listen to the name you supply, and try to locate the number automatically.

Pointing Devices

A **pointing device** gives users control over the movements of an on-screen **pointer.** The pointer is an on-screen symbol that signifies the type of command, input, or response you can give (see Figure 2C.5). Pointing devices also enable users to initiate actions, such as clicking, double-clicking, selecting, and dragging (see Figure 2C.6). By means of these actions, users can give commands and responses to the program that the computer is running. Pointing devices can also be used to provide input. For example, pointing devices can be used in graphics programs to draw and paint on-screen, as if you were using a pencil or brush.

Figure 2C.5

Standard pointers (Microsoft Windows).

Pointer Name	Purpose
Normal Select	Selects an item on-screen.
Help Select	Shows help for this item.
Working	Informs you that the computer is busy.
Text Select	Moves the cursor to the pointer's location within text, or selects text by dragging.
Precision Select	Allows for exact on-screen selection.
Unavailable	Informs you that this item is not available now.
Vertical Resize	Resizes vertically as you drag the mouse.
Horizontal Resize	Resizes horizontally as you drag the mouse.
Diagonal Resize	Resizes diagonally as you drag the mouse.
Move	Moves the whole item when you drag the mouse.
Link Select	Moves to this item.

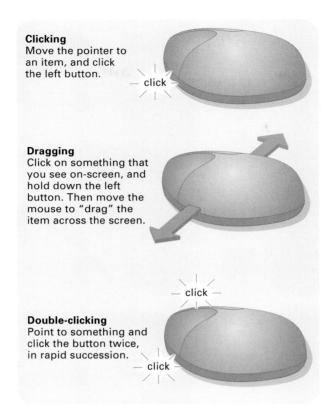

Clicking
Move the pointer to an item, and click the left button.

— click —

Dragging
Click on something that you see on-screen, and hold down the left button. Then move the mouse to "drag" the item across the screen.

— click —

Double-clicking
Point to something and click the button twice, in rapid succession.

— click —

Figure 2C.6

Using a mouse.

Action	Procedure
Point	Move the mouse across the flat surface until the tip of the selection pointer (the arrow) rests on the desired item.
Click	Press and release the button (Macintosh) or the left mouse button (PC).
Double-click	In quick succession, press and release the button (Macintosh) or the left mouse button (PC) two times. If the double-click action doesn't work, try again, but do it faster.
Right-click	Press and hold the button (Macintosh) or the right mouse button (PC).
Drag	Move the pointer to an item. On a Macintosh, hold down the button. On a PC, hold down the left button. Then drag the item to its new location, and release the button.

The most-widely used pointing device is the mouse, which is standard equipment on today's computer systems. However, many users prefer to use mouse alternatives, such as trackballs, pointing sticks, or touchpads. These pointing devices are discussed in this section.

Mouse

A **mouse** is a palm-sized pointing device that is designed to move about on a clean, flat surface (refer to Figure 2C.7a). As you move the mouse, the mouse's movements are mirrored by the on-screen pointer. To initiate actions, use the mouse buttons. On the Macintosh, the mouse has just one button. On the PC, the mouse typically has two buttons. Linux systems may be equipped with a three-button mouse. Some applications use the middle mouse button for certain

(a)

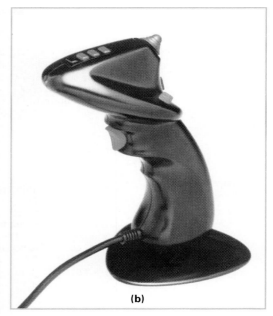

(b)

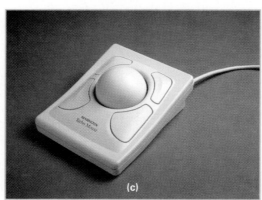

(c)

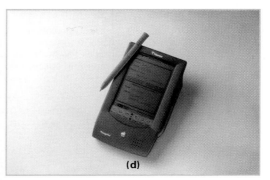

(d)

(e)

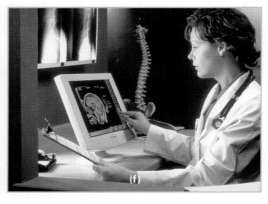

(f)

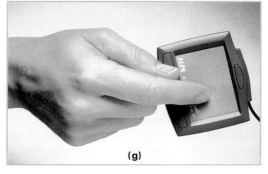

(g)

Figure 2C.7 a–g

Common pointing devices:
(a) Mouse
(b) Joystick
(c) Trackball
(d) Pen
(e) Pointing stick
(f) Touchscreen
(g) Touchpad

purposes. If you're using a Linux system equipped with a two-button mouse, you may be able to emulate the middle button's action by pressing both buttons at the same time.

Types of Mice

Mice connect to computers in different ways. **PS/2 mice** connect to the computer's PS/2 port. Most of the mice sold today are PS/2 mice. Less-commonly used, but still available, are **serial mice,** which connect to a disused serial port. **Bus mice,** an obsolete design, connect to an expansion card that fits into the computer's expansion bus. **Cordless mice** use invisible infrared signals to connect to the computer's infrared (IrDA port). Although cordless mice eliminate the clutter caused by the mouse's cord, the infrared transmitter must be in a direct line of sight with the receiving port on the computer's case. For more information on ports and connectors, see Module 2A.

Mice use two different technologies. **Mechanical mice** use a rotating ball to generate information about the mouse's position. One drawback is that the ball can get dirty, which interferes with the mouse's ability to determine its position. **Optical mice** use a low-power laser to determine the mouse's position. However, you must use this type of mouse on a special mousepad, which uses a grid to determine the mouse's location. Some mice combine the two technologies by using a laser to monitor the mechanical ball's movements.

Developed by Microsoft, the **wheel mouse** includes a rotating wheel that can be used to scroll text vertically within a document or Web page (see Figure 2C.8).

Health Risks of Mouse Usage

Like keyboards, mice are associated with cumulative trauma disorders. Be sure to safeguard your health when you use the computer. If you are unable to use a mouse due to cumulative trauma disorder, you may be able to use a **foot mouse.** A foot mouse uses two interchangeable foot pedals to control the pointer (see Figure 2C.9). One pedal enables the user to control the pointer's location, while the second is used as a clicking device. See Module 10B for more information.

Alternative Pointing Devices

Although the mouse is by far the most popular pointing device, some people prefer alternatives such as trackballs, touchpads, or pointing sticks. These alternatives are especially attractive when desktop space is limited—or nonexistent, as in most of the places where people use notebook computers (such as airline seats).

Trackballs   Trackballs are mice flipped on their backs (refer to Figure 2C.7c). Instead of moving the mouse directly, you move the ball directly. Although some people like trackballs, they are not popular. The ball can be difficult to control with precision. Furthermore, the ball gets dirty from oils on the user's fingers. Frequent cleaning is required.

Pointing Sticks   A **pointing stick** is a small, stubby pointing device that protrudes from the computer's keyboard (refer to Figure 2C.7e). To use the pointing stick, push the stick in various directions with your finger. Separate buttons are used to initiate actions, such as clicking and dragging. Developed by IBM

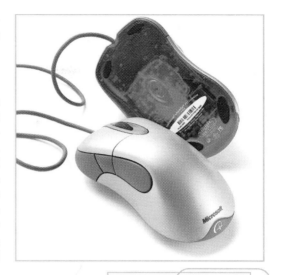

Figure **2C.8**

A wheel mouse.

Destinations

Looking for a foot mouse? Visit the NoHands Mouse home page (**http://www. footmouse.com**) for information on these pointing devices.

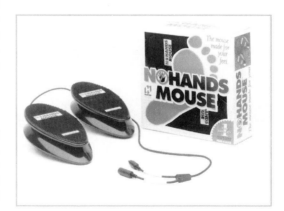

Figure **2C.9**

Victims of cumulative trauma disorders attributed to mouse usage can purchase a foot mouse to avoid further injury.

Figure 2C.10

Some desktop computer keyboards include touchpads.

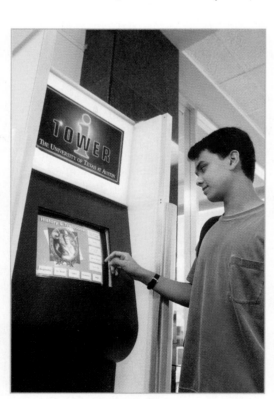

Figure 2C.11

Kiosks use touch screens to provide information and services to the public.

for its notebook computers, the pointing stick is now available for desktop computer keyboards as well.

Touchpads Many notebook computers use a **touchpad** for a pointing device (refer to Figure 2C.7g). The touchpad is a pressure-sensitive device that responds to your finger's movement over the pad's surface. For example, you can move the pointer to the right by placing your finger on the pad and sliding it to the right. To emulate a mouse click, tap the pad with the tip of your finger. To emulate a double-click, tap twice. You can also use the buttons that are situated near the touchpad's surface. Some notebook users like touchpads so much that they prefer them for desktop use, too. You can purchase desktop computer keyboards that are equipped with built-in touchpads (see Figure 2C.10). Having the same type of pointing device on all the computers you use helps to reduce confusion when you move from one computer to the next.

More Ways to Control the Computer

Most users control their computers by using the keyboard and a pointing device, such as a mouse, trackball, or touchpad. For special purposes, such as playing games or using a computer that is made available for use by the public, additional input devices are available, including joysticks, touch screens, pens, and graphics tablets. The following sections discuss these input devices.

Joysticks

A **joystick** is an input device with a large vertical lever that can be moved in any direction (refer to Figure 2C.7b). Although joysticks can be used as a pointing device, they are most often used to control the motion of an on-screen object in a computer game. A variety of buttons are available for initiating actions, such as firing weapons.

Joysticks aren't all fun and games. In industry and manufacturing, joysticks are used to control robots. Flight simulators and other training simulators also use joysticks to simulate vehicle controls.

Touch Screens

A **touch screen** uses a transparent, pressure-sensitive panel to detect where users have tapped the display screen with the tip of a finger (refer to Figure 2C.7f). Touch screens are easy to use. In addition, they are more reliable than keyboards and pointing devices—and virtually impossible to steal. All these characteristics make touch screens an excellent choice for publicly-accessible computers, such as those placed in **kiosks.** A kiosk is a booth that provides a computer service of some type. An example of a kiosk is an **automated teller machine (ATM),** which provides bank customers with 24-hour access to their funds. Kiosks are used for many purposes, such as providing information to tourists (see Figure 2C.11).

Although touch screens are easy to use, human fingers are much bigger than an on-screen pointer. As a result, software designers must provide fewer options and larger, on-screen buttons. These characteristics of touch screens make them best suited to simple, special-purpose programs. For more detailed work, **light pens** can be used. A light pen contains a light source that triggers the touch screen's detection mechanism (see Figure 2C.12).

Pen Computing

Pens, which look like ordinary pens except that their tips are equipped with electronics instead of ink (refer to Figure 2C.7d) are commonly found on **personal digital assistants (PDAs).** When you touch the pen's tip to the PDA's screen, you can use the pen like a pointing device. Most PDAs are equipped with **handwriting recognition** capabilities, which enables them to detect handwritten characters and transform these characters into text. The term **pen computing** refers collectively to the branch of computing that involves PDAs, pens, and handwriting recognition.

Will handwriting recognition take over other methods of providing input? Today's handwriting recognition technology is imperfect, at best. To get the PDA to understand the letters you are writing, you may need to write them in a special way (Figure 2C.13). Most experts believe that handwriting recognition will become one of the more popular methods for getting information into the computer, but keyboards will continue to be used. The main reason? People with good typing skills can enter information much more quickly with a keyboard.

Figure 2C.12

Light pens provide a way to get input into a touch screen system.

Graphics Tablets

A tool used in CAD applications and other graphics applications is a **graphics tablet.** A digitizing tablet consists of a grid on which designs and drawings can be entered. Most tablets are pressure-sensitive, and the user draws directly on the tablet using a special pen called a **stylus** (also called a puck). Digitizing tablets are used to design such things as cars, buildings, medical devices, and robots.

More Ways to Get Data Into the Computer

You can equip personal computers with many additional input devices. The following section begins with the computer's "ears" and moves to its "eyes."

Sound Cards

Computers equipped with **sound cards** can accept sound input from a microphone. In PCs, a sound card is an expansion board (see Module 2A) designed to record and play back **sound files.** (Sound is built into Macintosh computers.) Sound files contain digitized sound data, which is saved to one of several standardized sound formats. These formats specify how sounds should be digitally-represented, and generally include some type of **data compression** that reduces the size of the file. Examples of popular sound file formats are the Windows WAV format (the standard Microsoft Windows stereo sound file format), AU sounds (a low-quality, monaural sound format often encountered on the Internet), and **Moving Pictures Experts Group (MPEG)** audio formats (called MP-2 and MP-3). The MPEG formats reduce file size significantly without sacrificing audio quality.

Figure 2C.13

To enter letters into a personal digital assistant, you may need to write them in a special way.

Video Capture Boards

A **video capture board** is an expansion board designed to accept analog or digital video signals and transform them into digital data, which is then compressed and stored. (Some Macintoshes have video capture circuitry built

Destinations

To get the latest on hand-writing recognition and pen computing, visit the Pen and Mobile Computing page (**http://hwr.nici.kun. nl/pen-computing/ index.html**).

in.) Video applications process and save the video input. Some can display this input on-screen.

Video capture boards enable computers to display **full-motion video,** a "movie" that gives the illusion of smooth, continuous action. Like actual movies, digitized video consists of a series of still photographs, called frames, that are flashed on-screen at a rapid rate. A rate of at least 24 frames per second (fps) is needed to produce an illusion of smooth, continuous action.

What can you "capture" with a video capture board? You can use just about any video source, including TV broadcasts, taped video, or live video from video cameras. Low-cost video cameras, called **WebCams,** are popular items for low-resolution **videoconferencing** through the Internet (see Figure 2C.14). In a videoconference, two or more people can have a virtual face-to-face "meeting," even though they are separated by thousands of miles. WebCams don't have a fast enough frame rate to give an illusion of full-motion video, but they enable people to exchange "jerky" videos even if they're dialing into the Internet over slow phone lines. Effective long-distance videoconferencing awaits improvements in the Internet's signal-carrying capacity.

Figure 2C.14

WebCams are popular for low-resolution videoconferencing.

Because digitized video consumes huge amounts of disk space, compression is used to reduce the size of stored video files. The most popular compression technique is the **Moving Pictures Experts Group (MPEG)** video compression standard, which can compress video data by as much as 100 to 1. The tradeoff is while compression reduces file size, it places a greater demand on the computer's processor. Digital video works best in systems that have **hardware MPEG support** built into the computer's video circuitry rather than relying on software to decompress and process the video images.

Digital Cameras

Figure 2C.15

A digital camera.

A **digital camera** uses a lens to capture an image, but stores it in digital form rather than recording the image on film (see Figure 2C.15). The least expensive, point-and-shoot digital cameras cannot take professional-quality pictures, but they are adequate for snapshots and Web page images. However, a new generation of high-resolution (and very expensive) cameras is available that can take outstanding photographs. Some experts believe that digital cameras will replace film-based cameras someday.

Most digital cameras use a **charge-coupled device (CCD)** to record the image. A CCD consists of a grid containing light-sensitive elements. Each element converts the incoming light into a voltage that is proportional to the light's brightness. The digital camera's picture quality is determined by how many elements the CCD has: the more elements, the sharper the picture. A digital camera that uses 1,440 elements horizontally and 1,080 vertically is said to have a resolution (sharpness) of $1,440 \times 1,080$. These cameras can produce a much sharper image than a camera with a resolution of 640×480. However, high-resolution CCDs are expensive.

The better cameras, called **megapixel** cameras, have CCDs or comparable light-sensitive devices with at least one million elements. These cameras can produce reasonably-sharp images up to an enlargement of 4 by 6 inches. **Two-megapixel** cameras can produce sharp images at higher enlargements, such as 8 by 10 inches.

Since digital cameras have no film, the shots you take need to be stored in the camera until you can transfer them to a computer for long-term storage or printing. The two most popular methods of storing images in the camera are called **CompactFlash** and **SmartMedia.** Both use flash memory technologies to store from 4 to 128 megabytes of image data. About 12MB of flash memory is the equivalent of a standard, 12-exposure film roll. However, most cameras enable you to select from a variety of resolutions, so the number of shots you get will vary depending on the memory your camera contains.

When you've used up all the available memory on your camera, you'll need to transfer the images to your computer or to a specially-equipped printer. This operation is called **downloading.** Early digital cameras required you to connect your computer to a disused serial port (see Module 2A) to perform the downloading operation. The use of the serial port for this purpose was not convenient because you had to shut down your computer before making the connection. More recent digital cameras use the Universal Serial Bus (USB) for downloading connections. USB is advantageous because it is not necessary to switch off the computer before making the connection. Other cameras connect by means of a PC Card, while still others can record images on floppy disks.

Destinations

For an introduction to digital photography, see the Digital Camera Guide (**http://www.zdnet. com/zdhelp/filters/quick start/camera/**). Explore the latest digital camera technology at CNET's Digital Camera page (**http://www. computers.cnet.com/ hardware/0-1078.html**).

Scanners

Scanners use charge-coupled devices (CCDs) to digitize an image formed by a lens. Scanners are designed to copy anything that's printed on a sheet of paper, including artwork, handwriting, printed documents, or typed documents. **Flatbed scanners** work on a single sheet of paper at a time. **Sheetfed scanners** draw in the sheets to be copied by means of a roller mechanism. **Handheld scanners** can be used to copy smaller originals, such as photographs (see Figure 2C.16).

Scanners have varying **optical resolutions,** depending on the number of distinct light-sensitive elements packed into the scanner's CCD. Scanners may use image enhancement techniques to simulate higher resolutions. Scanners also vary in **bit depth,** the number of bits used to represent each dot (pixel). A 24-bit scanner can capture up to 16.7 million colors.

Most scanners come with **optical character recognition (OCR)** software that automatically decodes imaged text into a text file. This technology has improved to the point that most printed or typed documents can be scanned into text files, eliminating the need to retype such documents to get them into the computer.

Fax Input

Facsimile machines (also called **fax machines**) transmit scanned images of documents via the telephone system. Fax machines do not require the use of a computer. However, you can set up a computer to simulate a fax machine. To do so, you'll need **fax software,** which enables the computer to send and receive faxes. You'll also need a **fax modem.** A fax modem is a communications device that enables a computer to send and receive faxes via the telephone system. When the fax modem is connected to a telephone line and the fax software is running, the computer can receive incoming faxes. The incoming document is displayed on-screen, and it can be printed or saved.

Figure   2C.16

Handheld scanners are used most often to scan images into a microcomputer.

Input Devices in Business, Industry, and Science

Source data automation is the process of capturing data at its source, eliminating the need to file paper documents or to record the data by keying it manually. The result is lower costs and fewer errors. For example, many businesses use **image processing systems** to file incoming paper documents electronically. The documents are scanned, and the images are stored on the computer, where it's easier and faster to retrieve them. Railroads, for example, use scanners to record and track the location of hundreds of thousands of freight cars.

The banking industry developed one of the earliest scanning systems in the 1950s for processing checks. The **magnetic-ink character recognition (MICR)** system is used throughout the banking industry. The bank, branch, account number, and check number are encoded on the check before it is sent to the customer. After the customer has used the check and it comes back to the bank, all that needs to be entered manually is the amount. MICR has not been adopted by other industries because the character set has only fourteen symbols.

Figure 2C.17

Many retail stores use a bar code reader to determine what's being sold and to retrieve the item's price from a computer system.

Of all the scanning devices used in business, you are probably most familiar with **bar code readers.** Many retail and grocery stores use some form of bar code readers to determine the item being sold and to retrieve the item price from a computer system (see Figure 2C.17). The code reader may be a handheld unit or embedded in a countertop. The bar code reader reads the **universal product code (UPC),** a pattern of bars printed on merchandise. The UPC has gained wide acceptance since its introduction in the 1970s. Initially, workers resisted the use of the code because the system was used to check their accuracy and speed. Today, bar codes are used to update inventory and ensure correct pricing. Federal Express uses a unique bar code to identify and track each package. Federal Express employees can usually tell a customer within minutes the location of any package.

From taking exams, you are already familiar with **Mark Sense Character Recognition** systems. Every time you take a test with a "fill in the bubble" Scantron form and use a #2 lead pencil, you are creating input suitable for an **optical mark reader (OMR)** (see Figure 2C.18). A #2 lead pencil works best because of the number of magnetic particles in that weight lead. The OMR senses the magnetized marks, enabling the reader to determine which responses are marked. OMR is helpful to researchers who need to tabulate responses to large surveys. Almost any type of survey or questionnaire can be designed for OMR devices.

Figure 2C.18

Optical mark readers are useful for tabulating responses to large surveys.

Biological Feedback Devices

Biological feedback devices translate eye movements, body movements, and even brain waves into computer input. **Eye-gaze response systems** enable quadriplegics to control the computer by moving their eyes around the screen. A special camera tracks eye movements and moves the cursor in response.

Three-dimensional **virtual reality** programs use helmets and sensor-equipped gloves to enable users to "move" through a simulated "world." The helmet contains two miniature television screens that display the world in what appears to be three dimensions (see Figure 2C.19). A turn of the head

Figure 2C.19

Three-dimensional virtual reality programs use helmets to enable users to "move" through a simulated "world." The helmet contains two miniature television screens that display the world in what appears to be three dimensions.

moves your view of the world accordingly. Using a **data glove,** users can touch and manipulate simulated "objects."

Can you control a computer by *thinking?* Not yet, but it *is* possible to do so by altering brain wave patterns. Two types of brain waves, called alpha waves and mu waves, are easy to control. For instance, you can increase alpha wave output dramatically by closing your eyes and letting your mind go blank. Mu waves can be controlled by visualizing activities such as smiling, chewing, or swallowing. These waves can be picked up by sensors and used to control computers. Currently, these technologies are being developed to benefit those with physical disabilities, but they may have wider potential.

Chemical Detectors

What about the computer's sense of smell? The human nose can detect remarkably minute traces of chemicals in the air. And increasingly, so can computers. If you've visited an airport recently, you may already have been "sniffed" by a computer input device designed to detect minute traces of explosives. Some patrons are asked to step into a special booth, where air jets dislodge chemicals adhering to a person's clothes and hands. The air is then sucked through a chemical sensor that can identify many types of explosives. A computer screen displays the results of the test, and instructs the operator if explosives are detected.

UNDERSTANDING OUTPUT: MAKING DATA MEANINGFUL

Output refers to the results of the computer's processing operations, which transform unorganized (or disorganized) data into useful information.

Word processing software provides an example of output in action. When you're using a word processing program, tools and utilities transform the data—a document's raw text—in many ways. When you sort a table in alphabetical order, the output is the sorted table. When you choose the command that numbers the pages, the output is the document's page numbers. When you change the typeface (font), the output shows up in the document's changed appearance. When you print your document, the output is a stream of data that's designed to produce the results you want with the specific brand and model of printer you're using.

SPOTLIGHT

▶Computers transform unorganized data into information, which is useful and meaningful to people. But information isn't the same thing as knowledge. Knowledge involves grasping the truth about something. Often, there's a huge gap between getting information and knowing the truth—and nowhere is this better illustrated than in the controversy surrounding the 1999 crash of EgyptAir flight 990, a tragedy that took 217 lives.

On November 1, 1999, EgyptAir flight 990 was cruising normally at 33,000 feet after taking off from New York's JFK International Airport. The plane's captain had left the cockpit. Evidence from the plane's data recorder suggests that, soon afterward, the co-pilot (Gameel Batouti) switched off the autopilot, and sent the plane into a sudden, out-of-control dive. The pilot, returning to the cabin, tried to regain control of the aircraft. Apparently, the two pilots struggled at cross-purposes, with the pilot pulling up on the stabilizer and the co-pilot pushing down. At 15,000 feet, the aircraft stabilized and began a brief ascent, but one of the pilots switched off the engines, and the plane resumed a deep, out-of-control dive—this time with fatal results. The aircraft plunged into the cold waters of the Atlantic Ocean. At the speed the plane was traveling, the plane may as well have struck solid stone. There were no survivors.

After an extensive and costly search of the debris field, 250 feet under the ocean's surface off Nantucket, divers recovered the cockpit voice recorder. Engineers at the laboratories of the U.S. National Transportation Safety Board (NTSB) used computers to extract all of the information that the recorder contained, including everything uttered by the pilots—including their whispers and prayers. NTSB researchers hoped to produce a complete, accurate transcript of everything said in the cockpit during the flight's final minutes. This task would not be a simple one, since EgyptAir pilots normally converse in Arabic, a language that is not widely-spoken by U.S. nationals. Still NTSB officials leaked to the press the startling news that Batouti, moments before sending the aircraft into its fatal dive, whispered "I've made my decision now," followed by an Islamic prayer. The U.S. press speculated that Batouti was a "religious fanatic" who committed suicide, taking more than two hundred lives with him.

There was just one problem with these reports: they were false. Batouti never said anything like "I've made my decision now." What he said was "Tawakilt ala Allah (I entrust myself to God)." According to Islamic scholars and Arabic speakers, this is a minor prayer, one that a religious person might utter as many as 200 times per day. It's frequently spoken, almost as a matter of habit, before initiating an action, such as sticking a key in a car's ignition or lighting the stove in the kitchen. Angered by what they perceived as the NTSB's rush to judgment, Egyptian government officials demanded an immediate stop to speculation regarding the cause of the crash. In turn, Muslims were angered by what they saw as Western misunderstanding of their religion.

In the following weeks, another plausible scenario emerged. Flight 990's dive could have been caused by a mechanical failure—specifically, a runaway stabilizer. Located on the aircraft's tail, the stabilizer is a control surface that determines the aircraft's upward or downward motion. A runaway stabilizer could have forced the plane into a steep dive. To deal with the problem, the pilots needed to shut down the hydraulic pressure to the stabilizer by flipping two stabilizer trim switches to the "cut out" setting. However, the Boeing 767's controls also contain two switches labeled "cut off." These switches shut down the engines. Some airline safety experts speculated that the pilots, in a panic, used the wrong switches, plunging the plane into its last, fatal dive. Still, the aircraft's data recorders provided no evidence of any problem with the aircraft's stabilizers. At this writing, the cause of Flight 990's fatal plunge is still unknown.

What's the lesson here? The NTSB's audio processing capabilities did an excellent job of generating the information crash investigators needed: a complete, detailed transcript of cockpit conversations. But cockpit voice recordings are seldom able to disclose the truth about the cause of a crash. The voice recording must be synchronized with output from the flight's data recorder. In addition, researchers need to examine the physical evidence, the wreckage recovered from the ocean's floor.

Output devices enable people to see, hear, and even feel the results of processing operations. The most-commonly used output devices are monitors and printers, which are detailed in subsequent sections.

Output falls into two major categories: output that you can see, and output that you can hear. Visible output includes the following examples:

- **Text output** consists of characters (letters, numbers, and punctuation marks), but text output isn't just a bunch of disorganized verbiage: it's *organized* in some way. Examples include a sorted list of names and addresses or a document that's been formatted for attractive printing.

- **Graphics output** consists of visual images, including charts and pictures. Once again, graphics output isn't output unless it has been processed in some way. For example, photo editing programs can remove "red eye" or speckles from photographs. The result is graphics output.

- **Video output** consists of a series of still images that are played back at a fast enough **frame rate** to give the illusion of continuous motion. (Frame rate refers to the number of images displayed per second.)

Audible output consists of sound, music, or synthesized speech. Again, sounds aren't output unless they're the results of processing operations.

Output devices enable our senses to perceive the results of computer processing—to see these results, to hear them, and even to feel them. This section begins with the visual output media with which you're most familiar: the computer's visual display system. Subsequent sections examine printers, sound systems, and cutting-edge output systems that engage our sense of touch.

OUTPUT DEVICES: ENGAGING OUR SENSES

An output device is a computer peripheral that can make output accessible to people. The most-widely used output devices are visual display systems and printers.

Visual Display Systems

The computer's visual display system is its most important output system. Two components are required to generate the visual display: the video adapter and the monitor, which are covered in the following sections.

Video Adapters

The image displayed on a monitor is generated by a **video adapter** (also called **display adapter**), an expansion board that plugs into one of the computer's expansion slots. (On some computers, the video adapter circuitry is built into the motherboard.) The video adapter determines the overall quality of the image that the monitor displays. Video adapters contain their own processing circuitry as well as their own memory, which is called **video RAM (VRAM).** Adapters with fast processors are called **accelerators** because they can speed up the image's display.

The amount of VRAM determines the maximum **resolution** that can be displayed. The term *resolution* generally refers to an image's sharpness. Video adapters conform to standard resolutions that are expressed by the number of dots (pixels) that can be displayed horizontally and vertically. For example, the **Video Graphics Adapter (VGA)** defines a resolution of 640 dots horizontally by 480 vertically (640 × 480), which requires enough memory to store over 300,000 dots. To display a **Super VGA** resolution (1024 × 768), the video adapter must have enough memory to store more than twice as many dots. Table 2C.4 lists common PC resolutions.

Table 2C.4

Common PC Resolutions
640 × 480
800 × 600
1024 × 768
1600 × 1200

Table 2C.5

Common Color Depth	
Color Depth	**Number of Colors**
VGA (4 bits)	16
256-color mode (8 bits)	256
High color (16 bits)	65,536
True Color (24 bits)	16,777,216

Also requiring memory is the information needed to display color. The term **color depth** refers to the number of colors that can be displayed at one time. To display a maximum of 16 colors, only 4 bits of data are required for each screen pixel. To display 16.7 million colors, however, the adapter's memory must store 24 bits of information for each displayed pixel (see Table 2C.5).

How do resolution and color depth relate to each other when it comes to a given video adapter's performance? With 2MB of installed VRAM, an adapter can display 16.7 million pixels only at lower resolutions (such as 800 × 600). To display 16.7 million colors at higher resolutions, more memory is needed. Some video adapters can be upgraded with additional VRAM (see Module 10A).

Adapters also vary in how many colors they can display. Another important measurement of video adapter quality is the **refresh rate** generated at a given resolution. Refresh rate refers to the frequency with which the screen image is updated, and it's measured in hertz (Hz), or cycles per second. Below 60 Hz, most people notice an annoying, eye-straining **flicker.** Very few people notice flicker when the refresh rate exceeds 72 Hz.

Monitors

Monitors (also called **displays**) display the video adapter's output. The on-screen display enables you to see how applications are processing your data, but it's important to remember that the screen display isn't a permanent record. To drive home this point, screen output is sometimes called **soft copy,** as opposed to **hard copy** (printed output). To make permanent copies of your work, you need to save it to a storage device (see Module 2B) or print it.

Monitors are categorized by the technology used to generate its images, the colors they display, their screen size, and additional performance characteristics.

Types of Monitors

Monitors that look like television screens use the TV's **cathode-ray tube (CRT)** technology, in which the image is formed by an electron "gun" shooting a stream of electrons at the screen's phosphorescent surface. Although the term *CRT* is sometimes used to mean "monitor," it's properly used to refer to only the "picture tube" that generates the display. In a color monitor, three guns corresponding to the three primary colors (red, green, and blue) are combined in varying intensities to produce on-screen colors (see Figure 2C.20). CRT monitors are inexpensive compared to other types of monitors, but they consume more energy and take up more room on the desk.

The thinner monitors used on notebook and other small computers are known as **flat-panel displays.** Compared to CRT-based monitors, flat-panel displays consume less electricity and take up much less room. Some believe that flat-panel displays will replace CRTs for desktop systems, but several problems remain to be solved, including expense (large LCD displays are much more expensive than CRTs). At their best, flat-panel displays have many advantages, including elimination of screen flicker (an annoying CRT problem that can cause eye strain). When prices drop sufficiently, flat-panel displays will start eating into CRT sales for desktop systems.

Most flat-panel displays use **liquid crystal display (LCD)** technology (see Figure 2C.21). LCD displays sandwich cells containing tiny crystals between two transparent surfaces. By varying the electrical current supplied to each crystal, an image forms. The least expensive LCDs are called **passive-matrix LCDs** (also called **dual scans**). Passive-matrix LCDs may generate image flaws, such as an unwanted shadow next to a column of color, and they are too slow for full-motion video. **Active-matrix LCDs** (also called **thin film transistors [TFTs]**) use transistors to control the color of each on-screen pixel. Speed and color quality improves, but active-matrix displays are more expensive. Other flat-panel display technologies include **gas plasma displays** and **field emission displays (FEDs).** An intriguing new technology, FED displays look like LCDs, except a tiny CRT produces each on-screen pixel.

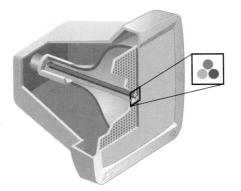

Figure 2C.20

Monitors use cathode-ray tube (CRT) technology, in which the image is formed by an electron "gun" shooting a stream of electrons at the screen's phosphorescent surface. In a color monitor, three guns corresponding to the three primary colors (red, green, and blue) are combined in varying intensities to produce on-screen colors.

Monochrome and Color Monitors

Monochrome monitors typically display only two colors: green or amber characters against a black background. **Grayscale monitors** display black, white, and various shades of gray, and are used to prepare copy for noncolor printing. Color monitors display colors, but the number of colors they can display depends on the video adapter's capabilities as well as the monitor's. Most of the monitors used with today's PCs are color monitors capable of displaying 16.7 million colors.

The large monitors that you see connected to desktop computers are cathode-ray tube (CRT) monitors (see Figure 2C.22).

Figure 2C.21

A crystal-clear laptop color LCD display.

Screen Size

Monitors are also categorized by their size. In CRTs, the quoted size is the size of the CRT's front surface measured diagonally. But some of this surface is hidden and unavailable for display purposes. For this reason, it's important to distinguish between the monitor's quoted size and the **viewable area,** the area available for viewing. Table 2C.6 shows typical relationships between quoted size and viewable area. Vendors now provide both sizes, thanks to a consumer lawsuit.

Figure 2C.22

Desktop computers use cathode-ray tube technology.

How big should your monitor be? Increasingly, 17-inch monitors are considered standard. For desktop publishing and other applications where full-page displays are needed, 21-inch monitors are preferred. An alternative to a 21-inch display is the type of 17-inch display that can rotate to a vertical position and display a full page.

Additional Monitor Characteristics

Although the monitor's resolution is determined by the video adapter's output, every monitor has a maximum resolution that it cannot go beyond, even if the video adapter can do so. In addition, monitor quality is strongly affected by **dot pitch,** the space—measured in millimeters (mm)—between each physical dot on the screen. A dot pitch of .28mm or lower is considered good. Older **interlaced monitors** cut costs by refreshing every other line on each pass of the cathode gun, but this resulted in screen flicker. Most of today's monitors are **noninterlaced monitors,** which update the entire screen on each pass (see Figure 2C.23). Finally, monitors vary in the maximum refresh rate they can accept. Some monitors are designed to run at a fixed refresh rate, but most monitors in use today are **multiscan monitors.** These monitors automatically adjust their refresh rate to the video adapter's output. If the monitor cannot display output at a refresh rate of 72 Hz or higher, eye fatigue may result.

Data Projectors

Data projectors take a computer's video output and project this output onto a screen, so that an audience can see it. Some data projectors are relatively inexpensive, portable devices, while others are more expensive devices that are built into an auditorium's audio-visual system.

For presentations to small audiences, **LCD projectors** are increasingly popular. An LCD projector enables a speaker to project the computer's screen display on a screen similar to the one used with a slide projector. Some units have their own built-in projectors; others are designed for use with an overhead projector. LCD projectors are acceptable for relatively-small audiences (up to approximately 25 people), but the image they generate isn't sharp enough to enlarge to a size that a larger audience could read.

Digital light processing (DLP) projectors employ millions of microscopic mirrors embedded in a microchip to produce a bright, sharp image. Each mirror corresponds to a pixel, and switches on and off to generate the image. Computer-controlled light beams reflect the image through a lens, which projects the image to a screen. This image is visible even in a brightly-lit room, and it's sharp enough to be used with very large screens, such as those found at rock concerts and large auditoriums.

Table 2C.6

Quoted Monitor Size and Actual Viewable Area	
Monitor Size	**Viewable Area**
21 inches	20 inches
17 inches	16 inches
15 inches	14 inches

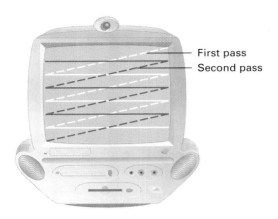

Interlaced monitors
Refresh every other line on each pass of the cathode gun, but this results in screen flicker

Noninterlaced monitors
Update the entire screen on each pass

First pass
Second pass

Figure   2C.23

Interlaced vs. noninterlaced monitors.

Headsets

A **headset** (also called **head-mounted display**) is a wearable output device that includes twin LCD panels. When used with special applications that generate stereo output, headsets can create the illusion that an individual is walking through a three-dimensional, simulated environment.

The **Cave Automated Virtual Environment (CAVE)** enables virtual reality explorers to dispense with the headsets in favor of 3-D glasses. In the CAVE environment, the walls, ceiling, and floor display projected three-dimensional images. More than 50 CAVEs exist, enabling researchers to study topics as diverse as the human heart and the next generation of sports cars.

Printers

Printers produce permanent versions (called hard copy) of the output that's visible on the computer's display screen. Two basic technologies dominate the world of computer printers: impact and nonimpact printers.

Impact Printers

When part of the printer presses the paper to form the character, the printer is considered an **impact printer.** Impact printers can produce carbon copies and are noisy, although covers are available to muffle the noise. Impact printers can produce a page, a line, or a character at a time. Large computers use **line printers** that can crank out hard copy at a rate of 3,000 lines per minute. Print quality is low, but these printers are mainly used for printing backup copies of large amounts of data. **Letter-quality printers,** which closely resemble office typewriters (except that they are controlled by the computer), are still used in some law offices.

Dot-matrix printers (see Figure 2C.24), which were once the most popular type of printer used with PCs are decreasing in use. If you use a magnifying glass to look at a report created with a dot-matrix printer, you can see the small dots forming each character. The least-expensive dot-matrix printers print using a matrix of 9 pins and produce poor quality printouts. Better dot-matrix printers use a 24-pin printhead and can produce **near-letter-quality printouts** (printouts that look almost as good as printed text). Quality may still be poor, however, if the ribbon needs replacing, which is often the case for dot-matrix printers located in college computer labs. Some professors will not accept papers printed on any kind of dot-matrix printer because the output is so difficult to read.

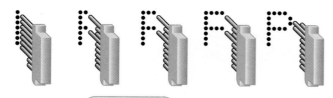

Figure **2C.24**

Dot-matrix printers use a matrix of pins to create images in a dot pattern.

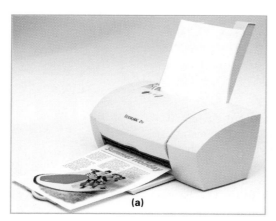

(a)

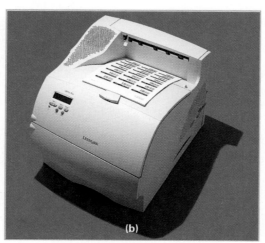

(b)

Figure **2C.25**

Nonimpact printers can produce both text and graphics and are quiet: (a) inkjet printer and (b) laser printer.

Nonimpact Printers

In contrast to impact printers, nonimpact printers are quiet. However, since nothing presses on the page, a **nonimpact printer** can't produce carbon copies. This is usually not a problem because it's easy to produce multiple originals, but sometimes carbons are required for legal purposes.

Nonimpact printers are the most-widely used printers for PCs today. Nonimpact printers can produce both text and graphics. Some of the most-popular nonimpact printers are laser printers and inkjet printers (see Figure 2C.25).

Inkjet printers (also called bubble-jet printers) are the least-expensive (and most popular) nonimpact printers. Like dot-matrix printers, inkjet printers work by forming an image that is composed of tiny dots, but the dots are much smaller and more numerous. The result is a printout that's difficult to distinguish from the fully-formed characters printed by laser printers. Inkjet printers can also print in color, which makes them popular choices for home users. Earlier inkjets had problems with smudging, but new ink formulations have all but eliminated this problem. Although inkjet printers are inexpensive and produce excellent output, they are slow, and per-page costs may exceed the costs of running a laser printer due to the generally-high cost of ink cartridges.

Laser printers work like copy machines. Under the printer's computerized control, a laser beam creates electrical charges on a rotating print drum. These charges attract toner, which is transferred to the paper and fused to its surface by a heat process. In contrast to inkjets, laser printers print faster; some can crank out 18 or more pages per minute. Although they are more expensive initially than inkjet printers, laser printers generally have lower per-page costs.

Laser printers come in a variety of sizes. Generally, the larger and faster the printer, the more expensive it is. Large laser printers are used on mainframes and minicomputers where high-quality graphic output is required. In corporate networks (see Module 6B), high-volume **network laser printers** take care of the printing needs of entire departments. Smaller, **personal laser printers** are available for individual use. **Color laser printers** are available, but they are expensive. Laser printer quality is judged by the number of dots per inch (dpi) that the printer can produce. The least-expensive laser printers can generate 300 dpi, which is adequate for text (but not for graphics). The best laser printers can produce 600 dpi or more.

The best color printers are **thermal transfer printers.** These printers use a heat process to transfer colored dyes or inks to the paper's surface. Because the colors run together, thermal transfer printers do a much better job of printing photographs and artwork than other computer printers. The best results, however, require glossy paper, which is expensive. The best thermal transfer printers are called **dye sublimation printers** (see Figure 2C.26). These printers are slow and expensive, but they produce results that are difficult to distinguish from high-quality color photographs. Less expensive are **snapshot printers,** which are thermal transfer printers designed to print the output of digital cameras at a maximum size of 4 by 6 inches.

   Multifunction printers combine inkjet or laser printers with a scanner, a fax machine, and a copier, enabling home office users to obtain all these devices without spending a great deal of money.

Plotters

A **plotter,** like a printer, produces hard-copy output. Most form an image by physically moving a pen over a sheet of paper. A continuous-curve plotter is used to draw maps from stored data (see Figure 2C.27). Computer-generated maps can be retrieved and plotted or used to show changes over time. Plotters are generally more expensive than printers, ranging from about $1,000 to $75,000 (or even more).

Figure   2C.26

The best thermal transfer printers are dye sublimation printers. They produce results similar to high-quality photographs.

Fax Output

As you learned earlier in this module, computers equipped with a fax modem and fax software can receive incoming faxes. They can also send faxes as output. To send a fax with the computer, save your document using a special format that is compatible with the fax program. The fax program can then send this document through the telephone system to a distant fax machine. It is not necessary to print the document locally in order to send it as a fax.

   If the document you want to fax is available only in hard copy, computer faxing is not as convenient. You must first scan the document (see "Scanners," earlier in this module). Then you can fax it through the computer.

Audio Output: Sound Cards and Speakers

Sound cards and speakers, the two accessories needed to listen to computer-generated sound, are increasingly found on new computer systems. Such sounds include various system beeps and warnings, the output of recorded sound files, and even synthesized speech. In **speech synthesis,** a program "reads" a text file out loud. Speech synthesis enables people who are blind or have low vision to access huge amounts of text-based material that would otherwise be inaccessible to them.

Figure   2C.27

Plotters are ideal for engineering, drafting, and many other applications that require intricate graphics.

   Like audio compact disc players, sound cards can play the contents of digitized recordings, such as music recorded in the Windows WAV or MPEG sound file formats. Some do this job better than others. Quality enters into the picture most noticeably when the sound card reproduces files containing **Musical Instrument Digital Interface (MIDI)** information. MIDI files are text files that tell a **synthesizer** when and how to play individual musical notes. (A synthesizer produces music by generating musical tones.) The least expensive sound cards use **FM synthesis,** an older technique that produces a sound associated with cheap electronic keyboards or the music accompanying old computer games. Better sound cards use **wavetable synthesis,** in which the sound card generates sounds using ROM-based recordings of actual musical instruments. The latest sound cards include surround-sound effects.

Tactile Feedback

You've seen how output devices engage our eyes and ears. What about our sense of touch? If researchers in a new field called **haptics** have their way, you'll be able to feel computer output as well as see and hear it. (The term *haptics* refers to the sense of touch.) Haptics researchers are developing a

CURRENTS

Which Computer Would You Like to Wear Today?

Anyone who has grown up in the age of electronics knows that every electronic device keeps shrinking. Radios that took up space in the corner now fit on a wristwatch. Televisions have followed suit, and can now easily fit into your shirt pocket. Telephones will keep getting smaller and lighter, until you can conceal a cell phone just about anywhere.

Computers are no different. In their early days, computers took up entire rooms. Now you can fit just as much computing power into the palm of your hand. Why stop there? If you can make computers even smaller and more powerful, you can wear them like clothing or jewelry.

Those days are now here. Powerful computers are being designed into rings, stuffed in brooches, and concealed in eyeglasses. Computers are even being placed inside prosthetics that replace amputated arms or legs.

The effects of these wearable computers have not fully hit society yet but are poised to do so in the next few years. Business people will be able to augment their memory with a wearable computer that keeps track of their contacts and recalls information without visible prompting. Journalists can record what goes on around them and annotate the information as necessary to accomplish their jobs.

Imagine how wearable computers can affect the lives of maintenance workers. A computer on the belt could easily be connected to a display monitor concealed in an ordinary pair of eyeglasses. As the worker looks at the inside of some equipment being fixed, the computer pops up a schematic for the equipment. The schematic, shown on the inside of the eyeglass lens, can be positioned over the real layout for the equipment. The result is the ability to quickly pinpoint the name, purpose, and condition of each component in the equipment.

This blending of virtual reality with the real world, known as *augmented reality,* is not science fiction. It's already underway in some large corporations. Taken to another level, the schematics shown in the worker's field of vision can be interfaced with motion and position sensors so that when the worker moves his or her head, the schematics projected by the computer change to reflect whatever is being looked at.

New uses for augmented reality are being discovered all the time. For instance, agents for the U.S. Customs Service are using special wearable computers that utilize voice-recognition software and full-color monitors. The agents, looking for stolen vehicles, use the computers to recall the license number of any vehicle in the United States. This happens as the agent strolls through a parking lot or along a lane of traffic.

The biggest drawbacks in wearable computers at the present time are twofold: batteries and communications. Batteries, which must be used to power wearable computers, are still large and bulky for any extended use of the electronics. The classic tradeoff is to either limit the usable life of the electronics (without recharging) or wear a large battery pack on the belt or in a backpack.

Wearable computers are often configured as a collection of small components, and communications between those components can be a problem. For instance, when a belt-worn computer needs to communicate with a head-mounted monitor, the natural way is through a cable running between the two. Although this may make electrical sense, it may not be acceptable in some surroundings and for some uses. Some cutting-edge wearable computers are now using wireless components, but this adds to power consumption and potentially shortens battery life.

The potential uses for wearable computers are unlimited. As components continue to shrink, capabilities continue to expand, and technology rushes to meet imagination, each of us may add a computer to our wardrobe.

A wearable computer.

variety of technologies, including **tactile displays** that stimulate the skin to generate a sensation of contact. Stimulation techniques include vibration, pressure, and temperature changes. When used in virtual reality environments, these technologies enhance the sense of "being there" and physically interacting with displayed virtual objects.

TAKEAWAY POINTS

- Input refers to the software, data, or user-supplied information that is entered into the computer's memory. The four types of input are software transferred from storage devices, unorganized data that needs to be processed, commands that tell programs what to do, and user responses to a program's messages.
- Computer keyboards differ from typewriter keyboards in the following ways: some keys on the computer keyboard, such as the Enter key, work differently than they do on a typewriter keyboard. In addition, some computer keyboard keys perform different functions at different times. Another difference is that computer keyboards have many more keys.
- The computer keyboard's special keys include cursor movement keys (arrow keys and additional keys such as Home and End), the numeric keypad (for entering numerical data), toggle keys (for switching keyboard modes on and off, such as Num Lock and Caps Lock), function keys (defined for different purposes by application programs), modifier keys such as Ctrl and Alt (for use with keyboard shortcuts), and special keys for use with Microsoft Windows.
- Speech recognition software and a microphone enable users to dictate words to a computer. The words may be commands, or data to be entered as text in a document. Although speech recognition benefits users who cannot or should not type, the software makes many errors.
- The most popular pointing devices are mice, trackballs, trackpoints, and touchpads. The latter three are preferred when space is limited.
- Mouse types include mice that connect in different ways (PS/2 mice, serial mice, bus mice, and cordless mice) and those that use one of two available technologies (optical and mechanical).
- To get sound, video, and images into the computer, you can use the microphone input of a sound card, a video capture board, a digital camera, a scanner, or a fax modem.
- The two major types of output are visual and auditory. Types of visual output are text output, graphics output, and video output.
- Factors determining a computer's video output quality are the amount of VRAM on the video card and the adapter's refresh rate.
- CRT monitors are inexpensive compared to other types of monitors, but they consume more energy and take up more room on the desk. Flat-panel displays are more expensive, but they take up much less room and are easier on the eyes.
- A monitor's quality is determined by its screen size (the larger, the better), its dot pitch (a dot pitch of .28mm or lower is good), the use of interlacing (noninterlaced monitors are better), and its ability to work with adapters that have a high refresh rate (72 Hz or higher).

MODULE REVIEW

KEY TERMS AND CONCEPTS

accelerators
active-matrix LCDs, or thin film transistors (TFTs)
automated teller machine (ATM)
autorepeat
bar code readers
biological feedback devices
bit depth
bus mice
Caps Lock
cathode-ray tube (CRT)
Cave Automated Virtual Environment (CAVE)
character
charge-coupled device (CCD)

color depth
color laser printers
command
CompactFlash
continuous speech recognition
cordless mice
cumulative trauma disorder (CTD), or repetitive strain injury (RSI)
cursor, or insertion point
cursor-movement keys, or arrow keys
data
data compression
data glove

data projectors
dead keys
diacritical marks
digital camera
digital light processing (DLP) projectors
discrete speech recognition
dot-matrix printers
dot pitch
downloading
dye sublimation printers
enhanced keyboard
ergonomic keyboards
Esc
extended keyboard

eye-gaze response systems
facsimile machines (fax machines)
fax modem
fax software
field emission displays (FED)
flatbed scanner
flat-panel displays
flicker
FM synthesis
foot mouse
frame rate
full-motion video
function keys
gas plasma displays
graphics output
graphics tablet
grayscale monitors
handheld scanners
handwriting recognition
haptics
hard copy
hardware MPEG support
headset or head-mounted display
image processing systems
impact printer
inkjet printers
input
input devices
interlaced monitors
joystick
keyboard
keyboard shortcuts
kiosks
laser printers
letter-quality printers
light pens
line printers
liquid crystal display (LCD)
LCD projectors

magnetic-ink character recognition (MICR)
Mark Sense Character Recognition
megapixel
mechanical mice
modifier keys
monitors or displays
monochrome monitors
mouse
Moving Pictures Experts Group (MPEG)
multifunction printers
multiscan monitors
Musical Instrument Digital Interface (MIDI)
near-letter-quality printout
network laser printers
nonimpact printer
noninterlaced monitors
numeric keypad
Num Lock
optical character recognition (OCR)
optical mark reader (OMR)
optical mice
optical resolutions
output
output devices
passive matrix LCDs, or dual scans
pen computing
pens
personal digital assistants (PDAs)
personal laser printers
plotter
pointer
pointing device
pointing stick
printers
PS/2 mice

QWERTY keyboard
refresh rate
resolution
scanners
serial mice
sheetfed scanners
SmartMedia
snapshot printers
soft copy
sound cards
sound files
source data automation
speech recognition or voice recognition
speech synthesis
status indicators
stylus
Super VGA
synthesizer
tactile displays
text output
thermal transfer printers
toggle key
touchpad
touch screen
trackball
two-megapixel
universal product code (UPC)
video adapter, or display adapter
video capture board
videoconferencing
video graphics adapter (VCA)
video output
video RAM (VRAM)
viewable area
virtual reality
wavetable synthesis
WebCams
wheel mouse
wireless keyboard

TRUE/FALSE

Indicate whether the following statements are true or false.

1. Storage devices can function as input devices when they're used to transfer software from storage to the computer's memory.

2. Computer keyboards have fewer keys than an electronic typewriter keyboard.

3. Trained operators use the function keys on a keyboard to enter numbers quickly.

4. Touchpads enable users to select options by pressing a specific part of the screen.

5. Today's continuous speech recognition software enables users to speak without pausing between words.

6. WebCams are a popular input device used for low-resolution videoconferencing.

7. Source data automation involves filing paper documents or recording data by keying it manually.

8. Monitors that resemble television screens use CRT technology.

9. Nonimpact printers such as inkjet and laser printers are the most popular printers in use today.

10. Interlaced monitors update the entire screen on each pass of the cathode gun.

MATCHING

Match each key term from the left column to the most accurate definition in the right column.

_____ 1. input device

_____ 2. toggle key

_____ 3. dead key

_____ 4. speech recognition

_____ 5. kiosk

_____ 6. pen computing

_____ 7. sound card

_____ 8. data compression

_____ 9. output device

_____ 10. refresh rate

a. a type of input where the computer recognizes spoken words

b. hardware component that makes output accessible and includes printers and monitors

c. the branch of computing that involves PDAs and handwriting recognition

d. the frequency with which a screen image is updated

e. hardware component that enables you to get programs, data, commands, and responses into the computer's memory

f. reduces the size of a file

g. a keyboard shortcut that adds a diacritical mark to the next letter you type

h. a booth that provides a computer service and often includes a touch screen

i. a key that has two positions (on and off)

j. an expansion board that can record and play sound files

MULTIPLE CHOICE

Circle the letter of the correct choice for each of the following.

1. Which of the following is a popular input device?
   a. monitor
   b. mouse
   c. plotter
   d. synthesizer

2. Which of the following describes the function of toggle keys on the keyboard?
   a. adds diacritical marks to the next letter you type
   b. interrupts or cancels an operation
   c. moves the cursor
   d. switches the keyboard between all caps and normal mode

3. Prolonged keyboard use can result in which of the following?
   a. cumulative trauma disorder
   b. malfunction of the mouse and other input devices
   c. a keyboard that becomes inoperable over time
   d. dead keys

4. Which of the following mice uses a rotating ball to generate information about the mouse's position?
   a. bus mouse
   b. foot mouse
   c. mechanical mouse
   d. optical mouse

5. Which of the following devices uses handwriting recognition software?
   a. touchpad
   b. trackpoint
   c. personal digital assistant
   d. touch screen

6. Which of the following expansion boards accepts analog or digital video signals and transforms them into digital data?
   a. accelerator
   b. sound card
   c. WebCam
   d. video capture board

7. What kind of software accompanies most scanners and automatically decodes imaged text into a text file?
   a. optical character recognition (OCR)
   b. source data automation
   c. image processing software
   d. fax software

8. Which of the following does not generally apply to monitors?
   a. Monitors that look like TV screens use cathode-ray tube (CRT) technology.
   b. Monitors display "soft," or temporary, copy.
   c. Most monitors are wearable output devices that include twin LCD panels.

   d. Monitor quality is strongly affected by dot pitch.

9. Which output device can be used to print carbon copies?
   a. dot-matrix printer
   b. laser printer
   c. plotter
   d. inkjet printer

10. Which of the following printers is considered the best color printer?
    a. multifunction printer
    b. thermal transfer printer
    c. line printer
    d. color laser printer

FILL-IN

In the blank provided, write the correct answer for each of the following.

1. _____ marks include accent marks, tildes, and umlauts.

2. _____ enable users to initiate actions such as clicking, double-clicking, selecting, and dragging.

3. A(n) _____ uses a transparent, pressure-sensitive panel to detect where users have tapped the display screen with their finger.

4. Personal digital assistants are equipped with _____ capabilities, which enables them to detect handwritten characters.

5. A(n) _____ uses a lens to capture an image, but stores it in digital form rather than recording the image on film.

6. _____ use charge-coupled devices (CCD) to digitize an image formed by a lens

and are designed to copy anything that's printed on a sheet of paper.

7. Video adapters contain their own memory which is called _____ .

8. The thinner monitors used on notebook and other small computers are known as _____ displays.

9. Most of today's monitors are _____ monitors, which update the entire screen on each pass.

10. _____ printers combine inkjet or laser printers with a scanner, a fax machine, and a copier.

SHORT ANSWER

On a separate sheet of paper, answer the following questions.

1. Describe two examples of source data automation.

2. What are the advantages and disadvantages of modern speech recognition technology?

3. Identify four types of pointing devices. What is their major advantage over a keyboard?

4. How are biological feedback devices used today?

5. What types of operations can a PDA perform?

6. What are the different types of technologies associated with flat-panel displays? Why aren't these types of displays more common for desktop computer systems?

7. List three types of scanners. Describe how a computer scans a document.

8. What are the pros and cons of inkjet printers vs. laser printers?

9. List and briefly describe the functions of four output devices.

10. What is tactile feedback and how might it be used?

PFSweb, Inc.

Mike Willoughby gets to play with toys. Ok, so maybe the "toys" are really computers. But in his job as Vice President of E-Commerce Technologies at PFSweb, Mike keeps up with all the changes occurring in the computer hardware and software markets. He has to, since PFSweb is in the e-commerce business, with customers that demand top-end, state-of-the-art systems to help run their own e-commerce web sites.

The computers used by PFSweb run the range from PCs to IBM AS/400 midrange computers. The personal computers are used for PFSweb's "business-to-consumer," or B2C, activities. You know, like selling CDs to music lovers. These computers are very cost-effective as web servers. The AS/400 computers serve the needs of "business-to-business," or B2B clients. These computers work as "applica-

tions" servers, handling the work of customer shopping carts, merchandise catalogs, order management, credit card authorizations, fraud checks and more. PFSweb also has a number of computers for running its own business. AS/400 machines serve the company's billing, web design, computer system development, communications, and other day-to-day needs. And what's cool about all the hardware is that everything is fully redundant. So, if one of the servers goes down, another computer right next to it kicks in to keep the web activity going. After all, it can be costly to have a client lose business because of a broken machine. For added security, PFSweb also has a full back-up site in Philadelphia, ready to go in case of disaster at the main data center in Plano, Texas.

Mike says that the choice of hardware is critical, because the technology must support every client's needs. In other words, by playing with the newest developments in technology, he can be sure PFSweb always has the latest and best components to serve up both stability and flexibility to even the most demanding clients.

What do you think? How long will it be before people are making most of their purchases over the web? What technologies need to be in place for this to happen?

WebLink Go to **www.prenhall.com/ pfaffenberger** to see the video of PFSweb's computer data center and explore the Web.

E-COMMERCE IN ACTION

CHAPTER 3

The World of Computer Software

U.S. cruising sailor Kathy Mix has a string of accomplishments under her belt, including designing and constructing a 55-foot sailboat named Myth. *But she ran into a challenge during a Caribbean cruise: too many charts—more than 200 of them. When you're at sea, you may need to put your finger on the chart you need without delay, and fumbling through a disorganized stack of charts can eat up precious time. Kathy's solution? A notebook computer equipped with a database management program. To determine which chart she needs, Kathy plugs in* Myth's *current location, and the database software instantly shows the name of the chart that covers this area.*

As this example illustrates, the key to the computer's usefulness is software, the instructions that tell the computer what to do. Software transforms a hunk of useless electronic junk into a useful tool. Every day, people are discovering new ways to apply computers, often using off-the-shelf application software, such as the database management software that's used aboard Myth.

Software defines what a computer can do, right down to the fundamentals—including what happens when you flip the switch to turn the power on. The term system software *encompasses all the programs that enable the computer to function. In contrast,* application software *refers to all the programs that transform the computer into a tool that's useful to people. Both are necessary, and they're introduced in this chapter, beginning with system software.*

145

3A

SYSTEM SOFTWARE: KEEPING THE COMPUTER RUNNING SMOOTHLY

WHAT YOU WILL LEARN . . .

When you have finished reading this module, you will be able to:

1. List the two major components of a computer's system software.

2. Explain why a computer cannot function without an operating system.

3. List the four major functions of an operating system.

4. List the three major types of user interfaces.

5. Discuss the strengths and weaknesses of the most popular operating systems.

6. Explain what happens when you turn on the computer.

7. List six system utilities that are considered essential.

8. Discuss data backup procedures.

Without system software, a computer is just an expensive hunk of junk. The most important parts of any computer's software system are the two components of system software: the operating system (OS) and essential system utilities, such as backup programs. Learning how to use an operating system and system utilities is the first step you need to take toward mastery of any computer system. In this module, you'll learn what operating systems do, look at the most popular operating systems, and learn which utilities you should use to ensure that your computing experience is safe and enjoyable.

OPERATING SYSTEM (OS): THE COMPUTER'S TRAFFIC COP

Imagine the traffic in a downtown New York City intersection at rush hour, and you'll have a good idea of what it's like inside a computer. Electrons are whizzing around at incredible speeds transported this way and that by the electronic equivalent of a harried traffic cop. Impatient peripherals and programs are honking electronic "horns," trying to get the cop's attention. As if the scene weren't chaotic enough, the "mayor" (the user) wants to come through *right now*. Somehow, everyone gets through.

Explore IT Lab

Operating Systems

The computer's **operating system (OS)** keeps traffic running smoothly. You can think of the operating system as a computerized version of a traffic cop, standing at the intersection of the computer's hardware, application programs, and the user (see Figure 3A.1).

A computer can't run without an operating system. The operating system is usually stored on the computer's hard disk. When you turn on a computer, the computer copies the essential portions of the operating system, called the **kernel** or the **supervisor program,** into the computer's memory, where they remain during the entire operating session. The kernel is called **memory resident** because it "resides" in memory at all times. Because the kernel is memory resident, it must be kept as small as possible. Less frequently-used portions of the operating system, called **nonresident,** are copied from the disk as needed.

Because operating systems work closely with the computer's hardware and with application programs, all of these components must be designed to work together harmoniously. The operating system requires a specific type or family of processors. For example, Microsoft Windows 98 requires Intel processors, such as the Pentium. Similarly, application programs must be designed to work with a specific operating system. A Macintosh program requires Mac OS and will not run on Microsoft Windows. (Some Windows programs will run on Macintoshes that are running a program that emulates Windows, but performance suffers.)

All operating systems perform certain basic functions. The operating system manages programs, parcels out memory, deals with input and output devices, and provides a means of interacting with the user (see Figure 3A.2).

Figure 3A.1

Like a computerized version of a traffic cop, standing at the intersection of the computer's hardware, application programs, and the user, the computer's operating system keeps traffic running smoothly.

Figure 3A.2

Figure 3A.2

The operating system manages programs, parcels out memory, deals with input and output devices, and provides a means of interacting with the user.

Managing Programs

An important operating system function—and the one that most dramatically affects an operating system's overall quality—is the way it manages program execution. **Single-tasking** operating systems can run only one application program at one time, which users find very inconvenient. Many users work with five or more applications in a single session. To switch programs with a single-tasking operating system, you must quit one program and start the second one. Today, **multitasking** operating systems are the norm.

Multitasking operating systems enable a single user to work with two or more programs at once. (Note that multitasking isn't the same thing as *time-sharing,* in which two or more users use the same computer simultaneously.) The CPU doesn't actually run two programs at once; rather, it switches between them as needed. From the user's perspective, one application (called the **foreground application**) is active, while another (the **background application**) is inactive (see Figure 3A.3).

A clear measure of the stability of different operating systems is the technique used to handle multitasking.

In an early form of multitasking, **cooperative multitasking,** users can run two or more programs. The foreground application gains control of the CPU and keeps this control until the program's task is finished. Only then does it relinquish the CPU to other applications. But what happens if the foreground application **crashes** (stops working)? The crashed program never relinquishes the CPU. In consequence, the computer "freezes," or "hangs," and the user must restart the computer, losing any unsaved work in any of the applications. Microsoft Windows 3.1 and all but the most recent version of Mac OS (including Mac OS 8) use this type of multitasking.

A better and more recent type of multitasking, called **preemptive multitasking,** enables the operating system to regain control if an application stops running. You lose any unsaved work in the application that crashed, but the failure of one application does not bring the whole system down. Personal computer operating systems that use preemptive multitasking

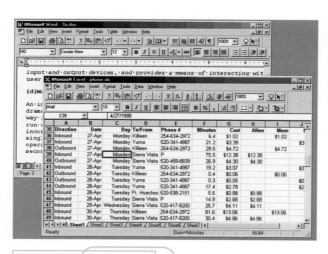

Figure 3A.3

Multitasking operating systems enable a single user to work with two or more programs at once. Here, the user is switching between a word processing application and a spreadsheet application.

include Linux, the next major version of Mac OS, Windows 95, Windows 98, and Windows NT.

A recent development in multitasking, **multithreading,** enables the computer to execute more than one task in a *single* program. To facilitate multithreading, programmers must divide a program into distinct tasks, called **threads.** For example, one thread could handle printing, while another handles file retrieval. With multithreading, users can work on one task in an application while other tasks keep running in the background. Multithreading also brings benefits when more than one application is running. With multithreading, the background application's threads keep running even when the user is working with the foreground application. Personal computer operating systems that can handle multithreaded applications include Linux, Mac OS 8, Windows 95, Windows 98, and Windows NT. The best operating systems combine multithreading with preemptive multitasking so that multiple thread execution is less likely to crash the computer.

Some operating systems are designed to facilitate **multiprocessing,** the use of two or more processors at a time. *Symmetric multiprocessing (SMP),* the easiest type of multiprocessing to implement, is designed to work with multithreading. When a program needs to execute a thread, the operating system finds an idle processor and assigns the thread to this processor. Personal computer operating systems that support multiprocessing include Linux, Microsoft Windows NT, and Mac OS 8.

Managing Memory

A second operating system function involves managing the computer's memory. For example, the operating system gives each running program its own portion of the memory, called a **partition.**

The best operating systems implement **virtual memory,** a method of using the computer's hard disk as an extension of random-access memory (RAM). In virtual memory, program instructions and data are divided into units of fixed size, called **pages.** If memory is full, the operating system starts storing copies of pages in a hard disk file, called the **swap file.** When the pages are needed, they are copied back into memory (see Figure 3A.4). Although virtual memory enables users to work with more memory than the amount installed on the computer's motherboard, the paging operations—called **swapping**—slow the computer down.

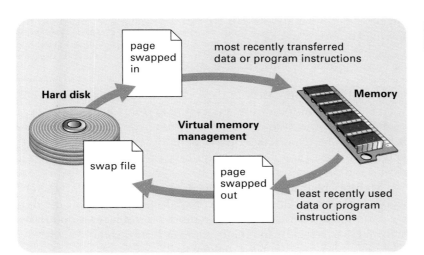

page swapped in

most recently transferred data or program instructions

Hard disk

Memory

Virtual memory management

swap file

page swapped out

least recently used data or program instructions

Figure 3A.4

In virtual memory, program instructions and data are divided into units of fixed size, called pages. If memory is full, the operating system starts storing copies of pages in a hard disk file, called the swap file. When the pages are needed, they are copied back into memory.

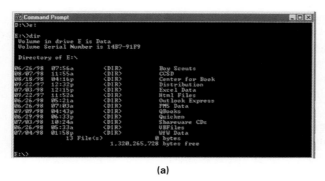

(a)

(b)

(c)

Figure 3A.5

Examples of (a) command-line, (b) menu-driven, and (c) graphical interfaces.

Handling Input and Output

A third operating system function involves dealing with input and output devices. For example, these devices generate interrupts, signals that inform the operating system that something has happened (for example, the user has pressed a key, the mouse has moved to a new position, or a document has finished printing). The operating system provides *interrupt handlers,* miniprograms that kick in immediately when an interrupt occurs.

As you know, many brands and models are available for input and output devices such as monitors, modems, and sound cards. Because each brand and model of a given device has its own unique characteristics, the operating system needs **device drivers.** Device drivers contain specific information about a particular brand and model. Most operating systems come with device drivers for popular input and output devices. Additional device drivers are supplied by the device manufacturers themselves.

User Interface

From the user's perspective, what makes or breaks an operating system is the quality of the **user interface,** the part of the operating system that interacts with the user. Sometimes the user interface is called the **shell,** suggesting the idea that the user interface (shell) "surrounds" the operating system (the kernel within the shell). The three types of user interfaces are command-line, menu-driven, and graphical interfaces (see Figure 3A.5).

Types of User Interfaces

A **command-line user interface** requires the user to type commands using *keywords* that tell the operating system what to do (such as "format" or "copy"). You must observe rules of **syntax,** a set of regulations that specify exactly what you can type in a given place. For example, the following command

```
copy a:myfile.txt c:myfile.doc
```

copies a file from the disk in drive A to the disk in drive C, not the other way around. Command-line operating systems aren't popular with most users because they require memorization, and it is easy to make a typing mistake. Some experienced users actually prefer them, however, because you can operate the computer quickly after you've memorized the keywords and syntax.

Menu-driven user interfaces enable the user to avoid memorizing keywords and syntax. On-screen, text-based menus show all the options available at a given point. With most systems, you select an option by using the arrow keys to select it, and then you press Enter. Some systems enable you to click the desired option with the mouse.

S P O T L I G H T

GNOME: MAKING UNIX AND LINUX EASY TO USE

▶Operating systems based on UNIX aren't easy to love, unless you've got some special affection for command-line interfaces. But that's about to change, thanks to GNOME. Currently available for Linux and several other UNIX-like operating systems, GNOME is an easy-to-use desktop environment that's immediately familiar to anyone who has used Mac OS or Microsoft Windows. Best of all, it's free. Distributed under a license that makes the software freely redistributable, GNOME offers a user experience that's sufficiently attractive to tempt growing numbers of users away from the market-leading Microsoft Windows.

The brainchild of twenty-something Miguel de Icaza, GNOME began as a labor of social conscience as well as love. Then a programmer affiliated with the National Autonomous University of Mexico in Mexico City, de Icaza realized that only four percent of the world's population used computers—and of the remaining 96 percent, few would be able to pay for commercial operating system software. The growing availability of free, high-quality UNIX-derived operating systems, such as Linux, was creating a genuine opportunity to reduce the digital divide, de Icaza realized, but Linux—sans GNOME—was too hard to use.

By making Linux user-friendly, GNOME makes Linux accessible—and because it's free, it promises to bring computing to places where computers are currently hard to come by. One example: the Mexican schools. Thanks to Linux and GNOME, the Mexican government has been able to embark on an ambitious program to place computers in every one of the country's schoolrooms. If the Mexican government had to fork over money for a commercial operating system such as Microsoft Windows, far less money would have been available for PC purchases.

GNOME promises to bring computing to places where computers are currently hard to come by.

Graphical user interfaces (GUIs) are by far the most popular. In an operating system, GUIs are used to create the **desktop environment,** which appears after the operating system starts. In a desktop environment, computer resources (such as programs, data files, and network connections) are represented by small pictures, called **icons.** You can initiate many actions by clicking an icon. Programs run within sizeable on-screen windows, making it easy to switch from one program to another (see Figure 3A.6). Within programs, you can give commands by choosing items from pull-down menus, some of which display **dialog boxes.** In a dialog box, you can supply additional information that the program needs (see Figure 3A.7). If a program needs to give you a warning message, you see an **alert box** that tells you what might happen if you proceed. Although GUIs are easy to use, they make heavy demands on a computer's processing circuitry and slow the computer down considerably.

Figure 3A.6

Programs run within windows. You can initiate actions by clicking an icon. Within programs you can give commands by selecting items from pull-down menus.

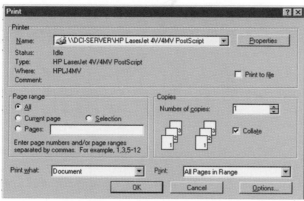

A dialog box enables you to provide additional information that a program needs. This is the print dialog box.

Directories, Folders, and Files

Default and Alternative User Interfaces

Every operating system provides a **default user interface,** which accepts user commands and provides messages in response. But it's often possible to use a different user interface than the default one. For example, MS-DOS uses a default command-line interface. But many programs are available that provide a menu-driven interface for MS-DOS. In UNIX, many users become confused because so many different shells are available. For example, the version of UNIX for Intel processors, Linux, can work with three different command-line user interfaces and dozens of graphical user interfaces.

User Interface Functions

All three types of user interfaces typically enable the user to do the following:

- Gain access **(log in)** to the system by providing a **user ID** (also called a user name) and a **password.** Many personal computers aren't secured in this way, but most can be.

- Start (also called **launch**) application programs.

- Manage disks and files. You can format new disks, display a list of files in a directory, create new directories, rename directories, delete empty directories, copy files from one directory or disk to another, rename files, and delete files.

- Shut down the computer safely by following an orderly shutdown procedure. You shouldn't just switch the computer off; doing so may leave scrambled data on the computer's hard disk.

EXPLORING POPULAR OPERATING SYSTEMS: A GUIDED TOUR

The place where two rivers come together is called a confluence, and it's a good metaphor for understanding the variety of operating systems available. As you'll see, all of today's popular operating systems are strongly influenced by two very different predecessors: UNIX, and the first GUI-based operating system developed at Xerox's Palo Alto Research Center (PARC). In various ways, all current operating systems represent variously successful attempts to pull together the ideas pioneered in these systems.

UNIX

Developed at AT&T's Bell Laboratories in the early 1970s, **UNIX** is a pioneering operating system that continues to define what an operating system should do and how it should work. UNIX was the first operating system with preemptive multitasking, and it was designed to work efficiently in a secure, centrally-administered computer network. Other important UNIX innovations include the concepts of file directories and path names (see Module 2B). It also supports multiprocessing, making it ideal for use with high-powered minicomputers equipped with several CPUs.

If UNIX is so great, why didn't it take over the computer world? One reason is the lack of compatibility among the many different versions, or *flavors,* of UNIX. Another reason is its difficulty of use. UNIX defaults to a command-line user interface, which is challenging for new computer users.

Recently, a number of GUI interfaces have been developed for UNIX, improving the usability picture (see Figure 3A.8).

UNIX's greatest success lies in **client/server computing,** a type of computer usage that is widely found in corporations today. In client/server computing, programs are broken into two parts, called the *client* program and the *server* program. The client program handles interaction with the user and is installed on users' desktop systems. The server program runs on a high-powered, centralized minicomputer that everyone on the network can access (if they have the appropriate security clearance). Examples of such programs include massive databases that track all of a company's financial data. UNIX-based client/server systems have enough sheer number-crunching capabilities to replace much more expensive mainframe systems, and they are very popular in corporations.

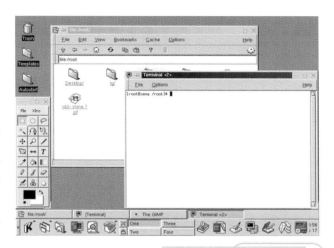

Figure 3A.8

UNIX's greatest success lies in client/server computing, a type of computer usage that is widely found in corporations today. Recently, a number of GUI interfaces have been developed for UNIX, improving the usability picture.

Xerox PARC and the First GUI

While UNIX was defining how operating systems should manage computer resources, work at Xerox Corporation's Palo Alto Research Center (PARC) established how an OS should look. In the mid- to late-1970s, PARC researchers originated every aspect of the now-familiar GUI interface, including the idea of the screen as a "desktop," icons, on-screen fonts, windows, and pull-down windows. Although Xerox released a GUI-based computer (called the Star) in 1981, the company was never able to capitalize on its researchers' innovations.

MS-DOS

MS-DOS (or DOS for short) is an operating system for Intel-based PCs that uses a command-line user interface. Developed for the original IBM PC in 1981, MS-DOS was marketed by IBM in a virtually-identical version, called PC-DOS. Like every operating system discussed in this module, MS-DOS shows the influence of UNIX. DOS commands for managing and navigating directories, for example, are almost identical to those in UNIX.

Because DOS was developed for early 16-bit Intel microprocessors, it can't take full advantage of the advanced capabilities of Intel's 32-bit microprocessors (beginning with the 80386). For example, DOS runs in the Intel processors' *real mode,* in which the operating system cannot prevent applications from invading each others' memory space (which causes crashes). In addition, DOS can work with only 640KB of RAM at a time. Although some users still run DOS to take advantage of applications that aren't available for other operating systems, its use is declining.

Mac OS

Just as MS-DOS brought key UNIX ideas to personal computing, **Mac OS** introduced the graphical user interface to the world. Closely modeled on the system developed at Xerox PARC, the original Macintosh operating system was released in 1984. It consisted of the operating system (called System) and a separate shell (called the Finder). By the late-1980s, the Mac's operating system was the most technologically-advanced in personal computing, but Apple Computer was unable to capitalize on its lead and the Mac OS (as it came to be

Figure ⟨3A.9⟩

Released in 2000, Mac OS X brings Mac OS up to the technical standards of Microsoft Windows.

called after System 7.5) fell behind Microsoft Windows. Still, Mac OS is widely-considered to be the easiest operating system for beginning computer users. In 1998, Apple was reinvigorated by the return of founder Steve Jobs and released a much-improved, more-stable version of Mac OS (currently in version 8.1), and announced a new version that would bring Mac OS up to the technical standard set by Microsoft Windows 98. A new version called Mac OS X, released in 2000, brought Mac OS up to the technical standards of Microsoft Windows (see Figure 3A.9).

Microsoft Windows 3.x

Early versions of Microsoft Windows did not attract much attention, even though they helped to introduce the graphical user interface (GUI) to PC users. The release of Windows 3.0 changed the face of computing forever. Windows 3.0 was the first version of Windows to enable users to take full advantage of Intel's new 32-bit microprocessor, the 80386. This microprocessor offered a new processing mode, called *protected mode*, that enabled users to access virtually unlimited amounts of memory.

The various versions of Microsoft Windows 3.0 (including Windows 3.1, 3.11, and Windows for Workgroups 3.1), collectively known as **Microsoft Windows 3.x,** are not actually operating systems. In reality, they are MS-DOS applications that "switch" Intel processors into protected mode. To work with MS-DOS, these programs can work with only 16 bits of data at a time. As a result, they cannot take full advantage of the 32-bit processing capabilities of the Intel 80386 and higher microprocessors. Although Windows 3.x can run more than one program at a time, it uses cooperative multitasking, which means that the failure of any one application is likely to crash the whole system.

Windows 3.x is still in use. Some corporations ran into huge training and equipment upgrade costs when they migrated from MS-DOS to Windows 3.x, and they remain unconvinced that more recent versions of Windows offer enough improvement to warrant another round of costs.

Microsoft Windows 95 and 98

Unlike Windows 3.x, **Microsoft Windows 95** (called **Win 95** for short) is a true operating system, not merely a DOS application. (A version of DOS is included for downward compatibility.) Technically, Windows 95 is a major advance because it fully supports the 32-bit processing capabilities of Intel 80386 and later microprocessors. In addition, it also supports a key feature of UNIX, preemptive multitasking, which enables the operating system to regain control if an application crashes.

Despite its attractive features, Win 95 is best understood as a transitional operating system, poised between Windows 3.x (a 16-bit operating system) and Windows NT (a true 32-bit operating system with advanced features). Win 95 is designed to run the many existing 16-bit applications designed for Windows 3.x, as well as new 32-bit applications. Many corporate information technology (IT) managers decided to skip Windows 95 in favor of upgrading eventually to Windows NT, which Microsoft describes as the operating system of the future. Win 95 did very well in the consumer market, though, thanks to the fact that millions of new PCs included Win 95.

Microsoft Windows 98, or **Win 98,** released in 1998, is an improved version of Win 95 that offers better stability, improved Internet connectivity, updated drivers for new peripherals, including DVD-ROM discs and devices that use universal serial bus port (USB) connections (see Figure 3A.10). Despite these improvements, businesses have not been eager to upgrade to Win 98, and most of the operating system's sales reflect the system's installation in brand new PCs. An upgraded edition, **Microsoft Windows 98 SE** (short for "Second Edition"), was released in 2000. According to Microsoft, Windows 98 SE is still the best choice for home computing because it offers the best support for multimedia, PC gaming, home networking, and popular peripherals.

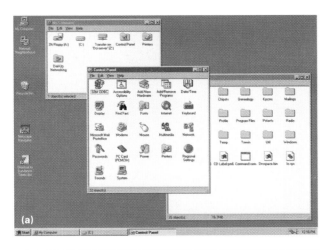

Microsoft Windows CE

Designed for hot-selling palmtop computers (also called personal digital assistants, or PDAs), **Microsoft Windows CE** is a "light" version of Windows. Unlike other palmtop operating systems, Windows CE is designed to run simplified versions of Windows 95 and Windows 98 programs, such as Microsoft's own office applications, which are available in "pocket" versions for Windows CE. This enables users to create documents on a palmtop and transfer them to a desktop computer for further processing and printing.

For mobile computing, Windows CE includes an interactive scheduling calendar, an address book for contacts, electronic mail, and Web browsing. By means of an automatic active synchronization program, users can quickly synchronize the corresponding utilities on their desktop computers. CE includes handwriting recognition and support for voice recording as well (see Figure 3A.11).

Microsoft Windows NT

Corporations have largely left Win 95 and Win 98 to the consumer market, but that's not the case for **Microsoft Windows NT,** a true 32-bit operating system. Unlike Win 95 and Win 98, Windows NT is specifically designed for client/server systems, formerly a stronghold of UNIX. To support client/server computing, Windows NT is made up of two components, called **Windows NT Workstation** and **Windows NT Server.**

The Windows NT Workstation module is designed for individual desktop computers. It looks just like Win 95 or Win 98, but it's a more sophisticated operating system oriented to business needs. It's faster than Win 95 and Win 98 (by as much as 30 percent). But the real benefits of Windows NT Workstation emerge in a networked corporate environment, where NT desktops link to servers running Windows NT Server.

In a corporate network, Windows NT Server provides the following benefits:

- **Security** Controls individual workstation access to networked resources, such as a database containing sensitive financial information.

- **Remote administration** Enables network administrator to set options remotely for each user's computer, such as specifying which applications the user can start.

Figure **3A.10**

(a) Windows 95.
(b) Windows 98.
Win 95 did very well in the consumer market because millions of PCs included Win 95. Although Win 98 is an improved version of Win 95, most of the operating system's sales reflect the system's installation in brand new PCs.

Techtalk

blue screen of death
A feared error message with a blue background that appears when Microsoft Windows NT has encountered an error condition—which is, unfortunately, resolvable in most cases only by rebooting the system.

Figure 3A.11

Windows CE includes an interactive scheduling calendar, an address book for contacts, electronic mail, and Web browsing. CE also includes handwriting recognition and support for voice recording.

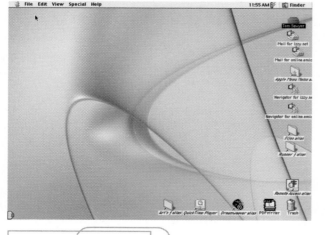

Figure 3A.12

Microsoft Windows 2000 Professional combines the attractive, easy-to-use interface of Windows 98 with the security features of Windows NT Workstation.

Destinations

Explore the features of Microsoft's latest Windows offerings at the Windows Home Page (**http://www.microsoft.com/windows**).

- **Directory services** Provides a "map" to all the files and applications available on the network.

- **Web server** Makes Web pages available to internal intranet users or the external World Wide Web. (For more information on intranets, see Module 7A.)

In corporate computing, Microsoft Windows NT is making rapid inroads into a market once dominated by much more expensive UNIX-based systems. Why? Windows NT enables companies to use inexpensive Intel-based hardware. However, Microsoft still needs to convince companies that Windows NT has the security and number-crunching power to rival high-end UNIX systems.

Microsoft Windows 2000

Microsoft's latest operating system offerings, **Microsoft Windows 2000 Professional** and **Microsoft Windows 2000 Server,** combine the benefits of the firm's previous products. Intended for users' computers, Microsoft Windows 2000 Professional combines the attractive, easy-to-use interface of Windows 98 with the security features of Windows NT Workstation (see Figure 3A.12). Microsoft Windows 2000 Server is the newest version of Windows NT, and is designed to run on professionally-administered server systems.

Linux

Just as Microsoft Windows NT is invading UNIX's territory in corporate computing, UNIX appears to be returning the compliment—specifically, by invading Windows' bread-and-butter territory, the Intel-based PC. A new "flavor" of UNIX, called **Linux,** is the fastest-growing operating system for Intel-based personal computers. (Versions of Linux have also been created for other PCs, including Macintoshes.) If you saw the movie *Titanic*, you saw some of Linux's work: Linux powered the PC on which the movie's animations were created. According to one estimate, more than 257 million systems are running Linux (see Figure 3A.13).

What makes Linux so attractive? Two things: it's powerful, and it's free. Let's tackle "powerful" first. Linux brings all the maturity and sophistication of UNIX to the PC. Created in 1991 by a Finnish university student named Linus Torvalds, Linux has since been developed by thousands of the world's best programmers, who have willingly donated their time to make sure that Linux is a very good version of UNIX. According to Linux backers, they may have created the *best* version of UNIX in existence. Linux includes all the respected features of UNIX, including multitasking, virtual memory, Internet support, multiprocessor support, and graphical user interfaces. Recently, researchers at Los Alamos National Laboratories created a "bargain-basement supercomputer" by hooking up 68 microprocessors in a Linux-based system. The computer took only three days to assemble using off-the-shelf components. The result? One of the 500 fastest computers in the world, capable of performing 19.2 billion operations per second.

And now for the free part. Linux is distributed using the Open Software Foundation's **General Public License (GPL),** which specifies that you can obtain and use Linux for free, as long as you do not turn around and try to sell it to somebody. In practice, most people buy a **Linux distribution,** a CD-ROM containing Linux and a collection of drivers, utilities, GUI interfaces, and application programs. Although most of the software on these CD-ROM discs is governed by GPL, what's being sold is the considerable effort that goes into collecting all the Linux drivers and utilities, organizing them coherently, and providing a setup utility that makes it easy for novices to get Linux running.

Although Linux is powerful and free, many corporate information officers (CIO) shy away from adopting Linux precisely because it isn't a commercial product with a stable company behind it. Also, Linux can't run the popular Microsoft Office applications, which most corporate users prefer. But Linux is gaining increasing acceptance. A big reason is a Web server called Apache. (A Web server is a program that makes Web pages available on the Internet.) Apache is currently the most popular Web server available, and it's also a GPL-distributed freebie. Because Linux is so powerful, many companies are finding that they can take disused Intel hardware, such as PCs based on the Intel 486, install Linux and Apache, and presto! They have a Web server that equals the performance of systems costing $10,000 or more.

Figure 3A.13

Linux is the fastest-growing operating system for Intel-based personal computers. Linux includes all the respected features of UNIX and it's free.

STARTING THE COMPUTER

When you start or reset a computer, it reloads the operating system into the computer's memory. This process is called **booting,** after the notion that the computer "pulls itself up by its bootstraps." In a **cold boot,** you start the computer after the power has been switched off. In a **warm boot,** you restart a computer that is already on. Warm boots are often necessary after installing new software or after an application crashes. In PCs, you can initiate a warm boot by pressing Ctrl + Alt + Del (all three keys simultaneously).

Destinations

For the latest news and developments in Linux, visit Linux Today **(http://linuxtoday.com)**. Linux beginners can get assistance at Linuxnewbie. org **(http://www.linuxnewbie.org)** and Linux Start **(http:www.linuxstart.com)**.

The BIOS Screen and Setup Program

When you first turn on or reset a PC, you'll see the **BIOS screen,** which provides information about the BIOS software encoded in the computer's ROM. BIOS stands for **basic input/output system.** As its name suggests, it equips the computer with the software needed to accept keyboard output and display information on-screen. At this point, you can access the computer's **setup program** by pressing a special key, such as Del. (You'll see an on-screen message indicating which key to press to access the setup program.) The setup program includes many settings that control the computer's hardware. You should not alter or change any of these settings unless you are instructed to do so by technical support personnel.

The Power-On Self-Test (POST)

After the BIOS loads, this software executes a series of tests to make sure that the computer and associated peripherals are operating correctly. Collectively, these tests are known as the **power-on self-test (POST).** Among the components tested are the computer's main memory (RAM), the keyboard, floppy disk drives, and the hard disk. If the computer encounters an error, you'll hear a beep and see an on-screen message. Often, you can correct such problems by making sure components such as keyboards are plugged in securely.

MOVERS & SHAKERS

Linus Torvalds

In the world of computers, operating systems are typically created by large teams of software engineers working for large corporations. That concept was turned upside down in 1991 when Linux was unleashed on the world. Linux, a derivation of UNIX, is a freeware operating system. Not only is the operating system free, but so too is the source code on which the operating system is based.

The story of Linux began with a simple student at Helsinki University in Finland. Linus Torvalds was first introduced to UNIX and learned how to program in C in 1990. Like many other computer geeks, he coveted the capability to run UNIX on his home computer. Unfortunately, starting prices for UNIX were $5,000, and it required a $10,000 workstation. So he decided to write his own version from scratch.

Torvalds had the kernel of his new operating system working in early 1991. After a few more changes, he posted his fledgling operating system, named Linux version .02, on an Internet newsgroup and invited people to download it and try to make it better. They did, on both counts.

As people downloaded Linux, they used their expertise to make modifications or improvements in various parts of the system. A few people worked on the file I/O routines, while a few others worked on the user interface, and still others worked on printer drivers.

With thousands of volunteer programmers around the world working on Linux, the improvements were made at a frenetic pace. Large corporations had a hard time mustering the wherewithal to get their operating systems out the door on time, but Linux just kept getting better and better each month.

The beauty of Linux, and its development model, is that it doesn't run on any particular type of computer: it runs on them all. Linux has been ported (translated) to run on systems as small as 3Com's PalmPilot computer or as large as homegrown supercomputers. It has won many awards and plaudits from the popular computer press, being rated as the best operating system of 1996 by InfoWorld magazine.

The community approach to Linux has made it a marvel of the computer world, and made Linus Torvalds a folk legend. While he doesn't make a cent from Linux, he is viewed as a demigod by many of the seven or eight million people using the operating system.

Indeed, Torvalds must gain quite a bit of satisfaction from what he launched only a few years ago. His creation is now the fastest-growing operating system for Intel-based PCs. As is often the story, he was in the right place at the right time to change history. Without the communications power of the Internet, Linux may never have made it out of the university. And without the contributions of thousands of Linux devotees, Linus Torvalds may never have become a legend in his own time.

Linus Torvalds.

Loading the OS

Once the power-on self-test is completed, the BIOS initiates a search for the operating system. When it finds the operating system, it **loads** the software into the computer's memory. (To load a program means to transfer it from a storage device to memory.) Settings in the setup program determine where BIOS looks. On most PCs, BIOS first looks for the operating system on the computer's hard disk. On newer PCs, it's possible to load an operating system from a CD-ROM. The BIOS can also be set to look for the operating system on the floppy disk drive. If your computer fails to start normally, you may be able to get your computer running by choosing the setup program option that loads from Drive A, and inserting the **emergency disk** in the disk drive. The emergency disk loads a reduced version of the operating system that can be used for troubleshooting purposes.

Authentication

When the operating system finishes loading, you may see a dialog box asking you to type a user name and password. This process is called **authentication** (also called **login**). In authentication, you verify that you are indeed the person who is authorized to use the computer. If the computer is connected to a network, the authentication you provide enables you to access network resources.

Consumer-oriented operating systems such as Microsoft Windows and Mac OS do not demand that you supply a user name and password to use the computer. However, you can set up **profiles** on these systems. Associated with a user name and optionally a password, a profile is a record of a specific user's preferences. If you set up a profile for yourself, you will see your preferences on-screen after you log in. Other users will see their preferences, without disturbing yours.

On multi-user computer systems, you must have an **account** on the computer that is created by the computer's **system administrator,** the person who is responsible for the computer. Your account consists of your user name, your password, and your storage space, called a **home directory.** To access your account, you must supply your user name and password.

If you are given a user name and password that enables you to access network resources at your school, it's very important that you safeguard this information. Don't write it down where others could read it, and never give your password to others. If you do, somebody could use your account in such a way that the actions they perform will seem as if they were done by you. If such actions involve playing pranks or engaging in illegal activities, you could lose your computer privileges.

SYSTEM UTILITIES: TOOLS FOR HOUSEKEEPING

System utility programs provide a necessary addition to an operating system's basic system-management tools. Sometimes these programs are included in the operating system, and sometimes they're provided by third-party suppliers. The following utilities are considered essential.

File Management

Perhaps the most important of all system utilities is the **file manager,** a utility program that enables you to deal with the data stored on your disk (see Figure 3A.14). The file manager enables you to perform various housekeeping operations on the files and folders created on your computer's storage devices.

Your data (as well as the programs installed on your computer) is stored in **files,** which are named units in which related data is stored. For example, your first college essay could be stored in a file called essay1.doc. A filename such as this one often consists of two parts, the **filename** proper (essay1), a period, and an **extension** (doc). The extension indicates the type of data that is contained in a file (in this case, the file is a Microsoft Word document).

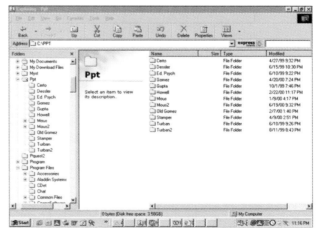

Figure 3A.14

A file manager such as Windows Explorer enables you to organize your files and folders.

Files are organized using **directories** (also called **folders**). In Microsoft Windows, important directories include My Documents (a directory containing the work you create with application programs), Program Files (a directory containing the software installed on your system), and Windows (a directory containing the Windows operating system).

A file manager such as Windows Explorer, the standard file manager in Microsoft Windows 98, enables you to visualize the arrangement of folders on a given storage device, such as the computer's hard disk. When you select a folder, you see the folder's contents in the panel to the right. For each file, you see the file's name, size, type, and date of last modification. (If this information isn't visible, click Views until it's displayed.)

You can use a file manager to perform any of the following tasks:

- Creating new folders.

- Moving and copying items between folders.

- Examining the contents of files using **file viewers,** which are mini-programs designed to give you a quick view of a file.

- Deleting files and folders.

- Moving or copying items to other disks, including a floppy disk.

- Launching application programs.

When you organize files and folders with a file manager, be sure to limit your actions to the data files you create with application programs. Never move or delete files or folders in the Program Files or Windows folders! If you do, the computer may fail to operate correctly until you reinstall all the software.

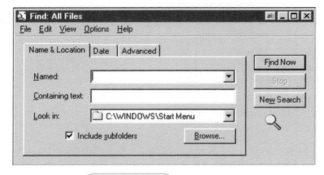

Figure 3A.15

Use a file finder when you can't locate a needed file.

File Finders

On a large hard disk with thousands of files, the task of finding a needed file can be time-consuming and frustrating if attempted manually. For this reason, most operating systems include a **file finder** utility, which enables you to search an entire hard disk for a missing file. In Microsoft Windows, the Find enables you to search for files in a number of ways, including name, date, and size (see Figure 3A.15). A similar Mac OS utility, called Find File, offers the same features.

Backup Utilities

Backup utilities are an essential part of safe, efficient computer usage. They copy data from the computer's hard disk to backup media, such as tape cartridges or a ZIP drive. Should the hard disk fail, you can recover the data from the backup disk.

A backup begins with a **full backup,** in which a "mirror image" is made of the entire hard disk's contents. Subsequently, the software performs an **incremental backup** at specified intervals (such as once per day). In an incremental backup, the backup software copies only those files that have been created or changed since the last backup occurred. In this way, the backup media always contain an up-to-date copy of all programs and data. In the event of a hard disk or computer system failure, the backup tape can be used to restore the data by copying it from the tape to a new hard disk.

Backup utilities are an essential part of computing. Always make backups of your important files.

Even if you don't have backup software, you can still make backup copies of your important files: just copy them to a floppy disk. When you finish working on an assignment, *always* copy the data to a floppy disk, and put the floppy disk away for safekeeping. Don't ever rely on a hard disk to keep the only copy of a college paper!

Antivirus Software

Antivirus programs (also called *vaccines*) protect a computer from computer viruses (see Figure 3A.16). These programs work by examining all the files on a disk, looking for the tell-tale "signatures" of virus code. One limitation of such programs is that they can detect only those viruses whose "signatures" are in their databases. Most antivirus programs enable you to download the signatures of new viruses from a Web site. New viruses, however, appear every day. If your system becomes infected by a program that's not in the system's database, the program may not detect it. Due to this shortcoming, many antivirus programs also include monitoring programs that can detect and stop the destructive operations of unknown viruses. You'll learn more about computer viruses and antivirus programs in Module 9B.

Figure 3A.16

Norton Antivirus is a utility that works by examining all the files on a disk, looking for the tell-tale "signatures" of virus code.

File Compression Utilities

To exchange programs and data efficiently, particularly by means of the Internet, **file compression utilities** are needed (see Figure 3A.17). These programs can reduce the size of a file by as much as 50 percent without harming the data. Most work by searching the file for frequently-repeated but lengthy data patterns, and substituting short codes for these patterns. When the file is decompressed, the utility restores the lengthier pattern where each code is encountered. Popular compression utilities include WinZip for the PC and StuffIt for Macintosh systems.

Most compression utilities can also create **archives.** An archive is a single file that contains two or more files, stored in a special format. Archives are handy for storage as well as file exchange purposes because as many as several hundred separate files can be stored in a single, easily handled unit. WinZip combines compression and archiving functions.

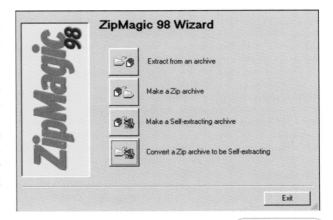

Figure 3A.17

A file compression utility enables you to create archives and compressed files.

Disk Scanning Utilities

A **disk scanner** can detect and resolve a number of physical and logical problems that occur as your computer stores files on a disk. A physical problem involves an irregularity in the drive's surface, which results in a **bad sector** (a portion of the disk that is unable to store data reliably). The scanner can fix the problem by locking out the bad sector so that it is no longer used. Logical problems are usually caused by a power outage that occurs before the computer is able to finish writing data to the disk. **Disk cleanup utilities**

Figure 3A.18

Periodically, you should defragment your hard disk to ensure top performance.

can save disk space by removing temporary files that are no longer needed.

File Defragmentation Programs

As you use a computer, it creates and erases files on the hard disk. The result is that the disk soon becomes a patchwork of files, with portions of files scattered here and there. This slows the hard disk because the read/write head must go to several locations to find all of a file's data. A disk with data scattered around in this way is referred to as **fragmented.** Fragmentation isn't dangerous—the location of all the data is known thanks to the disk's tracking mechanisms—but periodic maintenance is required to restore the disk's performance. File defragmentation utilities (see Figure 3A.18) are used for this purpose.

TAKEAWAY POINTS

- An operating system works at the intersection of application software, the user, and the computer's hardware. It manages programs, parcels out memory to applications, deals with internal messages from input and output devices, and provides a means of communicating with the user.

- Multitasking enables users to work with more than one program at a time. Preemptive multitasking is much safer to use than the earlier type, cooperative multitasking.

- The three basic types of user interfaces are command-line interfaces, menu-driven interfaces, and graphical user interfaces (GUIs). GUI is the easiest to use, but some experienced users like the speed of command-line interfaces.

- UNIX is popular in high-end client/server systems, in which a powerful computer called a server makes data available to users through a computer network.

- Based on user interface ideas developed at Xerox Corporation's research center, the Mac OS (formerly called System) introduced the GUI to personal computing. Although Mac OS supports multithreading, by 1998 it still did not support preemptive multitasking.

- Early versions of Microsoft Windows were essentially MS-DOS applications, but Microsoft Windows 95 and 98 brought all the benefits of GUI and preemptive multitasking to PC users. Windows 95 and 98 have had their greatest success in the consumer market.

- Microsoft Windows NT Workstation and Windows NT Server are eating into UNIX's market share in client/server computing. At the same time, however, a free version of UNIX, called Linux, is gaining ground in Microsoft's home territory, the PC. A new version of NT, called Windows 2000, is available in two versions: Windows 2000 Professional (the successor to NT Workstation) and Windows 2000 Server (the successor to NT Server).

- Essential system utilities include backup software, file managers, file finders, disk scanning programs, antivirus software, file compression utilities, and defragmentation programs.

- A sound backup procedure begins with a full backup of an entire hard disk, and periodic incremental backups of just those files that have been created or altered since the last backup occurred.

MODULE REVIEW

KEY TERMS AND CONCEPTS

account	disk scanner	loads
alert box	emergency disk	log in
antivirus programs	extension	Mac OS
archives	files	memory resident
authentication or login	file compression utilities	menu-driven user interfaces
background application	file finder	Microsoft Windows CE
backup utilities	file manager	Microsoft Windows 3.x
bad sector	filename	Microsoft Windows 95, or
BIOS (basic input/output	file viewers	Win 95
system) screen	folders	Microsoft Windows 98, or
booting	foreground application	Win 98
client/server computing	fragmented	Microsoft Windows 98 SE
cold boot	full backup	Microsoft Windows NT
command-line user interface	General Public License (GPL)	Microsoft Windows NT Server
cooperative multitasking	graphical user interfaces (GUIs)	Microsoft Windows NT
crashes	home directory	Workstation
default user interface	icons	Microsoft Windows 2000
desktop environment	incremental backup	Professional
device drivers	kernel, or supervisor program	Microsoft Windows 2000 Server
dialog boxes	launch	MS-DOS
directories	Linux	multiprocessing
disk cleanup utilities	Linux distribution	multitasking

multithreading	preemptive multitasking	system administrator
nonresident	profiles	threads
operating system (OS)	setup program	UNIX
pages	single-tasking	user ID, or shell
partition	swap file	user interface
password	swapping	virtual memory
power-on self test (POST)	syntax	warm boot

TRUE/FALSE

Indicate whether the following statements are true or false.

1. A computer cannot run without an operating system.

2. A background application is considered active and a foreground application is considered inactive.

3. Cooperative multitasking is more prone to system problems than preemptive multitasking.

4. Multithreading enables the computer to execute more than one task at a time.

5. A menu-driven interface is the most popular type of user interface.

6. MS-DOS developed to take full advantage of 32-bit processors.

7. Microsoft Windows 95 is considered a true operating system rather than just a DOS application.

8. Microsoft Windows CE runs on palmtop computers.

9. A file compression utility is the most important system utility.

10. Backup utilities are an essential part of safe, efficient computer usage.

MATCHING

Match each key term from the left column to the most accurate definition in the right column.

_____ 1. operating system

_____ 2. multitasking

_____ 3. multiprocessing

_____ 4. kernel

_____ 5. warm boot

_____ 6. file manager

_____ 7. file viewers

_____ 8. archives

_____ 9. disk scanner

_____ 10. fragmented

a. mini-programs designed to give you a quick view of a file

b. restarting a computer that's already on

c. describes a disk whose data is scattered

d. a single file that contains two or more files stored in a special format

e. the use of two or more processors at a time

f. manages programs, parcels out memory, deals with input and output devices, and provides a means of interacting with the user

g. a utility that can detect and resolve physical and logical problems on a disk

h. enable a single user to work with two or more programs

i. a utility program that enables you to deal with the data stored on your disk

j. essential portions of an operating system

MULTIPLE CHOICE

Circle the letter of the correct choice for each of the following.

1. What does memory resident mean?
   a. a program that resides in memory at all times.
   b. a program that monitors memory to make sure it is used efficiently.
   c. a measure of the amount of memory in a computer system.
   d. any program residing in memory.

2. Which of the following is not something typically handled by the operating system?
   a. managing programs
   b. dealing with I/O devices
   c. publishing Web pages
   d. interacting with the user

3. What is the name given to a distinct task running in a system relying on multithreading?
   a. unithread
   b. process
   c. program
   d. thread

4. Which of the following operating systems does not support multiprocessing?
   a. Mac OS 8
   b. Windows 98
   c. Linux
   d. Windows NT

5. Which of the following is a type of user interface?
   a. command-line
   b. BIOS
   c. dialog box
   d. none of the above

6. Which of the following is a key component of a graphical user interface?
   a. command words
   b. icons
   c. cursors
   d. shell

7. Which of the following operating systems is ideally suited for a networked corporate environment?
   a. Windows 3
   b. Windows 95
   c. Windows NT
   d. Windows 98

8. Which company developed the first graphical user interface?
   a. Microsoft
   b. AT&T
   c. IBM
   d. Xerox PARC

9. Which is the fastest growing operating system for Intel PCs?
   a. Linux
   b. UNIX
   c. Windows NT
   d. Windows CE

10. Which of the following is not a system utility program?
    a. antivirus software
    b. file defragmentation
    c. multitasking
    d. file compression

FILL-IN

In the blank provided, write the correct answer for each of the following.

1. A computer's _____ is usually stored on a hard disk and works closely with the computer's hardware and application programs.

2. When multiple programs are running on a computer system, the one being used at the current time is known as the _____ application.

3. If an operating system uses virtual memory, when memory is full, the operating system starts storing parts of memory in a(n) _____ on the hard drive.

4. Every operating system provides a(n) _____ user interface, which accepts user commands and provides messages in response.

5. The first graphical user interface was developed at _____ .

6. To support client/server computing, Windows NT is made up of two components called Windows NT _____ and Windows NT _____ .

7. _____ is a free and powerful operating system that brings all the maturity and sophistication of UNIX to the PC.

8. Files are organized using _____ .

9. _____ are programs that can reduce the size of a file by as much as 50 percent without harming the data.

10. If a file's data is not stored in contiguous locations on a disk, it's said to be _____ .

SHORT ANSWER

On a separate sheet of paper, answer the following questions.

1. What are the different functions of an operating system?

2. What are the differences between single-tasking, multitasking, multithreading, and multiprocessing?

3. Explain how virtual memory is implemented in an operating system.

4. What is the purpose of a device driver? Why are they necessary?

5. What are the pros and cons of using a command-line user interface?

6. What is a GUI? Why is it important?

7. Explain why UNIX did not become popular on personal computers.

8. Discuss the genealogy of Windows and when it became one of the most popular operating systems on the market.

9. What factors contribute to Linux not being readily adopted in the corporate marketplace?

10. What types of system utilities are mandatory for a smoothly-operating computer system?

3B

MODULE

OUTLINE

WHAT YOU WILL LEARN . . .

When you have finished reading this module, you will be able to:

1. Differentiate between horizontal and vertical applications.

2. List the most popular types of horizontal applications.

3. Differentiate between commercial software, shareware, freeware, and public domain software.

4. Explain software versions.

5. Discuss the advantages and disadvantages of standalone programs, integrated programs, and suites.

6. Describe the essential concepts and skills of using application software, including installing applications, launching applications, understanding and using application windows, getting on-screen help, using menus and toolbars, and working with documents.

7. Discuss the advantages of Web integration.

Medical offices use vertical applications to handle their billing.

Explore IT Lab

Application Software

The term **application software** generally refers to all the programs that enable computer users to *apply* the computer to the work they do. In this sense, application software is in contrast to system software, the programs that help the computer to function properly. Application software enables people to work efficiently with documents created in almost any line of work, including invoices, letters, reports, proposals, presentations, customer lists, newsletters, tables, and flyers. In this module, you'll learn how to make sense of the world of application software.

HORIZONTAL VS. VERTICAL APPLICATIONS

Application programs fall into two categories: horizontal applications and vertical applications.

Horizontal applications are used *across* the functional divisions of a company (and are also popular in the consumer market). They are general-purpose programs that address the needs of many people, such as writing (word processing), working with numbers (spreadsheets), and keeping track of information (databases).

Vertical applications are designed for a particular line of business or for a division in a company (see Figure 3B.1). For example, programs are available to handle the billing needs of medical offices, manage restaurants, and track occupational injuries. Many of the estimated 350,000 programs available for Microsoft Windows are vertical applications.

Vertical applications designed for professional and business use may cost much more than horizontal applications. In fact, some of these programs cost $10,000 or more. The high price is due to the small size of most vertical markets.

If the right application isn't available, **custom software** might hold the key. Custom software requires the services of a professional programmer (or programming team) and is expensive.

TYPES OF APPLICATION SOFTWARE

The most popular horizontal applications are called **personal productivity programs.** This category usually includes word processing software, spreadsheet programs, database programs, and sometimes additional programs such as personal information managers (electronic address books and scheduling). Also included in this category are presentation graphics programs, which enable you to develop slides and transparencies for presentations. These programs help individuals do their work more effectively and efficiently. You'll learn about personal productivity programs in Chapter 4.

A second type of horizontal software includes multimedia and graphics software, including desktop publishing programs, photo-editing programs, and three-dimensional rendering programs.

A third type includes programs for using the Internet, such as email programs and Web browsers, which you'll learn about in Chapter 7.

All three types of horizontal applications—personal productivity, multimedia and graphics software, and Internet programs—are likely to be found on business users' personal computers.

A fourth type of application software includes programs developed for the home and educational markets, including personal finance software, tax preparation software, personal desktop publishing programs, image-editing programs, home design and landscaping software, computer-assisted tutorials, computerized reference information (such as encyclopedias and street maps), and games.

SYSTEM REQUIREMENTS

Programs require that your system meet its minimum **system requirements,** the minimum level of equipment that a program needs in order to run. For example, a given program may be designed to run on a PC with a Pentium microprocessor, a CD-ROM drive, at least 16MB of RAM, and 125MB of free hard disk space. If you're shopping for commercial software, you'll find the system requirements printed somewhere on the outside of the box. Although a program will run on a system that meets the minimum requirements, you will be wise to exceed them, especially when it comes to memory and disk space.

COMMERCIAL PROGRAMS, SHAREWARE, AND FREEWARE

Most computer programs are copyrighted, which means that you cannot make copies for other people without infringing on the program's copyright (such infringements are called **software piracy** and are a Federal offense in the United States). **Commercial software** is copyrighted software that you must pay for before you can use it. **Shareware** refers to copyrighted software that you can use on a "try before you buy" basis. If you like the program after using it for a specified trial period, you must pay the **registration fee,** or you violate the copyright. **Freeware** refers to copyrighted software given away for free, with the understanding that you can't turn around and sell it for profit. Included in the freeware category are programs distributed under the GNU Projects **General Public License (GPU),** such as the Linux operating system.

Very few programs are in the **public domain.** These programs are expressly free from copyright, and you can do anything you want with them, including modifying them or selling them to others.

Some software is **copy protected,** which means the program includes some type of measure to ensure that you don't make unauthorized copies of it. Copy protection schemes aren't popular with users because they often impose performance penalties or require you to add a piece of hardware, called a **dongle,** to your system. Dongles generally attach to a serial or parallel port. If the dongle stops working, you can't use the program. Most users avoid purchasing copy-protected software unless they have no alternative. Although software piracy is a serious problem, most users believe that the answer is not to impose restrictions that would result in a potential loss of software use for people who have purchased the software legally.

On the Internet, software publishers sometimes offer **time-limited** trial versions of commercial programs. You can download, install, and use these programs for free, but they are set to expire when the trial period ends. After the program expires, you can no longer use it. Also available for free are **beta versions** of some forthcoming programs. A beta version is a preliminary version of a program in the final phases of testing. Beta software is known to contain bugs (errors) and should be installed and used only with caution. Like time-limited trial versions, beta software is also set to expire after a set period of time.

SOFTWARE LICENSES

When you purchase a commercial or shareware program, you're not really purchasing the software, as you'll discover if you read the **software license** (a document distributed with the program). Generally, a license gives you the right to install and use the program on only *one* computer. If you want to install the

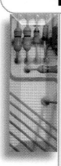

IMPACTS

Software Piracy: "Warez" Can Get You Into Big Trouble

It's called *warez*, and there's one important thing to know about it: it's illegal. The term *warez* (pronounced "wares") is widely used in the computer underground to describe illegal copies of commercial programs, such as Adobe Photoshop or Microsoft Office. Thanks to the Internet, trafficking in illegally-duplicated software is rampant, and increasing rapidly. According to a recent estimate, U.S. software firms lose $3 billion per year due to unauthorized software duplication. At this pace, the cost to the U.S. economy amounts to more than 100,000 jobs and $1 billion in lost tax revenues.

Faced with mounting losses, the commercial software industry is pressuring law enforcement to take a tougher stance—and it's getting results. Recently, a Jacksonville, Florida man was sentenced to 2 1/2 years in jail following his conviction for distributing illegally-duplicated software over the Internet. In a search of his home, investigators found more than 1,000 programs that they suspected were illegally duplicated, with a retail value of $52,000. Youth isn't necessarily an excuse, as a 16-year-old Connecticut man learned. Youth Bureau investigators arrested him after a four-month investigation and accused him of selling pirated software and music CDs.

Much of the warez trafficking on the Internet takes place on Internet Relay Chat (IRC), in which it's harder to trace the actions of individuals. It's harder, but not impossible, as 25 individuals learned recently. All 25 were named in a lawsuit filed by the Business Software Association (BSA), an industry association that fights software piracy. The lawsuit's filing was accompanied by FBI-conducted raids at residences throughout the U.S., in which computer equipment and software were confiscated. In addition to their civil liability under the lawsuit, each of the accused individuals was subject to up to $100,000 in civil penalties for *each* case of infringement that could be proven by prosecutors. Criminal penalties include fines of up to $250,000 and jail terms of up to 5 years.

What about casual trading—just sharing programs without asking for money? That's illegal, too—and equally dangerous. Thanks to the No Electronic Theft (NET) Act, signed into law by President Clinton in 1997, it's no longer necessary for prosecutors to prove a profit motive in cases of criminal copyright infringement.

Myths about warez don't help. Many Internet users believe that it's okay to download illegally-duplicated software and try it for 24 hours. If you decide to keep it, you can purchase a legal copy. However, this is false. It's always illegal to use copyrighted software in a way that violates the software license.

Despite enforcement efforts, software piracy is still rampant in the U.S., where an estimated 25 percent of all business software programs in current use are thought to be illegally-obtained. But the situation is much worse overseas. In China, as much as 96 percent of the software in current use is illegally-obtained, thanks to the existence of several dozen large CD duplication factories that, until recently, operated with impunity. More recently, China's bid to gain entry into international trade associations has led to a crackdown against the duplication factories, but unauthorized software duplication is still the norm, rather than the exception. Unauthorized duplication is hurting China's emerging software industry, too. Beijing's Kingsoft Company, one of China's largest software producers, estimates that for every legal copy of its software, three pirated copies are in existence. As a result of piracy, the Chinese software market isn't growing and many publishers are driven into bankruptcy.

program on more than one computer, you must purchase additional licenses. Otherwise, you will violate the publisher's copyright. Organizations such as colleges and universities often purchase **site licenses,** which enable them to install copies of the program on a specified number of computers.

Looking for a warranty? Forget it. Most software publishers will be happy to replace the program disk if it's defective, but that's it. The license expressly denies any liability on the publisher's part for any damages or losses suffered through the use of the software. If you buy a program containing bugs, and if these bugs wipe out your data and destroy your business, it's your problem. Or that's what software companies would like you to believe. In the past, these licenses haven't stood up in court. Judges and juries have agreed that the products were sold with an implied warranty of fitness for a particular use. Under consideration by U.S. state legislatures is a

Destinations

How will UCITA affect you? Learn more about the UCITA controversy at UCITA Online **(http://www.ucitaonline.com)**.

controversial model act, called the Uniform Computer Information Transactions Act (UCITA), which would give these licenses the force of law.

DISTRIBUTION METHODS

Before the Internet came along, most software was available only in shrink-wrapped boxes. Now, many software publishers are taking their cue from free-ware and shareware publishers and using the Internet as a means of distributing programs and program updates. Doing so is much cheaper than physically delivering a program in a box. Users of Microsoft Windows and Microsoft Office, for example, can get free product updates by accessing Microsoft's Web site (see Figure 3B.2).

DOCUMENTATION

If you buy software in a shrink-wrapped package, you typically get at least some printed **documentation** in the form of tutorials and reference manuals that explain how to use the program. You'll also find **help screens** in the program that enable you to consult all or part of the documentation on-screen. You may also find additional information at the software publisher's Web site.

SOFTWARE VERSIONS

You'll notice that most program names include a number, such as 6.0. Software publishers often bring out new versions of their programs, and these numbers enable you to determine whether you have the latest version of the program. In a version number, the whole number (such as 6 in 6.0) indicates a major program revision. A decimal number indicates a **maintenance release** (a minor revision that corrects bugs or adds minor features). Recently, some software publishers have started identifying product versions by using the year of the product's release (such as Microsoft Office 2000).

INSTALLATION

Before you can use an application program, you must install it on your computer. Most programs come with an installation or setup utility, which makes this job quite easy. After the program has been installed, you will see its name in menus or on the desktop, and you can start using it.

If the software was obtained from the Internet, you must first decompress it. Fortunately, many programs from the Internet include decompression software. You simply launch the file you obtained, and the decompression occurs automatically.

Should you decide to stop using a Microsoft Windows program, don't simply erase the program from your hard disk. You need to **uninstall** the program by using the special tools provided for this purpose.

REGISTRATION

When you purchase a commercial or shareware program, you'll be asked to **register** your software by filling out a registration form. (If your computer is connected to the Internet, you can sometimes do this on-screen. Otherwise, you have to mail the registration form to the software publisher.)

Generally, registration is worth the trouble. After you're registered, you'll receive automatic notification of software upgrades. Sometimes, you'll have a chance to upgrade to the new version at a price lower than the one offered to the general public.

Figure 3B.2

Many software publishers use the Internet to deliver software updates. For example, you can get free product updates of Microsoft Windows and Microsoft Office by accessing Microsoft's Web site.

CURRENTS

It's a Small Software World

The marriage of the computer and communications technology has resulted in a world that is shrinking more and more every day. Using the Internet, it is just as easy to send a computer file around the globe as it is to send one across town.

The worldwide advent of computers, however, has led to a communications problem. Original computer encoding methods did not envision the global use of computers and thus the need for different character sets for different languages. The most common method of encoding text, ASCII, defines a mere 128 characters and symbols. Other computer manufacturers defined different sets of additional characters, which added another 128 characters. These additional characters, however, were not standardized.

One solution to the increasing use of multiple languages in computers is the Unicode standard. This standard, devised and promoted by the Unicode Consortium, allows for the display of most unique language characters in the world. The development of Unicode was performed by a team of computer professionals, linguists, and scholars.

Normal ASCII encoding schemes use 8-bit characters. Thus, up to 256 unique individual characters can be encoded and displayed on the computer. The Unicode standard requires the allocation of 16 bits (2 bytes) for encoding each character. This means 65,536 unique characters can be defined.

The amount of unique character codes means Unicode can be used to encode most of the characters in the world's major languages. An extension mechanism built into the standard means that it is possible to encode close to a million more characters, if necessary. This capability should be sufficient for all known language requirements, plus the encoding of all the historic scripts of the world, including languages and symbols no longer in use.

As presently defined, Unicode includes codes for characters used in the major written languages of the world, including Arabic, Armenian, Bengali, Cyrillic, Devanagari, Georgian, Greek, Gujarati, Hebrew, Japanese kana, Kannada, Korean hangul, Lao, Latin, Malayalam, Oriya, Tamil, Telugu, Thai, and Tibetan. Work is progressing to add more characters, including those from languages such as Braille, Burmese, Cherokee, Ethiopic, Khmer, Sinhalese, and Syriac.

An analysis of the languages of the world shows many character duplications from one language to another. Many Germanic and Romance languages, for example, essentially use a common character set. Unicode defines only unique characters. Each character is assigned a unique 16-bit code. (This is similar to how characters are encoded in other schemes.) When referred to in written text, the code is shown in 4-digit hexadecimal, with a leading U. For example, U+0041 is the Unicode value for the uppercase letter A. Unicode also assigns a unique name to each character encoded. For example, U+0041 is also assigned the name Latin capital letter A.

The advantages of Unicode-compliant systems and software are immediately available to people who work with more than a single language. Such an encoding system is also beneficial to those who work with complex symbols, such as in mathematics or other technical fields. Such symbols are treated the same as any other language characters and built directly into the code. This comprehensiveness was not possible with earlier encoding schemes, such as ASCII.

Unicode is receiving greater acceptance among major software publishers. In the future, it is expected that most (if not all) of the world's software will support Unicode and thereby promote a freer exchange of data. You can find out more about Unicode by visiting the Unicode Web page at **http://www.unicode.org/.**

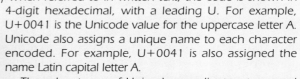

Original computer encoding methods did not envision the global use of computers.

VISUAL METAPHORS: WORKING IN FAMILIAR WAYS

What makes a great personal productivity program? Judging from the preferences of millions of buyers in a huge, worldwide software marketplace, it's not simply the richness of a program's features. Successful programs do a good job of fitting into the way we're accustomed to doing things (see Figure 3B.3).

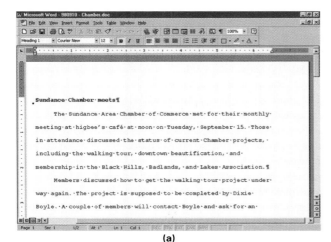

(a)

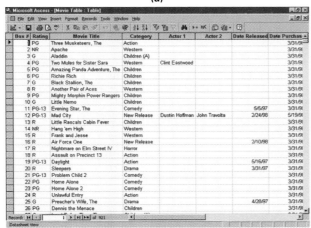

(c)

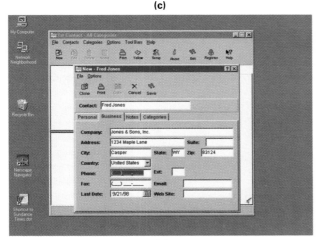

(e)

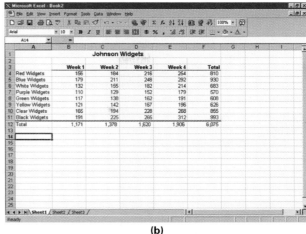

(b)

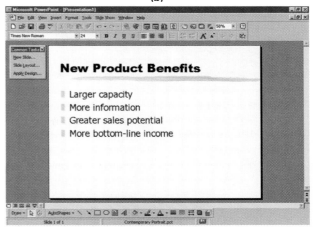

(d)

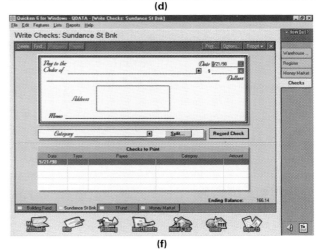

(f)

Figure 3B.3

Successful programs do a good job of fitting into the way we're accustomed to doing things. (a) Word processing programs simulate a sheet of paper and show how the document will look when it's printed. (b) Spreadsheet programs simulate an accountant's worksheet. (c) Database programs simulate a file card. (d) Presentation graphics programs look like an overhead. (e) Contact managers simulate an address book. (f) Personal finance programs simulate a checkbook.

Figure 3B.4

Microsoft Office is a popular office suite.

INTEGRATED PROGRAMS AND SUITES: THE ALL-IN-ONE APPROACH

Individual productivity applications, called **standalone programs,** are giving way to packages that combine two or more programs. **Integrated programs** offer all the functions of the leading productivity programs in a single, easy-to-use program. **Software suites** (also called *office suites*) combine individual programs in a box that may include as many as five or more productivity applications. Unlike integrated programs, software suites include separate programs, but they're integrated by means of a management tool (such as Microsoft Office Manager) that enables quick access to any of the suite's programs. Today, most personal productivity software is sold in office suites, such as Corel's WordPerfect Suite, Lotus's SmartSuite, and the market leader, Microsoft Office (see Figure 3B.4).

Few standalone programs are top sellers in the personal productivity area, largely because buyers can often get the entire suite for little more than the cost of one of the individual programs.

Integrated programs such as Microsoft Works or AppleWorks are generally aimed at beginning users. They offer easy-to-learn and easy-to-use versions of basic productivity software functions. All the functions, called *modules,* share the same interface, and you can switch between them quickly. The individual modules, however, may be short on features compared to standalone programs or office suites. The lack of features may make these easy programs seem more difficult when you start exploring the program's more advanced capabilities.

Office suites typically include a full-featured version of leading word processing, spreadsheet, database, presentation graphics, and personal information manager (PIM) programs (see Table 3B.1). Ideally, the programs in an office suite offer some degree of interface consistency, but that's not always the case. In some suites, the programs were developed by two or more different companies, and it shows. The best suites include tools that enable you to switch quickly from one program to another. For example, Microsoft Office includes the Explorer bar, a toolbar that remains on your computer's desktop and enables you to start any office program quickly.

Table 3B.1

Office Suites (Microsoft Windows)			
	Corel Office	**Lotus SmartSuite**	**Microsoft Office**
Word Processing	WordPerfect	Word Pro	Microsoft Word
Spreadsheet	Corel Quattro	Lotus 1-2-3	Microsoft Excel Pro
Database	Paradox	Lotus Approach	Microsoft Access
Presentation Graphics	Corel	Freelance Graphics	Microsoft Power-point Presentations
Personal Information Managers (PIMs)	Corel	Lotus Organizer	Microsoft Outlook InfoCentral

SPOTLIGHT

LIVING THE EASY LIFE

▶Have computers made life easier? The answer is a resounding yes, according to a 1997 survey in the United States of more than one thousand adults. Of those surveyed, 77 percent said that computer technology has made their lives easier over the past decade. One important reason cited was that high-quality application software (including word processing and spreadsheet software) enabled them to work at least part of the time at home, in closer contact with their families. More than one-fourth of those surveyed already did some or all of their work on home computers, and more than half expected to do so by the year 2000. Application software enables people to work efficiently with documents created in almost any line of work, including invoices, letters, reports, proposals, presentations, customer lists, newsletters, tables, and flyers.

High-powered PCs and high-quality application software are fueling a boom in the SOHO (small office/home office) market. In 1998, nearly 50 million SOHO workers in the United States planned to spend an average of $2,500 on computer hardware and software. PCs and application software are also finding their way into executive suites, completing a corporate conquest that began twenty years ago. Martha Stewart, chief executive officer (CEO) of a huge homemaking media empire (including the TV show Martha Stewart Living), uses a Power Macintosh for writing and editing. Currently, more than half of the CEOs of United States corporations are computer-literate, and the rest are scrambling to learn. A "computer boot camp" for CEOs, sponsored by a leading software firm, has attracted over 500 high-powered executives to a Colorado retreat, where they learn much of what you're learning right now. As is the case wherever PCs are found, application software is the key. The CEOs are pecking away at keyboards learning how to use word processing and spreadsheet software, as well as surf the Web and use email. And how are they doing? One of the teachers told a TV interviewer, "He had a little trouble with mouse double-clicking initially, but right now it's under control."

Most CEOs know how to use word processing and spreadsheet software, as well as surf the Web and use email.

The best office suites offer a **document-centric** approach, made possible by **object linking and embedding (OLE).** In a document-centric approach, your focus is the document you're creating. This can contain word processing text, presentation graphics, portions of a database, or data from a spreadsheet. When you select any of these components, the window changes to show the menus and toolbar relevant to the type of data you're working with. This process is made possible by OLE, which enables applications to exchange data and work with one another.

USING APPLICATION SOFTWARE

Applications transform your computer into a useful tool for a huge variety of tasks, spanning the gamut of human activities. To use your computer successfully, you'll find it useful to acquire the essential concepts and skills of using application software, including installing applications, launching applications, understanding and using application windows, getting on-screen help, using menus and toolbars, and working with documents. The following sections briefly outline these concepts and skills.

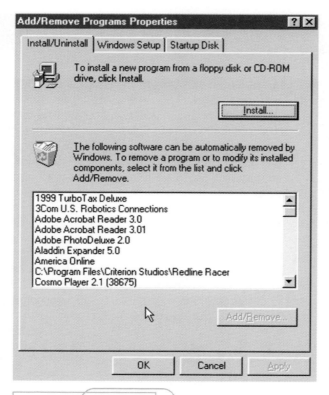

Figure 3B.5

In Microsoft Windows, you should always use this utility to remove unwanted software.

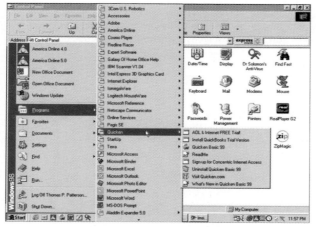

Figure 3B.6

To launch an application with Microsoft Windows, click Start, point to Programs, and choose the application you want.

Installing Applications

Before you can use an application, you must install it. To **install** an application involves more than transferring the software from the distribution media, such as a CD-ROM, to your computer's hard disk. The program must also be configured properly to run on your system. Installation software makes sure that this configuration is done properly.

In Microsoft Windows, configuration includes making modifications to the **registry,** a configuration database that is stored within the Windows folder. If you later decide that you do not want to use an application, you should not merely delete it from your hard disk. You should uninstall the application using the Windows utility (called Add and Remove Programs) that is provided for this purpose (see Figure 3B.5). Uninstalling removes the program from the registry as well as removing the application's files from your disk.

Launching Applications

Once you install an application, you can **launch** the application. When you launch an application (also called starting an application), your computer transfers the program code from your computer's hard disk to the memory, and the application's default window appears on-screen. To launch an application with Microsoft Windows, you can click the Start menu, point to Programs, and choose the application you want to launch (see Figure 3B.6). In Mac OS, you locate the program's folder, and double-click the program's icon.

Understanding the Application's Window

When the application appears on-screen (see Figure 3B.7), you'll see some or all of the following features:

- **Title bar** The **title bar** usually contains the name of the application as well as the name of the file you are working on, if any. If you haven't yet saved the file, you'll see a generic file name, such as Untitled or Document1. To reposition the window on-screen, drag the title bar. When the window is active, the title bar is highlighted. If the title bar isn't highlighted, click within the window to activate it.

- **Window controls** Within the title bar, you will also find **window controls.** These enable you to **maximize** the window (enlarge it so that it fills the whole screen), **minimize** the window (hide the window so that it is reduced to the size of an icon or button), **restore** the window (change to the previous unmaximized size), and **close** the window once you're finished using it.

- **Window borders** In Microsoft Windows, you can change the size of a window by dragging a vertical border left or right, or a horizontal

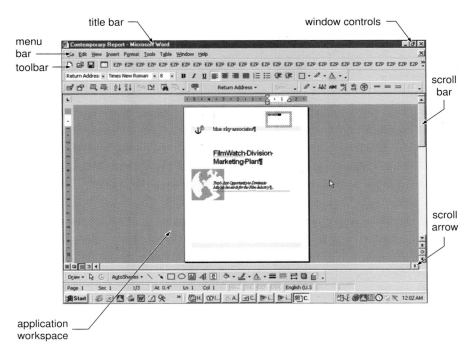

title bar ⌐

window controls ⌐

menu bar ⌐

toolbar ⌐

scroll bar

scroll arrow

application workspace

Figure 3B.7

These window features are found in most Microsoft Windows applications.

border up or down. If you click and drag on a window corner, you can size the window horizontally and vertically at the same time. In Mac OS, you can click and drag on the size box, which is positioned in the window's lower right corner, to size the window on-screen.

- **Menu bar**   The **menu bar** contains the names of **pull-down menus,** which are rectangular lists containing the names of the **commands** you can use with this application. A command performs a specific type of action, such as printing or formatting text. In Microsoft Windows, the menu bar is positioned beneath the title bar. In Mac OS, the menu bar is positioned at the top of the screen.

- **Toolbar**   The **toolbar** contains pictures, called **icons,** that depict the actions performed by the most commonly-used commands. Some applications have more than one toolbar. If you see a ribbed control at the edge of the toolbar, you can drag the toolbar to a different location.

- **Application workspace**   The **application workspace** displays the **document** you are working on. In computing, the term document refers to any type of work you do with the computer, including written work, an electronic spreadsheet, or a graphic. Most applications display a blank document by default. If you wish to work on an existing document, you use the Open command to locate the document and load it into the workspace.

- **Scroll bars, scroll boxes, and scroll arrows**   If the document with which you are working is larger than the application workspace, you will see one or more **scroll bars.** A scroll bar provides tools that enable you to **scroll** through the document. The term scroll refers to the appearance of most documents on-screen: they seem to be continuous, like a roll of shelf paper. However, some programs enable you to view a multi-page document using an on-screen representation of the printed page. In such applications, you may **page** through

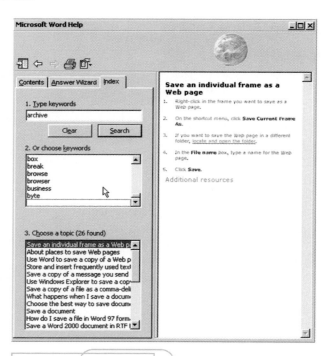

Figure 3B.8

If you have trouble remembering how to use an application, remember to use the on-screen help utilities.

the document rather than scrolling. Whether you are scrolling or paging, you can use the **scroll box** and **scroll arrows** to move through the document. Typically, you can click the scroll arrows to move line-by-line, and drag the scroll box to move larger distances.

■ **Status bar**   The **status bar,** located at the bottom of the document window, displays information about the program as well as the program's messages to you, the user.

Getting Help

Most applications provide on-screen **help** utilities, which typically include a table of contents to frequently requested items and a searchable index to all available items (Figure 3B.8). Some applications provide animated assistants that enable you to type a question and view a list of possibly-relevant responses. If the assistant annoys you, you can hide it.

Understanding Menus

Although applications organize menus in varying ways, many applications make use of the following standard menu names:

■ **File**   On the **File menu,** you will find options for creating new documents, opening existing documents, closing documents, saving documents, saving documents with a new file name or new location, printing documents, and exiting the application.

■ **Edit**   On the **Edit menu,** you will find options for deleting text, cutting text to a temporary storage location called the **clipboard,** pasting text from the clipboard to the cursor's location, undoing and redoing actions, and finding text within the document. In Mac OS, this menu also contains the Preferences options, which enables you to choose program preferences.

■ **View**   The **View menu** contains options that enable you to choose how your document is displayed. Typically included are **zoom** options, expressed as a magnification percentage; **normal layout** (no pagination) or **page layout** (on-screen representation of pages as they will print); and options that enable you to hide or display toolbars.

■ **Tools**   The **Tools menu** typically includes useful utilities, such as a spelling checker. In Microsoft Windows, it also includes Options, a command that enables you to choose program preferences.

■ **Help**   On the **Help menu,** you will find the various options available for getting help with the program. If you are connected to the Internet, you may be able to access additional help resources on the Web.

Choosing Preferences

Applications typically enable you to choose **preferences,** which are your choices for the way you want the program to operate (see Figure 3B.9). These choices affect the program's **defaults,** which are the settings that are in effect unless you deliberately change them. For example, Microsoft Word enables you to display white text against a blue background, a setting that some writers find is a bit easier on the eyes.

When you start working with a newly-installed application, check the preferences menu for an option (usually called **autosave**) that automatically saves your work at a specified interval. With this option enabled by default, you will be assured that you'll never lose more than a few minutes' worth of work should the computer fail for some reason.

Using Popup Menus

In addition to menus and toolbars, most applications enable you to display **popup menus,** also called **context menus** (see Figure 3B.10). Typically, a popup menu appears when you click the right mouse button. (On the Macintosh, you can display a popup menu by holding the mouse button down.) Popup menus list the commands that are available for the area where you clicked the mouse button. For example, if you right-click the application workspace within Microsoft Word, you will see a menu of text-editing and text-formatting commands.

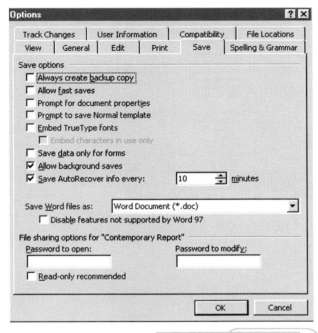

Figure   3B.9

Most applications enable you to choose your preferences for program defaults.

Using Wizards

To guide you through lengthy or complex operations, some applications display **wizards.** A wizard is a series of dialog boxes that guides you through a step-by-step procedure. When you finish making choices in one dialog box, click Next to go on to the next step.

Creating New Documents

When you create a new document, you can start with a new, blank document or a **template.** A template is a generic version of a document that has already been started for you. For example, word processing programs typically include templates for faxes, letters, memos, reports, manuals, brochures, and many more. The template may include text, appropriate formats, graphics, or all of these.

Opening an Existing Document

To **open** an existing document means to locate the document and load it into the application workspace. To do so, you'll use the Open dialog box. Figure 3B.11 shows the typical appearance of an Open dialog box in Microsoft Windows. Begin by selecting the folder that contains the document. Next, highlight the document's name. Click OK to transfer the document to the application workspace.

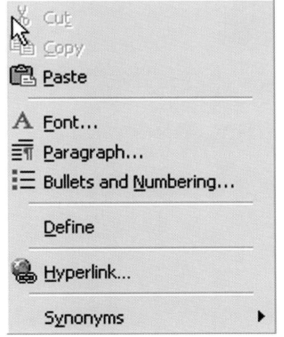

Figure   3B.10

Popup menus display the options available for the context in which you displayed the menu.

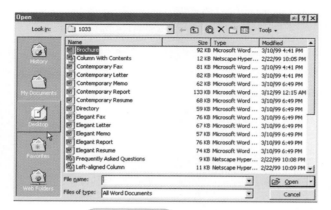

Figure 3B.11

To open a document, begin by selecting the folder that contains the document. Then highlight the document's name, and click OK.

Figure 3B.12

To save your document, choose a storage location and file name.

Saving Your Work

Saving your work refers to the process of transferring the document from the computer's volatile memory to a non-volatile storage device, such as a hard disk. In Microsoft Windows, documents are saved by default to a folder called My Documents.

When you save your work for the first time, you will need to give your document a **file name** (see Figure 3B.12). This is the name that the storage device uses to identify the file uniquely, so the name must differ from all the other file names used within the same folder or directory. In Microsoft Windows, you can use up to 250 characters in a file name, and it's possible to use spaces. File names cannot include any of the following characters: forward slash (/), backslash (\), greater-than sign (>), less-than sign (<), asterisk (*), question mark (?), quotation mark ("), pipe symbol (|), colon (:), or semicolon (;). In Mac OS, you can use up to 31 characters in a file name, including spaces.

Microsoft Windows file names typically include a period and an **extension,** an addition to the file name of up to three characters in length. Typically, file names are used to identify the type of data that the file contains, and sometimes, the application that created the file. Many applications will automatically assign an extension when you save your document for the first time. For example, Microsoft Word automatically assigns the .doc extension. In Mac OS, extensions are not needed because Macintosh files include a code representing the name of the application that created the file.

Once you have successfully saved your document to the default document folder (such as My Documents), you can save another copy elsewhere by using the **Save as** command. This command enables you to save the document using a new file name, a new location, or both.

Exiting the Application

When you are finished using the application, don't just switch off the computer. Exit the application by choosing the appropriate command from the File menu. By doing so, you can assure that the application will warn you if you have failed to save some of your work. In addition, you will save the configuration choices you made while using the program, if any.

Shutting Down Your System

When you are finished using the computer, be sure to exit properly. In Microsoft Windows, click Start, and choose Shut Down. In Mac OS, click Special, and choose Shut Down. Don't just switch off the power without going through the shut down procedure properly. If you switch the power off without shutting down, the operating system may fail to write certain system files to the hard disk. The next time you start the computer, the operating system will need to run the file checking utility to repair the resulting damage, which may take a few minutes to complete.

WEB INTEGRATION: A NEW WAY TO GET THE WORD OUT

The new wave in office suites is Web integration, which, for application software, means the capability to save your files in the HTML codes that underlie World Wide Web documents (see Chapter 7). Why save in HTML? The answer boils down to one costly process: file conversion.

Many large organizations have been spending millions of dollars dealing with file incompatibility problems caused by the use of proprietary file formats. If you don't have Microsoft Word installed on your system, for example, you can't view a Word file unless you have a conversion program. The use of proprietary file formats imposes severe burdens, unless everyone in the company is using the same product. Even then, you may get file incompatibility problems because publishers introduce new file formats with new versions to support new features. Programs that can save data to HTML eliminate file conversion costs because the file can be read by anyone with a Web browser.

File conversion costs come into play, too, when companies want to publish documents on the Web for use on the Internet or on internal corporate intranets (see Module 7A). To put any document on the Web generally requires saving the document in plain ASCII text and then reformatting it from scratch for Web publishing. The capability to save documents in HTML format eliminates these costs.

TAKEAWAY POINTS

- Application software includes two categories of programs: horizontal and vertical.
- Horizontal programs are used across all the divisions of an organization and are also popular in the consumer market.
- Vertical programs are developed for use in a specialized field or business, such as a medical office or a restaurant.
- The four types of horizontal applications are personal productivity programs, multimedia and graphics software, Internet programs, and home/educational software.
- You must pay for commercial programs before you can use them. Shareware programs are copyrighted but distributed on a "try before you buy" basis. Freeware programs are copyrighted but available for free, as long as you don't turn around and sell them. Public domain programs are not copyrighted.
- In a software version, the whole number refers to a major program upgrade, and the decimal number refers to a bug fix (maintenance upgrade). Recently, software publishers have started to use the year of product release rather than version numbers.
- Most people get personal productivity software by purchasing an office suite because they can save money by doing so. Integrated programs are aimed at beginning users and may not include features some users will want later.
- To use your computer successfully, you need to acquire the essential concepts and skills of using application software, including installing applications, launching applications, understanding and using application windows, getting on-screen help, using menus and toolbars, and working with documents.
- Programs that can save data to HTML eliminate file conversion costs because the file can be read by anyone with a Web browser.

MODULE REVIEW

KEY TERMS AND CONCEPTS

application software	horizontal applications	save as
application workspace	icons	scroll
autosave	integrated programs	scroll arrows
beta versions	install	scroll bars
clipboard	launch	scroll box
close	maintenance release	shareware
commands	maximize	site licenses
commercial software	menu bar	software license
copy protected	minimize	software piracy
custom software	normal layout	software suites
defaults	object linking and embedding	standalone programs
document	(OLE)	status bar
document-centric	open	system requirements
documentation	page	template
dongle	page layout	time-limited
edit menu	personal productivity programs	title bar
extension	popup menus or context menus	toolbar
file menu	preferences	tools menu
file name	public domain	uninstall
freeware	pull-down menus	vertical applications
general public license (GPL)	register	view menu
help	registration fee	window controls
help menu	registry	wizards
help screens	restore	zoom

TRUE/FALSE

Indicate whether the following statements are true or false.

1. The operating system of your computer is a primary example of application software.
2. Personal productivity programs help individuals do their work more effectively and efficiently.
3. Billing software is an example of a vertical application.
4. Horizontal applications are designed for a particular line of business.
5. Software piracy is a U.S. Federal offense.
6. Shareware is copyrighted software you must pay for before using.

7. Before you can use a program, you must install it on your system.
8. A document-centric approach to software focuses on the document being created rather than the application used to do the creating.
9. A window is a document that has already been started for you.
10. Web integration describes the capability of application software to save your files in HTML code.

MATCHING

Match each key term from the left column to the most accurate definition in the right column.

_____ 1. application software
_____ 2. horizontal application
_____ 3. vertical application
_____ 4. personal productivity programs
_____ 5. shareware
_____ 6. freeware
_____ 7. status bar
_____ 8. software license
_____ 9. site license
_____ 10. documentation

a. software that's designed for a particular line of business or for a division
b. copyrighted software that's free
c. gives you the right to install and use a program on one computer
d. all the programs that enable computer users to apply the computer to the work they do
e. gives you permission to install copies of a program on a specified number of computers
f. word processing, spreadsheet, and database programs, for example
g. copyrighted software that you can use on a "try before you buy" basis
h. software that's used across the functional divisions of a company
i. printed or online material that explains how to use a program
j. displays information about the program as well as the program's messages to the user

MULTIPLE CHOICE

Circle the letter of the correct choice for each of the following.

1. What is a horizontal application?
   a. an application that can be used properly only in the prone position.
   b. an application used across the functional divisions of a company.
   c. an application whose packaging is wider than it is tall.
   d. an application designed for a particular line of business or for a division within a company.

2. Which of the following is a horizontal application?
   a. CAD software
   b. software to manage a video store
   c. motel management software
   d. word-processing programs

3. Which of the following is not an example of personal productivity software?
   a. custom software
   b. spreadsheet programs
   c. database programs
   d. presentation graphics software

4. What are the advantages of shareware?
   a. It is not copyrighted.
   b. You don't have to pay for it.
   c. You can try it before you buy it.
   d. All of the above.

5. What is a dongle?
   a. a hardware device used to enforce copy protection.
   b. the power supply leads used in a PC.

c. a pejorative term used to describe renegade programmers.

d. a type of vertical application.

6. What do you purchase when you buy a software program?
   a. the unlimited rights to the program and its source code.
   b. the right to use the software in accordance with the publisher's software license.
   c. a box and a distribution media such as a disk or CD-ROM.
   d. a warranty that guarantees the software will do what you want it to do.

7. Which of the following can be considered software documentation?
   a. the software license
   b. reference manuals that accompany the software
   c. the beta version of the software
   d. the site license

8. Microsoft Office is an example of what type of program?
   a. standalone
   b. integrated
   c. software suite
   d. vertical

9. Which of the following programs are typically not included in software suites?
   a. ftp client
   b. word processing
   c. database
   d. spreadsheet

10. The capability to save application files in HTML provides which of the following benefits?
    a. a common format for sharing data with others.
    b. the capability to publish on the Web.
    c. no need to convert application files.
    d. all of the above.

FILL-IN

In the blank provided, write the correct answer for each of the following.

1. The category of programs that enable computer users to apply the computer to the work they do is called _____ software.

2. The most popular horizontal applications are called _____ programs.

3. _____ applications are typically more expensive than horizontal applications.

4. _____ software requires the services of a professional programmer or programming team and is expensive.

5. _____ is copyrighted software given away for free.

6. A(n) _____ is a preliminary version of a program in the final phases of testing.

7. When software is _____ the program includes some type of measure to ensure that you don't make unauthorized copies of it.

8. If you want to install a program on a number of machines in your organization, you can purchase individual copies of a(n) _____ .

9. To guide you through lengthy or complex operations, some applications display _____ , which are a series of dialog boxes that guides you through a step-by-step procedure.

10. On the _____ menu, you will find options for deleting text, cutting and pasting text, finding text, and undoing and redoing actions.

SHORT ANSWER

On a separate sheet of paper, answer the following questions.

1. What are the differences between horizontal and vertical applications?

2. Discuss the three categories of horizontal applications.

3. Name a business where vertical applications are used. What are the applications?

4. How do system requirements affect the software used in an organization?

5. What are the differences between shareware and freeware?

6. How does software copy-protection work? How is it generally viewed by users?

7. What warranty provisions are there in relation to software?

8. What are the benefits of registering your software?

9. Identify the differences between standalone programs, integrated programs, and software suites.

10. Describe the features in an application window. What are they used for?

PFSweb, Inc.

If there was one word to sum up the incredible growth of e-commerce on the Web, what would it be? Graphics? Choice? Bandwidth? How about "standards"? It may not sound very flashy, but standards for everything from communications to how Web pages display have helped to streamline business activity on the Web.

Mike Willoughby, Vice President of E-Commerce Technologies at PFSweb, has been part of the e-commerce movement from its inception. Prior to the mid-90s, companies that wanted to do business online often found that they had to create the software from scratch to do what they wanted. Mike has been there, done that. The "from scratch" approach was expensive, and proved to be affordable only to a few large organizations. Then, around the late 1990s, standards for Internet communications emerged. ActiveX and Java became popular for Web-based interactivity, allowing customers to perform inventory queries ("Is Aerosmith's latest CD in stock?") and check order status in real time ("When was my CD shipped?"). Today, a new standard for Web-based communications has emerged called XML. XML-based communications packaging lets computers seamlessly pass data such as customer order information or

queries between servers and systems in different locations. This means time and money saved in both creating and operating e-commerce Web sites.

PFSweb runs a lot of different software programs on its computer hardware. There is software for hosting Web sites. Special software is used for credit card authorizations and fraud checks. Tax calculations and reporting have their own software programs. Freight calculations for shipping require separate program instructions. Programs for shipping with FedEx, UPS, Airborne, and USPS also exist. The back-end inventory management and customer order management is handled by yet another program. The Memphis distribution center (where all the physical goods people buy on the Web come from) requires special software for its management. And of course, there are e-mail and chat programs. Every last program relies on standards to function properly.

For actually running PFSweb's own business, separate AS/400 computers run enterprise resource planning software by JD Edwards. Separate software modules for accounts receivable and payable, invoicing, cash management, customer sales reporting, and more are in place. All told, there are dozens of different software programs running on PFSweb's computer hardware in the data center.

What do you think? Why are so many different software programs needed to operate an e-commerce Web site? Why doesn't software companies write one big e-commerce program that does everything? What effect might e-commerce Web site buyers see if standards such as XML were not in place?

WebLink Go to **www.prenhall.com/ pfaffenberger** to see the video of Mark Willoughby and explore the Web.

E-COMMERCE IN ACTION

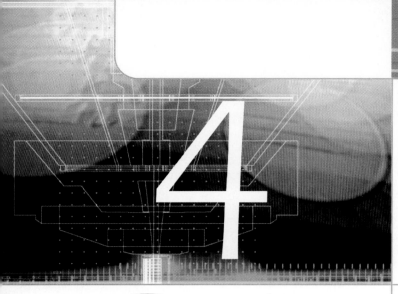

4

Concepts of Application Software

No matter which line of work or career you're planning to pursue, you will be wise to learn the essentials of office suite applications (including word processing, electronic spreadsheet, presentation graphics, and database software). Increasingly, knowledge of these applications is a prerequisite for the better-paying jobs, and such knowledge pays off well in your studies, too. Still, you'll be wise to avoid limiting your knowledge to "which key to press" for a specific program, such as Microsoft Word 2000. Of course, such knowledge provides an indispensable point of departure for your journey into computer fluency. You need to know how to use at least one of each type of software provided in an office suite. But you also need to learn the deeper knowledge that will enable you to learn new programs quickly.

How can you acquire this deeper knowledge of office applications? By fully understanding the concepts that underlie application software design. For example, most office suite programs offer a feature that enables you to select a variety of formats, including font, font size, indentation, alignment, and line spacing, and save all these formats together as a named style (such as "Body Text" or "Normal Paragraph.") Subsequently, you can enter all these styles at once by choosing the style you created. Once you understand the concept of named styles, and why named styles are so useful, you will eagerly look for style-like features in any new program. And you'll instantly recognize them, even if they're named differently or located on a different menu.

A computer-fluent person knows how to use an office suite well, and also knows how to learn new programs quickly. To develop computer fluency, you need to explore. Chances are that you'll first learn the specifics of market-dominant software, such as Microsoft Office 97 or 2000 for Windows. But don't limit yourself. Sit down at a Macintosh, and try using the Mac OS version of Microsoft Office—which, incidentally, has some very nice capabilities that aren't found in the Windows version. Better yet, try using Sun Microsystem's Star Office software on a computer running Linux. Push yourself, explore, and compare—and in time, you'll find that you can learn software so quickly that people who watch you will say, "You're a whiz at this, aren't you!"

Don't look for the specifics of office software usage in the modules to follow. If the course you're taking involves hands-on office software instruction, your instructor will provide a supplementary textbook or lab manuals. What you'll find here is the conceptual knowledge that will enable you to learn any new office program in short order.

MODULES

187

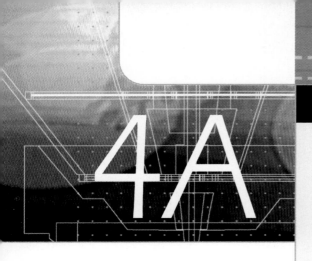

WRITING WITH WORD PROCESSING SOFTWARE

4A

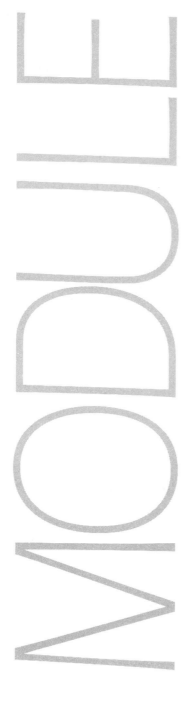

MODULE

WHAT YOU WILL LEARN . . .

When you have finished reading this module, you will be able to:

1. List the four basic functions of word processing programs and explain why word processing is more efficient than previous writing technologies.

2. Describe the various ways in which you can view your document while you work with its text.

3. List the basic text editing functions.

4. Differentiate between text selection and text editing.

5. Explain why spelling and grammar checkers cannot find all the errors that may appear in your document.

6. List the four levels of formatting and provide examples of the formats controlled at each level.

7. Explain the use of styles in a word processing program and explain why they provide a more efficient way of formatting than assigning formats individually.

8. State the advantage of typing tabular material in a table format rather than relying on tabs for alignment.

9. Differentiate between word processing and desktop publishing software.

WORD PROCESSING SOFTWARE: THE ELECTRONIC SCRIBE

Word processing programs enable you to write, edit, format, and print a document with ease. Using word processing software, you can produce a high-quality document in much less time than if you used a typewriter. The reason lies in the ability of word processing software to separate document creation from document printing. With a typewriter, as soon as you type a word, that word appears on paper. If you need to correct a word in a typewritten document, you must erase the word somehow and then type the correction in the same spot. A word processing program, in contrast, enables you to create a document, check it for spelling, edit it for style, format it for presentation, and save it for later retrieval. You can do all these tasks before you print your document. If you take full advantage of these opportunities to organize and revise your work, the results may be superior to work produced on a typewriter.

Destinations

Can a computer make you a better poet? Visit the Word Together Rhyming Dictionary (**http: www.together software.com**, and follow the Rhyming link) to find rhymes for any word you type in the search word text box.

You need not perform the four steps of word processing—writing, editing, formatting, and printing—in order. Many writers do a bit of writing and editing, and then print the document so they can see how it's developing. Then they go back and do more writing and editing (and perhaps throw in some formatting now and then).

Composing Your Document

Writing with a word processing program is easier than using a typewriter, but writing can be challenging in itself. Beginning writers often make the mistake of trying to start writing without developing some sort of plan. If you find yourself having a tough time getting started, try a prewriting technique such as outlining, block diagramming, or brainstorming—all of which are better done with a paper and pencil than with the computer.

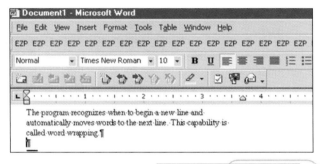

Figure 4A.1

In word wrapping, word processing software automatically starts a new line when needed. Press Enter only when you want to start a new paragraph.

Word Wrapping

Once you've developed a plan for your document, it's time to start writing. With a word processing program, you can enter your work without being concerned about how the document will look. Instead of listening for a typewriter's warning bell to tell you when to begin a new line, you can continue to type. The program recognizes when to begin a new line and automatically moves words to the next line. This capability is called **word wrapping.** The only time you need to press the Enter key is at the end of a paragraph. In word processing, the term **paragraph** simply means a unit of text that begins and ends with an Enter keystroke (Figure 4A.1).

Symbols and Special Characters

Should you need to insert a technical symbol or a special character (such as a copyright mark), you can do so by choosing a special command that enables you to choose the symbol or character from a menu. In Microsoft Word 2000, you can display the available symbols and special characters by clicking Insert on the menu bar and choosing Symbol. In the Symbol dialog box, you can choose Symbol or Special Character to look for and select the character you want (see Figure 4A.2).

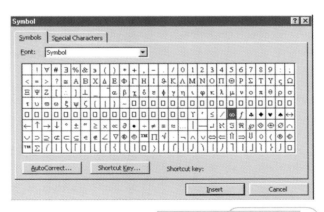

Figure 4A.2

In Microsoft Word 2000, use the Symbol dialog box to enter symbols or special characters.

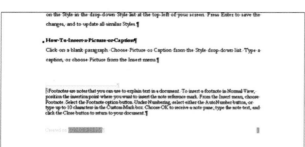

Figure 4A.3

Word processing software automatically lays out all the elements of a page and determines the location of page breaks automatically.

Pagination

In addition, a word processing program automatically determines when to begin a new page. When you include footnotes, footers, or headers, the software adjusts the size of the page and begins each new page correctly (see Figure 4A.3).

Autocorrect

Most of today's leading word processing programs include an **autocorrect** feature, which automatically corrects certain mistakes while you're typing. Examples of such mistakes include the failure to capitalize the first letter of a sentence, capitalizing two letters at the beginning of a sentence, or making certain common spelling errors (such as *recieve* or *acomodate*). Although this feature is useful, it can be annoying. For example, suppose you are typing a table in which the entries begin with a lowercase letter. Although you do not want these entries capitalized, the program will automatically correct the capitalization, since it appears that you are starting a new sentence. When this feature gets in your way, disable it. With Microsoft Word 2000, you do so by choosing Autocorrect from the Tools menu, and disabling the correction feature that you do not wish to use.

Autosave

When you create text with a word processing program, it's kept in the computer's **RAM** (random-access memory). Because this memory isn't a permanent storage medium, you need to save your work (store a copy on a floppy disk or hard disk). Should the power fail (or the computer crash) before you save your work, you'll lose everything you've accomplished since the last time you saved. Experienced word processing users know that it's important to save your work every few minutes.

The best programs have an **autosave** that automatically saves your work at an interval you specify, such as every five minutes. If you're using a program that has an autosave feature, learn how to turn it on. In most programs, the autosave feature is turned off by default. In Microsoft Word 2000, you can enable autosave by clicking Tools on the menu bar, choosing Options, clicking the Save tab, and checking Save Autorecover Info. Type a save interval in the text box, and click OK.

Outlining

To help you organize your writing, the best programs offer **outlining,** a special document viewing mode that enables you to view your document as an outline (in which only the headings appear). In addition to using the document to give you a better view of your document's structure, you can also use outlining to reorganize your document. When you move an outline heading within outline view, all the associated text moves with it. In Microsoft Word, you can quickly organize your document into an outline by applying the predefined Heading styles (such as Heading 1, Heading 2, and Heading 3) to your document. When you view your document as an outline, these headings correspond to the various outlining levels (see Figure 4A.4). For more information on styles, see "Formatting," later in this chapter.

When you are viewing your document as an outline, you can use special commands to **demote** an outline level (move it to the right and lower its importance) or **promote** an outline level (move it to the left and raise its importance).

Views

While you're writing, you can choose the type of document view you prefer (Figure 4A.5). Typically, you can choose from **normal view** (you see your document as if it were a continuous scroll), **print layout view** (you see your document as it will appear when printed, complete with on-screen representations of the page), and **Web layout** (you see your document as it would appear on the World Wide Web).

Most word processing programs enable you to split the document window, enabling you to see two portions of your document at once (see Figure 4A.6). You can display your document's outline in one window and the text in the other, or you can look at two different portions of your document at the same time. Microsoft Word also enables you to display a **document map,** in which the document's outline appears in a window to the left of the document text (see Figure 4A.7).

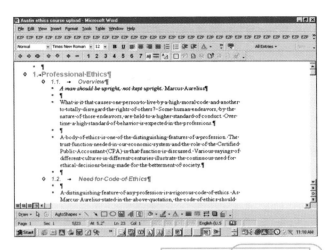

Figure   4A.4

In Microsoft Word, you can quickly organize your document into an outline by using heading styles.

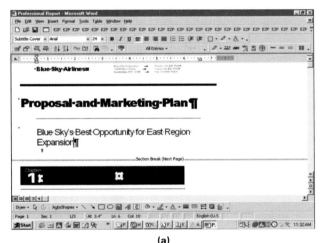

(a)

(b)

(c)

Figure   4A.5

You can choose from any of these views: (a) normal, (b) print layout, or (c) Web layout.

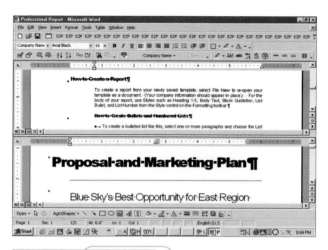

Figure 4A.6

In Microsoft Word, you can split the screen by dragging or double-clicking the split bar.

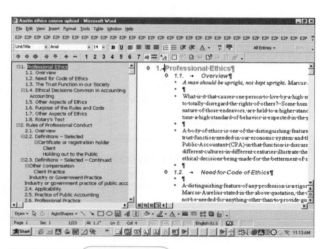

Figure 4A.7

Microsoft Word 2000 enables you to display a document map, in which the document's outline appears in a window positioned to the left of the text window.

Experiment with various **zoom levels,** which are expressed as a percentage of the normal document size (100%). At higher magnifications, the characters are larger, so the text is easier to read. However, you see less text on-screen, so it's hard to get a sense of your document's overall flow.

Footnotes and Endnotes

When you write papers in college, you will typically need to document your work by **citing** sources. When you cite sources, you give enough information about the sources so that a curious or critical reader could locate them independently. You do so by writing a **citation** (a footnote or endnote) in a proper **citation format,** a template for writing a citation that is approved by a professional association (such as the Modern Language Association) or a recognized authority (such as the University of Chicago Press's *Manual of Style*). **Footnotes** appear at the bottom of the page, while **endnotes** are collected at the end of a document **section** (for more information on sections, see "Formatting," later in this module). Make sure you fully understand just what your instructor requires you to document and which citation format you should use. Typically, you need to provide sources for all of the following:

- A direct quotation, in which you reproduce another author's words.

- A paraphrase, in which you draw from another author's words but make some changes.

- Facts that are not common knowledge, such as those contained in a college-level encyclopedia.

Failure to document your sources could lead to charges of plagiarism, which is a serious offense. Be sure you clearly understand the rules concerning plagiarism.

Footnotes and endnotes consist of two parts, the **reference mark** (a number or symbol that appears in the text) and the *citation* (the text of the footnote or endnote). To insert a footnote with Microsoft Word 2000, position the cursor where you want the footnote or endnote to appear, click Insert on the menu bar, and choose Footnote. In the dialog box that appears, you can select the type of citation (footnote or endnote) as well as the type of reference mark (an automatically-inserted number or a symbol). After you click OK, the screen will scroll to the footnote or endnote location (in Print Layout view) or a special window (Normal view), where you may type the citation text.

Some assignments may require you to type a bibliography at the end of your paper. Note that bibliographies typically use a slightly-different type of citation format than footnotes or endnotes. Typically, each bibliographic entry begins with the author's last name. Type each bibliographic item in its own paragraph. With Microsoft Word, you can quickly alphabetize such a bibliography by selecting all the paragraphs in the bibliography, clicking Table on the menu bar, and choosing Sort. Click OK to sort the paragraphs in alphabetical order.

Pictures

Most word processing programs enable you to insert pictures into your document. You can insert **clip art** (ready-to-use pictures that are included with the program) or pictures stored in graphics files on your computer's disk. To insert the picture, the picture must be stored in a graphics file format that the program recognizes. After you insert the picture, you will see **drag handles** that indicate that the picture is selected (see Figure 4A.8). By dragging the handles, you can **size** the picture (change its size) by dragging one of the drag handles. You can also **scale** it (change the size in a way that preserves the **aspect ratio,** the ratio between the picture's horizontal and vertical dimensions). To scale a picture in Microsoft Word 2000, hold down the Shift key while you drag one of the corner drag handles.

Objects

In addition to text and pictures, you can insert objects within your document. An **object** is a type of data that is inserted along with the programming code needed to manipulate the object. For example, when you insert a picture into a Microsoft Word document, the program also inserts the graphics code that is needed to edit and manipulate the picture. To work with an object you have inserted in a Word document, just double-click on the object. Word will start the appropriate program and display the object in the program's application workspace. In some cases, the object's programming code becomes part of the word processing application. Among the objects that can be inserted in Word documents are Microsoft Excel charts, Microsoft PowerPoint slides, media clips, sounds, and more. The objects available are dependent on which applications are installed on your system.

Field Codes

A **field code** is a special code that is entered into your document in order to display certain types of automatically-inserted information, such as the current date and time. When you are viewing your document in the normal field code display mode, in which the codes themselves are hidden, you see the results of the code, rather than the code itself.

Page Numbers

Most word processing programs do not number your document's pages on the printout unless you deliberately turn page numbering on. You should do so whenever you prepare and print a document longer than one page. In Microsoft Word 2000, you can enable page numbering by clicking Insert on the menu bar and choosing Page Numbers. In the Page Numbers dialog box, you can select where you want the page numbers to appear. If you plan to insert headers or footers in your document (see "Formatting," later in this module), you can add page numbers to these formats.

Editing Your Document

Editing your document is much easier and more efficient with a word processing program than with a typewriter. Be aware, though, that most writers

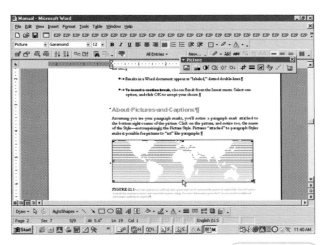

Figure 4A.8

Drag handles appear when you select a picture that has been inserted into your document.

Table **4A.1**

Selecting Text with Microsoft Word	
To Do This	**Use This Technique**
Select a word	Double-click the word.
Select a line	Move the pointer to the left of the line, and click the left mouse button.
Select a paragraph	Move the pointer to the left of the paragraph, and double-click the left mouse button.

Destinations

If you're planning to write an undergraduate or graduate thesis, you'll need to develop and manage a large bibliography. Favored by research scholars is EndNote (**http://www.endnote.com**), a utility that searches online bibliographic databases, organizes references in your personal bibliographic database, and constructs bibliographies automatically.

find it easier to edit on **hard copy** (a printed version of the document) than on-screen. Why this is so is the subject of much debate; it seems that, for most writers, it's easier to get some distance on the document—to view it more impersonally and critically—when it has been printed. Mark up a printed version of your work, and use the marked-up version for on-screen editing.

Basic Editing Concepts

Learn to use the following procedures to ensure your word processing proficiency:

- **Deleting text**   As you write, you can use the Backspace key to delete characters to the left of the cursor. In addition, you can go back to text you've already entered, and insert and delete text as you please. When the cursor is positioned within existing text, you can press the Delete key to delete characters to the right of the cursor.

- **Inserting text**   You can insert new text within text you've already typed. The new text will appear at the cursor's location. Note, though, that most word processing programs handle text insertions in two different ways, and you need to decide which one you prefer. In **insert mode,** the software moves the rest of the text to the right (and down) as you type the new material. In **typeover mode** (also called **overtype mode**), the new material replaces (types over) existing text. Most programs work in insert mode by default. To insert text within text you've already typed, position the cursor where you want the new text to appear, and then start typing. If you're uncertain which mode you're using, look at the status bar. In Microsoft Word, OVR is highlighted when you're using the typeover mode.

- **Selecting text**   Many editing operations require you to **select** text before you choose an editing command. To select text means to highlight it on-screen. To do so, hold down the mouse button and drag over the text. You can also select text by using mouse shortcuts. Refer to Table 4A.1 for selecting text with Microsoft Word.

- **Copying and moving text**   To reorganize your text, you can move blocks of text using an operation called **cut and paste** (see Figure 4A.9). You begin by selecting the text and choosing the **Copy** or **Cut** command, which places the text on the **clipboard,** a temporary storage location. You then move the cursor to the place you want the text to appear, and you choose a command—called **Paste**—that inserts the clipboard contents in this location.

- **Undoing and redoing revisions**   If you've just made an editing change and don't like the results, you can use the **Undo** command to restore your document's previous appearance. Some programs offer

Typical Keyboard Shortcuts for Text Editing		Table 4A.2
To Do This	**Press This Key**	
Select all	Ctrl + A	
Bold	Ctrl + B	
Italic	Ctrl + I	
Copy to clipboard	Ctrl + C	
Paste from clipboard	Ctrl + V	
Undo	Ctrl + Z	
Cut to clipboard	Ctrl + X	

multiple undo features that enable you to retrace your steps through recent editing changes. Microsoft Word 2000 offers this feature. In addition, you can selectively undo any of your recent editing changes by clicking the Undo button on the Formatting toolbar and choosing the editing change from a drop-down menu. The **Redo** command repeats the last editing change. Refer to Table 4A.2 for editing text with Microsoft Word.

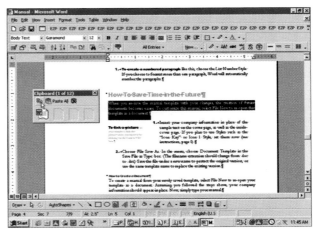

Figure 4A.9

The cut and paste feature enables you to move blocks of text.

Checking Spelling and Grammar

Most word processing programs include the following additional tools for editing your text:

■ **Spelling checkers** match your document against a built-in dictionary. Recent word processing programs can check spelling while you're typing and highlight any errors you make. If a word is flagged as a possible error, you right-click on the word. From the popup menu, you'll see options that enable you to correct it, ignore it, or add the word to the dictionary. You can also run the spell-checking command on your entire document. As you do, you'll need to make decisions about each word that the spell-checker flags (see Figure 4A.10).

■ **Grammar and style checkers** use a variety of algorithms to detect grammatical errors (such incomplete sentences) and usage problems (such as overuse of the passive voice).

Note that both spell checkers and grammar and style checkers have limitations. Spelling checkers can't detect errors that involve the use of correctly-spelled words in the wrong location ("You are deer to me," he said, lovingly). Grammar and style checkers may fail to detect serious grammatical errors and usage problems. There's no substitute for a final proofreading—by hand.

Callouts to buttons on right include:

Ignore All Ignore this instance of the word and all other instances in the document.

Add Add this correctly-spelled word to the dictionary so that it is not flagged in the future.

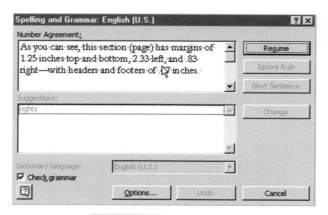

Figure 4A.10

Using spell-checking options.

Change   Replace the word with the word that is highlighted in the Suggestions area.

Change All   Replace this instance of the word and all additional instances of this word with the word that is highlighted in the Suggestions area.

Autocorrect   Add this correction to the Autocorrect list so that it will be corrected automatically when you type.

Tracking Changes

In most organizations, written work is usually produced collaboratively. Often a lead author creates the first draft. Subsequently, other authors or editors will add comments to the document, and they also propose insertions or deletions. To produce the final draft, the lead author must go through the document and approve or reject each of the proposed changes. This is tedious work when done by hand, but it's much easier thanks to computers and features such as Microsoft Word's ability to track editing changes (see Figure 4A.11). Word's Track Changes feature

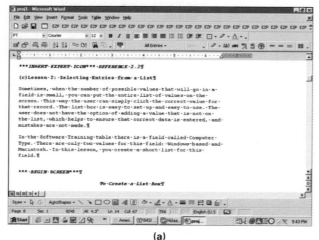

(a)

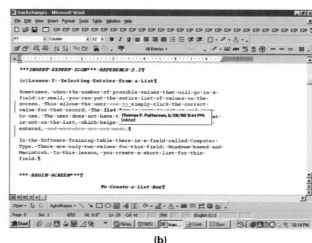

(b)

Figure 4A.11

Microsoft Word's ability to track editing changes facilitates collaborative writing: (a) Original document. (b) Track Changes (revision) feature is on, showing inserts and deletions and tool tip with author name and date of change. (c) Original author approves or rejects each change.

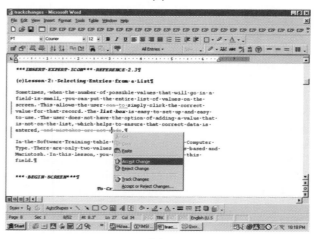

(c)

S P O T L I G H T

WORD PROCESSING AND WRITING QUALITY

▶In the mid-1980s, an English professor wrote an essay criticizing the growing use of word processing software in colleges and universities. While admitting that word processing programs made editing and revision tasks easier, the professor challenged readers to name *one* critically-acclaimed novelist who used the technology in favor of the old writer's standby, the typewriter. Her implication was that something about word processing harms writing quality.

Fast-forward to the present, and you'll need to ask a different question: which of today's critically-acclaimed novelists *don't* use word processing? Some don't, actually. But for writers, it's not a question of using a good or bad technology for writing—each uses what is right for him or her. For writers, a favorite writing tool becomes linked, in their minds, with the creative process itself. British author Liza Cody can't imagine writing without a sharp pencil and paper, and James Michener—who knew how to use a computer and had one around—preferred to type out his 900-page novels on a big, noisy, office typewriter. After all, as best-selling novelist Walter Mosley points out, the only tool really needed for writing is a brain.

Still, almost all writers use word processors now (including Mosley, a former computer programmer). However, experienced writers are on the lookout for word processing's pitfalls—and chief among them is the ease with which you can insert text within existing sentences. The result, all too often, is a bloated sentence that's worse than the original. Sometimes, the best cure for a poorly-written paragraph is the Delete key and a fresh start.

Another pitfall of word processing software involves organization, particularly when you're writing lengthy documents (more than two or three pages). When you're viewing only one-third of a page at a time, it's difficult to keep the overall flow of your writing in mind. The result, all too often, is a poorly-organized paper. Here again, though, technology offers a cure. Increasingly, writing teachers advise students to make use of a nifty Microsoft Word outlining feature that automatically displays the first line of each paragraph. By switching back and forth between the first line and normal document views, you can keep the overall flow of your document in mind—and the result is likely to be a significantly-better paper.

(called Revision Marks in older versions of the program) is a major reason for the program's dominance in publishing houses throughout the world.

When you're working on a document that a lead author has created, you can turn on change-tracking by clicking Tools on the menu bar, pointing to Highlight Changes, and choosing Track Changes. After you've turned on change-tracking, Word highlights the text you've inserted with a distinctive color. It also marks this text with your name and the date of the change. Deletions aren't removed from the text; instead, they're shown with strikeout characters, so the lead author can see what you've deleted. (If the formatting distracts you, it's possible to hide the special change-tracking formats so that they aren't visible while you're working.) When the lead author gets the document back from you, the Accept or Reject Changes option—also accessible by clicking Tools and pointing to Track Changes—enables this author to go through the document change-by-change, and approve each one selectively. It's also possible to accept all the changes without further review.

Formatting

When you're writing and editing text, you're concerned with the content of what you're writing. In **formatting,** you specify the appearance of the text as it will later be printed. In "what-you-see-is-what-you-get" (**WYSIWYG**) programs, you see the results of your formatting choices on-screen.

Some formatting occurs by default. Most word processing software includes default settings for margins (top, bottom, left, and right), tabs, and line spacing. You can change the settings, if you want.

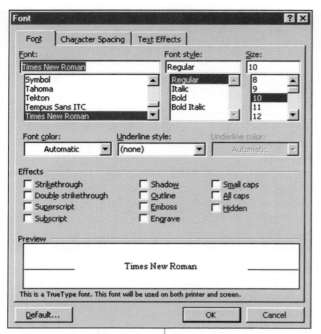

Typically, sans serif fonts are used for display type, while serif fonts are used for body type. Avoid using more than two fonts in the same document.

Your document is formatted at four levels: characters, paragraphs, sections, and pages, as the following sections explain.

Character Formatting

In **character formatting,** you can choose the following:

- **Character size** is measured in **points.** One inch is equal to 72 points. 10 points or 12 points is considered appropriate for normally-sized text.

- **Typefaces** (also called **fonts**) are described by the font's name (such as Times Roman, Helvetica, or Avant Garde). The term typeface refers to the overall design of the character set, which gives it a distinctive appearance. Typefaces fall into two major categories: **serif typefaces** (typefaces with finishing strokes) and **sans serif typefaces** (typefaces without finishing strokes). Generally, serif typefaces are preferred for the document's **body type** (text paragraphs), and sans serif typefaces are often used for **display type** (titles and headings). Some typefaces are **monospace typefaces,** which use the same amount of horizontal space for each character. Others are **proportionally-spaced typefaces,** which use more space for wider letters (such as *m* and *w*) and less for thinner ones.

- **Weight** refers to the thickness or darkness of a character. **Regular weight** characters are used for ordinary body text. **Bold** characters are thicker and darker, and are used for emphasis.

- **Slant** refers to the vertical alignment of a character. **Italic** characters slant to the right, while *oblique* characters slant to the left.

- The term **effects** sums up a variety of additional character formatting options, including **small caps** (a format in which lowercase letters are displayed and printed in small capital letters), **shadow** (a format in which the character is shown with a background shadow), and **outline** (a format in which the character is drawn with an outline rather than a solid fill).

- **Position** formats control the location of a character with respect to the **baseline,** the line on which characters are positioned. **Superscript** refers to characters positioned above the baseline, and **subscript** refers to characters positioned below the baseline.

- **Spacing** refers to the distance between characters. In **expanded spacing,** extra space is added between characters, so that they look stretched out horizontally. In **condensed spacing,** space is removed between characters, so that they look squashed together. In **kerning,** the space between wide and narrow characters is automatically adjusted so that the spacing appears more balanced.

Paragraph Formatting

In **paragraph formatting,** you can choose the following:

- **Alignment** specifies the evenness of the beginning or ends of the lines of a paragraph. **Flush left alignment** aligns the text on the left and

Techtalk

font

In printing, the term **font** refers to a collection of characters in a distinctive typeface and of a certain size. For example, Times New Roman 12 is a font. In computing, the term font is used synonymously with **typeface** to refer to the distinctive design of a set of characters.

leaves the right margin ragged. The opposite is **flush right alignment,** which aligns the right margin but leaves the left ragged. **Centered alignment** centers the lines, leaving both margins ragged. **Justified alignment** aligns both the left and the right margins. Text aligned flush left is the easiest to read.

- **Spacing** (also called **leading**) refers to the amount of space between lines. You can choose single-line spacing or double-line spacing, or specify the amount of space in points.

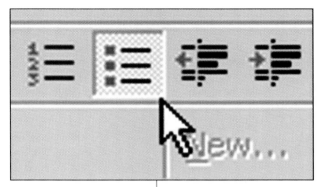

Bulleted lists provide a useful way to break up the text on the page. To create a bulleted list item with Microsoft Word 2000, click the Bullets icon on the Formatting toolbar.

- **Indents** enable you to indent the text from the left margin, the right margin, or both. With Microsoft Word, you can indent text quickly by selecting a paragraph and clicking Increase Indent or Decrease Indent on the Formatting toolbar. A **hanging indent** isn't indented on the first line, but second and subsequent lines (called **turnover lines**) are indented by a default amount (usually, one tab stop) or by an amount you specify.

- **Tab settings** are associated with paragraphs in most word processing programs, which means you can create paragraphs with varying tab settings (called **tab stops**). Most programs create flush left tab stops by default. Generally, you can also create flush right (right-aligned) or decimal (decimal-aligned) tab stops, and choose **leaders** (lines of dots or dashes that are automatically inserted up to the tab stop). To view and manipulate the tab stops, display the **ruler** (a bar across the top of the screen that measures across the width of the page).

- **Bulleted** and **numbered lists** are useful for listing items or giving instructions. To create a bulleted list with Microsoft Word, click Bullets on the toolbar. To create a numbered list (with automatic item numbering), click Numbering on the toolbar.

- **Borders** and **shading** enable you to add special effects to a paragraph. With borders, you can add a line (called a **rule**) to the top, bottom, left, or right side of the paragraph. You can also add a **fill** (a color or shade) or a pattern (such as a herringbone pattern) to the paragraph's background.

- **Frames** are rectangular areas that are attached to a specific, absolute area of the page, such as a two-inch square that is positioned four inches from the top of the page and three inches from the left margin. You can use frames to position **text boxes** (rectangular boxes containing text) or graphics on the page.

Section Formatting

A **section** is a portion of a document that the writer arbitrarily designates by means of **section breaks.** Section breaks are used to begin and end certain formats that apply throughout an entire section. In Microsoft Word, these formats include endnotes and **columns.** Columns are a section format in which the text is broken up into two or more vertical columns on the page, each of which is separated by white space. Columns are often called newspaper columns because they look like the columns in a newspaper or magazine. They are also called snaking columns because the text automatically "snakes" from the bottom of one column to the top of the next as you add and delete text.

In Microsoft Word 2000, you control page formats by clicking File on the menu bar and choosing Page Setup.

Page Formatting

In **page formatting,** you can choose the following:

- **Headers and footers** are zones of text appearing within the top or bottom margins, respectively. Within the headers and footers, you can insert automatic page numbers, dates, and text.

- **Margins** can be specified for the top, bottom, left, and right of the document.

- **Gutters** are extra spaces that are added to make room for binding when you're printing on both sides of the page. On right-hand (odd-numbered) pages, the gutter is added to the left margin; on left-hand (right-numbered) pages, the gutter is added to the right margin.

- **Paper size** can be changed. Options include all the standard paper sizes as well as custom sizes you specify.

- **Orientation** can also be changed. Your options are the default, called **portrait** (the text runs down the narrow orientation of the page), or **landscape** (the text runs across the wide orientation of the page).

Styles

A **style** is a collection of formats that you've saved with a distinctive name (see Figure 4A.12). For example, you can create your own style named Bulleted List which incorporates the following: a 1.0 inch hanging indent, 10 pt. Times New Roman text, a blank line before and after, and justified alignment. Styles provide an extremely convenient and efficient way to format your document because they enter two or more formats at once. The real convenience comes when you need to change a style's format. When you make a change to the underlying style by accessing the document's **style sheet,** a list of all the styles available for the document, the change is automatically reflected in every unit of text that you have applied to text throughout your document.

Microsoft Word comes with an assortment of predefined styles, all of which are contained in the style sheet associated with the default document template, called Normal. You can create new styles by clicking Format on the menu bar, choosing Style, and clicking New in the Styles dialog box. To make working with your styles more convenient, you can assign frequently-used styles to keyboard shortcut keys.

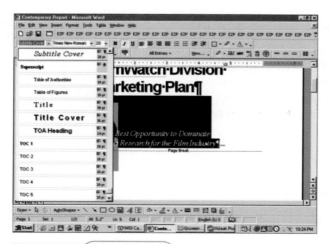

Figure 4A.12

You can create your own styles, which enable you to apply two or more formats with one command.

Tables

In a word processing program, a **table** is a special type of format that consists of horizontal rows and vertical columns, each of which intersect to form **cells.** What makes tables so useful is the ability of cells to expand or contract

CURRENTS

"Take a Letter, Please"

Imagine sitting in front of your computer, but it has no keyboard. Instead of typing, you speak to the computer. You give it commands or start to dictate. The computer quickly obeys, acting on your commands or transcribing as you speak.

The past decade or so has seen great progress in the area of speech recognition by computers, although the scenario just cited is true only in a limited sense. Error rates (how many mistakes the computer makes), however, continue to drop by a factor of two every other year.

Until recently, the best speech recognition was performed by using a process called discrete speech recognition or isolated-word speech recognition. This process requires that the speaker insert a short pause between each word. This is an unnatural way to speak, and it sounds stilted to those listening. However, discrete speech recognition is easy to implement because the computer can quickly tell where one word ends and another begins.

Continuous speech recognition, on the other hand, is just becoming practical on a wide scale. This type of speech recognition is more difficult to implement. The primary reason is that when we speak, the sound of a word is affected by the words surrounding it and how fast it is spoken. This effect is called co-articulation. Humans, particularly those speaking a language since a very young age, are able to compensate for the nuances of continuous speech. Computers are not so capable. Error rates in a continuous speech recognition system are still high.

Other variables can affect the accuracy of speech recognition systems. For example, it is possible to develop or adapt a speech recognition system so that it works with a particular speaker. This is accomplished by storing samples of words spoken by the person, and then using those in parsing the person's speech later. These types of systems tend to be relatively error-free (over time) because they are specialized for use by one person.

Independent systems—those that are designed to be used by numerous people—are much more difficult to develop and more expensive. This is to be expected, however, when a program has to compensate for different dialects, vocal patterns, and pitches.

The improvements in speech recognition over the past several years have led to some handy applications. A big selling feature in luxury cars is the hands-free cellular phone. Simply tell the phone whom you want to call, and it does so. For instance, you might say "call home," and the phone understands and makes the call. This is accomplished through a process of training the phone so that it knows your voice and associates a particular phone number with a particular command (such as "call home").

Another common application is for use in phone companies. Many large phone companies have computerized directory assistance services, removing the human operator from the picture. When you dial the number for information, a computerized voice asks you for the city and the name you want. When you respond, the computer uses speech recognition technology to locate the number and deliver it to you.

As speech recognition systems continue to develop, it won't be many years until you can quickly dictate your term paper or a letter to Uncle Bob. Until then, it's best to leave your keyboard plugged in and brush up on your typing.

Great progress has occurred in the area of computerized speech recognition.

dynamically as you add or delete text. This ability puts an end to one of the most dreaded of all typists' tasks, the chore of typing a complex table using nothing but tab stops.

To insert a table with Microsoft Word, click Table on the menu bar, point to Insert, and choose Table. In the Insert Table dialog box, you can choose

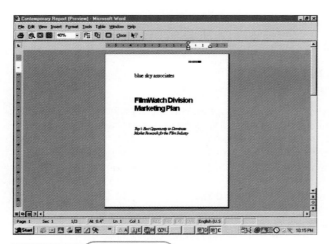

Figure 4A.13

Microsoft Word 2000's Print Preview feature enables you to view your document's printed appearance before printing.

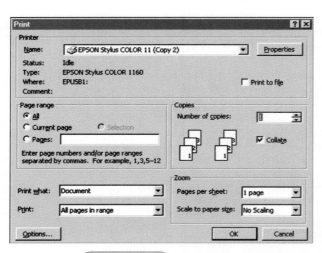

Figure 4A.14

In the Print Dialog box, you can generally initiate printing just by clicking OK. Optionally, you can select a different printer or choose from a variety of options, including number of copies.

how many columns and rows you want to insert. After you click OK, Word creates the table, and you can start typing within it. To add a new row, go to the last cell in the table, and press Tab.

Once you've inserted a table, you can edit the table structure by adding or deleting rows and columns. You can also merge cells together.

PRINTING

When you're ready to print your document, you can display a preview of your document's printed appearance, if you wish (see Figure 4A.13). This feature, called **Print Preview,** enables you to see all of your document formats precisely as they will appear when printed. Use Print Preview to make sure page breaks and other formats will look good when printed. A useful feature of Microsoft Word is the Shrink to Fit button on the Print Preview toolbar. This button automatically adjusts the font size and margins in an attempt to get a document to print on just one page. This feature comes in very handy for letters.

After you've decided to print your document, choose the print command. In the Print Dialog box, you can choose several options, including the number of copies you want to print, the pages you want to print, and (with most printers) the print quality (see Figure 4A.14).

THE INTERNET CONNECTION

The latest programs can save your work to the HTML file format, using the codes that underlie World Wide Web documents. This means you can publish your documents on the Web without having to learn HTML or translate the files for Web publishing purposes. In addition, HTML files are easy to exchange with other people—just about everybody has a Web browser!

DESKTOP PUBLISHING

Desktop publishing (DTP) combines text, graphics, and advanced formatting to create a visually-appealing printed document, such as a newsletter, a flyer, a brochure, a magazine, or a book. Although many word processing programs can do much of what desktop publishing programs do, the difference between the two lies in emphasis. In a word processing program, the emphasis is placed on writing and editing the text. In a desktop publishing program, the emphasis is placed on the text's *appearance*. (You can create the text in a desktop publishing program, but these programs enable you to import text and graphics from other applications.)

What's the payoff of using desktop publishing software? Compared to manual layout methods, desktop publishing saves a great deal of time, and it also enables many publishers to produce high-quality output in-house instead of outsourcing the work to professional layout studios. Unlike most word processing programs, desktop publishing programs are designed to produce output for professional typesetting machines, called *imagesetters*, that can print at resolutions of more than 2500 dpi. High-end desktop publishing software is routinely used to produce most (if not all) of the magazines you see in a magazine rack.

When you desktop-publish a document, you do five basic tasks. First, you determine the layout of the page. Next, you enter the text and graphics, or you import them from other sources. Then you format the document, save it, and print it. Much of this process closely resembles what you do with a word processing program, with one major exception. Before you begin working with the text, you determine how you want the page layout to look. (It's helpful to sketch this out in pencil.) You then create your basic page design by building a **master page,** using graphical on-screen tools. The master page is a template for how all the pages will appear. Included on the master page are areas for text columns, headers and footers, titles, and graphics. The areas you've created, called *frames,* are like containers for text or graphics. You can fill these areas with text by typing, but it's more common to import text that's been created and edited in a word processing program. When you import text, it flows into the container.

You can also import graphics. You can anchor a graphic to a fixed position on the page so that text flows around the graphic (you see this effect all the time in magazine layouts).

Black-and-white desktop publishing is so easy to do that many individuals and small businesses now produce their own newsletters, flyers, and magazines. Working with color is more difficult. When you're working with color, you need to know how to specify color so that the printer knows what you want, and this requires learning specialized terminology and procedures.

Desktop publishing combines text, graphics, and advanced formatting to create visually-appealing printed documents, such as newsletters, flyers, brochures, and magazines.

TAKEAWAY POINTS

- Word processing programs provide tools for writing, editing, formatting, and composing textual documents. Word processing is more efficient than non-computer writing technologies (such as pen-and-paper or typewriters) because text entry and editing are separated from printing functions, enabling low-cost revision.

- Because your work is temporarily stored in the computer's volatile RAM before you save it, a power outage could wipe out hours of effort. Be sure to save your work regularly. If the program you are using has an Autosave function, be sure to enable it.

- Leading word processing programs such as Microsoft Word enable you to view your document in a variety of ways, including outlining (in which document headings become outline headings), a document map (in which the document outline is positioned in a window beside the normal text), a normal view (in which you can scroll through the document), a print layout view (in which you can page through the document), and a Web view (in which you can view your document as it will appear when published on the World Wide Web).

- The basic text editing functions in a word processing program include commands for deleting text, inserting text, selecting text, copying text, moving text, undoing editing changes, and redoing editing changes.

- Text selection refers to the process of highlighting text on-screen. Once the text is highlighted, you can perform editing and formatting operations on this text.

- Spelling and grammar checkers rely on algorithms that inevitably miss some types of errors. There is no substitute for a final, hand proofreading of your written work.

- Formatting occurs at the character, paragraph, section, and document levels. Character formats include character size, typefaces, weight, slant, effects, position, and spacing. Paragraph formats include alignments, indents, tabs, bulleted and numbered lists, borders and shading, and frames. Section formats include newspaper columns and endnotes. Page formats include headers and footers, margins, paper size, and orientation.

- Styles enable you to collect and save two or more formats under a style name. You can then apply all the stored formats by choosing the style. If you change the style after applying it, your changes automatically affect all of the text that has been formatted with that style throughout your document.

- For typing tabular data, tables are easy to use because each cell dynamically expands or contracts to accommodate the text you type.

- Desktop publishing (DTP) combines text, graphics, and advanced formatting to create a visually-appealing printed document. Desktop publishing saves time by enabling publishers to produce high-quality output in-house instead of outsourcing the work to professional layout studios.

MODULE REVIEW

KEY TERMS AND CONCEPTS

alignment	columns	fonts
aspect ratio	condensed spacing	footers
autocorrect	copy	footnotes
autosave	cut	formatting
baseline	cut and paste	frames
body type	demote	gutters
bold	desktop publishing (DTP)	hanging indent
borders	display type	hard copy
bulleted lists	document map	headers
cells	drag handles	indents
centered alignment	effects	insert mode
character formatting	endnotes	italic
citation	expanded spacing	justified alignment
citation format	field code	kerning
citing	fill	landscape
clip art	flush left alignment	leaders
clipboard	flush right alignment	leading

margins
master page
monospace fonts
multiple undo
normal view
numbered lists
object
outlining
orientation
page formatting
paper size
paragraph
paragraph formatting
paste
points
portrait
position
print layout view
print preview

promote
proportionally-spaced fonts
redo
reference mark
regular weight
rule
ruler
sans serif fonts
scale
section
section breaks
select
serif fonts
size
shadow
shading
slant
small caps
spacing

style
style sheet
subscript
superscript
tab settings
tab stops
table
text boxes
turnover lines
typefaces
typeover mode (or overtype
   mode)
undo
Web layout
weight
word wrapping
WYSIWYG
zoom levels

TRUE/FALSE

Indicate whether the following statements are true or false.

1. Using word processing software, you can produce a high-quality document in about the same time as using a typewriter.

2. You don't need to perform the four steps of word processing, writing, editing, formatting, and printing, in that order.

3. To start a new line in a document, it's important that you press the Enter key at the end of each line.

4. A word processing program automatically determines when to begin a new page.

5. The autocorrect feature automatically saves your work at an interval you specify.

6. Footnotes appear at the end of a document and endnotes appear at the bottom of a page.

7. You need special software to insert pictures into a document.

8. To number the pages in a document, you need to turn on the page numbering feature because most word processing programs won't do this automatically.

9. Formatting enables you to specify the appearance of your text when it's finally printed.

10. In a desktop publishing program, the emphasis is on the document's appearance rather than writing and editing text.

MATCHING

Match each key term from the left column to the most accurate definition in the right column.

_____ 1. autosave

_____ 2. outlining

_____ 3. document map

_____ 4. reference mark

_____ 5. clip art

_____ 6. drag handles

_____ 7. hard copy

_____ 8. redo

_____ 9. typeface

_____ 10. spacing

a. the distance between characters

b. ready-to-use pictures included with a program

c. repeats the last editing change

d. visible indications that a picture has been selected

e. a feature that saves your work at a specified interval

f. overall design of the character set

g. a special document viewing mode that enables you to view your document's headings

h. a document's outline that is displayed in a window to the left of the document text

i. a printed version of a document

j. a number or symbol that appears in text

MULTIPLE CHOICE

Circle the letter of the correct choice for each of the following.

1. What are the four basic steps of word processing?
   a. conceiving, writing, editing, printing
   b. planning, writing, formatting, printing
   c. outlining, writing, revising, saving
   d. formatting, printing, writing, editing

2. As you edit your text, which key do you use to delete the character to the left of the cursor?
   a. Backspace
   b. Delete
   c. Alt
   d. F9

3. Which editing mode results in existing text moving to the right of new text?
   a. typeover mode
   b. add mode
   c. insert mode
   d. edit mode

4. Which of the following is not a common editing tool in word processors?
   a. outlining
   b. spelling checker
   c. grammar checker
   d. style checker

5. Which of the following types of formatting results in moving characters above the baseline?
   a. subscript
   b. emphasis
   c. font change
   d. superscript

6. Which of the following is an example of paragraph-level formatting?
   a. character size
   b. indent
   c. spacing
   d. subscript

7. Which of the following is *not* a type of paragraph justification?
   a. flush left
   b. centered
   c. radial
   d. justified

8. What is another name for line spacing?
   a. white space
   b. horizontal value
   c. justification
   d. leading

9. Which of the following is an example of page formatting?
   a. tables
   b. styles
   c. margins
   d. section breaks

10. When using desktop publishing software, you create your basic page design by building what?
   a. a master page
   b. a layout guide
   c. a mock-up
   d. a style guide

FILL-IN

In the blank provided, write the correct answer for each of the following.

1. The capability to move words to the next line, as necessary, is called _____ .

2. A(n) _____ is a unit of text that begins and ends with an Enter keystroke.

3. The _____ feature automatically corrects certain mistakes as you're typing.

4. To view your document as if it were a continuous scroll, you choose _____ view.

5. A(n) _____ is a type of data that is inserted with the programming code needed to manipulate it.

6. In _____ programs, you see the results of your formatting choices on-screen.

7. _____ alignment aligns both the left and right margins of a paragraph.

8. A(n) _____ allows you to save formatting characteristics with a distinctive name and then later apply those characteristics, as a whole, to any text you choose.

9. A(n) _____ is a special type of format consisting of horizontal rows and vertical columns, each of which intersect to form cells.

10. The _____ feature enables you to see all of your document formats precisely as they will appear when printed.

SHORT ANSWER

On a separate sheet of paper, answer the following questions.

1. What are the four steps of using a word processor?

2. What features of a good word processor are designed to assist with the writing process?

3. What is the difference between normal view, print layout view, and Web layout view?

4. What are the two editing modes (for adding text) in most word processors?

5. What are the differences between a thesaurus, a spell checker, and a grammar checker?

6. What are the common formatting options for word processors?

7. What is a hanging indent, and how is it created?

8. What is the difference between portrait and landscape orientations?

9. What are the advantages of being able to save your work to HTML file formats?

10. What are the major differences between word processing and desktop publishing software?

4B

MODULE

OUTLINE

WHAT YOU WILL LEARN . . .

When you have finished reading this module, you will be able to:

1. List four uses for electronic spreadsheet software.
2. Identify the components of a spreadsheet.
3. List and discuss the six basic skills you use to build a worksheet.
4. List the types of information you can type in a cell.
5. State the order of evaluation used in Microsoft Excel and explain why it is important to understand this order.
6. Explain how replication works.
7. Identify situations in which you need to use absolute cell references.
8. Explain how to design a spreadsheet in a way that avoids common errors.
9. Describe the types of charts that can be produced with a spreadsheet program and which types of data are best represented with each.
10. List some of the risks of using a spreadsheet.

Here's a scene that could occur in just about any contemporary business or nonprofit organization. Two managers are huddled over a notebook computer, looking at tables of numbers on-screen. One says, "What would happen if we could cut shipping costs by just 5 percent?" A few keys are pressed, and the other manager says, "Looks good. If we can get the shipper to agree to this, we can double our sales volume—and everyone wins."

You're watching a **what-if scenario,** in which people plug in test data to see how it affects an outcome (in this case, sales volume). In the past, what-if scenarios involved long hours of adding up tables of numbers and then recalculating them after you changed an input value. Now, such calculations are easy thanks to electronic spreadsheet software, one of the most popular productivity programs available. Using spreadsheets, computer users can create numerical **simulations** of anything that can be described with numbers, ranging from a family's monthly budget to the world's population. (A simulation is a small-scale model of something in the real world. By manipulating the model, you can learn more about the larger reality you're modeling.) Spreadsheets have found uses in every area of human endeavor, including the arts and humanities as well as science and business.

As you learn how to use spreadsheet software, remember that spreadsheet simulation—like all simulation—has limitations and risks. This module explores the essentials of spreadsheet usage and examines the benefits and risks of spreadsheet simulation.

INTRODUCING SPREADSHEET SOFTWARE

A **spreadsheet** is a program designed to process information in the form of tables. You can type a table of numbers in a word processing program, of course. But what makes spreadsheet software so desirable is its capacity to hide mathematical formulas "under" the numbers, so that some of the numbers you're seeing on-screen are actually generated by the underlying formula. One such formula could say, in effect, "add this column of numbers and show the result here." If you make a change to the column of numbers, the software automatically recalculates the sum and displays the result. Working with a spreadsheet is fun because it's as if the table is live: you make changes to the data and see recalculated results almost instantly.

The capability to recalculate complex tables of numbers quickly makes spreadsheets ideal for what-if scenarios. But they're also useful for simpler mathematical tasks, such as summing a long list of numbers. Because spreadsheets accept text as well as numbers, you can provide text headings for the quantities you enter so that you can later remember what they mean.

Another important use for spreadsheets use involves business charts, such as pie charts, line charts, and bar charts. Most spreadsheet programs can generate such charts almost automatically from the numerical data you supply. For anyone who needs to create such charts for reports or presentations, spreadsheet programs are a genuine productivity booster.

Spreadsheets are also used for storing and analyzing data. Although database software is generally considered more appropriate for such purposes, you can set aside part of a spreadsheet for a small database. This is particularly useful when you want to analyze data frequently.

EXPLORING THE WORKSHEET

In this section, you'll take a closer look at a typical spreadsheet program and learn to identify what you're seeing. Microsoft Excel, the leading electronic spreadsheet program, is described here.

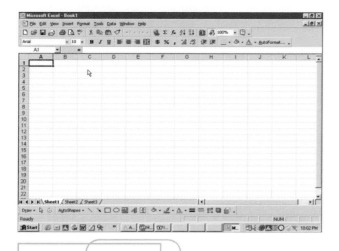

Figure 4B.1

A typical spreadsheet program.

Cell A1   Row 1

Column A   Scroll bars   Window boundary

Figure 4B.2

Some worksheets need more space than the window provides. To bring additional portions of the worksheet into view, use the scroll bars and scroll arrows.

When you launch Excel, you'll see the features that are normally found in an application window, including the title bar, menu bar, toolbars, application workspace, scroll bar, and status bar. The following special features appear in the Excel window (see Figure 4B.1):

■ **Worksheet** A worksheet is an on-screen grid of **rows** and **columns.** An intersection of a row and a column is called a **cell.** Each cell has a unique name composed of its column letter and row number, such as B2 or E6. A worksheet can be much larger than the window (see Figure 4B.2). Some worksheets need more space than the window provides. To bring additional portions of the worksheet into view, use the scroll bars and scroll arrows.

■ **Cell pointer** When you move the mouse pointer over the worksheet, it becomes a **cell pointer,** shaped like a cross. You can use the cell pointer to select one or more cells.

■ **Active cell** On the worksheet, the **active cell** is highlighted. The active cell is the one where text or figures will appear when you start typing.

■ **Name box** The **name box** displays the name of the active cell.

■ **Formula bar** The **formula bar** serves as an editing scratchpad for entering data or formulas into a cell. When you start typing anything into a cell, you'll see an **enter button** and a **cancel button** appear to the left of the formula bar. As you type, you can correct a mistake by clicking within the formula bar and using Delete or Backspace to correct the error. When you are finished typing, you can click the enter button to confirm the cell's contents, or click the cancel button to abandon your changes. You can also confirm your entry in a cell by pressing a navigation key such as Tab, Enter, or an arrow key (see Table 4B.1 for a list of the navigation keys you can use).

■ **Worksheet tabs** Located in the lower left corner of the screen, the **worksheet tabs** enable you to select which **worksheet** you want to use. A single file (called a **workbook**) can contain more than one spreadsheet. By default, new workbooks contain three worksheets, titled Sheet1, Sheet2, and Sheet3.

■ **Horizontal scroll bar** The **horizontal scroll bar,** positioned at the lower left of the window, enables you to bring hidden columns into view.

USING A SPREADSHEET PROGRAM

When you use a spreadsheet program, you will typically use all or most of the following skills:

Selecting cells You can select an individual cell or a **range** of two or more cells.

Table **4B.1**

Keyboard Shortcuts for Worksheet Navigation (Microsoft Excel)

Table **4B.1**

To Do This	Press This Key
Go to the next cell right	Tab or right arrow
Go to the next cell left	Shift + tab or left arrow
Go to the next cell down	Enter or down arrow
Go to the next cell up	Shift + Enter or up arrow
Go to column A of the current row	Home
Go to cell A1	Ctrl + Home
Scroll up one screen	Page Up
Scroll down one screen	Page Down
Scroll right one screen	Alt + Page Down
Scroll left one screen	Alt + Page Up
Go to the last cell that contains data	Ctrl + End
Reposition the worksheet to show the selection	Ctrl + Backspace
Go to a cell you specify	F5

Entering data You can enter numbers, text, dates, and times, and the program will automatically recognize the type of data you have entered.

Editing data Once you have entered data, you can change or delete the data.

Formatting data You can choose fonts, font sizes, colors, borders, and shading. In addition, you can choose from a variety of numeric data formats, which affect the way values are displayed.

Entering formulas A **formula** is an equation that calculates a new value (and shows it on-screen) based on existing values.

Editing the worksheet structure You can add or remove columns and rows. In addition, you can change the width of columns and the height of rows.

The following sections detail the knowledge and skills you will need to perform these tasks successfully.

Selecting Cells

To select any individual cell on the worksheet, simply click it with the cell pointer. You'll see the cell's name in the Name box.

You can also select a range of two or more cells. Ranges are always rectangular in shape, and they are defined by stating the name of the cell in the upper left corner and the lower right corner, separated by a colon. For example, the range A1:C10 defines a range consisting of thirty cells (see Figure 4B.3). You will often use ranges in spreadsheet formulas.

To select a range with the mouse, position the cell pointer over the first cell you want to select, and drag the mouse over the remaining cells. Release the mouse when you've finished selecting the range.

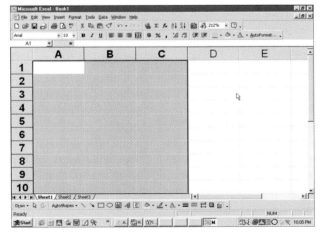

Figure **4B.3**

All ranges, such as this one (A1:C10), are rectangular in shape.

To select a range with the keyboard, position the cell pointer in the first cell you want to select, hold down the Shift key, and press the arrow keys to expand the selection until you have finished selecting the range.

Entering Data in the Worksheet

What makes spreadsheets so useful is their capability to accept a variety of different types of input into each cell. The program automatically determines which type of data you are entering and formats the data accordingly.

Types of Input Data

Microsoft Excel automatically recognizes the following types of data when you start typing them in the worksheet:

- **Numbers** You can type any number, large or small. In spreadsheets, numbers are called **values.** When you type numbers, you can type an **integer** (a whole number, such as 55), a decimal number (such as 321.9), a fraction (such as 4¾), or a number in scientific notation (such as 5.09E+16). You can also use mathematical symbols such as plus (+), minus (−), percent (%), fraction (/), exponent (E), and dollar sign ($). Note: If you see a number in scientific notation that you didn't type that way, or a series of hash marks (#########), the column isn't wide enough for the number. Widen the column to bring the number into display.

- **Text** You can enter explanatory text. In spreadsheets, text entries are called **labels** because they are most often used to explain the numbers you've entered. Excel automatically recognizes text when you start entering it, and formats the text so that it is aligned flush left in the cell. If no information appears in adjacent cells, the label is allowed to overlap the cells to the right. Otherwise, you may need to widen the column to see all the text. Sometimes you may want to enter a number and have it treated like text. To do so, type an apostrophe followed by the number.

- **Dates and times** You can type dates and times, and they will be recognized and stored as dates and times rather than values or labels. In Excel, you can type any of the following to indicate September 26, 2002: 9/26/02 or 26-Sep-02. The following indicate 10:15 PM: 10:15 PM or 22:15. You can combine dates and times, as in the following example: 9/26/02 10:15 PM or 26-Sep-02 22:15.

Using Fill to Enter Data Quickly

Special features in Microsoft Excel enable you to copy data quickly. Suppose you have entered a column of figures, and you want to copy the figures to the next column to the right. You can do so using Excel's **fill** command. This command fills a range of cells with values from selected cells. To use fill, select the column of figures. Note the **fill handle** at the lower right corner of the selection (see Figure 4B.4). To fill the next column with these figures, drag the fill handle so that you select the next column. When you release the mouse button, the program fills the next column with the data from the original column.

Using AutoFill to Enter a Data Series

Spreadsheets enable you to enter data in a **series** automatically. A series is a sequence of numbers, times, or dates that are increased or decreased by a set value. For example, the series consisting of the following values increases by 10: 10, 20, 30. In this series, the amount by which each value is increased, called the **increment,** is 10. (If the value was reduced, it would be called a **decrement.**) With Microsoft Excel, you can enter a series automatically by typing the first two values in the series. When you select the cells, you'll see the fill handle at the lower right corner of the selection box. Drag this handle down or right to extend the series.

Editing Data

Once you've entered data into the worksheet, you can edit the data using some of the same techniques you would use in a word processing program. However, spreadsheet editing commands work somewhat differently, as this section explains. When you edit spreadsheet data, you work with one or more cells at a time.

To edit an individual cell, select the cell with the cell pointer, and click within the formula bar. You can then use the Backspace and Delete keys to remove unwanted characters. To insert new data, click the cursor where you want new text to appear and start typing. Click the enter button, or press a navigation key, to confirm the change.

To edit more than one cell at a time, select a range. Once you've selected the range, you can do any of the following:

- **Clear the cells** To clear cells means to remove the data that you entered. In Excel, you can clear the cell by pressing Delete. Note that clearing the cell does not erase any formats you have chosen. It does not erase formulas, either. To clear formats and formulas, click Edit on the menu bar, choose Clear, and select the information you want to remove.

- **Deleting the cells** In contrast to clearing the cells, to delete cells means to take the computer equivalent of a knife and "cut" the cells out of the spreadsheet. When you delete cells, the program will need to know how to shift the remaining cells. You'll see a dialog box asking you to specify whether to shift cells left or up, or delete the entire column or row. To delete cells, click Edit on the menu bar, and choose Delete.

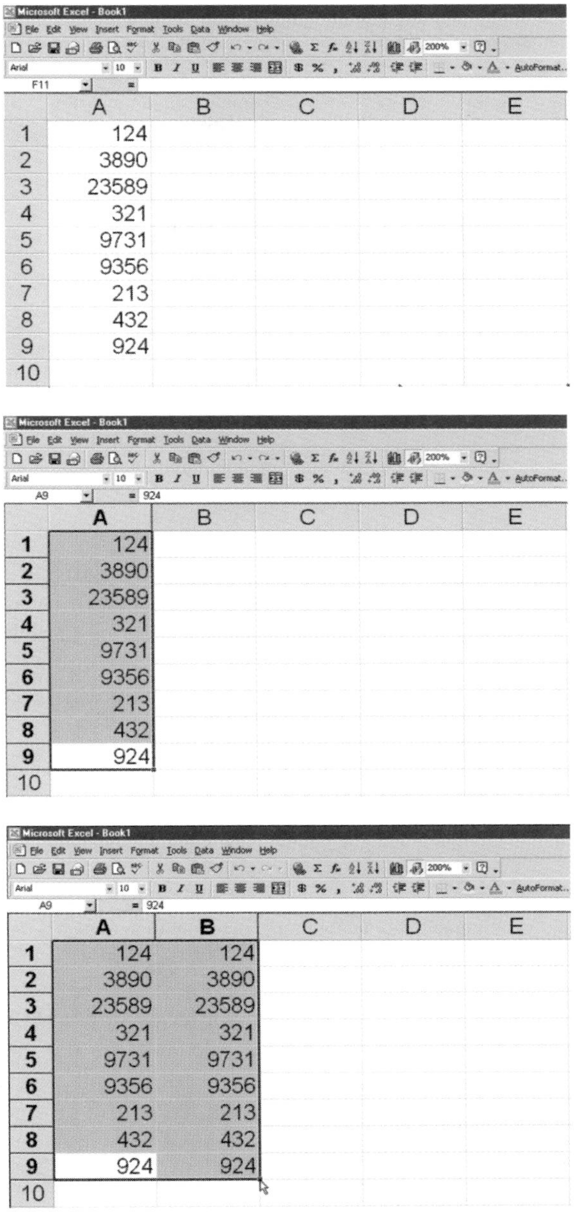

Figure 4B.4

You can use the fill command to copy data quickly.

Keyboard Shortcuts for Filling Data (Microsoft Excel)	
To Do This	**Follow These Instructions**
Fill down	Begin the selection with the cell that contains the value to copy, and expand the selection down. Press Ctrl + D to fill the selection.
Fill right	Begin the selection with the cell that contains the value to copy, and expand the selection right. Press Ctrl + R to fill the selection.

Table 4B.2

Table **4B.3**

Numeric Format Options (Microsoft Excel)

Category	Examples	Purpose
General	20.82, 20388	Default numeric format
Currency	$10.42, ($1000)	Currency format. Negative numbers are shown in parentheses.
Accounting	$10.42 5.40	Currency format. Aligns values by their decimal point.
Percentage	175%	Multiply the entered value by 100 and displays the value with a percentage symbol
Fraction	13 3/16	Displays decimal values as fractions
Scientific	1.55E10	Shows numbers in scientific notation

- **Copying and moving cells** You can use copy and paste techniques to copy or move data within your worksheet. Begin by selecting one cell or a range of cells, and choose Copy or Cut from the Edit menu. The program surrounds the cell or cells with a dotted-line highlight. Click the cell where you want to copy or move the data. If you are copying or moving a range, click in the upper left corner of the range. Press Enter to complete the editing action. You can also use drag and drop to move cells. To use drag and drop, select a range, and then drag the range to its new location.

Formatting Data

When you enter data into a cell, you can also choose formats, including the formats you'd choose in a word processing program, such as font, font size, font color, and text alignment.

Spreadsheet programs also have **numeric formats,** which enable you to specify how values will appear in a cell. For example, if you choose the currency format, values appear with a currency sign and currency punctuation (for example, the value 102585.4 appears as $102,585.40). See Table 4B.3 for a list of the numeric formats you can use.

Be aware that spreadsheet programs calculate based on the underlying value, which may differ from the displayed value after you choose certain formats. For example, suppose you choose a numeric format that rounds numbers to two decimal points, but the underlying value has five numbers after the decimal point. It is the underlying value, not the displayed one, that is used for calculation purposes.

Entering Formulas

The heart of any worksheet's capabilities lies in the formulas you create. Without formulas, a worksheet isn't any more useful than a table created in a word processing program.

In Microsoft Excel, formulas always begin with an equals sign (=). This sign alerts the program that the typing to follow describes a formula. As you type the formula, you see the formula in the formula bar. After you press Enter, the formula disappears. Instead, what you see on-screen is the value that is calculated by the formula.

If the formula doesn't work, look for the message "Error in Formula." This message means that you typed something incorrectly. Check your typing, and try again. If the formula looks like a text entry, you made a common error:

SPOTLIGHT   ONLINE TRADING

▶Equity ownership has always been a hallmark of capitalism. Nowhere is that fact more evident than on Wall Street, the financial bastion for corporate America. For close to two centuries, the barons of commerce have gathered and traded stock in the country's largest businesses.

The swift-moving information revolution has finally met the money markets, and we are witnessing a fundamental change in how stocks and bonds are traded. Before the widespread use of personal computers, most trading was performed through brokers. These are essentially intermediaries you hire to buy or sell stocks on your behalf. Using a full-service broker is expensive, because you pay a commission on each transaction.

As computers started making inroads into homes, discount brokerages appeared on the scene. These companies offer fewer services than full-service brokers, but also charge quite a bit less. They still serve, however, as your intermediary to the stock market.

When the Internet arrived on the consumer scene, the brokerage world was turned on its head by the marriage of deep-discount brokers and direct electronic access. Now those interested in trading stocks can do so around the clock using the World Wide Web—without a broker.

Besides the ability to control your own financial destiny, online stock trading offers a potentially-huge benefit: speed. If you deal with a human broker, from the time you initiate your transaction to when it is completed could be several minutes (or longer, depending on whether you play phone tag). With online trading, your financial transactions are completed in a minute or less. This may not sound like a big deal, but in a rapidly-moving market, it can represent the difference between prime rib and hamburger for dinner.

The largest online stock-trading service is E*TRADE GROUP INC., located in Palo Alto, California. Their Web site is **www.etrade.com.** E*TRADE GROUP INC. is not the only online brokerage firm; about 60 or 70 such firms are available. The services offered and prices charged by each firm can differ greatly. Some focus on low commissions; others focus on extremely-fast trades. You should research the companies to discover which is best for your stock trading needs, or you may want to open accounts with more than one firm.

Riskiest of all is a practice known as *day trading,* in which investors use online tools to buy and sell stocks for quick, short-term profit. Although some investors make money in day trading, as many as 70 percent of them may not only lose money, but they'll lose everything they invested—and that's true even when the general market trend is upward.

Online brokerages have been criticized for encouraging customers to buy on the margin, a practice in which the brokerage lends an investor the funds needed for a large share purchase. If the shares appreciate, the investor can pay back the loan easily. If the stock goes down, the money won't be available to pay back the loan. For this reason, securities regulations enable brokerages to "call" the margin loan, which means they can sell an investor's other stocks to pay back the outstanding loan. In a declining market, this can translate into huge losses for an investor because the sold stocks are probably also down—but they will probably bounce back once the downturn is over.

Although trading stocks online is revolutionizing the financial markets, and it may sound appealing, there are two caveats. First, doing your own trading shifts the knowledge of burden from your broker to you. Second, the temptation to make knee-jerk financial decisions is greater when you do your own trading. Analysts have known for years that the best market returns are gained by staying in for the long run. If you see one of your stocks taking a downturn, the initial reaction is to sell the stock. After all, it takes only a few seconds online. Such a course, however, may not be the most prudent.

Regardless of any potential pitfalls, online trading is here to stay. You can benefit by using this new financial tool to your advantage.

E*TRADE GROUP INC. is one of the largest online stock-trading services.

Table 4B.4

Order of Evaluation (Microsoft Excel)

Order	Operator	Description	Example	Result
First	−	Negation	=−5+2	3
Second	%	Percent	=10%*100	10
Third	^	Exponentiation	10^3+2	1002
Fourth	*, /	Multiplication or Division	10*3+2	32
Fifth	+, −	Addition or Subtraction	10+3−2	11

You can override the default order of evaluation by using parentheses. In the following example, the default order of evaluation requires the program to perform multiplication before addition:

$$= 10 * 3 + 2$$

The result is 32. By using parentheses, you can force the program to perform the addition first, as in this example:

$$= 10 * (3 + 2)$$

The result is 50.

forgetting to type the equals sign. Select the cell, click within the formula bar, and add the equals sign.

Simple Formulas

Many spreadsheets contain little more than simple formulas, which use nothing fancier than the basic **arithmetic operators:** addition (+), subtraction (−), multiplication (*), and division (/).

These arithmetic operators need something to work with. You can include values, for example:

$$= 2 + 2$$

If you place this formula into a cell, you see 4 in the cell.

Order of Evaluation and Parentheses

To write spreadsheet formulas correctly, make sure you understand the **order of evaluation,** which specifies how the program reads the formulas. In Table 4B.4 you see the order of evaluation used by Microsoft Excel. Evaluated first is a negation (a minus sign placed in front of a number), followed by percents, exponents, multiplication or division, and addition or subtraction. If the program encounters operators with the same level of **precedence** (the same status in the order of evaluation), the program reads the expression from left to right. Study the examples to make sure you understand how the order of evaluation affects the result.

If you specify an uneven number of opening and closing parentheses, you'll see the message "Parentheses Do Not Match" or "Error in Formula." You can correct this mistake on the formula bar.

Cell References

In the examples you've examined thus far, you've seen formulas that contain values. However, it isn't a good idea to use values within the formulas themselves. Because formulas are hidden from view, you might not realize that

Destinations

John Walkenbach's The Spreadsheet Page is the ultimate Web destination for anyone interested in every aspect of spreadsheets—including spreadsheet jokes! It's located at **http://www.j-walk. com/ss/.**

you had typed the wrong value, and as a result, your spreadsheet could produce an incorrect answer. To keep all the values in your spreadsheet in plain sight, it's best to build formulas using cell references.

In a **cell reference,** you type a **cell address** (such as C9 or B2) instead of a value. The program goes to that cell, gets the value stored in the specified cell, and uses that value within the formula.

Now suppose you have two cells that contain values: cell B9 contains 2, and cell C9 contains 2. In cell C10, you enter the following formula:

```
= B9 + B10
```

The answer, 4, appears in cell C10.

With Microsoft Excel, you can easily create cell references in a formula by using the mouse or the arrow keys. Begin by selecting the cell in which you want to place the formula. Then type an equals sign to start the formula. Click the mouse in the first cell you want to reference, or use the arrow keys to select this cell. You will see the cell reference in the formula bar. Then type an arithmetic operator, such as a plus sign. Now use the mouse or arrow keys to select the second cell; you will see the cell reference in the formula bar. You can continue constructing the formula this way, or you can click Enter (or press a navigation key) to complete the formula.

You can also refer to a cell in another worksheet in the same workbook. To do so, type an equals sign followed by the name of the worksheet, an exclamation point, and the name of the cell in the other worksheet. Here's an example:

```
= Sheet2!B9
```

This cell reference produces the value contained in cell B9 in Sheet2.

Replication

What you're about to learn will explain why spreadsheets are so popular and easy to use. **Replication** enables you to *copy* a formula to a range of cells. The program adjusts the formulas so that they work perfectly in the new location.

Here's an example that explains how replication works. Suppose you have a simple spreadsheet, like the following:

	A	B	C	D
1		January	February	March
2	Standard	10	8	6
3	Super	9	13	29

This spreadsheet lists the sales for two products, Standard and Super. In February, for example, 8 Standards were sold. You want totals for all three columns (B, C, and D).

Start by writing the formula that totals the numbers in Column B. You can do this by inserting the following simple formula (in Microsoft Excel format) in cell B4:

```
= B2 + B3
```

This produces the correct total, 19.

Now you select cell B4, and you replicate (copy) this formula to cells C4 and D4. (In Microsoft Excel, you do this by clicking within B4, and expanding the selection to cells C4 and D4, then you choose Fill Right from the Edit menu.) You see the following:

	A	B	C	D
1		January	February	March
2	Standard	10	8	6
3	Super	9	13	29
4	TOTAL	19	21	35

Techtalk

Easter egg

In a computer program, a hidden feature inserted by programmers to give themselves credit or provide an entertaining, undocumented feature. Microsoft Excel 2000 contains a hidden auto racing game (see **http://www. j-walk.com/ss/excel/ eastereg.htm for instructions**). For information on Easter eggs in other programs, see The Easter Egg Archive (**http://www.eeggs. com**).

Cells C4 and D4 now contain the correct totals. How did *that* happen? If you examine the formula in C4, you'll see that the program automatically changed the formula to reflect its new location. The original formula was B2 + B3. When copied to cell C4, the formula was changed to C2 + C3. Similarly, when copied to cell D4, the formula was changed to D2 + D3. When you replicate a formula, the program looks at all the cell references in the formula, and automatically adds or subtracts column or row numbers, as necessary.

To understand why replication works this way, you need to know that the program does not actually store cell references in the way you type them. For example, in the original formula, you typed two cell references: B2 and B3. But the program didn't actually store "B2" and "B3." For B2, it stored information that says, in effect, "get the value from two rows up, in the same column." For B3, it stored "get the value from *one* row up, in the same column."

Now can you see how replication works? When you copy the formula in B4 to C4 and D4, you aren't copying the cell references you typed. Instead, you're copying information that tells the program where to get a value *relative to the current cell's position.* For this reason, this type of cell reference is called a **relative cell reference.**

Absolute Cell References

As you've just learned, spreadsheet programs automatically adjust cell references in copied formulas to reflect the copied formula's new position. But sometimes you need to "lock down" a cell reference so that it doesn't change when you copy or move the formula. Consider this example:

*	A	B	C	D
1	Amount to save:	10 percent		
2	January income:	$200	Savings:	$20
3	February income:	$400	Savings:	$40

To figure out how much you should save in January, put the following formula in cell D2:

$$=B1 * B2$$

This says, "Multiply my January income by the percentage I want to try to save each month." You get the right answer.

Look what happens, though, if you replicate the formula one row down to D3:

$$=B2 * B3$$

The program did what it was supposed to do. When you moved the formula down one row, it added 1 to each cell reference's row number. However, the formula doesn't work correctly. It says you're supposed to save $80,000! (Good luck.)

What went wrong? It's okay that the program adjusted the reference to cell C3—you want that to happen. Unfortunately, the program also adjusted the reference to cell B2, changing it to B3. So you're now multiplying $200 × $400.

You don't want the program to adjust the reference to cell B2, which contains the percentage amount to save. To prevent this from happening, you should use an **absolute cell reference.** An absolute cell reference says, "Don't change this."

In Microsoft Excel, you use a dollar sign ($) to indicate an absolute column or row reference. Here's an absolute reference to both the column and the row that form cell B2:

```
$B$1
```

And here's the correct formula for D2:

```
$B$1 * B2
```

When you replicate this formula to D3, you get the following:

```
$B$1 * B3
```

Just remember these simple rules: use relative cell referencing when you want the program to adjust cell references in copied formulas, and use an absolute cell reference when you want copied formulas to refer to one cell in a fixed location.

Note that you can specify relative or absolute references to column and row locations individually. The reference $B1 refers absolutely to column B, but the reference to row 1 is relative. Similarly, the reference B$1 refers relatively to column B, but the reference to row 1 is absolute. Remember to precede both parts of the cell reference with dollar signs if you want to type an absolute reference to a particular cell (such as B1).

Functions

To help you write complex formulas more quickly, spreadsheet programs have **built-in functions** (or *functions*, for short). For example, suppose you are trying to add a huge column of numbers. Instead of typing B2 + B3 + B4 + B5 (and so on), you can use the SUM function, as in the following example:

```
=SUM(B2:B35)
```

This function sums all the data in the range of cells B2 to B35. Functions have **syntax** requirements that specify how you must type them. In this example, you must type the correct function **keyword** (SUM) and enclose the range in parentheses. The keyword must be followed by an *argument*, which consists of additional information that is required by the function. For the SUM function, you must also supply the range of values to be added, and you must type the range expression correctly. In the above example, the

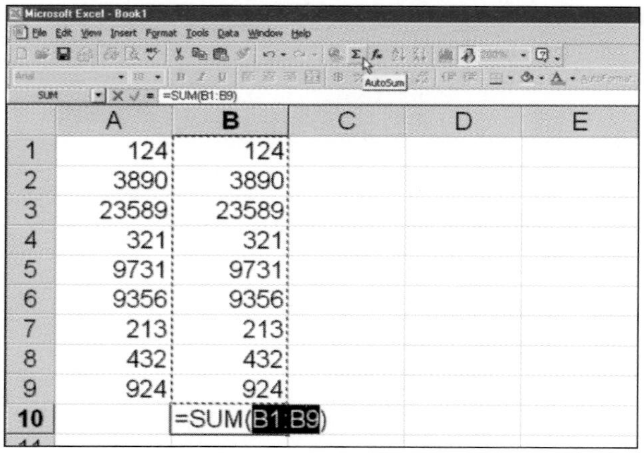

Figure 4B.5

When you use Excel's AutoSum button, make sure the program has selected the correct range of data.

range described is B2 to B35. Don't forget the colon, which is needed to tell the program that what you've typed is a range.

Because you use the SUM function so often, Microsoft Excel includes an AutoSum button on the toolbar that makes summing especially easy. To use AutoSum, select the cell where you want the sum to appear, such as the cell directly below the last number in a column of numbers. Then click AutoSum on the toolbar. If possible, Excel automatically determines which numbers you're trying to add up. Be sure to inspect the proposed selection to make sure the program has made the correct decision (see Figure 4B.5)

Some functions require multiple arguments. For example, the PMT function determines the periodic payment on a loan. To calculate the payment, you must supply (at the minimum) the interest rate, the number of payments, and the amount financed (the value of the principal). The function's syntax looks like this:

```
PMT (rate,nper,pv,fv,type)
```

In this function, the required arguments (rate, nper, and pv) are shown in bold; the other two (fv and type) are optional. In place of these arguments, you need to supply values or cell references. The *rate* is the interest rate, expressed as a percentage. *Nper* refers to the number of payments. *Pv* refers to the principal amount. Note that the arguments must be separated by commas; do not insert additional spaces. To calculate the loan payment on a $21,000 automobile, assuming 60 monthly payments and a 9.5% annual interest rate, you type the following formula:

```
=PMT(9.5%/12,60,21000)
```

After you confirm this formula, the program returns the loan payment. The answer is negative (shown in parentheses) because this is money that you must pay out. Note that this formula divides the annual interest rate by the number of months in a year (12), producing the monthly interest rate.

When you type arguments, you can use cell references instead of values—and it's a wise idea to do so. Consider the following example:

	A	B
1	Interest rate	9.5%
2	Number of payments	60
3	Amount financed	21000
4	PAYMENT	441.04

In this example, cell B4 contains the following formula:

```
PMT(B1/12,B2,B3)
```

Now you can try some "what-if" scenarios. How would the payment change if you could get an 8.5% rate instead of 9.5%? What if you pay the loan off in 72 months instead of 60?

As you design your worksheets, always separate data entry areas from calculation areas, as the preceding example illustrates. You can see the values with which you're working, so you're less likely to make a silly mistake. In addition, you can type in new values without disturbing the formula—and this capability transforms your worksheet into the "what-if" tool that makes spreadsheet software so useful.

Using the Insert Function Command

Because Microsoft Excel has so many functions, you may find it helpful to work with the Function command, one of the options on the Insert menu. To use this command, select the cell where you want to insert the function, click Insert on the menu bar, and choose Function. You'll see a menu of available functions. Try selecting PMT from the Financial functions. You'll see the dialog box shown in Figure 4B.6. This dialog box helps you construct the function; you can type the arguments in the text boxes. To enter a cell reference, click the cell reference icon at the right edge of the text box. The program hides the dialog box and enables you to select the cell that you want to enter. Press Enter to return to the dialog box after identifying the cell. To find out what the argument abbreviations mean, click the Help button. When you're finished providing the arguments, click OK. Table 4B.5 lists the categories of functions and their purposes.

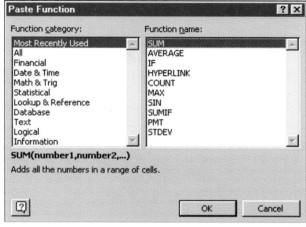

Figure 4B.6

Because Microsoft Excel has so many functions, you may find it helpful to work with the Function command, an option on the Insert menu.

Function Categories (Microsoft Excel)	

Table 4B.5

Category	Purpose
Database	Producing counts or sums or determining the maximum or minimum values in a range of data.
Date and Time	Displaying dates or times, such as showing today's date.
Engineering	Performing engineering analyses, such as working with complex numbers, converting one form of measurement to another, and converting numbers between one type of number system and another.
Financial	Calculating loan payments, appreciation of investments, and depreciation of property.
Information	Determining the type of information shown in a cell. These functions can be used to test for errors.
Logical	Determining whether a condition is true or false.
Lookup and Reference	Retrieving values from a list or table.
Math and Trigonometry	Performing mathematical and trigonometry calculations like those found on a scientific calculator.
Statistical	Performs statistical calculations on a range of data, such as finding the average or standard deviation.
Text	Changing text (for example, converting uppercase letters to lowercase).

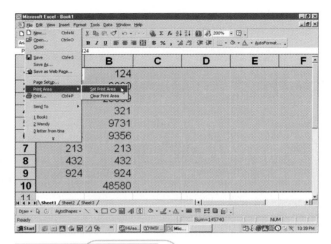

Figure **4B.7**

Once you define a print area, the program will print this area (and this area only) unless you subsequently change it.

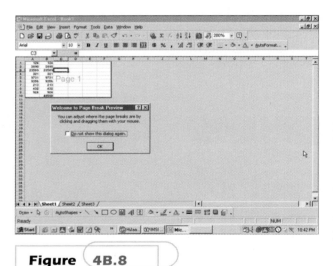

Figure **4B.8**

In Page Break Preview, you can adjust page breaks by dragging the page break lines.

Editing the Worksheet Structure

As you work with your worksheet, you may need to change the worksheet's matrix of rows and columns. You can add and delete rows and columns. In addition, you can change column width and row height. The following briefly summarizes the Excel procedures you can use to accomplish these tasks.

- **Adding rows and columns to the worksheet** Select the row below the place where you want to add a new row, or select the column to the right of the place where you want to add a new column. Then click Insert on the menu bar, and choose Rows or Columns.

- **Deleting an entire row or column** Click the row or column header button (the one that contains the column letter or row number). This selects the column. Then click Edit on the menu bar, and choose Delete.

- **Changing column width or row height** You can change width or height by dragging on a row or column border. You can also use AutoFit to size the row or column to accommodate the largest entry. To use AutoFit, click Format on the menu bar, point to Column or Row, and choose AutoFit.

Printing Your Worksheet

The worksheet printing process is much like printing with other types of application programs, but there are some key differences.

First, you can define a **print area** before you initiate printing. The print area is a range that you identify by selecting it before you choose the print area command (in Excel, you choose this command by clicking File on the menu bar, pointing to Print Area, and choosing Set Print Area). Once you have defined a print area, the program will print this area by default. If you enlarge the spreadsheet beyond the print area, you should change it before printing, or some of your data may not print (see Figure 4B.7).

A second difference lies in the use of repeating titles. Most spreadsheets contain rows, columns, or both that contain helpful labels that explain what the figures are about. To have these labels repeat on each page of the printout, you can select rows, columns, or both to be printed at the top or left of the page. With Microsoft Excel, you do so by clicking File on the menu bar, clicking Page Setup, clicking the Sheet tab, and filling out the areas called Rows To Repeat At Top or Columns To Repeat At Left.

Consider using the landscape printing orientation for your spreadsheet. In any case, be sure to preview the page breaks before printing to make sure that the printout will look good. In Microsoft Excel, you can preview page breaks by using the Print Preview command (an option on the File menu), and clicking the Page Break Preview button. When you see the page break preview, you can adjust page breaks by dragging the page break lines (see Figure 4B.8).

DESIGNING AN EFFECTIVE WORKSHEET

To create an effective worksheet, you'll be wise to spend some time developing a good, overall design. Admittedly, few people create spreadsheets this way. Instead, they just sit down and start typing in labels, formulas, and data.

But as many as one-third of the spreadsheets developed this way contain errors, as you'll learn in the discussion of spreadsheet risks later in this module. The following approach helps reduce these risks by encouraging you to think about what you want to accomplish before you begin creating the worksheet. It also produces a well-organized spreadsheet that is easy to proofread for errors.

Follow these steps to create an effective worksheet:

- **Define the worksheet's purpose** Suppose you have a new job managing a retail store. Your employees receive a base salary, plus a commission on their sales. Each month, you must calculate the commission each employee receives.

- **Plan how the output will look** Now that you know the purpose of your spreadsheet, it's simple to predict the output you need: a list of employee names and the amount of commission each should receive.

- **Define the user's input** To calculate the commission, you need two types of data: the commission rate and each employee's total monthly sales. Be sure to add explanatory text that explains how to supply the needed data.

- **Define the calculations** To calculate the monthly commission, you use the following simple formula:

```
monthly sales X commission rate = commission
```

Suppose Steve sold $1,500 this month, and the commission rate is 7.5 percent. Here's the formula for Steve:

```
$1500.00 X .075 = 112.50
```

Always test your formula with a pocket calculator before building your spreadsheet around it. If you get an incorrect answer, find out why before proceeding. You may need to use parentheses to override the default evaluation order.

- **Build formulas using cell references rather than values** By doing so, you keep data entry and calculation areas separate, and that helps to cut down on errors. Here's an example of a good design:

	A	B	C
1	Commission Rate:	7.5%	
2	Name	Sales	Commission
3	Steve	1500	$112.50
4	Antonio	2000	$150.00
5	Kyung	1250	$93.75

In this example, you type the commission rate in B1, and you type the salesperson's monthly sales in B3, B4, and B5. To calculate the commissions, you enter the following formula in cell C3:

```
=$B$1*B3
```

Note the use of the absolute cell reference (B1), which points to the cell in which you type the commission rate. When you fill this formula down to cells C4 and C5, the formula copies as follows:

```
C4:  $B$1*B4
C5:  $B$1*B5
```

- **Protect formulas from accidental erasure**   When you *protect* cells, their content cannot be changed unless you deliberately turn protection off. Because cells containing formulas look just like cells containing values, it is a very good idea to protect these cells. Doing so prevents you or some other user from typing over the formula inadvertently. In the above example, cell C4 contains the result of a formula ($150.00). If someone typed $175.00 in the cell, the formula would be destroyed. To protect a cell with Excel, click Format on the menu bar, choose Cell, click the Protection tab, and click Protect. Note that protection doesn't work until you've protected the entire worksheet by clicking Tools on the menu bar, pointing to Protection, and choosing Protect Sheet.

CREATING WORKSHEET CHARTS

Most people find it difficult to interpret a table of numbers. The chart generating capabilities of spreadsheet programs present numbers in a far more understandable form.

What's involved in generating a chart from a spreadsheet? You begin by identifying a range of values, which is called a **series.** Next, you choose the command that starts building a chart and then choose the **chart type** you want. Most programs offer you the choice of bar, column, line, and pie charts. After you make your choice, the program displays the chart. You can then add titles and other embellishments to make the chart more attractive.

Which type of chart should you use? Here's a quick guide (see Figure 4B.9):

- **Column chart**   A column chart provides a ready comparison among separate items. It can be used also to show changes over time (called a **time series**). For example, you can use a column chart to show the sales for each month of the year.

- **Bar chart**   Because the bars are stacked vertically, a bar chart is not a good choice for a time series. Use a bar chart to compare separate, distinct items. For example, you can use a bar chart to show the total sales for Models 101, 102, and 103.

- **Line chart**   This type of chart is designed for time series use, showing fluctuations in on-going, continuous trends over time. You could use a line chart to show how basic production costs, including the cost of raw materials and utility charges, have fluctuated over a one-year period.

- **Pie chart**   A pie chart shows the parts of a whole. Use this type of chart to show relative percentages when everything adds up to 100 percent. You could use a pie chart to show how Models 101, 102, and 103 contribute differently to the total sales picture.

Here are some ways to get fancy with charts:

- **Multiple series**   You can define more than one data series in any chart except a pie chart. For example, you could create a column chart that shows sales for eight product lines over a four-week period.

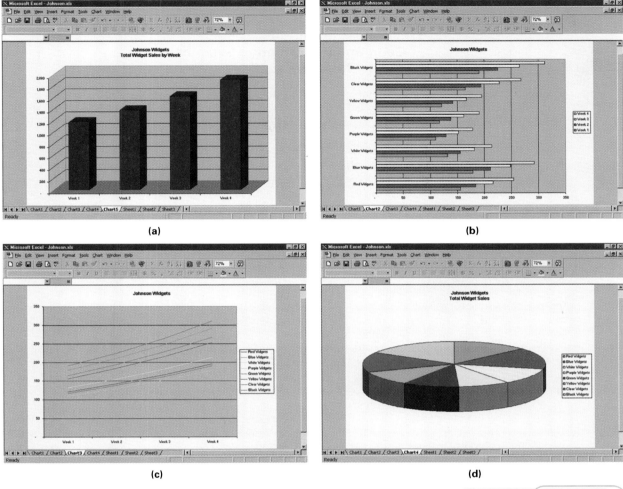

(a)

(b)

(c)

(d)

Figure   4B.9

Charts bring numbers to life:
(a) column chart, (b) bar chart,
(c) line chart, and (d) pie chart.

- **Legend**   A **legend** provides a key to what the different colors or shades mean. A legend comes in handy when you have a complex chart with lots of pie slices or different data series.

- **Scaling**   Spreadsheet programs adjust the scale of a chart automatically, but sometimes you need to adjust the scale manually to avoid giving a false impression. If a line chart shows sales rising too steeply, you can make the increase seem more gradual by changing the scale.

ADVANCED SPREADSHEET FEATURES

Most spreadsheet programs enable users to develop **macros.** A macro is a set of operations that accomplishes a specific task. When you make a macro, you save the macro's keystrokes under a name that you provide. Later, when you issue the macro name, the entire set of operations is executed. Macros themselves are stored in a remote part of the spreadsheet that is not needed for data and are saved along with the spreadsheet. Examples of tasks that can be saved as macros include printing a block of the spreadsheet, inserting a row into the spreadsheet, and copying appropriate formulas and functions into the new row.

Many new spreadsheets offer statistical analysis capabilities. These programs can quickly perform analysis of variance, regression analysis, and other complex statistical operations with a minimum of work by the user. You can then graph the results of these operations.

IMPACTS

Geographic Information Systems: Nowhere to Hide?

It looks like a map—but it's also a database. Called a *geographic information system (GIS)*, this new technology is revolutionizing the way we understand and navigate through the world around us. The benefits are undeniable—but there are risks, too, especially now that GIS data is becoming accessible on the Internet.

What's a GIS? In brief, it's a computer system that displays what looks like a map—except that it's linked to a database that contains all sorts of information about the geographical points shown on the map. For example, suppose you're using a GIS to view a map of lakes, rivers, and streams in an area affected by acid rainfall. If you click on a lake, you'll see the water acidity data that's stored along with the lake's image. And there's more. Using *overlays,* images such as colors that are superimposed on the map, you could quickly see which of the bodies of water is the most affected by acid rain pollution. Using *topological modeling,* you could quickly see how many more bodies of water would be affected if pollution levels were to increase.

Unquestionably, geographic information systems are a beneficial technology—and they've even saved lives. In New Zealand, public health officials are using a GIS to reduce the risks of meningitis, a potentially fatal disease. When an outbreak occurs, it's plotted on the system's maps, which are accessible to community health practitioners. Armed with an early warning that there's an outbreak in their area, practitioners are on the lookout for the early warning signs of a meningitis infection. The earlier meningitis is diagnoses, the greater the patient's chance of survival—and thanks to the GIS, meningitis outbreak notifications increased by 40 percent after the system was installed.

Police investigators are using GIS systems to track and solve crimes. In Brooklyn, New York, a series of slashing stumped detectives until they plotted the crimes on a GIS, which also contained information about areas where gang members gather. When the system was asked to compare the slashings with gang areas, there was a near-perfect match. It turns out that one of the area's gangs was initiating new members by asking them to slash passers-by, and arrests followed.

Among the most enthusiastic GIS adopters are city and county governments, which are using GIS systems for a variety of applications, including emergency response management, land use planning, and environmental impact assessment. A fully developed city or county GIS may contain dozens of layers of information, including election wards, bird habitats, sewer lines, drug arrests, septic systems, traffic accidents, and school districts. The information is useful to planners, and it can help local governments beat back the tide of urban sprawl, as planners in a Massachusetts town discovered. A GIS-developed map clearly showed how a proposed housing development would adversely affect groundwater quality, wetland areas, wildlife habitats, and historic structures, and helped persuade the town council to veto the plan.

Increasingly, local governments are making GIS information available to the public, generally by means of printed maps that are specially prepared on request. But there's a new trend afoot: Putting the data on the Internet. In Dakota County, Minnesota, law enforcement agents and judges were shocked to learn that anyone—including convicted criminals accessing the Internet from jail—could locate their homes and families by searching the county's online GIS. County officials defended the system by pointing out that it duplicates information that anyone could access by walking into the county courthouse.

But there's a big difference between county courthouse records and Internet-accessible data. To get the information at the courthouse, you have to travel there, go in the door, ask for the documents, and—in most cities or counties—you have to sign a form. What's more, you'll be in for some tedious research with unwieldy, paper-based documents. You wouldn't be likely to do such a thing on a spur-of-the-moment impulse. On the Internet, you can access the data quickly and anonymously—and that's why it's a different matter entirely. After a protest, Dakota County officials removed information about law enforcement personnel from the GIS, but many other local governments are still making this information available online.

Some state governments try to protect police officers and judges by prohibiting the publication of their home addresses and telephone numbers on the Internet—which is why you won't find such information on any Internet-accessible GIS in the state of California. But California's laws apply only to governmental bodies, not to the private sector. With no-holds-barred private firms jumping into the growing market for Internet-accessible geographic data, the fight to conceal the addresses of law enforcement officials seems destined to fail.

Another special feature of many spreadsheet packages is data management. The data management capabilities of spreadsheets include creating a simple database, sorting records, and searching the database for a particular item. Each row of the spreadsheet becomes a record in the database, and each cell in the row is a field of the record. Database management is covered in detail in module 4D.

SPREADSHEET RISKS

Although spreadsheets are an indispensable tool, they are also risky to use if you don't check your work.

Many problems arise from the all-too-common practice of burying important assumptions inside cells, where formulas containing mistakes are hidden from view. According to some studies, as many as one-third of the spreadsheets in use by a typical company contain one or more errors. Sometimes the consequences of these errors are serious. In Texas, for example, several oil company executives were fired after a multimillion dollar loss was traced to a faulty spreadsheet.

A lot can go wrong with a poorly-designed spreadsheet. If the person who created the spreadsheet wants a key value input as a percentage, for example, but doesn't document this and doesn't choose the percentage format for the input cell, subsequent users could easily type a value that is *way* off. For example, suppose you think you're supposed to type 7.5 for 7.5 percent. In an unformatted cell, you must first convert this percentage to a decimal value (0.075). If you type 7.5, the formula will assume that you mean 750 percent!

A third problem is that cells containing formulas look like any other cell; that is, they show a value. Someone might type a value into a cell containing a formula in an effort to change a value. Instead, the person erases a key formula and ruins the entire spreadsheet!

How can you avoid spreadsheet errors? Try these strategies:

- Audit your spreadsheet by testing all the formulas with a hand calculator.

- Make use of the auditing tools provided with your spreadsheet program. For example, Microsoft Excel includes an auditing toolbar. Among the available commands is Trace Precedents, which enables you to see which cells feed values into a formula.

- Clearly separate data input areas from data output areas.

- Document your spreadsheet well. Explain its purpose and indicate what type of data is needed in each data input cell. Even if you will be the only person using this worksheet, documenting is still worthwhile. Months from now, even you will forget your assumptions!

- Don't bury key values or assumptions in formulas. Put them in input cells so that they're clear to everyone (and available for alteration if circumstances change).

- For each important formula, check at least one of the calculations on a handheld calculator. If there's a discrepancy, something is wrong.

- Use cell protection for cells containing formulas. Cell protection prevents users from altering the cell's contents.

- Consider using input validation techniques to make sure users type values that lie within an appropriate range. You can use the spreadsheet's logical functions for this purpose.

TAKEAWAY POINTS

- Spreadsheet programs are commonly used for "what-if" scenarios, for working with lengthy tables of numbers, for generating charts from tables of numbers and, less frequently, for storing and analyzing data.

- In addition to the usual features of an application's window, a spreadsheet program such as Microsoft Excel includes a worksheet (a matrix of rows and columns), a cell pointer, an active cell, a formula bar, worksheet tabs, and a horizontal scroll bar.

- To build a worksheet, you will use all or most of these skills: selecting data, entering data, editing data, formatting data, entering formulas, and editing the worksheet structure.

- A range is a rectangular portion of the spreadsheet, demarcated by the upper right and lower left corners. To indicate a range in a formula, type a cell reference to the upper right and lower left corners, separated by a colon (A1:B9).

- In a cell, you can enter values, including integers, decimal numbers, fractions, percentages, or numbers typed in scientific notation (such as $5.09E+16$). You can also enter labels, dates (such as 9/26/02 or 26-Sep-02), and times (such as 10:15PM or 22:15).

- In Microsoft Excel, operators within formulas are evaluated in the following order: negation, percents, exponentiation, multiplication or division, and addition or subtraction. When operators are equal in precedence, evaluation proceeds from left to right. If you do not understand the order of evaluation, you could accidentally write a formula that produces the wrong answer.

- Replication can successfully copy formulas in a table so that they work in a new location. This works because, in a relative cell reference, what is actually stored is the location of a cell relative to the current cell, rather than an absolute cell reference.

- Use an absolute cell reference when you want copied formulas to refer to one cell in a fixed location.

- To build an effective worksheet and avoid common errors, define the worksheet's purpose, plan how the outlook should look, define the user's input, define the calculations, build formulas using cell references rather than values, and protect formulas from accidental erasure.

- You can create the following types of charts by selecting data and using the program's built-in charting wizard: column charts (useful for showing changes over time), bar charts (useful for comparing items), line charts (useful for showing continuous trends over time), and pie charts (useful for showing how the parts contribute to the whole).

- Spreadsheets can cause errors if they are poorly documented so that users enter data in the wrong format. They can also produce errors if users inadvertently type a value in a cell containing an unprotected formula.

MODULE REVIEW

KEY TERMS AND CONCEPTS

absolute cell reference	formula	print area
active cell	formula bar	range
arithmetic operators	horizontal scroll bar	relative cell references
bar chart	increment	replication
built-in functions	integer	rows
cancel button	keyword	scaling
cell	labels	series
cell address	legend	simulations
cell pointer	line chart	spreadsheet
cell reference	macros	syntax
chart type	multiple series	time series
column chart	name box	values
columns	numeric formats	what-if scenario
decrement	order of evaluation	workbook
enter button	pie chart	worksheet
fill	precedence	worksheet tab
fill handle		

TRUE/FALSE

Indicate whether the following statements are true or false.

1. Spreadsheets are helpful for creating "what-if" scenarios.
2. To generate charts from spreadsheet data, you typically use a presentation graphics program.
3. The active cell is the one where text or figures will appear when you start typing.
4. Numeric formats allow you to control how a number appears.
5. Cell referencing is not important in creating formulas.
6. Built-in functions allow you to quickly and easily create complex formulas.
7. A legend is for identifying the various slices of a complex pie chart.
8. A bar chart is a great way to show trends over time.
9. A macro is a set of operations that accomplishes a specific task.
10. The data management features of a spreadsheet allow you to create complex database applications.

MATCHING

Match each key term from the left column to the most accurate definition in the right column.

_____ 1. spreadsheet
_____ 2. syntax
_____ 3. macro
_____ 4. value
_____ 5. label
_____ 6. cell
_____ 7. worksheet
_____ 8. formula
_____ 9. active cell
_____ 10. ranges

a. an intersection of rows and columns in a worksheet
b. The area where text or figures will appear when you start typing
c. an on-screen grid of rows and columns
d. these are defined by stating the name of the cell in the upper left corner and the lower right corner, separated by a colon
e. an equation that calculates a new value (and shows it on-screen) based on existing values
f. a program designed to process information in the form of tables
g. a number in a spreadsheet
h. the requirements specifying how you must type functions
i. a set of operations that accomplishes a specific task
j. text entry in a spreadsheet

MULTIPLE CHOICE

Circle the letter of the correct choice for each of the following.

1. What is the secret to a spreadsheet's usefulness?
   a. It allows you to enter formulas and display their results.
   b. It allows you to enter large tables of numbers.
   c. You can save information between sessions.
   d. You can print results in several different formats.
2. Every cell in a spreadsheet has a unique identifier called what?
   a. a tag
   b. a cell name
   c. a cell address
   d. a location
3. When you enter a formula in a cell, what do you see displayed in the formula bar?
   a. the results of the formula
   b. the formula
   c. a label
   d. a value
4. How does the spreadsheet program know you are entering a formula in a cell?
   a. You choose a special formula option from a menu.
   b. You enter your information using the formula bar.
   c. It just knows without the need to do anything special.
   d. You start the formula with an equals (=) sign.

5. The requirement that functions be entered in a specific way is known as what?
   a. syntax
   b. built-in
   c. keyword
   d. integrity

6. When creating a spreadsheet, what is it helpful to know first?
   a. how your charts will look
   b. the purpose of the spreadsheet
   c. the formulas you will use
   d. the input available

7. Which type of chart is designed for displaying a time series?
   a. line
   b. bar
   c. pie
   d. graphical

8. Which symbol do you use to indicate an absolute column or row reference?
   a. @
   b. =
   c. +
   d. $

9. What is the key problem when it comes to spreadsheet errors?
   a. typographical errors
   b. important assumptions buried in cell formulas
   c. wrong input data
   d. poorly-defined output needs

10. What is one way to check the formulas in your spreadsheet?
    a. Make sure your charts look right.
    b. Double-check your input values.
    c. Use the Function command.
    d. Use a handheld calculator.

FILL-IN

In the blank provided, write the correct answer for each of the following.

1. Using spreadsheets, computer users can create numerical _____ of anything that can be described with numbers.

2. The intersection of a row and column is known as a(n) _____ .

3. A number entered into a cell is also called a(n) _____ .

4. A(n) _____ is another name for text stored in a cell.

5. _____ specify how values will appear in a cell.

6. The _____ specifies how the spreadsheet program reads the formula.

7. _____ allows you to copy a formula to a range of cells.

8. Use a(n) _____ when you want the program to adjust cell references in copied formulas.

9. Use a(n) _____ when you want copied formulas to refer to one cell in a fixed location.

10. A(n) _____ chart shows fluctuations in on-going, continuous trends over time.

SHORT ANSWER

On a separate sheet of paper, answer the following questions.

1. Discuss the major features and benefits of spreadsheet programs.

2. What are the different types of information you can enter in a cell?

3. What is meant by cell referencing?

4. How does replication work?

5. How are functions valuable when used in formulas?

6. Distinguish between relative and absolute cell references.

7. What steps should you follow to create an error-free spreadsheet?

8. How does a pie chart differ from a bar chart? A line chart?

9. What is the purpose of developing macros?

10. Describe some of the risks associated with spreadsheets.

MODULE

4C

DESIGNING PRESENTATIONS

WHAT YOU WILL LEARN . . .

When you have finished reading this module, you will be able to:

1. Explain why you should use visual aids when you give an oral presentation.
2. Explain and discuss the difference between presentation graphics and analytical graphics.
3. List the various ways you can view your presentation in a presentation graphics program and discuss the uses of each view.
4. Identify the six basic skills you need to use a presentation graphics program.
5. List the three ways you can begin a PowerPoint presentation and discuss the strengths and weaknesses of each.
6. List the slide layouts from which you can choose when you compose slides, and discuss how each is used.
7. Describe the general procedure you follow to add a chart to a PowerPoint presentation.
8. Discuss the benefits of using conceptual illustrations in your presentation, and list the PowerPoint tools you can use to create such illustrations.
9. List and discuss your options for producing output media for your presentation.
10. Discuss ways to make your visuals more effective.

The evidence is overwhelming. If you want your audience to remember your presentation, be sure to use **visual aids,** such as overhead transparencies, 35mm slides, or computer-aided presentations. In one study, audience retention was a paltry 14 percent without visuals, but jumped to 38 percent when visuals were added. What accounts for the difference? Experts agree that visual aids engage the audience—and an engaged audience is better able to comprehend what you're saying.

Preparing visual aids for a presentation used to require time and money. Professional graphic artists needed a lot of lead time to prepare visuals for managers and executives. If you needed a change within 24 hours of the presentation, you were out of luck. Today, presentation graphics packages enable any computer user to prepare great-looking visual aids for any presentation. To convert the program output to 35mm slides, you need at least 24 hours of lead time. You can prepare overhead transparencies, however, by printing them on a laser or ink-jet printer, and you can make changes just minutes before your presentation, if necessary.

Presentation graphics programs are popular, and it's no surprise why. The few minutes you spend giving a presentation are crucial to shaping the audience's impression of you and your capabilities. You will be wise to learn the essential skills of presentation graphics software usage and put these skills to work every time you give a presentation.

INTRODUCING PRESENTATION GRAPHICS SOFTWARE

Presentation graphics software, like other top-selling productivity programs, uses a visual metaphor: here, a simulation of the media (such as a 35mm slide or transparency) that you'll use for your presentation. Each page of the presentation is called a **slide,** even if you plan to produce other kinds of output.

Presentation Graphics vs. Analytical Graphics

Today, presentation graphics packages enable any computer user to prepare visual aids for any presentation.

The term **presentation graphics** tells you a great deal about what these programs are designed to do—and what they are *not* designed to do. Presentation graphics are the opposite of **analytical graphics.** In analytical graphics, you portray *all* of the data so that you can see overall patterns. In presentation graphics, you remove all the unnecessary detail. You boil the presentation down to just those points that your audience needs to see.

Presentation graphics programs enable you to create simple, easily-read slides that you can share with an audience. Remember to keep it simple! Do not try to pack your entire talk into your slides.

The use of the term *presentation graphics* to describe this type of software does not imply that every slide must contain a picture. In fact, most presentations are made up of **text slides,** in which points are listed by means of a bulleted list. Rather, the use of this term is intended to highlight the most important principle of effective presentation graphics: keep it simple.

Exploring the Application Window

This module illustrates the use of presentation graphics software with examples drawn from Microsoft PowerPoint, the best-selling presentation graphics package.

Like other office applications, PowerPoint has the usual features you'd expect to see in the application window, including the title bar, menu bar, toolbars, scroll bars, and a status bar. But there are some important differences, too (see Figure 4C.1). For example, PowerPoint displays a Drawing toolbar by default. This toolbar contains useful tools for adding visual interest and illustrations to your slides.

When you start PowerPoint for the first time, you'll see a dialog box that enables you to choose which action you want to perform (for example, using the AutoContent wizard, developing a new presentation using a template, or creating a blank presentation). You can also open an existing presentation, if you wish (see Figure 4C.2). Click Cancel to close this dialog box.

Perhaps the most striking difference between a presentation graphics program and other applications lies in the variety of ways you can view your data. In Microsoft PowerPoint, you can choose among the following views:

- In the **Slide view,** you see your slides, one by one. You use this view to create and edit your slides.

- The **Outline view** shows an outline of your presentation's text. This view enables you to build your presentation quickly and in an organized manner. Choose this view when you need to improve your presentation's organization and logical structure.

- In PowerPoint's **Normal view,** you see the Outline view on the left, and the Slide view on the right (refer again to Figure 4C.1).

- The **Slide Sorter view** displays **thumbnails** (small graphical images) of each slide, enabling you to change their order. This view comes in handy when you want to rearrange the slides in your presentation.

- The **Notes Page view** enables you to add speaker notes to each slide. You can view and print the notes separately, if you wish.

- The **Slide Show view** enables you to view an on-screen slide show consisting of the slides you've created for your presentation. It's a great way to review your work. You can also use this view for automated presentations that you can give to small groups of two or three people.

- Like the master pages in a desktop publishing program, each presentation has a **master slide** that contains the basic slide layout. The **Master view** enables you to view and edit the master slide. Your changes will appear on all the slides in your presentation.

Figure 4C.3 walks you through the various slide views in Microsoft PowerPoint, the best-selling presentation graphics package.

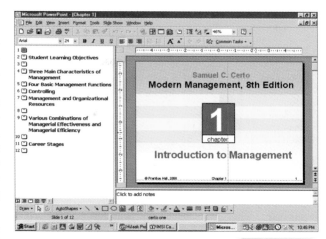

Figure 4C.1

Microsoft PowerPoint's Normal view displays your presentation's outline on the left and your slides on the right.

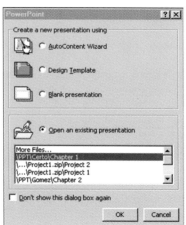

Figure 4C.2

When you start PowerPoint, you'll see this dialog box. You can use it to start a new presentation or load an existing one.

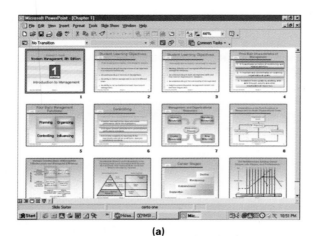

(a)

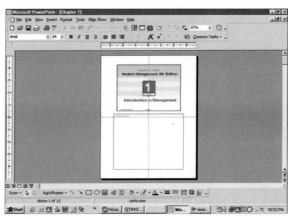

(b)

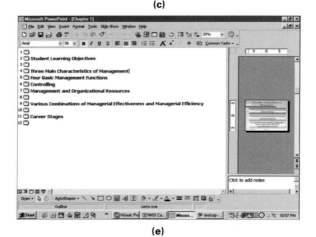

(c)

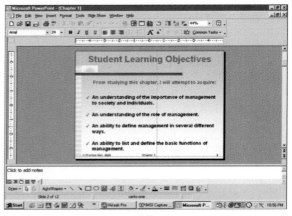

(d)

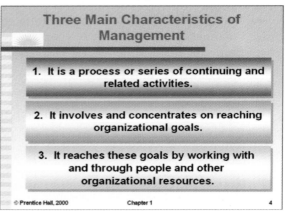

(e)

Three Main Characteristics of Management

1. It is a process or series of continuing and related activities.

2. It involves and concentrates on reaching organizational goals.

3. It reaches these goals by working with and through people and other organizational resources.

⊕ Prentice Hall, 2000   Chapter 1   4

(f)

Figure 4C.3

Slide views: (a) Slide Sorter, (b) Notes Page, (c) Master, (d) Slide, (e) Outline, (f) Slide Show, and (g) Normal.

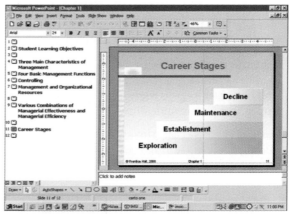

(g)

CREATING A PRESENTATION

To create a presentation with Microsoft PowerPoint, you will need to acquire the following skills:

Destinations

Would you like to inform rather than infuriate your audience? David Coder's *Presentation Graphics: The Good, the Bad, and the Ugly* provides an excellent series of tips for creative effective slides (**http://nucleus.immunol. washington.edu/ graphics/graph_1pg.htm**).

- **Choosing a template**   A **template** provides an attractive, ready-to-use design for your presentation that includes a theme, a balanced color scheme, appropriate fonts, and well-chosen font sizes.

- **Choosing the slide layout**   You can choose from a wide variety of **slide layouts** (called AutoLayouts in PowerPoint), which consist of prepared areas for data entry called **placeholders.** Examples of slide layouts include a title slide or a slide with a title and a bulleted list.

- **Working with placeholders**   You can quickly develop your presentation by clicking placeholder areas within the slide layouts. After you click the placeholder, PowerPoint will provide the tools you need to add the type of data that the placeholder requires.

- **Inserting charts, graphics, and drawings**   Text-only presentations quickly lose their audiences. You should enliven your presentation by adding graphics, such as **clip art** (prepared, ready-to-use images), pictures from graphics files, and conceptual illustrations that you can create using the program's drawing tools.

- **Viewing and organizing your presentation**   You can use the outline and slide sorter view to improve your presentation's organization.

- **Producing the output media**   You can print your slides on regular or transparency paper, or send them to a service bureau to be made into 35mm slides. You can also output your presentation as a Web page and make it available to Web users.

Choosing a Template

You can choose from the following ways to begin your PowerPoint presentation:

- **AutoContent Wizard**   This wizard enables you to choose from a variety of prepared presentations on a variety of themes, such as "Brainstorming Session," or "Project Post-Mortem." Be aware that many people use PowerPoint, so many people in your audience will know where your presentation came from.

- **Template**   Most presenters prefer to construct their own presentations using one of PowerPoint's built-in templates. Each template comes with its own distinctive color scheme, font choices, graphics, and overall layout. Again, since so many people use PowerPoint, it is likely that some people in your audience will have seen the template before, so your presentation may appear somewhat lacking in originality.

- **Blank presentation**   Building a presentation from a blank presentation is much more work than using a template, but this choice may be appropriate if you want a "no-frills" look. This method is also a good choice if you want to make sure your presentation appears as original as possible.

Figure 4C.4

Begin your presentation by choosing a design template.

To begin a new presentation with a template, click File on the menu bar, choose New, click the Design Templates tab, and choose a design template (see Figure 4C.4).

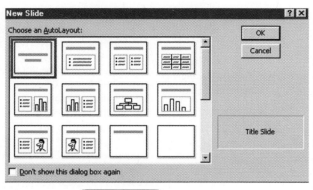

Figure 4C.5

In this dialog box, you choose a slide layout for the next slide you will create.

Choosing the Slide Layout

Once you've chosen a design template for your presentation, you'll see the New Slide dialog box (Figure 4C.5). This dialog box shows miniature versions of the slide layouts, called AutoLayouts, from which you can choose. To begin your presentation, choose Title Slide.

- **Bulleted list**   Use this AutoLayout to list items or points that you will discuss.

- **Two-column bulleted list**   Use this option to compare two things or two ideas.

- **Table**   This is a good choice when you want to summarize a small amount of numerical data.

- **Text and chart**   This design gives you a great way to show a simple chart with the points you want to make about the chart.

- **Organization chart**   This is just the ticket for describing the outcome of the next reorganization. If you choose this AutoLayout, you will be able to use special tools that make it easier to create the organization chart.

- **Chart**   You can generate a chart from numerical data you supply or import a spreadsheet chart.

- **Text and clip art**   Use this option to add some visual interest in the form of clip art, graphical images, and cartoons provided with the program.

- **Title only**   This slide contains nothing but a title text area, but you can add other content, if you wish. This is a good choice for a slide containing a conceptual illustration that you create with PowerPoint's drawing tools.

- **Blank**   This slide contains nothing at all. It's a good choice if you need an entire slide for a large picture or drawing.

- **Text and Media Clip**   This is a good choice only if you're giving an on-screen (computer) slide show. In the Media Clip area, you can add a sound or video.

- **Object and Text**   You can also include an object in your presentation. An object is data produced by a program other than PowerPoint. Examples of objects include a Microsoft Excel chart, a Microsoft Word table, or a sound.

Using Placeholders

When you've chosen an AutoLayout that contains text areas, you'll see a message within the placeholder such as "Click to add title" or "Click to add text." Recall that a placeholder is an area within the slide layout that is designed to accept a certain type of data, such as text or a picture. Just click within the text placeholder to add text. Don't worry about deleting the "Click to add text" message; it automatically disappears when you start typing. These text areas are preformatted with fonts, alignment, and font size choices that are appropriate to the design you're using.

If you make a spelling mistake, the misspelled word will have a wavy red line under it. Right-click the word to see a list of suggested corrections. To

Techtalk

Web ring
A Web ring (also spelled Webring) is a series of sites that have been grouped together so that you can navigate from one to the next easily. If you're looking for original clip art for your next presentation, try the Original Graphics on the Net Web ring, located at **http://nav.webring. org/cgi-bin/navcgi?ring-abloom;list**). You'll find a list of dozens of sites offering free, original graphics.

insert symbols, click Insert on the menu bar, click Symbols, and choose a symbol from the Symbols dialog box.

Should you type more text than the placeholder can accommodate, click the placeholder border and drag one of the drag handles to enlarge the placeholder. If there isn't enough room, click the placeholder to select the entire area, click Format on the menu bar, click Font, and select a smaller font size. However, bear in mind that people in the back of an audience of 25 to 50 people may not be able to read fonts smaller than about 24 points.

Inserting Charts, Clip Art, and Drawings

If you have chosen an AutoLayout that includes an area for a chart, double-click the chart placeholder. You'll see a Datasheet window, which looks like a spreadsheet (see Module 4B), and a sample chart (see Figure 4C.6). You can change the values and labels in the datasheet window to suit the data you are presenting. If you would like to change the chart type, click Chart on the menu bar, and choose Chart Type.

If you have created a chart with Microsoft Excel, you can import it into your PowerPoint presentation. However, you should think twice before doing so. Chances are that your Excel chart is an analytical graphic, one that shows all the underlying data. In presentation graphics, you should omit all unnecessary detail. It's better to build a simple chart using PowerPoint's tools rather than import a complex Excel chart that may confuse your audience. The same goes for tables. Although you can import a Word table into your presentation, it's much better to use PowerPoint's table editor. It automatically encourages you to create a much simpler table (and one with much larger fonts) than the tables you create with Word.

If you have chosen an AutoLayout that includes a clip art placeholder, double-click the placeholder to view your clip art options in the Clip Art Gallery (see Figure 4C.7). You can choose from a variety of clip art categories. When you've selected the clip art image that you want to insert, click Insert.

Be aware that millions of people use PowerPoint and you will often see these very same images in other presentations. If you would like your presentation to look more original, consider using clip art drawn from another source. You can insert a picture from any graphics file that PowerPoint can read. To do so, click Insert on the menu bar, point to Picture, and choose From File.

Consider adding a conceptual illustration to your presentation. Professional presenters know that a picture is worth a thousand words. If you can think of a simple drawing that expresses a concept you are trying to explain, by all means try to create such a drawing. Even if you do not think your artistic talents are all that great, you can successfully use PowerPoint's drawing tools to create good-looking illustrations.

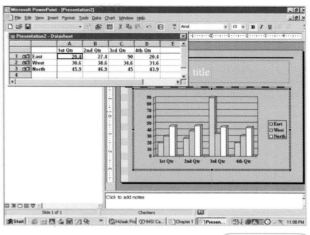

Figure  **4C.6**

To add a chart to your presentation, you can modify the sample chart that automatically appears when you click the chart placeholder.

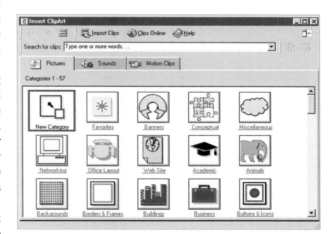

Figure  **4C.7**

You can choose clip art from the Clip Art Gallery, but PowerPoint has so many users that your slides may appear unoriginal.

Figure 4C.8

You can use PowerPoint's built-in AutoShapes to add visual interest to your slides.

To create a drawing, choose a slide layout with a blank area. You can use the following tools to build your drawing:

- **Drawing Toolbar** Click one of the icons on the drawing toolbar to enter lines, lines with arrows, boxes, circles and ovals, text boxes, decorative text (with WordArt), or clip art. For the drawing objects you enter, you can choose line and fill colors, line widths, arrow styles, shadowing, and three-dimensional effects.

- **Autoshapes** Click the AutoShapes button on the Drawing toolbar (or display the AutoShapes toolbar) to choose from a wide variety of prepared shapes, including banners, arrows, borders and frames, buttons and icons, conceptual diagrams, and much more (see Figure 4C.8). Once you've inserted an AutoShape, you can independently select the shape, size it, move it, copy it, change fill colors, and add text.

Viewing and Organizing Your Presentation

Once you've finished your presentation, you can use the automated slide show to preview your presentation's appearance on-screen. Should you need to revise the presentation's text, switch to the Outline view, which enables you to work with the overall flow of your presentation's text slides (see Figure 4C.9). Should you need to rearrange the order in which slides appear, switch to the Slide Sorter view, in which you can drag and drop slides to a new location (see Figure 4C.10).

Producing the Output Media

With most presentation graphics programs, you have the following output options:

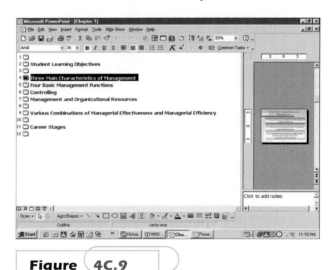

Figure 4C.9

Use the Outline view to reorganize your presentation's text.

- **On-screen show** With this option, you can turn a computer into a presentation medium. This isn't a good choice for an audience larger than two or three people unless the computer is equipped with an output projector.

- **Transparencies** You can print directly to transparency sheets, which are designed for use with an overhead projector. Be sure to get blank transparency sheets designed for your printer (laser or ink jet). Use transparencies with small- to medium-sized audiences (up to 30 to 50 people).

- **35mm slides** This is the best bet for large audiences, but you'll need lead time—perhaps as much as a week—as well as a room you can darken and a good slide projector.

- **Audience handouts** Most programs can print audience handouts, which contain reduced-size printouts of your slides along with room for notes.

- **Speaker notes** If you added speaker notes to your slides, you can print these, too.

Additional Features for On-Screen Presentations

If you're planning to create a computer-based slide show, you can use a variety of tricks, including the following:

- **Transition effect** This includes fades, dissolves, and cut-throughs. Transition effects come into play when you show the next slide.

- **Expansion** Suppose you present a bulleted list that shows the next three topics you are going to discuss. The expansion tool automatically creates and inserts three new slides, with each slide's title corresponding to the list items.

Figure 4C.10

Use the Slide Sorter view to change the order in which slides appear within the presentation.

- **Build** A **build** is a type of bulleted list in which the bulleted items appear one by one. Animation effects enable the new items to slide in from the side.

- **Multimedia** With the latest programs, you can include videos and animations on your slides, such as an airplane that takes off and flies right off the slide.

- **Automatic presentation** You can create automated presentations that run by themselves. This is a great way to get your message out in a trade booth; you're free to talk to customers while others are watching the show. You'll need to consider slide timing and decide whether you want viewers to be able to choose navigation options. For continuous viewing, the presentation can loop endlessly. In the latest versions of popular programs, you can even include voice recordings so that it seems as if you're really giving the presentation. You can add music, too.

Using an overhead projector to display transparencies is one of several presentation options.

If you're thinking about doing a computer-based presentation, be aware that it is risky. If you try to use somebody else's computer, you may find that it doesn't have the right version of the software installed. (You can save most presentations as a **runtime** version that enables you to run the presentation even if the software isn't installed, but you may not have all the control features you need.) Remember, you might be nervous before your presentation. Will you have a mental lapse and have trouble finding your file? For beginning presenters, it's best to use overhead transparencies or slides.

The Internet Connection

The latest presentation graphics programs can generate output to HTML and Internet graphics formats. They can even generate an entire Web presentation, including a title page, a table of contents, and a Web version of your slide show.

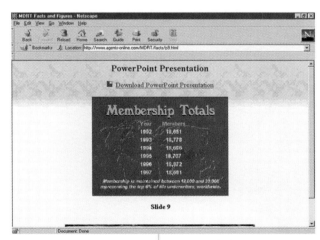

A PowerPoint presentation on the Web.

SPOTLIGHT

TOOLS FOR ROAD WARRIORS

▶ Everyone knows the image: a tired salesperson returns to a lonely motel room at the end of the day, only to be faced with calls to the office, clients, and home. Business is tough, and this front-line soldier has definitely been through a ferocious battle. This is the road warrior, battling to make sure that the company is first in the minds of clients across the land.

Technology won't provide a second wind or remove the need to be on the road in the first place, but it is quickly becoming an indispensable tool in making sure the road warrior is as efficient as possible. Beginning in the early 1980s, technology allowed road warriors to take more and more of their office with them. Before that time, a mobile office often consisted of a briefcase in the front seat of the car and a literature bin in the trunk. With the advent of mobile electronics, however, the briefcase has often been relegated to the back seat as other devices become the first choice for communications and productivity.

Over the years, four devices have become the workhorses of mobiles offices: the laptop computer, a cellular phone, a pager, and a personal digital assistant (PDA). Each device has undergone extensive and radical changes in the past decade, and to a degree each is becoming interchangeable.

The laptop computer is the focal point of any mobile office. These devices, once the size and weight

of a brick-lined suitcase, have become smaller and lighter. These computers are powerful as well, often outstripping the capabilities of their desktop relatives. Large, bright screens and powerful processors run the latest software and accessories, including high-powered multimedia presentation software. When the mobile professional is back in the home office, the computer can be quickly docked to a stationary system and connected to the company network.

In the past, those on the road relied on the telephone as their main communications medium, but the calling had to be one way. The mobile professional would need to stop at a pay phone or duck into a motel room and place their calls. Those days ended with the introduction of car phones and, later, cellular phone service, which allowed people to be in touch at any time and from any place.

These days, it's important to remain connected to the home office and the Internet while on the road. Traditional connection methods through modems are always available, but you have more cutting-edge solutions, as well. You can now plug your cellular phone into your laptop and immediately be connected, without any unsightly phone cord, even while driving down the road. Many companies offer devices that integrate a large amount of wireless communications capability in the once-isolated laptop.

Pagers, perhaps the oldest technological tool of today's road warrior, are also progressing towards tomorrow. Today's pagers not only let you know when you have a message, but also access and display your email and allow you to respond. Nationwide coverage means your pager can keep you in touch wherever you go. Many people use pagers to help screen calls and keep in touch with support personnel at the office, without using the high-cost airtime of some cellular phone systems.

The newest tool for road warriors is the personal digital assistant. These devices are nothing more than small computers, some of which can fit in your jacket pocket. They are great for keeping track of your appointment schedule, maintaining a database of contacts, and taking notes in a meeting. You can easily connect them to a laptop to upload or download necessary information in a flash.

In the future, more connections will be available on airplanes, in airports, in motels, and in cars for digital computing and communicating devices. As more and more of the workplace becomes mobile, new solutions for professionals will continue to evolve.

The laptop computer is the focal point of any mobile office.

The PowerPoint Backlash:
Please Leave Your Slides at the Door

You'll be wise to create visual aids for your next speech—but you'll also be wise to realize that there's a growing tide of resentment towards presentation graphics software in general (and PowerPoint in particular). How much resentment? Try this: U.S. General Hugh Shelton won't allow junior officers to use PowerPoint in their presentations. Increasing numbers of conference facilitators are warning participants that they'll have to leave their PowerPoint slides at the door, like guns outside a saloon in the Old West. If visual aids are such a plus for a presentation, why is there a backlash against PowerPoint?

Partly, the program is a victim of its own success. PowerPoint overwhelmingly dominates the presentation graphics software market—which means that, in a conference where you'll listen to ten speakers, you'll see ten sets of PowerPoint slides, each with the same, corny, click-art graphics. Worse, about one in eight speakers make use of PowerPoint's canned, ready-to-modify presentations, which are designed for a variety of purposes (such as conveying bad news). If you've got three speakers conveying bad news, you might wind up with three speeches with nearly-identical slides—and that's not likely to please an audience. Irritatingly, speakers overuse PowerPoint's animation tricks, such as letters dropping into place and slides fading into one another. The first time you see them, they look cool—but they become *very* annoying when you see them over and over.

Another reason for the backlash against PowerPoint is the poor quality of many of the visuals produced by untrained presenters. In the old days, only well-heeled managers and executives could afford to have slides produced by pricey graphics specialists. These slides generally looked great, assuming the graphics specialists knew what they were doing.

Today, with copies of PowerPoint installed on nearly everyone's computer, amateurs are getting into the act—and with predictable results, say PowerPoint's critics. One example: about one in eight adults is color-blind to some degree—which means you should avoid contrasting information using red vs. green, a color difference that some people in your audience may not be able to see.

Out-of-control color combinations are just the beginning. Too many presenters have absolutely no idea which type of chart to use to convey a certain type of information. As a result, they confuse their audiences—and the results can be catastrophic. After reviewing the slides prepared by Morton Thiokol engineers in their effort to delay the space shuttle *Challenger*'s fatal launch, graphics expert Edward R. Tufte concluded that the slides themselves may be partly responsible for the astronauts' deaths: The poorly-prepared charts obscured vital data that might have persuaded management to abort the launch.

Other PowerPoint critics warn darkly that the software itself might be responsible for the rash of bad presentations. Creating a presentation with PowerPoint is more like filling out a form than creating something unique—and what you'll create, most of the time, will be bulleted list charts. But that's only one way of organizing information, and in many cases, it's not the best. Can you imagine Lincoln delivering the Gettysburg Address with a series of bulleted list charts?

Despite all the criticism, PowerPoint is still a useful tool for presenters who aspire only to convey information clearly—a goal that's somewhat short of giving a Gettysburg Address-quality speech. And if you're afraid of boring your audiences, just remember this: With so many PowerPoint users around who can't keep their mouse off the animation and click-art menus, the key to originality lies in keeping it simple.

USING VISUAL AIDS EFFECTIVELY

Using visual aids won't transform a terrible speech into a brilliant one, so you'll be wise to take a public speaking course or read a book on presentation skills. Remember, too, that poorly-prepared visual aids can hurt even a good presentation. Be sure to follow these suggestions:

- **One concept per slide**   Don't try to pack all your points into a single slide. Use many slides and express one concept for each.

- **Keep your language simple**   In text slides, use plain, everyday language and avoid jargon.

Destinations

The Art of Communicating Effectively (**http://www. presentingsolutions.com /effectivepresentations. html**) offers tips for all aspects of a successful presentation. Take a look before your next speech!

- **Don't tell everything** In text slides, use no more than six or seven words per bulleted item. Suggest your point, but don't explain it all. Otherwise, you'll have nothing to say.

- **Hide unnecessary detail** Don't hit your audience with overly-complex graphics or tables of data.

- **Use a variety of slide formats** Don't use a long series of slides made up of only bulleted lists. Add visual interest with conceptual illustrations.

- **Make sure your slides are legible** The templates you'll use have nice, big fonts, so this probably won't be a problem unless you import charts or tables. Don't use font sizes smaller than 24 points.

TAKEAWAY POINTS

- Visual aids enhance your audience's interest in your presentation and increase their ability to comprehend and retain what you're saying.
- Analytical graphics render all of the underlying data visually so that an expert analyst can discern the underlying patterns. Presentation graphics omit unnecessary detail and show only the patterns that the audience needs to see.
- You can view your presentation in Slide view (useful for creating and editing slides), Outline view (useful for improving the organization of your presentation's text), Slide Sorter view (useful for changing the order in which slides appear), Notes Page view (useful for creating speaker notes), and Master view (useful for making changes to the underlying template).
- To use a presentation graphics program successfully, you need to know how to choose a template; choose a slide layout; work with the various types of placeholders; insert charts, graphics, and drawings; view and organize your presentation; and produce the output media.
- You can begin a PowerPoint presentation using AutoContent (presentations containing sample text as well as an overall design), a template (a well-designed slide background), or a blank presentation. Starting with AutoContent is the least work, but your presentation will lack in originality. Using a blank presentation is the most work, but ensures originality. Starting with a template provides a good balance between the two extremes.
- When you create a new slide, you can choose from bulleted lists (useful for listing items or points), two-column bulleted lists (useful for comparing two things or two ideas), a table (useful for summarizing a small amount of numerical data), text and charts (useful for showing a chart and listing points about it), an organizational chart (useful for discussing changes to an organization), chart (useful for creating simple presentation charts), text and clip art (useful for adding visual interest to text slides), title only (useful for creating conceptual illustrations), blank (useful for large drawings or pictures), text and media clips (useful for on-screen presentations that incorporate sound or video), or object and text (useful for importing content from Word or Excel).
- To add a chart to a PowerPoint presentation, click the chart placeholder and make changes to the sample chart.
- Conceptual illustrations help an audience grasp complex subjects quickly. To create conceptual illustrations, you can use PowerPoint's Drawing toolbar and AutoShapes.
- To produce output, you can choose an on-screen slide show (useful for small audiences only, unless you have output to a projector), transparencies (useful for audiences of up to 50 people), 35mm slides (useful for larger audiences), and Web output (useful for Web-based presentations).
- A computer-based slide show enables you to use a variety of eye-catching effects, but it raises the risk that something will go wrong.
- To make your visuals effective, develop one slide per concept, keep your language simple, don't tell everything on the slides, hide unnecessary detail, use a variety of slide formats, and make sure your slides are legible.

MODULE REVIEW

KEY TERMS AND CONCEPTS

analytical graphics	Outline view	Slide Show view
build	placeholders	Slide Sorter view
clip art	presentation graphics	Slide view
Master view	presentation graphics software	templates
master slide	runtime	text slides
Normal view	slide	thumbnails
Notes Page view	slide layouts	visual aids

TRUE/FALSE

Indicate whether the following statements are true or false.

1. Most presentations are made up of graphical slides rather than text-based slides.

2. Slide Show view displays thumbnails of each slide, enabling you to change their sequence.

3. It's better to use a variety of slide formats rather than a long series of slides consisting of only bulleted lists.

4. A template provides an attractive, easy-to-use design for your presentation.

5. An on-screen show is a good choice for an audience of 10 or more.

6. Most presentations will run on any computer, so a rehearsal before your actual presentation is seldom necessary.

7. Use a two-column bulleted list to compare two things or two ideas.

8. To make your presentation look more original, consider using clip art from other sources.

9. The more concepts you can pack into a slide, the more impressive and effective the presentation.

10. A simple presentation can often be the most effective.

MATCHING

Match each key term from the left column to the most accurate definition in the right column.

_____ 1. text slides
_____ 2. Slide view
_____ 3. Notes Page view
_____ 4. transition effect
_____ 5. build
_____ 6. presentation graphics software
_____ 7. Master view
_____ 8. blank
_____ 9. AutoShapes
_____ 10. audience handouts

a. a type of bulleted list in which the bullet items appear one by one
b. enables you to create simple, easily-read slides
c. contains reduced-size printouts of your slides along with room for notes
d. enables you to add speaker notes
e. describes a slide that's a good choice for adding a large picture or drawing
f. includes fades, dissolves, and cut-throughs
g. enables you to see your slides one by one
h. describes a presentation where points are listed by means of a bulleted list
i. a button on the Drawing toolbar
j. enables you to view and edit the master slide

MULTIPLE CHOICE

Circle the letter of the correct choice for each of the following.

1. A presentation package cannot produce which of the following as output?
   a. slides
   b. speaker notes
   c. faxes
   d. audience handouts

2. Which of the following helps your audience remember your presentation?
   a. AutoContent wizard
   b. analytical graphics
   c. visual aids
   d. placeholders

3. A presentation template typically contains which of the following?
   a. layout, font choices, and color schemes
   b. color schemes, text items, sounds
   c. animations, font choices, and layout
   d. video clips, sounds, and clip art

4. Which of the following is not a view available in Microsoft PowerPoint?
   a. slide view
   b. page layout view
   c. outline view
   d. notes view

5. What is a thumbnail?
   a. a small graphical representation of a slide
   b. an on-screen icon for moving to the next slide
   c. a printout of a slide
   d. a way of condensing speaker notes

6. When should you use a table to present information in a slide?
   a. to present a large amount of numerical data
   b. to show comparisons between two sets of data
   c. to summarize a small amount of numerical data
   d. to combine text and graphics in a seamless presentation

7. A type of bulleted list in which each bullet appears one-by-one is called what?
   a. expansion
   b. growth
   c. limited display
   d. build

8. To allow for use with the Internet, some presentation software will do what?
   a. generate HTML files
   b. use Internet graphic formats
   c. create an entire Web presentation
   d. all of the above

9. What should you do if you are going to use someone else's computer for your presentation?
   a. make sure the same version of software you use is available

   b. make sure the hardware you need is available
   c. do a practice run on the hardware before your presentation
   d. none of the above

10. Which of the following is a good rule of thumb for creating slides?
    a. Use many slides with verbose explanations on each slide.
    b. Use only a few slides with lots of information on each slide.
    c. Use many slides with only a single concept per slide.
    d. Use no more than ten slides in an entire presentation.

FILL-IN

In the blank provided, write the correct answer for each of the following.

1. _____ significantly increase an audience's retention level.

2. _____ graphics portray all of the data so you can see overall patterns.

3. _____ are clear sheets of plastic designed for use with an overhead projector.

4. _____ slides can be effective in a presentation, but often take several days or a week to prepare.

5. To see the Outline view on the left and the Slide view on the right, select _____ view.

6. In Microsoft PowerPoint, _____ view allows you to use thumbnails to arrange the order of your slides.

7. The _____ enables you to choose from a variety of prepared presentations on a variety of themes.

8. Graphical images and cartoons provided with a program are called _____ .

9. A(n) _____ is an area within the slide layout that's designed to accept a certain type of data.

10. You can save most presentations as a(n) _____ version so you can run the presentation even if the software isn't installed.

SHORT ANSWER

On a separate sheet of paper, answer the following questions.

1. What are the different types of output you can create with a typical presentation program?

2. What are the benefits of using presentation templates?

3. What are the common ways you can view your presentation while you are developing it?

4. What options are available for presenting information in a typical presentation program?

5. What criteria would you use to determine whether you should present information in a table or a chart?

6. What different multimedia effects can you include in a computer-based presentation?

7. How is expansion used in developing a presentation?

8. What are the pros and cons of doing a computer-based presentation?

9. How can presentations be targeted for the Internet?

10. What are the points to remember for the effective use of visual aids in a presentation?

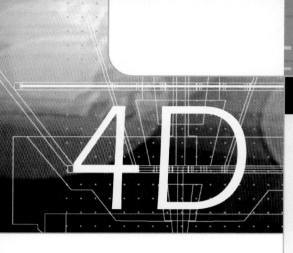

BUILDING DATABASES

OUTLINE

WHAT YOU WILL LEARN . . .

When you have finished reading this module, you will be able to:

1. Recognize potential uses of a database program.

2. Describe the basic components of a database.

3. Describe the five capabilities of a good database management system.

4. Distinguish between flat file and relational database management programs and explain the advantages and disadvantages of each.

5. List the major database objects that can be created with Microsoft Access and briefly discuss their uses.

6. List and briefly discuss the steps involved in designing a database.

7. Explain the concept of data types and give examples of the most commonly-used types.

8. Briefly describe the process used to create tables, forms, queries, and reports using Microsoft Access wizards.

9. Explain what database servers do and how Access can work with a database server.

Information isn't useful if you're buried in it. For computers to deliver on the promise to help us cope with information more efficiently, they must cut information down to a manageable size. And that's precisely what database programs are designed to do. **Database programs** store information so that you can quickly locate, organize, and display (or print) information you need while keeping unwanted information out of your way.

Because database programs are so valuable, they're found on all types of computers, large and small. PC users set up personal databases to track collections, research notes, and more. In large corporations, a trend has emerged toward ever-larger databases called **data warehouses,** which are capable of storing all the information that a corporation possesses. The payoff could be huge. Lucent Technologies in Murray Hill, New Jersey, for example, is reported to have saved $10 million the first day a new data warehouse went into operation—the software found $10 million worth of transactions that had been shipped without follow-up billing. The company previously used smaller, separate databases for billing and shipping, and nobody ever discovered the foul-up.

Understanding database concepts is a prerequisite for membership in an information society. No matter what line of work you pursue, you'll wind up working with databases sooner or later. Internet search services, discussed in Module 7A, enable you to search the entire World Wide Web as if it were one enormous database! After you grasp the essential database concepts, you may see ways to put database software to work for you, helping you to become more effective. As you'll learn in this module, you can easily create personal databases with tools such as Microsoft Access, which is part of the Microsoft Office suite of software applications. This chapter introduces Access after discussing the essential database concepts.

DATABASE CONCEPTS: THE ESSENTIALS

A **database** is any collection of information data stored in an organized way. Databases existed before computers. The card catalogs that you still see in some libraries, for example, provide an excellent example. Let's see what's in a database, and then look at the ideal database systems.

Records and Fields

A database can consist of one or more files. In a library, for example, you will find a subject catalog and also an author-title catalog. Similarly, some databases are stored in one large file or many smaller ones. In a computer database, the files we're talking about are computer files; specifically, files created by database software.

A database file is made up of **records.** A database record is a unit of information about something. In a library card catalog, each card provides a record of information about a single book.

Within a record, you generally find information organized into distinct **fields.** A field is a separate area designed to store a certain type of data. For example, on a library's catalog cards, you find fields for the book's author, title, publisher, date of publication, and so on. Within each field, only a certain type of information is permitted (called the **data type**). For example, in the date of publication field, you need to enter a date. Figure 4D.1 summarizes the structure of a database (files, records, and fields).

So what's so special about computer databases? We've been talking about noncomputer databases so far, but the computerized version isn't all that different. What makes them stand head-and-shoulders above their paper

Figure **4D.1**

A database consists of one or more files. A file is made up of records, and within a record, you find information organized into distinct fields.

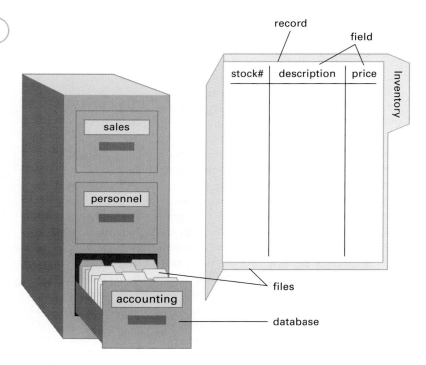

predecessors is the speed with which they can find needed information, group and organize this information for rapid comprehension, and output this information in a readable form.

The Ideal Database System

The ideal database provides rapid access to the data you need. A good database system also preserves data integrity, promotes data independence, avoids data redundancy, ensures data security, and provides procedures for data maintenance.

Data Integrity

The term **data integrity** refers to the validity of the data contained in a database. Data integrity can be reduced in many ways, including input typing errors, hardware malfunctions, and data transmission errors. To avoid data integrity errors, database programs should use **data validation** procedures, which define acceptable input ranges for each field in the record. If the user tries to input data that is out of this range, an error message is displayed.

Data Independence

The term **data independence** refers to the storage of data in such a way that it is not locked into its use by a particular application. To ensure data independence, it's important to avoid software that uses proprietary file storage techniques. Otherwise if the database software vendor goes out of business or refuses to support new types of computers, your software will be unsupported.

Avoidance of Data Redundancy

Data should be entered once. **Data redundancy** (repetition of data) is a characteristic of poorly-designed systems. For example, in many companies, customer names and addresses may appear in two different, unrelated databases. This not only doubles the amount of work needed to update the customer's records should the customer move, but also increases the chance of an error. Will the data be typed the same way twice?

Data Security

The data stored in a database shouldn't be accessible to people who might misuse it, particularly when the collected data is sensitive. Sensitive data includes data about people, such as their health records, and data about an organization's finances. Equally important is the protection of data against losses due to equipment failure or power outages. Regular backup procedures are needed so that the data can be restored after an equipment failure.

Data Maintenance

Good database management involves having a system in place for data maintenance. This system includes procedures for adding records, updating records, and deleting records.

TYPES OF DATABASE PROGRAMS

Two types of application software have been developed to work with database files. File management programs can work with only one file at a time. Database management systems can work with several separate files at a time. This section describes both types of software.

File Management Programs

So far, this module has discussed file management programs. A **file management program** enables users to create customized databases, and to store and retrieve data from these databases. File management programs come in handy when an individual or small business needs to set up a computerized information storage and retrieval system. The owner of a baseball card store, for example, could create a database of available baseball cards for customer reference.

Because file management programs are less complex than database management systems, they are also less expensive and easier to use than database management systems. The ease of use comes at a price, though. File management programs create **flat files.** (You can also create a flat file database with Microsoft Excel.) Flat files can be accessed sequentially when most of the records need to be processed, accessed randomly to retrieve a specific record, or sorted (so that the records can be accessed sequentially in a different order). The information stored in a flat file cannot, however, be linked to data in other files.

Database Management Systems

A database management system (DBMS) can link data from several files. A DBMS is usually more expensive and more difficult to learn than a file management program. The most widely-used type of DBMS is called a relational database, but object-oriented databases may be the wave of the future.

In a **relational database,** data in several files is related through the use of a common key field. Each record in the file has the same key field but unique key field contents, enabling the field to be used to identify a record. The computer uses this key field as an index to locate records without having to read all the records in the files. (In computer science, the term *relational database* has a more restricted meaning, but this meaning isn't relevant to the way the term is understood in the general computer industry.)

A relational DBMS is best envisioned as a collection of two-dimensional tables. Each row in the table corresponds to a record, and each column

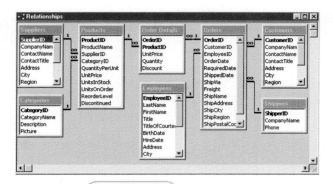

Figure **4D.2**

In this Microsoft Access database, eight tables are related by means of common fields.

corresponds to a field. A relational database structure can link a customer table and an accounts payable table, for example, through the use of a common field, such as a customer account number field. The user can then request a report consisting of fields from both the customer record and the accounts payable record (see Figure 4D.2).

What's the advantage of using a relational DBMS instead of a file management program? Before DBMS software came along, it wasn't unusual for companies to have dozens of database files, each with incompatible formats. This violated the rule of avoiding data redundancy (data typed in two or more places), and because it multiplies the possibilities for errors, it also violated the rule of data integrity. With relational database programs, it's possible to design the database using two or more tables so that data redundancy is eliminated. This process is called **normalization.**

Object-oriented databases are the newest type of database structure and are likely to gain in popularity. In an object-oriented database, the result of a retrieval operation is an object of some kind, such as a document. Within this object are miniprograms that enable the object to perform tasks, such as display a graphic. Object-oriented databases can incorporate sound, video, text, and graphics into a single database record. This type of database is well-suited for multimedia applications. A search of a health-related database, for example, could display a document that included pictures of healthful foods, videos of exercise techniques, and recorded lectures from health professionals.

Data Warehousing and Data Mining

Nuggets is a data mining system from Data Mining Technologies.

A data warehouse is not intended to replace database management systems developed to support the functional divisions of an organization, such as marketing or accounting. Instead, a data warehouse supplements them by bringing all the data together into a massive database (often containing one trillion bytes of data or more). Data warehouses collect data in a more primitive, less organized way to support management decision-making (see Module 8A). By means of a data exploration technique called **data mining,** managers can explore data in an attempt to discover previously-unknown patterns. Less ambitious data warehouse projects, intended to support one division of an organization rather than the entire enterprise, are called **data marts.**

INTRODUCING DATABASE SOFTWARE

Computerized database systems are a world apart from precomputer database techniques. Human effort is no longer required to sort and organize records, to comb through thousands or even millions of records to find and display information. All these tasks are accomplished with the computer's impressive capabilities to examine and organize huge amounts of digitized data at fast speeds.

Relational database programs were once the exclusive possessions of medium- to large-sized organizations, staffed with the trained experts needed to use and maintain the not-very-user-friendly software. All that's

SPOTLIGHT

MINING THE DATA

▶ Retail leader Wal-Mart is creating a data warehouse capable of storing the ultimate primitive data for a huge enterprise: precise records of what was sold, for what price, and when, in all its retail stores. Such a database would easily beat the record for the largest database in existence. This data warehouse is designed with no particular purpose in mind, but that's the point. Data warehouses are intended to support exploration and discovery of data patterns that aren't obvious even to experienced managers and executives. Less ambitious data warehouse projects, intended to support one division of an organization rather than the entire enterprise, are called data marts.

What's the point of keeping billions of records of primitive data? Wal-Mart will use its gigantic data warehouse to figure out what's selling and what's not. Other companies use data warehouses to eliminate fraud, the costs of which are inevitably passed on to consumers. WorldCom, the nation's fourth-largest long-distance telephone company, uses a gigantic data warehouse to track every call placed on the company's worldwide system. The database grows by one billion records per month, and the entire database can be searched in a matter of seconds by using WorldCom's ultra-sophisticated database software and hardware. Here's an example of the payoff: a gang who had stolen a customer's calling card number placed calls within moments of one another in several different cities. WorldCom's analysis software detected the fraudulent use and notified the FBI. The thieves were arrested just minutes after they hung up the phone.

changed with the arrival of programs such as Microsoft Access, currently the leading database program for PCs. Like its predecessors, Access uses relational principles. However, it's much easier to use. Access makes use of wizards to guide you through each step of the database design process, so that non-experts can easily create useful databases.

This section introduces you to Microsoft Access and provides an overview of the database creation process. There's much more to learn about Access than this module can discuss—the following merely scratches the surface of Access's capabilities—but you'll find enough information to grasp the essentials of working with a high-quality relational database program.

Database Objects

Microsoft Access provides tools for both designing and using the following database components, which are called **database objects:**

- **Tables** A **table** stores information in a list of records, each of which has one or more fields. On-screen, an Access table looks like an Excel spreadsheet (see Figure 4D.3). However, there is an important difference. Each field can contain only one type of data, called the **data type,** such as text, numbers, or dates. You can directly view the data in a table by using the **Datasheet view.**

- **Forms** A **form** provides a customized display window for one record at a time (see Figure 4D.4). When you create a form, you have much more control over how the various fields are arranged than you do with the Datasheet view. A major advantage of viewing data with forms lies in the form's ability to pull in data from two or more tables.

Destinations

Looking for Microsoft Access information? Check out the Microsoft Access Webring (**http://www.webring. org/cgi-bin/webring?** ring-accessing; list). The ring includes more than 200 Web sites featuring Access tutorials, tricks, sample databases, and add-on software.

Figure 4D.3

Viewed in Datasheet view, an Access table looks like an Excel database.

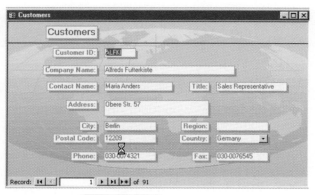

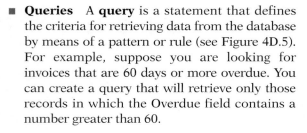

Figure 4D.4

Forms provide a convenient way to work with one record at a time.

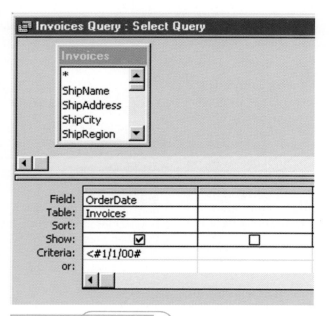

Figure 4D.5

Queries define the criteria for retrieving information from your database.

- **Queries** A **query** is a statement that defines the criteria for retrieving data from the database by means of a pattern or rule (see Figure 4D.5). For example, suppose you are looking for invoices that are 60 days or more overdue. You can create a query that will retrieve only those records in which the Overdue field contains a number greater than 60.

- **Reports** A **report** is a template that is used to print information from your database. Like a form, a report can pull in data from two or more tables (see Figure 4D.6).

Because an Access database may consist of many tables, forms, queries, and reports, Access provides a window that conveniently groups all the resources in a database (see Figure 4D.7).

DESIGNING A DATABASE

Before you create a database with a relational program such as Microsoft Access, you need to do some planning. It's best to do this planning with old-fashioned technology—paper and a nice, sharp pencil. You'll need to define the following:

- **Fields** What type of information do you need to store? It's best to store *all* the available information, just in case you might need it. If you're creating a database of rare books, you'll certainly want publication data (such as author, title, and date of publication), but you may also want the name of the dealer from whom you bought it.

- **Data Types** Once you've decided which fields you need to create, you will next decide which data type to use for each field. You can choose from text, numbers, dates, logical (yes/no) fields, and others. For more information on data types, see "Understanding Data Types," later in this section.

- **Tables** Now that you've developed a list of field names and data types, you need to decide how to organize them into tables. You'll have the right design when it is necessary to type information.

- **Common fields** In order for the program to relate the data in two or more tables, you need to define common fields. This is usually done by creating ID fields. For example, the rare books table can contain a field called Vendor_ID, which gives the ID number or name of the vendor who sold you the book. In the Vendor table, the same field (Vendor_ID) appears, and it is used to link specific Vendor_ID codes with the names, addresses, and telephone numbers of specific vendors.

- **Primary key** The **primary key** is the field that is used to uniquely identify each record in a table. In the rare books database, for example, the primary key could be the book's title.

- **Index fields** An **index field** is a field containing information that you frequently search for by means of queries. If you designate a field as an index field, searches are faster. The primary key is an index field by default.

When you've defined the fields, data types, tables, common fields, primary keys, and index fields for your database, you're ready to start creating it using Access.

Understanding Data Types

Microsoft Access enables you to work with the following data types:

- **AutoNumber**   Inserts a new, unique number as each new record is added.

- **Currency**   Stores numerical data in a format appropriate for currency.

- **Date/Time**   Stores dates and times from the year 100 through the year 9999, and does so in a way that the dates and times can be sorted, calculated, and compared.

- **Hyperlink**   Stores a Web hyperlink.

- **Lookup Wizard**   Creates a drop-down list box containing valid values from a lookup table.

- **Memo**   Stores up to 64KB of text.

- **Number**   Stores numeric values that can be used for calculations.

- **OLE Object**   Stores an object created with another application, such as a Word document, an Excel spreadsheet, or a picture.

- **Text**   Stores up to 255 characters of text. This is the default data type.

- **Yes/No**   Stores a single value that is either true (yes) or false (no).

Creating a Table with the Table Wizard

To create a table for your database, you can use a special Access feature that enables you to perform this task quickly: the **Table Wizard** (see Figure 4D.8). This wizard enables you to choose from a variety of ready-to-use tables. Each table also includes a variety of ready-to-use fields. For example, the Contacts table contains all the fields needed for a contacts table including FirstName, LastName, Address, and many more. You can build your own table quickly by adding fields from any of the ready-to-use tables.

To use the Table Wizard, click New on the menu bar, type a name for your new database, click Table in the Objects bar, and double-click Create Table By Using Wizard.

Once you've created your table, you can view it on-screen. To do so, open the Database window for

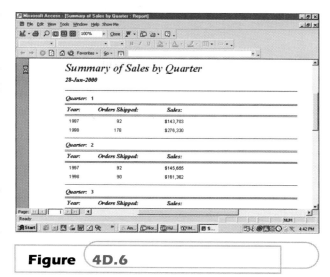

Figure 4D.6

Reports provide templates for printing data neatly.

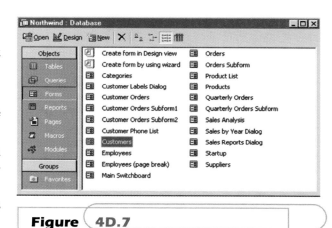

Figure 4D.7

The Database window conveniently groups all of a database's objects so that they are easily accessed.

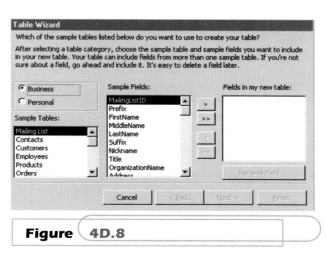

Figure 4D.8

With the Table Wizard, you can quickly create a table by adding ready-to-use fields.

enterprise resource planning (ERP)
A computer-based planning system that integrates all aspects of a business, including design, resource allocation, scheduling, manufacturing, and marketing. ERP systems typically include a high-performance database management system. The market leader in ERP software is SAP AG, a German firm.

the database you're creating (if necessary), click Tables on the Object bar, and double-click the table you just created. You'll see your table on-screen.

When you're viewing your table, or any other database object, you can alternate between two views: the **Datasheet view** and the **Design view.** In the Datasheet view, you see your data (see Figure 4D.9). You can view the data, edit the data, and add new records. In the Design view, you can change the structure of your database by adding fields, changing existing fields, or deleting fields (see Figure 4D.10). To switch between the two views, open a database object, and click View on the toolbar.

To refine your table, you can add some or all of the following for each field you have created:

■ **Input masks** to make sure that users enter valid data. An input mask controls what type of information can be entered in a field. For example, an input mask of 99/99/00 is commonly-used in date fields. In this expression, the number 9 means that the user can type a number in that place, but the number is not required. The 0 means that a number *must* be typed in that place.

■ **Default values** are entered automatically as a starting point for data entry.

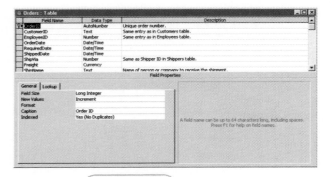

Figure 4D.9

In the Datasheet view, you can work with the data contained in an object (shown here is a table).

■ **Required fields** must contain data before the record can be processed and added to the database.

■ **Validation rules** are like input masks, but they give you more ways to make sure users enter valid data. For example, you could type Between 25 and 50 in the Validation Rule area to make sure that users enter a value between 25 and 50. In the Validation Text area, you can specify the text to display if the user enters an incorrect value.

These and other field properties are added by displaying the table in Design view, selecting the field in the Field Name list, and clicking the General tab.

Creating a Form with the Form Wizard

Once you've created a table, you can quickly create a form by using the **Form Wizard** (see Figure 4D.11). This wizard creates the form automatically based on fields you select from one or more tables in your database. To use the Form Wizard, click Form in the object bar, and double-click Create Form By Using Wizard.

When you've finished creating your form, you can use it to view and edit the data in your database. At the bottom of the form, you'll see controls that enable you to page through the records in your database (see Figure 4D.12). To add new records, click the New Record button on the toolbar.

Figure 4D.10

In the Design view, you can change the underlying structure of the object (shown here is the design of a table).

If you display your form in Design view, you can jazz it up in ways far too numerous to discuss here. For example, you can change or customize the **controls** used to enter data in your form. Controls are data input tools, such as option buttons, command buttons, text boxes, check boxes, and list boxes. You can also choose fonts, font sizes, alignments, colors, lines, and borders.

Creating a Query with the Query Wizard

The whole point of creating a database lies in transforming all that data into information—and that means boiling down the data to just the patterns you're looking for. You can do this by creating a query. In Microsoft Access, a query consists of the following:

- **A list of the fields you want to display** You can include fields from two or more tables, if you wish. You should display only the fields that you really need to see. Remember, the whole point of the query is to cut the data down to just what's needed.

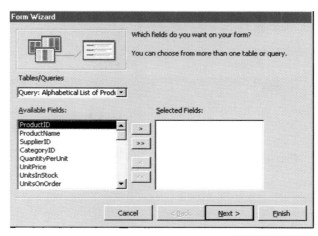

- **Criteria for selecting records** To retrieve just the data you want, you can specify **criteria** for selecting records from your database. (The singular is criterion.)

Figure 4D.11

The Form Wizard enables you to create a form by including fields from as many tables as you wish.

You can use wizards to create a query in a two-step process, starting with selecting the fields you want to display. To create a query using the Query Wizard in Microsoft Access 97, open the Database window for the database you are creating, select Queries in the Objects bar, and click New. In the New query dialog box, choose Simple Query Wizard.

You can use the Simple Query Wizard to select the fields to include in the query output. Click Next, and choose Detail. When you click Next again, click Modify the Query Design. You'll see your query in the Design view (see Figure 4D.13).

In the Design view of your query, you can add criteria for selecting data from the database. A criterion consists of the following:

- **Selection field** You need to specify which field should be searched when the program tries to select records that match the criteria you're specifying.

Figure 4D.12

Forms provide a convenient way to view and edit the data in your database. If you click New Record, you'll see a new, blank form, which you can use to add new data.

- **Operator** The **query operator** specifies what type of selection operation you want to perform. For numbers, dates, and times, you can use the comparison operators shown in Table 4D.1.

- **Value** In a query, the **value** indicates the data to be matched or compared. A value can be text, a number, a time, or a date. Text values need to be enclosed within quotation marks, while dates and times need to be enclosed within pound signs (#).

Specifying Criteria

To add a criterion to your query, click within the Criteria box under the field you want to search, and type a criterion. Here are some tips for writing criteria:

- If you omit the operator, Access assumes you mean "equals" (=). In the rare books database, you could type "London" in the criteria box of the Author field to find books by Jack London.

- Text criteria are case-sensitive. You must type the capitalization pattern used to record data in the table.

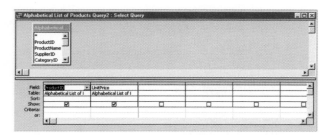

> ■ You can use wildcards with text criteria. The asterisk (*) stands for any character or characters, while the question mark (?) stands for any one character. For example, you could type "Super*" in the Hero field of a comics books database to retrieve all the comic book heroes whose names start with "Super."

Figure 4D.13

After you use the Query Wizard, you'll see the fields you've selected for inclusion in your query. Shown here is the Design view of your query.

Adding Additional Criteria

Sometimes you may wish to specify more than one criterion for a query. To do so, you will need to use logical operators (see Table 4D.2). In brief, a **logical operator** gives you a way to create more refined queries by linking two or more query criteria. You can broaden the scope of a query by using the OR operator. You can narrow the scope of a query by using the AND operator, and you can further narrow it by adding a NOT operator.

When you're viewing your query in Design view, you can easily add OR criteria by typing an additional criterion on the OR line. Figure 4D.14 shows a query that uses an OR expression.

To use the AND operator, add a criterion to another field. For example, in the rare books database, you could type "Shakespeare" under the Author field and "Excellent" under the Condition field. Access will retrieve only those records where the Author is *Shakespeare* and the Condition is *Excellent*. If you would like to use the NOT operator, you can append this operator to one of the criteria in the Criteria field.

Table 4D.1

Comparison Operators (Microsoft Access)		
Operator	**Description**	**Example**
=	Equals	="London"
<	Less than	<#02/09/02#
<=	Less than or equal to	<=22901
>	Greater than	>#12/31/03#
>=	Greater than or equal to	>=125.25
<>	Not equal to	<>"paid"
Between x and y	Between value x and value y	between 25 and 50

Table 4D.2

Selected Logical Operators (Microsoft Access)		
Operator	**Description**	**Example**
OR	Retrieves a record only if EITHER criterion is true	"Shakespeare" OR "Dickens"
AND	Retrieves a record only if BOTH criteria are true	Author="Shakespeare" AND Condition="Excellent"
NOT	Retrieves only those records that do NOT match the specified criterion	NOT "Shakespeare"

To run your query, just click the View button on the toolbar to switch to the Datasheet view. Doing so runs the query automatically. The result of a query is a new table that contains only those records that match the criteria you specified. Access saves your query along with the other objects in your database, so you can run it again as it's needed.

Advanced Queries

You can do much more with Access queries than this section has space to discuss, including the following:

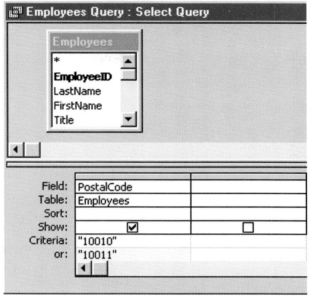

■ **Aggregating Data**   An **aggregate query** performs a calculation on the numerical data in the database. For example, you can produce sums, averages, and counts. In the rare books database, you could use this feature to calculate the total price of all the Jack London novels in your collection.

■ **Calculated Fields**   A **calculated field** performs a calculation on all the data contained in a specified field, and shows the result of these calculations. For example, you could use this feature to calculate how much those Jack London novels would cost if you offered them at a 10 percent discount.

Figure   4D.14

This query will match either of the specified conditions (implicit OR operator).

■ **Grouping**   A **grouped query** organizes the query results in groups. For example, you could display the contents of the rare books database grouped by Publisher, and then by Author.

■ **Sorting**   You can specify the way records are sorted in the query results. By default, Access sorts the records in Ascending order (A to Z, 0 to 9, earliest to latest), but you can choose Descending or Not Sorted if you wish.

■ **Crosstabs**   A **crosstab** query produces sums, averages, and other statistics for grouped data. For example, you could compare the average price of paperbacks vs. hardcover books in your rare books database.

■ **Updates**   An **update query** changes the data in a field according to the criteria you specify. For example, you could use this feature to increase all the prices in your rare books database by 10 percent.

■ **Deleting Data**   A **delete query** will remove all the data in your tables that conform to the criteria you specify—which is dangerous, so don't use this type of query unless you're sure you know what you're doing. As an example, you could use this feature to delete all the records in the rare books database that contain "Sold" in the Status field.

■ **Making New Tables**   A **make-table query** creates a new, valid table based on the results of your query. This is a good way to back up your database.

Creating Reports with the Report Wizard

Unlike queries, reports are designed to be printed rather than viewed on-screen. You can create a variety of reports with Microsoft Access. Here, you'll learn about the two simplest types of reports: *columnar reports* and *tabular reports*. A **columnar report** prints the records in your database in a format that looks like a form (see Figure 4D.15). A **tabular report** organizes the information in a list format (see Figure 4D.16).

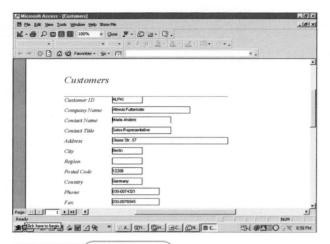

Figure 4D.15

A columnar report prints information in a format similar to a form, with one page per record.

Figure 4D.16

A tabular report summarizes information by means of headings that correspond to database fields.

Using the AutoReports

To create either of these standard report formats quickly, open the Database window for your database, select Reports in the Object bar, and click New. In the New Report dialog box, select AutoReport: Columnar or AutoReport: Tabular, and select the table or query that you want to use. Click OK to create the report.

Advanced Reports

To create customized reports, you can use the Report Wizard, which enables you to specify your report's format in greater detail than the AutoReport formats allow. With the Report Wizard, you can produce printouts that group records by field, sort the records in various ways, and produce sums or averages. You can also customize the report format with fonts, font sizes, colors, borders, shading, and more.

CLIENT/SERVER DATABASE SYSTEMS

When you create a database with Microsoft Access using the techniques just discussed, the result is a local database, one that's stored on the same computer that runs Access. However, Access is also capable of working with **database servers.** In brief, a database server is a professionally-administered program that runs on a local area network (LAN) and is designed to respond to external requests for data. A database server is not designed to be easy to use—and that's because users never contact the server directly. To access the data in the database, users run a **client** program, a user-friendly program that enables them to add data to the database, maintain existing records, perform queries, and generate reports. Because these database systems draw a distinction between the database server and client, they are often called **client/server** systems. They are designed so that many users—hundreds or even thousands of them—can access the database simultaneously. Examples of database servers include the market-leading DB2 (IBM) and Oracle (Oracle Corporation).

When used with most database servers, clients frame query requests using a **query language** called **SQL** (pronounced "sequel"). Query languages enable you to compose simple or complex requests for data. Short for Structured Query Language, SQL enables users to phrase queries in a way that the server can understand. SQL is not difficult to learn. However, most users prefer to use clients that provide user-friendly tools for constructing SQL queries. One such client is Microsoft Access. With Access, you can build queries that, in the background, are transformed into SQL queries, which can be sent to a database server. In sum, Access can be used to build local databases. It can also be used as a client to access database servers.

MOVERS & SHAKERS

Larry Ellison, Oracle Corporation

Dozens, if not hundreds, of database programs are on the market. Many of these products are produced by small companies, and some products are produced by large companies that also produce other software. Only a handful of companies, however, grew solely on the basis of a database program. One such company—and the largest in the marketplace—is Oracle Corporation.

Oracle was the brainchild of Larry Ellison, who was born in 1944 in the ghettos on the South Side of Chicago. As a child, he dreamed of being a builder and a scientist, and creating something special. He studied mathematics at the University of Chicago, but never finished his formal college education. Lurking in Ellison's mind was a powerful conviction that the abstract concepts of mathematics could work powerful magic in our everyday lives. Silicon Valley beckoned. Instead of sticking it out until graduation, Ellison headed West and got a job at Amdahl Corporation as a programmer.

Inspiration was soon to follow. In 1976, Ellison read a research paper published by IBM about their decade of work in relational databases. The paper was an eye-opener for Ellison, who was fascinated by the mathematically consistent and complete way in which the paper described how information could be managed and retrieved. And it wasn't all theory. The paper described a language called SQL that could be used to access the data stored in the revolutionary new data architectures that IBM's brilliant scientists had developed.

Why didn't anyone else see the opportunity that Ellison perceived? The theory of relational databases was not new; it had been around for about ten years. Extensive research by database experts had convinced many people that relational databases were nothing but an idealistic dream of how data should be handled. Many people considered that dream unattainable because accessing data stored in a truly-relational model would be too slow and overtax available hardware systems. But Ellison knew that computers were becoming more and more powerful. Soon, they would be able to handle the heavy demands of a relational database—and Ellison was determined to be out in front of everyone else when it happened.

Ellison concluded that IBM didn't fully realize what they had. His goal was to beat IBM to the punch and come out with a product before they could release their own. With a paltry investment of $2,000 and two years of development, Oracle was born. Additional funding came from consulting work performed by Ellison and others at the company.

The first version of Oracle was sold and installed in November of 1979 at Wright-Patterson Air Force Base in Dayton, Ohio. In subsequent years, Oracle has grown into a hugely-profitable multibillion-dollar company with over 34,000 employees. The quality of its database product (now up to version 8) and Ellison's charisma and relentless competitive nature propelled the company to the top of its industry. Oracle is now the most popular database product in the world.

As far as databases go, Oracle is not for everyone. For instance, it would not be a good choice for keeping track of your coin collection or your audio CDs. Instead, Oracle is targeted at medium-to-large businesses, or those with a specific need for a robust relational database program. Oracle is a database server program that is very powerful and exceptionally well-suited for large databases with many, many users. Oracle software has been used in everything from traditional business applications such as accounting to cutting-edge servers for on-demand video systems. But it isn't user-friendly. Installing, configuring, and administering Oracle requires professional expertise. To make use of the data in an Oracle database, users run user-friendly client programs, which enable them to frame SQL queries without having to learn the language.

Oracle software runs on all sorts of hardware, including networked computers, personal digital assistants, personal computers, workstations, minicomputers, mainframes, and massively-parallel supercomputers. It relies on the SQL language to store, change, and access information in a database.

It's interesting to see how the fortunes of computer companies develop. Oracle is one such company that has successfully exploited a niche in the computer market. And along the way, the dream of a poor kid from the South Side of Chicago came true as he built both a company and a remarkable product. And what about IBM? Perhaps they were slow on the uptake, but Oracle's success taught them their lesson. IBM's relational database software is ranked No. 2 in the market—but Oracle's still in the lead.

Larry Ellison.

THE INTERNET CONNECTION: GOING PUBLIC WITH DATA

The latest trend in database software is **Web integration,** a name for a variety of techniques used to make information stored in databases available through Internet or intranet connections. Web integration enables customers of the express shipping giant FedEx to access shipping information through its Web site. You don't have to learn SQL or any other query language to use this or similar sites. The Web server accepts your input and translates it into a query sent to the database. The database responds with the requested information, and the server generates a new Web page on-the-fly, containing the information you've requested.

What kind of hardware is involved? From the company's Web server, information requests are routed to a massive IBM System/390 mainframe networked with several high-end UNIX systems. Many other companies are venturing into online commerce by making enormous internal resources available to the public through the Internet. At AMP, Inc., a Pennsylvania-based electronics components manufacturer, an enormous online catalog of nearly 90,000 components is made accessible by means of a Web server linked to an Oracle relational database. The payoff for AMP is an annual savings of $2 million in expenses related to catalog production, telephone calls, and customer support.

TAKEAWAY POINTS

- Database management software comes in handy whenever you're dealing with more data than you can work with conveniently. Database software transforms data into information by showing just the information required for a task.

- A database is any collection of data stored in an organized way. A database file is made up of records, which are units of information about something. Each record has one or more fields; each field stores a certain type of data.

- A good database system ensures data integrity (validity of the data), promotes data independence (usefulness with more than one application), avoids data redundancy (entry of the same data in two or more places), ensures data security (protection from loss of confidentiality), and provides procedures for data maintenance (procedures for adding, updating, and deleting records).

- File management programs work with only one database file, called flat files, at a time. As a result, they cannot eliminate data redundancy. Relational databases work with two or more database files, called tables, at a time. The data in the various tables can be related together by means of common fields. Through a process called normalization, it is possible to design a relational database so that data redundancy is eliminated.

- The major database objects used in Microsoft Access include tables (lists of records with one or more fields), forms (customized display windows for one record at a time), queries (statements that define criteria for retrieving information from the database), and reports (templates for printing database information).

- To design a database, begin by listing the fields and data types you want to use. Then figure out how to place the fields into two or more separate tables so that data redundancy is eliminated. Create common fields to link the data in the various tables. Define primary keys to uniquely identify the records in each table, and identify index fields to speed sorts and queries.

- To create tables, forms, queries, and reports using Microsoft Access, use the wizards provided for this purpose. When you create tables, you can make use of the sample tables and fields provided with Access. To create a form quickly, let Access create the form automatically from the fields present in one or more tables. To create queries, select the fields you want to display, and type one or more conditions. To create reports quickly, you can use the built-in, automatic columnar or tabular reports.

- Database servers make databases available to two or more users simultaneously on a local area network (LAN). To access the data made available by a database server, users run user-friendly client programs, which provide graphical tools for constructing queries. Microsoft Access can function as a client for database servers.

MODULE REVIEW

KEY TERMS AND CONCEPTS

aggregate query	data type	form
calculated field	data validation	Form Wizard
client	data warehouses	grouped query
client/server	database	index field
columnar report	database objects	logical operator
controls	database programs	make-table query
criteria	database servers	normalization
crosstab	Datasheet view	primary key
data independence	delete query	query
data integrity	Design view	query language
data marts	fields	query operator
data mining	file management program	records
data redundancy	flat files	relational database

report	Table Wizard	update query
Structured Query Language	Tabular report	value
(SQL)	time fields	Web integration
table		

TRUE/FALSE

Indicate whether the following statements are true or false.

1. Regardless of what line of work you pursue, you'll end up working with databases sooner or later.

2. Databases are collections of data stored in a random fashion.

3. A database record is a unit of information about something.

4. To avoid data integrity errors, database programs should use data validation procedures.

5. Data redundancy is a characteristic of well-designed databases.

6. A file management program is usually more expensive and more difficult to learn than a database management program.

7. Object-oriented databases are the latest type of database structure and are likely to gain in popularity.

8. A form stores information in a list of records, each of which has one or more fields.

9. Logical operators help you specify more than one criterion for a query.

10. Web integration allows information stored in databases to be available through Internet or intranet connections.

MATCHING

Match each key term from the left column with its most accurate definition in the right column.

_____ 1. field

_____ 2. flat file

_____ 3. normalization

_____ 4. query

_____ 5. report

_____ 6. primary key

_____ 7. controls

_____ 8. aggregate query

_____ 9. columnar report

_____ 10. client/server

a. a field that is used to uniquely identify each record in a table

b. performs a calculation on the numerical data in a database

c. information stored in this cannot be linked to data in other files

d. a system that's designed so that many users can access data simultaneously

e. a separate area designed to store a certain type of data

f. data input tools used to enter data in a form

g. a process that eliminates data redundancy

h. a statement that defines criteria for retrieving data

i. a template that's used to print information from your database

j. prints the records in a database in a format that looks like a form

MULTIPLE CHOICE

Circle the letter of the correct choice for each of the following.

1. A database file is made up of what?
   a. characters
   b. fields
   c. records
   d. text

2. Which of the following is analogous to a record in a database?
   a. a single phone number from the phone book

   b. a single card in a card catalog
   c. a single drawer in a filing cabinet
   d. a single book from a bookshelf

3. The type of information permitted to be stored in a field is known as what?
   a. data type
   b. character
   c. record
   d. variable

4. What do data validation procedures do?
   a. allow automatic data entry
   b. make sure data is correct
   c. introduce complexity into a database
   d. define acceptable input ranges for a field

5. If a ZIP code is entered in a field intended for a phone number, this is an example of violating which principle of good database design?
   a. data independence
   b. data redundancy
   c. data integrity
   d. data security

6. If a database contains the same information more than once, this is an example of what?
   a. data independence
   b. data redundancy
   c. data integrity
   d. data security

7. Which database object provides a customized display window for one record at a time?
   a. table
   b. form
   c. query
   d. report

8. What data type creates a drop-down list box containing valid values from a lookup table?
   a. AutoNumber
   b. hyperlink
   c. OLE object
   d. Lookup Wizard

9. For what type of applications is an object-oriented database well-suited?
   a. general applications
   b. horizontal applications
   c. financial applications
   d. multimedia applications

10. What is the latest trend in database software?
    a. data warehousing
    b. Web integration
    c. object-oriented design
    d. standalone modules

FILL-IN

In the blank provided, write the correct answer for each of the following.

1. A(n) _____ is any collection of information stored in some organized way.

2. A database record is made up of _____ .

3. Data _____ refers to the validity of the data contained in a database.

4. Data _____ refers to the storage of data in such a way that it is not locked into use by a particular application.

5. A(n) _____ program enables users to create customized databases and to store and retrieve data from these databases.

6. In a(n) _____ database, data in several files is related through the use of a common key field.

7. Data _____ are intended to collect data in a primitive, less-organized way than traditional databases.

8. _____ enables managers to explore data in an attempt to discover previously-unknown patterns.

9. Smaller data warehouse projects designed for use in a single division of an organization are called _____.

10. A(n) _____ field is a field containing information that you frequently search for by means of queries.

SHORT ANSWER

On a separate sheet of paper, answer the following questions.

1. What is the purpose of a database?
2. How does a computerized database differ from non-computerized databases?
3. What are the qualities of a good database?
4. Provide an example of how data independence works and why it is desirable.
5. How does data redundancy affect a database?
6. Describe how to construct a simple query using SQL.
7. What are the two major types of database programs?
8. How does a key field work in a relational database?
9. How do relational databases differ from object-oriented databases?
10. What is the purpose of data warehousing? Data mining?

PFSweb, Inc.

What do you think makes a good Web site interface? Maybe it's speed or lots of graphics. Perhaps an email link for asking questions is important to you. For e-commerce companies, knowing what elements rank highly with customers can make or break the success of a Web venture. You've really got to know your customer! For business-to-business (B2B) e-commerce sites, the big deal is functionality, not flash. In other words, the site must make it easy for corporate buyers to quickly and easily make purchases. Fancy graphics, animations, and long wait times just don't cut it with busy professional buyers.

If you're tailoring your Web site to consumers for the business-to-consumer (B2C) market, the requirements change. Emphasis needs to be placed on the merchandising, as well as easing the entire buying process. Graphics such as photos or illustrations take on more relevance. One simple way for an organization to get a handle on what works and what doesn't, is to visit other Web sites—especially those of competitors. By doing a little research before building your Web site's interface, you'll not only discover some cool features that are "must haves," but you'll also see some of problems you'll want to avoid.

What do you think? Think about your own Web experiences. When you use the Web, what Web site features are most important to you? What features are annoying? How long are you willing to wait for a site's graphics to load? Does the speed of a site determine whether you'll revisit it later?

Web Link Go to **www.prenhall.com/ pfaffenberger** to see the video of PFSweb's Valarie Remmers talking about how new clients get started with an e-commerce Web site.

E-COMMERCE IN ACTION

5

Multimedia and Virtual Reality

It's one of the hottest sites on the Web—and one of the strangest. At Ananova's home page **(http://www.ananova.com),** you can click on a graphic image to see a video of an attractive-looking young woman reading the news to you—that is, if your definition of "attractive" includes a short-cropped shock of green hair But Ananova isn't a woman. She's a computer-generated graphic, and what you're hearing is a computer-generated voice. Ananova is the world's first virtual newscaster, and her appearance in the summer of 2000 caused a sensation. Ananova's home page was deluged with millions of visitors, her face graced the pages of newspapers and magazines worldwide, and she even made the pages of Vogue only two months after her debut—which isn't bad for a new media personality.

Ananova is made possible through multimedia, which involves blending two or more media to create a richer, more engrossing experience for viewers. Multimedia has been around for a while, but it's much easier to implement with computer and Internet technology—an obvious point, if you think about the difficulties of delivering real-time video with the morning newspaper. But that's child's play on a Web page. In Module 5A, you'll learn how professional graphics artists develop their work using the tools of digital media production—a booming field in which artistic and professional opportunities abound. In Module 5B, you'll also consider the fascinating and often-disturbing potential of computer-based multimedia to draw us into immersive, computer-based environments, such as three-dimensional virtual realities that you can explore endlessly, graphics-intensive action and role-playing games, communities of simulated people that exist only on the Internet, and much more.

MODULES

5A

MODULE

OUTLINE

WHAT YOU WILL LEARN . . .

When you have finished reading this module, you will be able to:

1. Define multimedia, interactive media, and hypermedia.

2. Distinguish between the hardware needed for multimedia viewing and the hardware needed for multimedia production.

3. Explain the difference between paint programs and draw programs.

4. Discuss the role of codecs in multimedia use.

5. Briefly explain what multimedia authoring systems do.

The big moment is almost here. You've assembled the cast, set the stage, and written the script. The curtain is about to go up.

If you think we're talking about theater, guess again. What's about to transpire is a multimedia presentation. The cast consists of graphics, animation, video, and sound files. The stage is a computer screen. The script is a play-by-play scenario that determines when and where the cast appears on the stage. As you'll learn in this module, you can write such a script with a multimedia authoring package or an authoring language such as the Synchronized Multimedia Integration Language (SMIL), which was developed for Web presentations.

Like other visual metaphors that help us understand software, the theater metaphor makes sense of multimedia's complexities. In this module, you'll find an introduction to multimedia and go on to explore the applications that help multimedia authors develop the cast, such as image, sound, and video editors. You'll then explore multimedia authoring packages and languages. Along the way, you'll learn how multimedia presentations are developed. You'll also learn a good deal about the multimedia aspects of Web publishing, because many of the same technologies come into play when developers create interactive, multimedia-enriched Web pages (see Module 7D). If you've been wondering whether there's room in computing for artistically-minded people, this module should put your doubts to rest!

INTRODUCING MULTIMEDIA

What's **multimedia?** The standard definition is any presentation that involves two or more media, such as text, graphics, or sound (see Figure 5A.1). By this ho-hum definition, any TV show or movie is a multimedia experience. What makes multimedia *exciting* is another characteristic altogether: interactivity. In **interactive multimedia,** users can choose their own path through the presentation. The interactive dimension makes computer-based multimedia a non-couch-potato technology; instead of sitting back and letting someone else determine the presentation's flow, you're in control.

Interactivity has helped make the World Wide Web popular, as the Web can be viewed as a gigantic multimedia presentation. Most Web pages include graphics along with the text, and many also offer animations, videos, and sounds. The Web's navigation method, called **hypertext,** enables users to browse as they please. (In a hypertext world, you choose where you want to go by clicking a link to another document.) By blending multimedia with the Web, **hypermedia** becomes possible. In many Web pages, for instance, you can click parts of a graphic to access a different page. In hypermedia, media other than text becomes the vehicle for navigating to new material.

Multimedia Hardware

Just a few years ago, most personal computers needed additional equipment to run multimedia presentations. Today, this equipment—a sound card, a CD-ROM drive, and speakers—is standard issue. If you want to go into serious multimedia production, you may need additional equipment, such as a pen-based graphics tablet, stereo microphones, a digital camera, and a video adapter. If you enjoy playing games, you'll want a 3-D video accelerator,

Figure 5A.1

Multimedia is any presentation that involves two or more media, such as text, graphics, or sound.

Techtalk

skins
Computer graphics for decorating your Web browser or PC music player are called "skins." Skins are colorful graphical icons that computer users can download from the Internet to replace boring buttons and music player bars.

Figure 5A.2

In businesses, multimedia is finding its way into automated presentation systems.

Explore IT Lab

Multimedia

which is an add-on video adapter that works with your current video card. For 3-D sound, you'll need a sound card capable of reproducing these sounds. And while you're at it, pick up a few extra speakers and a subwoofer.

Multimedia Applications

Multimedia is used for any computer application in which text alone won't do. Arguably, this category includes just about *every* computer application, because graphics, sounds, animations, and video can often do a more effective job of involving the user (and conveying information) than text alone.

Multimedia is a prerequisite for computer games of all kinds, but it's also finding growing use in computer-based education (CBE) and computer-based training (CBT). Hot sellers in the CD-ROM market include multimedia versions of reference works, such as dictionaries (which include recordings that tell you how to pronounce difficult words), encyclopedias (replete with sound and video clips from famous moments in history), and how-to guides, which use multimedia to show you how to do just about anything around the home.

In businesses, multimedia is finding its way into **information kiosks** (automated presentation systems used for public information or employee training) and even into corporate databases (see Figure 5A.2). A major wholesale electronics firm is developing an object-oriented database to store complex images of engineering designs, which can't be stored in a text-only database. By making these designs accessible to buyers, the firm can help buyers determine quickly whether a given design is appropriate for their needs.

MULTIMEDIA RESOURCES: INTRODUCING THE CAST

A multimedia presentation may involve some or all of the following: bitmapped graphics, vector graphics, edited photographs, rendered three-dimensional images, edited videos, and synthesized sound. The following sections briefly introduce some of the software used to create the cast of a multimedia production.

Compression and Decompression (Codecs)

Computers can work with art, photographs, videos, and sounds, but they can do so only when these multimedia resources are stored in digitized files. These files, however, require huge amounts of storage space. For example, an average-sized hard disk could store only a dozen audio CDs, and there wouldn't be much room left for system software or applications. To reduce the size of multimedia files, most software uses compression/decompression algorithms called **codecs.**

Codecs use two different approaches to compression, called **lossless compression** and **lossy compression.** In lossless compression, the original file is compressed so that it can be completely restored, without flaw, when decompression occurs. In lossy compression, the original file is processed so that some information is permanently removed. However, you probably won't notice the loss. Lossy compression techniques eliminate information that isn't perceived when people see pictures or hear sounds.

CURRENTS

New Media: Pushing the Boundaries of Art

Fiorella Terenzi, an Italian astrophysicist and composer, uses radio telescopes to retrieve radio waves from galaxies millions of light-years away. Then she feeds the data into a computer and uses a sound-synthesis program to assign the data's patterns to synthesized musical instruments, such as violins. What does the result sound like? You can hear for yourself on Fiorella Terenzi's Music from the Galaxies (Island Records). Critics find the recording beautiful, ethereal, and strange. But is it music?

Terenzi's disc illustrates an important point about the role of computers in new media, a term that refers generally to the use of computers and computer-controlled video and music technology to process and present works of art. Computers assist artists in many ways, for example, by making the tasks of creating art more convenient. But computers are also pushing the boundaries of art, forcing us to question just what art really is.

If you think art museums are a series of rooms with paintings hung on the wall, you would have been shocked by the Whitney Museum of American Art's 2000 Bicentennial Exhibition. On view were several huge, computer-controlled video installations, including Doug Aitken's "Electric Earth," a four-room projected video installation that depicts an African-American youth dancing solo down abandoned Los Angeles streets. Viewers move through the installation seeing "walls" where, in fact, two projected images overlap. Aitken's work pushes the boundaries in ways other than sheer monumental size; some of the projected videos show Aitken himself, interacting with the devastated urban environment. What's Aitken's point? It's up to the viewer, but Aitken's deliberate self-inclusion forces us to bring the artist into the picture, something that's rare in traditional media.

Traditionally, museums strive to preserve art for future generations, and they're far from abandoning their goal. Still, it's hard to see how some complex installations will survive the vagaries of time. Consider Jason Rhoade's 1998 installation, titled "Creation Myth."

Occupying most of a huge room, the installation includes video cameras, computers, monitors, printers, mirrors, converter belts, and even an electric train set. The various components of the installation interact in a carefully designed sequence of chain reactions that appear to be almost accidental—and certainly meaningless. What's the point of "Creation Myth"? One of Rhoade's points is that a work of art isn't something that's going to be exhibited for eternity; it's simply too expensive and time-consuming to keep "Creation Myth" going, let alone preserve it for all time.

Some artists are using new media techniques to enable museum patrons to interact with art works. Toshio Iwai's "Piano-As Image Media" enables visitors to click a mouse, which creates random patterns of notes that cascade upwards to what appears to be a gigantic player piano, which transforms the notes into light patterns.

Sometimes new media artists push the boundaries too far, at least according to their critics. Some hip-hop (rap) groups use digitized sound samples of other artists' works as a mode of artistic expression in performances and recordings, but failure to obtain permission to use the samples can land the groups in court, as De La Soul found out in 1993 after using a lengthy sample of another musician's recording.

Traditionalists lament the role of computers in today's art world, pointing out that it's no longer necessary to spend years developing the type of skill possessed by a Bach, Rembrant, or Picasso. For example, a computer can help you compose and perform a symphony, even though you can't play more than one note at a time on a piano. Does art suffer when people can bypass the years of arduous training that go into a traditional artistic education? Perhaps, but it's well to remember that precisely the same arguments were heard a century ago when photography was developed. There were dire warnings about the coming demise of serious painting. A century later, it's clear that photography has influenced painting—there's even a genre of painting called Photo-Realism, which mimics the striking detail of a huge photographic enlargement—but painting hasn't disappeared. More than likely, old media and new media will continue to coexist and influence each other. The question that remains is just as difficult to answer as always: Which works—new media or old—are so significant, and so important, that they will be appreciated and venerated for generations to come?

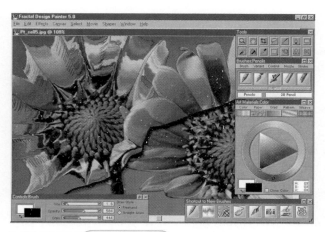

Figure 5A.3

Paint programs are used to create bit-mapped graphics, which are composed of tiny dots, each corresponding to one pixel on the computer's display.

Paint Programs

Paint programs are used to create **bit-mapped graphics** (also called *raster graphics*), which are composed of tiny dots, each corresponding to one pixel on the computer's display (see Figure 5A.3). Although paint programs enable artists to create pictures easily, the resulting bit-mapped image is difficult to edit. To do so, you must zoom the picture so that you can edit the individual pixels, and enlargement may produce an unattractive distortion called the *jaggies*. Professional paint programs such as Fractal Design Painter enable users to create beautiful painterly effects, even if they're not good at art!

Although most monitors can't display more than 72 dots per inch (dpi), paint programs can create and store bit-mapped graphics at higher resolutions, which comes in handy for printing.

The number of colors you can display depends on the amount of video RAM in your system (see Module 2C). The more colors shown on-screen, the more memory required to store them. A file that stores 8 bits of color information per pixel can display a **color depth** of only 256 colors. For realistic color photographs, a color depth of 16.7 million colors is needed (24 bits per pixel).

Paint programs can save your work to a variety of file formats, including the following standard formats:

- **Graphics Interchange Format (GIF)** (pronounced "jiff") A 256-color file format that uses lossless compression to reduce file size. It's best for simple images with large areas of solid colors. Because this file format is a Web standard, it's often used for Web pages.

- **Joint Photographic Experts Group (JPEG)** (pronounced "jay-peg") Files that can store up to 16.7 million colors and is best for complex images, such as photographs. This image format is also a Web standard. The JPEG file format uses lossy compression to reduce file size.

- **Portable Network Graphics (PNG)** (pronounced "ping") A new alternative to GIF that doesn't require companies to pay a royalty for the lossless compression technique used.

- **Windows Bitmap (BMP)** A standard bit-mapped graphics format developed for Microsoft Windows. Compression is optional, so BMP files tend to be very large.

Image Editors

Image editors are sophisticated versions of paint programs designed for editing and transforming—but not creating—complex bit-mapped images, such as photographs. These programs make use of automated image processing algorithms to add a variety of special effects to photographic images. They also enable skilled users to combine photographs in a way that leaves few traces behind.

Leading image editors such as Adobe Photoshop have been used by professional design studios for years, but image editors may soon capture a wider market due to the booming market for digital cameras. Programs such

Destinations

A popular paint program is Paint Shop Pro (Jasc Software). You can download a preview copy from Jasc's Web site (**http://www.jasc.com**).

as Adobe's PhotoDeluxe are designed for beginners who want to perform the most common image enhancement tasks quickly and easily and then print their pictures on a color printer. Among the image processing tasks that PhotoDeluxe can perform are removing red-eye from flash snapshots and adjusting the picture's overall color cast.

Drawing Programs

Drawing programs are used to create **vector graphics,** in which each on-screen object is stored as a complex mathematical description. What this means, in practice, is that every object in a vector graphic can be independently edited and resized without introducing edge distortions, the bane of bit-mapped graphics. To compose an image with a drawing program, you need to create independent lines and shapes. You can then add colors and textures to these shapes. Because the resulting image has no inherent resolution, you can choose any size you want. The picture will print using the output device's highest resolution.

Professional drawing programs, such as Macromedia Freehand and Adobe Illustrator, save files by outputting instructions in the **PostScript** language, which is an automated **page description language (PDL).** A page description language is a programming language capable of precisely describing the appearance of a printed page, including fonts and graphics. PostScript is an established PDL standard widely used in desktop publishing. To print PostScript files, you need a printer equipped with its own microprocessor and an interpreter capable of decoding PostScript instructions. PostScript graphics files are saved to the **Encapsulated PostScript (EPS)** format, which encapsulates the PostScript in a file that also contains a bit-mapped thumbnail image of the enclosed graphic. (The thumbnail image enables you to see the graphic on-screen.)

One drawback of drawing programs lies in the lack of Web support for vector graphics. Several proposals have been made for adopting a standard.

Animation Programs

When you see a movie at the theater, you're actually looking at still images shown at a sufficiently-high **frame rate** (images per second) so that the eye is tricked into seeing continuous motion. Like a movie, an **animation** consists of a series of still images displayed at a frame rate high enough to create the illusion of movement. Animators create each of the still images separately. In computer animation, the computer provides tools for creating the animation as well as running it.

It's easy to create a simple animation using the GIF graphics file format, which enables programs to store more than one image in a GIF file. Also stored in the file is a brief script that tells the application to play the images in a certain sequence and to display each for a set period of time. Because Web browsers can read GIF files and play the animations, **GIF animations** are common on the Web.

Professional animation programs provide more sophisticated tools for creating and controlling animations, but they create proprietary files. To view these files on the Web, you need a special viewer.

Destinations

Visit Adobe's Web site to learn more about Photoshop (**http://www. adobe.com**).

Destinations

Explore the leading animation software at Macromedia's Web site (**http://www.macro media.com**).

When you see a movie at the theater, you're looking at a series of still images shown at a high frame rate (images per second). The eye is tricked into seeing continuous motion.

SPOTLIGHT

MULTIMEDIA: THE NEW TEXTBOOKS

▶Imagine you are there: shivering with Washington at Valley Forge, riding with General Grant at Appomattox, performing with Mozart for the King of Prussia, walking on the moon with Neil Armstrong, fiddling with Nero as Rome burns.

Showing documentaries is a time-honored method of education. They allow the student to more easily visualize historical events and understand issues affecting those events. Traditional documentaries are taking a new twist, however, with the advent of interactive multimedia. The use of dramatic multimedia presentations earns high praise from teachers and school administrators worldwide. Studies indicate that programs such as these greatly improve student comprehension and retention.

Humans thrive on multiple input. Educators have long recognized that we remember only 10 percent of what we read, 20 percent of what we hear, 30 percent of what we see and hear, 50 percent of what we see someone do while explaining, and 90 percent of what we do ourselves, even if it's only a simulation. By using well-designed interactive multimedia software, students learn more in less time.

One of the most powerful applications of computer technology in the classroom is the creation of interactive tutorials. Many different tutorial programs allow students to create presentations using text, graphics, images, narration, sound, and video. A photo-editing program supports collages, and animation is an option. Robust programs of this type are available for both Macintosh and Windows systems.

The educational world—from preschools to professional schools—is adopting multimedia at various rates. The rate of technology-related spending in school systems has increased in recent years in an attempt to keep pace with the growth of computers.

Many schools are not only offering classes in how to use computers, but also utilizing computers to change the way in which instruction takes place.

One success story is at Bakersfield College in Bakersfield, California. College President Rick Wright and a colleague were the first to use multimedia as a teaching tool in their general psychology course. They captured digital audio from CDs or audio tape, digitized images from photos and slides, and even used full-motion videos culled from a twenty-year collection of psychology videotapes. "We try to sort out the best of the material to use as clips in our lectures," President Wright said. "This technology lets you clip the pertinent things and insert them in your lecture where you want them. Multimedia clip making is a stroke of genius, because if you can capture just what you need from the videotapes for each topic in your lecture, it gives you incredible power—everything is integrated."

In addition to creating homemade multimedia presentations, instructors can purchase thousands of commercially-prepared titles on CD-ROM and now DVD-ROM. Such titles are available from a variety of sources and cover a wide range of topics. You can locate multimedia educational software that covers everything from anatomy to zoology. The business of providing multimedia reference material and self-paced interactive instruction is booming. Many traditional textbook companies are starting to enter the multimedia field, as well.

Increases in the use of multimedia are also affecting traditional textbook creation. Some publishers are beginning to combine textbooks and multimedia CD-ROMs to create an integrated approach to teaching and learning. The student may use the textbook during class periods, but then rely on the supplemental material on the CD-ROM for greater understanding of core content or for quizzing on retention.

As more teachers become educated in multimedia techniques, students will benefit through more interesting lessons and greater retention of the material presented. This increases the student's interest in taking classes, and teachers can teach larger groups of students by using multimedia techniques.

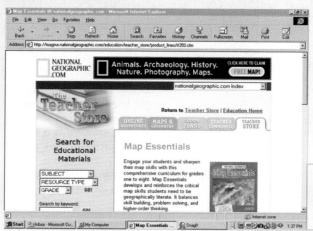

Instructors can purchase thousands of commercially-prepared titles on CD-ROM and now DVD-ROM. Such titles are available from a variety of sources and cover a wide range of topics.

3-D Rendering Programs

A **3-D rendering** program adds three-dimensional effects to computer graphic objects. The results are strikingly realistic and can be rotated in any direction to achieve just the result the artist is looking for.

In the past, rendering software required a high-powered engineering workstation, but today's top PCs are up to the task. One rendering technique, **ray tracing,** adds amazing realism to a simulated three-dimensional object by adding variations in color intensity that would be produced by light falling on the object from multiple directions (which is the norm in the real world).

Video Editors

Video editors enable you to modify digitized videos, such as videos imported from a video camera by means of a video capture board (see Module 2C). With a video editor, you can cut segments, resequence the video, add transitions, compress the file, and determine the video's frame rate (the number of still images displayed per second).

Video editors also enable you to save video files to some or all of the following video file formats:

- **Moving Pictures Experts Group (MPEG)**   A family of video file formats and lossy compression standards for full-motion video. The most recent version, MPEG-2, offers resolutions high enough to fill a monitor's screen at speeds of up to 60 frames per second (fps). MPEG-2 is the video format used by DVD-ROM discs (see Module 2B). MPEG-2 videos include CD-quality audio.

- **QuickTime**   A video file format developed by Apple Computer. The latest version, QuickTime-3, plays full-screen, broadcast-quality video as well as CD-quality audio and is widely used in multimedia CD-ROM productions.

- **Video for Windows**   The native video file format for Microsoft Windows (often called AVI because these files use the .avi file name extension). This format isn't adequate for full-screen, broadcast-quality video.

Because a huge amount of data must be stored to create realistic-looking video on a computer, all video file formats use compression/decompression (codec) techniques. For the best playback, special video adapters are required also. These adapters have hardware support for decoding videos at high speed.

To make video available on the Internet, **streaming video** formats have been developed. These formats enable the video picture to start playing almost immediately after the user clicks the video link. (With non-streaming video, the user has to wait for the entire file to be transferred to the user's computer before playing begins.) Streaming video formats rely on compression, low frame rates, and small image size to deliver video over the Internet, which does not have sufficient **bandwidth** (signal-carrying capacity) to disseminate broadcast-quality video. A variety of competing streaming video formats are available; the most popular format is RealNetworks' RealVideo format.

Audio Software

A variety of programs are available for capturing and processing sound for multimedia presentations, including sound mixers, compression software, bass enhancers, synthesized stereo, and even on-screen music composition programs. You won't see any tape recorders in today's recording studios—just computers!

Destinations

Learn some more about rendering and see some pretty awesome examples by visiting Webreference.com's 3-D Animation Workshop (**http://www.web reference.com/3d/**). Hint: start with Lesson 1. If you're thinking about a career in computer animation and 3-D graphics, don't miss 3D Ark, which has tons of information about getting started in this new field (**http://www.3dark.com**).

A variety of software is available for capturing and processing sound for multimedia presentations.

Destinations

The leading vendor of streaming audio and video software, RealNetworks, enables you to download free versions of its audio and video players (**http://www.real.com**).

Digital audio **waveforms** (recorded live sounds or music) can be saved in a variety of file formats. Here are the most popular ones:

- **MP3** A sound file format with almost unbelievable characteristics: using MP3 (also known as MPEG3), you can compress CD-quality digital audio by a factor of 12:1 with no perceptible loss in sound quality.

- **Sun/Next (AU) sounds** A low-fidelity monoaural format developed for Sun and Next workstations and now widely-used due to the small size of AU files. It's often used to distribute sample sounds over the Internet.

- **WAV sounds** The default Microsoft Windows sound file format (called WAV due to the .wav extension used to store these sounds). WAV sounds can be saved to a variety of quality levels, including low-fi mono all the way up to CD-quality stereo. WAV sounds usually aren't compressed, so they tend to take up a lot of disk space.

Streaming audio formats are available that enable Internet-accessed sounds to start playing almost immediately after the user clicks the audio link. The most popular streaming audio format, RealAudio, can deliver voice-quality audio over modem connections.

You'll also encounter **Musical Instrument Digital Interface (MIDI)** files, which don't contain waveforms. Instead, they contain a text-based description designed to drive **synthesizers,** electronic devices that simulate musical sounds. Sound cards have built-in synthesizers.

MULTIMEDIA AUTHORING SYSTEMS: WRITING THE SCRIPT

Now that you've met the cast, take a look at the tools you use to write the script. To create multimedia presentations, you use **authoring tools.** These tools enable you to specify which multimedia objects to use (such as text, pictures, videos, or animations), how to display them in relation to each other, how long to display them, and how to enable the user to interact with the presentation. To take full advantage of an authoring tool's capabilities, it's often necessary to learn a **scripting language** (an easy-to-learn programming language). A leading authoring package is Macromedia Director.

Commercial authoring tools such as Macromedia Director save output in proprietary file formats, which has impeded the delivery of complex multimedia presentations on the Web. To view Macromedia presentations on a Web site, it's necessary to download and install a **plug-in program** (software that extends a browser's capabilities), but few users spend the time to do this. To counter this problem, the Web's standards-setting body, the World Wide Web Consortium (W3C), recently approved the **Synchronized Multimedia Integration Language (SMIL),** a simple multimedia scripting language designed for Web pages. If SMIL is supported by Web browsers, Internet users will be able to enjoy enhanced multimedia without having to download plug-in programs.

IMPACTS

Computers and Art

The fine arts—including painting, drawing, illustration, and sculpture—are changing as artists increasingly see the computer as an artistic medium. And the result? New technologies are opening doors—and challenging basic assumptions.

Making Art More Accessible

Thanks to the Internet and CD-ROM-based multimedia, fine art is more accessible than ever. On the Internet, Web Museums currently attract thousands of visitors per week. You'll find thousands of graphics files containing scanned images of art masterpieces.

Corbis, funded by Microsoft billionaire Bill Gates, has been buying the digital rights to art masterpieces from museums around the world. Recent acquisitions include the entire contents of the Philadelphia Museum of Art, Ansel Adams' photographs, and the entire contents of the Bettman Archive, a 16-million-image library of classic photographs. Currently, the company's archive includes 18 million digitized images. Among the company's CD-ROM publications are *A Passion for Art: Renoir, Cézanne, Matisse, and Dr. Barnes*, and *Leonardo da Vinci.*

Is there something sinister about Corbis? In making stock photographs available for purchase, Corbis is doing what stock photography companies have been doing for years. (Corbis is now the leading provider of stock photographic images to the magazine and book publishing industries.) In attempting to obtain the digital rights to virtually the entire world's collection of fine art, however, Corbis has ruffled some feathers. Museum curators don't like the idea of Corbis trying to collect 25 cents for every use of an image derived from their collections. In the hands of a profit-seeking commercial firm, art masterpieces could be trivialized into a schmaltzy, Hollywood-like production. Museum directors, however, see a much-needed source of revenue in Corbis' licensing fees.

Restoring Art

Even as Internet art museums and CD-ROM discs are making fine art more accessible, computers are helping restore original works of art that have been damaged by the ravages of time. In Italy, computers played an important role in the restoration of Michelangelo's sublime frescoes in the Sistine Chapel. Originally developed by NASA engineers to enhance satellite photographs, advanced imaging techniques enabled the restoration team to detect color and detail beneath centuries of grime, oxygenation, and abuse.

Creating Art

Increasingly, amateur and professional artists alike are forsaking the traditional tools of their medium and turning to computer tools. A standard in professional illustration is Adobe Illustrator. The program's drawing tools enable illustrators to create precise drawings in a fraction of the time required by traditional methods. In the fine arts, MetaCreation's Painter 5 software gives artists and designers hundreds of brushes that behave the way real brushes do. A wet brush, for example, stains the screen in a realistic way.

Generating Art

The visual arts have their own version of David Cope's music-generating software: programs that instruct the computer to generate art with minimal human intervention—or none at all. The term *algorithmic art* refers broadly to the use of an unfolding algorithm as a means of artistic expression. An example is the use of *fractal geometry* to create ultra-realistic landscape images. A *fractal* is an irregular geometric shape, the components of which have shapes similar to the whole. If you examine a fractal shape more closely, the shape's components look just like the larger shape. What's fascinating about fractals is their frequent occurrence in nature: snowflakes, tree bark, and mountain peaks all exhibit fractal characteristics. A program that can generate fractal shapes can be used to create images that are startlingly natural and realistic because the program uses the same logic that underlies the generation of shapes in nature.

Computers have played an important role in restoring Michelangelo's frescoes in the Sistine Chapel.

TAKEAWAY POINTS

- Multimedia refers to the use of two or more media in presenting information. Interactive multimedia enables users to choose their own path through the presentation; hypermedia uses media other than text as a means of accessing alternative navigation paths.

- Most of today's PCs are equipped with the hardware needed for multimedia viewing, but multimedia production requires input devices for graphics, sound, photographs, and video.

- Paint programs are used to create bit-mapped pictures consisting of individual dots. Draw programs create vector graphics images composed of individually-selectable objects. Bit-mapped graphics are good for complex images but are difficult to edit and cannot be enlarged without introducing unattractive edge distortions. Vector graphics images can be sized without introducing such distortions.

- Compression/decompression (codec) schemes are needed for digitized audio and video files due to their very large size.

- A multimedia authoring system enables you to write a script specifying when and where multimedia objects will appear on-screen.

MODULE REVIEW

KEY TERMS AND CONCEPT

3-D rendering
animation
authoring tools
bandwidth
bit-mapped graphics
codecs
color depth
drawing programs
Encapsulated PostScript (EPS)
frame rate
GIF animations
Graphics Interchange Format (GIF)
hypermedia
hypertext
image editors
information kiosks

interactive multimedia
Joint Photographic Experts Group (JPEG)
lossless compression
lossy compression
Moving Pictures Experts Group (MPEG)
multimedia
Musical Instrument Digital Interface (MIDI)
page description language (PDL)
paint programs
plug-in program
Portable Network Graphics (PNG)

PostScript
QuickTime
ray tracing
scripting language
streaming audio
streaming video
Synchronized Multimedia Integration Language (SMIL)
synthesizers
vector graphics
video editors
Video for Windows
waveforms
Windows Bitmap (BMP)

TRUE/FALSE

Indicate whether the following statements are true or false.

1. Multimedia is any presentation that involves two or more media.

2. In lossless compression, the original file is processed so that some information is permanently removed.

3. Another name for bit-mapped graphics is raster graphics.

4. The number of colors you can display on a monitor depends on the amount of video ROM you have in your system.

5. JPEG is a graphics file format in wide use on the World Wide Web.

6. Drawing programs are used to create raster images.

7. Frame rate describes the number of individual images displayed per minute.

8. A 3-D rendering program adds three-dimensional effects to computer graphics.

9. RealAudio can be used to deliver voice-quality audio over modem connections.

10. To use a multimedia authoring tool, you often need to learn a foreign language.

MATCHING

Match each key term from the left column to the most accurate definition in the right column.

_____ 1. multimedia

_____ 2. hypertext

_____ 3. hypermedia

_____ 4. codecs

_____ 5. lossless compression

_____ 6. lossy compression

_____ 7. bit-mapped graphics

_____ 8. image editors

_____ 9. animation

_____ 10. streaming video

a. the act of processing an original file so that some information is permanently removed

b. images that are composed of tiny dots, each corresponding to one pixel on the computer's display

c. a format that enables a video picture to begin playing after the user clicks the video link

d. a graphic you can click on to access a different Web page

e. a presentation involving two or more media

f. a series of still images displayed at a frame rate high enough to create the illusion of movement

g. compression/decompression algorithms

h. the compression of a file so that it can be completely restored when decompression occurs

i. a link you can click on to access a different Web page

j. sophisticated versions of paint programs designed for editing and transforming complex bit-mapped images

MULTIPLE CHOICE

Circle the letter of the correct choice for each of the following.

1. The number of colors that can be displayed on your computer monitor is dependent on what?
   a. How the graphic was created.
   b. The speed of your video card.
   c. The amount of video **RAM** in your system.
   d. The type of monitor you have.

2. Which of the following is the color depth when you use 24 bits of color information per pixel?
   a. 16 colors
   b. 256 colors
   c. 32,767 colors
   d. 16.7 million colors

3. Which of the following is not a standard graphics file format?
   a. ACX
   b. GIF
   c. JPEG
   d. BMP

4. Which of the following is an example of a drawing program?
   a. Photoshop
   b. Paint Shop Pro
   c. Macromedia Freehand
   d. PageMaker

5. Which technology is often used to add realism to a simulated three-dimensional object by adding color variations?

   a. ray tracing
   b. depth conversion
   c. visual extension
   d. heuristic rendering

6. A codec is used for what purpose?
   a. The compression and decompression of video data.
   b. To produce realistic sounds.
   c. To move information quickly over the Internet.
   d. To provide a reference standard for multimedia data files.

7. Which of the following terms describes the signal-carrying capacity of a communications channel?
   a. spectrum
   b. bandwidth
   c. data rate
   d. streaming

8. What type of compression ratios can be achieved for CD-quality audio using the MP3 format?
   a. 5:1
   b. 10:1
   c. 12:1
   d. 15:2

9. SMIL is an acronym meaning what?
   a. standard multimedia implementation layer
   b. synchronized multimedia integration language
   c. single media integration layer
   d. small media Internet language

10. Which of the following is necessary to use when working with an authoring tool?
    a. MP3
    b. WAV Sounds
    c. Sun/Next (AU) Sounds
    d. scripting language

FILL-IN

In the blank provided, write the correct answer for each of the following.

1. Paint programs are used to create _____ graphics.

2. Drawing programs are used to create _____ graphics.

3. PostScript is an example of a(n) _____.

4. A(n) _____ enables you to modify digitized videos by means of a video capture board.

5. The video file format developed by Apple Computer is known as _____.

6. To make video available on the Internet, _____ formats have been developed.

7. RealAudio is a popular _____ format.

8. To create multimedia presentations, you use _____ tools.

9. To take full advantage of an authoring tool's capabilities, it's often necessary to use a(n) _____.

10. To view Macromedia presentations on a Web site, it's necessary to download and install a(n) _____ program.

SHORT ANSWER

On a separate sheet of paper, answer the following questions.

1. What is the difference between multimedia, interactive multimedia, hypertext, and hypermedia?

2. What types of applications are being developed with multimedia techniques?

3. What's the difference between lossy and lossless compression?

4. What are the primary differences between paint programs and image editors?

5. What graphics file formats are in common use on the Internet?

6. What is the purpose of a video editor program? How do programs of this type work?

7. What are the major types of video file formats in use?

8. How does streaming video work?

9. What are the major types of audio compression formats in use?

10. Describe the ways in which multimedia presentations are created.

5B

MODULE

VIRTUAL ENVIRONMENTS

OUTLINE

WHAT YOU WILL LEARN . . .

When you have finished reading this module, you will be able to:

1. List three types of virtual reality presentations.
2. Identify examples of virtual reality applications.
3. Describe the most popular virtual reality application and discuss its primary criticism.
4. Distinguish between MUDs and gMUDs.

Techtalk

tele-immersion

Tele-immersion is coming! With the implementation of Internet2 (a testing-ground network for university collaboration), people in different geographic locations will be able to meet in a simulated environment. Users will feel as though they're actually looking, talking, and meeting face-to-face in the same room. It requires use of multiple cameras taking rapid sequential shots of the same object, running continuous distance calculations, and then reconstructing the 3-D image in the simulated environment to replicate real-time movement.

If you're headed to the Rossetti Archives, a comprehensive collection of 19th century painter Gabriel Rossetti, you won't be taking the subway—or for that matter, a car or taxi. That's because the Rossetti Archives isn't a brick-and-mortar building. Instead, it's a Web site, accessible on the electronic grounds of the University of Virginia **(http://jefferson.village.virginia.edu/:2020).** Described as a hypermedia archive, this site enables you to experience Rossetti's life and work from a variety of angles, including digitized reproductions of Rossetti's paintings and writings, scholarly commentaries and criticism, translations, biographical materials, and much more. If you prefer the experience of visiting a museum to see Rossetti's paintings, try visiting the Rossetti Room **(http://urizen.village.virginia.edu/dgr/dgr_stories.html),** a three-dimensional, virtual reality "museum" in which you can "stroll" around and view reproductions of Rossetti's work.

The Rossetti Room illustrates a powerful new set of possibilities that are enabled by the rise of powerful desktop computers with equally-impressive graphics capabilities. Experiments such as the Rossetti Room create *immersive* environments, which draw you in and give you a sense of "being there." That the experience can be profound is attested to by the growing numbers of people who are hooked on three-dimensional multiplayer Internet games. That it can also be somewhat disquieting is attested to by the smaller numbers of people who, once having experienced a virtual environment, find themselves so strongly drawn to it that they show signs of addiction. It's increasingly clear that the computer can offer a tantalizing alternative to reality. What's far from clear, as yet, are the questions of how this powerful new medium will be profitably used, and how it will impact society.

VIRTUAL REALITY: TOWARD THE HOLODECK?

You've probably seen one of the episodes of *Star Trek: The Next Generation* where the crew takes some time off in the Holodeck, an immersive virtual reality environment. (One of the show's standard plots is that the crew gets trapped in the Holodeck and has to fight for their lives against virtual creatures that suddenly become deadly.) **Virtual reality (VR)** refers to the creation of an immersive, three-dimensional world that appears as if you can actually go inside and explore it.

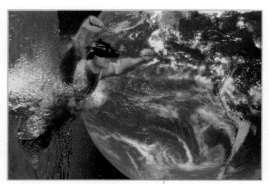

Virtual reality refers to the creation of a three-dimensional world that appears as if you can go inside and explore it. Navigation controls enable you to walk around or fly within the simulated world.

Enhancing the Immersive Experience: VR Hardware

Displayed on a two-dimensional computer screen, virtual reality environments are lots of fun. You can use navigation controls that enable you to walk around or fly, if you prefer, in the simulated world. But virtual reality comes into its own when you don a **head-mounted display (HMD),** a helmet-like contraption equipped with stereo LCD displays. You can then physically explore what appears to be a complex virtual environment, even though you're really walking around in a big, empty room.

The most advanced (and expensive) immersive technology to date is the **Cave Automatic Virtual Environment (CAVE),** which projects stereo images on walls to give the illusion of a virtual environment. To create the illusion of objects inside the environment, explorers wear special shutter glasses that alternately block the left and right eyes in synchronization with the projection sequence, which similarly alternates between left and right stereo vision seen from the person's location. The effect is so realistic that explorers can't tell the difference between real and simulated objects in the room unless they touch them.

Bringing VR to the Internet: VRML

On the World Wide Web, virtual realities can be created by means of the **Virtual Reality Modeling Language** (**VRML,** pronounced "vir-mal"). VRML enables programmers to define the characteristics of Web-accessible, three-dimensional worlds, through which visitors can journey. To visit a VRML site on the Web, you'll need to equip your Web browser with a VRML plug-in, such as the Microsoft VRML Viewer for Internet Explorer, or WorldView (Intervista Software), a VRML plug-in for Netscape Navigator. After installing the plug-in and accessing a VRML "world" (a Web site with the .wrl extension), you can walk or even "fly" through the three-dimensional construct. In some virtual worlds, you'll see other explorers who are virtually represented by means of an **avatar,** a graphical representation of a computer user who is exploring the world. You can choose your own avatar as well as interact with other users' avatars.

Practical Applications of VR

What's the use of virtual reality? For consumers, the answer is simple: games. Almost all top-selling computer games offer three-dimensional virtual realities. But virtual reality (VR) isn't all fun and games. In the military, VR systems are being used to train fighter pilots and combat soldiers. In architecture, VR simulations enable clients to preview and walk through an architect's design. In medicine, VR is being used to train surgeons in delicate and dangerous surgical techniques. In manufacturing, VR is being used to analyze complex, three-dimensional structures to make sure that they have been correctly designed and can be manufactured in a cost-effective way.

COMPUTER GAMES

By any standard, it's a big business. In the U.S., computer games bring in sales at a clip of $6 billion per year, and the market shows no signs of shrinking.

This highly-profitable industry got its start in the 1970s, when the earliest computer video games (such as Pong) appeared in bars and gaming arcades. Next, video games came to the living room with the advent of Atari, Nintendo, and Sega console game players, which are special-purpose computers designed to display their output on a TV screen. Games soon migrated to personal computers—and from there, to the Internet.

A new wrinkle on the gaming scene is **multiplayer online gaming,** an Internet-based gaming service that enables players to engage other characters—and in this case, they're controlled by other players rather than the computer. Combining a rich, graphical virtual environment with multi-player thrills, these services are attracting increasing numbers of users. There's a technical problem, though, caused by the Internet's inherent latency, which can cause characters to freeze up momentarily (or even disappear, if the user's connection is lost).

The VR Factor

Taking a cue from virtual reality, the hottest computer games offer three-dimensional, graphical environments that players can explore. They've helped to fuel explosive growth in the computer gaming market. One of the earliest three-dimensional, VR-type games, Doom, has sold over 2.7 million copies, and it's believed that some 20 million

Destinations

Like to try a virtual world? Try The Palace (**http://www.thepalace. com**) or ActiveWorlds (**http://www.active-worlds.com**). Active-Worlds has thousands of kilometers of virtual territory, in which hundreds of thousands of virtual explorers are constructing abodes of various sorts on their "property." If your tastes run toward the Gothic, try TombTown (**http:// www.tombtown.com**), the Web's only virtual cemetery.

Destinations

A great way to tour some of the best VRML sites on the Web is the VRML Web Ring, a series of Web sites linked together to provide an introduction to virtual reality. You'll find the VRML Web Ring headquarters at **http://www. avatara.com/ring/.**

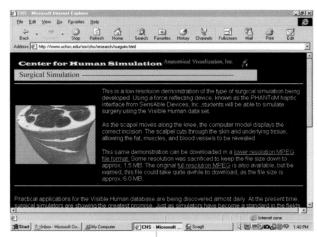

In medicine, VR is being used to train surgeons in surgical techniques.

MOVERS & SHAKERS

Merce Cunningham

Choreographers plan dance performances. Today, they're getting a lot of help from computers. The most popular choreography software, LifeForms (Credo Interactive, Inc.), creates animated sequences useful for visualizing a dance and presenting dance ideas. A pioneer of modern dance, Merce Cunningham, has used LifeForms since 1989, creating more than a dozen dances with the software. In 1994, Cunningham premiered a 90-minute dance called "Ocean," created entirely with LifeForms. The program comes equipped with a huge database of dance animations, which collectively encompass the language of dance. Of LifeForms, Cunningham says that the program enables him to explore possibilities that aren't possible on the dance floor. You can't ask a dancer, for example, to do a difficult jump 20 times in a row, just so you can investigate different ways of doing it.

Computers are helping choreographers shape dance, as you've just learned. But people are turning the tables on the computer. In a new technology called performance animation (also called motion capture), human dancers, puppeteers, and even athletes dress in special suits containing sensors and go through the motions planned for an animated cartoon's character. Transferred to a computer, the data generates animation sequences instantly, and the result is a high degree of realism. Among some motion-captured people you've probably seen are 40 extras hired to mill about the deck of the *Titanic* in 1998's box-office blockbuster.

Cunningham's recent work folds performance animation back on itself in a way that audiences have found especially fascinating. In *Biped*, 14 dancers are joined by disembodied, motion-captured images of dancers that are projected onto a thin, transparent screen of gauze at the front of the stage. By placing live dancers and performance animation images on the same stage, Cunningham invites the audience to consider just what we gain—and what we lose—by digitizing the motions of the human form.

copies of the game are in use worldwide. 3-D games have also driven computer video card manufacturers to new feats of technical innovation. Today's 3-D video cards offer sophisticated, ultra-fast graphics processing that, only a few years ago, would have required a research supercomputer to equal.

Too Much Violence?

Computer gaming isn't universally admired. More than one-third of all games fall into the action category. Among these, the most popular are so-called "splatter" games, which emphasize all-out violence of an especially-bloody sort. Parents and politicians express the concern that kids who play these games may be learning aggressive behaviors that will prove dysfunctional in real life—and they may be right.

In a study of 210 college students before and after playing an especially-violent computer game, researchers found an increase in aggressive reactions and hostility. Another study found that young men who played violent computer games during their teenage years were more likely to commit crimes. Fears concerning the impact of violent computer games were heightened by the Columbine High School tragedy, in which two Littleton, Colorado teenagers opened fire on teachers and fellow students before committing suicide. Subsequently, investigators learned that the boys were great fans of splatter games such as Doom and Quake, and may have patterned their massacre after their gaming experiences.

Still, psychologists disagree on the effect of violent computer games. Some point out that they're little more than an extension of the World War II "combat" games that kids used to play on streetcorners before the television—and the computer—came along. Others claim that violent video games provide an outlet for aggression that might otherwise materialize in homes and schools.

One thing's for certain: computer games keep getting more violent. Just after the Columbine massacre, the video game industry released a slew of new titles that offered a smoother gaming experience, particularly when you're connected to the Internet in multi-player mode—and, of course, much more realistic beheadings, amputations, and disembowelments.

MUDs

The non-computer-based Dungeons and Dragons role-playing game, in which players can take on the personalities and powers of fantasy characters, including elves, sorcerers, and muscle-bound adventurers as they interact with other players has been popular among gamers for years. Role-playing games are a natural for Internet-connected computers, which enable players to participate even if they're not physically present in the same room. Although there are several types of Internet-mediated role-playing games in existence, they're generally called **MUDs,** an acronym for **multi-user dungeons.**

MUDs and their various offshoots offer users a text-only environment, consisting (generally) of a number of rooms—sometimes thousands of them—inhabited by various online characters. You can ask for a description of the room, a list of players present in the room, and additional facts. You interact with other players by means of text chatting, very much like the chat rooms on America Online or the channels to be found on Internet Relay Chat (IRC).

If MUDs are text-only, what's so engrossing about them? Just ask the regulars. It's a matter of using your imagination. Most MUDs focus on themes derived from popular books (such as Rober Zelazny's *Amber* novels or Anne McCaffrey's *Pern* series), movies (such as *Babylon 5* or *Star Wars*), or role-playing games. Within a MUD, you can construct a persona for yourself, build a fantasy environment around you, and share the experience with other players.

MUDs aren't necessarily all fun and games. On most MUDs, player killing is allowed or tolerated, which means that your character might get suddenly zapped. You'll have to invent a new character, and you may lose all the possessions and powers your character has acquired. In addition, women often complain that male players harass them online to the point that they give up and log off.

The latest MUD development, **graphical MUDs (gMUD),** brings the virtual environment to life with three-dimensional, graphical environments. Many are directly accessible online with no special equipment other than a Web browser, but a new trend is a commercial gMUD that relies on a locally-installed game package to speed up processing. Examples include Ultima Online and EverQuest. Players may fork over up to $40 for the locally-installed software and $10 per month for online usage.

Destinations

For a list of publicly-accessible MUDs, visit the MUD Connection (**http://www. mudconnect.com**).

SPOTLIGHT

THE COMPUTER IN TINSELTOWN

▶Computers have starred on both sides of the Hollywood movie camera for a few decades now. Although computer-literate viewers can easily find inconsistencies and glitches in how computers are depicted and used on-screen, behind the scenes it is a different story.

It's hard to imagine moviemaking these days without the use of computers. They affect every aspect of production, from creating storyboards to editing and mixing the final scenes. They are used for fantastic special effects, as well as subtle changes to scenes you would never guess a computer had touched.

Perhaps the biggest effects of computers are in editing, audio, and special effects. The last area has the biggest visual impact, but the other two are where the filmmaker's talent shines.

For many movies, editing—the process of taking raw footage and making a movie from it—is performed digitally on a computer. Instead of working with rolls and rolls of celluloid strewn around the editing suite, the editor sits in front of a computer workstation and views the movie, frame-by-frame, as it's played back from a hard drive. (A single second of video has thirty frames.) Individual scenes are quickly located and combined with other scenes. With the click of a mouse, the editor can instruct the computer to make the edits previously performed by hand.

The computerized approach to editing is such a different process from the way editing used to be performed that it's changing the work habits of the industry. Instead of editorial teams viewing movie clips and working together to splice the final footage, editors are doing individual work more and more. With the computer workstation approach, editors are isolated and must rely on themselves rather than the team. This isolation results in greater individual pressures and stress.

The audio track created for a movie is also greatly affected by computers. A separate voice track is created while the video is shot. The voice track is then synchronized and combined with the video footage into a coherent mix. Only toward the end are sound effects and music added to create the final audio track.

The process of audio-to-video synchronization is similar to the video editing process. Digital manipulation allows audio technicians to identify the exact frame where the audio should begin or end. The results of the synchronization can then be viewed and quickly changed, if necessary.

For the movie-viewing public, special effects is where the computer has made a huge impact. Computers allow filmmakers to create shots and scenes that would be impossible in real life. From movies such as *Star Wars* (LucasFilms, 1977) to *Terminator 2: Judgment Day* (Carolco Pictures, 1991) to *Armageddon* (Touchstone Pictures, 1998), the computer has been used to create strange new worlds and drastically change the mundane world in which we live. Computers have even been used to create entire new worlds, as in the animated *Toy Story* (Disney, 1995).

It isn't just animation or science fiction movies where special effects shine, either. Fantasy movies, romances, action flicks, and traditional dramas all use special effects to change the way in which explosions occur, leaves fall, or actors appear. Computers are used to add reflections in windows or increase the way the stars appear on a moonless night. Who can forget Lt. Dan Taylor in the movie *Forrest Gump?* During the course of the movie, the character lost his legs in Vietnam. Lt. Taylor was played by Gary Sinise, an actor with two good legs. Fantasy became reality as his legs were "surgically removed" by the special effects crew for the movie.

As filmmakers use computers in ever-more-complex ways to help create the movies we view, the public's expectations become greater. The movie viewer accepts fantasy as reality, without even overtly realizing it is fantasy. We want to see the impossible look real. As filmmakers race to deliver this expectation, computers—and technicians who can effectively use those computers—will play a bigger role in Hollywood.

Computers were used to generate the characters and scenery in Disney's *Toy Story*.

TAKEAWAY POINTS

- The three types of virtual reality presentations are two-dimensional displays of 3-D environments, head-mounted display systems, and CAVEs.
- Virtual reality is popular in computer games, and it has many useful applications in military training, architecture, medicine, and manufacturing.
- Computer games are by far the most popular application of virtual reality. More than one-third of all computer games fall into the action category; among these, the most popular are so-called "splatter" games, which emphasize violence. Parents and politicians express concern that kids who play these games may be learning aggressive behaviors that will prove dysfunctional in real life.
- Multi-user dungeons, or MUDs, are Internet-mediated role-playing games. MUDs offer users a text-only environment, consisting of a number of rooms—sometimes thousands of them—inhabited by various online characters. The latest MUD development, graphical MUDs (gMUD), brings the virtual environment to life with three-dimensional, graphical environments.

MODULE REVIEW

KEY TERMS AND CONCEPTS

avatar
Cave Automatic Virtual
    Environment (CAVE)
graphical MUDs (gMUD)

head-mounted display (HMD)
multiplayer online gaming
MUDs (multi-user dungeons)

virtual reality (VR)
Virtual Reality Modeling
    Language (VRML)

TRUE/FALSE

Indicate whether the following statements are true or false.

1. The most immersive and most expensive VR technology to date is the Cave Automatic Virtual Environment (CAVE).
2. Head-mounted displays do not enhance a virtual reality experience very much.
3. Virtual reality is used to train fighter pilots and combat soldiers.
4. MUDs offer users a graphics-only environment consisting of a couple of rooms inhabited by four or fewer online characters.
5. Violence is not a pressing issue in the computer game industry.

MATCHING

Match each key term from the left column to the most accurate definition in the right column.

_____ 1. virtual reality

_____ 2. Cave Automatic Virtual Environment (CAVE)

_____ 3. Virtual Reality Modeling Language (VRML)

_____ 4. multiplayer online gaming

_____ 5. Graphical MUDs (gMUD)

a. an immersive technology that projects stereo images on walls to give the illusion of a virtual environment

b. the latest development that brings the virtual environment to life with three-dimensional, graphical environments

c. the creation of an immersive, three-dimensional world that appears as if you can actually go inside it and explore it

d. an Internet-based gaming service that enables players to engage other characters

e. enables programmers to define the characteristics of Web-accessible, three-dimensional worlds

MULTIPLE CHOICE

Circle the letter of the correct choice for each of the following.

1. Which technology represents the most realistic virtual reality experience?
   a. HMD
   b. VRI
   c. CAVE
   d. JPEG

2. Which accessory would you wear to explore a complex virtual environment?
   a. headphones
   b. head-mounted display
   c. goggles
   d. 3-D glasses

3. If you want to visit a virtual reality modeling language (VRML) site on the Web, which of the following would you need?
   a. a VRML plug-in
   b. a virtual reality modeling language
   c. an avatar
   d. permission from Microsoft

4. Which technical problem is associated with multi-player online gaming?
   a. The games may be too violent for some, which might cause some players to drop out of the game.
   b. Not all players will necessarily have the same VR hardware.
   c. Not all players will necessarily have the same version of the VR software.
   d. The Internet's latency can cause characters to momentarily freeze up or disappear altogether.

5. Which of the following relies, in some cases, on a locally-installed game package to speed up processing?
   a. MUD
   b. head-mounted display
   c. gMUD
   d. CAVE

FILL-IN

In the blank provided, write the correct answer for each of the following.

1. _____ refers to the creation of an immersive, three-dimensional world that appears as if you can actually go inside and explore it.

2. A graphical representation of a computer user who is exploring the world is called a(n) _____ .

3. On the World Wide Web, virtual realities can be created by means of the _____ .

4. _____ offer users a text-only environment consisting of a number of rooms inhabited by various online characters.

5. The latest MUD development, _____, brings the virtual environment to life with three-dimensional, graphical environments.

SHORT ANSWER

On a separate sheet of paper, answer the following questions.

1. How does virtual reality work?
2. How is virtual reality being used today?
3. What are the controversies associated with computer games?

4. What's the difference between a MUD and a gMUD?
5. What is a Virtual Reality Modeling Language and what do you need to visit a VRML site on the Web?

PFSweb, Inc.

Most e-commerce Web sites have two components: the front-end marketing piece and the back-end transaction-processing piece. The front-end usually contains the home page, marketing/brand development information, company information, and other pages designed to inform the user about the e-commerce company and its products or services. You know, the flashy stuff. The back-end piece is where money changes hands. The product catalog with search capability, shopping cart, payment processing, fraud checks, and final bill calculation are performed here.

For a business-to-consumer (B2C) Web site, graphics usually are contained in two places: the marketing front-end, and the catalog. Graphics take a lot of time to load relative to plain text, and the last thing any company wants to do is make the customer wait, especially if they're ready to buy! In fact, most customers will only wait a few seconds before giv-

ing up and canceling the purchase transaction. So most B2C sites pay careful attention to their use of graphics and multimedia elements, and design them so you can make your purchases quickly.

PFSweb's experience is revealing an interesting trend in the use of graphics. Most business-to-business (B2B) client sites are cutting back on graphics in favor of faster content delivery and streamlined order processing. B2C sites are even re-thinking their use of graphics. When graphics on the Web was a new concept, lots of sites tossed in every conceivable item—sound, color, dancing animals, you name it. But consumers are smarter now, and don't have the time or patience for irrelevant fluff. What's more, the competition in both arenas is forcing e-commerce companies to get to know their competitors and customers much better, leading to Web sites that better suit their preferences. Does this mean the sizzle has gone out of the e-commerce steak? Not at all, it just may mean you get your steak the way you want it!

What do you think? What types of Web site graphics do you find most useful? As a consumer, are you willing to trade off fewer graphics for faster site download time? What if you were buying industrial components for a manufacturer? Do your answers change? Why or why not?

WebLink Go to **www.prenhall.com/ pfaffenberger** to see the video of Mike Willoughby of PFSweb tell what graphical elements are most important in Web sites today.

E-COMMERCE IN ACTION

6

CHAPTER

Data Communications

Imagine a world in which only two telephones exist. You wouldn't have much choice concerning who you're going to call! Now start squaring the number: 4 telephones, 16 telephones, 256 telephones. . . and eventually, billions of them. Does their value increase? You bet, says Bob Metcalfe, inventor of the Ethernet technology that powers local area networks worldwide. The telephone system's value increases as more people use it, to the point that it becomes an indispensable resource. That's why more than 95 percent of U.S. homes have telephone service. Can you imagine dealing with today's economy without the aid of a telephone?

What happens when you bring computers into the picture? The telephone system makes computers more valuable by giving them a means to exchange data over telephone lines. Telecommunications, the use of the telephone system to transmit computer data, is an everyday fact. In the U.S., more than half of the country's residences connect to the Internet by means of a home computer, a modem, and a telephone line. Module 6A explores the use of the public telephone system for telecommunications.

Designed for voice, the telephone system isn't ideal for transferring computer data. Computer networks provide connections that are optimized for high-speed data transfer. In Module 6B, you'll learn about the two types of computer networks that are in common use today: local area networks (LANs), which connect computers in a limited geographical area, and wide area networks (WANs), which can connect computers separated by continental and even transcontinental distances.

All the evidence suggests that data communications will become just as indispensable as the telephone is right now. Already, businesses can't survive in a highly-competitive marketplace without high-speed, long-distance data communications services—and in the future, individuals are increasingly likely to consider network connectivity to be just as important as today's telephone. If you watch the crowds lining up to check email at airport data centers, you'll become convinced that the future is already here—and you'll understand why it's so important to understand the technology that underlies data communications.

M O D U L E S

6A

MODULE

OUTLINE

WHAT YOU WILL LEARN . . . .

When you have finished reading this module, you will be able to:

1. Explain the limitations of the public switched telephone network (PSTN) for sending and receiving computer data.

2. Discuss how modems transform digital computer signals into the analog tones suited for the telephone system.

3. Define *bandwidth* and discuss the bandwidth needs of typical users.

4. List two digital telephony standards that can bring digital connections into homes and offices using existing wiring.

5. Provide examples of how convergence is blurring the boundaries among popular communication devices, including phones, computers, and TVs.

6. Discuss the prospects for telephony through the Internet.

Suppose that you're on a business trip and need to access your electronic mail. You hook up your notebook computer to the telephone system, which enables you to access the distant computer that's been collecting and storing your messages. You're experiencing the realities of **telecommunications.** Defined broadly, this term refers to the transmission of information of any type using the telephone system. Your interest is in the transmission of computer data (your email) through the telephone system, which is the focus of this module.

Although it's common to use the telephone system to send and receive computer data, it's important to understand the phone system's limitations for this purpose. Most telephone connections in homes and offices offer analog service, which isn't ideal for data communication. In this module, you'll learn why analog connections are still so common, what's needed to hook up computers to phone lines, and how this situation is changing as new digital telephone services become available.

In the short run, faster connections to computer-based services such as the Internet will become available. And in the long run, the distinctions between the telephone system and computer networks may disappear as all our familiar communications gadgets and systems join the digital age.

Destinations

Want to learn more about PSTN and fast-breaking new telecommunication technologies? A great place to start is HelloDirect.com's tutorials (**http://static.hellodirect.net/1086.htm**).

UNDERSTANDING THE TELEPHONE SYSTEM

Let's start with the beginning: the **public switched telephone network (PSTN),** derisively (and somewhat unfairly) called Plain Old Telephone Service (POTS) by some computer users. The derision comes from the fact that most telephone lines provide an analog connection, based on standards that date back more than a century (see Figure 6A.1). As you'll see, though, it's not true that the PSTN is an entirely-analog network. In this section, you learn enough about how PSTN works to realize that it's on the verge of becoming a digital network, which will mean big, positive changes for data communication.

Quality of Service

Any discussion of the telephone system should begin with praise for its accomplishments. Today's telephone system uses advanced switching technology to create an end-to-end circuit between *any* two telephones in the world. What's amazing about this system is the number of telephones that can be directly and almost instantly connected. Nearly one-half billion telephones are in existence today, and most are accessible by means of direct dialing (see Figure 6A.2). In the United States alone, nearly one billion telephone calls are made every day. Despite infrequent service outages, PSTN is able to pull off these feats with a guaranteed **quality of service (QoS).** When you need to make a call, you can, and the audio quality is good.

Figure 6A.1

Most telephone lines provide an analog connection, based on standards that date back more than a century.

Local Exchange Carriers (LECs)

Telephone services are provided by **local exchange carriers (LECs),** also called *telcos,* which provide directly-wired services between the homes and offices of subscribers. This network of local connections is called the **local access and transport area (LATA).** Within the LATA, you can place a call without accessing a long-distance carrier.

Let's explore the local exchange by starting with your home telephone. Most telephones in use today are *analog* devices, which transmit and

Figure 6A.2

Nearly one-half billion telephones are in existence today, and most are accessible by means of direct dialing. In the U.S. alone, nearly one billion telephone calls are made every day.

Destinations

Fiber Optics Online (**http://www.fiberoptics online.com**) is a trade journal specializing in the fiber optics industry. The journal's Web site is a great place to learn about new fiber-optics technologies.

Destinations

To learn more about the ITU and international telecommunications standards, visit the ITU's home page at **http:// www.itu.int/.**

receive a continuously-changing electrical signal that matches the acoustics of the human voice. These telephones are linked to *subscriber loop carriers (SLCs)* by means of copper wires (called **twisted pair,** that are twisted around each other to prevent interference (called noise) from electrical circuits. An SLC is a small, waist-high installation that connects as many as 96 subscribers; you've probably seen one in your neighborhood. The area served by an SLC is called the **local loop.**

In most local exchanges in the United States, only the local loop is stuck with analog technology, thanks largely to the fact that nearly all existing buildings were constructed with built-in twisted-pair wiring. The expense required to rewire all this construction is simply too great. From the SLC on, though, the telephone system is increasingly a digital network. The SLC transforms local analog calls into digital signals, routing them through high-capacity, fiber-optic cables to the *local exchange switch,* which is also based on the digital technology capable of handling thousands of calls. The local exchange switch is located in the local telephone company's central office.

Long-Distance Transmission Media

If you place a call outside the local transport area, an **interexchange carrier (IXC)**—a long-distance telephone company—comes into play. In the United States, long-distance service is open to competition.

A variety of transmission facilities are used to provide regional and long-distance service between local telephone exchanges, including the following:

- **Copper wire** Specially-conditioned copper wires called *T1 carriers* can handle as many as 24 voice calls simultaneously (or up to 1.544 Mbps of computer data).

- **Fiber-optic cables** Fiber-optic cables consist of thin strands of glass that transmit data by means of pulses of light (see Figure 6A.3). *T3 carriers* can handle 672 voice calls or 43 Mbps of computer data.

- **Microwaves** High-frequency radio waves called *microwaves* handled much of the long-distance telephone service until the recent growth of fiber-optic networks. Because microwaves must travel in a straight line, relay stations were built at a distance of approximately every 30 miles (the line-of-sight distance to the horizon) or closer if the terrain blocks transmission.

- **Satellites** Essentially microwave relay stations suspended in space, communications satellites are positioned in *geosynchronous orbits,* which match the speed of the earth's rotation and therefore are permanently positioned with respect to the ground (see Figure 6A.4).

Because long-distance lines must handle thousands of calls simultaneously, techniques called **multiplexing** have been developed to send more than one call on a single line. The electrical and physical characteristics of copper wire place a limit of 24 multiplexed calls per wire, but fiber-optic cables can carry as many as 48,384 digital voice channels simultaneously. In contrast to the analog local loop, most long-distance carriers use digital signals so that they can pack the greatest number of calls in a single circuit.

Standards and Regulations

The public switched telephone network isn't purely a technological creation. It's based also on internationally-recognized standards and important legal and political concepts.

Standards

Because telephone services are offered by thousands of companies in hundreds of countries, standards are needed to ensure that one company's subscriber can communicate with another's. Telephone and other telecommunications standards are governed by the Geneva, Switzerland-based **International Telecommunications Union (ITU),** a division of the United Nations.

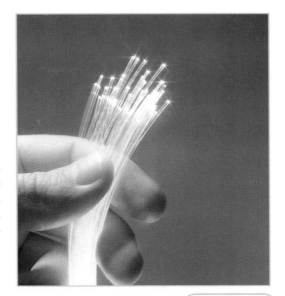

Figure   6A.3

Fiber-optic cables consist of thin strands of glass that transmit data by means of pulses of light. They can carry as many as 48,384 digital voice channels simultaneously.

Universal Service

In the United States, the concept of **universal service** underlies the legislation that regulates telephone service. This concept recognizes that telephone service is vital to public safety and economic welfare, but it also recognizes that profit-seeking telephone companies will not provide service in unprofitable areas (such as remote rural locales) unless they are provided with financial incentives. Telecommunications laws specify that subscribers and phone companies should pay access fees and other fees to cover the cost of construction and maintenance of telephone systems in remote or otherwise unprofitable areas. Universal service isn't an issue in most other nations, where telephone service is a state-run monopoly.

Common Carrier Immunity

Another important concept underlying the telephone system is **common carrier immunity. A common carrier** is a transportation or communications company that provides vital public services. In return, legislation holds these carriers immune from civil or criminal liability for the actions of individuals who misuse these services. If you make a harassing telephone call, for example, you are personally liable, not the phone company.

Deregulation

In the United States, an important development in telephony is **deregulation,** in which laws and regulations circumscribing telephone company actions have been altered or removed. In 1983, a court decision broke up telephone monopoly AT&T and created a competitive market for long-distance services. AT&T was restricted to providing long-distance service, while local telephone service would be provided by **Regional Bell Operating Companies (RBOCs),** also called Baby Bells, which retained a monopoly in their service areas. The Telecommunications Act of 1996 deregulated RBOCs, exposing them to local competition while enabling them to compete for long-distance service.

Figure   6A.4

This astronaut is servicing a communications satellite.

More Ways to Access the System

As you've already learned, most phones are analog devices tied to the local loop's twisted-pair wiring. That's unsatisfactory for many, so alternative ways have been devised to gain access to telephone services, such as private branch exchanges, wireless (cellular) telephones, and leased lines.

Private Branch Exchange (PBX)

Most of the phones in the local loop are analog devices, prone to noise and interference. Digital phones, however, offer noise-free transmission and high-quality audio. You've probably already used one: large organizations, such as corporations and universities, typically install their own internal digital telephone systems, called a **private branch exchange (PBX).** By using a PBX, an organization can avoid the high cost of paying for a line for each employee to the local telephone company's exchange switch. Calls to the outside must be translated into analog signals to connect to the PSTN.

Cellular Telephones

The PSTN isn't the only analog phone technology around. Increasingly popular are **cellular telephones,** which enable subscribers to place calls through a wireless communications system (see Figure 6A.5).

World War II proved the usefulness of the walkie-talkie, a **wireless** communications service that enables mobile, two-way communication. (A wireless communications medium uses radio or infrared signals.) But a walkie-talkie signal weakens, and finally disappears, as you get out of the range of the transmitting unit. In 1971, AT&T discovered a way to solve this problem: build a network of automatic repeating transmitters (called a **cell site**), each of which would broadcast a signal throughout a limited geographic area (called a **cell**). As a caller moves from one area to another, a new cell site automatically steps in to keep the signal strength strong. All cell sites are connected to a Mobile Telephone Switching Office (MTSO), which in turn is connected to the standard PSTN telephone system (see Figure 6A.6). Originally (and still predominantly) an analog system, cellular telephone service was introduced commercially in 1983. Current projections call for a worldwide subscriber base of nearly 500 million by 2005.

Figure 6A.5

Cellular telephones enable subscribers to place calls through a wireless communications system.

Leased Lines

To get around the analog limitations of the local loop, companies that need long-distance data communication obtain **leased lines.** These specially-conditioned telephone lines provide direct digital access to long-distance carriers. Unlike switched local connections, leased lines are permanently connected and always available. You will learn more about leased lines in Module 6B.

The PSTN in Perspective

Because the PSTN forces computer users to transform digital data into analog form, it's of limited use for data communication. The analog connections are vulnerable to line noise and can't surpass a theoretical limit of 56 Kbps

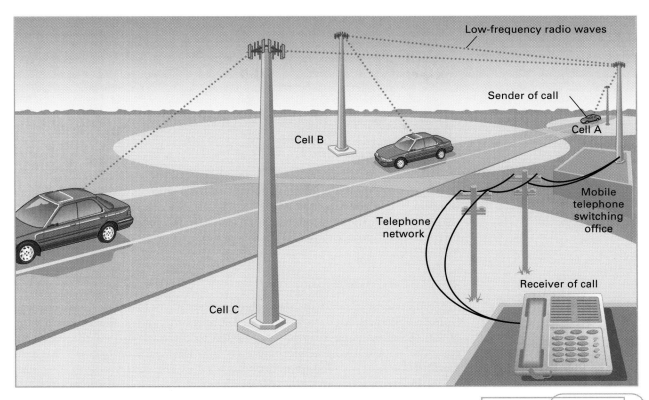

Low-frequency radio waves

Sender of call

Cell A

Cell B

Mobile
telephone
switching
office

Telephone
network

Cell C

Receiver of call

Figure   6A.6

As a caller moves from one area to another, a new cell site automatically steps in to keep the signal strength strong. All cell sites are connected to a Mobile Telephone Switching Office (MTSO), which in turn is connected to the standard PSTN telephone system.

for analog services on twisted pair. But most people don't realize that the PSTN in advanced industrial countries is already a predominantly *digital* network, as you've just learned. The local loop becomes analog in the last mile of service delivery, which is why it's called the **last mile problem.** The solution appears easy: just rip out the twisted pair and put in fiber-optic cable. But you're forgetting the price tag. To replace all the twisted pair that currently delivers phone service to homes and offices worldwide, a capital investment of an estimated $325 billion is required. That's not going to happen anytime soon.

MODEMS: FROM DIGITAL TO ANALOG AND BACK

As long as your telephone company is still using analog equipment in the local loop, all your messages, whether voice or data, must be sent as analog sounds that fall within the range of the human voice, for which the phone system was designed. Linking two computers through the analog telephone system requires that both computers be equipped with **modems,** devices that transform digital signals into analog form for transmission through the telephone network.

How Modems Work

Using a process called **modulation,** a modem transforms the computer's digital signals into analog tones that can be conveyed through the telephone system. On the receiving end, the process used is **demodulation,** in which the other modem transforms this signal from analog back to digital. Modems can play both roles, modulation and demodulation, which is where the name *modem* comes from: it's short for modulator/demodulator (see Figure 6A.7).

A modem transforms the computer's digital signals into analog tones that can be conveyed through the telephone system.

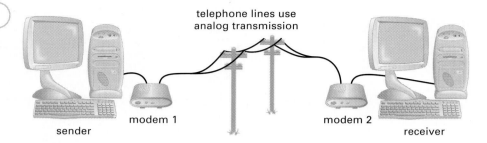

telephone lines use
analog transmission

sender   modem 1   modem 2   receiver

Two types of modems are available: internal and external. An **internal modem** is designed to fit in one of your computer's expansion slots. It gets its power from the computer's expansion bus. An **external modem** has its own case and power supply. For this reason, external modems are slightly more expensive.

Asynchronous Communication

Modems use a method of networking called **asynchronous communication.** In this method, data is sent one bit at a time, in a series (one after the other). Start bits and stop bits are added to the data so that the receiving computer can tell where one byte ends and the next one begins. This networking method is called asynchronous because the start and stop bits eliminate the need for some kind of synchronization signal. In **synchronous communication,** data exchange requires a synchronization signal that identifies the units of data being exchanged.

Modulation Protocols

To establish communications, modems must conform to standards called **modulation protocols.** These protocols, set by international standards organizations, ensure that your modem can communicate with another modem, even if the second modem was made by a different manufacturer.

Several modulation protocols are in common use. Each protocol specifies all the necessary details of communication, including the **data transfer rate.** This is the rate by which the two modems can exchange data. The rate is measured in **bits per second (bps).** You may encounter the term *baud rate* when a modem's data transfer rate is discussed, but the technical definitions of baud rate and bps rate differ. The correct measurement of a modem's data transfer rate is the bps rate. The baud rate is the maximum number of changes that can occur per second in the electrical state of a communications circuit.

Modem protocols are governed by the International Telecommunications Union (ITU). The most recent modulation protocol, called **V.90,** enables modems to communicate at a maximum rate of 56 Kbps. (In practice, V.90 modems rarely achieve speeds higher than 42 Kbps.) The protocol also includes standards for data compression and error checking. The previous protocol, **V.34,** enables a rate of 28,800 bits per second. An earlier standard, V.32, established a rate of 14,400 bps. Standards before V.32 regulated communication at 9,600, 2,400, 1,200, and 300 bps.

Two modems can communicate only if both follow the same modulation protocol. If your modem follows the V.34 protocol, your modem cannot communicate at 28,800 bps unless the modem on the other end observes the same protocol. Most modems, however, can **fall back** to a lower rate. When a modem attempts to establish a connection, it automatically negotiates with the modem on the other end. The two modems try to establish which proto-

Techtalk

negotiation
When you use your computer's modem to connect to a network, the funny screeching noises and static you hear is called "negotiation." Your modem is communicating with the modem on the other end of the line, figuring out how fast each modem can go, and how the bits to be exchanged are going to be handled.

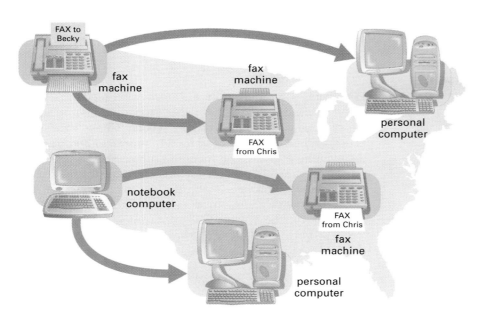

Figure   6A.8

Facsimile transmission enables you to send an image of a document over the telephone lines to anyone who has a fax machine. If your computer has a fax modem, you can send and receive faxes from your computer instead of a fax machine.

cols they share, and then they use the fastest rate that both modems have. If a computer with a 9,600 bps modem is connected to a computer with a 14,400 bps modem, data is transferred between the two computers at 9,600 bps.

Fax

Facsimile transmission—or **fax,** as it is popularly known—enables you to send an image of a document over the telephone lines to anyone who has a fax machine. The sending fax machine makes a digital image of the document. Using a built-in modem, the sending fax machine converts the image to an analog representation so that it can be transmitted through the analog telephone system. The receiving fax machine converts the analog signals to digital signals, converts the digital signals to an image of the document, and prints that image.

Fax usage didn't take off until the ITU established modulation protocol standards for facsimile transmission. These standards differ from modem protocols. Fax protocols govern transmission at 9.6 Kbps (V.29) and 14.4 Kbps (V.17).

Some modems, called **fax modems,** support fax as well as data modulation protocols. Figure 6A.8 illustrates the concepts of facsimile transmission. If your computer has a fax modem, you can send and receive faxes from your computer instead of a fax machine. However, you'll also need a scanner if you want to fax something that's printed or sketched on paper.

DIGITAL TELEPHONY: LIVING WITH TWISTED PAIR

Because twisted-pair wiring will be with us for many years, engineers have developed a number of interim digital telephony technologies that make use of twisted-pair wiring. Sometimes called *last mile technologies,* these solutions include digital telephone standards (such as ISDN and DSL) that can use twisted-pair wiring, as well as technologies that dispense with the local loop entirely, such as cable and satellite systems.

To understand new digital telephone technologies (as well as computer networks, the subject of Module 6B), you'll find it helpful to learn how engineers express the data transfer capacity (called **bandwidth**) of a given transmission medium. This section introduces the bandwidth concept and

Network-based delivery of high-quality videoconferencing requires a bandwidth of at least 10 Mbps.

goes on to examine the new technologies that can deliver digital telephone service directly to homes and offices.

Bandwidth

For digital communication, a transmission medium's bandwidth is measured in kilobits per second (Kbps), megabits per second (Mbps), or gigabits per second (Gbps). Bandwidth is determined by the method used to represent and transmit data via the transmission medium, subject to an upper limit imposed by the physical characteristics of the medium.

So how much bandwidth do you need? For text, you can get by with a slow modem (14.4 or 28.8 Kbps). That rate, however, is too slow for the World Wide Web (unless you're patient). Exploring the Web is a more pleasant proposition at 128 Kbps. But even 128 Kbps is far too slow for tomorrow's digital services, such as digital television, on-demand movies, and videoconferencing. These services require **broadband** digital transmission, conventionally defined to refer to connections with speeds of at least 1.5 Mbps. Network-based delivery of high-quality videoconferencing requires a bandwidth of at least 10 Mbps, the speed of a slow hard disk or standard Ethernet local area network (see Module 6B). High-definition television (HDTV), an emerging standard for digital TV, requires 11 Mbps.

Broadband digital connections aren't expected to be widely available soon. According to one estimate, by 2005 only about 5 percent of households in the United States will have digital connections operating at speeds of 1.5 Mbps or greater.

Last Mile Technologies

Thanks to the Telecommunications Act of 1996, local telephone services are facing competition for the first time. Cable TV companies, satellite firms, and other phone companies are invading their turf and offering improved service. In response, local phone companies are increasingly offering digital telephone services, including ISDN and ADSL. In this section, you learn what's available and what's coming, as phone companies finally solve the last mile problem by delivering digital telephony directly to homes, offices, and businesses.

Integrated Services Digital Network (ISDN)

Integrated Services Digital Network (ISDN) is an ITU-defined standard that provides digital telephone and data service. Three types of ISDN services follow:

- **Basic Rate ISDN (BRI)**   Designed for home and small business users, this service offers one or two 64 Kbps channels, as well as a 16 Kbps signaling channel. If you obtain service with two 64 Mbps channels, you can connect your computer at 128 Mbps (the service automatically cuts back to 64 Mbps when a voice call arrives). BRI can use twisted-pair wiring.

- **Primary Rate ISDN (PRI)**   Designed for organizations, this service includes 23 channels operating at 64 Kbps each as well as one signaling channel. PRI requires a T1 carrier (1.544 Mbps).

- **Broadband ISDN (BISDN)**   Still on the drawing boards, this high-bandwidth technology can't work with twisted pair; it requires fiber-optic cable. Its data transfer capacities vary, with a maximum bandwidth of 622 Mbps.

Basic Rate ISDN (BRI) is widely available in the United States, Japan, and Europe. In the U.S., the number of ISDN lines is expected to grow to 3.9 million by 2000.

The cost of an ISDN line is often two or three times that of an analog phone line, but there's a payoff: with 128-Kbps ISDN services, you get two telephone numbers with one ISDN account. You can use one for computer data and another one for voice or fax. When you're using the connection for computer data only, the system automatically uses both data channels to give you the maximum data transfer rate. If a phone call comes in, the connection automatically drops back to 64 Kbps to accommodate the incoming call. What's more, connection is nearly instantaneous. Unlike analog connections with a modem, there's no lengthy dial-in procedure and connection delay.

To hook up computers to BRI or PRI ISDN lines, you'll need an **ISDN adapter** (also called a *digital modem,* although ISDN modems aren't actually modems). ISDN adapters are 100 percent digital. Increasingly, small businesses and even homeowners are installing ISDN-capable *routers,* which enable them to link the ISDN circuit to a local area network (LAN). Routers and LANs are discussed in Module 6B. Using an ISDN router, a small business can connect as many as 32 PCs and provide all with on-demand Internet service.

ISDN is the first widely-available digital telephone service, but it may have a limited life, thanks to Digital Subscriber Line technologies discussed in the next section.

Digital Subscriber Line (DSL)

Digital Subscriber Line (DSL, also called xDSL) is a blanket term for a group of related technologies, including **Asymmetric Digital Subscriber Line (ADSL).** Already available in major metropolitan markets, ADSL is akin to ISDN in that it uses existing copper wiring. But ADSL is much faster: typically, up to 1.5 Mbps when you're downloading data and up to 256 Kbps when you're uploading data. (Note that downloading speeds are much faster than uploading speeds, which explains why the service is called *asymmetric.* ADSL isn't the best choice if you need to upload huge amounts of data.) DSL technologies are capable of higher bandwidth, but local loop wiring problems limit DSL to 1.5 Mbps (or less).

To connect to a DSL line, your computer needs a DSL "modem," as well as a DSL phone line and an Internet service subscription that includes DSL service. One problem is that DSL service isn't standardized, so you'll need to select a modem that's compatible with your telephone company's particular type of DSL service. Standardization efforts are underway, however, and these efforts will reduce the cost and complexity of DSL installations.

DSL isn't likely to be available in rural areas anytime soon. To connect with DSL, your computer must be positioned within one or two miles of a local switching station.

Destinations

BellSouth **(http://www. bellsouth.net)** is one of the first RBOCs to offer ADSL service. Follow the links to FastAccess to learn more about ADSL services and costs.

SONET

Requiring fiber-optic cable, **Synchronous Optical Network (SONET)** promises to break bandwidth restrictions wide open. The slowest SONET standard calls for data transfer rates of 52 Mbps; some enable rates of 1 Gbps or faster. Outside the United States, SONET is known as *Synchronous Digital Hierarchy (SDH).* SONET is expected to provide the fiber-optic cable services for Broadband ISDN (BISDN), but this service isn't expected to benefit homes and small businesses.

ALTERNATIVES TO DIGITAL TELEPHONY

Protected from local competition until 1996, local telephone companies have been slow to offer high-bandwidth digital telephone services. Now they're facing competition from satellite and cable TV systems and even the local power company.

Direct Broadcast Satellite (DBS)

Digital satellite systems, called **Direct Broadcast Satellite (DBS),** use an 18- or 21-inch reception disk to receive digital TV signals broadcast at a bandwidth of 12 Mbps. Increasingly, DBS operators offer Internet access as well as digital TV service, but at much less bandwidth. Currently, Hughes Network Systems offers satellite Internet access at 400 Kbps, but there's a rub: satellite systems can't handle uploaded data, so you'll still need a modem and telephone line to send requests to the server and upload files.

Cable Modems

Figure 6A.9

In contrast to twisted pair, coaxial cable makes it easy to achieve very-high-bandwidth data communication.

Currently, the leading contender in the high-bandwidth sweepstakes is your local cable TV company, which has probably already wired your home with **coaxial cable** (see Figure 6A.9). In contrast to twisted pair, coaxial cable makes it easy to achieve very-high-bandwidth data communication. What's more, about 73 million homes in the United States now subscribe to cable TV service, and an additional 35 million are within easy reach of cable systems.

Does the cable TV industry's huge installed base of coaxial cable hold the key to high-bandwidth digital service delivery? Not yet. The cable TV system was designed as a couch-potato service, in which customers would sit back and choose from a fixed number of channels. So most cable systems are designed to run signals in one direction only: toward the house, not away from it. However, data communication requires two-way communication. Only about one-eighth of the homes in the United States have cable service delivery that's capable of two-way data communication (the cable industry is busily upgrading the rest of its infrastructure to provide this capability). And increasingly, they're offering data communications services, specifically Internet access (see Module 7A).

For computer users, these services offer data transfer rates that leave ISDN in the dust and rival those of DSL. **Cable modems** now deliver data at bandwidths of 500 Kbps to 1 Mbps or more, depending on how many subscribers are connected to a local cable segment. You'll hear figures stating that cable modems are capable of bandwidths of 30 Mbps or more, but this bandwidth must be divided among the 2000 or more subscribers in the cable company's equivalent of the local loop.

Electrical Power Systems

Yes, you read the heading correctly: data communications can be sent over electrical power lines. Recent research has solved the problem of noise and interference generated by power fluctuations and surges. Current technology enables data transfer rates of 1 Mbps, comparable to DSL and cable modems. This approach, however, isn't readily compatible with the U.S. power grid. It's expected to attract users in Asia and Europe, which lack the

IMPACTS

The Digital Divide: It Isn't All Black and White

The survey results were disquieting, and they made headlines. A 1996 U.S. Commerce Department study disclosed significant differences in Internet access and usage among U.S. ethnic groups: 27 percent of white households had a PC and access to the Internet compared to only 10 percent of black households. Dubbed the "Digital Divide," the disparity was particularly disturbing because the pattern held up even when family income was held constant. As familiarity with PCs and the Internet translates into greater economic opportunity, there's a lot at stake here. For example, high-tech workers in Virginia receive more than twice the average wage for all private sector employees. If African-Americans are behind the curve when it comes to computer and Internet skills, they could find themselves at a competitive disadvantage.

Four years later, it's increasingly clear that the 1996 findings were something of a fluke. Since that time, African-American households have taken to the PC and Internet with a vengeance. Among households with incomes higher than $90,000, for example, eighty-three percent of black households are connected, a number higher than white households of similar incomes. Another study found that black households were investing 16 times more of their income in PCs and Internet connections than white households. These efforts are narrowing the gap: according to a recent projection, 64 percent of African-American households will have PCs and Internet connections by 2005, compared to 76 percent of white households, 68 percent of Latino households, and 84 percent of Asian households.

There's still a Digital Divide, but it's now understood to be a matter of income and geography rather than ethnic affiliation. It's still a serious problem: among households earning between $50,000 and $75,000 annually, Internet access jumped from 47 percent to 62 percent in just one year (1999–2000). In the same period, households earning $15,000 or less improved their numbers by only 2 percentage points, from 9 to 11. Wealthy U.S. households are 20 times likelier to have Internet access than poor ones. Geography matters, too. Some 25 percent of Americans live in rural areas where Internet access is slow or unavailable. If this imbalance isn't remedied, entire neighborhoods and regions could experience "cyber-lag," characterized by low wages, diminished opportunities, and isolation from the economic mainstream.

As the Digital Divide's patterns have come into clearer focus, so too have the proposed remedies. Recently, the Bill and Melinda Gates Foundation—the Microsoft billionaire's charitable fund—donated $4 million in cash and Microsoft services to low-income regions in Tennessee, where fewer than one third of public libraries had Internet access. Others call for the investment of public funds to make computers, Internet connections, and high-speed access more widely available in poor and rural areas.

What accounts for the African-American lag in the 1996 data? According to black entrepreneurs who led the way in creating black-oriented Web sites, it's partly a matter of the Web's learning to speak the right language. Back then, you'd search for days without finding a black-oriented site. One reason: initially, venture capitalists weren't interested in funding sites addressed to an unproven market. But pioneering sites such as NetNoir (**http://www.netnoir.com**) changed this picture very rapidly. Founded in 1995, NetNoir receives tens of millions of page hits per month, and it has plenty of company. Today, there are numerous, high-quality sites focusing on black history and culture (such as **http://www.africana.com, http://www.blackvoices.com**) and several portals oriented to African-American themes, such as The Black World Today (**http://www.tbwt.com**) and Black Planet (**http://www.blackplanet.com**).

It's not surprising that African-Americans are now taking to the Internet with such enthusiasm. Yvette Moyo, founder of MOBE (Marketing Opportunities in Black Entertainment, located at **http://www.mobe.com**) explains, "We have Web sites that allow us to see ourselves in so many different ways. . . . They give you a vision of what the future will be. They basically say, 'No limit'." That may be the Internet's most appealing characteristic, says Cheryl L. Savers, Ph.D., a black woman who was appointed U.S. Undersecretary of Commerce for Technology in the Clinton Administration. According to Savers, "Technology is one of the last frontiers where you can be certainly judged by ability and talent."

U.S. tradition of unlimited local telephone service and use power systems more amenable to data communication delivery. Some technical problems still need to be solved, however. In a Manchester, England test of this delivery method, researchers found that street light poles acted as transmitting antennas and interferred with local radio reception.

Digitization enables convergence, a process of technological morphing in which previously-distinct devices lose their sharply-defined boundaries and blend together.

CONVERGENCE: IS IT A PHONE OR A COMPUTER?

The phone system's going digital, and that's enabling new technologies that can carry computer data over voice lines. At the core of this process, however, is a more fundamental change: *digitization,* the transformation of all the media we've been discussing into digital systems. Digitization enables *convergence,* a process of technological morphing in which previously-distinct devices lose their sharply-defined boundaries and blend together. This section explores some of the dimensions of computer-telephony convergence. As you'll see, it's creating some interesting hybrids.

The Everything PC

It *looks* like a computer, but it's much more: it's also an audiophile-quality stereo, a TV, a DVD player, and even an answering machine. That's the pitch for a new series of multimedia-enhanced PCs that combine huge monitors (27 or even 31 inches), DVD drives, high-fidelity speakers with surround sound, and voice-capable 56 Kbps modems. Equipped with a microphone and the right software, you can even use this PC to place free, long-distance phone calls over the Internet. This could be the ultimate machine for cramped dorm rooms!

TV Internet Set-Tops

Imagine you're sitting in front of your TV, and your eyes never leave the screen. The show you're watching is boring, so you spend some time checking your email and surfing the Web. While you're on the Web, you check an interactive channel guide featuring your local cable TV listings, jump to some TV-related Web sites, and finally find something worth watching. All these tasks are accomplished on your TV set, thanks to WebTV (WebTV is a trademark of WebTV Networks, Inc.), an Internet service that you access using an inexpensive **set-top appliance** that enables you to access the Internet using your TV as a display (see Figure 6A.10). To navigate the Web, you use a wireless keyboard or a remote control unit. Using a built-in modem, the WebTV service requires a phone line and a monthly subscription. The latest version of WebTV, called WebTV Plus, enables you to view TV and the Web simultaneously, thanks to a picture-in-picture function. You can also equip WebTV Plus with a color printer, if you want.

WebTV isn't just a no-hassle way to access the Internet. It's specifically designed to make watching TV more interesting by placing Internet-accessible resources at your fingertips while you're watching TV. Suppose you're watching a show and you'd like to see more information about it. If you see an on-screen icon, you can click this icon to view a list of Web pages related to this show and its subject. Email, chatting, and Usenet access enable you to voice your opinions about what you're watching and get into discussions with other viewers. (For more information on these Internet services, see Module 7A.)

Personal Communication Service (PCS)

Digitization is bringing the same rapid change to cellular phone service that you're seeing in other media. **Personal Communication Service (PCS)** refers collectively to a group of related digital cellular telephone service technologies, which are rapidly supplanting analog cellular services. Digital cellular phones offer noise-free sound and improved coverage, but that's just the beginning.

Destinations

WebTV's Web site (**http://www.webtv.com**) explains WebTV service options and how WebTV can enhance the TV viewing experience.

PCS offers protection from eavesdropping and cellular phone fraud, two problems that plague analog cellular technologies. It also offers a spate of new, computer-based telephony services, such as voice recognition technology, that enables users to screen incoming calls or to place calls without dialing a phone number. In short, PCS enables computers and cellular phones to combine, and the result will be a profusion of technologies that transform the way we communicate.

PCS promises to transform mobile computing into a reality for millions of people. Because PCS technology is digital, it's much more amenable to data communication than analog cellular services. It's possible to access the Internet by means of a modem connected to an analog cellular phone, but data transfer rates are as low as 4 Kbps due to line noise and poor connections. Emerging PCS standards will enable speeds of up to 384 Kbps for downloads. Expect to see a new generation of PCS-enabled devices for mobile computing, including personal digital assistants (PDAs) that can keep you in touch with your email wherever you go.

Internet Telephony

Here's the good news: you can place low-cost (even free), long-distance telephone calls over the Internet. Now for the bad news: the quality ranges from barely acceptable to just plain awful.

You'll learn more about how the Internet works in Module 7A, but here's a quick introduction that points out the shortcomings of **Internet telephony,** the use of the Internet for real-time voice communication. Unlike the public switched network, the public Internet doesn't establish a point-to-point, switched connection with a guaranteed quality of service. It was never designed for real-time use. When you place telephone calls over the public Internet, network congestion often causes garbled messages, delays, and echoes. Still, using the Internet for phone calls has a major advantage over the public switched telephone network: providers can route dozens, hundreds, or even thousands of calls over the same circuit.

You can place calls via the Internet in a variety of ways. To place free long distance calls, you'll need a computer equipped with a microphone, speakers, an Internet connection, and a telephony-enabled program such as Microsoft's NetMeeting. Your calls are limited to people using similarly-equipped computers—and they need to be online.

What about placing a call to an ordinary telephone? Although you can't do it for free, **Internet telephony service providers (ITSPs)** such as Net2Phone are stepping into the act by offering computer-to-phone and phone-to-phone services that use the Internet for long-distance transmission. Rates are cheap, but the quality isn't always what subscribers expect.

Still, the basic idea of Internet telephony has an enormous advantage. Because the Internet doesn't rely on switches to route messages, it's cheaper to operate. According to one estimate, routing data over a switched network costs more than three times as much as sending the same data over a switch-free computer network (such as the Internet). New technologies, such as advanced compression, are making Internet telephony sound better, but you'll still run into delays when you're calling.

A different approach is being taken by Qwest Communications International, Inc., a Denver, Colorado-based multimedia communications company that's busily constructing a 18,449-mile network of high-speed

Figure 6A.10

WebTV allows you to access the Internet using your television set as a display.

SPOTLIGHT

JACK IN AND YACK— AND SAVE BIG BUCKS

►Even if Internet telephony can't deliver "clear as a bell" sound quality, that's not stopping the growing millions of users who are signing up for Internet-based long-distance services. Worldwide, more than 40 million people are already using Internet-based long-distance telephone services, and the number is expected to grow to more than 400 million by 2003.

What's responsible for Internet telephony's stunning success? It's the low cost. Hackensack, N.J.-based Net2Phone offers long-distance services that cost as little as one-fifth the charges levied by conventional long-distance carriers. Net2Phone routes calls from one telephone to another via the Internet. You can save even more by placing a call from your computer to another telephony-enabled computer— in fact, you can place such calls for free, provided that both computers are connected to the Internet.

For large organizations, such as school districts and corporations, the savings add up fast. In Spokane, Oregon, the local school district saved $100,000 in telephone and Internet-access fee charges by moving to Internet telephony for all internal calls. In Peru, a mining equipment company cut its international phone bill by 90 percent after switching to an Internet-based long-distance service.

Because Internet telephony is fully digitized, it opens up a world of new possibilities for convergence between telephones and computers—and people are already finding ways to take advantage of this fact. In the Spokane schools, the availability of cost-free, high-bandwidth Internet telephone service enables teachers to collaborate with teams of geographically-separated students, who interact with the teachers while sitting at classroom computers. Web sites are eager to build voice-enabled features into e-commerce sites, a feature that may help deal with shoppers' frustrations and insecurities about ordering online.

Conventional long-distance carriers are watching Internet telephony warily, but telephone giant AT&T has decided to jump right in by recently concluding a $1.4 billion deal to purchase Internet telephony pioneer Net2Phone. AT&T chairman and CEO C. Michael Armstrong told a reporter that voice over the Internet is an "inevitable outcome of technology"—a fact already appreciated by millions of people worldwide.

Because Internet telephony is fully digitized, it opens up a world of new possibilities for convergence between telephones and computers.

fiber-optic cable. Essentially a private Internet, the Qwest network uses some of the same technology that underlies the public Internet, but because it's private, Qwest can make sure the network isn't overloaded. In addition, Qwest is using additional technologies that will make the Qwest network arguably the best Internet network in the world. As a result, Qwest is able to guarantee service quality. Qwest's first voice-over IP phone-to-phone long-distance service, available in 125 U.S. cities, charged 7.5 cents per long-distance minute, compared to the 10 cents or more charged by conventional long-distance providers.

Because it's cheaper to build telephone networks with Internet technology rather than with switching circuits, some experts believe that the term *telecommunications* will become obsolete. Computer data won't be routed over voice networks: instead, voice will be routed over computer networks, the only type of network that will exist once the obsolete switching technology is dismantled.

CURRENTS

Universal Service: The End of an Era?

It's called *universal service*—and thanks to the rise of Internet telephony, it may very well be coming to an end. An outgrowth of Depression-era New Deal legislation, universal service has long been a cornerstone of U.S. telecommunications policy. In the telecommunications industry, universal service assures that people in all parts of the country have equal access to "reasonably-priced" telephone services.

There's just one problem: it's much more expensive to provide telephone service in lightly-populated rural areas, where wires must be strung dozens or hundreds of miles just to serve a few houses. To pay for local phone service, long-distance companies collect surcharges from their customers, and kick back most of these surcharges to local telephone companies in the form of *access fees*. In turn, the local telephone companies use these fees—more than $25 billion per year—to hold down the cost of residential telephone services.

But all that's changing. Thanks to the U.S. Telecommunications Act of 1996, competitive access providers (CAPs) can sell direct access to the long-distance market without paying access fees—and that's one of the reasons Internet telephony is booming. Internet telephony service providers (ITSPs) such as Net2Phone don't pay access fees. According to conventional long-distance providers, that isn't fair. Long-distance, regional, and local telephone companies want the U.S. Congress to hit ITSPs with access fee charges—or abandon the idea of universal service altogether.

The 1996 Telecommunications Act does give telephone companies a break. The legislation calls for gradual reductions in access fees until they're completely eliminated. But it doesn't let consumers off the hook. Universal service must still be paid for somehow, so the Telecommunications Act extended the concept of universal service to digital-based services such as the Internet. For now, consumers are taking the hit, as you'll discover if you examine your next phone bill: there's a welter of incomprehensibly-named taxes, such as the Presubscribed Interexchange Carrier Charge, the Federal Access Charge, state-imposed Universal Service charges, and—chances are—several more. The various taxes and fees can add up to 60% to the cost of your monthly phone bill.

At least there's one tax you won't be paying any more. In 2000, the U.S. Congress voted to terminate the Federal Excise Tax on telephone service—a tax that was initially created in 1898 to pay for the Spanish-American War.

Internet Faxing

If the Internet isn't perfect for voice calls, it has none of those shortcomings for faxes. Faxes don't have to be delivered in real time, like voice does, so slight service delays don't cause a problem. But faxing through the PSTN is expensive, particularly for international calls. With annual worldwide fax volume nearing the 400 billion page mark in 1998, it's clear that many organizations could save a great deal of money by routing faxes over the Internet.

How does Internet faxing work? You'll need an Internet connection and an account with an Internet fax service provider. From a fax machine or computer, you can send the fax through the Internet to the fax service provider, which then automatically routes the fax through the Internet to a local telephone near your fax's destination. The service isn't free, but it's 25- to 50-percent cheaper than sending the fax through the phone system.

TAKEAWAY POINTS

- The public switched telephone network (PSTN) is predominantly digital, except for the local loop, which uses low-bandwidth twisted-pair wire connected to analog telephones.
- To send digital data over the telephone system, it's necessary to modulate the signal (transform it into analog form). On the receiving end, the signal must be demodulated (transformed back into digital form). Modems (modulators/demodulators) perform this service.
- The term *bandwidth* refers to the data transfer capacity of a communications channel and is measured in bits per second (bps).
- Modulation protocols are standards that define how modems work. The latest protocol is called V.90, and it enables data transfer rates of up to 56 Kbps.
- 56 Kbps isn't sufficient for real-time video-conferencing or other advanced multimedia

applications. For these applications, bandwidths of 1 Mbps or more are needed for good quality.

- ISDN and ADSL are two digital telephony services that can bring digital service directly to homes and offices using twisted-pair wiring. Basic ISDN services can provide data transfer rates of up to 128 Kbps. ADSL is expected to provide 1 Mbps or more.
- Digitization is blurring the boundaries between phones, computers, and TVs. WebTV brings Internet capabilities to TV viewing, and PCS enables high-bandwidth data communications through cellular telephones.
- In Internet telephony, voice is routed over the public Internet or private networks constructed using Internet standards. But these networks cannot guarantee PSTN's quality of service.

MODULE REVIEW

KEY TERMS AND CONCEPTS

Asymmetric Digital Subscriber
   Line (ADSL)
asynchronous communication
bandwidth
Basic Rate ISDN (BRI)
bits per second (bps)
broadband
Broadband ISDN (BISDN)
cable modems
cell
cell site
cellular telephones
coaxial cable
common carrier
common carrier immunity
copper wire
data transfer rate
demodulation
deregulation
Digital Subscriber Line (DSL)
Direct Broadcast Satellite
   (DBS)
external modem

facsimile transmission (fax)
fall back
fax modems
fiber-optic cables
Integrated Services Digital
   Network (ISDN)
interexchange carrier (IXC)
internal modem
International
   Telecommunications Union
   (ITU)
Internet telephony
Internet telephony service
   providers (ITSPs)
ISDN adapter
last mile problem
leased lines
local access and transport area
   (LATA)
local exchange carriers (LECs)
local loop
microwaves
modems

modulation
modulation protocols
multiplexing
Personal Communication
   Service (PCS)
Primary Rate ISDN (PRI)
private branch exchange (PBX)
public switched telephone
   network (PSTN)
quality of service (QoS)
Regional Bell Operating
   Companies (RBOCs)
satellites
set-top appliance
synchronous communication
Synchronous Optical Network
   (SONET)
telecommunications
twisted pair
universal service
V.34
V.90
wireless

TRUE/FALSE

Indicate whether the following statements are true or false.

1. Most telephone lines provide an analog connection, which is based on standards that date back more than a century.

2. Most telephones in use today are digital devices, which transmit and receive a distinct electrical signal.

3. Telephone and telecommunications standards are governed by the International Telecommunications Union (ITU), a division of the United Nations.

4. In the United States, the concept of multiplexing underlies the legislation that regulates telephone service.

5. A private branch exchange is a transportation or communications company that provides vital public services.

6. Leased lines give companies direct digital access to long-distance carriers.

7. To establish communications, modems must conform to standards called modulation protocols.

8. For digital communications, a transmission medium's broadband is measured in kilobits, megabits, or gigabits per second.

9. The three types of ISDN services are Basic Rate, Primary Rate, and Broadband.

10. When used for real-time voice communication, the Internet establishes a point-to-point, switched connection with a guaranteed quality of service.

MATCHING

Match each key term from the left column to the most accurate definition in the right column.

_____ 1. local exchange carriers

_____ 2. universal service

_____ 3. wireless

_____ 4. leased lines

_____ 5. modulation

_____ 6. asynchronous communication

_____ 7. bandwidth

_____ 8. set-top appliance

_____ 9. Internet telephony

_____ 10. multiplexing

a. a communications medium that uses radio or infrared signals

b. the data transfer capacity

c. a process that describes a modem transforming a computer's digital signals into analog tones

d. to provide directly-wired services between the homes and offices of subscribers

e. a method of networking in which data is sent one bit at a time in a series

f. specially-conditioned telephone lines that provide direct digital access to long distance carriers

g. using the Internet for real-time voice communication

h. a concept that recognizes that telephone service is vital to public safety and economic welfare

i. techniques that enable one to send more than one call on a single line

j. enables you to access the Internet using your TV as a display

MULTIPLE CHOICE

Circle the letter of the correct choice for each of the following.

1. Which of the following provides basic telephone services?
   a. operators
   b. local exchange carriers (LECs)
   c. cable modems
   d. International Telecommunications Union

2. Which of the following is not a transmission medium used to provide regional and long-distance service between local telephone exchanges?
   a. microwaves
   b. fiber-optic cables
   c. common carrier
   d. copper wire

3. Which of the following techniques can send more than one call on a single line?
   a. multiplexing
   b. local loop
   c. interexchange carrier
   d. modulation

4. What do you call a transportation or communications company that provides vital public services?
   a. common carrier
   b. private branch exchange (PBX)
   c. Digital Subscriber Line (DSL)
   d. Synchronous Optical Network (SONET)

5. When someone makes a cellular phone call, all the cell sites are connected to which of the following?
   a. public switched telephone network
   b. Mobile Optical Network (MONET)
   c. Mobile Digital Subscriber Line (MDSL)
   d. Mobile Telephone Switching Office (MTSO)

6. Which concept recognizes that telephone service is vital to public safety and economic welfare?
   a. quality of service
   b. universal service
   c. telecommunications
   d. convergence

7. Which of the following enables two modems to exchange data?
   a. modulation rate
   b. demodulation rate
   c. data transfer rate
   d. baud rate

8. Which of the following services requires broadband digital transmission?
   a. faxing
   b. digital television
   c. sending email
   d. none of the above

9. Which of the following technologies requires fiber-optic cable and promises to break bandwidth restrictions wide open?
   a. cable modems
   b. Synchronous Optical Network (SONET)
   c. Direct Broadcast Satellite
   d. WebTV

10. Using the Internet for real-time voice communication is known as what?
    a. Internet faxing
    b. Personal Communications Service
    c. Internet telephony
    d. convergence

FILL-IN

In the blank provided, write the correct answer for each of the following.

1. _____ refers to the transmission of information of any type through the telephone system.

2. Telephone services are provided by _____ , which provide directly-wired services between subscribers and customers' homes and offices.

3. Large organizations typically install their own internal digital telephone systems, called _____ .

4. Cellular telephones enable subscribers to place calls using a(n) _____ communications system.

5. Using a process called _____ , a modem transforms the computer's digital signals into analog tones that can be conveyed through the telephone system.

6. To establish communications, modems must conform to standards called _____ .

7. The rate by which two modems exchange data is measured in _____ .

8. If your computer is equipped with a(n) _____ , you can send and receive faxes from your computer instead of a fax machine.

9. _____ refers collectively to a group of related digital cellular telephone service technologies.

10. _____ offer computer-to-phone and phone-to-phone services that use the Internet for long-distance transmission.

SHORT ANSWER

On a separate sheet of paper, answer the following questions.

1. What is meant by the term *quality of service* as it relates to the modern telephone system?

2. Explain the limitations of the public switched telephone network (PSTN) for sending and receiving computer data.

3. Describe the various functions of telecommunications transmission media such as copper wire, fiber-optic cable, microwaves, and satellites.

4. Define the concepts of universal service and common carrier immunity. Why are these concepts important?

5. What are the various alternatives for accessing telephone services besides the local loop's twisted-pair wiring configuration?

6. What is meant by the "last mile problem?"

7. Describe how modems work. What are the various modem protocols governed by the International Telecommunications Union?

8. Define the concepts of bandwidth and broadband.

9. List and describe the three types of Integrated Services Digital Network (ISDN) services.

10. Cite examples of how convergence is blurring the boundaries among popular communication devices, including phones, computers, and TVs.

NETWORKS: SUPERHIGHWAYS FOR DIGITAL INFORMATION

6B

MODULE

OUTLINE

WHAT YOU WILL LEARN . . .

When you have finished reading this module, you will be able to:

1. List the three main types of computer networks.
2. Discuss the ways that connecting computers increase the value of an organization's information technology investment.
3. Explain the importance of protocols in a computer network.
4. Contrast circuit switching and packet switching networks and explain their respective strengths and weaknesses.
5. Discuss the difference between peer-to-peer and client/server LANs.
6. Name the most-widely used LAN protocol and discuss its benefits.
7. Discuss three business applications of WANs.

Fast forward a few years, and imagine yourself building a house. Everyone in your five-person family wants a computer, a printer, and an Internet connection. You could pay for five computers, five printers, and five Internet accounts. Or you could pay for five computers, one really good printer, one Internet account, and inexpensive local area network (LAN) hardware that enables everyone to share the printer and Internet connection. If you think the LAN route makes sense, you've just joined the huge and growing number of people who have discovered the benefits of computer networking. A new trend, home networking, is already a $100 million annual market in the United States and is slated to grow to $1.1 billion in the next five years.

Businesses of all sizes are already convinced that networking is a great idea. They're spending $26 billion annually on computer networking equipment right now. The benefits go far beyond saving money on shared peripherals: networks enable organizations to create massive, centralized pools of information, which are vital to performing their mission. And networks enable people to communicate and collaborate in ways that aren't possible without some means of connecting the computers they're using.

Although computer networking is increasingly important, most people consider this topic to be highly technical. As this module makes clear, however, the *concepts* of computer networking are easy to understand. As an informed and literate computer user, you need to know enough about networking to understand the benefits and possibilities of connecting computers. In addition, learning about computer networking is a good idea for anyone looking for a job these days. Employers like to hire workers who can grasp networking concepts. This module explains the essential concepts of computer networking and teaches the basic networking terms you'll need to discuss the subject intelligently.

INTRODUCING COMPUTER NETWORKS: SYNERGY AT WORK

As composers working individually, former Beatles John Lennon and Paul McCartney penned many fine songs. But most rock critics agree that their solo efforts can't match the magic that happened when Lennon and McCartney worked together. This magic is called *synergy*. Synergy occurs when the performance of two or more components working together exceeds the performance of the same components working alone. And as you'll see in this module, synergy sums up nicely what happens when you connect two or more computers.

What Is a Computer Network?

A **computer network** links two or more computers so that they can exchange data and share resources, including expensive peripherals such as high-performance laser printers.

By this definition, mainframe-based timesharing systems aren't networks. In timesharing systems, a series of **terminals** are hooked up to a single, large computer system. Terminals aren't computers. They lack their own processing or storage capabilities. The essence of computer networking is that it enables two or more *computers* to work together.

What's the difference between computer networks and data communications using the telephone system ? It boils down to speed. Computer networks are optimized for transmitting computer data, and some experimental networks are so fast that they could transfer the entire contents of the Library of Congress in a matter of minutes. The public switched telephone network (PSTN) is optimized for voice communication and can't match the speed of data-only networks. Some computer networks use PSTN for local-access to long-distance data networks, but the fastest computer networks bypass PSTN entirely or use special, data-only lines leased from the long-distance telephone companies.

Types of Computer Networks: LANs and WANs

Computer networks fall into three categories: **local area networks (LANs), metropolitan area networks (MANs),** and **wide area networks (WANs):**

- A local area network uses direct cables or localized wireless radio or infrared signals to link computers within a small geographic area, such as a building or a group of buildings.

- A metropolitan area network uses high-speed fiber-optic lines to connect computers located at various places within a major urban region, such as the San Francisco Bay Area. A Scottish MAN, called FatMAN, links universities in Scotland with 155-Mbps fiber-optic cables.

- A wide area network uses long-distance transmission media, including telecommunications networks (see Module 6A), to link computers separated by a few miles or even thousands of miles. The Internet (covered in Chapter 7) is a wide area network open to public use. (As you'll see, other WANs, including some that use the same technology that the Internet uses, aren't public.)

Although the Internet is technically a wide area network, the term *WAN* is generally used to refer to other long-distance networks, called public data networks (PDNs), that are leased to business and government customers. PDNs offer the security and guaranteed bandwidth that the Internet cannot yet ensure. This module discusses LANs, PDNs, and other WANs that businesses use. Chapter 7 explores the public Internet.

Networking Synergies in a Nutshell

What's the point of having a computer network? When you connect two or more computers, you see gains in every aspect of computing:

- **Reducing hardware costs** Computer networks enable users to share expensive equipment and reduce costs. In a LAN, for example, dozens of users can share a single high-capacity printer. In a WAN, users of underpowered computers can connect to a supercomputer, which can process their data much more rapidly. At Stroh Brewing Co. plants throughout the United States, networking software enables the company to dispense with up to ten high-cost printers for each of the company's brewing locations.

- **Enabling shared applications** Computer networks enable users to share software. For example, **network versions** of applications are designed to be installed on a high-powered computer, called a **file server,** that makes these applications available to more than one user at a time. At Everett Wholesale Paper Co., a Washington-based industrial paper supply firm, sales representatives upload orders from notebook computers to an order-tracking program installed on the company's file server. After installing the network, employees found that they had up to 20 percent more time to focus on their customers' needs.

- **Building massive information resources** Computer networks enable users to create common pools of data, which employees can access to obtain the data they need. For example, at Prentice-Hall, a textbook publisher, a company-wide network makes a vast archive of illustrations available to book designers and greatly reduces the amount of time spent tracking down appropriate photographs for textbooks and other publishing projects.

- **Connecting people** Computers create powerful new ways for people to work together. For example, **group-ware** applications enable workers to create a shared calendar for scheduling purposes. Team members can see instantly who is available at a given day and time. What's more, these people don't have to work together in the same building. They could be located at various places around the world and still function effectively as a team.

NETWORK FUNDAMENTALS

A computer network's basic components include physical media such as cables, switches or routers that guide messages to their destination, and standards (called protocols) that specify how computers can communicate over the network. The following sections introduce these network fundamentals; subsequently, you'll learn more specifics about how LANs and WANs work.

Computer networks enable users to create common pools of data, which employees can access to obtain the data they need.

Physical Media

Most people think of computer networks in terms of cabling, but the physical medium is actually the least-important part of a computer network. To be sure, some media place restrictions on the amount of data that can be transferred through a network, but even the simplest and least-expensive cable-twisted pair can transfer as much as 1.5 Mbps. Network signals can traverse any type of telecommunications medium, including telephone lines, coaxial cable, microwave relay systems, satellites, wireless (radio and infrared), and fiber-optic cable. (For a discussion of physical media in telecommunications, see Module 6A.) Often, a single message travels over several different physical media before arriving at its destination.

Explore IT Lab

Building a Network

Switching and Routing Techniques

Networks can work with an amazing variety of physical media. But how does the message get through the maze of cables to the right place? Who sorts the mail en route? Networks funnel messages to the correct destination using two basic technologies: **circuit switching** and **packet switching.**

Circuit Switching

In circuit switching, the network creates a physical, end-to-end circuit between the sending and receiving computers. This is the same technology used in voice networks, discussed in Module 6A. It can be used for computer data, too. Circuit switching works best when it is essential to avoid delivery delays. That's why circuit switching is ideally suited to voice and real-time videoconferencing. In a circuit switching network, high-speed electronic switches handle the job of establishing and maintaining the connection.

Packet Switching

Packet switching works in a way that's radically different from the telephone system (see Figure 6B.1). In packet switching, an outgoing message

1. An outgoing message is divided up into data units of fixed size, called packets.

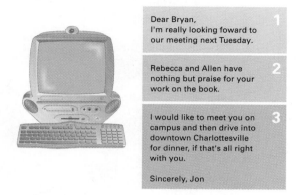

Dear Bryan,
I'm really looking foward to our meeting next Tuesday.

1

Rebecca and Allen have nothing but praise for your work on the book.

2

I would like to meet you on campus and then drive into downtown Charlottesville for dinner, if that's all right with you.

Sincerely, Jon

3

2. Each packet is numbered and addressed to the destination computer.

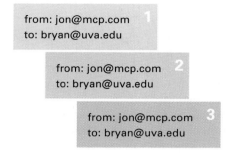

from: jon@mcp.com
to: bryan@uva.edu

1

from: jon@mcp.com
to: bryan@uva.edu

2

from: jon@mcp.com
to: bryan@uva.edu

3

3. After reading the packet's address, the router consults a table of possible pathways to the packet's destination. If more than one path exists, the router sends the packet along the path that is least congested.

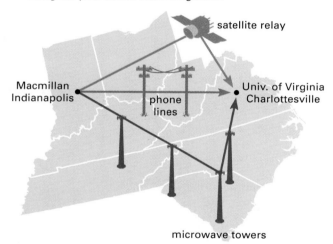

satellite relay

Macmillan
Indianapolis

phone
lines

Univ. of Virginia
Charlottesville

microwave towers

4. On the receiving computer, protocols come into play that put the packets in correct order and decode the message they contain.

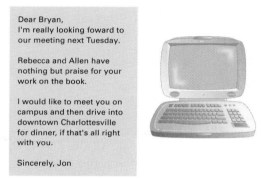

Dear Bryan,
I'm really looking foward to our meeting next Tuesday.

Rebecca and Allen have nothing but praise for your work on the book.

I would like to meet you on campus and then drive into downtown Charlottesville for dinner, if that's all right with you.

Sincerely, Jon

Figure 6B.1

Packet switching.

is divided into data units of a fixed size, called **packets.** Each packet is numbered and addressed to the destination computer. The sending computer pushes the packets onto the network, where they're examined by **routers.** Routers are computer-based devices that examine each packet they detect. After reading the packet's address, the router consults a table of possible pathways to the packet's destination. If more than one path exists, the router sends the packet along the path that is most free from congestion. There's no guarantee that the packets will arrive in the same order that they were sent, but that's no problem. On the receiving computer, protocols come into play that put the packets in the correct order and decode the message they contain. If any packets are missing, the receiving computer sends a message requesting retransmission.

Packet switching networks are often called **connectionless** because, unlike switched networks, it's not necessary to have an active, direct electrical connection for two computers to communicate. For example, the Internet is a packet switching network: you can send somebody an email message even if the destination computer isn't operating. If the message doesn't get through, the software keeps trying to send it for a set period of time, after which it gives up.

Which Is Best?

Compared to circuit switching, packet switching has many advantages. It's more efficient and less expensive than circuit switching. What's more, packet switching networks are more reliable. A packet switching network can continue to function even if portions of the network aren't working. Routers may be able to find alternative pathways so that the data reaches its destination.

Packet switching does have its drawbacks, however. As it examines a packet, a router delays the packet's progress by a tiny fraction of a second. In a huge packet switching network such as the Internet, any given packet may be examined by many routers, introducing a noticeable delay called **latency.** If the network experiences **congestion** (overloading), some of the packets may be further delayed, and the message can't be decoded until all its packets are received. That's why packet switching networks aren't ideal for real-time voice communication (see Module 6A).

Protocols

What makes a network function isn't merely the physical connections. Of fundamental importance are the standards that specify how the network functions. These standards are called **protocols.**

What are protocols? They're like the manners you were taught when you were a child. When you're growing up, you're taught to say certain fixed things, such as "How do you do?" when you meet someone in an unfamiliar, formal social situation. The other person replies, "Very good, thank you." Such exchanges show a certain amount of insincerity, but they do serve to get communication going. Networking protocols are similar. They are fixed, formalized exchanges that specify how two dissimilar network components can establish communication.

In the early years of computer networking, protocols were zealously-guarded trade secrets of computer hardware manufacturers. Because they were owned by a single company, such protocols were called **proprietary protocols.** But these early networks had the same problem of other proprietary systems: customers weren't happy with the restrictions they imposed. You couldn't set up a network unless you were willing to buy all your equipment from the same manufacturer. Without the development of nonproprietary protocols, called **open protocols,** networking may never have become so widespread. An open protocol is a networking standard that has been developed and published by an independent organization, such as a standards committee organized by a professional association.

Open protocols benefit everyone. After they are published, companies know that they can purchase networking equipment that supports these protocols without locking themselves into a single vendor's products. Similarly, vendors know that the market for networking products will grow as more companies offer equipment that supports the open protocols.

A specific type of network may use dozens of protocols, which cover the many different aspects of routing data communications correctly. For example, the Internet uses well over one hundred protocols that specify every aspect of Internet usage, such as retrieving documents through the World Wide Web or sending email to a distant computer. The total package of protocols that specify how a specific network functions is called a **protocol suite.** Collectively, a protocol suite specifies the network's overall

Techtalk

spiders
The World Wide Web contains more than just a vast network of information links. "Spiders" exist there, too. A spider is a small piece of software that crawls around the Web picking up URLs and information on the pages attached to them.

design, called the **network architecture.** The term *architecture* may sound daunting, but in the next section you will learn that the basic idea isn't much more complicated than a layer cake.

Network Layers

Networks aren't easy to design because they are complex systems, and a lot can go wrong. To make network design easier, engineers divide a network architecture into separate **layers,** each of which has a function that can be isolated and treated separately from other layers. Because each layer's protocols precisely define how each layer passes data to another layer, it's possible to make changes within a layer without having to redesign the entire network.

The Protocol Stack

How do layers work? To understand the layer concept, it's helpful to remember that protocols are like manners, which enable people to get communication going. Let's look at an example.

Suppose you're using a Web browser (see Module 7B), and you click a link that looks interesting. Now imagine that each protocol is a person, and each person has an office on a separate floor of a multistory office building. You're on the top floor, and the network connection is in the basement. When you initiate your request, your browser calls the person on the next floor down, "Pardon me, but would you be so kind as to translate this Web page request into a form the Web server can process?" The person on the floor below replies, "I am ever so pleased to do so," and then calls the person on the *next* floor down. "If it isn't too much trouble, would you please put this translated message in an envelope and address it to such-and-such computer?" And so it goes, until the message finally reaches the physical transmission medium that connects the computers in the network.

At the receiving computer, precisely the opposite happens. The message is received in the basement and is sent *up*. It's taken out of its envelope, translated, and finally handed up to the top floor, where it's acted on.

To summarize, a network message starts at the top of a pile or stack of layers and moves down through the various layers until it reaches the bottom (the physical media). Because the various layers are seen to be vertically arranged like the floors in an office building, and because each is governed by its own protocols, the layers are called a **protocol stack.** On the receiving end, the process is reversed: the received message goes up the protocol stack. First, the network's data envelope is opened, and the data is translated until it's usable by the receiving application (see Figure 6B.2).

Figure 6B.2

A network message starts at the top of a stack of layers and moves down through the various layers (protocol stack) until it reaches the bottom, or physical media. On the receiving end, the process is reversed.

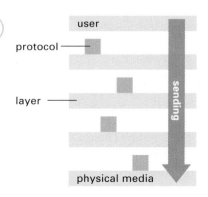
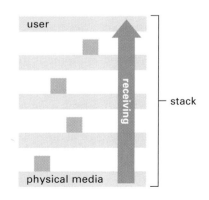

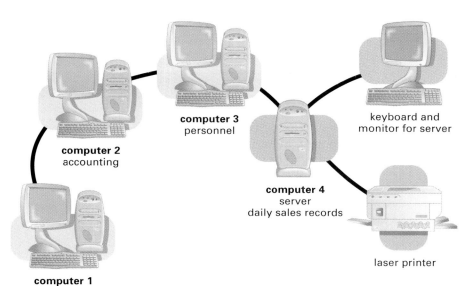

LANs transform an organization's hardware into what seems to users like one gigantic computer system.

computer 3
personnel

keyboard and
monitor for server

computer 2
accounting

computer 4
server
daily sales records

laser printer

computer 1
sales and marketing

LOCAL AREA NETWORKS (LANS): LIMITED REACH, FAST CONNECTIONS

LANs don't travel far—the maximum geographic reach of a LAN is about one mile—but they're fast. Even the least expensive LANs can transfer data at 10 Mbps, and speeds of 100 Mbps or more are increasingly common. The newest LAN technology, called **Gigabit Ethernet,** can transfer data at the amazing rate of 1,000 Mbps (that's 1 **gigabit** per second).

LANs transform an organization's hardware into what seems to users like one gigantic computer system. From any computer on the LAN, you can access any data, software, or peripherals (such as fax machines, printers, or scanners), as long as the network administrator has made these resources accessible (see Figure 6B.3).

Like all networks, LANs have all the basic network components—cabling, protocols, and a mechanism for routing information to the correct destination. As you'll see in the following sections, LANs require that connected computers have special hardware and software. LANs are primarily differentiated by the networking model they use (peer-to-peer or client/server), as well as their cabling, protocols, and spatial design (topology).

Networking Hardware: Network Interface Cards (NICs)

To connect to a LAN, a computer must be equipped with special hardware and software. In the hardware department, a computer needs a **network interface card (NIC),** an expansion board designed to fit into the computer's expansion slots (see Module 2A), to work with a LAN, unless this circuitry is part of the computer's design (see Figure 6B.4). Some NICs are designed to work with a specific type of LAN cabling and protocol, but others can work with more than one type.

When a PC is connected to a LAN, the PC is called a **workstation.** The term **node** is used to describe any computer or peripheral (such as a

A computer needs a network interface card (NIC) to work with a LAN. Some NICs are designed to work with a specific type of LAN cabling and protocol, but others work with more than one type.

printer) that's connected to the network. Every node on the LAN has a unique name that's visible to LAN users, as well as a unique, numerical network address.

Networking Software

Each computer on the LAN must also be equipped with additional system software that enables the computer to connect to the network and exchange data with other computers. Most operating systems, including UNIX, Linux, Windows 95, 98, NT, and 2000, as well as Mac OS now include such software in standard installations. You can set up a simple LAN, called a peer-to-peer network, by using this software, but you'll need additional software to set up a client/server network. Let's examine the differences between these two types of LANs.

Peer-to-Peer Networks

In a **peer-to-peer network,** all the computers on the network are equals—that's where the term *peer-to-peer* comes from—and there's no file server. In **file sharing,** each computer user decides which, if any, files will be accessible to other users on the network. Users may also choose to share entire directories, or even entire disks. They can also choose to share peripherals, such as printers and scanners.

Peer-to-peer networks are easy to set up. People who aren't networking experts do it all the time, generally to share an expensive laser printer or provide Internet access to all the workstations on the LAN. Peer-to-peer networks tend to slow down with heavy use, however, and keeping track of all the shared files and peripherals quickly becomes confusing. For this reason, peer-to-peer LANs aren't suitable for networks that connect more than one or two dozen computers.

Client/Server Networks

The typical corporate LAN is a **client/server network,** which includes one or more file servers as well as networked workstations (see Figure 6B.5). The file server is a high-capacity, high-speed computer with a large hard disk capacity. It contains the **network operating system,** the software required to run the network. The server also contains network versions of programs and large data files. **Clients** (all the computers that can access the server) send requests to the server. The client/server model works with any size or physical layout of LAN and does not tend to slow down with heavy use.

A network operating system (NOS), such as Novell Corporation's NetWare or Microsoft Windows NT Server, is a complex program that requires skilled technicians. NOS services include file directories that make it much easier to locate resources on the LAN, automated distribution of software updates to the PCs on the LAN, and support for Internet services such as the World Wide Web and email.

Media

LANs use a variety of physical media to carry network signals:

■ **Twisted pair** Twisted pair uses two insulated wires twisted around each other to provide a shield against electromagnetic interference, which is generated by electric motors, power lines, and powerful radio signals. The best type of unshielded twisted pair, called **category 5 (cat-5),** can support data transfer rates of 100 Mbps or more.

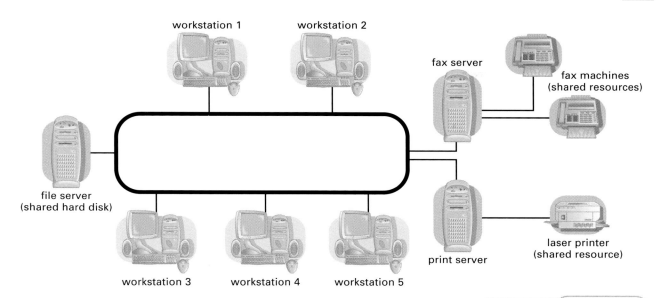

workstation 1 workstation 2

fax server

fax machines
(shared resources)

file server
(shared hard disk)

print server

laser printer
(shared resource)

workstation 3 workstation 4 workstation 5

Figure 6B.5

A client/server network
includes one or more file
servers as well as networked
workstations.

- **Coaxial cable** Familiar to cable TV users, this cable consists of a center wire surrounded by insulation, which is then surrounded by a layer of braided wire. The braided wire provides a shield against electrical interference.

- **Fiber-optic cable** A type of cable that transmits data in the form of light pulses, fiber-optic cable can carry more data for longer distances than twisted pair or coaxial cable.

- **Infrared** If you use a television remote control, you're already familiar with this wireless signaling technique. No wires are required, but the transmitter and receiver must be in the line of sight or the signal is lost. Infrared signals work within a maximum of about 100 feet.

- **Radio** Most wireless LANs use a radio transmission technique that ensures security by spreading the signal over a seemingly-random series of frequencies. Only the receiver knows the series, making it difficult to eavesdrop on the signals. Radio-based wireless LAN signals can traverse up to about 1,000 feet.

Wireless LANs come in handy when users must move around a building instead of staying put. In Veterans Administration hospitals, wireless LANs are helping hospital personnel track the distribution of controlled substances, a job that's both time-consuming and prone to error, without the computer's help. Now nurses use bedside computers, connected to the network through wireless signals, to track the use of these substances.

LAN Topologies

The physical layout of a local area network (called its **topology**) isn't just the arrangement of computers in space. Topologies also provide a solution to the problem of **contention,** which occurs when two workstations try to access the LAN at the same time. Contention could result in **collisions,** the corruption of network data caused by two workstations transmitting simultaneously.

The earliest LANs used a **bus topology,** also called a *daisy chain,* in which the network cable forms a single bus to which every workstation is attached. At the ends of the bus, special connectors called terminators configure the end of the circuit. To resolve the contention problem, bus networks

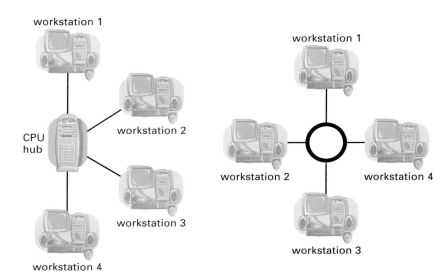

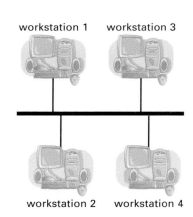

Bus topology
The network cable forms a single bus to which every workstation is attached.

Star topology
This network introduces a central wiring concentrator called a hub. It's easy to connect new users by running a cable to the hub.

Ring topology
All the nodes are attached in a circular wiring.

Figure **6B.6**

Most networks use a bus, star, or ring topology.

use some type of **contention management** technique, which specifies what happens when a collision occurs. (A common technique is to abandon any data that could have been corrupted by a collision.) The underlying design is simple, but bus networks are unwieldy in practice since it's difficult to add users in the middle of the circuit.

A **star topology** solves the expansion problems of the bus topology by introducing a central wiring concentrator, called a **hub.** Adding users is simple: you just run a cable to the hub and plug the new user into a vacant connector. Star networks generally use contention access to deal with collisions.

A **ring topology** has all its nodes attached in a circular wiring arrangement. This topology creates a unique way of preventing collisions. A workstation can transmit only when it possesses the **token,** a special unit of data that travels around this ring. Although ring topology networks are circular in that the token travels a circular path, they look more like star networks because all the wiring is routed to a central hub. Figure 6B.6 summarizes the bus, star, and ring topologies.

LAN Technologies

Although several LAN technologies specify functions at the lower layers of the protocol stack (see Table 6B.1), by far the most popular LAN standard is **Ethernet,** originally developed in the 1970s by Bob Metcalfe and other researchers at Xerox Corporation's Palo Alto Research Center (PARC). Various versions of Ethernet are used by approximately 80 percent of all LANs. Although early versions of Ethernet (called 10base2 and 10base5) used coaxial cable in bus networks, the most popular versions today are Ethernet star networks that use hubs and twisted-pair wire. Two versions are available: **10baseT** (10 Mbps) and **Fast Ethernet** (100 Mbps, also called 100baseT). The equipment used to create a 10baseT Ethernet for five PCs can cost as little as $200. A new version, called Gigabit Ethernet, will enable data transfer at 1000 Mbps (1 gigabit per second).

Destinations

Like to learn more about the Ethernet? Check out Charles Spurgeon's Ethernet Web site (**http://www.ots.utexas. edu/ethernet/**), which covers all the Ethernet technologies used today and includes a practical guide for do-it-yourselfers.

Popular Lower-Layer LAN Protocols			Table 6B.1
Protocol Name	**Data Transfer Rate**	**Physical Media**	**Topology**
LocalTalk	230.4 Kbps	Shielded twisted pair (phone connector cords)	Bus
Ethernet (10base5 and 10base2)	10 Mbps	Coaxial cable	Bus
Ethernet (10baseT)	10 Mbps	Twisted-pair cable	Star
Fast Ethernet (100baseT)	100 Mbps	Twisted-pair or fiber-optic cable	Star
Gigabit Ethernet	1000 Mbps	Fiber-optic cable	Star
IBM Token Ring Network	4-16 Mbps	Twisted pair	Star

Perhaps the simplest LAN technology is **LocalTalk,** the networking system built into every Macintosh computer. You can quickly create a LocalTalk network by buying some LocalTalk connectors and ordinary telephone cables.

LAN Protocols

LAN technologies such as Ethernet specify the nuts and bolts of the lower layers, including the physical and data link layers. These layers can work with a variety of higher-level protocols, which handle the network, transport, and higher layers. Following are examples of such higher-layer protocols:

- **AppleTalk**   This Apple Computer protocol provides the network routing and addressing functions for all Macintosh networks, whether they use LocalTalk, Ethernet, or token-ring networks at lower layers.

- **IPX/SPX**   These are the network and transport layer protocols used for Novell NetWare networks.

- **NetBEUI**   The NetBEUI protocols define Microsoft Windows NT-based networks.

- **TCP/IP**   These are the core Internet protocols (see Module 7A). Like AppleTalk, TCP/IP can be used with a variety of lower-level protocols, such as Ethernet. A LAN that uses TCP/IP is called an **intranet,** a term that suggests that it's an Internet designed for internal use in an organization. You'll examine intranets in Module 7A.

A single network can run more than one higher-level protocol at a time. Many LANs run IPX/SPX to access file servers, AppleTalk to provide support for the Macintoshes connected to the network, NetBEUI to connect with Windows NT servers, and TCP/IP for Internet access.

WIDE AREA NETWORKS (WANS): LONG-HAUL CARRIERS

Local area networks enable an organization to share computing resources within a single building or group of buildings. But a LAN's geographic limitations pose a problem. Today, most organizations need to share computing resources with distant branch offices, employees who are traveling, and even people outside the organization, including suppliers and customers. LANs

SPOTLIGHT

CONNECTING THE NAVAJO NATION

▶In the Southwest, straddling the borders of Arizona, New Mexico, and Utah is the Navajo Nation. Driving through the 26,000-square-mile area, one gets the sense of what the term *wide open spaces* really means. However, the large area and sparse population of the Navajo Nation presents special challenges for education and networking.

The Nation established Diné College in 1968 to help meet the educational needs of Navajo youth. The college has grown to seven campuses within the Nation, all of which are in small towns and separated by hundreds of miles. The college awards associate degrees and technical certifications in areas that are important to the economic and social development of the Nation.

Connecting the individual campuses to the Internet became a particularly-difficult task. Educators recognized that, in order to best serve the 2,000-plus students, Internet access is virtually a necessity. The problem, however, is that much of the Navajo Nation doesn't have a communication infrastructure. Approximately half of the households don't even have phone service, and those that do find the quality of that service sometimes lacking. For data communications, the maximum reliable data speed is often limited to 28.8 Kbps. In addition, Internet access through a private service provider is virtually always a long-distance call.

The low speeds, poor quality, and high cost of modem connections meant that using the Internet for education was largely unfeasible. Dr. David Basham, director of the Navajo Learning Network, took it as a personal challenge to overcome these obstacles. By working with educators in other state facilities, he came up with a possible solution: satellites.

Through the use of satellite technology, Dr. Basham was able to devise a way to receive Internet information quickly and inexpensively. He purchased a system called DirecPC Network Edition, which uses a small 18-inch satellite dish to receive information from the Internet, and regular telephone or data lines to send information. Because the majority of any Internet use in an educational environment involves massive amounts of downloaded information, the satellite solution seemed ideal.

DirecPC Network Edition works a little differently than a normal one-on-one Internet connection. In a regular dial-up connection to an Internet provider, a single computer requests information from the Internet and then receives it, all over the same phone line. The DirecPC solution, however, allows multiple computers, such as those in a classroom setting, to connect to the Internet simultaneously. Information is downloaded through the satellite dish at approximately 400 Kbps, much faster than is possible through regular phone lines.

Perhaps the only potential drawback to his solution is that the use of the satellite dish means information to and from the classroom computers cannot be transmitted over the same path. This is because the small satellite dishes are receive-only devices. To compensate, the students use regular phone lines to connect to the DirecPC computers and make requests, which are then delivered using the satellite. In areas where the Internet is only a local phone call away, this is a viable solution. Some Diné College campuses, however, are in remote areas that do not have local phone access to the Internet. For these campuses, funding from several grant sources allowed the establishment of an enterprise network for the campuses using dedicated low-speed data lines.

As a result of the satellite and the phone and data lines, Diné College and the Navajo Nation were able to get educational access to the Internet quickly and inexpensively. This has increased the quality of education and the opportunities available to students in the area.

The large area and sparse population of the Navajo Nation presents special challenges for education and networking.

foster internal communication, but they also threaten to insulate an organization, cutting it off from the outside world.

Outside contact is increasingly important. In the early 1990s, the 80/20 rule was often used for network planning purposes: 80 percent of the networking traffic would occur on internal LANs, while only 20 percent would go outside. Today, the rule is closer to 50/50. In addition, WANs are growing at an incredible rate—in excess of 75 percent per year, according to an MIT study.

Why don't companies simply use the Internet to link to the outside world? They do, but the Internet has two major limitations (as you'll learn in Module 7A): poor security and service interruptions due to network overload. Companies are increasingly using the Internet for low-security operations, as well as for exchanging data that isn't time-critical. But they are reluctant to use the public Internet for exchanging financial data or any other types of data that must arrive on time.

Destinations

Like to know the latest news about LANs? Check out *LAN Times,* the premiere trade journal in this area. LANTimes Online is located at **http://www.lantimes.com.**

How WANs Work

WANs are like long-distance telephone systems. In fact, much of the WAN traffic is carried by long-distance voice communication providers, such as AT&T, MCI, and Sprint. Like long-distance phone carriers, WANs have what amounts to a local access number, called a point of presence (POP), and long-distance trunk lines, called backbones.

Point of Presence (POP)

To carry computer data over the long haul, a WAN must be locally accessible. For this reason, WANs make a **point of presence (POP)** available in as many towns and cities as possible. A point of presence is a WAN network connection point that enables customers to access the WAN by means of a local analog telephone call (using a modem) or a direct digital hookup that enables a continuous, direct connection. A WAN called Tymnet has over 1,000 local points of presence in the United States.

The following physical media are often used to create permanent digital connections from an organization to a POP:

WANs are like long-distance telephone systems. In fact, a lot of WAN traffic is carried by long-distance voice communication providers.

- A 56-Kbps **leased line** is a specially-conditioned telephone line that enables continuous, end-to-end communication between two points. The earliest type of permanent digital connection, 56-Kbps leased lines are expected to decline in popularity as services such as ISDN and ADSL become more-widely available.

- As discussed in Module 6A, ISDN services offer connections ranging from 56 to 128 Kbps (Basic Rate ISDN) or 1.5 Mbps (Primary Rate ISDN) using ordinary twisted-pair telephone lines.

- Also discussed in Module 6A, ADSL and related Digital Subscriber Line (DSL) technologies are expected to provide 1-Mbps access, again using ordinary twisted-pair telephone lines.

- Larger organizations, such as Internet service providers, corporations, and universities, connect using a leased **T1** line. This is a costly service that isn't affordable for individuals and small businesses.

■ A new local connection service, called a **permanent virtual circuit (PVC),** uses a type of packet switching known as **frame relay.** Like leased 56-Kbps lines and leased T1 lines, a PVC establishes point-to-point data communication, but the use of packet switching enables more than one user's data to traverse the line simultaneously. Accordingly, costs are lower than private leased lines.

Backbones

The high-capacity transmission lines that carry WAN traffic are called **backbones.** Some are regional, connecting towns and cities in a region such as southern California or New England. Others are continental or even transcontinental in scope.

Whatever their scope, backbones are designed to carry huge amounts of data traffic. Cross-country Internet backbones, for example, can handle nearly 2.5 gigabits per second, and much higher speeds are on the way. A current U.S. government-funded research project is constructing a backbone network that will operate at speeds of 9.6 gigabits per second.

Some WANs use circuit switching network technology, but most use packet switching.

How WANs Are Organized

Most WAN traffic travels over connections leased from WAN service providers. The Internet is a WAN of massive proportions. Backbone providers receive compensation by charging fees to Internet service providers (ISPs), who in turn sell subscriptions to individual and organizational Internet users. As you'll learn in Module 7A, the Internet isn't secure, and the quality of service may not be acceptable for business use. Most businesses use WANs other than the Internet for sensitive financial transactions and time-sensitive data.

A **public data network (PDN)** is a for-profit data communications network available for use on a per-byte-transmitted fee basis. PDNs charge hefty fees, but they can assure good security and can guarantee that bandwidth (network capacity) is available when it's needed.

Large corporations, banks, and governments may construct private data networks, which aren't open to the public or to any other users. These are the most secure WANs, but they're also the most expensive to operate. An alternative developed in the 1980s, called the **virtual private network (VPN),** consists of lines that are exclusively leased to a single company, thus ensuring excellent security.

WAN Protocols

Like any computer network, WANs use protocols. The oldest packet switching protocol for WAN usage, called **X.25,** is optimized for dial-up connections over noisy telephone lines and is still in widespread use. Local connections generally offer speeds of 9.6 to 64 Kbps. It's best used to create a point-to-point connection with a single computer. X.25 is widely used for automated teller machines (ATMs) and credit card authorization devices. New protocols designed for 100 percent digital lines, such as Switched Multimegabit Data Service (SMDS) and Asynchronous Transfer Mode (ATM), enable much faster data transfer rates (up to 155 Mbps).

WAN Applications

WANs enable companies to use many of the same applications you'll use on the Internet, such as email, conferencing, document exchange, and remote

Destinations

If you'd like to explore cutting-edge WAN technologies such as SMDS and ATM, a good place to start is Pacific Bell's FasTrak Data and Video Services page (**http://www.pacbell. com/products/business/ fas-trak/index.html**).

The PARC Mystery: Why Did Xerox Fail to Capitalize on Its Own Technological Innovations?

It's one of the most amazing feats of sheer technical brilliance in the history of computing—and indeed, in the history of any technology. In the early 1970s, a talented team of researchers at Xerox Corporation's Palo Alto Research Center (PARC) invented just about every major technology that you'll find in today's desktop computers. Yet Xerox failed to recognize what the PARC researchers had achieved and couldn't market any of their innovations successfully. The story of Xerox PARC is carefully studied to this day by business management students who are hoping to avoid what is commonly seen as Xerox's colossal marketing blunder. Was it really a blunder—or were the PARC researchers simply ahead of their time?

What did the PARC researchers come up with? Here are a few highlights:

- The graphical user interface (GUI) replete with pull-down menus, dialog boxes, on-screen fonts that look the way they'll print, and on-screen graphic images.

- The mouse—which, in its earliest incarnations, was made out of a block of wood.

- Laser printers and the Postscript page description language, which today form the standard for business and personal printing with computers.

- Desktop publishing software and what-you-see-is-what-you-get (WYSIWYG) word processing software.

- The Ethernet networking standard for local area networks.

All these technologies came to fruition in Xerox's Star, a 1974 desktop computer system with 512K of RAM and a brilliant, page-white display. Xerox attempted to market the Star as a breakthrough product, one that would enable collaborating workgroups to share their work by means of a high-speed, local area network and produce beautifully-printed, richly-detailed documents. Unfortunately, Xerox sold very few Stars. However, within a few years, other companies took the PARC researchers' innovations to market, and made billions.

Where did Xerox go wrong? Part of the problem was the Star's high cost: each fully-equipped Star system cost more than $10,000. Yet Xerox probably would have failed to market the Star successfully even if it could have been manufactured for half that sum. The reason? When Xerox marketers tried to explain what the Star was supposed to do, nobody had the faintest idea what they were talking about. In those days, the cutting edge of office technology consisted of electric typewriters and photocopying machines. The leap to today's collaborative computer systems was simply too great for people to appreciate. If you're still skeptical, consider that an entire decade elapsed before Apple Computer was able to win market acceptance for the Macintosh, a PARC-influenced system—and Apple was not able to win more than 10 percent of the total computer marketplace. The PARC researchers' ideas did not win full acceptance until the release of Microsoft Windows 95 and 98, more than 20 years after the original innovations took place.

Xerox's dilemma can best be summed up in the philosophy of famous American industrial designer Raymond Loewy, whose accomplishments include the fabled 1961 Studebaker Avanti. If you're looking for the right design, said Loewy, choose the one that's the "most advanced yet most acceptable" to the public. He even coined an acronym, MAYA, to sum up this philosophy. PARC's technology was far too advanced for public acceptance in the early 1970s, and the subsequent history of this technology's slow marketplace start shows this clearly.

Still, it's a good thing that PARC's management didn't take Loewy's maxim to heart. They might have directed PARC researchers to work on less-advanced technology! In this case, Xerox's loss translated into enormous gains for computer users worldwide.

database access. (You'll explore these uses of the Internet in the next two chapters.) This section focuses on the ways to take advantage of a WAN's superior security.

LAN-to-LAN Connections

In corporate information systems, WANs are often used to connect the local area networks (LANs) at two or more geographically-separate locations. This use of WANs overcomes the major limitation of LAN technology: its incapability to link computers separated by more than a few thousand feet. New services from WAN service providers such as AT&T, Sprint, and MCI enable companies to connect their LANs at 100 Mbps, the same data transfer rate used in most companies' internal systems. With these connections, users get the impression that they're using one huge LAN that connects the entire company and all its branch offices.

Transaction Acquisition

When you make a purchase at retail chain stores such as Sears or Starbucks Coffee, information about your transaction is instantly relayed to central computers through WANs. That's because the "cash register" the clerk uses is actually a computer, called a **point of sale (POS) terminal,** that's linked to a data communications network. The acquired data is collected for accounting and also analyzed to reveal changing sales patterns.

Electronic Data Interchange (EDI)

A set of standards that specify how companies can set up business-to-business financial transactions, **electronic data interchange (EDI)** is widely used to speed ordering, invoicing, and payments. If two companies have compatible systems, they can establish a connection through which company A sends a purchase order to company B by means of EDI-computer to computer. When company B ships the product, company B sends an invoice by EDI to company A. Company A can then pay by electronic funds transfer through its bank. The entire operation occurs without any paper changing hands.

If two companies do not have compatible systems, they can use an intermediary EDI company to change the code so that the two companies can communicate. Very large manufacturing companies often require as a condition of purchase that their suppliers have EDI systems compatible with the company's system. The buyer can order parts to be delivered just in time to be used. This capability enables the buyer to shorten the length of time between buying the parts and selling the finished product and receiving payment.

EDI can reduce a company's costs, but the technology is cumbersome and comes with high start-up costs. In Module 7A, you'll learn how companies are using the Internet to enable low-cost transactions (and how they're reducing the security risks that Internet use entails).

TAKEAWAY POINTS

- Computer networks link two or more computers so that they can exchange data and share resources.
- The three types of computer networks are local area networks (LANs), metropolitan area networks (MANs), and wide area networks (WANs).
- Computer networks can reduce hardware costs, enable shared applications, create the means to pool all of an organization's mission-critical data, and foster teamwork and collaboration.
- Computer networks require physical media, but their most important component consists of the protocols that define how network devices can communicate with each other.
- A network requires many protocols to function smoothly. When a computer sends a message over the network, the application hands the message down the protocol stack, where a series of protocols prepares the message for transmission through the network. At the other end, the message goes up a similar stack.

- Circuit switching creates a permanent, end-to-end circuit that is optimal for voice and real-time data. Packet switching does not require a permanent switched circuit and can funnel more data through a medium with a given data transfer capacity. But packet switching introduces slight delays that make the technology less than optimal for voice or real-time data.
- A peer-to-peer LAN doesn't use a file server and is most appropriate for small networks. Client/server networks offer network navigation tools, shared applications, shared databases, groupware, and email, but trained technicians are required to configure and maintain them.
- By far the most-widely used LAN protocol is Ethernet, which is available in 10- or 100-Mbps star topology configurations that use hubs and twisted-pair wiring.
- Businesses use WANs for LAN-to-LAN connections, transaction acquisition, and electronic data interchange.

MODULE REVIEW

KEY TERMS AND CONCEPTS

10baseT	gigabit	peer-to-peer network
AppleTalk	Gigabit Ethernet	permanent virtual circuit (PVC)
backbones	groupware	point of presence (POP)
bus topology	hub	point of sale (POS) terminal
category 5 (cat-5)	infrared	proprietary protocols
circuit switching	intranet	protocols
clients	IPX/SPX	protocol stack
client/server network	latency	protocol suite
coaxial cable	layers	public data network (PDN)
collisions	leased line	radio
computer network	local area networks (LANs)	ring topology
congestion	LocalTalk	routers
connectionless	metropolitan area networks	star topology
contention	(MANs)	T1
contention management	NetBEUI	TCP/IP
electronic data interchange	network architecture	terminals
(EDI)	network interface card (NIC)	token
Ethernet	network operating system	topology
Fast Ethernet	network versions	twisted pair
fiber-optic cable	node	virtual private network (VPN)
file server	open protocols	wide area networks (WANs)
file sharing	packet switching	workstation
frame relay	packets	X.25

TRUE/FALSE

Indicate whether the following statements are true or false.

1. A computer network links two or more computers so they can exchange data and share resources.

2. A metropolitan network uses direct cables to localized wireless radio or infrared signals to link computers within a small geographic area.

3. The physical medium is the most important part of a computer network.

4. The standards that specify how a network functions are called protocols.

5. Networks are simple systems that are easy to design.

6. One technology that networks use to funnel messages to their correct destination is called packet switching.

7. The maximum geographic reach of a local area network (LAN) is about one mile.

8. The typical corporate LAN is a peer-to-peer network.

9. The most popular LAN standard is Ethernet.

10. The Internet is a wide area network (WAN) of massive proportions.

MATCHING

Match each key term from the left column with the most accurate definition in the right column.

_____ 1. metropolitan area network

_____ 2. groupware

_____ 3. routers

_____ 4. protocols

_____ 5. network architecture

_____ 6. node

_____ 7. network operating system

_____ 8. clients

_____ 9. token

_____ 10. TCP/IP

a. the network's overall design

b. the use of high-speed optic lines to connect computers located at various places within a major urban region

c. a computer or peripheral that's connected to the network

d. applications that enable workers to create a shared calendar for scheduling purposes

e. software required to run the network

f. the core Internet protocols

g. standards that specify how the network functions

h. a special unit of data that travels around the ring in a ring topology

i. all the computers that can access the server

j. computer-based devices that examine each packet they detect

MULTIPLE CHOICE

Circle the letter of the correct choice for each of the following.

1. Which of the following is not a computer network?
   a. local area network
   b. leased-line area network
   c. wide area network
   d. metropolitan area network

2. Which of the following is an advantage to having a computer network?
   a. increasing the number of hardware components
   b. fiber-optic cable
   c. sharing applications
   d. the network operating system

3. Which technology enables networks to funnel messages to the correct destination?
   a. circuit switching
   b. packet switching
   c. routers
   d. a and b

4. To connect to a LAN, a computer must be equipped with which of the following?
   a. network interface card
   b. backbone
   c. workstation
   d. node

5. Which of the following networks is rather easy to set up?
   a. wide area network
   b. public data network
   c. peer-to-peer network
   d. client/server network

6. Which of the following is not a LAN topology?
   a. ring
   b. star
   c. hub
   d. bus

7. Which of the following is not a characteristic of a WAN?
   a. A lot of WAN traffic is carried by long-distance voice communication providers.
   b. A WAN must be locally accessible.
   c. Most businesses use WANs other than the Internet for sensitive financial transactions.
   d. LocalTalk is a popular WAN technology.

8. Which of the following is a WAN network connection point that enables customers to access the WAN through a local phone call?
   a. point of presence
   b. leased line
   c. permanent virtual circuit
   d. frame relay

9. What do you call a for-profit data communications network available for use on a per-byte-transmitted fee basis?
   a. virtual private network
   b. public data network
   c. peer-to-peer network
   d. client/server network

10. Which of the following is the oldest and most-widely used packet switching protocol for WAN usage?
    a. 10baseT
    b. category 5 (cat-5)
    c. X.25
    d. T1

FILL-IN

In the blank provided, write the correct answer for each of the following.

1. A computer _____ links two or more computers together to enable data and resource exchange.

2. A(n) _____ uses direct cables, localized wireless radio, or infrared signals to link computers within a small geographic area.

3. A(n) _____ is a networking standard that has been developed and published by an independent organization such as a standards body.

4. In _____ , an outgoing message is divided into data units of fixed size called packets.

5. When a PC is connected to a LAN, it's called a(n) _____ .

6. The _____ is a high-capacity, high-speed computer with a large hard disk capacity.

7. The earliest LANs used a(n) _____ topology.

8. A LAN that uses TCP/IP is called a(n) _____ .

9. The high-capacity transmission lines that carry WAN traffic are called _____ .

10. _____ is widely used to speed ordering, invoicing, and payments.

SHORT ANSWER

On a separate sheet of paper, answer the following questions.

1. What's the difference between computer networks and telecommunications networks?

2. Discuss the ways that connecting computers increases the value of an organization's information technology investment.

3. What are the differences between local, wide, and metropolitan area networks?

4. What are protocols?

5. Contrast circuit switching and packet switching networks and describe their pros and cons.

6. Name the three types of LAN topologies and describe how they work.

7. What's the most-widely used LAN protocol? What are its benefits?

8. Identify some popular lower-layer LAN protocols and indicate their physical media and topologies.

9. How are WANs used? How are WANs organized?

10. Describe the various applications associated with WANs.

PFSweb, Inc.

What's your biggest frustration with the Web? If you're like most people, you said "waiting for stuff to load." The causes could be numerous: limited bandwidth to your computer, slow processors on the sending or receiving end, heavy use of graphics by the site, bottlenecks along the network path the site travels, and more. When PFSweb takes on a new e-commerce client, one of the major areas of concern has to do with the network resources it will use to support the client's Web-based business activity so frustrations are minimized.

There are several key questions each e-commerce client must consider. First, does the Web site need to be available 24 hours a day, seven days a week? Will there be a financial impact if not? Second, how much Web traffic is expected? What sort of trends and peaks are anticipated? These are not easy questions to

answer, especially if the e-commerce client is new at selling online. But they make a world of difference for success.

PFSweb uses two major telecommunications providers for its network traffic—GTE for primary access, and AT&T for backup. That way, if there's a network outage at GTE, all traffic automatically switches over to AT&T lines. No business is lost, and those customers who rely on 24/7 (24 hours a day, seven days a week) access can rest easy. PFSweb also has separate inbound and outbound communications lines. Like one-way streets, the data traffic can flow much better when directed this way. Another technique being used is the banding of multiple T1 (high bandwidth) lines to increase capacity and reliability. Getting all of these pieces working just right requires some network "tuning," but it's all worth it when both the client and their customers are happy.

What do you think? Consumers now have several choices for speedy Internet access. Call your local telephone service provider and find out the following: What plans do they offer for residential Internet access? Which one provides the fastest access? Will the phone company also act as your Internet service provider? What are the costs and benefits of each plan? Do any of the options appeal to you as a consumer? Why or why not?

WebLink Go to **www.prenhall.com/ pfaffenberger** to find out what future telecommunications advances hold the most promise for e-commerce.

E-COMMERCE IN ACTION

7

CHAPTER

The Internet and the Web: Welcome to Cyberspace

The Internet is so solidly lodged in the public's mind that it's hard to imagine a time when this globe-spanning network didn't exist. Today, millions of people use the Internet to find jobs, pick movies, read the latest news, get weather reports, locate recipes, trade stocks, auction off unwanted goods, and much more. Chances are you've already been using the Internet, perhaps for years: the under-16 crowd is taking to the Internet in greater percentages than any other age group.

Still, too many people use the Internet without fully understanding the technology they're using—and that's risky. Increasing numbers of people are shopping online, but they don't understand that the 40-bit encryption that most browsers use by default isn't sufficient for security—and they don't know how to download the security upgrade. The Internet is an unparalleled information treasure house, but too many people lack the knowledge needed to search the Internet effectively or evaluate the quality of the information they find. And far too many people fail to understand the limitations and peculiarities of email, a shortcoming that could cost them their friends—and even their jobs.

It's easy to use the Internet, but knowledge is needed to use the Internet wisely. This point nicely illustrates the distinction between computer literacy and computer fluency that was introduced in Module 1A. A computer-literate person knows how to browse the Web; a computer-fluent person knows how to do so safely, how to locate needed information with precision, and how to determine whether the located information is trustworthy. Chapter 7 teaches the fundamentals of Internet fluency, beginning with Module 7A, "Understanding the Internet." This module provides a plain-English introduction to the way the Internet works. You'll find this knowledge invaluable as you seek to grasp the Internet's potential for transforming our lives. Module 7B turns to the World Wide Web and the exploding world of e-commerce. You'll learn how to locate the information you need, how to judge the quality of material you find online, and how to safeguard your security and privacy while you're shopping online. Module 7C covers Internet email, which is fast becoming an indispensable tool for keeping in touch with friends, family, support networks, employers, and people with shared interests. It's also a complex and risky technology, one that's poorly understood by far too many users. Concluding this chapter's presentation, Module 7D provides a brief introduction to the language underlying the appearance of Web pages, called HTML. You'll learn how to create a simple Web page whether you're using HTML tags or a "what-you-see-is-what-you-get" editor such as Microsoft Front Page Express. The module doesn't go into all the details of Web publishing, but it's enough to get you started—so start planning that home page!

M O D U L E S

MODULE 7A

UNDERSTANDING THE INTERNET

WHAT YOU WILL LEARN . . .

When you have finished reading this module, you will be able to:

1. Define the Internet and discuss why it is so popular.
2. Differentiate the Internet from online services.
3. Explain the difference between client and server software.
4. List the most popular Internet services and explain what they do.
5. Explain the difference between Internet addresses and domain names.
6. Discuss the use of Internet-based networks within large organizations.
7. List the initiatives underway to improve the Internet's performance.

The Internet is a global computer network with hundreds of millions of users worldwide, and it's growing like crazy. According to one estimate, more than 300,000 new Web pages appear every seven days, and the total amount of information available on this worldwide network doubles every year. But defining the Internet as a fast-growing global network understates its significance. We're witnessing the birth of the first major mass medium since television. Already, more than 50 percent of United States residents between the ages of 16 and 34 are Internet users. What's more, the Internet isn't simply a new mass medium: it's the *first* mass medium that involves computers and uses digitized data. For this reason, it's more interactive than TV, radio, and newspapers, which limit user interaction to content selection. With the Internet, people can *create* information as well as consume it. For this reason, it's the first truly *democratic* mass medium, one that allows ordinary people to add their own content to the growing mass of information available online.

The Internet is the first mass medium that involves computers and uses digitized data. More than 50 percent of United States residents between the ages of 16 and 34 are Internet users.

Computers and digitization affect this new medium's possibilities in another important way: the potential for *media convergence*, the unification of *all* earlier media (including newspapers, TVs, radio, and telephones). Skeptical? The Internet is already a major source of breaking news for Internet users, rivaling such traditional sources as newspapers and the evening news on TV. Today, you can hear more radio stations on the Internet than you can with any conventional radio. More than 1,500 radio stations in 100 countries are now broadcasting live shows over the Internet. And according to a recent estimate, by 2002 over 5 percent of all long-distance voice telephone calls will travel over the Internet, creating a $9 billion industry and posing a genuine threat to the public switched telephone network (PSTN).

Traditional media aren't going to go away soon, but you can count on one thing: the Internet is transforming almost everything we do, including communicating, obtaining information, learning, looking for jobs, keeping up with a career or a profession, and even falling in love. And it's equally indispensable for businesses. According to a recent estimate, electronic commerce (e-commerce), facilitated by the Internet, will create a market worth billions in coming years. Just what *is* this network, and why is it growing at such explosive rates?

 **Destinations**

Looking for a radio station? Try Live Radio on the internet (**http://www. live-radio.net**), which lists more than 1,500 live internet radio stations worldwide. You need a player to listen to radio over the internet, but you can download one for free. Radio station home pages have links that enable you to obtain the software you need.

INTRODUCING THE INTERNET: THE NETWORK OF NETWORKS

To understand the Internet, it's important to begin with a solid grasp of just what differentiates the Internet from other networks that traverse huge distances, such as the wide area networks (WANs) discussed in Module 6B. Here's the most important point: technically, the **Internet** is best defined as a technology for linking local area networks (LANs) into a huge, distance-conquering network. (LANs are introduced in Module 6B.)

In this network of networks, every connected computer can directly exchange data with any other computer on the network. The LANs and computers connected to the Internet are maintained by large organizations, such as corporations and universities, as well as by **Internet service providers (ISPs),** who sell Internet subscriptions to the public (see Figure 7A.1). Today, hundreds of thousands of networks and nearly fifty-million computers are directly connected to the Internet.

 Explore IT Lab

Internet and WWW

Figure 7A.1

LANs and computers connected to the Internet are maintained by corporations and universities, as well as by Internet service providers (ISPs), who sell Internet subscriptions to the public.

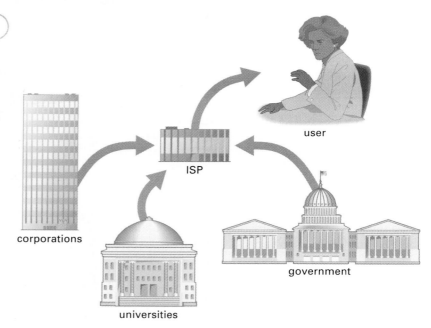

Techtalk

Internet or internet?

When people talk about the Internet with an upper-case "I," they're referring to the large, public Internet that had more than 300 million users in 2000. But the Internet isn't the only large-scale network that uses the same underlying technology. For example, the U.S. Department of Defense maintains a network called MILNET, which uses the same technology that's used in the public Internet. An internet, spelled with a lower-case "I," is a private network that uses Internet technology.

A Galactic Network

The Internet was first envisioned by MIT scientist J. C. R. Licklider in August 1962. Licklider, who was President Roosevelt's science advisor during World War II, headed the first computer research program at the Defense Advanced Research Projects Agency (DARPA, as it was then known), a unit of the U.S. Department of Defense. In a series of historic memos, Licklider spoke of a "galactic network," a globally-interconnected network through which any computer could directly access any other and exchange data. That's precisely what the Internet accomplishes.

In that it enables direct and immediate contact with any other computer on the network, the Internet bears some similarity to the world telephone system (although the Internet works on different principles). Every Internet computer has an **Internet address,** or **IP address** (similar to a phone number), and it can directly exchange data with any other Internet computer by "dialing" the other computer's address. The Internet works on packet-switching principles rather than the circuit-switching principles of the telephone system (see Module 6B for an explanation of these terms). Still, the Internet does for computers what the global telephone system does for phones: it enables any Internet-connected computer to connect almost instantly and effortlessly with *any* other Internet-connected computer anywhere in the world. The Internet is an incredible achievement: an enormous, worldwide information space in which every fully-connected computer has its own, unique address.

Interoperability

If the Internet merely allowed any one of millions of computers to exchange data with any other, it would be quite an achievement. But the Internet does more. It enables any connected computer to *operate* a remote computer by sending commands through the network. One key to the Internet's success is that such commands work even if the remote computer is a different brand and model. Called **interoperability,** this remarkable characteristic of the Internet comes into play every time you use the network. When you access the Web with a Macintosh, for example, you contact a variety of machines

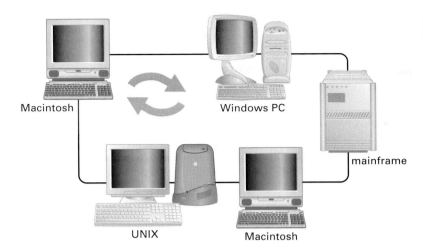

Figure 7A.2

The Internet is a cross-platform network. When you access the Web with a Macintosh, for example, you contact a variety of machines that may include other Macintoshes, Windows PCs, UNIX machines, and even mainframe computers.

that may include other Macintoshes, Windows PCs, UNIX machines, and even mainframe computers. You don't know what type of computer platform you're accessing, however, and it doesn't make any difference. (A *platform* is a distinct type of computer that uses a certain type of processor and operating system, such as an Intel-based Windows PC.) In other words, the Internet is a **cross-platform network** (see Figure 7A.2).

The Internet's cross-platform capability helps explain the network's popularity. No network could match the Internet's success if it forced people to use just one or two types of computers. Many home computer users have PCs, but others have Macintoshes and dozens of additional types of computers. All too many businesses have invested haphazardly in Windows PCs, UNIX workstations, and Macintoshes, only to find that, in the absence of the Internet, these computers don't work together well. Almost magically, the Internet enables these computers to exchange data and even to control each other's operations. As you'll see later in this module, this is a major reason for the explosive popularity of intranets, internal networks that use Internet technologies.

Leave the Lower Layers to the LANs and WANs

The Internet connects millions of LANs, but a key Internet design principle is that LANs do not all have to work the same way to connect to the Internet. The Internet protocols don't define the lower, nuts-and-bolts networking standards needed to transmit data physically over a certain transmission medium. (For an introduction to the concept of network layers, see Module 6B.) Instead, the Internet leaves this up to whatever network the Internet data is traveling on. This is an important key to the Internet's success because it means that an organization doesn't have to change its internal computer network to connect to the Internet. In the same way, Internet data can travel over any type of wide area network (WAN).

The Internet vs. Online Services

What's the difference between the Internet and an **online service,** such as Prodigy or America Online? An online service provides a proprietary network, accessed by means of WANs such as Tymnet, that offer email, chat rooms, discussions, and fee-based content, such as magazines and newspapers. To enable users to access the service, they distribute software that runs on users' computers, makes the connection to the service, and guides them through the available content and activities. As the Internet grew in popularity during the

Forty percent of home Internet users access the Internet through America Online (AOL).

mid-1990s, online services began to offer Internet access in an attempt to keep existing customers and attract new ones. While retaining their proprietary network and custom content, they have become Internet service providers. The leading online service, America Online (AOL), currently has 11 million paying subscribers. Forty percent of home Internet users access the Internet through AOL, preferring AOL's rich online content and guided experience to accessing the Internet by means of an independent Internet service provider (ISP).

ISPs generally do not make much effort to provide subscribers with rich content and a guided Internet experience, but new Web services called **portals** may give America Online some stiff competition. A portal is a gateway that provides a conveniently-organized subject guide to Internet content, fast-breaking news, local weather, stock quotes, sports scores, and free email.

The Internet's History

Where did the Internet come from? The Internet's origins date back to Licklider's idea of a galactic network, which led to 1960s-era work on packet-switching theory at the Massachusetts Institute of Technology (MIT). The Internet is also based on studies at a private-sector military think tank, the California-based Rand Corporation, that called for the construction of a military network that could continue to function even if enemies knocked out portions of the network. Rand researchers had independently concluded that a packet-switching network offered the best chance of survivability in wartime. Under the leadership of Lawrence G. Roberts at DARPA, these researchers formulated the specifications for the Advanced Research Projects Agency Network (ARPANET). In 1968, the agency requested bids for development work.

With DARPA's leadership and funding, university and corporate researchers developed the technologies we use today, including routers, wide area networks, and Internet protocols (standards). ARPANET went online in September, 1969, and connected four computers located in California and Utah. Although ARPANET access was initially restricted to universities or research centers with U.S. Defense Department contracts, the network grew rapidly. ARPANET became an international network in 1973, with the addition of computers at defense-related sites in England and Norway. By 1981, ARPANET connected 213 computers. By 1984, it connected 1,000 computers, and by 1987, this figure had risen to 10,000. Universities lacking ARPANET access were clamoring to get it.

The Importance of Communication and Socializing

Why did ARPANET grow so quickly? One reason is that network users came to see the network as an indispensable means of communication. Although ARPANET's designers thought the network would be used to exchange research data, users saw the network as a communications medium. Invented in 1972 by ARPANET researcher Ray Tomlinson, email quickly became the most-popular use of ARPANET. Researchers used email to stay in touch with colleagues at other institutions, and they felt that this contact was essential to their professional success. They also used ARPANET for socializing through discussion groups. Researchers who lacked ARPANET access felt shut out, so they pressured their universities to join the network.

From ARPANET to Internet

The ARPANET was a testbed network, designed to serve as the development platform for packet-switching technology. The original ARPANET protocols had many deficiencies. As ARPANET researchers Robert Kahn and Vincent Cerf worked to correct the network's shortcomings, they created the Internet protocols that are now in use throughout the world. On January 1, 1983, the Internet protocols went online for the first time.

As Internet technology took shape, ARPANET moved steadily away from its military origins. ARPANET was proving to be of great value to university research committees; at the same time, it was too widely available to be used safely for confidential military-related research. For this reason, in 1982 the civilian (ARPANET) network was separated from the military (MILNET) portions. Supervision of ARPANET passed to the U.S. National Science Foundation (NSF), which subsidized ARPANET to aid university researchers. NSF financed the construction of a new long-distance data transmission network, called NSFnet. The old ARPANET backbone was decommissioned in 1990, having performed its research function with spectacular success. Collectively, the NSFnet backbone and the various regional networks connected to it became known as the Internet.

By the late 1990s, the Internet was on its way to becoming a new mass medium of global proportions.

The Rise of a New Mass Medium

In the early 1990s, the Internet was still primarily a university network, used mainly for communication and file exchange. By the late 1990s, it was on its way to becoming a new mass medium of global proportions. Why?

Two factors spurred this transformation. The first is the World Wide Web, developed in 1989. The first graphical Web browsers, developed in 1994, transformed the Internet into something more than a communication and file exchange network: it became a medium for discovering and exploring information that even novices could enjoy. A second factor was the 1995 elimination of barriers to commercial activity on the Internet. Before 1995, commercial traffic was forbidden on the taxpayer-funded NSFnet backbone. When NSF shut down the backbone and eliminated all Internet subsidies, commercial Internet development took off.

Who controls the Internet today? Don't go looking for the headquarters of Internet, Inc., because you won't find it. Like the world telephone system, the Internet is a huge information space made up of thousands of privately-owned computers and networks, all of which agree to implement the Internet protocols and share resources on the network. A variety of organizations are responsible for differing aspects of the network. For example, the World Wide Web Consortium (W3C), based in Cambridge, Massachusetts, issues standards related to all aspects of the Web. Standards organizations cannot force vendors to follow these standards, but most Internet vendors understand that everyone loses if the standards are not followed.

Destinations

If you'd like to learn more about Internet history, the best place to start is the Internet Society's Internet Histories page **(http://www. isoc.org/internet/ history/)**. The Internet Society is a professional organization for anyone interested in supporting the Internet's technical development.

INTERNET SOFTWARE: CLIENTS AND SERVERS

The Internet is a network of networks. But a network without software and applications wouldn't attract millions of users. What makes the Internet so appealing for many is the variety of ways people can use the network. Made possible by special software, these uses are called Internet services.

An **Internet service** is best understood as a set of standards (protocols) that define how two types of programs, a **client** and a **server,** can

Table **7A.1**

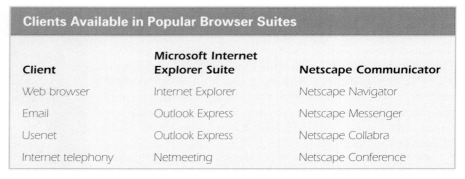

Client	Microsoft Internet Explorer Suite	Netscape Communicator
Web browser	Internet Explorer	Netscape Navigator
Email	Outlook Express	Netscape Messenger
Usenet	Outlook Express	Netscape Collabra
Internet telephony	Netmeeting	Netscape Conference

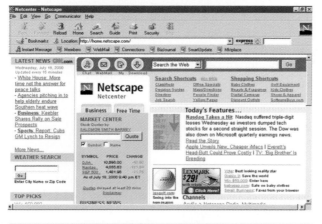

Netscape Navigator and Microsoft Internet Explorer are the two leading browsers.

communicate with each other through the Internet. A client, such as a Web browser, runs on the user's computer. Following the service's protocols, the client requests information from a server program, which is located on some other computer on the Internet. On the World Wide Web, content is made available by means of more than one million Web servers, located on computers all over the world. Other services require different types of servers (and different client programs).

To make use of the most-popular Internet services, you will need several client programs. That's why the two leading browsers, Netscape Navigator and Microsoft Internet Explorer, are available as software suites that include several popular clients in addition to the Web browser. Table 7A.1 lists the clients available in both suites, as well as the services they support. (You'll learn more about these services in a subsequent section.) Most Internet users obtain additional client software to make use of services that these suites don't support, such as Internet Relay Chat (IRC).

EXPLORING INTERNET SERVICES

The Internet's capacity to work with many types of computers enables users of all popular computers—Macs, PCs, and UNIX systems—to access the Internet. After you're connected, you can take advantage of a lengthy and growing list of Internet services, described in this section.

Electronic Mail (Email): Staying in Touch

To send email, you need to know the recipient's email address. When you receive email, you can reply to the message, forward it to someone else, store it for later action, or delete it. Usually, email arrives in a few seconds, but it's stored on the ISP's computer until the recipient logs on, downloads the message, and reads it. In addition to sending text messages, you can include attachments (files), such as a word processing document. You'll learn more about email in Module 7C.

The World Wide Web (WWW): Accessing Information

Second in popularity only to email, the World Wide Web is a global hypertext system implemented on the Internet. **Hypertext** provides an intuitive, fun way of browsing through information. In a hypertext document, certain words, called **hyperlinks,** are underlined or otherwise highlighted. When you click a hyperlink with your mouse, your Web client, called a **browser,** retrieves and displays the document associated with that hyperlink. This retrieval is possible because every Web page has its own unique address, called a **uniform resource locator (URL),** that specifies precisely where it is located on the Internet.

Email is fast becoming an indispensable communications addition to telephones, letters, and faxes.

The Web is so appealing not only because of its use of hypertext for browsing through information but also because of its graphical richness, made possible by the integration of text and graphics. Increasingly, documents available on the Web, called Web pages, look as well designed as the pages of commercial magazines, and they often feature the quality fonts you'd associate with desktop publishing.

FTP: Transferring Files

FTP (File Transfer Protocol) provides a way to transfer files through the Internet. With an FTP client, you can transfer files from an FTP server's file directories in an operation called **downloading.** In **uploading,** you transfer files *to* the server and write them to a directory on the remote computer. FTP can transfer two types of files: *ASCII* (text files)

This site is an example of a Web page that features interesting hyperlinks, fonts, and graphics.

and *binary* (program files, graphics, or documents saved in proprietary file formats).

To use FTP, you need a user name and a password. An exception is called **anonymous FTP.** In anonymous FTP, files are made publicly available for downloading. It's called anonymous FTP because you log on by typing the word *anonymous* instead of a user name, and you supply your email address as your password. The leading Web browsers, Microsoft Internet Explorer and Netscape Navigator, support file downloading from anonymous FTP sites, so you don't need any special skills to use anonymous FTP. Downloadable files are listed as hyperlinks; when you click such a hyperlink, downloading begins automatically.

Exercise caution when downloading executable program files and certain data files from the Web. (An *executable* program file is a file capable of running on your computer.) If you download software from a site that doesn't inspect files using up-to-date virus-checking software, you could infect your computer with a computer virus. Most Internet users believe that it's safe to download software from vendor sites (Web sites maintained by software companies) and from the leading shareware sites, such as http://www.shareware.com. However, you shouldn't download software to any computer that contains vital data. Also, be aware that many viruses are spread in the data files of productivity programs, such as Microsoft Word or Excel. These files may contain destructive viruses masquerading as *macros*, mini-programs that automatically carry out a series of program commands. If you download data files, be sure to check them with an antivirus program that can detect macro viruses.

Destinations

Leading Internet shareware sites include Shareware.com **(http://www.shareware.com)**, Filez **(http://www.freewarefilez.com)**, and Tucows **(http://www.tucows.com)**. From Download.com, you can download preview versions of commercial programs **(http://www.download.com)**.

Table 7A.2

Compression Software	
Extension	**Compression Software Needed**
.exe	None; this file is designed to decompress itself automatically
.zip	Winzip (http://www.winzip.com)
.hqx	BinHex encoding; decompress with Stuffit Expander
.sit	StuffIt; decompress with StuffIt Expander

ZipMagic is decompression software used for Windows systems.

Most downloadable software is *compressed*. In file compression, lengthy but frequently-used data patterns are replaced with a short code, enabling compression software to reduce the size of program files by as much as 50 percent. Compression enables faster downloads, but you must decompress the software after downloading it. In decompression, the compression software finds the short codes and replaces them with the longer data patterns. After decompressing the downloaded software, you can install it on your computer.

Some compressed files are designed to decompress automatically when you launch them. Others require you to obtain and install decompression software. On Windows systems, the most-widely used decompression software is WinZip (*http://www.winzip.com*). To survive the trip over the Internet, Macintosh software is encoded using BinHex and may also be compressed with a compression program called StuffIt. A free utility, called StuffIt Expander, decompresses and decodes the file in a one-step operation. You can tell how a file was compressed by looking at the file's extension (see Table 7A.2).

You can easily download publicly-accessible files by using a Web browser, but you'll need an FTP client to upload files. (An exception: Microsoft Internet Explorer 5.0 can upload as well as download.) If you would like to publish your own Web pages (see Module 7D), you need to use FTP to upload your pages to your Internet service provider's Web publishing directories so that your pages are available to other Internet users. The best FTP clients enable you to work with remote file directories as if those directories worked the same way your own computer does.

Usenet: Joining Online Discussions

Usenet is a discussion system accessible through the Internet. It consists of thousands of topically-named **newsgroups,** each of which contains **articles** that users have posted for all to see. Users can respond to specific articles by posting **follow-up articles,** and in time, a **thread** of discussion develops as people reply to the replies. A thread is a series of articles that offer a continuing commentary on the same general subject. To access Usenet, you use a Usenet client that communicates with a **Usenet server** (also called an **NNTP server**).

Usenet newsgroups are organized into categories called **hierarchies** (see Table 7A.3). These categories are further divided into several subcategories (also called hierarchies if they include more than one newsgroup). These subcategories include the **standard newsgroups,** the **alt newsgroups,** and

SPOTLIGHT

A TAXING QUESTION

▶The Internet has historically been viewed as an unregulated, unencumbered frontier—the "Wild West" of the late twentieth century. As more and more people use the Internet, the money transferred through the medium becomes larger and larger. Not only do ISPs make money, but so do other companies selling everything from underwear to trucks. Millions of people are starting to take the Internet seriously as a place to conduct commerce.

This means the amount of money being spent in traditional ways like the local store is not growing as fast as it could have been without the Internet on the scene. One side effect of this is that tax revenues, which are historically tied to traditional face-to-face sales, are not growing as quickly. The cost? According to one estimate, state and local governments stand to lose $8 billion by 2004. Retailing giant Wal-Mart recently announced that the firm was opening its own Web site to sell tax-free goods over the Internet. The reason? Unlike Internet retailers, Wal-Mart's physical stores must collect and pay state and local taxes, and Wal-Mart does not want to be at a competitive disadvantage. Looking at the prospect of declining tax coffers, state and local lawmakers are starting to seriously question how to tax Internet commerce.

Some states have already attempted to address taxation on the Internet. A few states passed laws requiring ISPs to collect taxes on the fees paid for Internet access. For instance, Tennessee and Texas have decided to assess taxes on those providing Internet-related services. In early 1997, Massachusetts passed a law requiring ISPs to collect their 5 percent sales tax on all Internet connection fees. The move forced many ISPs out of the state and caused others to rethink moving into the state. By August 1997, the Governor announced that the taxation was rescind-ed and that Massachusetts would become a tax-free Internet zone.

Other states have decided that the industry is too young to make any rulings. Still others have made a conscious decision to not tax the Internet. Some local jurisdictions have even tried to get into the act. One recent count indicated that the United States has more than 30,000 state and local taxing jurisdictions. Experts warn that hitting the Internet with thousands of varying taxes could cripple electronic commerce. Could you imagine starting a Web site if you had to deal with 30,000 different tax regulations and rates?

Recognizing a possibility for a taxing nightmare, the Federal government has passed the Internet Tax Freedom Act. This act essentially places a moratorium on taxing the Internet for a number of years. Those presently assessing taxes can continue, but no new state or local taxes can be imposed. The passage of the bill was hailed by many in the Internet industry as a victory.

The bill does not mean, however, that the Internet will never be taxed. During the moratorium, the different taxing authorities can sit and discuss how to best tax the Internet. When the moratorium is completed in October, 2001, the coordinated taxing plans can then be put into place—that is, if they can ever reach an agreement. Amid calls to extend the moratorium, a blue-ribbon committee charged with finding a solution to the problem was unable to agree on a recommendation.

Part of the problem with taxing the Internet is the fluid nature of the medium. The Massachusetts experience shows that companies can quickly and easily move to other places to avoid the effects of a tax. If the government decides to tax the Internet, even at a Federal level, it is conceivable that companies could simply move their base of operations to other countries. One of the ironies of the debate is that if the United States implements a poor tax policy, the country could end up at an economic disadvantage when compared with other countries, even though the United States conceived, developed, and delivered the Internet to the rest of the world.

As the Internet moves into the twenty-first century, it is clear that the taxation of Internet activities will remain one of the hottest topics around.

Millions of people are starting to take the Internet seriously as a place to conduct commerce. As a result, lawmakers are starting to seriously question how to tax Internet commerce.

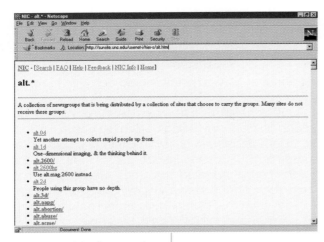

Anyone with the requisite technical knowledge can create an alt newsgroup, but servers aren't under any obligation to make them available.

the **biz newsgroups,** each of which include additional subcategories and hundreds of additional newsgroups.

- **Standard newsgroups** You're most likely to find rewarding, high-quality discussions in the standard newsgroups (also called world newsgroups), which can't be established without a formal voting procedure. Usenet servers are expected to carry all these newsgroups, with the exception of those in the talk hierarchy.

- **Alt newsgroups** The alt hierarchy is much more freewheeling. Anyone with the requisite technical knowledge can create an alt newsgroup (which explains why so many of them have silly or offensive names), but servers aren't under any obligation to make them available.

- **Biz newsgroups** These newsgroups are devoted to the commercial uses of the Internet.

In addition to the standard and alt newsgroups, most servers carry many **local newsgroups,** which are created to suit the needs of a specific community, such as a university. Some of these are of interest outside their context as well. For example, Symantec Corporation, a major software vendor, maintains the Symantec hierarchy. Technical support engineers monitor the groups and offer solutions to problems that users encounter with Symantec products.

To access Usenet, you need the Internet address of your service provider's Usenet server. You also need a Usenet client, software that comes with the two most popular browser suites. To begin using your Usenet client,

Table 7A.3

Standard Newsgroup Hierarchies	
Hierarchy Name	**Description of Topics Covered**
comp	Everything related to computers and computer networks, including applications, compression, databases, multimedia, and programming.
misc	Subjects that do not fit in other standard newsgroup hierarchies, including activism, books, business, consumer issues, health, investing, jobs, and law.
sci	The sciences and social sciences, including anthropology, archeology, chemistry, economics, math, physics, and statistics.
soc	Social issues, including adoption, college-related issues, feminism, human rights, and world cultures.
talk	Debate on controversial subjects, including abortion, atheism, euthanasia, gun control, and religion.
news	Usenet itself, including announcements and materials for new users.
rec	All aspects of recreation, including aviation, backcountry sports, bicycles, boats, gardening, and scouting.

download the entire list of newsgroups available on your ISP's server. Then *subscribe* to the newsgroups you want to follow. When you open the newsgroup, your client downloads the current article list, which may contain a few dozen to several thousand messages.

If you're sure you understand the newsgroup's mission, you can use your Usenet client to post your own messages. But be careful what you say on Usenet. When you post an article, you are publishing in a public medium. Although most Usenet servers erase messages more than a few days old, several Internet services store Usenet messages in Web-accessible archives. One such service, Deja News (**http://www.dejanews.com**), enables searchers to create an author profile, listing all the messages a given user has posted to Usenet within the past several years. Also, be aware that you'll be expected to follow the rules of **netiquette,** guidelines for good manners when you're communicating through Usenet. For example, some Usenet clients enable you to post messages using formatting, but this is considered bad manners because people who have text-only clients see a lot of meaningless formatting symbols. If you violate netiquette rules, you may receive *flames* (angry, critical messages).

Deja News enables searchers to create an author profile, listing all the messages a given user has posted to Usenet within the past several years.

IRC: Text Chatting in Real Time

Internet Relay Chat (IRC) is an Internet service that enables you to join chat groups, called **channels,** and get into real-time, text-based conversations. IRC servers typically make thousands of channels available; some cover a specific topic, and others are gathering places for groups of old friends.

When you join a channel, you'll find that others are already there, chatting away, with their messages appearing on-screen. Each message is prefaced with the participant's nickname. Sometimes IRC participants will send a special type of message, called an action, that describes a behavior (such as, "Walker shakes your hand"). Normally, your messages are seen by everyone in the channel, but it's possible to send a whisper, which is seen by only the one person to whom you send it.

Sometimes IRC isn't a friendly place. You may encounter various sorts of antisocial behaviors, including flooding (sending repeated messages so that no one else can get a word in edgewise) and nuking (exploiting bugs that cause your computer to crash). Bear in mind, too, that some of the "people" in channels aren't people at all, but rather mini-programs called *bots*. Bots are illegal on some servers, but on others they're used to greet newcomers (and sometimes to harass them). Also, every channel has a channel operator who can kick you out of the channel for any reason.

Internet Telephony: Real-Time Voice and Video

Although the Internet isn't ideal for real-time voice and video, you can place a "telephone" call to another Internet user, who must be online and have a computer equipped with a microphone and a sound card. If you and the person you're calling have a digital video camera, you can converse with real-time videoconferencing as well. Don't expect spectacular quality: you'll hear echoes and delays in the audio, and the picture will be small, grainy, and jerky. But there are no long distance charges! You can try Internet telephony by using the clients supplied with the two most popular browsers.

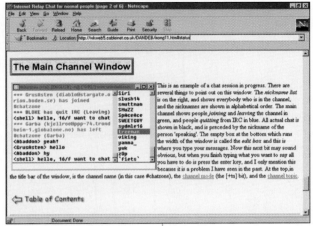

When you join an IRC channel, you'll find that others are already there, chatting away. The Main Channel Window screen here shows an example of a chat session in progress.

Microsoft's NetMeeting data conferencing features let you collaborate with a group of people through drawing on a shared whiteboard, sending text messages, and transferring data.

In addition to Internet voice and video calls, Internet telephony products support real-time conferencing with such features as a shared whiteboard (a space where callers can draw simple graphics or share pictures), file exchange, and text chatting. Current technology doesn't enable you to videoconference with more than one caller at a time, but you can create an audio conference with as many users as you want.

Until home users can obtain faster Internet connections, Internet telephony and videoconferencing will prove most useful on corporate intranets, where bandwidth is in ample supply.

More Internet Services

In addition to the services just mentioned, you may want to explore the following:

- **Buddy lists** This service's clients run in the background on your computer and let you know when friends or coworkers are online. Popular Internet paging programs includes ICQ (pronounced "I seek you") and AOL Instant Messenger.

- **MUDs** Short for multi-user dungeons, MUDs and several variants (including MUSHes and MOOs) offer text-based chatting environments based on a participatory theme, such as *Star Trek*.

- **Telnet** This service creates a virtual terminal, enabling you to control a remote computer.

- **Ping** This simple service enables you to determine whether your computer can connect to another computer on the Internet. It's often used to test whether Internet connections are working properly.

The following Internet services have declined in popularity since the rise of the World Wide Web, which offers a more convenient way to accomplish the same purposes:

- **Archie** This service enables you to search for files on anonymous FTP sites. It's easier to use Web-based services such as *http://www.freewarefilez.com*.

- **Gopher** This service presents text-based information (with some graphics) by means of menus. You can use a Web browser to access the information on Gopher servers, but most of the information on these servers has been moved to Web servers. As a result, the Web has largely supplanted Gopher.

- **Veronica** This service enables you to search for information available at Gopher sites. This same information is accessible also by using Web search services (see Module 8A).

One service that seemed to have a bright future in 1994, WAIS (short for Wide Area Information Server), is all but dead. Its functions have been supplanted by Web pages that interface with high-performance database management systems.

HOW THE INTERNET WORKS:
A GEOGRAPHY OF CYBERSPACE

You don't need a degree in electrical engineering to understand the basics of how the Internet works. In this section, you will explore the various components of the Internet, beginning with your computer.

Configuring Your Computer for Internet Access

To connect to the Internet, your computer must support Internet networking protocols (called TCP/IP). Today, this support is built into popular operating systems, such as Mac OS, Microsoft Windows, and Linux. You also need communications equipment, such as a modem, an ISDN adapter, or an Ethernet card, depending on how you're planning to access the Internet.

Accessing the Internet

You can access the Internet in the following ways:

- **Shell access** The least-expensive type of Internet access, this method requires a modem and a phone line. You get access to the shell (user interface) of a UNIX computer, enabling text-based applications such as email. UNIX knowledge is required for shell access. In this method, your computer isn't really connected to the Internet. You're using it as a terminal to access a computer that *is* connected to the Internet.

- **Dial-up access with Point-to-Point Protocol (PPP)** Most home users access the Internet this way. You need a modem and an analog phone line, or an ISDN adapter and an ISDN telephone line (see Module 6A for an explanation of these services). With this method, your computer is directly connected to the Internet, but it's usually assigned a temporary IP address. For this reason, you can't conveniently run server software on a computer connected to the Internet with PPP. To run a server, you need a system that has a fixed IP address and a registered domain name (see "The Domain Name System," later in this chapter). Some ISPs use an older protocol, called SLIP, which isn't as efficient as PPP.

- **Digital Subscriber Line (DSL)** Available in many urban areas, DSL connections offer high-speed access and a permanent online connection. Unlike ISDN, DSL does not require a special digital telephone line. One drawback of DSL is that service does not extend more than a few miles from telephone switching stations, so this service is unavailable in rural areas.

- **Cable and satellite access** Cable TV firms are increasingly offering Internet access at speeds much faster than dial-up modems. Satellite access enables fast downloads but requires a phone line and a modem for uploading data. Like modem access, these access methods give your computer a temporary IP address, so you can't run server programs in such a way that other Internet users can find your content.

- **LAN access** If the company you're working for has a LAN, or you're attending a university that provides Ethernet access in dorm rooms, you can access the Internet by means of the local area network. LAN access is generally much faster than dial-up access, but the performance you experience depends on how many LAN users are trying to access the Internet at the same time. With LAN access, your computer probably has a permanently-assigned IP address, and you may be able to run server programs.

Destinations

Looking for an ISP? A good place to start is The List **(http://thelist. internet.com)**, a buyer's guide to ISPs. You can search for an ISP by area code or country.

The List is a buyer's guide to ISPs that lists nearly 5,000 service providers.

TCG CERFnet provides a backbone network in the United States.

Destinations

Explore the Internet's physical structure at "An Atlas of Cyberspace" (**http://www.cyber geography.org/atlas/ atlas.html**), maintained by Martin Dodge at the Centre for Advanced Spatial Analysis, University of London.

Internet Service Providers (ISPs)

Internet service providers (ISPs) sell Internet subscriptions to home and business users. For home users, they offer dial-up access. Many ISPs also provide direct connections for businesses using leased lines (see Module 6B).

Backbones

To understand how data travels on the Internet, it's helpful to compare this journey to an interstate car trip. When you connect to the Internet and request access to a Web page, your request travels by local connections (the city streets) to your Internet service provider's local point of presence (POP). From there, your ISP relays your request to the regional backbone, a highway that connects your town to a larger metropolitan region. Your request then goes to a **network access point (NAP)** (a freeway on-ramp) where regional backbones connect to national backbone networks. And from there, the message gets on the national backbone network (the freeway). Near the destination, your message gets off the freeway and travels regional and local networks until it reaches its destination.

The Internet is becoming more complex every day as new backbone service providers expand the network and more ISPs sell this bandwidth to business and residential customers. How is this growth accommodated? Because the Internet isn't centrally administered, the network couldn't work without its automated routers, which route Internet messages to their destination (see module 6B for an introduction to routers). The Internet's routers are designed to share information with each other automatically. At any given moment, a router automatically possesses up-to-date information about the portion of the network to which it is directly connected. For this reason, new service providers can extend the Internet without obtaining permission from anyone. All that's needed is a registration process, discussed in the section "The Domain Name System" later in this module.

As local service providers extend the Internet, traffic grows rapidly. Backbone service providers are expanding capacity at a breakneck speed. For example, AT&T is doubling its Internet capacity every three months. Still, Internet experts worry that backbone service providers won't be able to construct bandwidth capacity rapidly enough to keep up with the Internet's burgeoning growth.

The Internet Protocols (TCP/IP)

As you learned in Module 6B, a network isn't just the physical transmission media that carry its signals, but also the standards (called protocols) that enable devices connected to the network to communicate with each other. The Internet protocols, collectively called **TCP/IP,** are open protocols that define how the Internet works. TCP/IP is an abbreviation for the two most important Internet protocols: the Transmission Control Protocol (TCP) and the Internet Protocol (IP). However, more than 100 protocols make up the entire Internet protocol suite, including the many protocols that define the Internet services discussed previously in this module.

Internet Protocol (IP)

Of all the Internet protocols, the most fundamental is the **Internet Protocol (IP).** IP defines the Internet's addressing scheme, which enables any Internet-connected computer to be uniquely identified. An Internet address, also called an IP address, is a four-part number, separated by periods (such 128.254.108.7). The IP protocol is a connectionless protocol (see Module 6B). With IP, two computers don't have to be online at the same time to exchange data. The sending computer just keeps trying until the message gets through.

Transmission Control Protocol (TCP)

Some Internet services (such as the Web) need two computers to communicate with each other. The **Transmission Control Protocol (TCP)** defines how one Internet-connected computer can contact another and exchange control and confirmation messages. You can see TCP in action when you're using the Web; just watch your browser's status line. You'll see messages such as "Contacting server," "Receiving data," and "Closing connection."

The Domain Name System

Because IP addresses are difficult to type and remember, the Internet uses a system called the **Domain Name System (DNS).** DNS enables users to type an address that includes letters as well as numbers. For example, you can type *www.mhv.net* to access the computer located at 199.0.0.2. A process called **domain name registration** enables individuals and organizations to register a domain name with a service organization called the **InterNIC.** Within large organizations, administrators can assign internal domain names without having to go through the InterNIC.

How do domain names work? The secret lies in computers called **domain name servers** (also called DNS servers). These computers maintain up-to-date lists that match local domain names with the correct IP addresses. Suppose you want to access the computer that houses the Internet Explorer home page at Microsoft Corporation. When you request this page, your local ISP's domain name server contacts Microsoft's domain name server and asks for this computer's IP address. In this way, you always get the correct IP address, even if Microsoft moves the content to a different machine.

Domain names can tell you a great deal about where a computer is located. For computers located in the United States, top-level domain names (the *last* part of the domain name) indicate the type of organization in which the computer is located:

- **gov** Government agencies
- **edu** Educational institutions
- **org** Organizations (nonprofit)
- **mil** Military
- **com** Commercial business
- **net** Network organizations (such as Internet service providers)

Outside the United States, the top-level domain indicates the name of the country in which the computer is located, such as ca (Canada), uk (Great Britain), and jp (Japan). A proposal to expand top-level domains would create the following: store (electronic shopping), arts (museums and culture), rec (recreational sites), info (information services), and nom (individuals).

Destinations

See for yourself how the domain name service operates. Access the NSLOOKUP page at **http://www.infobear.com/nslookup-form.cgi,** and type a domain name such as **http://www.microsoft.com.** Click the Run button, and you'll see a message showing the IP address associated with the domain name you typed.

INTRANETS: USING TCP/IP INSIDE THE ENTERPRISE

The Internet has developed into a mature technology, and millions of people know how to access and exchange information using Internet email, Web browsers, FTP, and discussion groups. And that's precisely why so many companies are building internal networks based on TCP/IP. Called **intranets,** these networks give users the same familiar tools they use on the Internet. However, these networks are intended for internal use only and are not accessible from the external Internet. To insulate the intranet from unwanted external access, computers equipped with *firewall* software screen incoming data, while allowing selected insiders to access external resources.

Intranets are transforming the way organizations produce and share information. Because it's so easy to create a Web page (see Module 7D), companies can distribute Web publishing duties throughout the enterprise. Previously, the Information Systems department would have to make information available. Now every department can maintain its own Web page, making its resources available to everyone. By moving expensive print-based publications to the internal Web, such as employee manuals and telephone books, companies can realize enormous savings and greatly reduce the amount of trash that goes to local landfills.

Some companies open their intranets to selected allies, such as research labs, suppliers, or key customers. Called **extranets,** these networks use the external Internet for connection, but the data traverses the Internet in encrypted form, safe from prying eyes.

THE FUTURE OF THE INTERNET

Assume there's a billion Internet users by the middle of the next decade. In addition, hundreds of millions of people will be connecting with super-fast connections, using technologies such as cable modems and ADSL (see Module 6A). Can the Internet handle this growth? According to Internet experts, key changes must take place to ensure that the Internet doesn't become overwhelmed by its own success.

More Internet Addresses

The IP protocol allows for a total of approximately 4 billion unique IP addresses, but that's not enough, due to the way the four-part IP addresses (such as 128.254.207.8) are broken up into distinct categories, called *classes.* Class A supports up to 127 large networks with up to 16 million addresses for each, class B supports up to 16,000 networks with up to 65,000 addresses for each, and class C supports 2 million networks with 254 addresses each. There aren't enough class A or B networks, and class C networks are too small. The solution lies in a new version of the Internet Protocol, called **IPv6,** but existing Internet equipment must be modified to work with the new protocol.

More Bandwidth

Internet 2 (I2) is a collaborative effort between more than 120 U.S. universities, several U.S. Government agencies, and leading computer and telecommunications companies. It is a project of the University Corporation for Advanced Internet Development (UCAID). The I2 project will develop and test high-performance network and telecommunications techniques. These improvements will eventually find their way to the public Internet. To test I2 ideas, universities participating in I2 are establishing **gigabits per second Points of Presence (gigaPoP).** These network connection points link to various high-speed networks that Federal government agencies have developed.

IMPACTS

The Internet: Fertile Soil for Hatred?

Thanks to the World Wide Web, individuals and organizations with little money can now get their message out cheaply. That's a wonderful thing about the Web, but it can also be terrifying as hate groups have been quick to seize the opportunity. Last year alone saw a 300 percent increase in the number of hate sites on the Internet, devoted to such causes as white supremacy, homophobia, Holocaust denials, and Neo-Nazism.

What's found at a hate site? Typical fare includes racist cartoons and jokes, links to other hate sites, and online books, including the *Turner Diaries*, a book described by the FBI as the "Bible of the racist right." The book is thought to have provided the inspiration for the Oklahoma City bombing.

Hate groups love the Internet. Formerly limited to pamphlet dropping, low-circulation publications, and street corner ranting, these groups can now get their message out to an audience that might never have seen their message otherwise. They're hoping to contact people who might be embarrassed to pick up an obviously-racist newspaper or pamphlet. These sites are accessible by kids, too. One offers a game called Concentration Camp Manager. The object: round up Jews. Growing numbers of educators report with dismay that school Internet connections provide students with their first exposure to hate groups.

Experts differ concerning the impact of hate sites. According to several organizations that monitor hate groups, the sites aren't succeeding in recruiting new members (membership in hate-oriented groups has been flat for several years). Indeed, the sites may be backfiring, because they are exposing these organizations and their ludicrous ideas to critical examination. But some worry that hate groups might provide the inspiration for "lone wolf" rampages. In the U.K., a 24-year-old self-professed Nazi killed three people and injured 79 others after a series of pub bombings, which were designed to start a "race war." The man found directions for building the bombs on the Internet.

But hate sites reach the entire Internet, including countries in which hate speech is illegal. In Canada, for example, a Canadian citizen is being tried by the Canadian Human Rights Commission because the man allegedly created and maintained a San Diego-based Web site denying the Holocaust's existence. In France, a judge fined Yahoo, Inc., for making neo-Nazi objects available in its online auction site.

Can hate sites be stopped—and more importantly, *should* they be stopped? One strategy to control them is to place pressure on Internet service providers (ISPs), who are free to create contracts that disallow hate speech on their sites. The Washington, D.C.-based Simon Weisenthal Center spends 80 percent of its time tracking down hate sites on the Internet. The Center contacts the sites' service providers and sends along the Center's code of online ethics, which calls for removing hate speech from the providers' systems. In Los Angeles, GeoCities, one of the country's largest Internet service providers, has adopted content guidelines that prohibit "blatant expressions of racism and hatred." However, other service providers won't go along, claiming that it's not their job to censor site content. Still others argue that hate speech, repellant as it is, nevertheless is protected speech under the U.S. Constitution's First Amendment. If a society cannot tolerate speech that some find repugnant, they say that society doesn't have free speech.

Many people feel that the Oklahoma City bombing was inspired by racist books such as the *Turner Diaries*, which is available in its entirety on the Internet.

TAKEAWAY POINTS

- The Internet is a network that connects hundreds of thousands of local area networks (LANs), creating a global medium in which millions of computers can directly dial each other and share resources.
- Internet protocols do not specify low-level network characteristics, so Internet data can travel on any type of network. In addition, networks do not have to be altered to carry Internet data.
- The Internet's popularity stems from its capability to foster communication and socializing, the fact that it can work with virtually all types of computers and networks, and the development of user-friendly tools such as Web browsers.
- Online services market a proprietary network that offers free and fee-based content, email, and chat groups. The Internet enables users to access any information available on millions of servers worldwide.
- Internet services are defined by protocols. Software includes clients (programs that access

information) and servers (programs that deliver requested information).
- Popular Internet services include email (communication), the World Wide Web (information browsing), FTP (file exchange), Internet Relay Chat (text chatting), and Internet telephony (phone calls through the Internet and video-conferencing).
- An Internet address (IP address) is a four-part number that uniquely identifies one of the millions of computers connected to the Internet. A domain name is an easy-to-type and easy-to-remember equivalent of the numerical address.
- Intranets enable companies to set up communication and information systems that use familiar Internet tools, such as email and Web browsers. They enable companies to also distribute publication tasks and save money by ceasing print publications.
- Tomorrow's Internet will feature a larger address space and higher bandwidth on backbone networks.

MODULE REVIEW

KEY TERMS AND CONCEPTS

alt newsgroups	gigabits per second Points of	local newsgroups
anonymous FTP	Presence (gigaPoP)	netiquette
articles	hierarchies	network access point (NAP)
biz newsgroups	hyperlinks	newsgroups
browser	hypertext	online service
channels	Internet	portals
client	Internet 2 (I2)	server
cross-platform network	Internet address, or IP address	standard newsgroups
domain name registration	Internet Protocol (IP)	TCP/IP
domain name servers	Internet Relay Chat (IRC)	thread
Domain Name System (DNS)	Internet service	Transmission Control Protocol
downloading	Internet service providers (ISPs)	(TCP)
electronic mail (email)	InterNIC	uniform resource locator (URL)
extranets	interoperability	uploading
follow-up articles	intranets	Usenet
FTP (File Transfer Protocol)	IPv6	Usenet server, or NNTP server

TRUE/FALSE

Indicate whether the following statements are true or false.

1. Today, hundreds of thousands of networks and nearly fifty million computers are directly connected to the Internet.

2. The Internet works on circuit-switching principles, just like the telephone system.

3. The Internet enables PCs, UNIX workstations, and Macintoshes to exchange data and to control each other's operations.

4. LANs must all work the same way to connect to the Internet.

5. Today, the World Wide Web Consortium (W3C) is responsible for controlling the Internet.

6. Email is the most popular Internet service.

7. The World Wide Web is a global hypertext system that's implemented on the Internet.

8. FTP (File Transfer Protocol) provides a way to transfer files through the Internet.

9. The Internet is ideal for real-time voice and videoconferencing.

10. Archie, Veronica, and Gopher are Internet services whose popularity is growing every year.

MATCHING

Match each key term from the left column with the most accurate definition in the right column.

_____ 1. Internet

_____ 2. interoperability

_____ 3. client

_____ 4. browser

_____ 5. local newsgroups

_____ 6. Biz newsgroups

_____ 7. Netiquette

_____ 8. TCP/IP

_____ 9. Veronica

_____ 10. Archie

a. a program that runs on the user's computer

b. guidelines for good manners when you're communicating through Usenet

c. Internet protocols that define how the Internet works

d. a technology that links LANs into a large, distance-conquering technology

e. an Internet service that enables you to search for information at gopher sites

f. a device that enables any connected computer to operate a remote computer by sending commands through the network

g. newsgroups created to suit the needs of a specific community

h. a Web client that retrieves and displays a document associated with a hyperlink

i. an Internet service that enables you to search for files on anonymous FTP sites

j. newsgroups devoted to the commercial use of the Internet

MULTIPLE CHOICE

Circle the letter of the correct choice for each of the following.

1. Which of the following maintains the LANs and computers connected to the Internet?
   a. Internet service providers
   b. corporations
   c. universities
   d. all of the above

2. Which of the following networks best describes the functional structure of the Internet?
   a. metropolitan area network
   b. cross-platform network
   c. local area network
   d. client/server network

3. Which of the following services is not typically provided by an online service?
   a. email
   b. chat rooms
   c. news services
   d. portals

4. Which of the following is a client program?
   a. hypertext
   b. ARPANET
   c. Internet address
   d. Web browser

5. Which of the following new Web services is giving online services such as America Online some stiff competition?
   a. ARPANET
   b. portals
   c. electronic mail
   d. Usenet

6. Which of the following factors is responsible for the rise of the Internet's popularity?
   a. the World Wide Web
   b. the elimination of barriers to commercial activity on the Internet
   c. online service providers
   d. a and b

7. Which of the following is necessary to access Usenet?
   a. Usenet client
   b. portal
   c. standard newsgroup
   d. local newsgroup

8. Which of the following is absolutely necessary to connect to the Internet?
   a. your computer must support the network access point protocols
   b. communications equipment such as a modem or ISDN adapter
   c. shell access
   d. LAN access

9. Which of the following Internet protocols is the most fundamental and defines the Internet's addressing scheme?
   a. Transmission Control Protocol (TCP)
   b. IP address protocol
   c. File Transfer Protocol (FTP)
   d. Internet Protocol (IP)

10. Which of the following is an internal network, based on TCP/IP, that gives users the same familiar tools they use on the Internet?
    a. local area network
    b. intranet
    c. extranet
    d. firewall

FILL-IN

In the blank provided, write the correct answer for each of the following.

1. The _____ is a technology for linking local area networks into a large, distance-conquering network in which every computer can directly exchange data with any other computer on the network.

2. A(n) _____ provides a proprietary network that offers email, chat rooms, discussions, and fee-based content.

3. A(n) _____ is a gateway that provides a conveniently-organized subject guide to Internet content.

4. To make use of the most popular Internet services, you need several _____ programs.

5. _____ is the most popular Internet service.

6. In a(n) _____ document, certain words, called _____, are underlined or otherwise highlighted.

7. Every Web page has a unique address, called a(n) _____.

8. _____ provides a way for users to transfer files through the Internet.

9. Usenet is a discussion system that consists of thousands of topically-named _____, each of which contains articles that users have posted for all to see.

10. _____ sell Internet subscriptions to home and business users.

SHORT ANSWER

On a separate sheet of paper, answer the following questions.

1. What is the Internet? Why is it so popular?

2. What is meant by interoperability?

3. List the differences between the Internet and online services.

4. Where did the Internet come from?

5. Who controls the Internet today?

6. What's the difference between client and server software?

7. List the most popular Internet services and explain what they do.

8. What's the difference between Internet addresses and domain names?

9. How do you access Usenet?

10. What kinds of initiatives are underway to improve the Internet's performance?

THE WORLD WIDE WEB AND E-COMMERCE

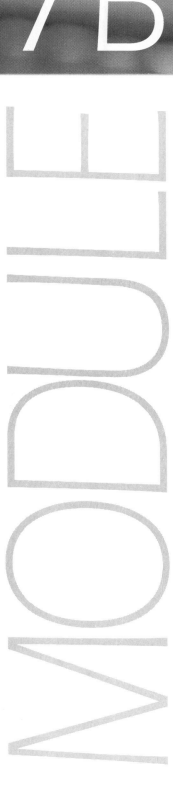

OUTLINE

WHAT YOU WILL LEARN . . .

When you have finished reading this module, you will be able to:

1. Explain the concept of hypertext.
2. Contrast Web browsers and Web servers.
3. Explain the parts of a URL.
4. Name the browser navigation buttons and their functions.
5. Contrast Web subject guides and search engines.
6. Explain how search operators can improve Web search results.
7. Evaluate the reliability of information on a Web page.
8. Define business-to-business e-commerce and explain why it's moving to the Internet.
9. List the fastest-growing public e-commerce applications and explain why customers like them.

Imagine an information source that contains billions of documents, each of them almost instantly accessible by means of the computer sitting on your desk. And imagine, too, that this information source is growing at an astonishing rate, with thousands of new documents appearing every day. This resource contains a wealth of useful information, and it's all available when you access the Internet. It's called the World Wide Web.

This module introduces the fundamental concepts of the Web, teaches the basics of using Web browsers, and explores the use of the Web for research. If you've never used the Web, you'll get a solid foundation in the essentials of productive Web usage. If you have used the Web and know how to use a browser, you'll learn how to search the Web much more effectively. You'll also learn how to evaluate the quality of the information you retrieve from the Web.

WELCOME TO THE WEB

Explore IT Lab

Internet and WWW

Second in popularity only to email, the **World Wide Web** is fast becoming an indispensable information resource. Increasing numbers of Internet users are turning to the Web to research product purchases, medical decisions, current events, and much more. In this section, you'll learn the fundamental concepts of the Web.

The Hypertext Concept

Hypertext is a way of presenting information so that the *sequence* of the information (the order in which the information is read) is left up to the reader. Hypertext works by means of **hyperlinks** (also called *links*). Links are underlined or highlighted words that you can click to bring another document into view (see Figure 7B.1). A **hypermedia** system enables users to retrieve multimedia resources, such as sounds and movies, as well as text.

Authors who write hypertext documents don't try to explain everything on one page. Instead, they provide links to additional documents that readers may consult. They create many concise documents (called chunks) that contain many links, instead of trying to explain everything in one place. Here's an example:

> Art historians consider **Monet** to be an **Impressionist.**

This sentence doesn't tell you anything about Monet or Impressionist. If you want to know more, you must click the underlined or highlighted text.

Creating a hypertext system for one computer is a lot of work. You must create a separate page explaining every concept for which you've created a link. That's why hypertext remained relatively obscure until the World Wide Web came along.

The Web is a **distributed hypermedia system.** In this system, the responsibility for creating content is distributed among many people. And the more people who create content, the easier hypertext development becomes. For example, if someone has created a document about Monet, and another person has created a document about Impressionism, you can link to these documents instead of writing them yourself.

The Web's distribution of content-creation responsibilities, however, has a drawback. You can link to any page you want, but you can't guarantee that the page's author will keep that page on the Web. The author can delete it or move it, and the author isn't under any obligation

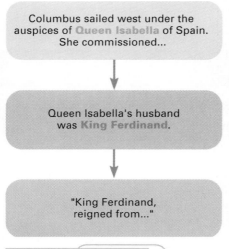

Columbus sailed west under the auspices of Queen Isabella of Spain. She commissioned...

Queen Isabella's husband was King Ferdinand.

"King Ferdinand, reigned from..."

Figure 7B.1

In hypertext, you follow the links to related information.

to notify other authors who have included links to the page. For this reason, **stale links,** which are links to documents that have disappeared, are common on the Web.

Figure 7B.2

Prentice Hall's home page.

Web Browsers and Web Servers

Like other Internet services (see Module 7A), Web software includes clients (browsers) as well as servers (called Web servers). This section introduces both; you'll look more closely at Web browsers next.

Web Browsers

A Web browser displays a Web document and enables users to access linked documents. When the user chooses a hyperlink, the browser originates a message to a Web server. This message asks the server to retrieve the requested information and send it back to the browser through the network. Browsers also contain navigation tools that enable the user to return to previously-viewed pages and to bookmark (that is, mark) favorite sites so that they can be redisplayed quickly.

The first Web browsers were **text-only browsers** that couldn't display graphics. The first successful **graphical browser,** Mosaic, helped launch the Web on its road to popularity. A graphical browser can display GIF and JPEG graphics as well as text. Developed by the National Center for Supercomputing Applications (NCSA) at the University of Illinois, Mosaic was followed by two commercial products, Netscape Navigator and Microsoft Internet Explorer, which have since captured virtually the entire browser market.

Web Servers

A **Web server** is a program that waits patiently for browsers to request a Web page. When the server receives a request for a specific resource, it looks for the requested file and sends it to the browser. If the file isn't found, the server sends an error message.

A **Web site** is a collection of related Web documents that a Web server makes available to the public. Typically, a Web site contains an **index page** (a default page, also called a *home page,* that's displayed automatically when a user enters the site at its top level). Figure 7B.2 shows the home page for Prentice Hall. Web sites generally include additional **Web pages,** which are individual Web documents.

Simple Web servers are easy to operate, but programming skills are needed to configure and maintain the industrial-strength servers used by popular Web sites. These complex servers use scripts and programs to enhance interactivity and provide access to information stored in databases.

Web Addresses (URLs)

To make the Web work, an addressing system is needed that precisely states where a resource (such as a Web page) is located. This system is provided by **Uniform Resource Locators (URLs),** a standard for describing the location of resources on the Web. You've undoubtedly seen plenty of URLs, which look like this:

Protocol	Server	Path	Resource Name
http://	**www.microsoft.com**	**/windows/ie**	**/default.htm**

A complete URL has four parts:

- **Protocol** The first part of a complete URL specifies the Internet standard to be used to access the document. For the Web, it's **http,** the *Hypertext Transfer Protocol.* Most browsers can also access information using FTP, Gopher, and other protocols. The protocol name is followed by a colon and two slash marks **(//).** With most Web browsers, you can omit the **http://** protocol when you're accessing Web pages by typing their address. For example, you can access **http://www.microsoft.com** by typing **www.microsoft.com.**

- **Server** The second part of a complete URL specifies the Internet domain name of the Web server on which the page is located.

- **Path** The third part of a complete URL specifies the location of the document on the Internet. It contains the domain name (see Module 7A) of the computer that's running the Web server. Also included is the location of the document on this computer, including the names of subfolders (if any).

- **Resource name** The last part of a complete URL gives the filename of the resource you're accessing. A resource is a computer file, which might be an HTML file, a sound file, a movie file, a graphics file, or something else. The resource's extension (the part of the filename that goes past the period) indicates the type of resource. HTML documents have the .html or .htm extension.

Many URLs don't include a resource name because they reference the server's default home page. For example, **www.microsoft.com/windows/ie** displays the default Internet Explorer home page. Other URLs omit both the path name and the resource name. These URLs reference the server's home page. For example, **www.microsoft.com** displays Microsoft's home page on the Web.

Web Protocols

Like other Internet services, the Web involves communication between clients and servers. The exact format of this communication is specified by the **Hypertext Transfer Protocol (HTTP).** This protocol specifies the format of URLs as well as the procedure clients and servers follow to establish communication.

Web Page Design Tools

To create a Web page, Web authors use a **markup language** called the **Hypertext Markup Language (HTML).** A markup language is a set of codes, called *elements,* that authors can use to identify portions of a document, such as a title or a heading. Most elements have two codes, called a *start tag* and an *end tag,* that surround the marked-up text. The following illustrates HTML markup for a level 1 (major) heading, a paragraph of text, and an indented quotation:

```
<h1>This is the text of a major heading.</h1>

<p>This is a paragraph of text. Most browsers display
paragraph text with a blank line before the paragraph and
flush left alignment.</p>

<BLOCKQUOTE>This is an indented quotation. Most browsers
display blockquote material with an indentation from the
left margin.</BLOCKQUOTE>
```

A document marked up with HTML contains nothing but plaintext (ASCII text) and is easy to exchange on a cross-platform network. When browsers access the document, they read the markup and position the various portions of the document in accordance with the browser's formatting settings.

You'll learn more about HTML in Module 7D. For now, it's important to understand that HTML's simplicity is an important reason for the Web's popularity. Anyone can learn how to create a simple Web page using HTML. As a result, it's possible for millions of people to contribute content to the Web.

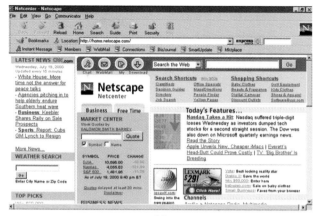

(a)

BROWSING THE WEB

The two most popular graphical browsers are Netscape Navigator (part of the Netscape Communicator suite) and Microsoft Internet Explorer (see Figure 7B.3). Learning to use one of these programs effectively is an essential component of computer and information literacy.

Exploring Your Browser's Window

Although browsers vary somewhat, you'll find the following features in the two most popular programs:

- **Navigation buttons**   On the browser's toolbar, you'll find frequently-used navigation buttons (Back, Forward, Home, and Refresh) that play an important role in Web navigation. You'll learn more about these tools in a subsequent section.

- **Address toolbar (also called location toolbar)**   This toolbar contains a text box that indicates the URL of the page you're currently viewing. If you type a URL in this text box and press Enter, the browser attempts to take you to the location you've entered.

- **Program icon**   This icon displays an animation when the browser is attempting to download information from the Web.

- **Status bar**   Here, you'll see messages about what the program is doing.

Within the application workspace area, you will see the page that's located at the URL indicated in the address toolbar. If the page is longer or wider than the window, you'll see scrollbars.

Default Start Page

When you start your Web browser, you will see the program's **default start page.** This page is located at the browser vendor's home server and generally offers the services you'd expect from a Web portal, such as free email, a subject guide to the Web, stock quotes, news, weather, and sports. (Web portals are introduced in Module 7A.) You can customize the program by changing the default start page.

If you get lost while exploring the Web, click the Home button on the browser's toolbar. This button redisplays the default home page.

(b)

Figure 7B.3

(a) Netscape Navigator and (b) Microsoft Internet Explorer are the two most popular graphical Web browsers.

In most Web pages, hyperlinks are under-lined, but sometimes they're embedded within graphics or highlighted in other ways.

Some Web pages include navigation aids, such as a column of subject links positioned on the left or right of the page.

Techtalk

clickstream

As you spend time on the World Wide Web, you leave a "clickstream" in your wake. A clickstream is a trail of Web links that you have followed to get to a particular site. Internet merchants are quite interested in analyz-ing clickstream activity so they can do a better job of targeting advertise-ments and tailoring Web pages to your liking.

Accessing Web Pages

To access a Web page, do any of the following:

- **Click a hyperlink** In most Web pages, hyperlinks are underlined, but sometimes they're embedded in graphics or highlighted in other ways. To tell whether a given portion of a Web page contains a hyperlink, position the mouse pointer over the area and watch for a change in its shape. Most browsers indicate the presence of a hyperlink by changing the mouse pointer to a hand shape.

- **Type a URL in the Address box (Internet Explorer) or Location box (Netscape Navigator)** You don't need to type *http://* when entering a URL. Watch for spelling errors, and don't insert spaces. A common mis-take users make is typing a comma instead of a period to separate the components of a URL.

- **Click a button on the Links toolbar** Both major browsers come with predefined links on a toolbar, which contain buttons linked to Web pages. You can customize this toolbar with pages you frequently access.

Using the Back and Forward Buttons

After you've accessed one or more Web pages, you may want to return to one you've seen previously. To return to the page you just viewed, click the "Back" button. To return to pages more than two or three clicks back, right-click the "Back" button and choose the page's name from the drop-down menu. (On a Macintosh, posi-tion the pointer over the "Back" button and hold down the mouse button until the menu appears.) After you've clicked the "Back" button, you can click the "Forward" button to go forward in the list of pages you've viewed.

Using Navigation Aids

When you're exploring a Web presentation that includes many pages, you'll probably find that the author has provided navigation aids, such as a column of subject links positioned on the left or right of the page. You can use these aids to explore the varying pages of this presentation.

History List

As you browse the Web, your browser keeps a list of the pages you've accessed. If you would like to return to a previously-viewed site and can't find it by clicking "Back," you can consult the history list and choose the page you want from this list. In Microsoft Internet Explorer, you can access this list by clicking the "History" button on the toolbar. In Netscape Navigator, you can choose the History option from the Communicator menu.

Favorites and Bookmarks

You'll soon find some Web pages to which you'll want to return frequently. To accomplish this easily, you can save these pages as favorites (Internet Explorer) or bookmarks (Netscape Navigator). After you've saved these pages as favorites or bookmarks, you will see the names of these pages in the "Favorites" menu (Internet Explorer) or the "Bookmarks" menu (Netscape Navigator).

In either program, you'll find that your list of favorite sites soon becomes unwieldy. You'll need to use the program's organization tools to categorize them by creating and naming folders. After you do this, the "Favorites" or "Bookmarks" menu shows folder names, and submenus pop up when you select a folder name.

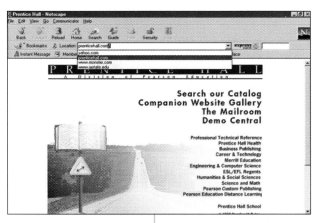

FINDING INFORMATION ON THE WEB

Although browsing by means of hyperlinks is easy and fun, it falls short as a means of information discovery. New Web users soon find themselves clicking link after link, searching for information that they never find. Some grow so frustrated that they stop using the Web. If you can't find the information you're looking for after a bit of browsing, try searching the Web. Although Web search tools are far from perfect, knowledge of their proper use (and their limitations) can greatly increase your chances of finding the information you want.

If you want to return to a previously-viewed site, you can consult the history list and choose the page from this list.

Understanding Information Discovery Tools

You've probably heard of search tools such as Yahoo!, AltaVista, and Lycos. What many Web users do not realize is that these tools differ, and some are more suitable for some purposes than others. Understanding these differences will help you increase your chances of success when you search for information on the Web.

Subject Guides

Most search services offer a **subject guide** to the Web, grouping Web pages under such headings as Business, News, or Travel. These services do not try to include every Web page in the subject categories. Instead, these companies offer a selection of useful, high-quality pages that they believe represent some of the more useful Web pages in a given category. If you're just beginning your search for information, a subject guide is an excellent place to start your search.

If you're looking for scholarly information on the Web, a good place to start is Infomine (**http://lib-www.ucr.edu**), a project sponsored by the University of California, Irvine. Also visit the Virtual Library (**http://www.vlib.org**), a subject guide maintained by volunteer specialists in their respective subject areas. Argus Clearinghouse (**http://www.clearinghouse.net**) is organized like the Virtual Library, and also includes site ratings.

You can use your browser's "Favorites" or "Bookmark" organization tools to categorize your favorite sites by creating and naming folders.

 **Destinations**

Researching a paper? Visit A Student's Guide to Research with the WWW (**http://www.slu.edu/departments/english/research/**), created by Craig Branham of St. Louis University.

Search Engines

If you can't find what you're looking for in a Web subject guide, you can try searching databases that claim to index the full Web. Called **search engines,** these services do not actually maintain databases of every Web page in existence, but the leading ones are known to have indexed about one-third of

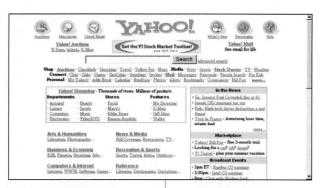

Yahoo! is one of the most extensive subject guides.

Destinations

Leading subject guides include Yahoo! **(http://www.yahoo. com)**, LookSmart **(http://www.looksmart. com)**, Snap! **(http:// www.snap.com)**, and NetGuide **(http://www. netguide.com)**. Most search sites offer subject guides, but Yahoo!'s is the most extensive.

Lycos is a popular search engine.

them. That's an enormous pool of information, and chances are that the use of these services will find some information relevant to the subject you're looking for. Unfortunately, few people know how to use these services effectively. All too often, people try search engines, only to see a lengthy list of irrelevant material.

To use a search engine, type one or more words that describe the subject you're looking for. Generally, it's a good idea to type several words (four or five) rather than one or two, as most Web searches produce far more results than you can use.

Why do search engines sometimes produce unsatisfactory results? The problem lies in the ambiguity of human language. Suppose you're searching for information on the Great Wall of China. You'll find some information on the ancient Chinese defensive installation, but you may also get the menu of the Great Wall of China (a Chinese restaurant), information on the Great Wall hotel in Beijing, and the lyrics to a song titled "Great Wall of China" by Billy Joel.

Although you can improve search effectiveness by learning the search techniques discussed in a subsequent section, Web searches will continue to be hampered by the lack of a framework to describe the content of Web documents. If such a framework existed, Web authors could describe their documents using such terms as *historical* or *commercial*. Searches would be much more effective because you could specify the type of document you want. Several proposals for such frameworks have been made, but no standard exists yet.

Specialized Search Engines

Full Web search engines generally do not index specialized information such as names and addresses, job advertisements, quotations, and newspaper articles. To find such information, you should access specialized search services. Examples of such services are Infomine (**http://lib-www.ucr.edu/vpainfo.html,** a database of information related to the visual and performing arts), BigBook (**http://www.bigbook. com,** a database of 16 million U.S. businesses), CareerBuilder (**http://www.careerbuilder.com,** a database of over 100,000 jobs uploaded weekly) and InformationPlease (**http://www.careerBuilder.com,** which contains the full text of an encyclopedia and an almanac).

SEARCH TECHNIQUES

By learning a few search techniques, you can greatly increase the accuracy of your Web searches. One problem with Web search services is that each uses its own unique set of **search operators,** symbols or words that you can use for advanced searches. A trend toward standardization, however, means that some or all of the following techniques will work with most search services. To find out which ones you can use in a given search service, look for a link to a page explaining search options.

Inclusion and Exclusion

In many search engines, you can improve search performance by specifying an **inclusion operator,** which is generally a plus sign. This operator states that you don't want a page retrieved unless it contains the specified word. By listing several key terms with this search operator, you can exclude many pages that do not contain one or more of the essential terms. The following, for example, will retrieve only those pages that contain all three of the words mentioned:

```
+kittens +care +Siamese
```

If the list of retrieved documents contains many items that you do not want, you can use the **exclusion operator,** which is generally a minus sign. For example, the preceding search retrieves many classified ads for Siamese kittens. You can exclude them by preceding the term *classified* with the exclusion operator, as follows:

```
+kittens +care +Siamese -classified
```

Wildcards

Many search engines enable you to use **wildcards,** which also help you improve the accuracy of your searches. In the preceding example, many unwanted pages contain the word *classifieds* and aren't excluded by the singular *classified.* A commonly-used wildcard is an asterisk, which stands for one or more characters in the position in which it is used. The following excludes any document containing the words *classified* or *classifieds:*

```
-classified*
```

Phrase and Boolean Searches

Another way to improve the accuracy of your searches involves **phrase searching,** which is generally performed by typing a phrase within quotation marks. This tells the search engine to retrieve only those documents that contain that exact phrase (rather than some or all of the words anywhere in the document).

Some search engines enable you to use **Boolean searches.** These searches use keywords (AND, OR, and NOT) to link the words you're searching for. Using Boolean operators, you can gain more precise control over your searches.

The AND, OR, and NOT Operators

When used to link two search words, the AND operator tells the search service to return only those documents that contain both words. For example, the search phrase "Jamaica AND geography" returns only those documents that contain both terms. You can use the AND operator to narrow your search so that it retrieves fewer documents.

If your search retrieves too few documents, try the OR operator. For example, the search phrase "pottery OR ceramics" retrieves documents that contain either or both of these words.

To exclude unwanted documents, you can use the NOT operator. This operator tells the search service to omit any documents containing the word preceded by NOT. For example, the search phrase "sailboats NOT yachts" retrieves pages that mention sailboats, but not those that mention yachts.

The NEAR Operator

Some search engines have a **proximity operator** (usually called NEAR), which enables you to specify that the two linked words appear close together (such as within ten words of each other). Consult the service's help page to find out whether such an operator is available and if so, what it's called

CareerBuilder.com is a specialized search engine that adds over 110,000 job listings each week.

Destinations

The leading search engines are HotBot (**http://www.hotbot. com**), AltaVista (**http:// altavista.digital.com**), GoTo.com (**http://www. goto.com**), Excite (**http://www.excite. com**), and InfoSeek (**http://www.infoseek. com**). Most of these also offer subject guides.

and how it works. The following example phrase retrieves only those documents that contain *browser* and *performance* within a few words of each other: "browser NEAR performance."

Using Parentheses

Many search engines that support Boolean operators enable you to use parentheses to nest Boolean expressions. Such expressions enable you to phrase a search question with unmatched accuracy.

In a search expression created with parentheses, the search engine evaluates the expression from left to right, except that material within parentheses is resolved first. Consider this example:

```
(growth OR increase OR development) NEAR (Internet OR Web)
```

This search question retrieves any document that mentions the words *growth*, *increase*, or *development* within a few words of *Internet* or *Web*.

EVALUATING THE INFORMATION YOU'VE FOUND

After you've found some information on the Web, it's time to evaluate it critically. Web pages are not subjected to the fact-checking standards found in newspapers or magazines, let alone the peer review process that safeguards the quality of scholarly and scientific publications. Although you can find excellent and reliable information on the Web, you can also find pages that are biased and self-serving. You will also encounter information that can be described only as the product of unbalanced minds. Beware!

Rules for Critically Evaluating Web Pages

As you're evaluating a Web page, carefully note the following:

- **Author** Who is the author of this page? Is the author affiliated with a recognized institution, such as a university or a well-known company? Is there any evidence that the author is qualified with respect to this topic? A page that isn't signed may signal an attempt to disguise the author's lack of qualifications.

- **Sources** Does the author indicate where the information's sources came from? If so, do they appear to be from recognized and respected publications?

- **Server** Who provides the server for publishing this Web page? Who pays for this page?

- **Objectivity** Does the presentation seem balanced and objective, or is it one-sided?

- **Style** Is the language objective and dispassionate, or is it strident and argumentative?

- **Purpose** What is the purpose of this page? Is the author trying to sell something or push a biased idea? Who would profit if this page's information were accepted?

- **Accuracy** Does the information appear to be accurate? Is the page free from sweeping generalizations or other signs of shoddy thinking? Do you see many misspellings or grammatical errors that would indicate a poor educational background?

- **Currency** Is this page up-to-date? When was it last maintained?

Locating Material in Published Works

Remember that the Web is only one of several sources you can and should use for research. Your best sources of information are found in respected publications that are likely to be found in the library. You can use the Internet, however, to locate publications that you can then obtain in your college's library. Check your library's home page to find out what Internet services are available. Also, visit UnCoverWeb (**http://uncweb.carl.org**), a free database service that enables you to search for quality articles from more than 17,000 published magazines and journals). After you search, you'll see article lists and titles. You can obtain the source in the library or order a copy directly from UnCoverWeb.

Need reliable information? UnCoverWeb is a free database service you can use to search for quality articles from over 17,000 published magazines and journals.

Authoritative Sources Online

Some respected magazines and journals have established Web sites that enable you to search back issues, giving you the best of both worlds: the power and convenience of the Internet, plus material that's more reliable than the average Web page. The following respected publications provide a valuable public service by providing free access to their back issue archives:

- *Christian Science Monitor* (**http://www.csmonitor.com/archive/p-archive.html**)

- *Time* magazine (**http://cgi.pathfinder.com/time/search/index.html**)

- *Scientific American* (**http://www.sciam.com/cgi-bin/search.cgi**)

ELECTRONIC COMMERCE

Electronic commerce, or **e-commerce,** is broadly defined as the use of telecommunications or the Internet to carry out business of any type. E-commerce isn't new: companies have used wide area networks (WANs) to do business with suppliers for years. What *is* new is that, thanks to the Internet and inexpensive PCs, e-commerce has become accessible to anyone equipped with an Internet connection and a Web browser. Increasingly, Internet users are shopping, opening bank accounts, and trading stocks online. In total dollars, e-commerce is still in its infancy—currently, 99 percent of retail sales occur in traditional, brick-and-mortar stores—but it's growing. By 2005, online retail sales are expected to reach 5 percent of the total U.S. figures. That's paltry compared to the mail-order business, but it's worth remembering that the mail-order business had to start from zero, too. According to a Microsoft Corporation executive, within a generation—25 to 30 years—approximately one-third of all consumer transactions will occur on the Internet, in the context of a massive global electronic marketplace for goods and services.

Business-to-Business E-Commerce

Although most people think of online shopping when they hear the term *e-commerce,* much of e-commerce's projected growth involves business-to-business links that customers won't see. According to one projection, business-to-business e-commerce will be a $66 billion market by 2000.

Why the rapid growth? Today, business-to-business e-commerce requires companies to lease network capacity from a **value-added network (VAN),** which charges a hefty per-byte fee. What's more, VANs aren't flexible. If a

Destinations

If you're using Web sources in a college paper, you'll need to cite your sources. A Style Sheet for Citing Internet Resources: MLA Style, located at **http://www.lib.berkeley.edu/TeachingLib/Guides/Internet/Style.html,** shows how to cite Internet sources using the Modern Language Association style, which is widely used in the humanities. For the American Psychological Association citation style for Internet sources, see The Columbia Guide to Online Style: APA-Style Citations of Electronic Sources, located at **http://www.columbia.edu/cu/cup/cgos/idx_basic.html.**

Explore IT Lab

E-Commerce

MOVERS & SHAKERS

Pioneers of the Web

Although the World Wide Web is just a single part of the Internet, it is the second-largest single part and is growing daily. Millions of users eagerly surf through millions of pages, all sharing information freely and openly.

It wasn't always that way, however. In the world of computing, the Web is not that old. It started as the brain-child of Tim Berners-Lee, a researcher at CERN in Geneva, Switzerland. Although many of the concepts behind the Web were laid out in a paper Berners-Lee authored at CERN in 1980, it wasn't until 1989 and 1990 that the protocols and programs were developed to make the Web a reality.

The original Web browsers were text-oriented programs designed for the UNIX environment. This approach more than fulfilled the development goals of Berners-Lee, who saw the Web as a way for researchers to communicate and collaborate. The lack of a graphical interface, however, was in stark contrast to the overwhelming success of Windows, the operating system that was taking the desktop world by storm.

In late 1992, two programmers at the National Center for Supercomputing Applications (NCSA) at the University of Illinois developed a new browser called Mosaic. The lead programmer on the project was an undergraduate student named Marc Andreessen. While working at the university's physics research lab, Andreessen saw the potential for bringing multimedia together with the capability to link global resources. At the time, the world had between thirty and fifty Web servers, but that didn't stop the development of Mosaic. The development effort consisted of many all-night sessions to get the C code put together and debugged. The result was released to the public as a free download in March 1993. It became extremely popular due to its easy-to-use point-and-click interface, and was quickly recognized as state-of-the-art in a very young World Wide Web.

In late 1993, Andreessen moved to California and accepted a job with Enterprise Integration Technologies. After three short months, Andreessen met with Jim Clark, founder of Silicon Graphics, and the two formed a new company named Netscape Communications Corporation. The focus of their company was the infant World Wide Web, and they decided to create a commercial Web browser that anyone could use.

Andreessen assembled a team of six programmers, most of whom had been involved with the development of Mosaic at NCSA. They developed the original Netscape Navigator in only three months, between May and July of 1994. After some testing and refinement, the product was released to the world in October 1994, just seventeen months after Mosaic was originally released.

Navigator featured several improvements over the original Mosaic. The biggest improvement was continuous document streaming, which meant users could view documents as they were being downloaded.

Netscape followed an unorthodox distribution program for their software: they gave it away. When released, Navigator was freely available to download for educational and non-profit uses. Others could use it for a time but then agree (on the honor system) to pay a modest licensing fee. In this respect, Netscape was following the popular distribution model of thousands of shareware authors.

The marketing model followed by Netscape was wildly successful. From the humble beginnings of Netscape in 1994, the company has grown into a powerhouse with annual revenues in excess of $525 million.

The most telling mark of Netscape's success was the entry of Microsoft into the Web arena. For a few years, the Redmond-based corporation had ignored the Web, but the dazzling growth and huge profits enjoyed by Netscape made them act quickly to catch up. That's just what Microsoft did; in fact, they moved so aggressively that they wound up in court accused of violating U.S. antitrust law. By bundling its Internet Explorer browser with the Windows operating system, Microsoft ate into Netscape's market share. Netscape was subsequently purchased by online giant America Online, where Andreessen worked briefly as the company's chief technology executive. Andreessen is now the CEO of a venture capital firm—and he's working as hard as ever.

Marc Andreessen, co-founder of Netscape Communications Corporation.

local dial-in (called a **point of presence**) doesn't exist, you can't connect without incurring long-distance charges. To exchange financial information, firms use a data standard called **electronic data interchange (EDI).** EDI requires partnering firms to collaborate in order to customize the various EDI documents, and it's a huge job. Despite the hassles of EDI, business-to-business commerce has been growing at a 15- to 20-percent annual clip.

With the Internet, business-to-business e-commerce is much easier to implement, far more flexible, and almost infinitely easier to use. One example is Boeing's Part Page, the aircraft manufacturer's password-protected Web site designed for

Increasingly, Internet users are shopping, opening bank accounts, and trading stocks online.

Boeing customers. In place of difficult-to-use EDI tools, Boeing customers can now use a familiar Web browser to search the massive parts inventory, place an order, and track shipments. Part Page also enables Boeing to offer quality service 24 hours per day, 7 days per week, in place of the former 8 hours a day, 5 days a week service. That's a key element of survival in a global economy. Boeing's Part Page uses SSL encryption to safeguard customer data. On the Internet, security is a concern, which is why the availability of strong encryption is so vital to the growth of Internet commerce (see Module 10C).

The latest wrinkle in business-to-business e-commerce is the **virtual private network (VPN),** a way of using the Internet to connect two physically-separate local area networks (LANs). Strong encryption is used to encode every message.

Online Shopping

Most people equate e-commerce with online shopping, which is made possible by the security and encryption features built into popular browsers. According to a recent survey, fewer than half of the Web's users have bought something online, but this percentage is growing each year. What's more, the same survey revealed that nearly three-quarters of Internet users used the Internet to research potential purchases before making them, even if they subsequently bought them in an old-fashioned real-world store. Businesses are concluding that they must be on the Internet or they'll soon be out of business.

One of the tremendous advantages of online shopping is the low capital investment needed to set up shop. For less than $2,000, a startup can open a Web storefront and start selling products online. For example, Amazon.com, the "world's largest bookstore," as it describes itself, is nothing more than a few offices in a Seattle office building. But don't be misled. Amazon.com saw its stock go through the roof in 1998, making it worth more than real-world competitors Barnes & Noble and Borders combined, even though it has only one-tenth of the sales. Were investors nuts? Perhaps, but they're betting that online bookstores are going to put their real-world counterparts out of business. Maybe they're right. Why go to a real bookstore, which offers as few as 10,000 titles (and rarely more than 40,000), when you can log on to Amazon.com, search a database of 3 *million* titles, get discounts of up to 40 percent, and have your books delivered in two or three days?

Don't make plans to drop out of college and set up shop just yet, though. Not every business succeeds on the Internet. What works best? The big winners thus far have been Amazon.com, autobytel.com (an online automobile information provider that enables car buyers to avoid showroom shakedowns), and

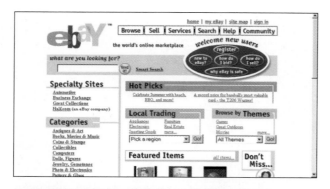

Autobytel.com and eBay are two highly-successful online businesses that put customers in direct contact with incredibly rich sources of information.

eBay (an online auction service that enables individuals to buy and sell collectibles through the Internet). In online shopping, you have to have the right angle.

Least successful of all e-commerce ventures are attempts to bring traditional retailing concepts to the Internet—and such efforts have already produced some spectacular failures, such as online fashion merchant Boo.com. Business experts believe part of the problem lies in poor customer service. Would-be customers are afraid something will go wrong with their order and they won't be able to talk to anyone about it. For this reason, **click-and-mortar** stores—retailers that have both an online and traditional retail store presence—are winning the consumer's confidence. Why? Shoppers can return products locally, or talk to an actual human being if there's something wrong with the order. During one recent holiday season, U.S. consumers returned more than 25 percent of the goods they purchased, representing more than $1 billion worth of merchandise. To survive, Internet-only retailers must make returning goods easier. For example, Road Runner Sports provides its online customers with a 30-day guaranteed return period, a shipping label, and a bag that can be used to return unwanted goods.

There's another reason for the click-and-mortar strategy's success: customers like to use the Internet to research products before they buy. Although less than 3 percent of new car sales are made online, more than 40 percent of new car buyers researched their purchase on the Internet.

Good site design matters, too. Studies show that 50 percent of online shoppers will immediately leave a site that takes more than eight seconds to download.

So what *does* work? The online shopping success stories give people something they can't get elsewhere. Amazon.com enables readers to choose from a massive inventory, most of which can be delivered to the customer's doorstep in two or three days. In addition, the site is rich in information, including reviews submitted by readers. If you search for a book on Amazon.com, you'll find it—if it exists—and you'll probably find others that will interest you. Autobytel.com offers great prices and a way to avoid haggling with dealers, an experience that virtually all car buyers detest. eBay puts collectors in contact with nearly one million collectors worldwide, and holds more than 10 million electronic auctions per month.

If one word could sum up what all these sites share, it's **disintermediation.** All three of these online success stories take intermediaries—booksellers, car salesmen, and auctioneers—out of the picture. These sites put customers in direct contact with incredibly-rich resources of information. They enable customers to make their own choices, without being restricted to stock-on-hand (or a salesperson's interference).

Secure Electronic Transactions (SET)

What about credit card fraud at online shopping sites? To protect both merchants and customers, Visa, MasterCard, and American Express got together to create an online shopping security standard called Secure Electronic Transactions (SET). SET's goal is to create a security infrastructure using

▶Initially, it sounds crazy. Why would anyone want to buy groceries on the Internet? If you'd like to know the answer, just ask anyone who's cash-rich and time-poor (and that category includes a fair share of a boom economy's population). Grocery shopping takes way too much time.

Once you start looking at the idea more closely, it doesn't sound so crazy. For the price of a good bottle of wine, you can select your groceries on the Internet and have them delivered to your home. What's more, the online supermarket "remembers" your last grocery list, so you can see what you needed to buy last time and what you will probably need to buy again. You can even set up recurrent transactions so that you receive needed perishables, such as

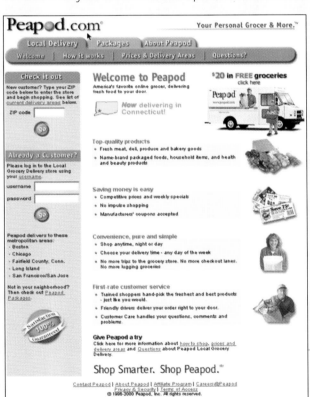

milk and eggs, on a fixed schedule. Some online supermarkets even offer budgeting, automatically tracking your expenditures so that you can stay within the limits you've set.

A leader in the online grocery business, Peapod (**http://www.peapod.com**) offers grocery delivery in several U.S. metropolitan areas. Peapod works with local grocery store retailers and employs a centralized distribution model to select and pack grocery orders in temperature-controlled bins. The bins are delivered to customers' homes in trucks that Peapod leases. Focusing on providing the services its customers want, Peapod enables customers to choose the time and date of delivery—an important matter for people with busy schedules. Peapod's online store offers prices that are competitive with those of local supermarkets, guarantees timely delivery, and promises fresh, damage-free produce and meat, selected with the customer's satisfaction in mind. If that's not attractive enough, consumers have found one very important advantage to online grocery shopping: it cuts down on impulse buying. The idea doesn't sound so crazy now, does it?

It's still far from certain whether companies such as Peapod can make money. The grocery business is one of the toughest around (profit margins are typically 3 percent or less) and supermarket chains haven't had much luck with the delivery services they've tried. Under a troubled financial cloud in the late nineties, Peapod had lost $28 million on $73 million of revenue, and investors were threatening to pull the plug. But earlier this year, international food provider Royal Ahold purchased a 51 percent stake in Peapod, and the company is now focusing its immediate growth along the East Coast, where many of Royal Ahold's retail brands have a strong presence.

Peapod's online store offers competitive prices, guarantees timely delivery, and promises fresh, damage-free produce and meat, selected with the customer's satisfaction in mind.

digital certificates for merchants and customers. To ensure that the certificates are valid, both certificates would have to be endorsed by a third-party **certificate authority (CA).** But very few online merchants are currently interested in SET because it requires customers to use cumbersome plug-in programs, which aren't popular with browser users.

Online banking allows customers to access their accounts and balance checkbooks online. About 10 to 12 million households make regular use of online banking.

Something like SET may be needed to get electronic commerce rolling, but it's overkill right now. Amazon.com reports that none of its 21 million customers has experienced any problems with credit card fraud. And just to make sure that consumers have full confidence, the company promises to cover your $50 liability should someone make fraudulent use of your credit card.

Online Banking

About 10 to 12 million households make regular use of online banking. In **online banking,** customers can use a Web browser to access their accounts, balance checkbooks, transfer funds, and even pay bills online. Currently, online banking offers a competitive advantage in attracting new customers. Soon, though, it will become an expected service, like ATMs. That's why a 1998 survey revealed that more than 93 percent of U.S.-based banks planned to deploy an Internet strategy within the next three years. An example of how online banking at Wachovia works appears on page 373.

Banks implement online banking in different ways. One method makes use of checkbook programs such as Microsoft Money or Intuit's Quicken, enabling customers to balance their checkbooks automatically. The drawback, however, is that you have to access your online banking account from the computer that has all the Money or Quicken data, and this data could be examined by anyone with access to your computer. An advantage is that Money and Quicken offer powerful features for budgeting your spending and analyzing your spending habits.

Newer Web-based systems that require only one program (a Web browser) are easier to use. All the data is stored on the bank's computer, not your own, which means you can access your account anywhere. Web-based online banking is also much easier to use. However, the Web-based systems don't offer advanced features such as budgeting and spending analysis. What's in it for the banks? Plenty: those bank branches and tellers cost a lot of money!

Many people who would like to use online banking are concerned about losing their money. As long as you follow certain precautions, however, you have little need for concern. Online banking is much safer than using an ATM.

When you access an online banking account, be sure you're doing so in your browser's **secure mode.** In the secure mode, the browser uses encryption to communicate with the bank's server. Check your browser's documentation to find out where the secure mode icon appears and how it looks. Also, be sure you're using the highest-level **128-bit domestic-level encryption,** which is invulnerable to decoding. Above all else, keep your password safe—don't give it to anyone or write it down where it could be seen.

Another concern is the security of the bank's **electronic vault,** a mainframe computer that stores account holders' information. Because no computer system is totally secure, it's reasonable to feel concerned that an intruder could gain access to the vault and steal a depositor's money. Still, the threat is small. Online banks use state-of-the-art security systems, including firewalls. An additional security measure is **active monitoring,** in which a security team constantly monitors the vault for the tell-tale signs of unauthorized access.

Online Stock Trading

Another area of e-commerce experiencing rapid growth is **online stock trading.** *Rapid* probably isn't strong enough; available only since 1996, online stock trading now accounts for one out of every six stock trades, making it

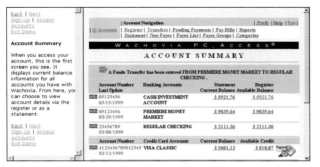

(a) Acccount summary

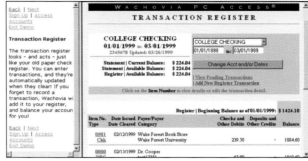

(b) Transaction register

(c) Select bills to pay

(d) Transfer funds

easily the fastest-growing application in consumer-based e-commerce. Offering secure connections through the customer's Web browser, online stock trading sites enable investors to buy and sell stocks online, without the aid of a broker.

The attraction of online stock trading can be summed up in one word: cost. Traditional, full-service brokerages charge up to $100 per trade, while discount brokerages charge about $50. The most aggressive online brokers, in contrast, have cut their charges to $10 per trade or less. Online brokers can offer such low prices because the trading is automatic—no human broker is involved—and because they can make money on the side on the investor's accounts. (You have to deposit at least $5,000 before you can start buying and selling stocks online.)

However, there is a downside, according to investment professionals. Most investors are wise to buy stocks and then hold on to them for the long term. Online trading appeals to an amateur investor's worst instincts—namely, buying when the market's at its peak of enthusiasm (and prices are also at their peak) and then selling when prices start to drop. This translates to buying high and selling low. You won't make money that way. That's true even when, overall, the market is going up. Most investment counselors believe that amateurs are well-advised to avoid frequent trading, because of the difficulty in getting through when trading is heavy. When the market plunged 554 points in October 1997, electronic investors received a rude shock: due to overloaded Internet servers, they couldn't unload their stocks until the market hit the bottom.

Online brokerages make up to 10 percent of their revenue from **margin loans,** which most online brokerages make available to their customers. These loans enable customers to purchase more stock than they could with their available cash alone. These loans can be dangerous. If the stock goes up, all's well. The customer can sell the stock, pay off the loan, and enjoy the profits. But what if the stock goes down? A 35-year-old Ohio electrician found out the hard way. Beginning with $6,000, he bought several risk Internet stocks on margin loans, eventually losing a total of $180,000.

**ONLINE BANKING
AT WACHOVIA**
(a) Your account summary shows the current status of all your accounts.
(b) The transaction register is just like a paper checkbook register, except it's automatically balanced when your checks clear! If you forget to write down a check, no problem. When the check comes in, it's automatically added to the register.
(c) You can set up dates and amounts for recurring bills, and they will be paid automatically.
(d) Need to transfer funds? Do it online and see the results instantly.

E-trading sites enable investors to buy and sell stocks online without going through a broker.

E-Postage

Postage meters, which are mechanical devices that crank out metered postage, are seen in business offices everywhere. If an experimental U.S. Postal Service program works out, you'll soon be able to obtain metered postage through the Internet, instead. Called SmartStamp, the program works in the following way: Once you access a virtual post office (a secure Web site), which enables you to purchase postage using a credit card, SmartStamp downloads the purchased postage to a security device attached to the computer's printer port. Whenever you print an envelope using a standard word processing program (such as Microsoft Word), SmartStamp verifies the address, calculates the correct postage amount, and automatically prints a valid stamp.

Don't expect anything fancy like an Elvis Presley stamp. The e-stamp is actually a bar code, but it's not like the UPC bar codes on supermarket items. Each stamp is unique: the code includes a digital signature that makes it all but impossible to forge the stamp.

TAKEAWAY POINTS

- Increasing numbers of Internet users are turning to the World Wide Web to research current events, general information, product information, scientific developments, and much more.

- In hypertext, related information is referenced by means of links instead of being fully explained or defined. On the Web, authors can link to information created by others.

- The Web is an Internet service that involves the use of a client (the browser) and a Web server, which retrieves documents requested by browsers.

- A URL consists of the protocol (such as **http://**), domain name (such as **www.microsoft.com**), the path (such as **/windows/ie**), and the resource name (such as **default.htm**). URLs enable Web authors to state the exact location of a resource available on the Internet.

- To create Web pages, Web authors use Hypertext Markup Language (HTML).

- Web subject guides index a limited number of high-quality pages, while full Web search engines enable you to search huge databases of Web documents.

- Most Web searches retrieve too many irrelevant documents. You can improve search results by using inclusion and exclusion operators, phrase searches, and Boolean operators.

- Anyone can publish anything on the Web. Don't accept any information you find until you have critically evaluated the author's credentials and purpose for publishing the page.

- Most e-commerce involves business-to-business links that currently require value-added networks (VANs) and Electronic Data Interchange (EDI). Many businesses are moving these transactions to the Internet to take advantage of the Internet's flexibility, widespread availability, and ease of use.

- Online shopping succeeds when it gives people something they can't get in traditional retail stores, such as an enormous selection or a way to avoid aggressive sales personnel.

- Online banking is growing rapidly, although some potential users are concerned about security.

- One of the most rapidly growing forms of e-commerce is online trading, but most investors would be well advised to stick with their investments rather than buying or selling too frequently.

MODULE REVIEW

KEY TERMS AND CONCEPTS

128-bit domestic-level
  encryption
active monitoring
Boolean searches
certificate authority (CA)
click-and-mortar
default start page
disintermediation
distributed hypermedia system
electronic commerce
  (e-commerce)
electronic data interchange
  (EDI)
electronic vault
exclusion operator
graphical browser

hyperlinks
hypermedia
hypertext
Hypertext Markup Language
  (HTML)
Hypertext Transfer Protocol
  (HTTP)
inclusion operator
index page
margin loans
markup language
online banking
online stock trading
phrase searching
point of presence
proximity operator

search engines
search operators
secure mode
stale links
subject guide
text-only browsers
Uniform Resource Locators
  (URLs)
value-added network (VAN)
virtual private network (VPN)
Web pages
Web server
Web site
wildcards
World Wide Web

TRUE/FALSE

Indicate whether the following statements are true or false.

1. The World Wide Web is a distributed hypermedia system.

2. A Web browser is a type of server software.

3. When using a browser, you always need to enter a protocol as part of a URL.

4. If Web page authors remove their Web pages, they're obligated to notify other authors who have included links to their pages.

5. As you browse the Web, your browser keeps track of only the currently-displayed page.

6. When using a search engine, it's a good idea to search for several words rather than one or two.

7. No checks exist on the quantity, quality, or value of information published on the Web.

8. Much of e-commerce's projected growth involves business-to-business links that customers don't see.

9. A disadvantage of online shopping is the high capital investment needed to set up shop.

10. The biggest attraction of online stock trading is its low cost.

MATCHING

Match each key term from the left column with the most accurate definition in the right column.

_____ 1. World Wide Web

_____ 2. hypertext

_____ 3. hypermedia

_____ 4. Web server

_____ 5. markup language

_____ 6. default start page

_____ 7. search operators

_____ 8. wildcard

_____ 9. electronic commerce

_____ 10. electronic vault

a. a set of codes that authors can use to identify portions of a document for a Web page

b. the use of telecommunications or wide area networking to carry out financial transactions

c. this helps you improve the accuracy of your searches on the Web

d. symbols or words that you can use for advanced searches

e. a mainframe computer that stores bank account holders' information

f. a way of presenting information so that its sequence is left up to the reader

g. this enables users to retrieve multimedia resources such as sounds and movies, as well as text

h. a program that waits patiently for browsers to request a Web page

i. an indispensable information resource on the Internet

j. a page that's located at the browser vendor's home server

MULTIPLE CHOICE

Circle the letter of the correct choice for each of the following.

1. Links to documents that have disappeared are known as what?
   a. unknown links
   b. stale links
   c. hyperlinks
   d. tenuous links

2. Which of the following is not a component of a URL?
   a. resource name
   b. protocol
   c. path
   d. language

3. If you click the Home button in a Web browser, what happens?
   a. The home page of the site you are visiting is displayed.
   b. The browser helps you create a home page.

   c. The default startup page for the browser is displayed.
   d. The displayed page becomes your home page.

4. Which Web browser button would you click to return to the Web page previously displayed?
   a. Home
   b. Back
   c. Forward
   d. Stop

5. Which of the following are not typically indexed in full Web search engines?
   a. resource information
   b. job advertisements
   c. magazines
   d. news stories

6. When using a search engine, a plus sign is an example of which of the following?
   a. an exclusion operator
   b. an addition operator
   c. a mathematical operator
   d. an inclusion operator

7. Which of the following is a commonly-used wildcard character?
   a. a plus sign
   b. an asterisk
   c. a minus sign
   d. a slash

8. Which of the following elements should not generally be considered when attempting to determine the value of Web page content?

a. author
b. style
c. sources
d. page size

9. Business-to-business e-commerce relies on which data standard?
   a. point of presence (PoP)
   b. electronic data interchange (EDI)
   c. value-added networks (VAN)
   d. virtual private network (VPN)

10. Which of the following can you typically not do with online banking?
    a. balance your checkbook
    b. pay bills electronically
    c. transfer funds
    d. secure a loan

FILL-IN

In the blank provided, write the correct answer for each of the following.

1. _____ is a way of presenting information so that the sequence of the information is left up to the reader.

2. A(n) _____ is a collection of related Web documents that a Web server makes available to the public.

3. To create a Web page, Web authors use a(n) _____.

4. Most Web search services offer a(n) _____ to the Web, grouping pages under descriptive headings.

5. If you can't find what you're looking for using a Web subject guide, you can try a(n) _____ such as Lycos or AltaVista.

6. _____ searches use key words such as AND, OR, and NOT.

7. Some search engines have a(n) _____, which enables you to specify that the two linked words appear close together.

8. Business-to-business e-commerce requires companies to lease network capacity from a(n) _____ network.

9. When you access an online banking account, be sure you're doing so in your browser's _____.

10. An additional security measure is _____, in which a security team constantly monitors the electronic vault for signs of unauthorized access.

SHORT ANSWER

On a separate sheet of paper, answer the following questions.

1. What factors contributed to the explosive growth of the Web in the mid-1990s?

2. What is the difference between a Web server and a Web browser?

3. What is the difference between a Web subject guide and a Web search engine?

4. Why do search engines sometimes produce unsatisfactory results?

5. What types of operators are typically used by search engines, and what are their purposes?

6. What are some rules of thumb for evaluating the value of content on the Web?

7. Discuss the benefits of online shopping to retailers. What is required to increase the probability of a successful online presence?

8. What is SET? Why has it been slow to catch on with retailers?

9. Briefly describe how online banking has grown in the past several years. What is the projected growth? What common banking transactions are available online?

10. Why has online stock trading been so successful? What are the potential pitfalls in online trading?

USING EMAIL

7C

MODULE

OUTLINE

WHAT YOU WILL LEARN . . .

When you have finished reading this module, you will be able to:

1. Explain how email works on the Internet.

2. Name the three parts of an email address.

3. Distinguish between the two leading messaging protocols (POP and IMAP).

4. Explain how to get an email account and configure an email client program.

5. Identify the parts of an email program's window.

6. Describe how to receive email messages, reply to messages, compose new messages, and forward messages to others.

7. Discuss the risks of email use.

You hear a lot about the Web, but email is the Internet's most-attractive application, and it's getting more popular every day. New email users are coming online at a phenomenal annual growth rate of 72 percent, compared with 42 percent for the total Internet market. In 2000, the number of email users in the U.S. alone is expected to exceeded 107 million, and they'll exchange a mind-boggling 6.9 *trillion* messages.

Why is email so popular? Two reasons: low cost and blistering speed. For the price of an Internet connection, you can send unlimited numbers of free messages to any of the millions of email users worldwide. And it's fast. Most email messages are delivered within five minutes of clicking the Send button.

Why should you learn about email? Email is an essential component of computer literacy. According to a recent survey, 93 percent of employers say that email skills are "important" or "very important" in hiring decisions. What's more, email is an indispensable part of anyone's career management strategy. Email enables you to contact prospective employers and submit your résumé. On the job, email is a great way to network with friends in the same line of work as well as with mentors who can help you cope with work-related issues. At the same time, you need to understand that email also poses certain risks, especially when you're using email at work.

EMAIL FUNDAMENTALS

To understand and use email, you need to learn a few basic terms and concepts.

Email Servers and Clients

Like other Internet services, email requires two types of software: an email server and an email client.

An **email server** runs on your Internet service provider's computer (see Figure 7C.1). However, you don't interact with the server directly—all of its functions are automatic. The server receives and stores incoming mail, waiting for you to log on and check your mail. When you do, you're told how many new messages you have, and you can read them, if you want. When you send mail, the server sends your mail over the Internet to its destination.

An **email client** (also called a **user agent**) runs on your computer (see Figure 7C.1). With this program, you can read the mail you've received. You can reply to received messages, compose new ones, and forward mail to a third party. Although you can buy **standalone email clients** such as Eudora, most people use the email capabilities built into the two leading Web browsers, Internet Explorer and Netscape Communicator.

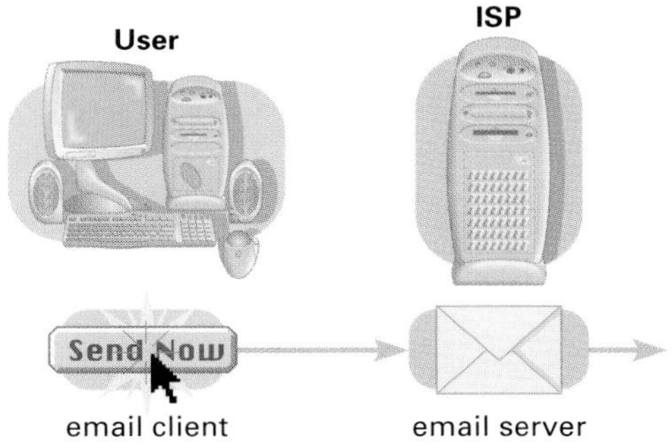

Figure 7C.1

An email server runs on your Internet service provider's computer. When you send mail, the server sends your mail over the Internet to its destination. An email client runs on your computer and enables you to read the mail you've received, reply to received messages, compose new ones, and forward mail to a third party.

Email Addresses

An Internet email address (such as **jsmith@jamestown.edu**) has three parts:

- **Mailbox name** The first part of an email address indicates the user's **mailbox name,** which identifies the user. Often, the mailbox name is the same as the user's **user name** (the name you supply when you log on to your account).

- **At sign (@)** This symbol separates the first and third parts of an email address.

- **Server address** The Internet address of the user's mail server.

Email messages can also include an **alias** (an additional name). Generally, this capability is used to indicate the user's real name in outgoing messages, as in the following example: John Smith **<jsmith@jamestown.edu>.** When you install your email client, you'll be asked to type your name. The program automatically adds your name as an alias to outgoing messages. When your message is received, the recipient's email client displays your message using your real name.

A major email shortcoming is that when you change Internet service providers, you can't leave a forwarding address. That can be a huge problem for college students. When you graduate, the academic computer center pulls the plug on your Internet account. If prospective employers try to contact you, they get a **bounce message** stating "no such user." Email servers return a bounce message if they're unable to deliver your message for some reason.

Email Protocols

Like other Internet services, Internet email requires **protocols** (communication standards). The **Simple Mail Transport Protocol (SMTP)** specifies how servers should send and receive plain-text messages across the Internet. It also describes the format of an email message, specifying that the message should include a **header.** The header supplies vital routing information, such as the sender's email address, the recipient's email address, and the message's subject. **Multipurpose Internet Mail Extensions (MIME)** specifies a way to send **binary files** as an **attachment** to email messages. (A binary file contains a program, a graphic, or a document formatted with nonstandard characters.)

The **Post Office Protocol (POP),** also called POP3, uses a server to store your incoming messages temporarily. When you access the server, your client program downloads all the messages to your computer and erases the server's copies. A major disadvantage of POP mail lies in its inconvenience. Once downloaded, your email isn't accessible when you're traveling and accessing the Internet from some other computer.

The **Internet Message Access Protocol (IMAP),** also called IMAP4, stores your messages on the server. Just as you can do with downloaded messages, you can read your mail, delete unwanted messages, organize mail into folders, compose mail, and send mail. However, everything's stored on the server. The major advantage of IMAP is mobility. In the morning, for example, you can check your email using the computer in your dorm room. Between classes, you stop by the computer lab and check your mail again. Surprise! One of your professors has cancelled an assignment. If you had waited until you got back to your room, you wouldn't have known, and you would have wasted your time. When you're home for vacation, you can check your mail using a home computer.

INTRODUCING EMAIL CLIENTS

Now that you know the essential email concepts and terms, let's take a closer look at the software you'll use to send and receive Internet mail.

Getting an Account

When you get your Internet account, your Internet service provider (ISP) will tell you your email address. You'll also receive your user name, your password, and the Internet address of your mail server. You need this information to access your mail. If you get an account at school or at work, you'll receive this information from the computer center.

Destinations

Among the most popular free email services are Angelfire (**http://email. angelfire.com**), Hotmail (**http://www.hotmail. com**), and Yahoo! Mail (**http://www.yahoo.com**).

You can also get into email using a **free email service,** such as Hotmail (**http://www.hotmail.com**). Free email services are Web-based companies that enable you to send and receive email using a Web browser. Supported by advertising that appears on the service's pages, these services are popular, even among users who have regular email accounts with an ISP, due to the convenience. With a free email service, you can access your mail anywhere that you can get a Web connection. Also, your email address doesn't change. This is a plus for college students who are hoping to network with prospective employers. Otherwise, how will they contact you after you've graduated and your campus account is closed? Free email services are also popular with business users because these services enable them to access POP or IMAP mail when they're traveling on business. College students enjoy the same benefit when they're home on holidays or for the summer.

No matter where you obtain your email account, carefully safeguard your email password. If you let someone else have it, they could send mail in your name—and that could get you in a lot of trouble.

Hotmail is a Web-based, free email service that gives you a permanent email address.

Setting Up Your Email Client

When you install your email program on your computer, you'll be asked to supply the following information:

- **POP3 or IMAP server**   This is the domain name of the server that stores your incoming mail until you access it.

- **SMTP server**   This is the domain name of the server that sends your outgoing mail. Sometimes the same server is used for both incoming and outgoing mail.

- **Your email address**   Be sure to type this carefully!

- **Your email password**   This is the password you use to access your email. It may differ from the password you use to connect to the Internet via a dial-up connection.

- **Your name**   This is the name that will show up in the From column of people to whom you send email. You can supply a nickname, if you prefer. However, avoid using a silly-sounding or slightly-obscene nickname because it will show up in all the messages you send, including the messages you send to your professors and potential employers!

In this dialog box, you can update or change your user information and the name you designate for the server.

To configure Microsoft Outlook Express, you can use the Internet Connection wizard that appears the first time you run the program. The wizard prompts you for all the necessary information and creates the account. To update or change email account information, click Tools on the menu bar, choose Accounts, and click the Mail tab.

In Hotmail's Options box, you can update or change your email account information.

Select your email account, and click Properties. Make your changes, and click OK.

If your computer will be used by anyone else, don't supply your password when you set up your email program. This makes email usage slightly less convenient because you'll be prompted to supply your password when you log on to the server. However, you'll be assured that nobody can get on your computer while you're out and send harassing mail in your name.

Exploring Your Email Client's Window

Although email programs vary, they all look and work pretty much the same. Within the program's window, you'll find the following:

- **Folder list** Your mail is organized into named folders. **Default folders** include an inbox folder (stores your incoming mail and any mail you haven't deleted or moved), sent mail folder (contains copies of mail that you've sent), and deleted mail folder. You can also create additional folders.

- **Message list** When you select a folder, this area shows a list of the messages the folder contains. Most programs indicate the sender, the subject, and the date received. Messages you haven't read appear in bold and have a distinctive icon.

- **Message window** Here you see the contents of the message currently selected in the message list. To view the message in a separate window, go back to the message list and double-click the selected message.

On the toolbar, you'll see the most-frequently used commands. These enable you to perform such actions as getting new mail, composing a new message, replying to a message, and printing a message.

COMPOSING, RECEIVING, AND FORWARDING EMAIL

After you've configured your email client to access your mail, you can log on to your mail server, read your mail, reply to messages, compose your own messages, and forward messages to others, as explained in the following sections. These procedures work the same whether you're using a POP or IMAP server.

Logging On to the Mail Server

To access your mail account, click the "New Mail" button on your email client's toolbar. (Your program may use a different name for this button.) If you didn't save your password when you configured your mail program, you'll be prompted to supply your password.

Receiving Email

After you've logged on, your email client downloads your new messages and displays your new mail as well as any older messages that you haven't deleted or moved. From here, you can read your messages, reply to a message, compose a message, or forward a message to someone.

Replying Directly to the Author

To reply to the author of a message, select the message in the message list and click the "Reply" button. (This might be named differently, depending on which program you're using.) You'll see a new message composition window. The software automatically fills in the recipient's email address and adds "Re:" in front of the original message's subject line. Most programs are set up to **quote** the message to which you're replying by copying the text to this window.

To type your message, move the cursor to the *top* of the window, above the quoted text. Recipients don't like scrolling down through quoted text to find your message at the bottom.

Replying to All

Some email messages are sent to more than one person. A quick way to determine this is if the "To:" and "Cc:" lines contain more than one email address. When you click the "Reply" button in this instance, your reply goes only to the person who sent you the message. However, if you click "Reply to All," a copy of the message goes to *everyone* listed in the message's "To:" and "Cc:" lines. One of those addresses might be a **group email address,** which could include dozens of people or even an entire company.

Do not use the Reply to All button unless you are absolutely sure you understand the consequences. A lot of people have found themselves in serious trouble and even lost their jobs by clicking "Reply to All" instead of "Reply to Author." These people thought they were writing back only to the author. Perhaps they made fun of their boss or used obscene language. They didn't realize that the "To:" line included a group email address that sent a copy of their reply to everyone in the company, including the boss.

Composing Email

To compose a new message to someone, click the "New Mail" button. (Just what this button is called depends on which email client you're using.) You'll see a composition window and will then need to type the recipient's email address. (If you want, you can use the program's built-in Address Book to store email addresses. When you do so, you can select the email address from the Address Book rather than type it each time.)

Before you send your message, you must type a subject line. Write a brief subject line (such as "Request for employment interview" or "Paper #1 extension request").

When you compose a message, you can choose from the following additional options:

- **Priority** Most email programs are configured to send messages using Normal priority. However, you can choose High or Low priority. Messages sent with these priority settings do not arrive sooner or later

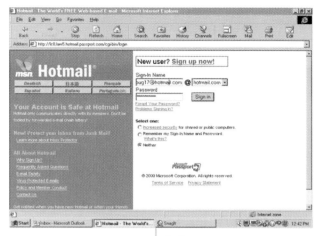

Before you can access your email account, you must enter your password.

The Inbox displays your new messages.

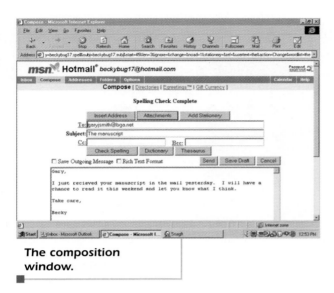

The composition window.

Techtalk

daemon
Have you ever received an email message that appears to be from someone named "demon?" No, your computer is not possessed. That message has actually come from "daemon," a program that hangs out in the background while your computer is operating. It only steps in when something requires attention, such as a misdirected email message that needs to be routed to its proper recipient.

than messages with Normal priority. Most email programs are configured to display these messages with special symbols that indicate a priority other than normal. In Outlook Express, messages sent with High Priority are preceded by a red exclamation point.

- **Digital signature** You can obtain a **digital signature** from a commercial certification agency, such as VeriSign (**http://www.verisign.com**) or from your employer. A digital signature uniquely and positively identifies your message as one that has been sent from your computer and your email account. A digital signature cannot be modified while your message is en-route without leaving signs that the receiving program can detect. For more information on digital signatures, see Module 9A.

- **Encryption** If you have obtained your correspondent's **public encryption key**, you can encrypt a message that you send to this correspondent. A public encryption key is a means of scrambling the message so that nobody but the intended recipient can read the message. For more information on encryption, see Module 9A.

Email Tips

- **Type a brief, descriptive subject line** If the subject line doesn't convey anything to your recipients, they may ignore your message. Also, put the important words first. Some email programs display only two or three subject words in message lists.

- **Send plain-text email, not HTML (formatted) mail** Some email programs are configured to send richly-formatted mail that incorporates the same HTML markup tags used to create Web pages. However, many people use email programs that do not read HTML tags, while others prefer to switch HTML capabilities off. To turn off HTML mail in Microsoft Outlook Express, click Tools on the menu bar, choose "Options," click the "Send" tag, and enable "Plain Text in the Mail Sending Format" area. Click OK to confirm your choice.

- **State your purpose immediately** Readers prefer to go through their mail quickly and don't like spending time figuring out why you're writing to them.

- **Edit quoted text** When you reply to email, most email programs will quote the text of the letter to which you are replying. If you are replying to just one or two points in the quoted text, delete the rest of it so your message is less lengthy and less complex.

- **Don't write in anger** Sometimes people send email messages that come across more harshly than they intended. If you receive a message that angers you, don't fire off a **flame** (an accusatory, hostile message). Take some time to cool off, pick up the telephone, call the sender, and talk it through.

- **Don't check your mail too often** Most email programs are configured to check your mail at set intervals, such as every 30 minutes, by accessing the incoming mail server. If too many users access their mail at more-frequent intervals, the result can bog down the server. Check your mail only once every half hour or hour.

Forwarding Email

The procedure you use to forward email closely resembles the procedure for replying to a message, except that you must supply the email address. The email software automatically places "Fwd:" before the original message's subject line and quotes the message text. Above the quoted text, insert a brief explanation of why you're forwarding the message.

Receiving Attachments: Beware!

Thanks to the MIME protocol, you can send and receive attachments, which are files that are included with the text message. Such files can include graphics, program files, and application software documents. And as millions of computer users have discovered to their dismay, they can also contain computer viruses.

Many of these viruses, such as the infamous "I Love You" virus that affected millions of computers worldwide, are programmed to replicate themselves by sending copies of destructive code to all the addresses in the affected user's address book. What this means is that recipients believe they're receiving a valid message from someone they know. However, when they double-click the attachment, the virus code goes to work, sending out even more copies of itself—and, in all likelihood, wiping out data on those computers.

Which attachment files can contain viruses? Any **executable file,** a file containing a program that can run on your computer, poses a special danger. However, documents created by other popular office application suites are dangerous, too. Word and Excel documents may contain **macro viruses,** which take advantage of the built-in programming language provided by these applications.

To avoid infecting your own computer and those of others, adopt the following rule: *never open an attachment within your email program, even if it looks perfectly innocent and comes from someone you know.* Instead, save the file to a floppy disk, if possible, and run a virus checker on the file before attempting to open it. In Outlook Express, you can do this by right-clicking the attachment icon and choosing Save As from the pop-up menu.

Sending Attachments: Be Courteous

You can send as well as receive attachments. To include an attachment with an Outlook Express message, click the Attach icon, locate and select the file you want to send, and click OK.

Be aware, though, that your recipient will have to endure a lengthy download when your message arrives, and your attachment will take up space on your recipient's hard drive. Don't send an attachment unless you are requested to do so or have otherwise cleared the matter in advance. When you receive a file that has an attachment, you'll see an icon informing you that the message contains more than text alone.

It's courteous to compress the attached file so that it doesn't take so long to download. Again, check with the recipients to see whether they'd like to get a compressed file, and if so, which compression program you should use. If you're sending the attachment to a Microsoft Windows user, compress the file using WinZip, the standard compression utility for Windows (see **http://www.winzip.com**).

Bear in mind that your recipients may not be able to use the attachment if they're using a different type of computer or don't have the program that created the attached file.

MANAGING EMAIL

Many email users quickly become overwhelmed by the number of messages they receive. It's not unusual, even for college students, to get dozens or even hundreds of messages per day. Here's how to handle the deluge.

Organizing Your Mail

Most email programs enable you to create your own mail folders. For example, you could create folders for each of the classes you're taking. In each folder, you can store mail from the teacher, as well as from other students in the same class. You could create another folder to store mail from your family.

If you're trying to find a message in a lengthy message list, remember that you can sort the mail in different ways. By default, your email program probably sorts mail in the order the messages were received. You can sort also by sender or recipient, and some programs give you even more ways to sort. With Microsoft Outlook Express, you can quickly sort messages by clicking one of the buttons at the top of the message list. For example, to sort messages by date, click the "Received" button. Click it again to sort the list in the opposite order.

Still can't find a message? Most email programs provide Find commands, which enable you to search for information in the header. The best programs enable you to also search for text in the message body. To search for a message with Outlook Express, click the "Find" button and choose the search options you want in the "Find Messages" dialog box.

Filtering Incoming Mail

After you have created mail folders, you may want to create **filters** that automatically route the incoming mail to one of these folders. A filter is a rule that tells the program what to do with incoming mail, such as this one: "If the incoming message contains 'CS110' in the subject line, move the message to the Computer Science 110 folder." With the leading email programs, it's easy to write filters by making choices in dialog boxes.

To create a filter in Outlook Express, click "Tools" on the menu bar, point to "Message Rules," and choose "Mail" from the popup menu. You'll see the "Message Rules" dialog box. Click "New" to create a new rule. You'll then see the "New Mail Rule" dialog box. In this dialog box, select the condition for the rule. For example, suppose you want to filter messages containing specific words in the subject line, such as "Student Council." To create a filter for such messages, check "Where the Subject Line Contains Specific Words." You'll see the new rule's text in the "Rule Description" area. To tell the program which words to look for, click the blue highlighted text, which says "contains specific words." In the dialog box that appears, type the words to search for, such as "Student Council," and click OK. The rule now says, "Where the subject line contains Student Council." In the "Select the Actions for Your Rule" area, check the action you want performed. For example, to move the message to a mailbox called Student Council, check "Move It to the Specified Folder." In the "Rule Description" area, type the blue text and choose the folder to which you want the message moved. When you're done, type a name for the rule, and click OK.

SPOTLIGHT

SPAM: CAN IT BE STOPPED?

▶Many email users receive unsolicited email advertising (called spam). This mail is sent by spammers, businesses that specialize in sending such mail. Spammers believe that they are only doing what direct marketing mail firms do: sending legitimate advertising. But they do not acknowledge a crucial difference between unsolicited postal advertising and spam. In postal advertising, the advertiser pays for the postage. In spam, the recipient pays the postage, in the form of Internet access fees. According to a coalition of Internet service providers, every Internet user is paying an average of $2 per month in additional fees because of costs directly attributable to the activities of spammers.

Most Internet users detest spam, and some find it so annoying that they stop using the Internet. For businesses, spam is a costly nuisance. On several occasions, spams of a gigantic scale have overwhelmed mail servers, resulting in impaired service for legitimate, paying customers.

Chances are that little or nothing of worth is being peddled: pornographic Web sites, phony get-rich-quick scams, bogus stock deals, rip-off work-at-home schemes, health and diet scams, and merchandise of questionable quality.

Can you filter out spam? You can try. Most spam, however, originates from a new account, which is almost immediately closed down after the service provider receives hundreds of thousands of outraged complaints. The spammer just moves on to a new account.

Don't reply to spam or request to be "removed" from a spammer's mailing list. All you accomplish is verifying that your email address is valid. A mailing list consisting of validated addresses is much more valuable than a "dirty" list, so all that will happen is that you'll get even more spam.

Increasingly, there are efforts to persuade legislatures—at both the state and Federal levels—to pass laws against spam. However, the Direct Marketing Association (DMA) believes that the appropriate solution is an "opt-out" system, in which spammed email users can request that the sender remove their names from the mailing list. Unfortunately, that's just what email users have been trained not to do, out of fear that they'll receive even more spam than before. In addition, efforts to outlaw spam run afoul of free speech guarantees under the U.S. Constitution's First Amendment, which applies to businesses as well as individuals. States that attempt to outlaw spam, as Washington did, may find that their laws are thrown out of court because they inhibit interstate commerce. But there's hope. Under consideration at this writing is a Congressional measure that would give Internet service providers the right to sue spammers for violating their spam policies.

For now, there's one thing to count on: if you haven't been spammed yet, you will be.

MAILING LISTS

As you explore the world of email, you will probably join one or more mailing lists, an email application that enables people to send messages to everyone who has subscribed to the list. Mailing lists are made possible by **list servers** (also called **reflectors**), programs that automatically send a copy of every submitted message to every subscriber's address. Topically-oriented mailing lists exist on every conceivable subject. For example, you may find that one of your classes has a mailing list that enables the students and teacher to continue their conversation outside of class.

Subscribing to a Mailing List

To join a mailing list, you must subscribe. To do so, you need to get specific instructions from the list's human administrator. (You may find this information on the mailing list's Web page.) Generally, subscribing involves sending an email message to the **list server's address** and including the word *subscribe* in the message's body, followed by the name of the mailing list and your name. You'll receive a confirmation message if everything goes well. (If not, you'll receive an error message indicating what you did wrong.)

Participating in a Mailing List

After subscribing to the mailing list, you'll start getting a lot of mail, which you should place in a folder. Open one of the messages and examine the "From:" line, which contains the mailing list's email address. Then write a filter that says, "If the incoming message contains the mailing list's email address, move it to the mailing list's folder." You'll have to fill in the specifics, but this is easy to do.

To reply to a mailing list message, just reply as you would normally. Sometimes, the reply goes to only the author. Most often, though, your reply goes to everyone. Check with the list's administrator if you're unsure who gets replies.

To send a new message to the list, compose a new message addressed to the **mailing list address.** Note that this differs from the list server address. For example, the list server address for the CS110 mailing list might be **majordomo@yourcollege.edu,** but the mailing list address might be **cs110@yourcollege.edu.**

Unsubscribing

If you no longer want to participate in the mailing list, please don't post a message to the list asking people to remove you from the list. This is unpopular with mailing list members, and you may get flames (angry letters) from some of them. Instead, find the mailing list's instructions and find out how to unsubscribe. Generally, you need to send mail to the list server with the word *unsubscribe*, followed by the name of the mailing list, in the message's body.

USING EMAIL RESPONSIBLY

Email cuts both ways. It's indispensable, but it can also get people in a lot of trouble.

Using Email at Work

Bear in mind that you have no right of privacy for your email when you're using your employer's computer system. Although your employer may not say so, every message you send might be read by another employee who alerts management if anything's amiss. You'll soon be packing your desk if you make fun of your boss, disclose inside information to competitors, threaten or harass other employees, or tell obscene or insulting jokes.

Be aware that email messages come across more harshly than spoken words. Never hide behind email to reprimand or criticize someone, as it will come across too harshly. Summon the courage to do so face-to-face. This is tough for people who don't like conflict, but there's no excuse for hiding behind email's facade. Don't use sarcasm because people might take you literally. Some email users like to use **smileys** (also called **emoticons**) to show that they're just joking, but some people do not believe that smileys are appropriate in business messages.

Backup Tapes

You should also be aware that most organizations keep backup copies of email, sometimes for several years. Even after you've deleted the messages from your machine, a copy is on a backup tape somewhere. If you get pulled into a lawsuit, attorneys can obtain copies of your email and bring these into the courtroom as evidence. The result could be a civil judgment against you for sexual harassment, defamation, discrimination, or disclosure of trade secrets.

Additional Risks

Don't fall for pyramid scams, which entice you to make money from new member's enrollment fees. These illegal schemes inevitably collapse, leaving "investors" with no returns while the originators flee to the Bahamas. Also, don't fall for email hoaxes, which are very common. You may receive a letter warning people not to open a message called "Join the Crew" or "Party Time" because doing so unleashes a virus that destroys your hard disk. This isn't possible: email messages can't do this. (Attachments, however, can contain computer viruses. It's the attachment you shouldn't open.) If you fall for the hoax and send a warning message to others, you'll look like a fool.

How to Stay Out of Trouble

To avoid email problems, follow these simple rules:

- Do not use your company's email for personal use. For personal email, get your own Internet account and access your personal mail only from home.

- Never respond to junk email (spam).

- Never use email to harass or intimidate anyone.

- When you are using your company's email system, never say anything in any email message unless you would be pleased and proud if your boss read it, because there's a chance your boss *will* read it!

Destinations

For an update on the latest email and other Internet hoaxes, see the U.S. Department of Energy's Internet Hoaxes page (**http://ciac.llnl. gov/ciac/CIACHoaxes. html**). The page is maintained by the Computer Incident Advisory Capability team. Also see Rob Rosenberger's Computer Virus Myths page, located at **http:// www.kumite.com/myths**.

IMPACTS

Is the Internet Bad for Your Mental Health?

The evidence discovered from a recent study seems clear enough: the more time interview subjects spent on the Internet, the less time they spent with family and friends. The study, conducted by researchers at Stanford University, examined the impact of Internet use on the way families spend their time. What's far from clear is the deeper question: Is Internet usage healthy?

According to an early study of the Internet's impact on mental health, it may be very unhealthy. Researchers at Carnegie-Mellon University were surprised to find that people who spent even a few hours per week on the Internet experienced higher levels of depression and loneliness than those who did not. These people interacted with other Internet users online, but this interaction seems to have been much shallower than the time formerly spent with friends and family. The result? According to these researchers, Internet use leads to unhealthy social isolation and a deadened, mechanized experience that is lacking in human emotion.

Still, there are conflicting studies—and one of them suggests an entirely-opposite conclusion. In a study of 3,533 adults, researchers at the Pew Internet and American Life project found that frequent Internet users visited family members more often, had more supportive social networks, and reported fewer feelings of social isolation than non-Internet users.

Why the difference in results? The answer may lie in the way the studies were conducted. Carnegie-Mellon researchers gave computers and Internet connections to the families they studied—and these families had never used the Internet before. Internet users often say that, during the first few months of Internet use, they spent far too much time online. After a while, they figured out that although the Internet is great, it isn't *that* great, and reduced the amount of their usage. In contrast, the Pew study interviewed experienced Internet users who had successfully integrated Internet use into their lives. For many, an advantage is email's ability to help family members keep in touch with each other. Nearly 60 percent of the women interviewed, and 44 percent of the men, said that email helped them communicate and keep in better touch with family members.

For some Internet users, there's a more serious danger than social isolation: addiction. According to a University of Florida study, Internet addiction can be just as serious as an addiction to drugs and alcohol. The study examined nearly a dozen men and women who spent up to 30 hours per week online during non-working hours. Several were flunking out of school, others were carrying out affairs that would lead to family break-ups, and still others were on the verge of losing their jobs. Another study indicated that nearly 200,000 U.S. Internet users were addicted to Internet porn sites and X-rated chat rooms.

According to psychologists who are increasingly concerned with this phenomenon, Internet addicts lie to their families about their usage, become devious and aggressive, lose sleep, and engage in compulsive and sometimes illegal activities, such as searching for online pornography at work. As many as 6 to 7 percent of all Internet users may be experiencing some form of addiction. Treatment for Internet addiction involves counseling, time management training, and attention to the underlying problem from which the addict is trying to escape.

TAKEAWAY POINTS

- People are increasingly turning to email in place of first class letters.
- Email servers work in the background, handling tasks such as receiving your mail from the Internet and sending your messages. You use an email client to send and receive messages.
- An email address has three parts: the mailbox name, the "at" symbol (@), and the server address.
- The two leading messaging protocols are Post Office Protocol, or POP (where you download messages to your computer), and Internet Message Access Protocol, or IMAP (where you keep your messages on the server).
- In your email client program's window, you'll see a folder list (containing an inbox, a sent mail folder, and a deleted mail folder), a message list, and a message window. When you select a folder, the message list shows the folder's contents. Similarly, when you select a message in the message list, the message window shows the message's content.
- Be careful when you reply to messages. If you click "Reply to All" instead of "Reply to Author," you may send your message to two or more recipients without realizing it.
- When you compose messages, be sure to use a descriptive but brief subject line.
- Before you send an attachment, discuss your plans with the recipient.
- To cope with email overload, create folders and write filters that route the mail to these folders.
- Do not use company email for personal purposes, and don't say anything in an email message that could get you or your company into trouble.

MODULE REVIEW

KEY TERMS AND CONCEPTS

alias
at sign (@)
attachment
binary files
bounce message
default folders
digital signature
email client, or user agent
email server
executable file
filters
flame
folder list

free email service
group email address
header
inbox
Internet Message Access
    Protocol (IMAP)
list servers, or reflectors
list server's address
macro viruses
mailbox name
mailing list address
message list
message window

Multipurpose Internet Mail
    Extensions (MIME)
Post Office Protocol (POP)
protocols
public encryption key
quote
server address
Simple Mail Transport Protocol
    (SMTP)
smileys, or emoticons
standalone email clients
user name

TRUE/FALSE

Indicate whether the following statements are true or false.

1. An email client runs on your Internet service provider's computer.

2. An alias is an additional name by which you can refer to your email address.

3. SMTP is an acronym for Sensible Mail Transfer Protocol.

4. If you allow someone access to your email password, he or she can read your email or send email using your name.

5. In an email client, a message list shows the messages contained in a folder.

6. It is not important to fill in the subject line on your outgoing email messages.

7. Email attachments can contain any type of computer file you would like to send.

8. A filter is a rule that tells an email client what to do with incoming mail.

9. Another name for a list server is a refractor.

10. Your email is private and protected by law under all circumstances.

MATCHING

Match each key term from the left column to the most accurate definition in the right column.

_____ 1. email server

_____ 2. email client

_____ 3. mailbox name

_____ 4. user name

_____ 5. Multipurpose Internet Mail Extensions

_____ 6. inbox

_____ 7. list server

_____ 8. message list

_____ 9. message window

_____ 10. server address

a. the name you supply when you log onto your email account

b. a program that automatically sends a copy of every submitted message to every mailing list subscriber's address

c. an area that shows a list of the messages a folder contains

d. the Internet address of the user's mail server

e. the area where you see the contents of a message

f. the first part of an email address that identifies the user

g. a method which specifies ways to send binary files as attachments to an email message

h. software that runs on your Internet service provider's computer

i. software that runs on your computer

j. area that displays your new mail as well as older messages that haven't been deleted or moved

MULTIPLE CHOICE

Circle the letter of the correct choice for each of the following.

1. Which of the following is another name for an email client?
   a. word processor
   b. database
   c. user agent
   d. email agent

2. What are the three parts of an email address?
   a. user id, at sign, and ISP
   b. mailbox name, at sign, and server address
   c. alias, at sign, and Web site
   d. mailbox name, at sign, and ISP

3. Which of the following is not a common protocol used for email systems?
   a. MIME
   b. SMTP
   c. POP
   d. JPEG

4. Which of the following is not a standard part of most email client user interfaces?
   a. postage account
   b. folder list
   c. message list
   d. message window

5. Which toolbar button in many email clients allows you to send a message back to the author and all other recipients of an original message?
   a. Broadcast
   b. Forward
   c. Reply to All
   d. Reply to Author

6. When you install your email program on your computer, you'll be asked to supply which of the following information.
   a. POP3 or IMAP server
   b. SMTP server
   c. list server address
   d. a and b

7. If you want to subscribe to a mailing list, you need to send an email message to which of the following?
   a. mailing list address
   b. administrator's address
   c. list server's address
   d. user's address

8. Which among the following do most email programs enable you to create?
   a. mail folders
   b. default folders
   c. backup tapes
   d. inboxes

9. In email terminology, what is a flame?
   a. a steamy message from an ardent admirer
   b. a message of support
   c. your high school sweetheart
   d. an angry message

10. Which of the following should you be careful about when working with email?
    a. filters
    b. list servers
    c. junk email
    d. default folders

FILL-IN

In the blank provided, write the correct answer for each of the following.

1. To use email, you need two software components called an email _____ and an email _____.

2. _____ are Web-based companies that enable you to send and receive email using a Web browser.

3. The _____ Protocol uses a server to store your incoming messages temporarily.

4. The _____ Protocol specifies how servers should send and receive plain-text messages across the Internet.

5. _____ folders include an inbox folder, sent mail folder, and deleted mail folder.

6. A(n) _____ address might include dozens of people or even an entire company.

7. _____ automatically route incoming mail to a particular folder.

8. A(n) _____ is a file containing a program that can run on your computer.

9. Mailing lists are made possible by _____.

10. Some people like to use _____ in their email to indicate an emotion.

SHORT ANSWER

On a separate sheet of paper, answer the following questions.

1. What are the parts of an email address, and what does each part do?

2. What are the different protocols used by email services?

3. Discuss the pros and cons of a Web-based email account as opposed to a regular email account.

4. What are the major features of an email client program's user interface?

5. Discuss the considerations you should make when sending attachments with your email.

6. Discuss the ways in which you can manage your email.

7. Discuss the purpose and benefits of mailing lists.

8. After you subscribe to a mailing list, how can you participate?

9. What precautions should you take when using email at work?

10. What commonsense steps can you take to stay out of trouble when using email?

7D

MODULE

CREATING A WEB PAGE

WHAT YOU WILL LEARN . . .

When you have finished reading this module, you will be able to:

1. Describe each step of the Web publishing process.
2. Describe the overall types of elements in HTML.
3. List the various tools for creating HTML.
4. Create a simple Web page with a background color or graphic, headings, text paragraphs, bulleted lists, hyperlinks and graphics.
5. Describe how Extensible Markup Language (XML) works and describe its advantages.

One reason for the Web's popularity lies in its democracy. Unlike "couch potato" media, users can originate content as well as consume it. Thanks to HTML, it's easy to create a simple Web page. While you're a student, you may want to create and publish a simple page to share your interests with others or make your résumé available to potential employers. After graduation, you'll find that employers will find your Web publishing skills an attractive item on your résumé. As you learned in Module 7A, companies with intranets are saving big money by distributing content-creation tasks throughout the enterprise. In this module, you'll learn how to create your own simple Web page using HTML.

THE WEB PUBLISHING PROCESS

To create a Web page, follow these steps:

Explore IT Lab

Building a Web Page

- **Define your purpose**   Begin by deciding why you want to publish your page. With a clear purpose, you will know what to include.

- **Define your audience**   After you've defined your purpose, you should define your audience. To whom are you addressing your message? How can you design your page so that your audience will appreciate your efforts?

- **Choose an HTML editor**   You can choose from a variety of programs to create your HTML page.

- **Make design decisions**   You can develop a look for your page and decide how and where you want material to appear.

- **Create your page**   In this step, you will create your page and add HTML.

- **Test your page**   To make sure your coding is correct, you can examine how your page looks by opening it with a Web browser.

- **Publish your page**   Most Web authors publish their page by placing it in the Web publishing directories of an Internet service provider. To send your page to the directory created for your use, use FTP.

The following sections show you how to follow these steps to create a simple Web page.

DEFINING YOUR PURPOSE

To communicate effectively, you should begin with a clear sense of purpose. As a student publishing a simple Web page, you can choose from a variety of purposes:

- **Making friends**   If you're attending a large college or university, it's hard to find people who share your interests. A Web page listing your interests and contact information may attract the interest of kindred spirits.

- **Making a point**   If you want to get your word out about a social or political issue that you care deeply about, the Web's a great place to do it.

- **Collecting links**   Have you performed some research on the Internet, only to find that no single page groups all the links on a specialized topic? Give something back to the Web by providing such a page.

SPOTLIGHT

A TRUE PUBLISHING STORY

▶The success of the Internet has caused many traditional businesses to reevaluate their perceptions of the world and their place in it. The reason for this is that it doesn't matter on the Internet whether you are large or small; it matters only how well you meet the needs of your customers.

Publishing is one such traditional industry where great changes are taking place. In the past, publishing has been a relatively-expensive business. In contrast, information can be published on the Internet to a vast array of consumers in just a matter of minutes and at a low cost.

One online publishing success story involves Randy Cassingham, a Colorado writer and humorist. Randy publishes a weekly email newsletter called *This is True* (**http://www.ThisisTrue.com**). Begun in 1994, the newsletter now reaches over 150,000 people in over 145 countries around the world. His electronic publishing efforts have led to four printed books and a syndicated weekly column in newspapers in four countries. He now makes a comfortable living through the newsletter, the books, and his speaking engagements.

Randy's newsletter is sent each weekend via email. He uses mailing list software to maintain his huge list of subscribers and to take care of sending out the newsletters automatically. People can visit his Web site or send email commands that allow them to automatically maintain their subscription.

This is True is nothing but plain text. It does not contain fancy graphics, sounds, or videos. Instead, Randy focuses completely on content. His audience eats it up. Each story he reports focuses on the bizarre and absurd in the real world. He scours news articles from scores of publications and wire services to find the eight or nine stories he writes about each week. One week he may be writing about inept burglars in Australia, while the next week a different story highlights the antics of politicians in a small town. The stories are all true (Randy will not publish stories simply on hearsay). He also stays clear of stories that only find their outlet in the weekly tabloids. He finishes each story with a one-line zinger that provides pointed commentary on the wacky world in which we live.

None of Randy's writing has a moralistic tone, nor does he take sides in political issues. He has been accused of being a conservative by liberals and a liberal by conservatives. Randy takes equal delight in shining a spotlight on the ludicrous activity all around us—regardless of the source.

The story of how Randy developed his small publishing empire is interesting. An aerospace worker in Southern California, Randy began *This is True* by writing commentary about news articles for a few friends. He sent his comments out by email and received a positive response. He officially began publishing in June, 1994. Within four months, he had over 10,000 subscribers, each anxious to hear Randy's witty take on the news of the day. He quit his day job in 1996 and moved to Colorado where his company, Freelance Communications, now focuses fully on *This is True.*

A subscription to *This is True* is free. Randy subsidizes his writing efforts through the sales of books that compile the content of the newsletters and from the sales of a single advertisement that appears in each issue. He also offers a premium subscription to *This is True* that provides twice as many stories to subscribers each week.

Randy is not alone in using the Internet to reach an online audience, nor is *This is True* the only newsletter being distributed via email. He is, however, one of the most successful. New online publishers are springing up every week, and the market for online newsletters is growing rapidly. Randy Cassingham, and publishers like him, represent a new type of publisher that we will see more of in the future.

- **Recruiting members for a campus organization** The Web is an ideal tool to get the word out about your club's activities.

- **Publishing your résumé** The Web's a good place to make your résumé available to prospective employers.

You may think of additional purposes, but bear one point in mind: a Web page should express just one purpose. The most-effective pages on the Web accomplish one well-defined goal. The least-effective ones try to accomplish too many goals or show very little thinking concerning the page's purpose.

Before you create your page, check with your college or university's information technology center to find out what types of Web pages students may publish. Every organization has **acceptable use policies (AUPs)** that specify appropriate uses of campus computing facilities. Make sure your objectives fit the guidelines; if you're not sure, ask.

DEFINING YOUR AUDIENCE: WHO'S READING YOUR PAGE?

After you define your purpose, you need to consider who will read your page. Your conception of audience affects what you'll say, how you say it, and how your page will look. For example, youth-oriented language and graphics are more appropriate for an audience of students than of prospective employers.

INTRODUCING HTML

As its name indicates, HTML is a **markup language.** A markup language defines how you insert special symbols into text so that the text can be processed by the computer. These symbols, called **tags,** surround a unit of text and define it in a certain way. For example, the <h1> tag defines the text that follows as a major heading (level 1 heading). To show the computer where the heading text stops, you insert a second tag, called a **close tag.** For level 1 heading, the close tag is </h1>. The slash mark indicates that the markup stops at that point.

A markup language is different from a programming language. A programming language tells the computer what to do. In contrast, a markup language tells the computer what a unit of text is. For example, the <h1> tag declares the following text to be a heading. For this reason, markup languages are part of a larger class of languages called **declarative languages.**

Markup languages such as HTML are designed to work on any computer platform (for this reason, they are called **cross-platform standards**). The text is ordinary ASCII text (or text conforming to an established international standard character set). The markup consists of nothing but standard punctuation symbols, such as greater-than (>) and less-than (<) signs. For this reason, marked-up text can be displayed and processed on any computer.

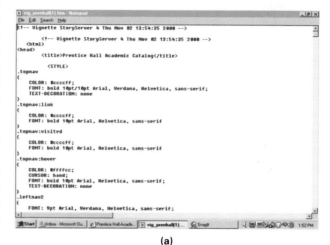

(a)

(b)

Content vs. Structure

In HTML and all markup languages, there is a basic distinction between **content** and **structure.** The term content refers to the *text* of the document. The term structure refers to the *parts* of the document, such as the title, headings, paragraphs, lists, and tables. HTML markup is used to identify the document's structure. The HTML is needed because the computer cannot otherwise tell the difference between parts of the document, such as the difference between a heading and an ordinary paragraph of text.

Web browsers are programmed to read HTML tags (see Figure 7D.1a). When a Web browser encounters the <title> tag, the program displays the text between the <title> tag and the </title> tag in a special area, usually the browser's title bar. The browser is programmed to detect and display the

Figure   7D.1

(a) A Web browser detects the HTML markup, formats the elements using its default settings, and (b) displays the page on-screen.

rest of the tags that are part of the standard HTML language, which is maintained by the **World Wide Web Consortium (W3C).** Headquartered in Cambridge, Mass., the W3C is an independent, international consortium of university scholars, technical experts, and Internet vendors that specifies standards which promote the growth of the Web.

Structure vs. Presentation

There's one additional general point to learn about HTML. When you mark up a document with HTML, you are supposed to be defining structure, but not the way that the structure will be *presented* by the Web browser when the document is displayed. For example, when you use the <h1> tag, a tag for major headings within a document, you are telling the browser that the text that follows is a heading, but you don't tell the browser anything about how to *display* the heading. Most browsers display major headings using a larger font and boldfaced type, but that's up to the browser.

To be sure, many Web authors can't restrain themselves from trying to use HTML to specify presentation. For example, the following HTML code displays a heading with centered, blinking text:

```
<blink> <center> <h1> Get Rich Fast!
</h1> </center> </blink>
```

As you can see, the above HTML is complicated—in fact, it's a mess, and it's a very expensive and tedious job to revise a document with such messy code. This is one very good reason to keep the structure and presentation separate. Another good reason: some people viewing the Web have limited vision. They need to define the way tags look so that they can see them more clearly.

Still, Web authors want to create good-looking pages with an attractive design. For this reason, the World Wide Web Consortium developed **Cascading Style Sheets (CSS),** another markup language that provides a way to define the presentation styles of the tags in a document. CSS provides a way to include or attach a **style sheet** to a Web document. A style sheet is a list of elements that includes specific presentation information for each, such as font, font size, font color, text alignment, and indentation.

Why don't style sheets violate the rule that Web authors should avoid including presentation information? Because CSS separates the presentation markup from the structural markup. All the CSS markup goes in special tags, a certain area within the document, or in a separate document altogether. Because the CSS information is kept separate, users can choose to ignore the CSS information if they wish. They can also substitute their own style sheet. People with limited vision use special style sheets that enlarge document fonts and increase color contrast.

HTML Markup vs. Word Processing Formats

In some ways, using HTML is like using a word processing program to format your document. Both can be used to shape the document's on-screen layout. Both use hidden codes to define the formats you choose. However, there are important differences. A word processing program's hidden codes focus on presentation—how the document should appear when displayed and printed. Also, a word processing program's codes are **proprietary,** which means that they are defined and copyrighted by the company which publishes the software. In addition, word processing codes are not designed to function in a cross-platform environment the way HTML is. If you create a Microsoft Word document, you can open that document on another platform only if a Word-compatible program is available. With HTML, your document is accessible on any computer that can run a browser.

Destinations

Visit the W3C's home page at **http://www. w3.com.** You'll find the latest news about Web standards, including HTML, and information about the issues facing the Web.

Introducing HTML Elements

In HTML terms, a document is made up of **elements,** which are portions of a document's structure such as titles, headings, lists, or paragraphs. Elements are defined by marking them up with tags.

There are two overall types of elements:

- **Block elements**   A block element defines a paragraph constructed broadly (including headings, lists, and ordinary text paragraphs). Browsers insert a blank line before a block element.

- **Inline elements**   An inline element defines a character style, such as bold or italic, or some other element that fits within a line.

Whether you're talking about block or inline elements, they both consist of some or all of the following components:

- **Start tag**   All elements begin with a start tag. The start tag is formed by typing a left angle bracket (<), the element name, and a right angle bracket (>). The tag may include one or more attributes, separated by a space.

- **Element name**   This is a code name such as <title> or <h2>. To make your HTML easier to read, you may want to type element names in uppercase.

- **Attributes**   Some elements enable you—or require you—to specify additional information. For example, the <img> element enables you to insert a graphic in your document. The <img> element's src attribute enables you to specify where the graphic is stored.

- **Value**   Most attributes require a **value,** which is usually surrounded by quotation marks and preceded by an equals sign (for example, src="portrait.jpg" specifies the image source and gives the filename).

- **Content**   Every element that accepts content has a **content model** that specifies what types of data can be included. It also specifies which tags can go within the element. For example, the <head> element cannot contain text—it can only contain tags, such as <title>. The <title> element, on the other hand, can contain text. Generally, you can include elements as well as text within the element. **Empty elements** do not accept any content. An example is the <br> element, which introduces a line break.

- **End tag**   The end tag repeats the element name. It surrounds the name with angle brackets, like a start tag, but also has a slash mark that comes after the first angle bracket (for example, </title>). This tells the browser when it has reached the end of the element.

The following example illustrates how these components look:

```
<h2 align="center">This is the element's content</h2>
```

Here's an explanation:

- **<h2>**   This is the start tag for a level two heading.

- **align = "center"**   This is an attribute. It governs the alignment of the title text. Here, the value is set to center and is surrounded by quotation marks. Note that the attribute fits within the start tag (<h2 align="center">).

- **This is the element's content**   The browser shows this text using the formatting it's programmed to display when it encounters an h2 heading, except that it takes the attribute align = "center" into account.

- **</h2>**   This is the end tag.

Destinations

Once you've created your Web page, you can get started with Cascading Style Sheets (CSS) with Eric Meyer's "Creating Your First Style Sheet," located at **http:// webreview.com/97/ 10/10/style/index.html.**

Destinations

For more information on the campaign to keep Web standards non-proprietary, visit the Web Standards Project (**http://www.web standards.org**), and Project Cool (**http://www. projectcool.com**).

Tools for Creating HTML

To create a Web page using HTML, you can choose from the following:

- **Text editors**   These are simple programs that enable you to enter and edit text. Most computers come with one. Windows computers come with NOTEPAD.EXE; Macs come with SimpleText. You can use these programs to write both your content and the HTML tags. The good thing about text editors is that you get total control over how the HTML is entered. The bad things are that you get no help and usually no spell checker.

- **Word processing programs**   Generally, it isn't a good idea to use a word processing program to create HTML files because these programs save text using proprietary file formats. These file formats won't work with most Web browsers (although recent versions of Microsoft Internet Explorer can read Microsoft Word files). The latest generation of word processing programs, however, enables you to save your work in HTML. Microsoft Word 2000, for example, works like a WYSIWYG editor for HTML pages as well as a word processing program.

- **HTML editors**   These are text editors with additional features designed to aid the HTML coding process. For example, they enable you to click the tags you want to enter, and then put them in your document automatically. The better ones include spelling checkers, as well as giving you a way to preview your document's appearance to see the way it will look on the Web. Many people create their Web documents using these programs. (Examples include HomeSite, Hot Dog Professional, and HTML Editor for the Macintosh.)

- **WYSIWYG editors**   These programs enable you to create HTML documents without typing any HTML tags. Instead, you create your document using word-processing-type commands, and see your document on-screen the way it will look on the Web. Examples include Netscape Page Composer (for Windows and Mac OS systems) and Microsoft FrontPage Express (for Windows systems).

- **Site managers**   These programs combine WYSIWYG editors with tools for managing multidocument Web sites. They are expensive and designed for the management of large or commercial Web sites. Examples include NetObjects Fusion (for Mac OS and Windows) and Microsoft FrontPage.

When you're learning HTML, it's a good idea to create your first pages by coding HTML directly. You can use a text or HTML editor for this purpose. By doing so, you'll grasp how HTML works, and you won't feel intimidated should you need to go into a coded page to make a correction. Later, you can use a WYSIWYG editor to code your pages more quickly. However, you'll probably find, as do most professional Web authors, that it's often necessary to get into the HTML code to solve a problem or add something that the WYSIWYG editor doesn't support. That's why it's smart to begin with a bit of direct HTML coding.

MAKING DESIGN DECISIONS

Your first design decision involves whether you'll create a presentation involving a single page or a welcome page that links to several subordinate pages. To make this decision, consider whether you can fit everything you want to say on one page. Generally, it's best to keep Web pages to a length of no more than two or three screenfuls, assuming people are viewing your pages on a 15-inch monitor with 800 by 600 resolution. (Sometimes it's justifiable to create lengthier pages, particularly when the material is unified and people want to print it out without hassles.)

Next, choose a look for your page. You can either choose a **background color** or a **background graphic.** Whichever you choose, be sure to use the same color or graphic on all pages of your presentation. This helps to give your presentation thematic unity. Also be aware that some colors and graphics make the text hard to read. Note that browsers **tile** background graphics so that they fill all the available background space. For this reason, you can use a small background graphic that contains a color or a pattern, and it will fill the entire background.

CREATING YOUR PAGE

In this section, you will learn how to create a simple HTML page. You can follow along by typing the examples as they're given. To prepare your page by typing HTML tags directly, you can use a text editor (such as the Windows Notepad) or an HTML editor. You'll also find instructions for preparing your page with Microsoft FrontPage Express, an easy-to-use WYSIWYG editor that is often installed with Microsoft Windows. Even if you go the WYSIWYG route, you'll find that it's helpful to understand the essentials of the underlying HTML code.

Choosing Your HTML Editor

If you would like to try entering HTML tags directly, you can use a text editor such as Microsoft's Notepad utility. The advantage of using a text editor is that this type of program automatically saves your document in plain (ASCII) text, which is required for Web publishing. If you use a word processing program, make sure you know how to save your file in plaintext. Save your work using the extension .htm or .html. Once you've created and saved the HTML document you write, you can use your browser's Open command (accessible on the File menu) to open and display the document.

Should you prefer to create your HTML page with a WYSIWYG editor (such as Microsoft FrontPage Express), there's no need to open the page in a Web browser. These programs display the pages the same way a browser does.

Entering the Global Structure

Every HTML document has a **global structure,** which informs the browser that it has encountered an HTML document. Additionally, the global structure divides the document into two components:

- **Head**   The information nested within the <head> element doesn't appear in the browser window, although <title> text does appear in the window's title bar.

- **Body**   The text and markup within the <body> element appear in the browser window.

If you're typing HTML tags directly with a text editor such as the Windows Notepad utility, you'll need to enter the head and body tags manually. Text-oriented HTML editors usually insert them automatically when you open a new document. If you're using FrontPage Express, they're also entered automatically when you start the program, which automatically displays a new Web page with the global structure already started for you.

Here's what the global structure looks like:

```
<html>
    <head>
        <title> Your document's title goes here</title>
    </head>
    <body>
    </body>
</html>
```

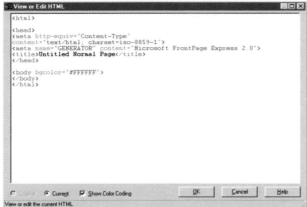

Figure 7D.2

Although FrontPage Express enables you to work with your Web page in a WYSIWYG environment, you can also display and directly edit the underlying HTML, if you wish.

If you're using an HTML editor or WYSIWYG program such as FrontPage Express, the global structure is entered automatically—but it may look slightly different. For example, FrontPage Express adds a few extra META tags that indicate the character set being used and the name of the program that created the page. To see the underlying HTML code that FrontPage Express enters, click "View" on the menu bar, and choose HTML. You'll see the View or Edit HTML window as shown in Figure 7D.2.

As the global structure shows, you can **nest** HTML elements. For example, the <title> element is nested in the <head>. Some elements can't be nested in certain areas, though. Notice how the indentations capture the nesting structure. For example, the <head> and <body> elements are nested in the HTML element (that's why they're indented). The <title> element is nested in the <head> element, and it's indented even more to show this. If you're typing HTML directly, use indents so that your HTML will be easier to proofread.

Defining the Head

For a simple HTML document, the only <head> element you'll use is the <title> element. This element's content appears on the browser's title bar. Choose your title carefully so that it describes your document well. Search engines give this text high priority for retrieval purposes. Here's what the code looks like after adding some text. In this example and the following ones, the newly-added or altered sections are marked in bold, so you can see what has been changed or added.

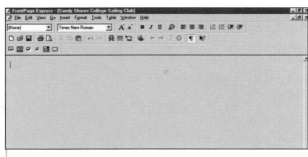

The <title> element's content appears on the browser's title bar.

```
<html>
    <head>
        <title>Sandy Shores College
        Sailing Club</title>
    </head>
    <body>
    </body>
</html>
```

To define a title for a FrontPage Express document, click "File" on the menu bar, and choose "Page Properties." In the "Page Properties" dialog box, click the "General" tab, if necessary (see Figure 7D.3). In the Title area, type your page's title, and click OK.

Creating the Body

The <body> element contains the text and markup that will appear in the browser window. You can use headings, paragraphs, bulleted lists, and a signature element to quickly create a simple but effective Web page.

Adding a Background Color or Graphic

If you'd like to add a background color or graphic, you can do so by adding an attribute to the <body> element. Use one of the following:

- **Background color**   Use the bgcolor attribute to specify the color. To name the color, you can use one of the sixteen common color names (see Figure 7D.4). You can also use one of the 216 color codes (for a list, see Joe Burn's Hex and Word Colors Codes page located at **http://www.htmlgoodies.com/basic_cl.html**).

- **Background graphic**   If you've located a graphic that you would like to use as a background, include it using the background attribute and the name of the file you want to use. You must place the graphic file in the directory that contains your Web page.

The following example specifies a background color:

```
<body bgcolor = "white">
```

The following example specifies a background graphic:

```
<body background = "parchment.jpg">
```

To add a background color or graphic with FrontPage Express, click "File" on the menu bar, choose "Page Properties," and click the "Background" tab. Choose a background graphic or color, and click OK.

Be aware that adding a background color or graphic may make your text difficult or impossible to read. To change your text's color, you can use the <font> element to surround all the text in the <body> element, as in the following example:

```
<body bgcolor = "black">
<font color = "white">

(put all the <body> content here)

</font>
</body>
```

When you use the <font> element's color attribute, specify colors the same way you specify background colors: by using one of the sixteen names or one of the 216 color codes.

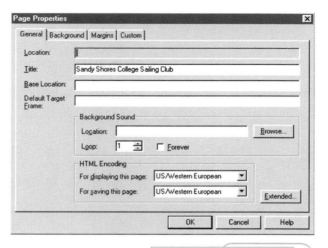

Figure 7D.3

Page Properties dialog box in FrontPage Express.

Aqua	Navy
Black	Olive
Blue	Purple
Fuschia	Red
Gray	Silver
Green	Teal
Lime	Yellow
Maroon	White

Figure 7D.4

Basic color names.

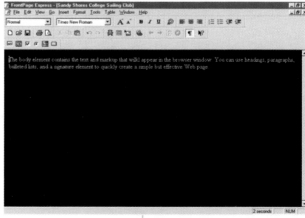

To change your text's color, you can use the <font> element to surround all the text in the <body> element.

Be aware that the use of the <font> tag and the bgcolor or background attributes is discouraged by the World Wide Web Consortium, which prefers that Web designers use CSS style sheets instead of adding presentation information to HTML.

Adding Headings

Many documents have headings and subheadings. HTML enables you to use up to six heading levels, although few Web authors use more than one or two. The top-level heading element (<h1>) generally appears in large, bold-faced type. In a document, this heading looks like the document's title. (Remember that the <title> element text appears on the browser's title bar, not in the browser window.) You can use the second-level element to divide the content in your document.

By adding the headings now, you can sketch out your page's overall structure. Here's an example:

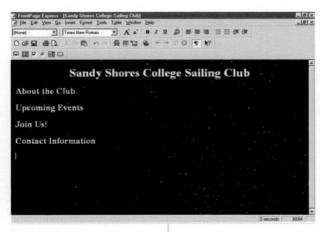

The page's overall structure.

```
<html>
    <head>
        <title>Sandy Shores College
        Sailing Club
        </title>
    </head>
    <body>
        <h1 align = "center"> Sandy
        Shores College Sailing
        Club</h1>
        <h2>About the Club</h2>
        <h2>Upcoming Events</h2>
        <h2>Join Us!</h2>
        <h2>Contact Information</h2>
    </body>
</html>
```

To add heading styles with FrontPage Express, click the down arrow in the style box, which is located on the Formatting toolbar, and choose the heading you want. You can choose from Heading 1 through Heading 7, which correspond to <h1> through <h7>.

Adding Text

Now is the time to add some text beneath your headings. Note the following:

- **Browsers ignore extra spaces** You can't format text (such as align text in columns) by pressing the spacebar. Browsers ignore any additional spaces you type and compress the text as if the spaces didn't exist.

- **Browsers ignore your line and paragraph breaks** To control line and paragraph breaks, you must use elements such as P and BR. You will learn about these in this section.

To create a paragraph of text, start the text with a <p> tag. (In the P element, the end tag is optional, but using it makes your document easier to proof-read.) When a browser encounters the P tag, it inserts a blank line in front of the paragraph. Here's an example:

```
<html>
     <head>
          <title>Sandy Shores College
          Sailing Club
          </title>
     </head>
     <body>
          <h1 align = "center" >
          Sandy Shores College Sailing
          Club</h1>

          <p>Welcome to the home page of
          the Sandy Shores College
          Sailing Club, a student
          organization designed to
          advance the sport of sailing
          in our beautiful bay. Members
          can use the club's Sunfish and
          Laser boats, participate in
          races, and enjoy our social
          events.</p>

          <h2>About the Club</h2>
          <h2>Upcoming Events</h2>
          <h2>Join Us!</h2>
          <h2>Contact Information</h2>
     </body>
</html>
```

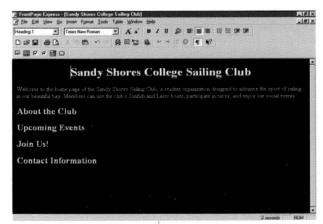

Creating a paragraph of text.

If you're using FrontPage Express, you start a new paragraph—and enter a P tag—by pressing Enter.

To start a new line without entering a blank line, use the BR element. If you're using FrontPage Express, you can start a new line by pressing Shift + Enter.

Adding a Bulleted List

Studies show that people don't like to read on the Web. Instead, they scan the screen for information they're looking for. You can aid them by breaking up the text so that the screen contains lots of white space and other visual cues for locating information. Bulleted lists (lists of items preceded by dots, called bullets) are a good way to make your page more readable.

To create a bulleted list, use the UL element. Within this element, you can include items by using the LI element. Browsers will supply the bullet automatically. Here's an example:

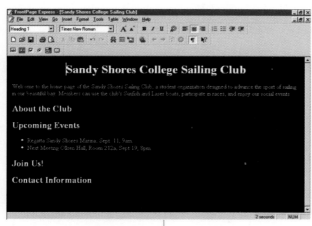

Creating a bulleted list.

```
<html>
    <head>
        <title>Sandy Shores College
        Sailing Club
        </title>
    </head>
    <body>
        <h1 align = "center" >Sandy
        Shores College Sailing
        Club</h1>

        <p>Welcome to the home page
        of the Sandy Shores College
        Sailing Club, a student
        organization designed to
        advance the sport of sailing
        in our beautiful bay. Members
        can use the club's Sunfish and
        Laser boats, participate in
        races, and enjoy our social
        events.</p>

        <h2>About the Club</h2>
        <h2>Upcoming Events</h2>

        <ul>
        <li>Regatta Sandy Shores
        Marina, Sept. 11, 9am. </li>
        <li>Next Meeting Ollsen Hall,
        Room 212a, Sept 19, 8pm.</li>
        </ul>

        <h2>Join Us!</h2>
        <h2>Contact Information</h2>
        </body>
</html>
```

To enter an unordered (bulleted) list with FrontPage Express, position the cursor where you want the list to appear, and click the "Bulleted List" button on the Formatting toolbar.

Adding Character Emphasis

You can use character emphases, such as bold or italic, to add more visual cues to your Web page. To add bold, use the B element. To add italics, use the I element. Both are inline elements, and you can place them within most block elements. In the following example, the words *Regatta* and *Next Meeting* have been emphasized in bold:

```html
<html>
    <head>
        <title>Sandy Shores College
        Sailing Club
        </title>
    </head>
    <body>
        <h1 align = "center" >
        Sandy Shores College Sailing
        Club</h1>

        <p>Welcome to the home page
        of the Sandy Shores College
        Sailing Club, a student
        organization designed to
        advance the sport of sailing
        in our beautiful bay. Members
        can use the club's Sunfish
        and Laser boats, participate
        in races, and enjoy our
        social events.</p>

        <h2>About the Club</h2>
        <h2>Upcoming Events</h2>

        <ul>
        <li><b>Regatta</b> Sandy
        Shores Marina, Sept. 11, 9am.
        <li><b>Next Meeting</b>
        Ollsen Hall, Room 212a, Sept
        19, 8pm.
        </ul>
    <h2>Join Us!</h2>
    <h2>Contact Information</h2>
    </body>
</html>
```

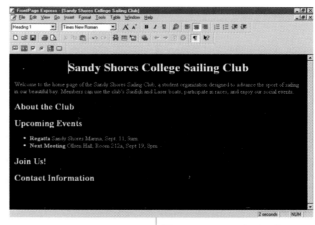

You can use character emphases such as bold or italics to add more visual cues to your Web page.

Adding character formatting to a FrontPage Express document is as easy as formatting a document with a word processing program. Just select the text you want to format, and click one of the character style buttons on the Formatting toolbar, such as "Bold" or "Italic."

Signing Your Page

To finish your page, be sure to sign it and provide contact information. Readers will also appreciate it if you include the date when you last modified the page. This will enable them to judge whether the information is up-to-date.

To sign your page, use the ADDRESS element, which is an inline element. Browsers generally format ADDRESS content using italics.

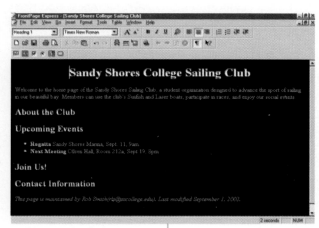

Be sure to sign your page and provide contact information. Readers will also appreciate it if you include the date you last modified the page.

```
<html>
    <head>
        <title>Sandy Shores College
        Sailing Club</title>
    </head>
    <body>
        <h1 align = "center"> Sandy
        Shores College Sailing
        Club</h1>

        <p>Welcome to the home page
        of the Sandy Shores College
        Sailing Club, a student
        organization designed to
        advance the sport of sailing
        in our beautiful bay. Members
        can use the club's Sunfish
        and Laser boats, participate
        in races, and enjoy our
        social events.</p>

        <h2>About the Club</h2>
        <h2>Upcoming Events</h2>

        <ul>
        <li><b>Regatta</b> Sandy
        Shores Marina, Sept. 11, 9am.
        <li><b>Next Meeting</b>
        Ollsen Hall, Room 212a, Sept
        19, 8pm.
        </ul>

        <h2>Join Us!</h2>
        <h2>Contact
Information</h2>

        <p><address>This page is
        maintained by Rob Smith
        (rls@sscollege.edu). Last
        modified September 1,
        2002.</address></p>
    </body>
</html>
```

To sign your page with FrontPage Express, position the cursor where you want the signature to appear, and choose "Address" from the style selection box on the Formatting toolbar.

Adding Hyperlinks

To add hyperlinks to your Web page, use the A element. This element has an important attribute called *href*. The href attribute enables you to supply the URL of another Web page. The A element's content appears on-screen with underlining, indicating that users can click this content to access another Web page. In the following section, you'll learn how to create three types of hyper-links: absolute hyperlinks (for accessing external URLs), relative hyperlinks (for accessing other pages located in the same computer as the page containing the link), and mailto URLs (for enabling easy-to-use email replies).

Absolute Hyperlinks

An **absolute hyperlink** contains a complete URL. You can use absolute hyperlinks to reference Web pages located on a Web server other than the one in which your Web pages are located for publishing. Here's an example:

```
<p>The best place to find sailing-related information on
the Web is <a href="http://www.apparent-wind.com/sailing-
page.html">Mark Rosenstein's Sailing Page</a>.</p>
```

Viewed in a browser, the preceding code looks like this:

```
The best place to find sailing-related information on the
Web is Mark Rosenstein's Sailing Page.
```

Note that the <a> tags enclose the **anchor text,** the text that is visible in the browser window as a hyperlink. By default, most browsers show anchor text with blue underlining.

Here are a few things to note about typing URLs:

- **Case sensitivity**   Some parts of the URL are case sensitive. The protocol name (such as **http://**) and domain name (here, **www.apparent-wind.com)** aren't case sensitive, but the path and resource names may be. Because it's often hard to tell the difference between the domain name and path name, it's best to treat the entire URL as if it were case sensitive. To insert the URL, it's a good idea to use a browser to locate the page, copy the URL from the Address or Location box, and paste it into your HTML page.

- **Spaces**   Don't include spaces in a URL.

- **Quotation marks**   When you're supplying a URL as a value for an attribute, be sure to enclose it all in quotation marks (for example, href = **"http://www.me.com/hi.html"**). A common mistake is forgetting to include the final quotation mark. If a link doesn't work, a missing quotation mark is the likely culprit.

To add an absolute hyperlink to your document with FrontPage Express, type and select the text that you want to hyperlink, click "Insert" on the menu bar, and choose "Hyperlink." You'll see the Create Hyperlink dialog box, shown in Figure 7D.5. Type the URL in the text box, but don't type quotation marks; the program inserts them automatically. Click OK to confirm.

If you are running Internet Explorer as well as FrontPage Express, you can enter hyperlinks quickly using drag-and-drop. In Internet Explorer, display a page that contains the hyperlink you want to add to your page. Click on the hyperlink and drag the link to the FrontPage Express window. When the cursor is positioned where you want the hyperlink to appear, release the mouse button.

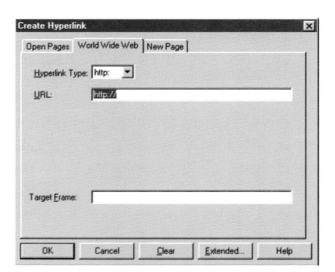

Figure   7D.5

Type the hyperlink text carefully—or better yet, enter the hyperlink using drag-and-drop.

Relative URLs

Relative URLs are used to link to documents on the same Internet computer. If you create a Web presentation with more than one Web page, you can use relative URLs to create links to these pages. When you upload your pages to the Web server, be sure to place all the pages in the same directory. Here's an example:

```
Please feel free to contact any of the club's
<a href="officers.html">officers</a>.
```

In a browser, this code appears as the following:

```
Please feel free to contact any of the club's officers.
```

Mailto URLs

A **mailto URL** enables reader feedback, as long as your page's readers are using a browser that includes email feedback capabilities (most do). When users click a hyperlink that contains a mailto URL, they see a mail composition window that enables them to send email to the person who maintains the page.

It's easy to write a mailto URL. Simply use the A element, as in the following example:

```
Write me at <a href="mailto:rmy@sscollege.edu>rmy
@sscollege.edu</a>.
```

In a browser, this code looks like the following:

```
Write me at rmy@sscollege.edu.
```

In case your page is accessed by somebody who isn't using a mail-enabled browser, it's a good idea to include your email address as the tag's content, as in this example. If you do, the link will work for people who do have mail-enabled browsers (most people do), and those who don't will see your email address, so they can write to you using a separate email program.

Adding Images

To include a GIF or JPEG graphic in your page, you should use the <img> element. This element has an important attribute called src. The src attribute enables you to specify the name of the graphics file you want to insert. For a simple Web page, you should refer to a graphic located in the same directory as your Web page. This means you must upload your graphics as well as your HTML pages when you publish your material.

To use the <img> element, position the cursor where you want the graphic to appear in your document and type the <img> tag with the src attribute. Note that the <img> tag is empty; it doesn't have any content, and it doesn't need an end tag.

```
<img src = "sailboat.jpg">
```

Be sure to enclose the file name in quotation marks.

To add a graphic to your page with FrontPage Express, click "Insert Image" on the Formatting toolbar. You'll see the Image dialog box, shown in

Figure 7D.6. Click the Other Location tab, if necessary, and type the name of the file in the "From File" box. Click OK to confirm.

TESTING YOUR PAGE

You can test your page by opening it with your Web browser. Just use the browser's "File Open" command, and use the "Browse" option to locate the file on your computer.

If something doesn't look right, it's probably due to one of the following common errors:

- **Typo** Perhaps you typed an element name incorrectly or made a mistake typing a URL.

- **Missing bracket** Perhaps you forgot to include an angle bracket. Your browser can't process the link correctly unless the start and end tags are fully formed.

- **Missing slash mark** Perhaps you forgot the slash mark on an end tag.

- **Missing end tag** Perhaps you neglected the end tag entirely. Most elements require end tags.

- **Missing quotation mark** Check to see whether you placed quotation marks at the beginning and end of URLs and other attribute values. It is particularly easy to forget the closing quotation mark.

PUBLISHING YOUR PAGE

To publish your page on your college's computer system or on a commercial ISP's server, you'll need a computer account, as well as specific instructions on how to upload your pages and graphics to your Web publishing directory. Ask your provider for specific instructions.

WEB PUBLISHING HORIZONS

In this module, you've learned how to create a simple Web page using HTML. However, there's more HTML to learn if you would like to get into Web authoring professionally. Also, be aware that there's a new markup language on the horizon, called XML, which promises to affect the way Web documents are prepared.

Learning More HTML

This module's brief introduction to HTML covers the basics, but there's much more to learn if you'd like to produce professional-looking pages. Here's an overview of some topics for further study:

- **Graphics positioning** The <img> element includes several attributes you can use to control the position and size of a graphic on a page (Figure 7D.7). You can also control graphic positioning using a style sheet language such as CSS.

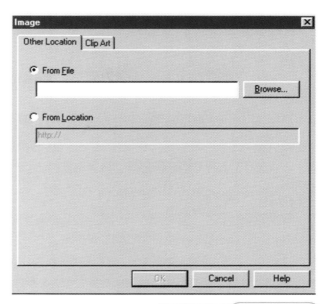

Figure 7D.6

Image dialog box.

Techtalk

link rot
When you search the Web for a certain site but encounter an error message that states the Web site no longer exists, you've experienced "link rot." Link rot describes the problem of constantly changing Web addresses. Since the Web is a collection of living documents, they have the ability to come and go with amazing frequency. That means a URL that worked last week may bring you to a dead-end this week.

Figure 7D.7

Image positioning tags and CSS can be used to specify a graphic's location on the page.

Figure 7D.8

HTML includes tags for creating tables similar to those you create with word processing programs.

Figure 7D.9

Frames enable browsers to display two or more HTML pages as if they were one integrated page.

- **Tables** HTML's table tags enable you to organize information into a matrix of rows and columns (see Figure 7D.8). Because the table tags aren't easy to use when you're typing HTML directly, it's best to use an HTML editor or WYSIWYG program to create tables.

- **Frames** With **frames,** a browser equipped with frames capabilities can show more than one HTML page simultaneously. Often, frames are used to create a panel of navigation aids, positioned on the right or left edge of the screen (see Figure 7D.9). When you click one of the hyperlinks in the navigation panel, you will see the document you requested in the document display frame.

- **Forms** HTML's **forms** element enables Web designers to create pages designed to accept user input (see Figure 7D.10). Programming is required to route the inputted data to a Web server, which then processes the submitted data.

- **Scripts** Professional Web designers use **scripting languages** such as **JavaScript** to build interactive features into their Web pages. A scripting language is a simplified programming language.

- **Multimedia** HTML's OBJECT element enables Web designers to embed a variety of multimedia files within Web pages, including sounds, videos, and animations.

XML: THE WEB'S NEXT LANGUAGE

HTML is a smashing success—and in large measure, it's due to it's simplicity. By learning just a few HTML tags, almost anyone can quickly create a Web page. But HTML's simplicity is also its major limitation. There are no HTML tags for several document elements that many people use, such as footnotes or bibliographic citations. HTML's shortcomings are more severe in specialized areas, such as the law, architecture, or medicine, where documents have unique elements not found elsewhere. What's the answer? Simple: a new language called XML.

Introducing XML

Short for **Extensible Markup Language,** XML is a simplified, easy-to-use version of the Standard Generalized Markup Language (SGML). SGML isn't a markup language, actually; it's a language for *creating* markup languages. And that's exactly what's so neat about XML. If you are frustrated because HTML doesn't include a tag you want, you can create your own using XML. For example, the following XML uses several newly-created tags to define part of a bibliographic citation:

```
<citation>
<last>Smith</last><first>Janet
</first>
<pubdate>2002</pubdate>
<title>Easy Guide to XML</title>
<publisher>Xdirections</publisher>
<place>Charlottesville, VA</place>
</citation>
```

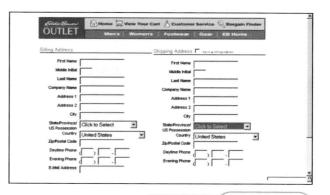

Figure 7D.10

Forms tags enable you to create fill-in forms for user input.

There's one problem, though. HTML works because browsers are programmed to recognize HTML tags. If you start making new tags with XML, how will the browser be able to read them?

The answer lies in XML's Chinese-box-like tag-nesting structure. In the above example, the bibliographic citation tags—such as <last> and <place>—are contained within <citation> tags. An XML-savvy browser doesn't know hooey about what these tags mean, but it *does* know that <last> and <place> (and the other tags) go within the <citation> element. An XML-capable browser, such as Microsoft Internet Explorer version 5 or Netscape Communicator version 6, can detect the nested structure of XML tags and display the structure in a navigation panel.

How XML Works

What's so great about a browser being able to detect the structure of XML tags? It means that it's possible for Web authors to invent all the tags they want, and still have them displayed in a meaningful fashion. And suddenly, the information presented on a Web page becomes *meaningful*. To understand why this is an advantage, suppose you are running an online art gallery, and you're exhibiting and selling works by Tom Smith—a great artist, but one with a very common name. People searching the Internet for "Tom Smith" will retrieve over 15,000 pages. On your page, the artist's name is coded with XML as follows: <artist>Smith, Tom (1956 -)</artist>. Thanks to XML, people can now search effectively for the very few Tom Smiths who are artists.

Although XML enables anyone to create new tags, there's much to be said for developing common XML **vocabularies,** which are sets of elements and tags designed for use in a particular field. Such efforts are going on in virtually every type of business and profession. For example, architects' associations are developing XML coding schemes for the special types of documents architects prepare.

What about presentation? You can specify presentation styles for your XML tags by using CSS, or a special style sheet language created especially for use with XML, called Extensible Style Language (XSL).

Introducing XHTML

The newest version of HTML, called XHTML 1.0, is almost exactly the same as HTML 4.0, but with one important difference: it's defined using XML, so that it becomes just as extensible as any markup language created with XML. To create HTML code that is compatible with XHTML-aware browsers, you need to observe a few rules:

- **Case sensitivity** Like XML, XHTML tags are case-sensitive. Be sure to type tag and attribute names in lowercase letters.

- **Close tags required** In HTML, you can omit certain close tags, such as </p> and </li>, and browsers will still format your page correctly. With XHTML, you can't leave the close tags out.

- **Close symbols in empty tags** Some HTML tags are *empty*, which means that they do not require a close tag. An example is <br>. In XHTML, you must type these tags with a close symbol after the tag name, as in this example: <br/>.

CURRENTS

The Pornography Factor

Of all the social impacts of the Internet, one of the least savory is the following: it's now the pornographer's distribution medium of choice. Almost everyone agrees that pornography is far too accessible on the Web. Kids can find it quite easily, and they do. Psychologists disagree about the impact of pornography on young, developing minds, but very few would argue that it's beneficial. Many people would like to put a stop to Internet-accessible pornography, or at least make it more difficult—or impossible—for kids to access it. The question is, how can this be accomplished without restricting freedom of speech?

The term *pornography* has no meaning in the law—at least not in U.S. law. The legal terms are obscenity and indecency. It's important to understand the difference because the U.S. Supreme Court has consistently held that indecency is protected speech under the U.S. Constitution but obscenity is not. In the United States, legislative attempts to ban pornography have run afoul of this distinction. They've attempted to ban indecency as well as obscenity, and the courts have consistently concluded that doing so would violate fundamental First Amendment rights.

Just what *is* obscenity? It's hard to define because what's obscene to one community isn't obscene for another. Without a cautious definition of obscenity, anti-pornography crusaders can succeed in suppressing "obscene" works of art or literature that turn out to have substantial artistic merit.

In a landmark 1973 decision, the U.S. Supreme Court developed a three-pronged definition of obscenity. To be judged obscene, the court argued, a work of art or literature would have to be *prurient*—that is, intentionally designed to produce sexual arousal—in a "patently offensive" way that lacked any serious artistic, political, literary, or scientific value. But the Court threw in an important condition: all these judgments—whether the work is prurient, offensive, or lacking in value—had to be viewed in accordance with *community standards*. What's offensive in a small Iowa town, for example, might be accepted in San Francisco.

In contrast to obscenity, indecency is a failure to conform to accepted moral standards, such as using four-letter words or referring explicitly and offensively to sexual organs or excretory acts in a public television or radio broadcast. Indecent speech or art may justifiably occur in the context of a work that is not obscene. For example, anatomy textbooks may contain explicit pictures or drawings of sexual organs. Although the U.S. Supreme Court holds that indecent speech is protected by the U.S. Constitution, it also says that indecent speech has no place in broadcast media, such as television and radio, which intrude into the home and can be accessed by children.

In 1996, by overwhelming margins in both houses, the U.S. Congress passed the Communications Decency Act (CDA), which was subsequently signed into law by President Clinton. Essentially, the CDA would have held the Internet and everything on it to the same decency standards as broadcast TV and radio.

The bill, strongly backed by the Christian Coalition and other conservative groups, imposed penalties of up to $250,000 in fines and prison terms for anyone posting obscene or indecent material on the Internet in such a way that made these materials accessible to minors.

According to CDA critics, the CDA's criminalization of indecent speech would effectively "dumb down" the Internet to a level acceptable to a 7-year-old child, which would destroy the Internet's value as a medium for education, commerce, and public communications. What would happen in a future in which virtually all information, including news reports and scientific publications, migrated from paper-based media to the Internet, as seems inevitable? Would scientists be jailed for publishing papers on reproductive disorders? According to scholars concerned with free speech issues, the CDA represents the single-greatest challenge to fundamental Constitutional free speech protections that has ever been mounted in the United States.

In 1997, the U.S. Supreme Court unanimously overturned the provisions of the CDA that criminalized indecent speech. In its decision, the Court compared the CDA to "burning the house to roast the pig." By giving Internet speech the highest constitutional protection, the Supreme Court rejected the CDA backers' contention that the Internet resembled broadcast television or radio, whose airwaves reach intrusively and invisibly into every home. The Internet is more like a library in the Court's view. Libraries are known to contain indecent material, but this material is protected for its educational and scientific value (Otherwise, your anatomy textbook wouldn't have that chapter on the reproductive system). It is up to librarians and parents to keep this material out of children's hands.

Although the CDA's indecency provisions were overturned, conservative legislators aren't about to quit. An ostensibly more carefully crafted bill, called the Child Online Protection Act (COPA), was passed in 1999, but it was also thrown out by a judge—for the same reason the CDA was overturned. These decisions affirm that the Internet is so vital to society that free speech must be protected, even at the cost of exposing children to indecency.

TAKEAWAY POINTS

- The Web publishing process involves defining your purpose, defining your audience, choosing an HTML editor, making design decisions, creating and testing your page, and publishing your page.

- You can use a variety of programs to create HTML pages, such as text editors, HTML editors, word processing programs, WYSIWYG editors, and site managers.

- HTML consists of block elements and inline elements that enable you to mark up the text in your document.

- When you finish your Web page, be sure to sign it and provide contact information. Including the date of when you last modified the page will help readers judge the timeliness of the information.

- Extensible Markup Language (XML) is a new markup language that enables Web authors to create and use their own elements.

MODULE REVIEW

KEY TERMS AND CONCEPTS

absolute hyperlink	declarative languages	markup language
acceptable use policies (AUPs)	element name	nest
anchor text	elements	proprietary
attributes	empty elements	relative URLs
background color	end tag	start tag
background graphic	Extensible Markup Language	structure
block elements	(XML)	style sheet
body	forms	tags
cascading style sheets (CSS)	frames	tile
close tag	global structure	value
content	head	vocabularies
content model	inline elements	World Wide Web Consortium
cross-platform standards	mailto URL	(W3C)

TRUE/FALSE

Indicate whether the following statements are true or false.

1. The first step in the Web publishing process is choosing an HTML editor.

2. A markup language is similar to a programming language.

3. Markup languages are designed to work on any computer platform.

4. It's a good idea to define your document's presentation as you define its structure.

5. Word processing codes aren't designed to function in a cross-platform environment like HTML is.

6. FrontPage Express is an easy-to-use WYSIWYG editor that is often installed with Microsoft Windows.

7. A background color or graphic should be used only on your first Web page, not on subsequent ones.

8. You can include up to six heading levels in your HTML documents.

9. Browsers ignore white space, such as extra spaces and lines, in an HTML document.

10. Parts of URLs are case sensitive, so you must be careful when typing them.

MATCHING

Match each key term from the left column to the most accurate definition in the right column.

_____ 1. markup language

_____ 2. close tag

_____ 3. declarative languages

_____ 4. style sheet

_____ 5. elements

_____ 6. end tag

_____ 7. site managers

_____ 8. absolute hyperlink

_____ 9. mailto URL

_____ 10. frames

a. a larger class of languages

b. portions of a document's structure

c. a complete URL

d. enables reader feedback as long as your page's readers are using a browser that includes email feedback capabilities

e. a tag that shows where the heading text stops

f. defines how you insert special symbols into text so that the text can be processed by the computer

g. a list of elements that includes specific presentation information for each element

h. enables you to see more than one HTML page at once

i. a tag that repeats the element name

j. combines WYSIWYG editors with tools for managing multidocument Web sites

MULTIPLE CHOICE

Circle the letter of the correct choice for each of the following.

1. Which of the following is not a step in the Web publishing process.
   a. choosing an HTML editor
   b. defining your purpose
   c. testing your page
   d. creating multiple versions of the same page for different audiences

2. What is the purpose of an acceptable use policy (AUP)?
   a. to specify appropriate uses of computing facilities
   b. to indicate ways in which Web pages can be used
   c. to add to the bureaucracy at your school
   d. none of the above

3. An ordinary paragraph in an HTML document is which of the following?
   a. a default element
   b. an inline element
   c. a block element
   d. a special element

4. Which of the following is an example of a valid start tag?
   a. </h1>
   b. {BR}
   c. [H3]
   d. <h2>

5. Which of the following tags must be at the very beginning of any HTML document?
   a. <head>
   b. <body>
   c. <html>
   d. <title>

6. Which of the following does not help you create a Web page using HTML?
   a. authoring software
   b. word processing program
   c. WYSIWYG editor
   d. text editor

7. Which attribute do you use to specify a background color?
   a. background color
   b. bgcolor
   c. bground
   d. color

8. Which of the following is not a valid color for use with HTML elements?
   a. aqua
   b. olive
   c. peach
   d. teal

9. Which of the following tag pairs is used to create bold text?
   a. <BOLDTYPE></BOLDTYPE>
   b. <b></b>
   c. <STARTBOLD><ENDBOLD>
   d. <BLD></BLD>

10. Which of the following technologies allow Web page designers to create style sheets that define exactly how elements in the page appear?
    a. TCP
    b. SGML
    c. HTML
    d. CSS

FILL-IN

In the blank provided, write the correct answer for each of the following.

1. Every university has _____ that specify appropriate uses of campus computing facilities.

2. A(n) _____ defines how you insert special symbols into text so that the text can be processed by a computer; these symbols are called _____ .

3. _____ is another markup language that provides a way to define the presentation styles of the tags in a document.

4. A(n) _____ element defines a character style or some other element that fits within a line.

5. A(n) _____ element defines a paragraph.

6. Every element that accepts content has a(n) _____ that specifies what can be included.

7. _____ are programs that enable you to create HTML documents without typing any HTML tags.

8. Every HTML document has a(n) _____, which informs the browser that it has encountered an HTML document.

9. _____ URLs are used to link to documents on the same Internet computer.

10. _____ is a new markup language that enables Web authors to create and use their own elements.

SHORT ANSWER

On a separate sheet of paper, answer the following questions.

1. Describe the steps in the Web publishing process.

2. What are some different possible uses for a Web page created by a student?

3. What is an HTML editor?

4. What is the difference between an HTML element name and an HTML attribute?

5. What is the global structure used by every HTML document?

6. What is the difference between a title and a heading? How are they coded in HTML?

7. What are some of the HTML tools you can use to create a Web page?

8. How do you create a valid hyperlink in a Web page?

9. What are some of the things you should look for when testing your Web page?

10. How does XML differ from HTML?

PFSweb, Inc.

Cliff Defee is in charge of operations at PFSweb. This means the company's Memphis distribution center, customer call centers, and all aspects related to the smooth flow of business rests on his shoulders. If it happens each day, Cliff probably has something to do with it. When e-commerce clients ask PFSweb to provide e-commerce solutions, Cliff has to consider the effect on operations.

Sometimes a new client will have only a handful of products for sale, called stock-keeping units (SKUs), that must be added to the Memphis distribution center. In this case, it may only take a day to catalog all the items and get them entered into PFSweb's warehouse database system. For a client with thousands of inventory item SKUs, it can take weeks to get the product data loaded and ready for online purchases. Not only that, but the increase in physical inventory may mean increasing floor space at the distribution center. In one case, an entirely new warehouse was built to handle the product volume for one new client. Clients that will use the call center need to be evaluated to determine whether new operators are needed, when the call volume will be heaviest, and whether email support personnel will be needed.

There is an impact on PFSweb's computer systems, also. New clients require computer processing power, disk space, and network bandwidth. Depending on the volume of business a new client will bring, entirely new hardware and software must be added to be sure PFSweb can handle the business. The company aims to have its systems at 65–70% utilization, and when they add equipment for new customers, the addition is targeted to drop usage to 40% so there is room to grow back up to 65–70%. No slow Web servers this way!

Finally, new clients bring a need for more human resources. As business for the client grows, PFSweb must add people to develop the computer systems, manage customer call activity in the call center, and process customer orders in the distribution center. But if everything works as planned, customers won't ever have to think about any of these details. That's just the way Cliff wants it.

What do you think? Why do you think it's important for an e-commerce site to provide different ways to communicate with its customers? If you had a question while buying something from a Web site, which form of communication would you like best: email, advanced Web site search features to look up more information, or a telephone call to a live operator?

WebLink Go to **www.prenhall.com/ pfaffenberger** to find out more about the operational challenges of putting up new e-commerce Web sites.

E-COMMERCE IN ACTION

CHAPTER 8

Creating Information Systems

TOOLS FOR GLOBAL COMPETITIVENESS

In the 1970s, Chrysler Corporation, one of the Big Three U.S. automakers, was in trouble. Japanese automakers seemed poised to take over the U.S. market, and it seemed clear that Chrysler just couldn't compete. One major problem was that Chrysler couldn't get its new models out fast enough: by the time they hit the showroom, they already looked dated. The company wouldn't have survived without a U.S. government bailout and some subsequent good fortune (including the runaway success of Chrysler's minivan). But the 1970s clunker is running like a finely-tuned racing engine today. In a ferociously competitive market, the company has increased its market share from 12.2 to 15.9 percent, with a goal of 20 percent. In 1998, the company was racking up earnings at the pace of $1 billion per quarter, astonishing analysts who underestimated the impact of the company's hot new products. With profits like these, it's no wonder that suitors soon came calling. European-based Mercedes-Benz viewed Chrysler as a means to solidify its position in the highly-competitive global auto marketplace, and the two companies merged in 1999.

What's the secret to Chrysler's success? One factor—and it's an important one—is the company's intelligent use of information technology to speed production and cut costs. Today, Chrysler can bring a new model from design to the showroom in just 31 months. In an industry characterized by razor-thin profits, Chrysler is earning 8 percent on sales. In fact, the company is considered to be the lowest-cost producer of automobiles in the world.

Chrysler's not alone. In 1997, the 500 largest U.S. companies raked in a staggering $350 billion in profits. Economists attribute this stunning performance, in part, to U.S. companies' innovative uses of information technology. The payoff for the United States is the most prolonged economic boom in American history, an almost ridiculously low rate of inflation, and the highest employment of all industrialized nations. As a noted Japanese economist put it, with a touch of chagrin, "The 'American Age' is back."

This module introduces and explores the technology that produces business information systems. In Module 8A, you'll begin by exploring the fundamentals of information systems. Module 8B takes a closer look at the overall process used to design and implement information systems, while Module 8C zooms in even further to examine the programming languages and program development methods used to create information systems in today's businesses.

MODULES

Introducing Information Systems 422

Systems Analysis and Design 439

Programming Languages and Program Development 453

8A

MODULE

INTRODUCING INFORMATION SYSTEMS

WHAT YOU WILL LEARN . . .

When you have finished reading this module, you will be able to:

1. List the three basic characteristics of a computerized information system.
2. List the functional divisions of a typical organization.
3. List the four functions of managers.
4. List the characteristics of valuable information.
5. Explain why information reduction is necessary.
6. Discuss the major types of computerized information systems used in today's organizations.
7. List three ways that point-of-sale (POS) terminals in the retail sector are helping to reduce the incidence of fraud.
8. Explain how information systems contributed to Wal-Mart's success in the retail market.

TOOLS FOR GLOBAL COMPETITIVENESS

It isn't fun when an elevator breaks down. People have to hike up and down the stairs, and if you're in a wheelchair, you can't get off the ground floor. If you're running a business upstairs and the elevator has a problem, you want the repair personnel to show up—fast.

Hartford, Connecticut-based Otis Elevator knew this very well, but the company nonetheless wasn't happy with its repair response times. In some areas, repair personnel showed up, on average, within 15 minutes of a service call, but in other areas, the average was 2 to 3 hours. For Otis Elevator, this performance wasn't good enough, and management decided to do something about it.

The solution was the intelligent, creative, and *purposeful* use of an information system. Instead of handling service calls regionally, Otis rerouted them to a national center, where customer service agents could consult a huge database containing information on every one of the more than half million installed Otis elevators. An expert system (an artificial intelligence program capable of performing reasoning operations) chooses the right mechanic, and within seconds, a call goes out to the mechanic's beeper. A 5-line display tells the mechanic where the service is needed, and a radio telephone enables further communication. As a result, Otis brought its service performance up to the level desired by both Otis and the company's customers.

Like Otis Elevator, smart businesses know that information systems aren't merely a cost center. Viewed properly, information systems are a *value* center, a wealth-producing asset that enables a firm to compete more effectively. In this module, you'll take a closer look at information systems: what they are, how they relate to business organizations, and how advanced information technologies are reshaping the corporate landscape.

COMPUTERIZED INFORMATION SYSTEMS (CIS): SERVING AN ORGANIZATION'S NEEDS

You already know that an **information system** processes data to produce information. As the Otis Elevator example suggests, this information is useful for providing quality customer service (and for other needs, too, as you'll see in a moment). But what's the *system* part mean?

A **system** is a collection of components purposefully organized into a functioning whole to accomplish a goal. Systems occur in nature, but what we're talking about are **artificial systems,** systems deliberately constructed by people to serve some purpose. Systems are all around us. The air transport system, for example, is a complex system that does a remarkably good job of safely delivering millions of people to their destinations every day.

At the core of the system concept lies the recognition that various parts of the system need to be modified or adapted so they will function together smoothly. (After all, you wouldn't want to fly on an airplane that had the wrong type of wing installed.) A second important concept about systems is that they have a **life cycle:** they're born, go through a process of maturation, live an adult life, and become obsolete to the point that they have to be modified (or abandoned). Table 8A.1 summarizes the stages of a system's life cycle. If you think about yesterday's transportation systems, such as canals or the Pony Express, you'll see it's obvious that systems outlive their usefulness.

At this point, we could be talking about any kind of system, including a manufacturing system (such as an assembly line). What's special about *information* systems lies in their provision of essential information services to **organizations,** which are collections of resources (personnel and equipment) organized so that they can provide a product or a service. Essential services

Table 8A.1

System Life Cycle	
Life Cycle Stages	**Key Tasks**
Preliminary design stage	Identify system development goals
Detailed design stage	Design specific components
Fabrication, assembly, integration, and test stage	Putting it all together
Production and customer support stage	Using the system
Termination and disposal stage	Retiring the system

provided by information systems include recording and keeping track of **transactions** (exchanges of goods, services, or funds), assisting decision-makers by providing them with needed facts and figures, and providing documentation needed by customers and suppliers. No organization, not even a small one, can function without an information system of some kind, even if it isn't computer-based. All businesses, for example, are required to keep detailed business records for tax purposes.

Computerized information systems make use of the computer's special capabilities—namely, accepting input in the form of represented data, processing that data to produce information, and disseminating this information throughout the organization. Computerized information systems don't consist merely of computers and software. They also include some method of representing the data essential to the organization, the trained personnel who operate the system, and the procedures these people must follow to ensure that the system functions properly.

A complete definition of a **computerized information system (CIS)** recognizes all these characteristics. A computerized information system:

■ Provides essential services to organizations, including processing transactions and keeping exact records.

■ Collects mission-critical data, processes this data, stores the data and the results of processing, and disseminates information throughout the organization.

■ Includes data, hardware, software, trained personnel, and procedures.

UNDERSTANDING COMPLEX ORGANIZATIONS: THE POWER PYRAMID

How can information systems help organizations achieve their goals? This question can't be answered unless you begin by considering how organizations are structured. Most information systems are designed to fit into existing organizational structures and support their activities. Some new information systems are designed to *change* this organizational structure to make the organizations more efficient.

Functional Divisions of an Organization

In a one-person organization, only one person (usually the founder) deals with money matters, handles sales and marketing, keeps essential records, and supervises the firm's primary activities, such as providing services or making products. For example, consider a one-person taxi business: the CEO collects the fares, pays the bills, keeps the books, *and* drives the taxi.

In biology, when you compare a one-celled creature to more complex organisms, you can see one big difference: complex creatures develop specialized groups of cells, called organs, that perform a specialized function. The same goes for organizations. When an organization grows to the point that the founder can't handle all the tasks alone, specialized divisions appear to handle each of the organization's core functions (see Figure 8A.1). Consider what happens when that one-person taxi company grows into a fleet of 300 vehicles. Chances are that the company will have separate people focusing on the following:

- **Finance** Deals with money: getting it, tracking it, spending it, and accounting for it to external stakeholders, such as stockholders and tax agencies. A taxi business with 300 vehicles needs at least one full-time accountant and a part-time bookkeeper or two.

- **Marketing and sales** Promotes the organization's product or service and arranges sales with customers. For example, someone has to handle those high-profit ventures such as providing limousines for weddings.

- **Human resources** Hires and trains new employees, deals with pay and benefits, and tracks employee performance. Finding and keeping good drivers is a big job.

- **Operations** Performs the organization's primary function, such as manufacturing a product or delivering a service. In the taxi business, someone has to make sure that the drivers know where to go and guarantee that they actually get to where they're going.

- **Information systems** Manage the organization's computerized information systems, including planning and purchasing new systems, providing user training and support, and dealing with day-to-day operational problems. A taxi business is an information-intensive job, which is why today's fastest-growing taxi companies use computer-based systems and state-of-the-art communications systems.

No matter where organizations appear, they tend to develop this functionally-differentiated structure, which is sometimes called the **traditional organizational structure.** A similar structure develops in nonprofit organizations and government agencies.

CHAIN OF COMMAND

An organization develops because one person can't handle all the work, and the same is true for management-related tasks. In a large organization, the CEO hires *senior managers* who can handle a division such as finance or marketing. To senior managers, the CEO delegates not only the responsibility to manage these divisions properly, but the power to do so effectively. After delegating responsibility and power to senior management, the CEO doesn't have to worry about the time-consuming details of making these divisions work. The CEO's job is to worry about big picture issues, such as where the organization should go in the future and how it's likely to be affected by trends in the organization's external environment.

The delegation of responsibility proceeds down the organizational ladder. The senior managers of each division hire *middle managers,* who are responsible for subdivisions. Middle managers may further delegate responsibility to *operational managers,* who directly supervise nonmanagement personnel (production workers, clerical workers, and other employees). Note that this

Figure 8A.1

In an organization, specialized divisions handle each of the organization's core functions. The information systems division manages all of the organization's computerized information systems.

Techtalk

CIO or CTO

As information systems have grown in importance for modern organizations, so has the need for someone to guide and manage that growth. That person is generally at the same executive level as the chief financial officer or chief operations officer and called the "chief information officer" (CIO) or "chief technology officer" (CTO). The CIO or CTO is responsible for assuring the company's technology supports its strategic direction as well as its employees, customers, and daily operations.

Figure 8A.2

The delegation of responsibility in an organization resembles a pyramid. Divisional senior managers hire middle managers, who may delegate responsibility to operational managers. Operational managers supervise production workers, clerical workers, and other employees.

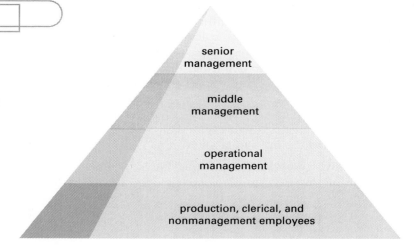

senior management

middle management

operational management

production, clerical, and nonmanagement employees

structure has a few people at the top and lots at the bottom. For this reason, it's called a *pyramid* (see Figure 8A.2). And because this organizational structure is a chain of command, with lots of power at the top and little at the bottom, it's also called a *hierarchy*. The hierarchical, pyramid-like qualities of an organization aren't as sharply formed as those of a military organization—corporations don't give death sentences for a failure to obey a command, for example—but there's no mistaking a basic fact: the higher up the ladder you go, the more power you have to determine what other people do.

What do all these managers do? **Managers** decide how best to use the organization's resources, including money, equipment, and people, so that the organization achieves its goals efficiently. All managers perform some or all of the following management functions:

- **Planning** Establishing goals and creating a strategy to achieve these goals.

- **Organizing** Putting resources together so that the goals are achieved.

- **Leading** Communicating goals and motivating people to achieve them.

- **Controlling** Assessing whether the goals are being met and taking corrective action if necessary.

Although all managers perform most or all of these functions, they do so in varying ways. Those in senior management (including the CEO) are more concerned with high-level planning and leadership. They make *strategic decisions* concerning the organization's overall goals and direction. Middle managers focus on planning their division's goals and organizing resources to achieve them. They make *tactical decisions* about how best to organize resources to achieve their division's goals. Operational managers focus on leadership and control, and they make *operational decisions* concerning localized issues (such as an inventory shortage) that need immediate action (see Table 8A.2).

One thing that all managers (and many employees) need is information. Every manager needs information to manage effectively. Without an accurate understanding of the organization's overall performance, for example, the CEO can't frame long-range plans or provide the right kind of leadership. The need for high-quality information is all the greater due to the organization's division into separate units, which may become isolated.

Types of Management Decisions		
Managers	**Decisions**	**Type**
Senior Managers	Strategic Decisions	Determining the organization's goals and direction
Middle Managers	Tactical Decisions	Deciding how to organize resources to achieve their division's goals
Operational Managers	Operational Decisions	Deciding how to handle localized issues requiring immediate action

Table 8A.2

INFORMATION: THE GOOD KIND AND THE OTHER KIND

Organizations need information. But not all information is valuable, and all too often, we're overwhelmed with more information than we can use. The result is a malady called **information overload,** a stress-induced incapacitation that is a threat to organizations and the people who work in them (see Figure 8A.3). An effective information system provides an organization with **valuable information** and uses one or more techniques of **information reduction.**

Figure 8A.3

Not all information is valuable, and all too often, we're overwhelmed with more information than we can use.

Characteristics of Valuable Information

Not all information is valuable, a fact you'll appreciate after doing some research on the Internet. To be valuable, information must be:

- **Accessible**   You can find it quickly and easily.

- **Accurate**   You're confident that it doesn't contain errors.

- **Complete**   The information doesn't omit anything important.

- **Economical**   The benefit exceeds the cost of producing the information.

- **Relevant**   It's related to the task you're trying to perform.

- **Reliable**   It's there every time you need it.

- **Secure**   Unauthorized people can't access the information.

- **Simple**   It doesn't overwhelm you.

- **Timely**   It's there when you need it.

- **Verifiable**   If necessary, you can confirm the facts and figures by double-checking them.

Techniques of Information Reduction

As pioneering computer scientist Grace Hopper stressed throughout her career, computers are indispensable, but they also pose the threat of producing too much information (information overload). To keep information from overwhelming people in an organization, it's important to control

SPOTLIGHT

DEALING WITH TECHNO-STRESS

▶Imagine you get up in the morning and turn on the TV. Immediately, you start seeing images on the morning news, accompanied by the babblings of reporters. You scan through the morning paper as you prepare a quick breakfast, then you hop into the car and drive to work with the radio blaring what seems to be more commercials than music. All the while, you may pass dozens of billboards and hundreds of traffic signs.

You arrive at work and turn on your computer. Your overnight email has deposited 54 new messages in your inbox, which is just the start of the day's deluge. You log on to the server and see that others in your workgroup are demanding your attention on three projects with looming deadlines. A quick check of your voice mail shows you already have 20 new messages, in addition to the 10 you didn't deal with yesterday. An office courier comes by and drops off a 15-page fax and three FedEx shipments. By lunchtime, you feel tired and drained, wishing for an escape.

You, like many other people, are suffering from information overload. We live in a society driven by information. Everywhere you look, information is coming at you faster and faster. To make matters worse, those generating the information are coming up with new, ingenious, and sometimes insidious ways to grab your attention. These are all part and parcel of information overload, a single factor in techno-stress, or computer-related stress.

Recent research performed in the United Kingdom by Benchmark Research has indicated that 43 percent of the 1,300 managers they surveyed suffer from techno-stress, which they labeled as Information Fatigue Syndrome. Symptoms include paralysis of analytical capacity, increased anxiety, greater self-doubt, and a tendency to blame others.

The most described feeling was that of drowning in a sea of information. People often feel out of control when it comes to dealing with the information glut they face. Many times, the stress induced by information overload leads to foolish decisions and flawed conclusions. This is ironic, given the fact that you would think more information should lead to better decisions.

The effects of overload can lead to even more serious problems. Many people report mental anguish and general anxiety from not being able to keep up with the incoming data. Others report physical illness, personal relationships that suffer, a lack of leisure time, and other problems.

Dealing with techno-stress is going to take a concerted effort on the parts of many people. Companies should introduce training designed to help managers and employees quickly determine the value of the information they receive. When they learn to quickly make that determination, it becomes easier to confidently press the "Delete" key and thereby become the master of the information they receive rather than the slave.

Improved communications skills (not communications technologies) can also help in dealing with techno-stress. As managers and others learn to communicate more quickly and concisely, they can avoid dealing with nonessential information. In addition, employees can cut to the chase and again make confident decisions on what is valuable and what is not.

Finally, organizations can help by using some type of information reduction measures. By reducing or digesting the information that employees need to deal with, the data becomes much more manageable.

As organizations move into the twenty-first century, the methods we have of communicating with each other are bound to increase. As these methods increase, so too will the messages transmitted over them. Members of organizations will need to learn to sink or swim, and the only difference between the two extremes will be how well the member can receive, process, and act upon information.

Everywhere you look, information is coming at you faster and faster.

information. With an information system, the following **control methods** are possible:

- Routing information so that it goes to only those people who really need to see the information.

- Summarizing information so that decision-makers do not drown in the details.

- Enabling selectivity so that people with specific information needs can get that information (and ignore the rest).

- Eliminating unnecessary information (exclusion) so that it doesn't take up time.

INFORMATION SYSTEMS IN ORGANIZATIONS: A SURVEY

To meet the information needs of an organization's employees, many different systems have been developed. In a very small business, a single computer might meet all of the business's information needs. Larger organizations supplement single-user systems with minicomputers, mainframe computers, local area networks (LANs), and wide area networks (WANs). (For an introduction to computer networks, see Module 6B.) Some of these larger systems are designed to assist **workgroups** (teams of two or more people working on the same project); others are **enterprise-wide systems,** available throughout an organization (including all of the organization's branch offices).

Transaction Processing System (TPS)

A **transaction processing system (TPS)** (also called an *operational system* or a *data processing system*) handles an organization's day-to-day accounting needs. It keeps a careful, verifiable record of every transaction involving money, including purchases, sales, and payroll payments. In businesses that sell products, a TPS is often linked with an inventory control system so that sales personnel will know whether an item is in stock. Transaction processing systems date to the earliest years of business computing, and the cost savings they introduced helped create a huge market for business computers. A TPS saves money by automating routine, labor-intensive record keeping.

Early transaction processing systems used **batch processing,** in which the data was gathered and processed at periodic intervals, such as once per week. With the rise of timesharing systems in the 1970s (see Module 1B), **online processing** systems were developed. These systems enabled operations personnel to enter transaction data and see totals and other results immediately.

Transaction processing systems provide useful tools for employees, such as sales and human resource personnel, but they're useful for managers, too. A well-designed TPS can produce periodic **summary reports** that provide managers with a quick overview of the organization's performance. They can also provide **exception reports** that alert managers to unexpected developments (such as high demand for a new product).

Management Information System (MIS)

A **management information system (MIS)** is a computer-based system that supports the information needs of different levels of management. This type of system is designed to help management make informed decisions. Most management information systems are designed to work with transaction

Figure 8A.4

A management information system produces reports that tell middle managers how well they are meeting goals.

processing systems. They produce reports that tell middle managers how well they are meeting goals (see Figure 8A.4).

Although management information systems continue to play an important role in organizations, they have drawbacks. They generate predefined reports that may not contain the information a manager wants. The information may not be available when it's needed, and it might also be buried within reams of printouts.

Decision Support System (DSS)

A **decision support system (DSS)** addresses the deficiencies of management information systems by enabling managers to ask questions that can't be answered by fixed, predefined MIS reports. For example, a retail chain manager can ask how an advertising campaign affected sales of advertised vs. nonadvertised items. Many DSS applications enable managers to create simulations that begin with real data and ask what-if questions, such as, "What would happen to profits if we went with a shipper who could cut our packaging costs by 2 percent?"

Online analytical processing (OLAP) provides decision support by enabling managers to import rich, up-to-the-minute data from transaction databases. For example, analysts at Pizzeria Uno, a chain of more than 100 pizza stores, obtain and analyze all the sales information from each of the firm's stores every morning. As a result, they can quickly spot trends that may be emerging in customer preferences and employee performance.

Executive Information System (EIS)

An **executive information system (EIS),** also known as an **executive support system (ESS),** supports management's strategic planning function. Although similar to a DSS, an EIS is designed to support decisions made by top-level management that will affect the entire company.

An executive information system filters critical information (including information about the firm's external environment) so that overall trends are apparent and presents this information in an easy-to-use graphical interface. Little training is required to use these systems.

Expert System

An **expert system** is a software package that deals with knowledge rather than information. Expert systems help in formulating a decision in the way an expert in the field might. Expert systems operate using principles of *artificial intelligence* (a field that attempts to endow a computer with intelligence). Expert systems are helping to improve service in one area in which organizations sometimes perform an unsatisfactory job: providing technical support for customers.

Knowledge Management System

Organizations are increasingly aware that knowledge is a valuable asset and are turning to technology to help them capture the knowledge employees create. A variety of information technologies are being used to create **knowledge management systems,** which capture such knowledge and make it available where it's needed. This process doesn't have to be high-tech: at Columbia/HCA, a nationwide hospital chain, a team visits each hospital and writes a report on the most successful business processes (best practices) found at each site. The reports are then made available on the company's internal Web server.

Computer-Supported Cooperative Work (CSCW)

Organizations that have networks can use **group-ware,** software that provides computerized support for the information needs of workgroups. Groupware applications are collectively known as **computer-supported cooperative work (CSCW).** These applications include electronic mail to help team members communicate, videoconferencing, group scheduling systems, customizable electronic forms, real-time shared applications, and shared information databases (see Figure 8A.5).

The first successful groupware, Lotus Notes, was designed to run on client/server systems (see Module 6B). Newer groupware products, such as Microsoft Exchange and new versions of Lotus Notes, are designed to run on intranets and extranets (see Module 6B). They make groupware applications available to workgroups that work at geographically-separated offices, and even enable organizations to bring in group members who work for other organizations (such as affiliated research labs).

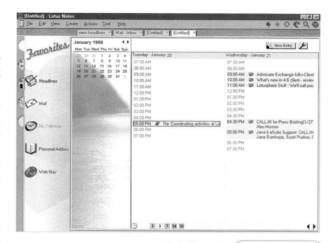

Figure 8A.5

Groupware applications such as Lotus Notes are collectively known as computer supported cooperative work (CSCW).

Workflow Automation

In many companies, important documents must go through a series of personnel for approval. For example, in an engineering firm, an engineer may prepare a proposal for an external contract. The proposal then goes to the engineer's supervisor for review and approval. The document may need to be seen by several other people until it is finally approved and sent. **Workflow automation** can greatly speed this process by automatically sending a document to the next person who needs to see and approve it.

Business Process Reengineering (BPR)

Business process reengineering (BPR), also known as **reengineering,** refers to the use of information technology to bring about major changes and cost savings in an organization's structure. At the core of reengineering is the principle that information technology (IT) doesn't bring big payoffs if you simply automate existing work processes. The key to big payoffs lies in using IT to *change* existing processes.

In BPR, designers ignore an organization's functional divisions and focus instead on work processes: activities that have an identifiable output and a value to the organization's customers. For example, product development is a process that often involves many functional divisions, including marketing, engineering, procurement, and finance. By using information technology such as groupware, an organization can be redesigned around work processes rather than functional divisions. The work is then carried out by a **cross-functional team,** in which team members perform functions that were formerly separated out among the company's functional units. For example, at Ford Motor Company, workers at the company's receiving dock note which items have been received, and forward the invoice to the accounting department. This process was reengineered through the simple expedient of placing accounting workstations right on the receiving dock and empowering the workers to enter the data directly. As a result, a major paperwork bottleneck was eliminated.

Reengineering can lead to big payoffs, but a high proportion of early BPR projects failed. Many companies came to see reengineering as a means

Destinations

To read more about how Lotus products, such as Notes, are helping to solve business challenges, check out the Industry Solutions at Lotus' home page of **http://www. lotus.com.**

Destinations

To learn more about workflow management, visit the Workflow Management Coalition's home page (**http:// www.aiim.org/wfmc/**).

IMPACTS

Computers in Manufacturing

Designing New Products

To compete in the global market, firms need to design new products quickly. A basic index of business performance is time-to-market: the time it takes to develop new products and get them to customers. If your time-to-market is too lengthy, you'll be out of business because your competitors will have made it to market before you.

In traditional U.S. manufacturing, companies got engineers, marketing people, and finance people together *after* the engineers came up with a product design. The result, all too often, was a shot-down design, and then a return to the drawing board. Chrysler Corporation, now Daimler Chrysler Corporation, was taking an average of 4.5 years to get new designs to dealer showrooms, which was too long. In the 1980s, Chrysler nearly went under again due to its lengthy design process. By the time its new, squarish cars hit the market, Ford had come out with its rounded-off Taurus, making Chrysler's newest offerings look like yesterday's styles.

To improve time-to-market, Chrysler introduced *cross-functional teams*, which created a new method of designing products. In a cross-functional team, a company puts the engineering, finance, and marketing people together from the beginning of the project. Instead of trying to shoot each other down, the team works together to come up with a design that's attractive to everyone. As a result, Chrysler cut time-to-market from 54 months to a record 31 months. Through new technologies and the continued focus to bring products to market faster, the company is currently moving toward a 24-month development time.

Streamlining Manufacturing

Companies have been using computers to cut manufacturing time and costs for more than two decades. *Computer-aided design (CAD)* applications enable engineers to create or modify designs for parts quickly. In CAD, the computer monitor replaces a manual drafting table and enables the designer to create three-dimensional images that can be rotated. Where manufacturing involves the use of industrial robots, *computer-aided manufacturing (CAM)* is possible. In CAM, also called art-to-part, the output from CAD programs directly drives the computer-controlled manufacturing equipment. If engineers need to change a part's design, they tweak it using CAD. Instantly, the equipment starts making the redesigned part.

CAD speeds the design process, but it's simply a faster version of what engineers did before computers. *Virtual manufacturing*, also called *computer-aided production engineering (CAPE)*, represents a new way of approaching the manufacturing process, and it's producing big. In virtual manufacturing, a powerful computer assembles all the digitally-drawn parts to see how they fit together. If some of the parts don't fit well, they can be modified before being manufactured, resulting in huge savings. Equally useful are programs that enable engineers to simulate an entire factory, revealing what's required to assemble the various components. If engineers using such a program discover a bottleneck, they can go back to the designers and request changes that lead to big improvements in production efficiency. Virtual reality models of a proposed design enable manufacturing engineers, marketing staff, and customers to walk through the product before it physically exists.

After the design has been finalized, computers can be woven into the entire production process. In *computer-integrated manufacturing (CIM)*, computers link the entire procedure, from order entry to production and from warehousing to distribution. On the factory floor, CIM software controls conveyors, robots, and *automatic guided vehicles (AGV)*, which zip around supplying components where they're needed. CIM compresses production times into amazingly brief spans. Production cycles that once required weeks or months can now be accomplished in days or hours.

Chrysler has cut time-to-market from 54 months to a record 31 months.

of **downsizing,** and employees learned to fear and resist BPR efforts. Most experts agree that it's best to use a more modest approach, building on existing information systems if possible.

Data Warehousing and Data Mining

Many large organizations have dozens or even hundreds of databases. Each was developed for a specific purpose and stored using proprietary file formats. For example, one health insurance firm had two large databases, one that kept track of financial transactions and another that recorded claims data. Because these two databases were separate and based on incompatible, proprietary data formats, the company's analysts couldn't ask a simple but important question: what types of claims are costing us the most money?

Increasingly, the contents of isolated, proprietary databases are being moved into **data warehouses,** a database of databases capable of bringing all of a firm's data together into one gigantic database that may contain as many as a trillion data records. Data warehouses are useful for operational employees and managers alike. The software enables operational employees to get detailed data but also produces summary data at whatever level interests a manager. Using a technique called **drill-down,** a manager can view performance data for the entire firm, and then drill down to lower levels (sales regions, offices, individual salespeople), viewing summaries at each level.

In a technique called **data mining,** analysts are exploring warehoused data to find previously-unknown patterns. At Merck-Medco, a division of pharmaceutical giant Merck that supplies drugs to health maintenance organizations (HMOs), a huge data warehouse enables analysts to discover hidden links between illnesses, types of patients, and drugs. The result has been more-effective, less-costly treatments. Using data mining, Merck-Medco has been able to cut prescription drug costs by 10 to 15 percent.

Increasingly, data warehousing is seen as a way to provide support to all the information systems discussed in this section.

Destinations

For more information on data warehousing, see the Data Warehousing Institute's home page at **http://www. dw-institute.com.**

COMPUTERS IN THE RETAIL SECTOR

In the retail sector, computers are indispensable for traditional applications such as automating the checkout process. But some companies have also figured out how to use computers for *strategic* purposes: getting an edge on their competitors. These companies have grown rapidly and made fortunes for their shareholders.

At the Checkout Stand

Today's cash registers are really computers—specifically, **point-of-sale (POS) terminals.** Clerks check items out by passing them over an optical scanner, which reads the item's **universal product code (UPC)** encoded on a label or a tag. The UPC identifies the item with a series of bars. The code is based on the width of the bars and the space between the bars. Use of the UPC code has resulted in a faster processing of items and fewer price errors. The latest POS terminals are fully integrated with a **credit card authorization** system, which automatically originates a call to a **call center,** a computer-based telephone routing system that connects to an authorization service, and cranks out an authorization number. Thanks to the volume of credit card authorization calls, firms that make call center equipment have watched their market grow from virtually nothing 25 years ago to a worldwide $200 billion bonanza today.

The UPC code has resulted in faster processing of items and fewer price errors.

Because point-of-sale terminals produce digitized data, they're useful for more purposes than determining the customer's bill. POS terminals are linked to the store's inventory database. When a customer buys an item, the database is automatically updated to reflect the lowered stock level. When the level gets too low, the software originates a restocking order.

Chain stores link their POS terminals to central computer systems using public data networks (PDNs). Disney, however, is taking POS data to the airwaves. At Walt Disney World, POS terminals at hundreds of retail carts supply data to company computers using **wireless communications,** a means of linking computers by radio signals. As a result, the *Lion King* cart never runs out of those cute stuffed animals, and that means bigger profits.

Point-of-sale terminals can also help reduce losses due to bad checks and credit card fraud. **Check-screening systems** read a check's account number, and access a database containing the numbers of delinquent accounts. These systems help reduce bad-check losses by up to 25 percent, translating into big savings for retail firms. According to one estimate, banks and retailers lose a staggering $58 billion annually due to bounced checks and check fraud.

Signature capture systems enable stores to capture a customer's signature digitally by having the customer sign the receipt on a pressure-sensitive pad using a special stylus. What's the point? The system cuts down on credit card disputes. With a receipt signed by the customer, the store can prove that the purchase was made. This system isn't popular with consumers, however, due to fears that a dishonest employee could use the captured signature for fraudulent purposes. **Photo checkout systems** access a database of customer photos, and display the customer's picture when a credit card is used. In a New York test, this system cut back credit card fraud by 94 percent.

Retail the Wal-Mart Way

Suppose your parents put $1,000 into Wal-Mart stock in 1970, when the company's stock was first offered to the public, and put the shares aside for the child they planned to have. You turn 18, your trust fund comes due, and guess what? You're a multimillionaire!

What's the secret of Wal-Mart's amazing success? Business analysts point to the retail chain's smart strategy of locating in populous but underserved semirural markets, good customer service, profit-sharing plans for employees (who are called associates), and low prices. Most of all, some say, Wal-Mart's innovative use of information technology is responsible for the company's success. Wal-Mart has poured billions of dollars into state-of-the-art information technology.

What's so special about the way Wal-Mart uses computers? For Wal-Mart, computers aren't simply a way of performing a task, such as keeping an inventory database up-to-date. Far more important, computers are a means of creating and cementing relationships with suppliers, the key business partner in any retail business. Instead of seeing suppliers as adversaries, Wal-Mart views them as partners and makes valuable information available to them, such as what's selling and what isn't selling in its huge chain of retail stores. (Wal-Mart collects this information by means of sophisticated checkout scanners, which quickly alert managers when sales patterns develop.)

In addition, Wal-Mart opens its inventory database to suppliers and tells them, "When you see that we're getting low on something, ship it." By trans-

Sophisticated checkout scanners that alert managers to sales patterns are partly responsible for Wal-Mart's and other retailers' success.

ferring the inventory maintenance responsibility to suppliers and creating the computer systems needed to do this, Wal-Mart cut inventory restocking time from the industry average of six weeks to just 36 hours. The result? When shoppers go to Wal-Mart, they find what they're looking for. That translates into customer loyalty and huge profits.

Not everyone is happy with Wal-Mart's success. In the suburbs and rural areas that Wal-Mart management favors for new stores, the coming of a new Wal-Mart generally spells the end of small, family-run businesses that cannot compete with Wal-Mart's pricing. In that respect, Wal-Mart's low prices don't come without costs of their own.

TAKEAWAY POINTS

- Human-engineered systems are organized collections of components designed to work together to accomplish a goal.
- A computerized information system is a system that provides essential services to organizations by collecting, processing, storing, and disseminating mission-critical data. The system includes data, hardware, software, trained personnel, and procedures.
- Typical functional divisions of an organization include finance, marketing and sales, human resources, operations, and information systems.
- Managers plan, organize, lead, and control. Senior management is more concerned with planning and leading; middle managers focus on planning and organizing; and operational managers focus on leadership and control.
- Managers and many employees need information that is accessible, accurate, complete, economical, relevant, reliable, secure, simple, timely, and verifiable.

- Techniques of information reduction include routing, summarizing, selectivity, and exclusion.
- Information systems include the transaction processing system (TPS), the management information system (MIS), the decision support system (DSS), the executive information system (EIS), the knowledge management system, groupware, workflow routing, and business process reengineering (BPR). Increasingly, data warehousing is seen as a way to provide all these systems with rich data.
- In the retail sector, point-of-sale (POS) terminals can reduce fraud through the use of check-screening systems, signature capture, and photo checkout systems.
- Wal-Mart revolutionized the retail industry by using information systems to share inventory information with suppliers. The result was a dramatic reduction in restocking time.

MODULE REVIEW

KEY TERMS AND CONCEPTS

artificial systems
batch processing
business process reengineering
   (BPR)
call center
check screening systems
computerized information
   system (CIS)
computer-supported
   cooperative work (CSCW)
control methods
credit card authorization
cross-functional team
data mining
data warehouses
decision support system (DSS)
downsizing
drill-down

enterprise-wide systems
exception reports
executive information system
   (EIS)
executive support system (ESS)
expert system
groupware
information overload
information reduction
information system
knowledge management
   systems
life cycle
management information
   system (MIS)
managers
online analytical processing
   (OLAP)

online processing
organizations
photo checkout systems
point-of-sale (POS) terminals
reengineering
signature capture
summary reports
system
traditional organizational
   structure
transaction processing system
   (TPS)
transactions
universal product code (UPC)
valuable information
wireless communications
workflow automation
workgroups

TRUE/FALSE

Indicate whether the following statements are true or false.

1. Information systems often consist of more than just hardware and software.

2. Information is only important to upper levels of management.

3. Not all information is valuable.

4. Summarizing information is one way to reduce the possibility of information overload.

5. Transaction processing systems handle the day-to-day production needs of an organization.

6. Management information systems provide decision support by enabling managers to import up-to-the minute data from transaction databases.

7. Executive information systems require quite a bit of training to use effectively.

8. Data mining allows analysts to explore large data sets to find previously-unknown patterns.

9. Point-of-sale terminals are effective at reducing losses due to bad checks and credit card fraud.

10. By using computer systems to transfer the inventory maintenance responsibility to suppliers, Wal-Mart cut inventory restocking time from the industry average of three weeks to one week.

MATCHING

Match each key term from the left column with the most accurate definition in the right column.

_____ 1. information system

_____ 2. system

_____ 3. organizations

_____ 4. managers

_____ 5. summary report

_____ 6. workgroups

_____ 7. batch processing

_____ 8. management information system

_____ 9. computer-supported cooperative work

_____ 10. data warehouse

a. data that is gathered and processed periodically

b. a computer-based system that supports the information needs of different management levels

c. this provides managers with an overview of the organization's performance

d. groupware applications that include email, videoconferencing, and shared information databases

e. a collection of components organized into a whole to accomplish a goal

f. a database of databases

g. collections of resources organized to provide a product or service

h. a system that processes data to produce information

i. teams of two or more people working on the same project

j. people who decide how best to use the organization's resources

MULTIPLE CHOICE

Circle the letter of the correct choice for each of the following.

1. Which of the following is not an essential service provided by an information system?
   a. recording and keeping track of transactions
   b. assisting decision-makers by providing information
   c. managing environmental units in physical facilities
   d. providing documentation needed by customers and suppliers

2. What type of organization structure is characterized by specialized departments?
   a. traditional organization
   b. lateral organization
   c. pyramid organization
   d. flat organization

3. Who typically makes strategic decisions for the organization?
   a. middle managers
   b. CEO

   c. operational managers
   d. supervisors

4. Which of the following are not characteristics of valuable information?
   a. plentiful, unstructured, free
   b. accurate, relevant, simple
   c. complete, reliable, timely
   d. accessible, economical, secure

5. What is another name for a transaction processing system?
   a. quality control system
   b. field management system
   c. management information system
   d. data processing system

6. Which of the following is a drawback to many management information systems?
   a. slow response time
   b. availability of information
   c. completeness of data
   d. system responsiveness

7. Which type of system is designed to support strategic planning?
   a. executive support system
   b. management information system
   c. decision support system
   d. transactional processing system

8. Which of the following is not an example of groupware?
   a. electronic mail
   b. videoconferencing
   c. word processing programs
   d. real time shared applications

9. In large organizations that collect a number of huge databases, which of the following tech- nologies can help organize, manage, and exploit all the data?
   a. trans-data analysis
   b. data warehousing
   c. business process reengineering
   d. knowledge management systems

10. Which of the following groups has access to Wal-Mart's inventory database?
    a. consumers
    b. competitors
    c. stockholders
    d. suppliers

FILL-IN

In the blank provided, write the correct answer for each of the following.

1. A(n) _____ is a collection of resources established to provide some kind of product or service.

2. An organization suffers from _____ when it is overwhelmed with more information than it can effectively or efficiently use.

3. _____ systems are systems deliberately constructed by people to serve some purpose.

4. A(n) _____ is a team of two or more people working on the same project.

5. A(n) _____ system saves money by automating routine, labor-intensive record keeping.

6. _____ systems allow managers to find information-based answers to questions that cannot be answered with fixed, prede- fined reports.

7. A(n) _____ is a software package that works with knowledge rather than infor- mation.

8. _____ can greatly speed an approval process by automatically sending a document to the next person who needs to see and approve it.

9. The use of information technology to imple- ment major changes and cost savings in an organization's structure is known as _____.

10. One technique used with data warehouses that allows managers to see underlying data at lower levels is known as _____.

SHORT ANSWER

On a separate sheet of paper, answer the following questions.

1. What are the characteristics of any informa- tion system?

2. What are the characteristics of a computerized information system?

3. What are the different phases of a system's life cycle?

4. How are organization structure and informa- tion systems related?

5. What are the typical levels of management and what are their responsibilities?

6. What are the characteristics of valuable information?

7. What techniques can an organization use to reduce the chances of information overload?

8. How do transaction processing systems save money for an organization?

9. What are the differences between a manage- ment information system and a decision sup- port system?

10. What are the reasons behind Wal-Mart's suc- cess in the retail sector?

8B

MODULE

SYSTEMS ANALYSIS AND DESIGN

WHAT YOU WILL LEARN . . .

When you have finished reading this module, you will be able to:

1. Explain what systems analysts do.
2. Discuss the reasons for the widespread use of the systems development life cycle (SDLC).
3. List the SDLC's five phases.
4. Describe the classic mistakes of failed information system development projects.
5. Discuss the activities in each of the SDLC's five phases.

Creating a computerized information system isn't something to take lightly. The benefits are great, but so are the risks. A poorly-planned information system can eat up profits, anger customers, and even cause companies to go bankrupt. Unfortunately, poor results are all too common. According to a recent study published in *PC Week,* nearly one-third of information projects are abandoned before completion because it is apparent that the project will fail. The price tag for these failures is $81 billion.

Is it too much to ask that information systems be finished on time and within budget, and do their intended job? Admittedly, information systems development is a difficult challenge, and it's not made any easier by the fact that every case is unique. (For example, a pizza delivery company needs a different information system than a pharmaceutical firm or an automaker.) In addition, users and clients may have difficulty communicating their needs clearly, leading to products that don't satisfy them. And too many time estimates are overly optimistic, typically by as much as 20 to 30 percent. Building an information system takes longer than most people care to admit.

In the face of such chaos, it makes good sense to try to get organized. **Systems analysis** is a field of knowledge concerning information system development. The field learns from previous development efforts and formulates strategies for improved planning, organization, control, and execution of information system development projects. Systems analysts have developed an organized procedure for planning and building information systems, called the systems development life cycle (SDLC), which is the focus of this module.

SYSTEM ANALYSTS: COMMUNICATION COUNTS

Computer professionals called **system analysts** are problem-solving professionals who work with users and management to determine an organization's information system needs. They define the requirements needed to modify an existing system or to develop a new one. System analysts don't ordinarily do the development; rather, they identify and evaluate alternative solutions, make formal presentations to management, and assist in the development of the system after an option has been chosen.

Much of a system analyst's job involves communication, including listening skills. System analysts must understand the organization's mission, including its strategic goals. They must talk to users and understand their needs. They must involve users in the project so that users feel some ownership of the project. They must keep in close contact with team project members so that they know how the project is doing. They must write voluminous documentation that explains, at every step, what was performed, why and how it was performed, and who did it.

THE SYSTEMS DEVELOPMENT LIFE CYCLE (SDLC): A PROBLEM-SOLVING APPROACH

In the early years of business computing, information system development was a disorganized, ad-hoc process, frequently producing discouraging results. Systems were typically delivered late, went over their budgets, and didn't provide the services users expected. The **systems development life cycle (SDLC)** approach was developed to improve the quality of information systems. By encouraging an organized approach to problem-solving, SDLC can produce better information systems, but it's no substitute for creativity and intelligence.

Destinations

If your company needs help in solving its business challenges, one of the world's leaders in figuring out solutions is an organization formerly referred to as Andersen Consulting. Their home page, **http://www. ac.com,** explains what they've done for others.

The Five Phases of SDLC

At the core of the SDLC model is a simple idea: you shouldn't go on to the next step until you're certain that the current one has been performed properly. Following are the model's five phases (steps or stages). Each is intended to address key issues and to produce **deliverables** (outcomes), which form the input for the next phase (see Figure 8B.1).

As outlined in Figure 8B.1, the five phases of the system development life cycle are as follows:

1. **Identifying the problem and opportunities**   What is the problem? What are the alternative solutions? How much will the solution cost? (Deliverable: a project proposal.)

2. **Analyzing and documenting existing systems**   What does the existing system do? What do users need? What should the new system do? (Deliverable: requirements statement.)

3. **Designing the system**   How will the new system work? (Deliverable: detailed specification of program design.)

4. **Implementing the system**   Does the system do what the programmer and users believe it should do? (Deliverable: finished and tested information system.)

5. **Supporting the system**   How can we best train users? How can we make this system easier to use and more efficient? (Deliverable: post-implementation reviews.)

Note that there are several different versions of the systems development life cycle. Some versions identify more phases than others, and use different names for individual phases. The five-part process described here represents the common practice.

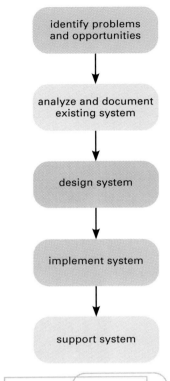

Figure   8B.1

The five phases of the system development life cycle.

Avoiding Mistakes

System analysts have learned, often through bitter experience, to avoid the classic mistakes of failed projects. Built into the SDLC model are the following essentials of system development wisdom:

- **User involvement is crucial**   Users include any person for whom the system is built, and that may include customers if, for example, you're creating a public Web site. Users are the ultimate judges of the system's usability. However, they may not know how to express their needs coherently. Without user involvement, the system may not meet user needs, and they may resist or even sabotage the new system.

- **A problem-solving approach works best**   To create an effective system, you must identify the problem, place the problem in context, define the solution, examine alternative solutions, and choose the best one. Without this approach, the system may not fully address the underlying shortcomings of the existing system.

- **Good project management skills are needed**   Many failed development projects are characterized by unrealistic expectations, overly-optimistic schedules, lack of solid backing from management, inability to make decisions and stick with them, lack of control over the insertion of new but unnecessary features, and interference from problem personnel. A poorly-managed project may become so chaotic that cancellation is necessary.

- **Documentation is required**   The term **documentation** refers to the recording of all information pertinent to the project, which is stored in

CURRENTS

Telemedicine

Can computers save lives? Definitely, through the use of telemedicine. Physicians at the University of North Carolina (UNC) Medical Center, one of the world's leading telemedicine centers, use computer network connections and sophisticated imaging technologies to extend a specialist's expertise into rural and remote areas, where such expertise isn't readily available. In one recent case, a young child living in an isolated rural community suffered a brain hemorrhage and couldn't be moved. By linking with other physicians via the Internet and videoconferencing connections, a local surgeon uploaded x-rays of the girl's brain and consulted with a UNC neurologist. The surgery was a success.

Telemedicine could bring dramatic quality gains to health care systems by making specialized expertise available at a low cost. The technology's possibilities were dramatically demonstrated during President Clinton's 1998 visit to China. Using the Internet, physicians at Stanford University consulted with Chinese doctors on a treatment plan for two seriously ill children located in a remote region of western China.

Although telemedicine sounds great, some major problems will have to be solved before its use becomes widespread. For example, state licensing programs forbid doctors to practice medicine outside the state in which they're licensed. And if a patient is misdiagnosed and then claims that a face-to-face meeting would have prevented the misdiagnosis, a malpractice lawsuit could result. Without regulation to address these and other issues, telemedicine will only grow slowly— and within state lines.

Among the most exciting innovations in technology is telemedicine, the use of computers and the Internet to make high-quality health care available to traditionally underserved populations.

Destinations

The business of solving organizational problems through technology is skillfully handled by a company called EDS. Examples of their successes can be found on their home page at **http:// www.eds.com.**

a **project notebook** (which may or may not be based on a computer system). The documentation enables everyone connected with the project to understand all the decisions that have been made. Documentation shouldn't be put off until the end of the project, when important information or key personnel might not be available. Without documentation, the system can't be properly supported or modified (especially after key development personnel have left).

■ **Use checkpoints to make sure the project's on track** At the end of each phase, the project must be critically and independently evaluated to make sure it's on track. An organization shouldn't be afraid to cancel the project (or repeat a phase) if the results aren't satisfactory. Some of the worst development disasters occurred when the project team concealed the fact that the system could not possibly work.

■ **Design for growth and change** If no room is left on a crucial data input screen, what happens when the firm introduces new products with more features? The system should be designed so that it won't break down or cause a major redesign in the event of change (including unanticipated increases in usage). Failure to anticipate change and growth could make the entire system useless in short order.

Avoiding mistakes doesn't guarantee success. On the other hand, making mistakes may very well guarantee failure!

The Waterfall Model

Although the systems development life cycle calls for a step-by-step process, it's not always wise to keep going if work in a later stage turns up problems with the work performed in an earlier one. For example, in the systems analysis phase, the team may discover that the problem hasn't been formulated correctly. The **waterfall model** builds correction pathways into the model that enable a return to a previous phase (see Figure 8B.2). It's the most-widely used way to implement the systems development life cycle.

PHASE 1: IDENTIFYING THE PROBLEM AND OPPORTUNITIES

In phase 1, an organization recognizes the need for an information system, defines the problem, identifies opportunities for change, and assesses the project's feasibility. The result is a project proposal submitted to senior management. If this phase is performed well, it assures that the right information system will be built and it assures, as importantly, that the wrong system won't be built.

Recognizing the Need for the System

New information systems (or modified ones) result from a recognition of deficiencies in performance (such as slow response time), information quality (out of date, inaccurate), economics (system costs too much to operate), security (too easy to break in), efficiency (wastes time, generates too much paper), or service (difficult to use, forces people to do things in an awkward way). Even if the current system doesn't have obvious deficiencies, it might still be judged worthwhile to replace it if a redesigned system could generate new business opportunities.

To get the project going, someone makes a formal request to the organization's information technology steering committee, which generally includes representatives from senior management, information systems personnel, users, and middle managers. The steering committee reviews requests and decides which ones to address.

If a project is approved, the steering committee appoints a project team. Goals for the first phase, planning, include determining the nature of the problem, examining alternative solutions, studying the project's feasibility, and creating a proposal for the overall project.

Defining the Problem

To solve a problem, you must first understand it, but that's not always as easy as it might seem. Problems can be masked by symptoms. A symptom is an unacceptable or undesirable result, whereas a problem is the underlying cause of the symptom. For example, people might complain about a symptom, such as the time it takes to get a response from the computer when entering a transaction. Users may demand more powerful computers. But the slow response time is just a symptom. If the problem lies in the slow speed of network transmission, it's a waste of money to buy faster computers!

Determining the exact problem is often a difficult task. Ideally, the problem definition stage identifies the features that need to be added to the information system to make it acceptable to users. Although users must be involved in defining the problem, they are not accustomed to looking at information systems in a structured, unbiased way. The system analyst talks to as many users as possible, and slowly a picture emerges of what these people do, when they do it, how they do it, and why they do it. The analyst then

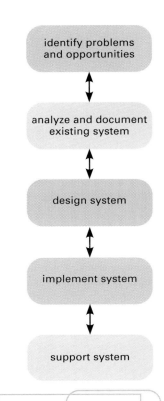

Figure 8B.2

The waterfall model builds correction pathways into the model that enable a return to a previous phase. It's the most-widely used implementation of the systems development life cycle.

To determine the exact problem, the system analyst must talk to as many users as possible to discover what they do, when they do it, how they do it, and why. The analyst then recommends new system features or an entirely new system.

derives from these facts a recommendation for new system features (if an existing system will be modified) or a new system built from scratch.

Identifying Opportunities

After the problem has been identified and the system requirements have been specified, the project team looks at a range of possible solutions, including internally-developed systems, off-the-shelf software, and externally-contracted solutions (called **outsourcing**). If the project team believes that a solution exists, the project proceeds.

Developing a Plan

When an appropriate solution has been identified, the project leader formulates a **project plan.** The plan identifies the project's goal and scope and specifies all the activities that must be completed for the project to succeed. For each activity, the plan specifies the estimated time that the project will require, as well as the estimated costs. The plan also identifies activities that must be completed before new ones can begin and indicates which activities can occur side-by-side. Project plans are often graphically summarized by means of a **Gantt chart,** a type of bar chart that shows how the activities are performed over time. Project management software (such as Microsoft Project) provides an excellent means of developing and modifying project plans (see Figure 8B.3).

Determining Feasibility

A feasible project can be completed successfully. Feasibility has three dimensions: technical, operational, and economic.

A project that's **technically feasible** can be accomplished with existing, proven technology. For example, consider a project that requires speech recognition. Although computers are getting much better at recognizing and transcribing human speech, they do make errors. If the error rate is unacceptable, the project isn't feasible until speech recognition technology is perfected.

A project that's **operationally feasible** can be accomplished with the organization's available resources. If some of the project's goals include changes beyond the organization's control (such as regulations in a foreign country), the project isn't operationally feasible.

The question of whether the project is **economically feasible** is usually answered by a **cost/benefit analysis,** where the costs are the expected costs to develop and run the new system. Cost estimates are general because they are estimated before the analysis. The purpose of cost estimates is to help clarify what the system is going to do.

The benefits include both tangible savings and intangible benefits. **Tangible savings** include labor costs, services, and materials that are need-

Figure 8B.3

A Gantt chart is a graphical summary of project plans that predicts activities performed over a period of time.

id	task name	duration	jan	feb	mar	apr	may	jun	jul	aug
1	planning	3w	1/26 ▬ 2/13							
2	analysis	10w	2/9 ▬▬▬▬▬▬ 4/17							
3	design	11w			3/23 ▬▬▬▬▬▬ 6/5					
4	implementation	4w						6/5 ▬▬ 7/3		

SPOTLIGHT

THE U.S. AIR TRAFFIC CONTROL SYSTEM: IS IT SAFE TO FLY?

▶Throughout the world, many large-scale organizations are facing a crisis brought on by *legacy systems,* information systems based on older-generation computers that can't handle today's demands. Replacing these systems isn't easy. For example, they may rely on programs written in languages that are no longer actively used. And all too often, the systems are so complex that the cost of replacing them is beyond the organization's means.

One of the best examples of an overloaded, obsolete information system is the U.S. Air Traffic Control (ATC) system. In the United States, the Federal Aviation Administration (FAA) runs the ATC system and hires and trains air traffic controllers. Given the ATC's importance, it's nothing short of amazing, say the FAA's critics, that the system is still using 30-year-old computers that break down with alarming frequency. Some of the FAA's computers are so old that they can be found only in one other place: computer museums.

In Chicago, an old ATC computer broke down seven times in 1997, disrupting air traffic. When failures occur, no immediate threat exists to public safety because backup systems step in to help controllers track aircraft locations. But these backup systems are slow and cumbersome to use, and controllers must increase spacing between flights to ensure safety, resulting in flight delays. The FAA concedes that

equipment failures cause air traffic slowdowns that cost airlines $5 billion annually.

Why has the FAA been so slow to update these critical systems? It's easy to point the finger of blame at plodding management and unresponsive bureaucrats. The biggest problem, however, lies in the enormous challenges of dealing with outmoded legacy systems. Just because these systems are old doesn't mean they're simple. The FAA's 250 computer systems run 23 million lines of code written in 50 different computer languages. What's worse, these systems and languages are so out-of-date that it's increasingly difficult to find qualified technicians and programmers who can help in the migration to modernized equipment.

Faced with a complex, safety-critical legacy system that's deteriorating rapidly, what should management do? One option is a completely new system, with new software and new computers. But shockingly few large-scale software projects succeed. Studies show that at least one-fourth of all large-scale software development projects are so riddled with bugs that they are eventually abandoned. The successful ones, however, overshoot their schedules by 50 percent. Of these, as many as three-quarters are operating failures that do not fully function as they were originally intended.

Recently, FAA officials admitted that a sweeping $7.5 billion upgrade program had failed, and the agency announced a much more modest (and much more successful) modernization program. The new program makes use of old software running on new machines, and therefore avoids the delays and cost overruns typically associated with new, massive software development programs.

The FAA concedes that the failures of outdated computer equipment result in air traffic delays that cost airlines $5 billion each year.

ed with the current system but can be eliminated if the new system is installed. It's common to sell a new system to a company's management based on **intangible benefits.** These benefits may include increased sales due to improved customer services or to managers having better information on which to base decisions. Bank managers, for example, may decide to install an automated teller machine (ATM) because they believe that many people will not deal with a bank that doesn't have one. Avoiding the loss of sales that would occur as a result of not installing the new system is an intangible benefit.

In many companies, managers request a study of the proposed system's **return on investment (ROI).** The money invested in the system should produce a return that is greater than alternative investments, such as putting the money in the bank.

Preparing the Project Proposal

At the conclusion of phase 1, the project leader writes a project proposal that introduces the nature of the existing system's problem, explains the proposed solution and its benefits, details the proposed project plan, and concludes with a recommendation. In response, management decides whether to continue the project.

PHASE 2: ANALYZING AND DOCUMENTING THE EXISTING INFORMATION SYSTEM

In phase 2, the systems analyst or the systems development team determines precisely what the new system should accomplish. Here, the emphasis is placed on *what* the system should do, not *how* (that comes later). This phase includes two steps: analyzing the existing system and determining the needs of the new system.

Analyzing the Existing System

A study of the existing system (whether computerized or manual) helps determine which activities currently being performed should be continued in the new system. This step can be simple if the current system is well documented. Unfortunately, most systems are not well documented, and that's especially true of updates to the original system. A major part of the analysis of the existing system is to document it. If the original system is computerized, the current hardware needs to be examined to see whether it is adequate to do the job.

An unexpected but valuable benefit of the systems analysis phase is that it often points out problems that weren't fully identified in phase 1. This analysis may be the first time a group of people has sat down in the same room and talked about the actual process. The discussion can result in new insights, and problems that were not part of the preliminary investigation can be solved.

Determining the New System's Requirements

After the existing system has been exhaustively documented, the new system's requirements are precisely stated. The requirements state the innovations that need to occur for the system to be acceptable to users. Here again, user involvement is crucial. System analysts obtain information about system requirements through interviews, surveys, and observations of the system's current uses.

PHASE 3: DESIGNING THE SYSTEM

In contrast to the previous phase, the system design phase, phase 3, is concerned with *how* the new information system will work. This phase isn't concerned with the nitty-gritty details of how the software will be coded. Instead, this phase's deliverable is a *logical design* that provides an overall picture of how the new system will work. Here, the project team uses the same tools developed to describe the existing system, such as entity-relationship diagrams, data flow diagrams, and data dictionaries. The team begins by specify-

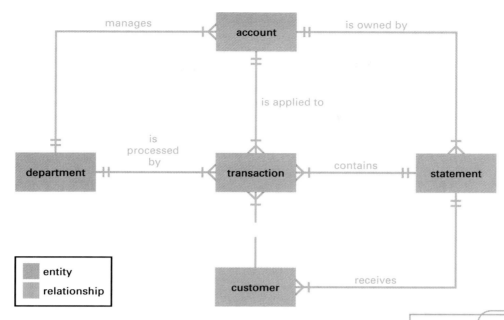

Figure 8B.4

An entity-relationship diagram depicts all the entities that play roles in the system.

ing how the new system's output will look—this is specified first because the output drives the rest of the design.

During this phase, it's important that analysts think about the system's logical requirements and don't start thinking about what can be accomplished (and what can't) with existing information systems and software. Such thinking might prevent them from realizing that they may need to create an entirely new type of system, one that's never been developed before. This is the reason phase 3 is clearly separated from phase 4, in which attention turns to the system's physical implementation. These two phases must be rigorously kept separate.

To describe the new information system, analysts can use **structural analysis and design tools.** These methods of graphical analysis help convey the analysts' findings to managers, programmers, and users alike. An **entity-relationship diagram (ERD)** shows all the entities (organizations, departments, users, programs, and data) that play roles in the system (see Figure 8B.4). A **data flow diagram** shows how data moves through the existing system using a set of graphical symbols (see Figure 8B.5). Also specified are the details of how this data is processed. Team members create a **project dictionary,** which explains all the terminology relevant to the project. They also develop a **data dictionary,** which precisely defines the type of data input into the system. The goal of this phase of the project is to specify in exact terms what data flows into the system, where it goes, how it's processed, who uses it, how it's stored, what data-entry forms are involved, and what procedures people follow.

Two new approaches, prototyping and computer-aided software engineering (CASE), are helping to improve the design phase. In **prototyping,** also called **joint application development (JAD),** a small-scale mock-up, or prototype, of the system is developed and shown to users (see Figure 8B.6). The prototype is developed at an early stage and isn't intended to be fully functional. It provides just enough functionality so that users can offer feedback. The advantage of prototyping lies in the fact that users don't have to imagine what the system specifications mean in terms of a working system. They can experience the system and thus find problems or enhancements that they may not have considered otherwise.

Techtalk

RAD

What would you think if the systems analyst working on your company's new information system told you that the project team will use "RAD" techniques to create the system? You might think it means some cool new approach is in the works. In actuality, RAD stands for "rapid application development," and it means that the development of the system will be greatly accelerated by combining prototyping, computer-based development tools such as CASE, special management practices, and extensive end-user involvement. That analyst was really telling you that you'll be seeing a lot of the project team, and that they'll be expecting you to help them work at light-speed to finish the system!

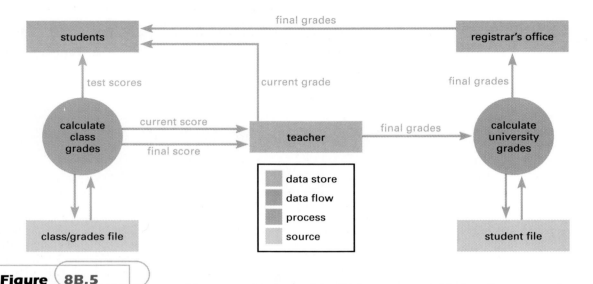

Figure 8B.5

A data flow diagram shows how data moves through the existing system.

The second new tool, called **computer-aided software engineering (CASE),** can help automate the often-tedious task of documenting entity relationships and data flows in a complex new system. Most CASE tools include project management, data dictionaries, documentation support, and graphical output. Some even generate prototype code automatically. CASE software, however, is expensive, requires extensive training, and is difficult to use.

PHASE 4: IMPLEMENTING THE SYSTEM

In phase 4, the systems implementation phase, the project team and management decide whether to create the physical system using internal expertise or to purchase it from outside vendors. In either case, hardware must be purchased and installed, and programs must be written. The system must be exhaustively tested, and users must be trained. When the team is confident that the new system is ready for use, the conversion to the new system takes place.

Figure 8B.6

A prototyping tool at work.

Deciding to Build or Buy

After the new system's requirements and logical design have been specified, the project team faces the **build-or-buy decision:** should the new system be developed in-house or purchased from an outside vendor?

If the decision is made to outsource the project, the project team sends out a **request for quotation (RFQ)** or a **request for proposal (RFP).** An RFQ is used if the specific components have been identified. An RFP is used if the project team wants a computer vendor or a **value-added reseller (VAR)** to select the system components. VARs are independent companies that combine and install equipment and software from several sources.

Developing the Software

To develop the software required for the new system, programmers use the **program development life cycle (PDLC),** described in Module 8C. Like the systems development life cycle, the PDLC is a step-by-step procedure that helps developers get good results.

Testing

Thorough testing is essential. The two basic types of testing are **application testing** and **acceptance testing.** In application testing, the programs are tested individually and then tested together. In acceptance testing, users evaluate the system to see whether it meets their needs and functions correctly. It's essential that errors or problems are detected before the system is released for general use in the organization.

Training

A computerized information system includes not only computer hardware and software but also knowledgeable users and procedures. A successful conclusion to the project requires training users to use the new system effectively. The best training methods involve sitting users down with the new system in one-on-one training sessions. Users will also need manuals that include tutorials as well as reference information. Increasingly popular is **computer-based training (CBT),** a form of computer-based education that uses multimedia, animation, and programmed learning to teach new skills.

PowerBuilder is a CASE tool that delivers a complete 4GL, RAD environment for building traditional client/server and multi-tier distributed applications.

Converting Systems

After the new system has been tested, conversion to the new system occurs. System conversion can be performed in any of the following ways:

- A **parallel conversion** involves running both systems for a while to check that the new system comes up with answers at least as good as those of the old system. This type of conversion is the safest, since the old system can carry the load until any problems with the new system are cleared up. This conversion is also the most expensive, however, because the work is duplicated.

- In a **pilot conversion,** one part of the organization converts to the new system while the rest of the organization continues to run the old system. When the pilot group is satisfied with the new system, the rest of the organization can start using it.

- A **phased conversion** occurs when the new system is implemented in different time periods, one part at a time. After one part of the new system is running, another piece is implemented.

- A **direct conversion,** sometimes called a crash conversion, requires stopping the old system and then starting the new system. A direct conversion is the most risky but may be necessary in some situations.

PHASE 5: SUPPORTING THE SYSTEM

In the final phase, the new system receives ongoing assistance to ensure that it has met its intended needs and works correctly. A **post-implementation system review** determines whether the system has met its goals. After conversion, widespread use may reveal errors that were not detected during testing, which must be corrected. In addition, changes will be needed as the business environment changes. For example, changes may be needed in data entry forms to deal with an expanded product line. In time, the system may be found to be so deficient that a new round of system development must take place—and the system development life cycle begins anew.

TAKEAWAY POINTS

- System analysts help determine an organization's information system needs by working closely with both users and management.
- The systems development life cycle (SDLC) was developed to impose order on earlier, haphazard development processes. It breaks information system development down into definite stages, each of which must be successfully completed before the project moves on to the next phase.
- The SDLC's five phases are identifying problems and opportunities, analyzing and documenting existing systems, designing the system,

implementing the system, and supporting the system.
- Each phase of the SDLC provides a deliverable, which serves as the input to the next phase. These deliverables are a project proposal, a graphical analysis of the current information system, a graphical and detailed analysis of the new information system, a finished and tested product, and a post-implementation review.
- The three classic mistakes of failed information system development projects are lack of user involvement, poor project management, and lack of documentation.

MODULE REVIEW

KEY TERMS AND CONCEPTS

acceptance testing	Gantt chart	project plan
application testing	intangible benefits	prototyping
build-or-buy decision	joint application development	request for proposal (RFP)
computer-aided software	(JAD)	request for quotation (RFQ)
engineering (CASE)	operationally feasible	return on investment (ROI)
computer-based training (CBT)	outsourcing	structural analysis and design
cost/benefit analysis	parallel conversion	tools
data dictionary	phased conversion	system analysts
data flow diagram	pilot conversion	systems analysis
deliverables	post-implementation system	systems development life cycle
direct conversion	review	(SDLC)
documentation	program development life cycle	tangible savings
economically feasible	(PDLC)	technically feasible
entity-relationship diagram	project dictionary	value-added reseller (VAR)
(ERD)	project notebook	waterfall model

TRUE/FALSE

Indicate whether the following statements are true or false.

1. System analysts help determine an organization's information system needs.

2. User involvement is beneficial, but not crucial, to successful system development.

3. A project notebook is used to store documentation about system development.

4. A Gantt chart identifies the project's goal and scope and specifies all the activities that must be completed for the project to succeed.

5. A cost/benefit analysis is usually used to determine the operational feasibility of a project.

6. The purpose of the second phase (analysis and documenting the current system) is to determine what the new system should do.

7. The system design phase is used to determine how the new system will work.

8. Prototyping is a tool that can help automate the often-tedious task of documenting data flows in a new system.

9. A VAR is an independent company that combines and installs equipment and software from several sources.

10. In a phased conversion, one part of the organization converts to the new system while the rest of the organization continues to run the old system.

MATCHING

Match each key term from the left column to the most accurate definition in the right column.

_____ 1. systems analysis

_____ 2. systems development life cycle

_____ 3. waterfall model

_____ 4. operationally feasible

_____ 5. return on investment (ROI)

_____ 6. data flow diagram

_____ 7. project dictionary

_____ 8. data dictionary

_____ 9. application testing

_____ 10. direct conversion

a. this describes how money invested in the system should produce a return greater than alternative investments

b. this shows how data moves through an existing system

c. this requires stopping the old system and starting the new system

d. the process where programs are tested individually and then tested together

e. the field of knowledge concerning information system development

f. this describes a project that can be accomplished with the organization's available resources

g. this precisely defines the type of data that is input in the system

h. an approach used to improve the quality of information systems

i. this explains all terminology relevant to the project

j. this builds correction pathways into the model that enable a return to the previous phase

MULTIPLE CHOICE

Circle the letter of the correct choice for each of the following.

1. What does SDLC stand for?
   a. Secondary Dynamic Life Cycle
   b. Simple Data Linear Compression
   c. Systems Development Life Cycle
   d. Synchronous Data Line Current

2. Which of the following is not a phase in the process followed by systems analysts?
   a. analyzing and documenting existing systems
   b. creating purchasing specifications
   c. implementing the system
   d. designing the system

3. Recognition of which of the following is not essential to sound system development?
   a. hiring value-added resellers
   b. good project management skills
   c. documentation
   d. user involvement

4. Which of the following doesn't need to be part of a project plan?
   a. résumés of key personnel
   b. goal
   c. scope
   d. necessary activities

5. Systems analysts obtain information about system requirements through which of the following?

   a. reading, surveys, and observations
   b. reading, studying, and guessing
   c. interviews, surveys, and observations
   d. interviews, studying, and observations

6. Which of the following tools is not a structural analysis and design tool?
   a. entity-relationship diagram
   b. Gantt chart
   c. data flow diagram
   d. project dictionary

7. Which of the following is used to define the type of data that is input into the system?
   a. project dictionary
   b. information gateway
   c. data dictionary
   d. data diagram

8. The acronym CASE stands for which of the following?
   a. computer-assisted system engineering
   b. community action for system engineering
   c. computer and system enterprises
   d. computer-aided software engineering

9. System training is a part of which development phase?
   a. phase 1
   b. phase 2
   c. phase 3
   d. phase 4

10. Which type of system conversion involves running two systems simultaneously to ensure that the new system produces output similar to, or better than, the old system?

    a. direct conversion
    b. parallel conversion
    c. pilot conversion
    d. phased conversion

FILL-IN

In the blank provided, write the correct answer for each of the following.

1. _____ is a field of knowledge concerning information system development.

2. The recording of all information pertinent to a project is called _____ .

3. The _____ builds correction pathways into the SDLC process that enables a return to a previous phase.

4. Contracting for goods and services external to an organization is called _____ .

5. Project plans are often graphically summarized by means of a(n) _____ .

6. A(n) _____ diagram shows all the entities that play roles in the system.

7. A(n) _____ is used to explain all the terminology relevant to a project.

8. Another name for joint application development (JAD) is _____ .

9. An increasingly-popular form of training is _____ training.

10. A(n) _____ conversion occurs when the new system is implemented in different time periods, one part at a time.

SHORT ANSWER

On a separate sheet of paper, answer the following questions.

1. What skills should a system analyst possess? Which skills are the most critical?

2. What are the five phases of SDLC?

3. Define the relationship between problems and symptoms. Give examples of each.

4. What are the three facets of a feasible project?

5. Describe the differences between tangible and intangible benefits.

6. Why is it important to document the existing system, regardless of whether it is computerized?

7. What are the advantages of prototyping at an early stage in the development of a system?

8. What are the advantages and drawbacks to using a CASE system?

9. What are the two types of testing performed on new systems? How do they differ?

10. What are the pros and cons of the different approaches to system conversion?

8C

MODULE

OUTLINE

WHAT YOU WILL LEARN . . .

When you have finished reading this module, you will be able to:

1. Explain what a programming language is.
2. Contrast machine language and assembly language.
3. Discuss the benefits of a high-level programming language.
4. List the measures taken to improve third-generation languages.
5. Identify the shortcomings of previous languages and explain how object-oriented languages may remedy these shortcomings.
6. List several popular programming languages and explain their advantages and disadvantages.
7. List the six phases of the program development life cycle (PDLC) and explain why it's needed.
8. Explain why top-down programming makes programs easier to debug and maintain.
9. List the three basic types of control structures.
10. Differentiate between syntax errors and logic errors in program testing.

Where does software come from? It's a programmer's dream to get computers to write software automatically, but this dream hasn't come true, yet. Computer software comes from the efforts of computer programmers, working individually or in groups, who use **programming languages** to do their job.

What's a programming language? It's not a natural language like the ones people speak. Rather, it's an artificial language, one that's deliberately created to tell the computer what to do. Typically, a programming language consists of a vocabulary and a set of rules (called **syntax**) that the programmer must learn. The vocabulary and rules are used to write a program, which, in most cases, must be translated before the computer can run it.

What's the best programming language? If you ask this question while you're talking to ten computer people, chances are you'll get ten different answers. The truth is that there isn't any one language that's best for all programming purposes. Every language has its advantages and disadvantages. The question is, which language is the right one for the job?

In this module, you'll learn how to make sense of the world of programming languages. You'll learn how these languages developed, and you'll take a look at today's hottest languages. You'll also learn how programs are developed by means of the **program development life cycle (PDLC)**, an organized method of software development that bears many similarities to the system development life cycle (SDLC) discussed in Module 8B. The PDLC is part of the SDLC's implementation phase.

If you don't plan to learn programming, this module will help you understand what the programming language debate is all about and will help you play a more-informed role in the companies you work for. And should you decide to give programming a try, you'll get the background you need to select a good language to learn.

FIRST-GENERATION LANGUAGES: 1S AND 0S

If the phrase "programming language" is taken to suggest a vocabulary that makes programming easy for humans, the earliest computers didn't have one. These computers had to be programmed in the computer's language, also known as machine language.

Machine language consists of binary numbers—0s and 1s—that directly correspond to the computer's electrical states. While tedious for humans to work with, machine language is the only programming language that the computer can understand directly without translation. The language must be written in accordance with the special characteristics of a given processor. Each type or family of processor requires its own machine language. For this reason, machine language is said to be **machine-dependent** (also called *hardware-dependent*).

In the computer's first generation, programmers had to use machine language because no other option was available (see Module 1B). Programmers had to know a great deal about the computer's design and how it functioned. As a result, programs were few in number and lacked complexity.

Although only a few people program directly in machine languages today, they are still in use. More recent programming languages give programmers easier ways to write programs, but as you will see, the code they write must still be translated into machine language to execute on a given processor.

SECOND-GENERATION LANGUAGES: A LITTLE EASIER

The first programming language to break programmers' dependence on machine language was **assembly language.** Assembly language closely resembles machine language, in that it's machine-dependent and closely tied to what goes on inside the computer. For this reason, it's called a **low-level**

Explore IT Lab

Introduction to Computer Programming

language (one that's not far removed from machine language in terms of its level of abstraction). To program in assembly language, programmers still need to know exactly how the computer works.

However, assembly language doesn't force you to program in binary. Instead, it enables programmers to use brief abbreviations for program instructions, as well as familiar, base-10 (decimal) numbers. The abbreviations are called **mnemonics** (pronounced "nih-MON-icks"). For example, the mnemonic COMPARE A,B tells the processor to compare the data stored in memory locations A and B.

Before an assembly-language program can be run on a computer, it must be translated into machine language. As it is written, the program is a text file called **source code.** The source code is translated into machine language by an **assembler.**

Assembly language is still used sometimes, especially when it is important to make a short program that runs as fast as possible. A good assembly-language programmer knows how to put a program together to provide fast execution on a given processor.

THIRD-GENERATION LANGUAGES: PROGRAMMING COMES OF AGE

Due to the shortcomings of machine and assembly language, **third-generation languages (3GL)** were developed. Although these languages are still **procedural languages,** in that they tell the computer what to do and how to do it, they are also **high-level languages.** A high-level language eliminates the need for programmers to understand the intimate details of how the computer processes data. They enable programmers to create programs at a high level of abstraction compared to machine and assembly language. For example, the programmer can write an instruction using familiar English words such as PRINT or DISPLAY. Each such instruction sums up many lines (sometimes hundreds of lines) of assembly or machine code. 3GL languages are much easier to read, write, and maintain than assembly language.

Compilers and Interpreters

Writing in a 3GL language, programmers create source code, just as they do when they write in assembly language. To be used on a specific type of computer system, this source code must be translated using a compiler or an interpreter (see Figure 8C.1).

A **compiler** is a translation program that translates all the source code into **object code,** a file that contains instructions in (or close to) a specific computer's machine language. With some compilers, it's necessary to use a program called a **linker** or **assembler** to transform the object code into an **executable program** (a program that runs on a certain type of computer). When the compiler translates the code, it checks the code for errors. If any errors are found, the program identifies the error's location and prints a **program listing** (a printout of the source code) that highlights the location and likely cause of the error.

An **interpreter** doesn't produce object code. Instead, it translates one line of the source code at a time and executes the translated instruction. Although interpreters run programs more slowly than programs compiled into object code, they are helpful tools for learning and **debugging** (ridding a program of errors, called **bugs**). As the program executes line-by-line, the programmer can see exactly what each line does.

For most programming languages, a programmer can use both an interpreter and a compiler. The interpreter comes in handy during the program development stage. When the program is finished, it's compiled for efficient use.

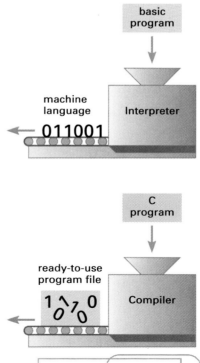

Figure 8C.1

An interpreter and compiler.

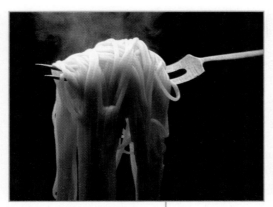

In a lengthy program, the use of many GOTO statements resulted in spaghetti code, or programs that were difficult to follow and consequently were prone to error.

Spaghetti Code and the Great Software Crisis

Although early third-generation languages such as Fortran and COBOL represented a major improvement over assembly and machine languages, they introduced a problem. To enable programs to branch out to new locations (depending on whether or not a condition was met), early third-generation languages used GOTO statements. This wasn't a problem for simple, short programs, but the advances of third-generation languages enabled programmers to tackle more ambitious projects. In a lengthy program, the use of many GOTO statements resulted in a **spaghetti code,** which were programs that were difficult to follow, and in consequence were prone to error.

The attempt to create larger and more complex programs led to the **software crisis** of the 1960s. Programs were not ready on time, exceeded their budgets, contained too many errors, and didn't satisfy customers. A study during the mid-1960s found that COBOL programmers were only able, on average, to produce ten error-free lines of code per day of work.

Structured Programming Languages

One response to spaghetti code's problems focused on improving the management of software development. Another response focused on improving the languages themselves. The earliest (late-1960s) product of such efforts was the concept of **structured programming** and languages that reflected structured programming concepts.

In structured programming, GOTO statements are forbidden, and programmers are required to construct the program using logical elements called *control structures.* For example, program branching is handled by an IF-THEN-ELSE control structure (called a *selection control structure*), rather than a GOTO statement. These elements are grouped in a block with an END statement, which results in more-readable code that's much easier to debug. Examples of structured languages include Algol and Pascal.

Modular Programming Languages

By the 1970s, it was clear that structured programming languages, although better than their predecessors, were not able to solve the problems encountered in the even-larger development projects underway at that time. That led to the development of the **modular programming** concept. In a modular language, the program is divided into separate modules, each of which takes care of a specific function that the program has to carry out. Each module requires a specified input and produces a specified output, so the programming job can be easily divided among members of the programming team. An important principle of modular programming is called **information hiding.** The author of one module doesn't have to be concerned with the details of what's inside another module. This information can remain hidden (and other programmers can ignore it) as long as a given module generates output in the specified form.

FOURTH-GENERATION LANGUAGES: GETTING AWAY FROM PROCEDURE

Although the transition from the second to the third generation of programming languages is reasonably clear, the same can't be said for the transition to **fourth-generation languages (4GL).** Various types of programming languages have been identified as "fourth generation," including **report generators** (languages for printing database reports) and **query languages** (languages for getting information out of databases). What all these languages share is that they are **nonprocedural;** that is, they do not force the programmer to consider the procedure that must be followed to obtain the desired result. For example, in **Structured Query Language,** or **SQL** (pronounced "sequel"), you can ask the following question of the information in a database:

```
SELECT employee-name
FROM employee-salary-table
WHERE salary > 50000
AND position = 'Engineer'
```

In everyday terms, "Get the names of all engineers who make more than $50,000." Note that this question isn't totally nonprocedural; you still have to know quite a bit about how the database is structured. (For example, you have to specify which table the information should come from.) The ultimate nonprocedural language would be **natural language,** the everyday language that people speak, but computers will need to be endowed with artificial intelligence before they can decode natural language.

OBJECT-ORIENTED PROGRAMMING: A REVOLUTION IN THE MAKING?

Although fourth-generation languages have given nonprogrammers useful tools for extracting information from databases, they aren't general-purpose programming languages. As a result, programmers kept on using third-generation languages. Structured and modular programming helped programmers do a better job, but they did not revolutionize programming. What's needed to take the next step is **component reusability,** the capability to develop well-designed program modules that perform a specific task, such as handling print output. If component reusability can be achieved, programmers could quickly construct a program by combining ready-to-use modules, in a process that would take a fraction of the time required to develop these modules from scratch.

Eliminating the Program vs. Data Distinction

A new approach to programming, called **object-oriented (OO) programming** (also known by the OOP acronym), promises to achieve the dream of component reusability. It does so by introducing a different philosophy of program design.

In traditional programming, the program and data are kept separate. If the data must change—for example, if a company decides that it needs to start tracking the exact time of orders as well as the date—all programs that access this data must also be changed. That's an expensive, time-consuming process.

In object-oriented programming, the problem of having to update numerous programs is solved by doing something unprecedented: eliminating the distinction between programs and data. In OOP, the data is stored, along with all the program procedures needed to access and use this data. If another program accesses the data, it immediately learns which procedures are available, including any new ones. This eliminates the need to go through and change numerous programs just because of some little change in the data. As explained in the next section, the term *object* is used to describe the units that store data along with the procedures available to access and use the data.

What Is an Object?

An **object** is a unit of computer information that contains data, as well as all the procedures or operations (called **methods**) that can process or manipulate this data. The object also contains information that defines its *interface,* or its means of exchanging messages with other objects. For example, one object can ask another object, in effect, "What methods do you have available?" and the object will describe them. With object-oriented programming, information hiding becomes a reality. Users (or other objects) don't have to know anything about the specifics of how the object was implemented internally. (In object-oriented programming, information hiding is called **encapsulation.)**

Here's an example to illustrate what an object is: suppose you're running a bike shop, and you've created an object called DASHER. This object contains all the data about Dasher bicycles (including inventory, pricing information, and performance characteristics). It also contains all the methods that can be used to process this data. You can use a program (which is itself an object) that can query DASHER to find out which methods are available. You'll find out that you can choose from many methods, including totaling the number of Dasher bicycles on hand, updating the inventory, listing available accessories, or computing a sale price including specified accessories.

Note that object-oriented programming encourages the programmer to start thinking *from the beginning* about the real-world environment in which the program will function. Proponents of object-oriented programming believe that this focus leads to more usable software.

Classes

An important feature of object-oriented programming is the concept of class, which is a category of objects. In the DASHER example just given, the DASHER object is part of a broader, more-abstract category of objects called BIKES. In other words, it's a *subclass* of the BIKES class. The BIKES class is a *superclass* of DASHER because it's more abstract and generic. Other lines of bikes carried by the same bike shop are SPEEDO and ZOOM-310. Objects exist for these, too, and they, like DASHER, are subclasses of BIKES.

Inheritance

One of the major objectives of object-oriented programming is reusability, the capability to create an object and then reuse it whenever it's needed. By means of inheritance, the possibilities for object reuse are multiplied.

Inheritance refers to an object's capacity to "pass on" its characteristics to its "children," or subclasses. To create objects for the bike shop, a programmer begins by creating the BIKES object. This object is then copied and modified to make the DASHER, SPEEDO, and ZOOM-310 objects, all of which inherit the BIKES object's properties (see Figure 8C.2).

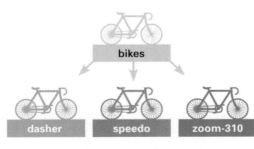

Figure 8C.2

DASHER, SPEEDO, and ZOOM-310 are subclasses of the BIKES object. They all inherit the BIKES object's properties.

Rapid Application Development (RAD)

Because objects can be so easily reused, object-oriented programming enables a fast method of program development, called **rapid application development (RAD).** In RAD, a programmer works with a library of prebuilt objects that have been created for a huge variety of applications.

Middleware (Objects Across the Enterprise)

One of the most appealing possibilities of object-oriented programming lies in its suitability for use in computer networks. Suppose you have hundreds or even thousands of objects accessible on the network, and each one contains data, as well as knowledge about how to use that data. It would be nice to be able to access these objects. But to do so, **middleware** is needed. The term middleware refers to standards that define how programs can find objects and query (ask) them about what kind of goodies they contain.

Middleware is a new concept, and its standards are only beginning to mature. One leading standard is the **Common Object Request Broker Architecture (CORBA).** CORBA defines how objects can communicate with each other across a network, even if the objects are written in dissimilar programming languages. For example, oil giant Chevron uses CORBA to give nearly 3,000 employees access to a variety of databases, which are written in many different languages. By means of the **Internet Inter-Orb Protocol (IIOP),** CORBA capabilities can be built into Web browsers, which transforms them into tools for requesting information from objects.

CORBA isn't the only middleware standard. Microsoft Corporation is pushing its own standard, called **Component Object Model (COM),** which works best when companies are running nothing but Windows machines.

A GUIDE TO PROGRAMMING LANGUAGES: ONE SIZE DOESN'T FIT ALL

In this section, you'll find a guide to the most popular programming languages in use today. As you'll see, each program has its pros and cons for particular purposes. A major part of programming success involves choosing the right language for the job.

COBOL and Fortran: For Some People, Retro Rules!

Imagine it's 1959. Cars have big fins. Dwight Eisenhower is the president of the United States. Hawaii becomes a state. And computer programmers are using COBOL and Fortran.

Now fast-forward. It's the beginning of the twenty-first century. Guess what? More than 50 percent of computer programmers are still using COBOL and Fortran. Are these really good languages, or do people have trouble learning new ones?

COBOL

COBOL is one of the earliest high-level programming languages, dating all the way back to 1959. It gets very little respect in university computer science departments—in fact, a leading computer scientist stated in 1982 that the teaching of COBOL should be made a criminal offense. People may yawn, laugh, or tell COBOL-bashing jokes, but guess what? The **Common Business-Oriented Language (COBOL)** is nonetheless the most-widely used business programming language in the world. What's more, thousands of jobs are available for COBOL programmers, and businesses are competing to hire COBOL talent. In the mid-1990s, COBOL accounted for more than 65 percent of all new application development. Why?

COBOL's success lies in the simple fact that it's a proven way to tackle the huge job of dealing with a large organization's accounting information, including inventory control, billing, and payroll. In addition, COBOL has some features that more recent programming languages would do well to imitate. For example, COBOL requires programmers to write in a style that explains what the program is doing at each step of the way. Anyone who knows COBOL can look at someone else's program and quickly figure out how it works.

That's what COBOL boosters say. Detractors say COBOL's longevity has more to do with the surprising survival of **legacy** (obsolete) mainframe computer systems, where COBOL programming dominates. Like other legacy programming languages, COBOL has been updated with structured and even object-oriented versions, so there remains a clear path into the future.

Fortran

Destinations

Learn more about COBOL by reading the COBOL FAQ (Frequently-Asked Questions), located on the Oxford University Library Automation Service (**http://www. lib.ox.ac.uk/internet/ news/faq/archive/ cobol-faq.html**).

Fortran, short for formula translator, is yet another survivor from the 1950s. It is so well-suited to scientific, mathematical, and engineering applications that even after all this time, it's very difficult to pry it out of engineers' hands. In many engineering schools, protracted battles arise over which programming language to teach engineering students: the computer science people want to teach C++, and the engineers want to teach Fortran.

What's so great about Fortran? The answer is in the name: "formula translator." If you need to solve a complex engineering equation, no other programming language comes close to Fortran's simplicity, economy, and ease of use. Fortran is most likely to be replaced not by another programming language, but a formula-solving program such as Wolfram Research's Mathematica, which can transform equations into complex (and often beautiful) graphics that reveal underlying mathematical patterns.

Structured and Modular Languages

COBOL and Fortran still have their places in mainframes and engineering shops, but large-scale program development requires structured and modular languages. The following languages are in widespread use among professional developers and software firms.

Ada

A high-level programming language incorporating modular programming principles, Ada is named after August Ada Byron (1815–1852), who helped nineteenth-century inventor Charles Babbage conceptualize what could have been the world's first digital computer. Ada's popularity is due in part to its role as the required language for most U.S. Defense Department projects until 1996. The major advantage of Ada is its suitability for the reliable control of real-time systems (such as missiles). The U.S. Navy's Seawolf submarine uses more than five million lines of Ada code running on more than 100 Motorola processors.

August Ada Byron helped nineteenth-century inventor Charles Babbage conceptualize what could have been the world's first digital computer.

Visual Basic

BASIC (Beginner's All-Purpose Symbolic Instruction Code) is an easy-to-use, high-level programming language available on many personal computers. Developed at Dartmouth College in the mid-1960s to teach programming basics to beginners, BASIC has become a language that many hobbyists use to create simple programs. It is also widely taught in high schools and some colleges in beginning programming courses. Many educators, however, believe that the original versions of BASIC taught flawed programming skills, due to BASIC's reliance on GOTO statements. More recent versions of BASIC incorporate the principles of structured, modular, and object-oriented programming.

BASIC was designed as an interpreted language so that beginners could create a program in an interactive mode, run the program, test it, and debug it. Interpreted languages are conducive to learning programming, but they run much more slowly than compiled programs. As a result, professional programmers avoided using BASIC. Newer versions of BASIC have since added compilers.

Is BASIC a kid's language, something you grow out of? No. **Microsoft's Visual Basic (VB)** is one of the world's most-widely used program development packages. In the United States, it's part of the programming toolkit of more than 50 percent of the country's 2.4 million professional programmers. The company has sold more than 1 million licenses for Visual Basic 5.0. What's the secret to Visual Basic's success? It's by far the most-successful rapid application development tool in existence for Microsoft Windows applications, and Windows is the operating system used in an estimated 80 percent of the world's computers (see Figure 8C.3).

Using an **event-driven** programming model, in which the program is designed to wait for the user to do something (such as click the mouse button), Visual Basic enables a programmer to develop an application quickly by designing the graphical user interface on-screen as the *first* step in program development. Each on-screen control, such as a text box or a radio button, can then be linked to a brief BASIC program that performs an action. The programmer doesn't have to worry about any of the code that generates the great-looking user interface: that's all handled automatically by the Visual Basic compiler, which creates an executable program capable of running on its own. Using Visual Basic, even a novice programmer can develop an impressive application in short order.

A huge variety of accessory tools enable Visual Basic programmers to quickly accomplish tasks such as building interfaces to databases and increasing the functionality of Web pages. **VBScript,** a **scripting language** based on Visual Basic, was created for writing **scripts** (short programs) that can be embedded in Web pages. A script isn't compiled; instead, it's interpreted by the Web browser, line-by-line.

ActiveX controls are miniprograms (mainly written in Visual Basic) that can be downloaded from Web pages and used to add functionality to Web browsers. However, VBScript and ActiveX controls require users to be running Microsoft Windows and Microsoft Internet Explorer.

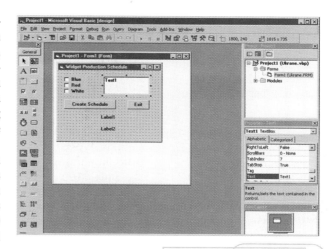

Figure 8C.3

Visual Basic enables a programmer to develop an application quickly by designing the graphical user interface on-screen as the first step in program development.

Pascal

Pascal, named after seventeenth-century mathematician Blaise Pascal, is a high-level programming language that encourages programmers to write well-structured programs. Pascal has gained wide acceptance as a teaching language, and is available in both interpreted and compiled versions.

Like most older programming languages, Pascal has been updated to reflect the new approaches to programming. An object-oriented version of Pascal provides the foundation for **Delphi,** a compiler created by Borland International (now called Inprise Corp.) that closely resembles Visual Basic. However, Delphi hasn't been able to match Visual Basic's success.

Object-Oriented (OO) Languages

Structured and modular languages are the workhorses of software development, but they're not the cutting edge. That honor goes to object-oriented (OO) languages.

Smalltalk

Developed in the early-1970s at Xerox Corporation's Palo Alto Research Center (PARC), the home of the graphical user interface (GUI) and many other key innovations in computing, **Smalltalk** is considered by many to be the only "100 percent pure" object-oriented (OO) programming language. Although the language is not often chosen for professional software development, more than a few corporations have chosen Smalltalk for mission-critical applications (including American Airlines, Federal Express, and Texas Instruments). But Smalltalk is facing stiff competition from the newest object-oriented language on the scene: Java.

C and C++

C is a high-level programming language developed by AT&T's Bell Labs in the 1970s. C combines the virtues of high-level programming languages with the efficiency of an assembly language. Using C, programmers can directly manipulate bits of data inside the processing unit. As a result, well-written C programs run significantly faster than programs written in other high-level programming languages. However, C is difficult to learn, and programming in C is a time-consuming activity. A more recent version of C, **C++**, incorporates object-oriented (OO) features, but doesn't force programmers to adhere to the OO model (see Figure 8C.4). Thanks to this flexibility and the high execution speed of compiled C++ programs, the C++ language is in widespread use for professional program development. For example, software giant Microsoft Corporation uses C++ for its application development.

Destinations

If you're thinking about a career in computer science or professional programming, C++ is the language to learn. For more information on C++, see C++ Virtual Library (**http://www. desy.de/user/projects/ C++.html**) and C++ FAQ Lite (**http://www. cerfnet.com/~mpcline/ c++-faq-lite/**).

```
# include <iostream.h>

void main ()
{
  cout <<"Hello
World!";
```

Figure 8C.4

A simple C++ program that prints "Hello World!" to the screen.

Java

Suppose you ask the computer industry's version of the magic mirror, "Who's the fairest of them all?" The answer will come quickly: Java. Developed by Sun Microsystems, **Java** is an object-oriented, high-level programming language with a new twist (see Figure 8C.5). According to Java backers, it is the world's first truly **cross-platform programming language,** a language that enables you to "write once, run anywhere." And it's gained acceptance faster than any programming language in the history of computing. Java is *hot*.

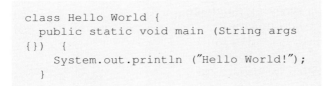

```
class Hello World {
  public static void main (String args
{})  {
    System.out.println ("Hello World!");
  }
```

Figure 8C.5

An example of sample Java code. Java has gained acceptance faster than any programming language in the history of computing.

Developed for consumer electronic devices, Java is a simplified version of C++ (and is much easier to learn than C++). But the feature "write once, run anywhere" is what's attracting attention. How is it possible to write one program and run it on any computer? As you've learned, language translators (compilers or interpreters) transform source code into executable programs, which are designed to run on a specific type of computer. But Java programs are designed to run on any computer in widespread use today, including computers using the Windows, Mac OS, or UNIX operating systems. The secret to this remarkable capability is the **Java Virtual Machine,** which needs to be installed on any computer that runs Java. The Virtual Machine is a program execution environment that provides a "home away from home" for Java, no matter what type of computer it's running on.

S P O T L I G H T

POSTSCRIPT AND THE DESKTOP PUBLISHING REVOLUTION

▶Programming languages allow humans to convey to machines what they want to accomplish. Many programming languages are on the market. Each has its strengths, weaknesses, proponents, and detractors.

One programming language that has been around for a while doesn't even need a computer to be useful—at least, not a computer in the traditional sense of the word. PostScript is a programming language that is used to describe how information should be placed on a printed page. In other words, it is a *page description language.* PostScript is used most often in printers but can be used in other types of output devices as well.

PostScript has its roots in work performed at Xerox's Palo Alto Research Center (PARC). Two researchers at the facility, John E. Warnock and Charles M. Geschke, developed the language. When Xerox failed to develop the potential of the language and settled on a different standard for page description, the two struck out on their own to form Adobe Systems, Inc., in 1982. By 1985, the first commercial product utilizing PostScript—the Apple LaserWriter printer—was released to the world. The result was the birth of a new revolution we have since termed *desktop publishing.*

Nothing about PostScript is mystical. By design, it is interpreted. Programming commands consisting of plain ASCII characters are sent and acted upon by a processor in a device. For instance, one set of commands might describe margins for the page, and another set might detail the type of fonts to be used. Still others can be used to create graphic designs or special artwork. In all, several hundred PostScript commands handle everything from creating a simple dot on the page to creating detailed output.

The PostScript language is considered a device-independent language. It does not require a specific type of computer, and can be implemented on any type of system. It has been embedded in printers, high-end typesetting equipment, and specialized manufacturing equipment. It can also be used to display information to a computer monitor. The language is considered device-independent because any PostScript file created on any system can be output on any device with a built-in PostScript-compliant interpreter.

Using special printer drivers, many programs can create output for PostScript devices. Programs such as word processors, spreadsheets, and graphics programs all typically generate PostScript output.

Since it was commercially introduced in 1985, PostScript has undergone two major revisions. The original PostScript, now known as PostScript Level 1, has been updated through Level 2 to the now-current Level 3. (Level 3 was introduced in early 1997.) Many computer programs produce PostScript output that utilizes only Level 1 commands, even though it is not the most recent PostScript version. In this lowest-common-denominator approach, they can be assured that their software will work with the widest array of output devices.

PostScript is a proprietary language owned and developed by Adobe. The company licenses the language to device manufacturers so that they can create PostScript interpreters for their output devices. The success of PostScript, and its worldwide adoption as a printing standard, have catapulted Adobe to the forefront of computing technology and ensured a place in computer history for Warnock and Geschke.

John Warnock.

Why is this capability so attractive? The answer is simple: reduced costs. Many companies are struggling with the fact that they've acquired computers helter-skelter over the years. They may have UNIX workstations, all kinds of Windows boxes, Macintoshes, and more. At the same time, they need to develop software tools that give all employees the ability to access mission-critical network resources. Java offers the possibility of writing only one program that can run on all the computers in a firm, without the considerable expense of making several versions of the original program for each type of computer it needs to be run on.

Java saves money in another way, too. When specially-designed Java mini-programs (called **applets**) are made available through a network, employees can obtain the program by accessing a Web page, clicking a link, and downloading the Java applet. The applet is soon running on the employee's computer, and the distribution costs are next to nothing. That's a different situation from traditional programs, which must be installed and configured on each employee's machine.

Despite Java's considerable advantages, the language has many of the same weaknesses of a young programming language that's still evolving. Downloaded applets pose a security risk, so they're limited to actions that don't involve storage devices. (To put this another way, Java applets run in a virtual "sandbox," where they can't get hold of any system features that could do damage.) Perhaps worst of all, though, is the fact that Java software is slow. Java programs aren't as slow as interpreted programs, but they're considerably slower than compiled programs.

JavaScript (ECMAScript)

Like VBScript, **JavaScript** is a scripting language designed for use on Web pages. Despite including "Java" in its name, JavaScript isn't actually based on Java, but instead was created by Netscape Communications. Recently standardized by the European Computer Manufacturers Association (ECMA), JavaScript is now properly known as ECMAScript. It's a simple, easy-to-learn language for writing scripts on Web pages, and it's in widespread use on the Web.

INTRODUCING THE PROGRAM DEVELOPMENT LIFE CYCLE (PDLC)

At the dawn of the modern computer era, no notion of managing the software development process existed. Programs were written for well-defined purposes, such as calculating missile trajectories. If the program didn't work, the programmer corrected it, so this approach came to be known as **code-and-fix** (or "cut-and-run," as detractors put it).

When businesses began using computers for more-complex purposes, problems appeared. Often, it turned out that programmers didn't really understand what managers wanted the program to do, and correcting problems often turned into an expensive, time-consuming nightmare. Other problems appeared, too: programmers didn't document their programs well (if at all), and some developed idiosyncratic programming styles so that they could assure their continued employment, since no one else could figure out what their code did! These early programs were almost impossible to debug and maintain (especially if the original programmer had left the company).

To address these problems, the program development life cycle (PDLC) was introduced in the 1970s, and is still in widespread use today. Like the software development life cycle, the PDLC provides an organized plan for breaking down the task of program development into manageable chunks, each of which must be successfully completed before moving on to the next phase (see Figure 8C.6). The six essential phases, or steps, in this life cycle are:

1. Defining the problem.
2. Designing the program.
3. Coding the program.
4. Testing and debugging the program.
5. Formalizing the solution.
6. Implementing and maintaining the program.

Phase 1: Defining the Problem

The first step in developing a program is to define the problem. This is a job for system analysts, who provide the results of their work to programmers in the form of a **program specification** (or "spec"). The specification precisely defines the input data, the processing that should occur, what the output should look like, and how the user interface should look. Depending on the size of the job, the program development might be handled by a single individual or by a team.

Phase 2: Designing the Program

An architect doesn't design a home by going to the site with a bunch of boards and bricks. After the architect has determined the home buyer's needs, the next step is an architectural drawing—a plan drawn up on paper that can be reviewed and discussed until everything's right. Similarly, programmers create program designs. Like an architect's drawing, the program design specifies the components that make the program work.

Top-Down Program Design

Program design begins by focusing on the main goal that the program is trying to achieve and then breaking the program into manageable components, each of which contributes to this goal. This approach is called structured programming (also called **top-down program design**). The first step in this approach involves identifying the *main routine*, which is the program's major activity. From there, programmers try to break down the various components of the main routine into smaller *subroutines*, also called *modules*, until each subroutine is highly-focused and accomplishes only one major task. Experience shows that this is the best way to ensure program quality. If a bug appears in a program designed this way, it is relatively easy to identify the module that must be causing the error.

Structured Design

Within each subroutine, the programmer draws on the programming equivalent of basic building materials, called **control structures,** to envision how the subroutine will do its job. These are combined to create an algorithm.

Three basic control structures, which are logical constructs that specify how the instructions in a program are to be executed, are available. Control structures are defined at a high level of abstraction, and are relevant to all programming languages (except very old ones).

In a **sequence control structure,** instructions to the computer are designed to be executed (performed by the computer) in the order in which they appear. Sequence control structures provide the basic building blocks

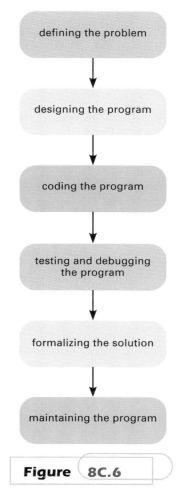

Figure 8C.6

The six phases of the program development life cycle.

for computer programs. If you can imagine yourself as a computer, here's an example of a sequence to follow to obtain pizza:

```
Go to the phone.
Dial the pizza place.
Order the pizza.
Hang up.
```

In a **selection control structure** (also called a *conditional*, or *branch*, control structure), the program branches off to different instructions depending on whether a condition is met. Most conditions are based on IF-THEN-ELSE logic. If a condition is true, one set of instructions is executed. If the condition is not true, a different set of instructions is executed. Here's an example that includes a *very* important test: making sure you have enough money for pizza!

```
Open your wallet.
IF you have enough money,
     THEN Go to the phone.
          Dial the pizza place.
          Order the pizza.
          Hang up.
     ELSE Forget the whole thing.
```

A variant of the selection control structure is the **case control structure.** In a case control structure, the condition is fundamental and each branch leads to its own, lengthy series of instructions. For example, the IRS processes tax returns differently depending on the taxpayer's marital status. A coded field indicates whether the taxpayer is married filing a joint return, married filing separately, single, head of household, or widowed. A case selection can be used so that the computer can determine which of those five categories a taxpayer belongs to, and then use the correct set of instructions to process the return.

In a **repetition control structure** (also called a *looping*, or *iteration*, control structure), the program repeats the same instructions over and over. The two types of repetitions are do-while and do-until. In a *do-while structure*, the program tests a condition at the beginning of the loop, and executes the specified instructions only if the condition is true. In a *do-until structure*, the program executes the instructions, and then tests to see whether a specified instruction is true. If not, the loop repeats.

Drawing on our pizza illustration once again, the following example illustrates a do-while structure:

```
DO gobble down pizza
WHILE there is still pizza.
```

Note that a do-while structure doesn't guarantee that the action will be performed even once. If the initial test condition is false, the action doesn't occur.

Here's a do-until structure:

```
DO gobble down pizza UNTIL none remains.
```

Developing an Algorithm

Programmers begin solving a problem by developing an **algorithm.** An algorithm is a step-by-step description of how to arrive at a solution. You can think of an algorithm as a recipe or a how-to sheet.

Algorithms aren't restricted to computers. In fact, we use them every day. Most people do long division by following an algorithm. Here's another example: suppose that you want to determine your car's gas mileage. You probably do this by filling the tank and noting your mileage. The next time you get gas, you note the mileage again, determine the number of miles you drove, and then divide the miles driven by the amount of gas you put in. The result tells you your car's mileage, at least for the type of driving you did between these two tankfuls.

In programming, coming up with an algorithm involves figuring out how to get the desired result by *nesting* control structures. To get programs to do useful things, programmers nest control structures within each other. Here's an example that remedies some of the unhealthy implications of the examples in the previous section:

```
WHILE there is still more pizza
Check to see whether you're still hungry
IF you are still hungry,
THEN gobble down pizza
ELSE put the rest in the fridge.
```

Program Design Tools

To help programmers develop well-structured programs, a variety of design tools exist.

Structure charts (also called **hierarchy charts**) show the top-down design of a program. Each box, or module, in the chart indicates a task that the program must accomplish (see Figure 8C.7). The top module, called the control module, oversees the transfer of control to the other modules.

A **flowchart** is a diagram that shows the logic of a program. Programmers create flowcharts either by hand using a flowcharting template or on the computer. Each flowcharting symbol has a meaning. A diamond, for example, is used to indicate a condition, a rectangle is used for a process, and a parallelogram indicates an input or output procedure (see Figure 8C.8).

Some programmers don't like flowcharting. **Pseudocode,** created in the 1970s as an alternative to flowcharts, is a stylized form of writing used to describe the logic of a program.

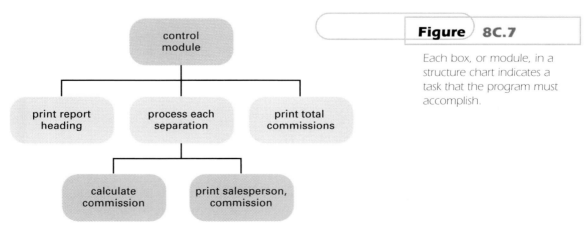

Figure 8C.7

Each box, or module, in a structure chart indicates a task that the program must accomplish.

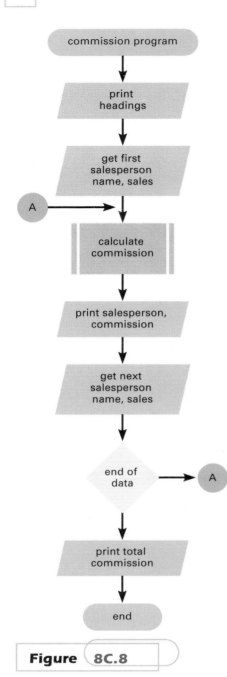

Figure 8C.8

A flowchart is a diagram that shows the logic of a program. Each flowcharting symbol has a meaning.

Phase 3: Coding the Program

Creating the code involves translating the algorithm into specific program language instructions. The programming team must choose an appropriate programming language and then create the program by typing the code. The programmers must carefully follow the language's rules of **syntax,** which specify precisely how to express certain operations. For example, different programming languages specify basic arithmetic operations in different ways. Program development tools can check for **syntax errors** while the program is being written. Syntax errors must then be eliminated before the program will run.

Phase 4: Testing and Debugging the Program

The fourth step in a programming project is to eliminate all errors. After the syntax errors are eliminated, the program will execute. The output may still not be correct, however, because the language translator cannot detect logic errors. A **logic error** is a mistake that the programmer made in designing the solution to the problem. For example, a programmer tells the computer to calculate net pay by adding (instead of subtracting) deductions to gross pay. The programmer must find and correct logic errors by carefully examining the program output. Syntax errors and logic errors are collectively known as bugs. The process of eliminating these errors is known as debugging.

After the visible logic errors have been eliminated, the programming team must test the program to find hidden errors. However, it's not always possible to examine every outcome for each program condition. Inevitably, some errors will surface only when the system is put into use.

Phase 5: Formalizing the Solution

Now the project is almost complete. The structure chart and pseudocode or flowchart developed during the design phase become documentation for others who will modify the program in the future. Other documentation should have been created as the program was being coded: lists of variable names and definitions, descriptions of files that the program needs to work with, and layouts of output that the program produces. All of this documentation needs to be saved and placed together for future reference.

Manuals still must be developed to thoroughly explain how the program works. These manuals will be given to the users when the program is installed or purchased. The manuals, along with the program design work, are known as documentation.

Phase 6: Implementing and Maintaining the Program

All that is left now is the sixth and last step: implementation. If the program has been developed for use by the company for whom the programmers work, the program will still need to be tested by the users. The best-written program is useless if the user does not understand how to work

An Issue of Timing

Some visionaries are way ahead of their time, particularly when it comes to software development. Sometimes these people raise issues that don't seem too important at the time, and they are subsequently ignored by the people around them. With the help of hindsight, it is easy to look back and feel that everyone really should have listened.

A case in point is Bill Schoen. A programmer working in Detroit, Schoen was the first to publicly point out what initially became known as the millennium bug, then as the year 2000 problem, and now simply as the Y2K problem. Schoen had the foresight (and the audacity) to bring the issue up in 1983. At the time, everyone thought that the new millennium was far, far away. They also thought that if there was a problem, it would be solved as old programming code faded away and new programs were developed.

Schoen was so passionate about the problem he foresaw that he devised a solution, quit his job, and formed the world's first Y2K consulting firm, Charmar Enterprises. The COBOL routine to correct the Y2K problem was developed on his Commodore 64 (an early personal computer) and named the Charmar Correction.

With his solution in hand, Schoen set out on a one-man crusade. He made numerous presentations, tried to get software companies to come up with their own solutions, and did a mass mailing to executives of the Fortune 500 companies. He tried to gain media exposure for the problem, but only ended up with a single article in print. (The editor at the magazine later admitted he ran with the story because it was a slow month and he figured that the Y2K issue was goofy enough to be interesting.)

At one point, Schoen made a management presentation about the problem to one of his clients, which also happened to be one of the world's largest corporations. The company subsequently canceled Schoen's contract and ignored the issue.

Eventually, Schoen drastically dropped the price of the Charmar Correction to under a thousand dollars. Many companies still scoffed at his predictions, and at a few companies he was booted out the door. Most companies were too concerned with their quarterly earnings to focus on a problem that was sixteen or seventeen years away.

Much to Schoen's dismay, his predictions and solutions were not well received by the computer world, either. His efforts led to only two sales of the Charmar Correction, and even those companies did not implement it systematically through their organizations. After a year of near-universal rejection, Charmar Enterprises closed its doors in 1984, and Schoen went back to programming at Ford Motor Company.

According to Schoen, a few simple corrections in the early 1980s could have solved 95 percent of the programming problems and averted the need to spend so much money in what has turned out to be a race against time. The Y2K problem has been characterized by Schoen as "the biggest technical screw-up in history." Many computer programmers and engineers would likely agree with him on that point, even though it was not seen as such in the early 1980s. In the 1990s, companies spent millions and even billions of dollars to correct the problem.

Bill Schoen used a Commodore 64 to develop a COBOL routine designed to correct the Y2K problem.

with it. What's more, users will discover program errors that weren't caught in the testing phase, no matter how exhaustively the program was tested.

The job isn't finished until the program is thoroughly documented. This requires writing a manual that provides an overview of the program's functionality, tutorials for beginning users, in-depth explanations of major program features, reference documentation of all program commands, and a thorough description of the error messages generated by the program.

Even after a program is complete, it needs to be maintained and evaluated regularly. In program maintenance, the programming team fixes program errors that users discover. In periodic evaluations, the team asks whether the program is fulfilling its objectives. The evaluation may lead to modifications to update the program or to add features for the user. It may even lead to a decision to abandon the current system and develop a new one. In that case, the program development life cycle begins anew.

TAKEAWAY POINTS

- A programming language is an artificial language consisting of a vocabulary and a set of rules.
- The earliest (and lowest-level) programming language is machine language, the binary instructions needed to control a particular brand and model of processor.
- Assembly language is easier to use than machine language because the programmer can use symbols to sum up program instructions. However, the programmer still needs to know a great deal about how a particular brand and model of processor works.
- High-level languages free the programmer from having to know the details of processors, but these languages still require the programmer to specify the procedure to be followed to solve the problem.
- Fourth-generation languages free programmers from having to worry about the procedure to be followed to solve a problem, but most are restricted to accessing databases.
- To solve the "spaghetti code" problems of early third-generation languages, new languages appeared that emphasized structure and modularity.
- Because third-generation languages failed in their goal of total modularity and information hiding, object-oriented languages appeared. These languages achieve these goals by combining procedures and data.

- An object is a computer resource that contains data, as well as a variety of procedures for making use of this data.
- The program development life cycle (PDLC) is needed because previous, ad-hoc programming techniques produced software that was riddled with errors and virtually impossible to debug or maintain.
- PDLC is part of the SDLC's implementation phase.
- The PDLC's six phases are defining the program, designing the program, coding the program, testing and debugging the program, formalizing the solution, and implementing and maintaining the program.
- Top-down programming makes programs easier to debug and maintain because program functions are divided into separate modules, each of which has a clear, simple function.
- Using the three basic types of control structures (sequence, selection, and repetition), a programmer can create an algorithm for performing any processing task. The use of these structures makes a program easy to read and maintain.
- The task of debugging a program requires finding and correcting not only syntax errors, which prevent execution, but also logic errors, which do not prevent execution but do prevent correct output.

MODULE REVIEW

KEY TERMS AND CONCEPTS

ActiveX controls
algorithm
applets
assembler
assembly language
BASIC (Beginner's All-Purpose Symbolic Instruction Code)
bugs
C
C++
case control structure
class
COBOL (Common Business-Oriented Language)
code-and-fix
Common Object Request Broker Architecture (CORBA)

compiler
Component Object Model (COM)
component reusability
control structures
cross-platform programming language
debugging
Delphi
encapsulation
event-driven
executable program
flowchart
Fortran
fourth-generation languages(4GL)
hierarchy charts

high-level languages
information hiding
inheritance
Internet Inter-Orb Protocol (IIOP)
interpreter
Java
Java Virtual Machine
JavaScript
legacy
linker
logic error
low-level language
machine language
machine-dependent
methods
Microsoft's Visual Basic (VB)

middleware	program specification	software crisis
mnemonics	programming languages	source code
modular programming	pseudocode	spaghetti code
natural language	query languages	structure charts
nonprocedural	rapid application development	structured programming
object	(RAD)	Structured Query Language
object code	repetition control structure	(SQL)
object-oriented (OO)	report generators	syntax
programming	scripting language	syntax errors
procedural languages	scripts	third-generation languages
program development life cycle	selection control structure	(3GL)
(PDLC)	sequence control structure	top-down program design
program listing	Smalltalk	VBScript

TRUE/FALSE

Indicate whether the following statements are true or false.

1. Machine language is a hardware-dependent programming language.

2. The output of a compiler is a program listing.

3. An interpreter runs programs just as quickly as when the programs are compiled.

4. Object-oriented programming allows the programmer to create reusable modules without being concerned about underlying data.

5. Visual Basic is a programming language used as a learning tool, but rarely used for commercial program development.

6. JavaScript is a version of the popular Java programming language.

7. The PDLC method of program development provides an organized plan for breaking down a programming task into manageable chunks.

8. At the beginning of PDLC, systems analysts provide programmers with a program specification.

9. In a selection control structure, instructions to the computer are designed to be executed in the order in which they appear.

10. Even after a program is complete, it needs to be maintained and evaluated regularly.

MATCHING

Match each key term from the left column to the most accurate definition in the right column.

_____ 1. low-level language

_____ 2. procedural language

_____ 3. interpreter

_____ 4. structured programming

_____ 5. component reusability

_____ 6. class

_____ 7. middleware

_____ 8. logic error

_____ 9. debugging

_____ 10. syntax

a. a category of objects

b. a mistake that the programmer made in designing the solution to the problem

c. standards that define how programs can find objects and query them

d. rules that specify precisely how to express certain operations

e. language that tells the computer what to do and how to do it

f. the capability to develop well-designed program modules that perform a specific task

g. the process of eliminating syntax and logic errors

h. a process of constructing a program so that it uses logical elements; GOTO statements are forbidden

i. a language that is similar to machine language in terms of its level of abstraction

j. a program that translates one line of source code at a time

MULTIPLE CHOICE

Circle the letter of the correct choice for each of the following.

1. Which programming language can a computer understand directly, without the need for translation?
   a. BASIC
   b. assembly language
   c. machine language
   d. C

2. Procedural languages were introduced in which generation of languages?
   a. first
   b. second
   c. third
   d. fourth

3. Which of the following is not a term used in object-oriented programming?
   a. encapsulation
   b. method
   c. class
   d. dataset

4. What is inheritance?
   a. The capacity of an object to transfer characteristics to an object in a subclass.
   b. How an object maintains cohesion from one program to another.
   c. The capability of an object to be encapsulated in a class.
   d. How concepts are passed from one language generation to the next.

5. Which of the following is considered by many to be the "purest" object-oriented programming language?
   a. Smalltalk
   b. C++

   c. Java
   d. Ada

6. Which of the following was not a problem evident in some early programming efforts?
   a. lack of programming documentation
   b. difficult to debug and maintain
   c. idiosyncratic programming styles
   d. using structured programming concepts to solve spaghetti code

7. Which of the following is not one of the six phases in PDLC?
   a. developing a prototype
   b. formalizing the solution
   c. specifying the problem
   d. testing and debugging

8. The first step in structured programming is identifying what?
   a. modules
   b. main routine
   c. subroutines
   d. desired output

9. Which of the following is not a program design tool?
   a. pseudocode
   b. flowchart
   c. structure chart
   d. program specification

10. In which PDLC phase is a programming language selected?
    a. phase 2
    b. phase 3
    c. phase 4
    d. phase 5

FILL-IN

In the blank provided, write the correct answer for each of the following.

1. _____ consists of binary numbers that directly correspond to a computer's electrical states.

2. Assembly language programs are translated into machine language by a(n) _____ .

3. A(n) _____ is a translation program that translates all the source code into object code.

4. _____ programming promises to achieve the dream of component reusability.

5. A(n) _____ is a unit of computer information that contains data as well as all the procedures or operations.

6. In _____ development, a programmer works with a library of prebuilt objects that have been created for a huge variety of applications.

7. A(n) _____ precisely defines the input data, the processing that should occur, what the output should look like, and how the user interface should look.

8. _____ show the top-down design of a program.

9. _____ is a stylized form of writing to describe the logic of a program.

10. A(n) _____ is a diagram that shows the logic of a program.

SHORT ANSWER

On a separate sheet of paper, answer the following questions.

1. What are the differences between natural and artificial languages?

2. What are the differences between an assembler, a compiler, and an interpreter?

3. What is the biggest difference between procedural and structured languages?

4. Discuss the elements of object-oriented programming, including classes, inheritance, and encapsulation.

5. Why are languages such as COBOL and Fortran still in wide use?

6. What are the major structured and modular languages being used today?

7. What are the six phases of PDLC?

8. What are the elements of a program specification?

9. Identify the basic control structures used in program development.

10. What are some of the different program design tools available to a programmer?

PFSweb, Inc.

PFSweb's Val Remmers likes puzzles, especially complex ones. Puzzles that make you think, puzzles that challenge your ability to solve them. She also likes the feeling of satisfaction that comes from successful completion. Her job is to help the company's current and prospective clients solve their e-commerce business problems—the puzzles that face them in doing business in the electronic marketplace.

There's a technique commonly used to help focus clients on reaching a solution: The systems development life cycle. When a client approaches PFSweb about providing back-end fulfillment services for its Web store (like taking orders and getting the goods to the customer), a team of analysts first meets with them to learn about their business. By listening to what the client says, Val and her team figure out client needs. What's the business problem to be solved? Does a new Web site need to be created? Does the marketing Web site exist, but now the company wants to start selling merchandise through the site? Does the existing Web site's transaction flows cause customers to abort orders before they are completed? Are customers simply losing inter-

est because the site takes too long to load, or doesn't have a way for customers to get more information via email?

With a handle on client needs, the team can prepare a prototype of the functional specifications required to solve the customer's problems. This prototype consists of computer screens that look and feel just like the real solution that will eventually be created, sort of like a building's façade. It looks real, but is missing all the technical details behind the buttons you click. The client can take a look at the screens and visualize how customers will interact. Often, this process reveals additional needs or preferences, such as a button for emailing questions to the company or changing the colors to better match the corporate image. Val's team goes back to the drawing board and refines the prototype with these changes, and brings them back to the client for another round of reviews.

When all the iterations of prototyping are complete, the actual software and hardware pieces needed for the solution are put in place. Programs are written, software is purchased, new hardware such as servers is installed, and Web site screens are updated for new functionality. With the help of the client, the pieces of the puzzle are put into place, and the completed picture emerges: the solution to the problem.

What do you think? If every business is unique, why does it make sense to use a **standard** approach to solving their e-commerce business problems? Can you think of another way PFSweb might help clients solve their business problems?

Web Link Go to **www.prenhall.com/ pfaffenberger** to hear Val Remmers talk about unusual requests from clients.

E-COMMERCE IN ACTION

9

Social and Ethical Issues of Computing

CHAPTER

Online shoppers didn't exactly beat a path to the virtual door of Toysmart, an online toy retailing business—despite the fact Toysmart seemed to get everything right. One of the site's plusses: a clearly worded privacy policy. If you registered on Toysmart, you'd be asked to reveal some very personal information, such as the names, ages, and interests of your kids. Toysmart assured its customers that this information would be kept strictly private, and never divulged to a third party. In the wave of bankruptcies that shutdown many struggling e-commerce sites in the summer of 2000, Toysmart folded up shop. A few days later, an advertisement appeared in a major financial newspaper offering Toysmart's assets for sale—including its database of information supplied by means of site registrations. Did Toysmart's liquidators break the law? That's debatable, because the U.S. has surprisingly few laws designed to protect consumer's privacy. There may be some on the way, thanks to the Toysmart episode. The e-commerce industry has insisted all along that laws aren't needed to protect consumer privacy, and that the industry is fully capable of regulating itself—but there were few takers for this position after Toysmart's databases went up for sale. How safe is your information when it's stored online? Even if online vendors honor their privacy promises, there's no guarantee that their systems are properly secured. Just to prove the point, a know-ledgeable intruder broke into a major e-commerce sites' systems and found 200,000 credit card numbers in a wide-open text file, one that could have been read by any employee (or anyone who succeeded at breaking into the firm's poorly secured computers). Is it any wonder that computer-based crime is skyrocketing?

In this chapter, you'll examine the many ways that computers are eroding the privacy of U.S. citizens. You'll also learn what's being done—and what still needs to be done—to safeguard computer systems from criminal attacks. You'll also explore the world of computer ethics, in which you'll learn what's right and what's wrong in the digital world—and why.

MODULES

 Privacy and Encryption   478

 Computer Crime and Security   494

 Ethics: Doing the Right Thing   514

PRIVACY AND ENCRYPTION

OUTLINE

WHAT YOU WILL LEARN . . .

When you have finished reading this module, you will be able to:

1. Explain the threat to privacy posed by the sale of sensitive personal information on the Internet.

2. Define anonymity and discuss how it can be abused.

3. Describe how technological developments are eroding privacy and anonymity.

4. Explain the reasons why many employers feel that they need to monitor their employees' computer usage.

5. State why U.S. security officials believe public-key encryption poses a threat to U.S. security, both foreign and domestic.

6. Describe the U.S. government's proposed key recovery plan and explain why it threatens the growth of Internet commerce.

The phone rings, and it's a collection agency. They're demanding immediate payment for a $5,000 stereo system bill that's past due. You can't believe what you're hearing! You always pay your bills on time, and what's more, you haven't purchased any stereo equipment lately. What's going on?

It's **identity theft,** one of the fastest-growing crimes in the United States and Canada. Criminals obtain enough information about you to open a credit account in your name and then max it out, leaving you with the bill. Although laws limit liability for each fraudulent charge to $50, victims of identity theft have found themselves saddled with years of agony. The bad marks on their credit reports prevent them from buying homes, obtaining telephone service, and getting jobs. Many victims of identity theft state that the crime completely ruined their lives.

What do criminals need to pull off an identity theft? They need only your address, Social Security number, and a little more information, such as the addresses you've lived at for the past few years. How does somebody get this information? Thanks to the Internet, it's easy—too easy, say privacy advocates. Dozens of Internet sites sell individuals' Social Security numbers for as little as $6 each. Is it any surprise that U.S. law enforcement officials say that identity theft is the fastest-growing type of crime and is already the leading type of consumer fraud?

PRIVACY AND ANONYMITY IN CYBERSPACE

Of all the social and ethical issues raised by the spread of ubiquitous, highly-networked computers, threats to privacy and anonymity are among the most contentious. This section introduces the basic concepts of privacy and anonymity, and shows how technology is eroding these basic rights.

Defined by U.S. Supreme Court Justice Louis Brandeis in 1928 as "the right to be left alone," **privacy** refers to an individual's ability to keep personal and family business away from prying eyes.

Sometimes people say that privacy isn't a concern unless you have something to hide. But this view is naive. It ignores the fact that individuals, governments, and corporations sometimes collect and use information in ways that harm people unnecessarily.

One example: stalking, another of the fastest-growing crimes. Sometimes, it's deadly. Rebecca Shaeffer, a California TV personality with a promising future, was murdered after an obsessed fan obtained her home address from state motor vehicle records. In the United Kingdom, one in every five women will be stalked at some point in their lifetimes. Typically, stalking incidents last an average of 7.5 years, and nearly 90 percent of all stalking cases involve ex-partners or acquaintances. Thanks to the easy availability of residential address information on the Internet, there's no place to hide.

Consider another example: DNA. As scientists unlock the genetic code, your DNA will reveal a great deal of information about you, including your susceptibility to alcoholism, cancer, heart disease, and many other genetically-influenced diseases that are very expensive to treat. If this information falls into the wrong hands, it could adversely and unfairly affect your chances for obtaining employment and health insurance. At most, one's genes reveal a propensity, usually only a very slight propensity, to develop a disease. People with such propensities generally lead healthy, productive lives. To exclude them from employment or health insurance benefits, privacy advocates insist, is as odious and unjust as racial or gender discrimination.

Techtalk

IP spoofing

Hackers have an entire toolkit filled with techniques for gaining unauthorized access to remote computer systems. One such technique is called "IP spoofing," where the intruder sends a message to a computer with an IP address disguised as an incoming message from a trusted source. The hacker must first locate and modify the message packet headers of a trusted source (called a port) and then manipulate the hacker's own communication so that it appears it came from the trusted port.

The Problem: Collection of Information Without Consent

Few people believe that privacy should be absolute. People are willing to divulge information when their consent is asked and they see a need for doing so. When you apply for a loan, the bank can reasonably ask you to list other creditors so that the bank can determine whether you pay your bills.

But most people are much less comfortable about divulging information when they see no clear need to do so—which is why marketers often solicit such information using tactics that can only be termed deceptive. For example, people often supply revealing personal information when they fill out product sweepstakes entry forms and warranty registration cards. The form or card says that the company needs the information in order to serve customers better. They do not disclose that this information will be sold to database marketing firms.

Much more information is collected from public agencies, many of which are under a legal obligation to make their records available to the public upon request. Again, this information is collected without your knowledge or consent. It finds its way into computerized databases—thousands of them—that track virtually every conceivable type of information about individuals. You are probably aware of credit reporting databases, which track your credit history. Other databases include information such as your current and former addresses, your current and former employers, other names you've used (and your previous name, if you're married and use a different name now), current and former spouses, bankruptcies, lawsuits, property ownership, driver's license information, criminal records, purchasing habits, and medical prescriptions.

You may also be surprised to learn that, in the United States, you have no right to keep sensitive personal information out of these databases, or to prevent database marketers from selling this information to whomever they please. Credit reporting databases are subject to Federal laws that require them to enable you to access and check the accuracy of credit files, but much of the rest of the industry is unregulated.

Hundreds of electronic databases track virtually every conceivable type of information about you. In the United States, you have no right to keep sensitive personal information out of these databases.

The Internet Factor

Who accesses this information? Most of the **database vendors** (companies that maintain these databases) claim that they sell only to bona fide customers, such as lending institutions, prospective employers, marketing firms, and licensed private investigators. They maintain that their databases do not pose a threat to the privacy of individuals because they are highly-ethical firms that would not release this information to the general public. However, they also state that, once the information is sold, they have no control over what someone else does with it.

According to privacy activists, what happens to information after it's sold is precisely the problem. Before the Internet came along, it was much more difficult for ordinary individuals to gain access to sensitive personal information, and doing so cost more money. Thanks to the Internet, it's much easier and much cheaper. Try browsing the Internet for "Social Security numbers." You'll find dozens of sites placed on the Web by private investigators who offer to find someone's Social Security number for a small fee, which can be charged to your credit card. Sites such as InfoUSA (**http://www.listbazaar.com**) offer information such as estimated income, marital status, buying habits, and hobbies for more than 120 million U.S. households. And this data could be accessed by jealous coworkers trying to get some dirt on you, stalkers hoping to hunt you down, and thieves who want to go on a shopping spree in your name.

PROTECTING PRIVACY: BASIC PRINCIPLES

How should governments protect the privacy of their citizens? Privacy advocates agree that the key lies in giving citizens the right to be informed when data is being collected about them—and what's more, the right to refuse to participate if they so desire. In the European Union, a basic human rights declaration gives all citizens the following privacy rights:

- Consumers must be informed when information is being collected about them. They must be told exactly what information is being collected and how it will be used.

- Consumers must be allowed to choose whether they want to divulge the requested information and to choose the uses that are made of this information.

- Consumers must be allowed to remove information about themselves from marketing and other databases, upon request.

In general, U.S. citizens do not enjoy these fundamental rights. Apart from the Fair Credit Reporting Act (FCRA), which provides limited privacy protection for credit information, no comprehensive Federal law governs the privacy rights of U.S. citizens. Instead, privacy is protected by a patchwork quilt of limited Federal and state laws and regulations. However, most of these laws regulate what government agencies can do. Except in limited areas covered by these laws, little exists to stop people and companies from acquiring information about you and selling this information to someone else. At work, you have no privacy when you are using your employer's computer system.

ANONYMITY

In Vernor Vinge's classic science fiction novella, *True Names*, computers are everywhere—but **anonymity** is illegal. The term anonymity refers to the ability to convey a message without disclosing one's name or identity.

A society in which anonymity is illegal would provide the perfect foundation for a totalitarian police state—a proposition that Adolf Hitler personally endorsed. "In the Third Reich," a Nazi apologist conceded, "there is no such thing as a private individual." In a democracy, anonymous speech functions as an important means by which people can make unpopular viewpoints heard without fear of reprisal.

To be sure, anonymity can be abused. Anonymity frees people from accountability, and as a result, they may abuse the privilege of anonymous speech. In particular, they may engage in **defamation,** the act of injuring someone's reputation by making false and malicious statements. When defamation occurs in writing, the term **libel** is used. Anonymous communications can also be used to threaten and harass, or to spread false and misleading information.

Still, the U.S. Supreme Court recently held that anonymity—despite its unpalatable aspects—must be preserved. In a democracy, what is essential is that citizens have access to the full range of possible ideas, so that they are best equipped to decide for themselves. By freeing authors from the need to be accountable for anonymous works, the Court argued, there is a potential that false or misleading ideas will be brought before the public, but the price is worth paying.

Destinations

An excellent source of information concerning all aspects of privacy is the Electronic Privacy Information Center (EPIC), located at **http://www. epic.org.**

Destinations

While you're browsing the Web, Web sites can collect information without your knowledge and consent. To see an example, visit the Center for Democracy and Technology's CDT Privacy Demonstration Page, which you can access from CDT's home page (**http://www.cdt.org**).

HOW IS TECHNOLOGY ERODING PRIVACY AND ANONYMITY?

Computers and the Internet enable marketing firms, snoops, and government officials to harness all the power of technology in order to collect information in ways that are hidden from the user's view. The same technology is also making it increasingly difficult for citizens to engage in anonymous speech. In this section, these two points are illustrated by looking at two technologies that are in increasingly common use: cookies and global unique identifiers (GUIDs).

Cookies

Imagine that you're shopping in your local supermarket. You notice that a clerk is following your every move and making detailed notes about which products you're examining, how long you look at them, and which products you buy. Would this constant surveillance make you uncomfortable? If so, you'd better think twice about shopping on the Web. Thanks to cookies, that's exactly what virtually all online retailing sites are doing.

Cookies are small files that are written to your computer's hard disk by many of the Web sites you visit. Essentially, cookies provide Web sites with a way of recording information so that it is available for future browsing sessions at the same site.

In many cases, cookies are used for legitimate purposes. For example, Internet retailing sites use cookies to implement "shopping carts," which enable you to make selections and then return to the online store for more browsing and shopping. What troubles privacy advocates is the use of cookies to gather data on Web user's browsing and shopping habits without their consent.

Several Internet **ad networks,** such as DoubleClick, Inc., use cookies to track user's browsing actions across thousands of the most-popular Internet sites. When you visit a Web site that has contracted with one of these firms, a cookie containing a unique identification number is deposited on your computer's hard drive. This cookie is used to track your browsing habits and preferences as you move among the hundreds of sites that contract with the ad network. As you visit another site, the cookie is detected, read, and matched with a profile of your previous browsing activity. On this basis, the ad network selects and displays a **banner ad,** a rectangular advertisement which is not actually a part of the Web page you are viewing, but is instead separately supplied by the ad network.

In response to concerns that their tracking violates Internet users' privacy, ad network companies claim that they do not attempt to link the collected information with users' names and addresses. However, current technology would enable these firms to do so—and some privacy advocates fear that some of them already have. A programmer named Richard M. Smith analyzed the data transmitted to the major Internet ad network, DoubleClick, Inc., and found that the following information was transmitted to DoubleClick from the Web sites he visited:

- Email address
- Full name
- Mailing address (street, city, state, and zip)
- Phone number
- Transactional data (names of products purchased online, details of plane trip reservations, and search phrases used at search engines)

Destinations

To see an online demonstration of how ad banner tracking can be paired with user names through site registrations, visit Privacy.net's demonstration page at **http://www.privacy.net/track.**

In early 2000, DoubleClick, Inc., put any doubts about its intentions to rest. The firm shelled out $1 billion to purchase Abacus Direct, a marketing database company that possessed detailed information on 120 million U.S. households. DoubleClick announced that it would begin a new program to combine its Internet and Abacus databases. Consumers who dislike such monitoring could "opt out" of the tracking by visiting the company's Web site, according to the firm.

DoubleClick's announcement made few friends for the firm. What resulted was a massive public outcry, a series of lawsuits, and the threat of an investigation from the U.S. Federal Trade Commission (FTC). After the firm's stock dropped precipitously in a massive bad-news selloff, the company's CEO, Kevin O'Connor, admitted that he had made a mistake, and vowed to hold off on linking names to Internet browsing habits until a "national consensus" on privacy emerged.

What's wrong with collecting information about a person's browsing habits? Internet marketing firms explain that, if they do collect such information, they could provide a "richer" marketing experience, one that's more closely tailored to an individual's interests. Privacy advocates reply that, once collected, this information could become valuable to others—including future employers. If you visited a number of sites specializing in information concerning worker's compensation, would this browsing behavior mark you as a "high risk" job candidate?

Global Unique Identifiers (GUIDs)

A **global unique identifier (GUID)** is a unique identification number that is generated by a computer hardware component or a program. Privacy advocates have discovered several instances in which popular computer components or programs made GUIDs available in such a way that anonymous usage of the Internet would become more difficult, if not impossible:

- To provide a better foundation for e-commerce, Intel Corporation designed a GUID into its Pentium III processors. The GUID could be used, the company said, to positively identify shoppers—an important step in the fight against online fraud. But analysts discovered that the Pentium III GUID can be accessed by Web servers, which holds out the threat that any site you visit on the Web could learn your identity. In response to a public outcry, Intel redesigned the Pentium III processor so that the GUID is turned off by default.

- A programmer who used a network traffic analysis device discovered that RealNetwork's RealJukeBox player was sending information back to the company when users accessed streaming audio or video content on the Internet, or played an audio CD. The information included the user's name, email address, and a description of the content being viewed.

- Microsoft Word 97 and Excel 97 embedded GUID information in every document users created with these applications. This information could have been used to trace an anonymous document back to a particular computer used on a university or corporate network.

Companies that introduce GUIDs into their products generally conceal this information from the public. When forced to admit to the use of a GUID, the firms typically remove the GUID-implanting code or enable users to opt out of their data collection systems. Advocates of online anonymity insist that these companies are missing the basic point: users, not corporations, should determine when and how they divulge their identities to third parties.

IS SELF-REGULATION SUFFICIENT?

As the previous sections illustrate, technology is posing a threat to basic privacy rights precisely because computer systems enable government and corporate snoops to automate the collection of marketing data—and what's more, the same systems also make it increasingly impossible to disguise one's identity so that such collection cannot take place. Still, marketing industry spokespeople and lobbyists argue that the U.S. government should not impose laws or regulations designed to protect consumers' privacy. They argue that the industry should be left free to regulate itself.

Privacy advocates counter that technology has outpaced the industry's capability to regulate itself, as evidenced by the widespread availability of highly-personal information on the Internet. Many of the most-aggressive Internet-based marketing firms have no ties or previous experience with traditional industry associations, such as the Direct Marketing Association (DMA), which claims to enforce a basic code of ethics among the companies that belong to the association. The DMA takes steps to assure that confidential information does not fall into the wrong hands and that consumers can opt out of marketing campaigns if they wish. According to privacy advocates, the reality of Internet marketing shows that self-regulation has failed. Confidential information is already easily and widely available on the Internet. And opt-out systems are already used for fraudulent purposes. For example, email spammers typically claim that recipients can "opt out" of mass email marketing campaigns. However, recipients who respond to such messages succeed only in validating their email address—and the result will be a major increase in the volume of unsolicited mail. Faced with such abuses, Internet users overwhelmingly agree—by a ratio of 3 to 1—that the U.S. government needs to adopt laws that will safeguard basic privacy rights.

Consumer fears regarding the use of information collected by Web sites may be impeding the growth of e-commerce. According to a recent survey by *Business Week* magazine, consumers not currently using the Internet cite privacy concerns as their primary reason for not going online. But online businesses don't seem to be getting the message. According to a recent study, more than two-thirds of the most-popular commercial Web sites displayed "privacy policy" pages that explained how they intended to collect and use personal information about site visitors—but only 10 percent of these sites gave visitors any meaningful control over the use of this information. Given that 82 percent of surveyed Internet users strongly object to the sale of their personal information, it's hardly surprising that the Internet retailer sector is growing more slowly than anticipated.

PRIVACY AT WORK

Increasingly, employees are given email accounts and Internet connections at work. They can't do business without it. According to a recent study, 80 percent of 1,000 surveyed employees in Fortune 500 firms say that email has replaced "snail mail" for the majority of their business correspondence. But the Internet can be a time-waster, too. One medium-sized company found that it lost $127,000 annually in lost time due to employees browsing the Web when they should have been working.

Employers are naturally concerned about getting their money's worth from employees. For this reason, more than three-quarters of large U.S. employers routinely monitor employees' phone calls, email, Web browsing habits, and computer files—and about one company in four has fired an employee based on what they've found. But the snooping is done for other reasons, too. Companies are concerned about employees who offer trade secrets to competitors in the hope of landing an attractive job offer. Another concern is sexual harassment lawsuits. Employees who access pornographic Web sites, or circulate offensive jokes via email, may be creating a hostile environment for female employees—and that could result in a huge lawsuit against the company. At an oil company subsidiary, email containing jokes such as "25 reasons why beer is better than women" resulted in a sexual harassment claim that was settled for $2.5 million.

Yet computer technology enables employers to monitor nearly everything an employee does, and many employees wonder whether the monitoring goes too far. While you're working with your employers' phone and computer systems, virtually everything you do may be monitored—right down to the keystrokes you type at the keyboard. Automated software combs your email for words such as "boss" and "jerk." Software that takes snapshots of your computer screen can defeat privacy measures such as encryption. At what point does employer snooping represent an unjustifiable intrusion into an employee's private affairs?

In the United States, few laws protect employees from intrusive monitoring. Your employer may be reading your email, listening to your phone conversations, and even viewing an exact copy of the computer screen you're looking at. If you send an email making disparaging remarks about your boss, chances are you'll be out of a job—and there won't be anything you can do about it.

When you're at work, remember the following rules:

Software from companies such as SpectorSoft provide people with a way to monitor their employees and family members.

- Except in the case of an emergency, never use your employer's telephone system for personal calls. Make all such calls from a pay telephone.

- Never use the email account your employer gives you for personal purposes. Get your own account with an Internet service provider (ISP), and be sure to send and receive all personal mail from your home computer.

- Assume that everything you do while you're at work—whether it's talking on the phone, using your computer, taking a break, or chatting with co-workers—is being monitored and recorded.

Protecting Your Privacy Online

To safeguard your privacy on the Internet, do the following:

- Browse anonymously by surfing from sites such as The Anonymizer (**http://www.anonymizer.com**) or The Cloak (**http://www.the-cloak.com**).

- Disable cookies on your Web browser or use cookie management software, such as Junkbuster (**http://www.junkbusters.com**).

- Use a "throw-away" email address on a free Web-based service such as Hotmail (**http://www.hotmail.com**) for the email address you place on Web pages, mailing lists, chat rooms, or other public Internet spaces that are scanned by email spammers.

- Tell children not to divulge any personal information to strangers online without first asking permission from a parent or a teacher.

- Don't fill out site registration forms unless you see a privacy policy statement indicating that the information you supply will not be sold to third parties.

THE ENCRYPTION DEBATE

An **encrypted** (coded) message cannot be read by anyone except the intended recipient. Until recently, encryption was used by intelligence services, militaries, and banks. But powerful encryption software is now available to the public, and U.S. law enforcement officials aren't happy about it.

Encryption Basics

To understand encryption, try this simple exercise: take a simple message, such as "I love you." For each character, substitute the letter exactly 13 positions to the right in the alphabet of 26 letters. (When you reach the end of the alphabet, start counting from the beginning.) You get a coded message, called ciphertext, that looks like this:

```
V YBIR LBH
```

Looks like gibberish, doesn't it? That's exactly the idea. If somebody intercepts this message, they won't be able to tell what it means. Your intended recipient, however, can tell what the message means if you give him or her the decoding key: in this case, counting 13 characters to the left (see Figure 9A.1). When your recipient gets the message and decodes it, your message reappears:

```
I LOVE YOU
```

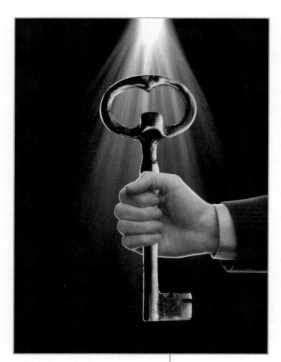

One way to break a code is to steal the key.

Congratulations! You just encrypted a message. You began with a readable message, called plaintext, and then encrypted the message by using an encoding key, a formula that specifies how to scramble the message so that no one can read it but the intended recipient. The recipient decrypts the message by applying the decoding key, which reverses the encoding key's action. This encryption technique is sometimes used in Usenet discussions. Called **rot-13,** it disguises text content that shouldn't be read by children.

The Problem of Key Interception

As you may have already concluded, rot-13 isn't a secure encryption method. If you study the ciphertext, you can find the key. Banks and military intelligence agencies use much more complex keys to encrypt their messages. Some of these keys are so complex that the world's most powerful computer would have to analyze the ciphertext for several hundred years to discover the key. The term *strong encryption* refers to encryption methods that are very difficult or impossible to break.

A code can be broken in another way: by stealing the key. This isn't as difficult as it sounds. In any single-key encryption method such as rot-13, you *must* give the key to your recipient. Without having received the key from you, the recipient cannot decrypt the message. Throughout his-

Figure 9A.1

Decoding key for "I Love You."

A	B	C	D	E	F	G	H	I	J	K	L	M	N	O	P	Q	R	S	T	U	V	W	X	Y	Z
1	2	3	4	5	6	7	8	9	10	11	12	13	14	15	16	17	18	19	20	21	22	23	24	25	26

tory, anyone wanting to send a secret message has also had to send the key by some means, such as by courier. Military victories have been won because the courier was intercepted and persuaded to act as a double agent, divulging the key to the enemy but delivering it as if nothing had happened.

Public-Key Encryption

Now that you understand the problem of key interception, you are prepared to grasp why **public-key cryptography** is considered one of the greatest (and most-troubling) scientific achievements of the twentieth century. In brief, public-key cryptography eliminates the need for people to exchange a key that could be used to decode the message.

In brief, here's how public-key cryptography works. You have a **public-key,** which you can freely give to anyone who wants it. Suppose your friend wants to send you a secret message. She uses your public key to encrypt her message, and sends it to you by email. If people intercept the message, they see nothing but gibberish. To read the message, they need the private key (which differs from the public key). But only *you* possess your private key, and you never give it to anyone. In short, no information is ever exchanged that would enable a third party to decode the message.

If you want to reply to your friend in secret, you obtain her public key and use this key to encode your message. When your friend receives your message, she uses *her* private key to decode it.

Experts in cryptography describe public-key cryptography as one of the major scientific revolutions of the twentieth century. It solves the problem of key interception. However, it also makes encryption much more convenient to use. And, as you'll see, it also concerns U.S. security officials.

Destinations

For more information concerning public-key encryption, visit the RSA Laboratories' Frequently Asked Questions on Cryptography page (**http://www.rsa.com/ rsalabs/newfaq/**).

Security Issues of Strong Encryption

Public-key cryptography sounds great, doesn't it? Not to everyone! U.S. Federal Bureau of Investigation Director Louis Freeh recently told the U.S. Congress that "the widespread use of robust unbreakable encryption ultimately will devastate our ability to fight crime and prevent terrorism. Unbreakable encryption will allow drug lords, spies, terrorists, and even violent gangs to communicate about their crimes and their conspiracies with impunity."

What's the concern here? In brief, public-key cryptography can be used not only in email messages but also on telephone conversations. It promises to put the FBI out of the wiretapping business. That's good news for organized crime. According to Freeh, court-ordered wiretapping is the single-most, effective tool used by law enforcement officials to combat the sale of illegal drugs, terrorism, violent crime, and espionage.

To enable investigators to intercept and decode encrypted communications, the U.S. administration and the FBI have proposed a number of initiatives. These include voluntary use of the Clipper Chip, a microprocessor that could be used to encrypt voice or data communications, but in such a way that investigators could intercept and decode the message (see Figure 9A.2). More recently, the Clinton administration proposed a **key escrow** plan, in which a user's private key would be held by an independent agency and divulged to investigators only when a valid court order is produced. In 1998, FBI director Freeh asked Congress to speed the development of key escrow by implementing a mandatory back door in computer-based encryption products. Called **key recovery,**

Figure 9A.2

The Clipper Chip can be used to encrypt voice or data communications.

this back door would be built into encryption products themselves and would enable investigators to decode almost any encrypted message without tipping off the message's sender or its intended recipient. Freeh also called for the criminalization of all encryption products that do not contain key recovery capabilities.

According to law enforcement officials, some type of key escrow system is needed to fight illegal drugs and terrorism. But the cost of key recovery would be very high, according to the plan's critics. It would leave citizens open to illegal monitoring for political reasons. Civil liberties advocates point out that, in the past, the U.S. government has too frequently used wiretapping for political purposes. During the 1960s, Dr. Martin Luther King was routinely wiretapped on the pretext that he posed a risk to national security. Former President Richard M. Nixon used illegal wiretaps to track the activities of his political opponents and the reporters and other individuals on his "Enemies List." Would a future Nixon monitor email, looking for evidence of political dissent? According to critics of key escrow, the government's proposals are similar to asking U.S. citizens to install a live video camera in their homes, which could be activated if investigators suspected criminal activity.

A key escrow system could be very costly in another way, too. It may impede the development of electronic commerce, which some see as the key to continued U.S. economic growth. Corporations and banks will not wholeheartedly embrace electronic commerce without secure encryption, but key escrow or key recovery involves tremendous security risks because the underlying algorithms are too complex and risky. For example, everyone's keys would have to be stored on some huge, central computer database, where investigators could access the keys after obtaining a warrant. However, no computer system can be 100 percent secure. Would criminals learn how to break into key databases and steal a bank's encryption keys? Would a disgruntled employee start selling keys to make extra money? Very few businesses will want to engage in Internet commerce if encryption is not secure.

Export Restrictions

The U.S. government wants to restrict domestic use of public-key encryption technology and also stop the spread of this technology overseas. Currently, the U.S. government encryption technologies are considered munitions (arms), which means that strong encryption tools cannot be exported without a license under the U.S. Department of Commerce's International Traffic in Arms Regulations (ITAR). Each application for an export license is required to go through a lengthy and expensive process that can take months or even years to complete.

What is a strong encryption tool? It all boils down to **bit length.** The greater number of bits in the key, the more difficult it is to break the code. 56-bit keys can be broken quite easily (a group of college students did so in 1997). For secure electronic commerce, a bit length of at least 128 is required. All banks require 128-bit encryption for online banking. The ITAR, however, define even 56-bit encryption tools as munitions. Currently, the U.S. Department of Commerce will grant permits for exporting programs containing insecure 56-bit encryption but only if the company promises to develop key recovery tools for domestic surveillance.

Even U.S. government officials admit that ITAR will not stop the spread of encryption technologies to other countries. The other countries already have them. The regulations serve only to keep U.S. firms from competing in what could be a lucrative international marketplace for software products

SPOTLIGHT   NAVAJO CODE TALKERS

▶ Suppose you're a Japanese intelligence officer in World War II, and you're trying to intercept U.S. Marine communications in the Pacific. If you can succeed, you'll know where the Americans are planning their next amphibious attack, and you'll give your country a tremendous advantage. However, the messages you're hearing are in some kind of code that you can't figure out.

What was the secret of U.S. Marine communications in the Pacific? A formidable secret weapon: the Navajo language and several hundred Navajo code talkers, who served with great distinction in the Pacific from 1942 to 1945. Transmitting coded messages in their native language, they served in all six Marine divisions, including Marine Raider battalions and Marine parachute units.

Navajo code talkers played a decisive role in the United States' Pacific victory. Major Howard Connor, 5th Marine Division signal officer, worked with six

Navajo code talkers during the invasion of Iwo Jima, which historians regard as the Pacific war's turning point. Working around the clock, the code talkers sent and received hundreds of messages, all without error. Connor declared, "Were it not for the Navajos, the Marines would never have taken Iwo Jima."

Who came up with the idea of using the Navajo language for secret communications? It was Philip Johnston, the son of a missionary and a fluent Navajo speaker who was raised on a Navajo reservation. Johnston knew that no dictionary of the Navajo language existed at that time and that the language was exceptionally difficult to learn. To express meanings in Navajo, you must learn a complicated syntax, including subtle tone generations that can alter a word's meaning. Knowledge of Navajo requires many years of training and direct exposure. Compounding the difficulty was the fact that code talkers used a special, memorized vocabulary consisting of Navajo translations of military and naval terms. These code words wouldn't make any sense even to a native Navajo speaker (for example, a submarine was an iron fish, while a fighter plane was a hummingbird).

After the war ended, the chief of Japanese Intelligence, Seizue Arisue, confirmed that the Japanese were never able to break the code, even after they captured a Navajo soldier and made him listen to the transmissions. Through the use of an ancient language and its application to modern needs, code talkers helped ensure the security of American forces at the height of the Pacific war.

Several Navajo code talkers served with great distinction in the Pacific from 1942 to 1945.

containing strong encryption. According to the U.S. Economic Strategy Institute, the total cost of continuing export controls on strong encryption products to the U.S. economy could hit $35 billion.

The Global Dimension

Outside the United States, few countries place restrictions on the use of encryption technologies. It is interesting to note that the few that do—including China and Singapore—are among the world's most authoritarian or totalitarian regimes. Until recently, an exception was France, which formerly had the world's most stringent controls on encryption technologies. However, France has recently relaxed its restrictions to enable French software companies to take advantage of the growing encryption marketplace.

 Destinations

To get the latest news and perspectives about cryptography issues, visit the Center for Democracy and Technology's Crypto Debate page (**http:// www.cdt.org/crypto**).

CURRENTS

Spies in the Sky?

Are U.S. national security agencies running an automated privacy-invasion system that spans the entire globe, one that's capable of eavesdropping on phone calls, faxes, or emails anywhere on the planet? No, this isn't an X-files rerun. Rumors about the existence of such a system have been floating around since 1988. U.S. security agencies strongly deny the existence of such a system, but there's increasing evidence that **something** like Echelon actually exists—not the least of which is the fact that several participating governments, including Australia and New Zealand, have confirmed the existence of at least some type of globe-spanning system for monitoring data transmissions.

What is Echelon? According to journalists and researchers who are trying to uncover the truth about the alleged global spying system, Echelon is a Cold War-era system that is designed to intercept and search phone calls, fax and Telex transmissions, email messages, Internet downloads, and satellite data transfers worldwide—some 3 billion messages per day, according to one estimate. Operated jointly by the United States, the United Kingdom, Canada, Australia, and New Zealand, the system uses ground-based listening devices and up to 120 satellites to intercept messages. It also uses sophisticated, artificial-intelligence-based software to comb through the huge volume of intercepted messages, looking for words and phrases such as "bomb," "terrorist," "Saddam Hussein," and other information of interest to intelligence agencies. Using these data-screening technologies, Echelon operators can allegedly hone in on specific organizations, individuals, and places at will.

If Echelon actually exists, is it such a bad thing? Most people would readily agree that the world isn't a particularly peaceful place, and countries need effective intelligence to protect their interests. Still, almost anyone familiar with the emerging facts about Echelon will find grounds for concern. In the United States, the agency most-deeply involved in Echelon, the National Security Agency (NSA), is prohibited from spying on U.S. citizens. However, Echelon critics believe that the NSA intercepts and scans up to 90 percent of the data transmitted on the domestic Internet, in direct violation of the agency's charter.

Europeans are alarmed by the prospect that Echelon has been used for industrial espionage. According to an accusation made by French government officials, Echelon was used to eavesdrop on a 1995 contract offer made by the European Airbus consortium to a prospective customer, and the information was passed on to U.S. aerospace giant Boeing—which subsequently used the information to win the contract.

The NSA denies these and other allegations concerning Echelon. It insists that the concept of a globe-spanning system capable of reading billions of messages per day is "sheer fantasy." Scholars who study the intelligence community tend to agree with the NSA. The technology probably doesn't exist to reliably transcribe millions of intercepted telephone calls into text. In fact, a former NSA director confessed that he had "wasted" millions of dollars of taxpayers' money trying to develop such a technology, only to meet with failure. Critics of the NSA portray it as a dysfunctional, overly-bureaucratic agency that is, if anything, woefully out of touch with the latest technology.

But Echelon's critics aren't convinced. In one of the most damaging revelations to date, the NSA conceded that the agency had obtained and compiled more than 1,000 pages of information on Diana, Princess of Wales, prior to her tragic death in an automobile accident. Just how the NSA obtained this information, and what it contains, is unknown—but some of the information was indeed obtained from "intercepted messages," according to an NSA spokesperson.

Echelon probably isn't as scary, or as effective, as the NSA's critics allege. But there are still grounds for concern. The Diana revelations prove that the NSA routinely engages in what one critic called "promiscuous" eavesdropping. And because the super-secret NSA is protected from public scrutiny, it's anyone's guess whether there's any truth to the mounting accusations concerning the system's misuse—including repeated allegations that the NSA is illegally using its technology to spy on U.S. citizens.

The NSA has conceded that they obtained and compiled more than 1,000 pages of information on Diana, Princess of Wales, prior to her death in 1997.

TAKEAWAY POINTS

- Because the United States has no comprehensive Federal regulations protecting an individual's privacy, highly-sensitive personal information, such as social security numbers, is now for sale on the Internet. Many Web sites collect personal information without informing their visitors.

- Anonymity refers to the ability to convey a message without disclosing one's name or identity. Anonymity may free people from accountability, and they may abuse the privilege of anonymous speech. They may injure someone's reputation by making false and malicious statements. Anonymous communications can also be used to threaten and harass, or to spread false and misleading information.

- Computers and the Internet enable marketing firms, snoops, and government officials to harness all the power of technology in order to collect information in ways that are hidden from the user's view. For example, cookies are small files that are written to your computer's hard disk by many of the Web sites you visit. Cookies provide Web sites with a way of recording information so that it is available for future browsing sessions at the same site. A global unique identifier (GUID) is a unique identification number that is generated by a computer hardware component or a program. Privacy advocates say that GUIDs make anonymous usage of the Internet more difficult, if not impossible.

- Because large U.S. employers want to make sure that they're getting their money's worth from employees, more than three-quarters of them routinely monitor employees' phone calls, email, Web browsing habits, and computer files. Companies are concerned about potential sexual harassment lawsuits and employees who offer trade secrets to competitors.

- U.S. security agencies fear that public-key encryption will prevent them from detecting the activities of terrorists, drug dealers, and organized crime syndicates.

- Encryption software containing key recovery features would enable investigators to read secret messages, but financial institutions fear that these features would open security holes.

MODULE REVIEW

KEY TERMS AND CONCEPTS

ad networks	defamation	libel
anonymity	encrypted	privacy
banner ad	global unique identifier (GUID)	public-key
bit length	identity theft	public-key cryptography
cookies	key escrow	rot-13
database vendors	key recovery	

TRUE/FALSE

Indicate whether the following statements are true or false.

1. Privacy is the right of a person to keep his or her personal and family business away from others.

2. A right to privacy is specifically granted by the U.S. Constitution.

3. Conducting personal business over the Internet can represent a threat to privacy.

4. Consumers not currently using the Internet don't consider privacy concerns as a primary reason for not going online.

5. Cookies are rarely used for legitimate purposes.

6. More than three-quarters of large U.S. employers routinely monitor employees' phone calls, email, and Web browsing habits.

7. The science of encoding messages so they cannot be read by anyone except the intended recipient is called cryptography.

8. Rot-13 is a secure encryption method.

9. Experts in cryptography describe public-key cryptography as one of the major scientific revolutions of the twentieth century.

10. Public-key cryptography cannot be used in telephone conversations.

MATCHING

Match each key term from the left column to the most accurate definition in the right column.

_____ 1. privacy

_____ 2. anonymity

_____ 3. libel

_____ 4. cookies

_____ 5. banner ad

_____ 6. global unique identifier

_____ 7. encrypted

_____ 8. public-key

_____ 9. public-key cryptography

_____ 10. key recovery

a. an encoding key that you make public so that people can read your encoded messages

b. a coded message

c. written defamation

d. the ability to convey a message without disclosing one's name or identity

e. an individual's ability to keep personal and family business away from prying eyes

f. a new encryption method that doesn't require the message's receiver to have received the decoding key in a separate transmission

g. a method of unlocking the key used to encrypt messages so that the message could be read by law enforcement officials conducting a lawful investigation

h. small files written to your computer's hard disk by many of the Web sites you visit

i. a rectangular advertisement

j. an identification number that is generated by a computer hardware component or a program

MULTIPLE CHOICE

Circle the letter of the correct choice for each of the following.

1. Who is responsible for regulating database vendors?
   a. database vendors
   b. Congress
   c. Federal Trade Commission
   d. state agencies

2. Database information is commonly collected through which of the following sources?
   a. loan applications
   b. product registration cards
   c. Web sites
   d. all of the above

3. The Fair Credit Reporting Act provides which of the following?
   a. Federal laws governing the privacy rights of U.S. citizens
   b. Limited privacy protection for credit information
   c. Extensive privacy protection for credit information
   d. None of the above

4. What is the act of injuring someone's reputation by making false and malicious statements called?

   a. libel
   b. anonymity
   c. perjury
   d. defamation

5. Which of the following uses cookies to track users' browsing actions across thousands of popular Internet sites?
   a. banner ads
   b. GUIDs
   c. Ad networks
   d. Email messages

6. Which of the following is the primary concern of those people who don't use the Internet?
   a. privacy
   b. anonymity
   c. libel
   d. encryption

7. What is a coded message called?
   a. RTF text
   b. encrypted
   c. plaintext
   d. ciphertext

8. Which of the following methods of compromising encryption were not proposed by those concerned with law enforcement?
   a. key recovery
   b. key escrow
   c. enemies list
   d. Clipper chip

9. What length of encryption key is currently required for electronic commerce?

   a. 40
   b. 128
   c. 64
   d. 56

10. What length of encryption key is currently approved for export under U.S. regulations?
    a. 40
    b. 128
    c. 64
    d. 56

FILL-IN

In the blank provided, write the correct answer for each of the following.

1. Most _____ claim that they sell only to bona fide customers.

2. The term _____ refers to one's ability to convey a message without disclosing a name or identity.

3. Several Internet _____ use _____ to track users' browsing actions across thousands of popular Internet sites.

4. Defamation in written form is called _____ .

5. A(n) _____ is not actually a part of the Web page you're viewing. It is separately supplied by the ad network.

6. A(n) _____ message cannot be read by anyone but the intended recipient.

7. _____ is an encryption technique that's sometimes used in Usenet discussions.

8. _____ cryptography eliminates the need for people to exchange a key that could be used to decode a message.

9. The greater number of _____ in a key, the more difficult it is to break the code.

10. _____ is proposed by law enforcement officials who are concerned that encryption would prevent the surveillance of criminal activities.

SHORT ANSWER

On a separate sheet of paper, answer the following questions.

1. Define the term *privacy*. In what ways does the computer revolution threaten privacy?

2. What efforts have been made to protect privacy in relation to computers?

3. Do you believe that the database vendor industry can adequately and effectively regulate itself? If not, who should do the regulation?

4. Can information collected by a credit bureau present a privacy threat?

5. What privacy rights do citizens have in the European Union? Do you think U.S. citizens should enjoy the same rights? Why or why not?

6. How can you best protect your privacy online? What steps can you take to ensure your privacy?

7. How might the use of information collected by Web sites be impeding the growth of e-commerce?

8. What are some of the reasons why material should be encrypted?

9. How do public-key encryption methods work?

10. Name the controversial issues associated with strong encryption techniques in the United States.

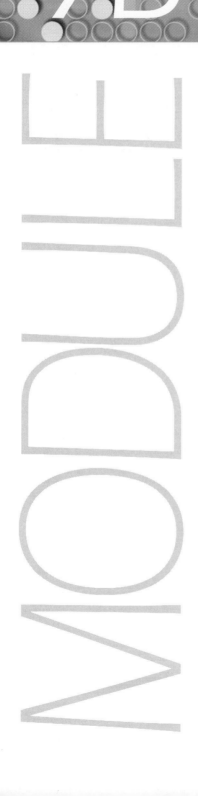

9B

COMPUTER CRIME AND SECURITY

WHAT YOU WILL LEARN . . .

When you have finished reading this module, you will be able to:

1. Explain how attackers and intruders can gain entry to computer systems and harm or destroy data.

2. List ways you can help system administrators keep a computer system safe from unauthorized accesses and computer viruses.

3. Identify the people who are most likely to attack or harm computer systems and explain their motives.

4. List the types of losses caused by computer system intrusions and attacks.

5. List and explain the tools and techniques used to defend computer systems against intruders and attackers.

On Christmas Day, 1995, Tsutomu Shimomura, a computational physicist, was about to leave for a skiing trip. Before doing so, he made a most-unwelcome discovery. By means of the Internet, an intruder broke into the computers he kept at his beach cottage near San Diego. Hundreds of pages of information concerning Shimomura's research on cellular phone security were stolen. That could be bad news for an industry experiencing nearly $1 billion per year in fraudulent calls.

Shimomura vowed that he'd bring the intruder to justice. Using his own considerable knowledge of Internet security, Shimomura tracked down the intruder to an apartment in Raleigh, North Carolina, where Federal authorities arrested Kevin D. Mitnick, a 31-year-old computer intruder who had previously been convicted of computer crimes. Subsequently, Mitnick was charged and convicted for charged with violating several Federal laws, including computer fraud, causing damage to computer systems, and interception of electronic communications.

Kevin D. Mitnick was charged with violating several Federal laws, including computer fraud and causing damage to computer systems.

In this module, you'll learn why computer crime is on the rise, and why improvements in computer security are needed. You'll learn about the tools and techniques attackers use to invade computer systems and steal or destroy computer data. You'll meet some of the people who are behind computer attacks, and learn about the motives that underlie their sometimes-devastating actions. You'll also examine the techniques security experts use to defend systems from intrusion and attack.

SCOPE OF THE PROBLEM

Shimomura's dogged and successful pursuit makes a great story. In fact, it was made into a movie (*Takedown*, by Miramar Productions). Unfortunately, very few computer attacks turn out so well for the victims. Most unauthorized intrusions go undetected and the attackers are never caught.

What *is* detected is financial loss. In a recent survey of United States and Canadian companies conducted by *Information Week*, more than half of the surveyed companies reported financial losses averaging in excess of $100,000 due to computer fraud. Seventeen companies reported losses of more than $1 million as the result of a single security incident. Just two years earlier, only 12 percent of the surveyed companies reported losses. Since many companies are reluctant to report losses out of fear that their customers will lose confidence in their security procedures the losses are probably much greater than reported. In short, computer crime is a serious problem, and it's getting worse. If ways are not found to counter computer crime, it could threaten the growth of electronic commerce.

More is at stake than financial loss. Consider this: if Mitnick could invade Shimomura's San Diego cottage from Raleigh, North Carolina, what's to stop foreign intelligence services from mounting similar attacks from abroad? The Internet, after all, is a global network. Advanced industrial economies are increasingly dependent on networked information systems to support vital infrastructures, such as finance, energy, and transportation. According to some experts, an enemy could bring the United States to its knees by means of electronic warfare without firing a single shot.

COMPUTER AND INTERNET CRIME: TOOLS AND TECHNIQUES

Anyone who wants to invade or harm a computer system can make use of a variety of tools and tricks, which are summarized in this section. Pay close attention, as you'll learn several facts that could help you avoid becoming a victim!

Tricks for Obtaining Passwords

The most-publicized computer security problems stem from **unauthorized access,** in which an unauthorized intruder gains entry to a supposedly-secure computer system. Typically, computer systems use some type of **authentication** technique—usually plain-text passwords—to protect the system from uninvited guests. It isn't difficult, though, to guess or obtain a password. In fact, many unauthorized access attempts target password lists.

Techniques used to obtain passwords include the following:

- **Password guessing** Computer users too often do not understand the need to choose secure passwords. In **password guessing,** they choose a password that's easily guessed, such as *password*! Other popular passwords are *qwerty*, obscene words, personal names, birthdays, celebrity names, and the names of cartoon characters such as Garfield.

- **Shoulder surfing** In a crowded computer lab, it's easy to peek over someone's shoulder, look at the keyboard, and obtain the person's password. Watch out for **shoulder surfing** when you're using an ATM machine, too.

- **Packet sniffers** A **packet sniffer** is a program that examines all the traffic on a section of a network. The program examines the data stream and looks for passwords, credit card numbers, and other valuable information.

- **Dumpster diving** Companies may unthinkingly discard documents that contain lists of user IDs and even passwords. In **dumpster diving,** intruders go through an organization's trash in the hope of finding such documents. It's wise to use a shredder!

- **Social engineering** Imagine that you get a call from a person who claims to be your network administrator. You're told, "We have a problem with our mail backup system. I need your password right now to save your mail." Without realizing what you're doing by answering, you're giving an intruder a means to gain entry to a secure system. You're a victim of **social engineering,** a form of deception designed to get people to divulge sensitive information.

- **Superuser status** Multiuser operating systems such as UNIX and Windows NT provide system administrators with **superuser status,** enabling them to access and modify virtually any file on the network. If intruders are able to obtain superuser status, they can obtain the passwords of everyone using the system.

Another widely-used technique involves exploiting well-known holes in obsolete email programs, which can be manipulated to disclose a user's password. Competent system administrators know better than to run these programs, but a tight job market and a huge increase in the number of networked systems makes it difficult to find well-trained people. As a result, too many computer systems are run by untrained people who leave gaping holes for intruders.

Salami Shaving and Data Diddling

Most computer crime is an inside job. In **salami shaving,** a programmer alters a program so that it subtracts a very small amount of money from each account—say, 2 cents—and diverts the funds to the embezzler's account. Ideally, the sum is so small that it's never noticed. In a business that handles thousands of accounts, an insider could skim tens of thousands of dollars per year using this method.

In **data diddling,** insiders modify data so that it's difficult or impossible to tell that they've stolen funds or equipment. In some cases, data diddling requires little more expertise than altering accounts or database records to disguise illegal activities. A Colorado supermarket chain learned a great deal about data diddling recently when it discovered nearly $2 million in unaccounted losses. Subsequently, the chain's computer manager and two clerks were arrested on suspicion of embezzlement. Although the highest salary they earned was $32,000, they had each purchased expensive new cars (including a Dodge Viper) and made several trips to Las Vegas, where they flashed wads of cash—$20,000 or more.

Forgery

Basic shortcomings in the Internet's technical design enable knowledgeable users to make data appear to come from one place when it's really coming from another. Pranksters can easily originate forged email messages, which can do a great deal of harm if the forgery is undetected. Spammers (marketers who send unsolicited email) use this technique to disguise the origin of their messages.

Security Loophole Detection Programs

Intruders can use a variety of programs that automatically search for unprotected or poorly-protected computer systems and notify them when a target is found. They can also use **SATAN,** a security loophole analysis program designed for use by system administrators. In the wrong hands, however, the program can tell an intruder how to get into a poorly-secured system.

Computer Viruses

A **computer virus** resembles a living virus in frightening ways. Like real viruses, computer viruses require a host (such as a program file), and they're designed to make copies of themselves.

How does a computer get infected by a virus? Typically, virus infections spread when somebody inserts a disk containing an infected program into a computer, and then starts the infected program. You might also get a virus by downloading an infected program from the Internet. Either way, starting the infected program causes the virus to start copying itself. The virus attaches itself to other programs and soon infects much or all of the software on your computer. Should you copy a program on your computer to a disk and give it to someone, the infection also spreads (see Figure 9B.1).

Although many viruses are best categorized as nuisances or pranks, all consume system memory and slow processing, while others damage data. For example, the Wazzu virus, one of the most-widespread in virus history, randomly relocates a word in a Microsoft Word document and sometimes inserts *wazzu* into the text. Still others—such as Disk Killer, authored by an individual who calls himself The Computer Ogre—are far more malicious: Disk Killer wipes out your hard drive.

The viruses we've been describing are called **file infectors** because they attach themselves to a program file. When the program is executed, the virus spreads to other programs on the user's hard disk. Most viruses are file infectors.

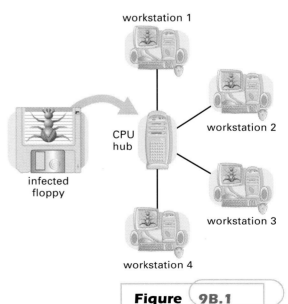

Figure 9B.1

Computer viruses can be passed from one computer to another on floppy disks and over networks.

A second type of virus is called a **boot sector virus.** A boot sector virus also propagates by means of an infected program, but it installs itself at the beginning of a hard drive, where code is stored that automatically executes every time you start the computer. Unlike file infectors, boot sector viruses don't require you to start a specific program to infect your computer: starting your system is sufficient. Boot sector viruses may lead to the destruction of all the data stored on the hard drive.

More recently, a third type of virus, called a **macro virus,** has appeared. Macro viruses take advantage of the automatic command execution capabilities (called **macros**) of productivity software, such as word processing and spreadsheet programs. Before macro viruses came along, the only type of file that could be infected by viruses (and cause them to spread) was an executable program file where the virus couldn't spread unless somebody ran the program. People have caught on to this and are more reluctant to exchange programs. What's scary about macro viruses is that they infect *data* files. Many people exchange data files; in fact, they *must* exchange data files to do their jobs. For example, most on-the-job writing you'll do will involve collaboration with one or more coworkers. When you exchange drafts of a report, will you infect your computer?

Viruses pose a serious threat to computer systems. Hundreds of viruses are in existence, and more are being written each day. In U.S. companies, they're causing serious financial losses. A recent 1997 survey of 563 firms revealed that nearly one-third experienced costs totaling nearly $12.4 million due to computer virus infestations. Two of the most famous and devastating viruses, the Melissa virus of 1999 and the "Love Bug" virus of 2000, are estimated to have cost businesses and individuals worldwide more than $10 *billion* in lost data, computer repairs, lost work time, and lost sales. And the threat is growing. Computer virus authors are hard at work trying to "improve" their programs. Some new viruses are self-modifying so that each new copy is slightly different from the previous one, making it difficult to protect the computer.

Most computer viruses spread by means of email attachments (see Module 7B). If you receive an email attachment that you weren't expecting, don't open it!

Destinations

With the proliferation of email viruses circulating on the Internet, whom can you trust? There are a couple of Web sites that offer information on computer viruses and debunk the myths surrounding them. For more information, go to **http://www.vmyths.com** or **http://www.symantec.com/avcenter/hoax.html.**

More Rogue Programs

Viruses aren't the only type of rogue program. Other destructive programs include time bombs, worms, and Trojan horses.

Time bombs, also called logic bombs, are designed to sit harmlessly on a system until a certain event or set of circumstances causes the program to become active. Disgruntled programmers may create a time bomb designed to detonate after they've left a firm's employment.

A **worm** resembles a computer virus in that it can spread from one computer to another. Unlike a virus, however, a worm can propagate over a computer network. It takes control of affected computers and uses their resources to attack other network-connected systems. In 1988, a worm set in motion by a Cornell University graduate student nearly brought the Internet to a standstill.

A **Trojan horse** is disguised as a useful program, but it contains hidden instructions to perform a malicious task instead. Sometimes a Trojan horse is disguised as a game or a utility program that users will find appealing. Then, when the users begin running the game, they discover that they have loaded another animal entirely. A Trojan horse may erase the data on the hard disk or cause other damage.

MEET THE ATTACKERS

Who wants to harm computer systems and computer users? As you'll see, a surprising variety of people can cause security problems, ranging from people with too much time on their hands to hardened criminals, such as the Russian intruders who recently made off with $10 million from Citibank. Motives vary, too. Some attackers are out for ego gratification and don't intend any harm. Others are out for money, and still others are just plain malicious.

The variety of attackers is a problem in itself. When intruders try to break into a system, administrators can't be sure initially where the problem's coming from. In 1998, U.S. Defense Department computers were besieged during a Gulf military action, and newspapers jumped to the conclusion that the attacks originated in Iraq and were intended to stymie the military's activities. The culprits turned out to be two California boys under the direction of a teenager computer intruder in Israel!

Crackers, Cyber Gangs, and Virus Authors

The most-celebrated intruders are computer hobbyists and computer experts, for whom unauthorized access is something of an irresistible intellectual game. The press tends to call all these hobbyists *hackers*, but this term is actually too broad. In this section, you'll learn more-focused terms to refer to the hobbyists who try to break into computer systems.

Hackers are computer hobbyists who enjoy pushing computer systems (and themselves) to their limits. They experiment with programs to try to discover **undocumented features,** capabilities that aren't mentioned in the systems' manuals. They modify systems to obtain the maximum possible performance. And sometimes, they try to track down all the weaknesses and loopholes in a system's security. When hackers attempt unauthorized access, they rarely damage data or steal assets. Hackers generally subscribe to an unwritten code of conduct, called the **hacker ethic,** that forbids the destruction of data. For hackers, unauthorized access is an intellectual diversion or game. (As you'll learn later in this module, the people who have to secure systems against hacker attacks don't think it's a game.) Hacker motives include ego gratification: hackers form communities, with a pecking order defined in terms of an individual's reputation for hacking prowess.

Crackers are hackers obsessed with gaining entry to highly-secure computer systems. Like hackers, they generally do not intend to harm or steal data, but the frequency and sophistication of their attacks cause major headaches for system administrators. A Pentagon official recently disclosed that the U.S. Department of Defense computer systems experience more than 1,000 detected unauthorized access attempts per day, and that as many as 96 percent of such attempts evade detection. Cracking appears to be one form of **computer addiction:** many crackers, such as Mitnick, confess that they feel compelled to return to cracking even if they have made an effort to stop. Like hackers, crackers are obsessed with their reputation in the hacking and cracking communities. To document their feats, they often leave calling cards, such as a prank message, on the systems they penetrate. Sometimes these traces enable law enforcement personnel to track crackers down. That's how Shimomura caught Mitnick.

Cyber gangs bring crackers together by means of the Internet and physical meetings. The group dynamics reinforce their immature and often destructive aims.

Computer virus authors, typically, are teenage males whose programming ability is much more developed than their ethical conscience.

Techtalk

phreaking
When a computer or other device is used to trick a telephone system, it's called "phreaking." When successful, a phone phreak will be able to make free telephone calls or have calls charged to a different account. Either way, they break into the phone system and steal time from the phone company.

They want to see how far they can push the boundaries of virus software. Often, they see no harm in what they are doing. They claim that all technological progress is inevitable, and that somebody else would eventually create the programs they write. Most eventually stop writing viruses after they've matured a bit and found something more worthwhile to do with their time.

More than a few hackers and crackers have turned pro, offering their services to companies hoping to use hacker expertise to shore up their computer system's defenses. (This practice is called *ethical hacking.*) And without doubt, some of them have crossed the line from hacking and cracking to intentional computer crime. This prospect sounds scary, but a far-greater threat exists inside the organizations that house computer systems, as the next section explains.

Disgruntled Employees

Computer intrusions make headlines, but a much-greater security risk stems from **disgruntled employees.** According to one estimate, 80 percent of all data loss comes from company insiders. Unlike intruders, employees have many opportunities to sabotage a company's computer system, often in ways that are difficult to trace. They may discover or deliberately create security holes called **trap doors** that, after leaving the firm, they can exploit to get even with the company. For example, they can divulge the company's trade secrets to a competitor or destroy crucial data.

A Texas firm learned the peril posed by disgruntled employees the hard way. Before leaving the firm, a fired programmer planted a **logic bomb** (a destructive program) that wiped out 168,000 critical financial records.

Spies

Corporate computer systems contain a great deal of information of interest to competitors, including product development plans, customer contact lists, product specification, manufacturing process knowledge, cost data, and strategic plans. According to computer security experts, **corporate espionage** is on the rise—so sharply that it may soon eclipse all other sources of unauthorized access.

How do spies gain entry to a corporation's computers? Some get help from hackers and crackers. More often, though, the perpetrators are ex-employees who have been hired by a competing firm precisely because of their knowledge of the computer system in their previous place of employment. Sometimes, employees who are planning to leave one company will create a trap door, which enables them to access the company's computers without detection after they have left the company and joined another.

Hacking and cracking skills are no longer the only means available for snooping on a company's data. In the mid-1980s, Wim van Eck, a Dutch electronics researcher, proved that it's possible to reconstruct the words on a computer display terminal from a distance by decoding the terminal's radio frequency emissions. What's even scarier is that the necessary device can be assembled from inexpensive, off-the-shelf components and mounted in an innocent-looking van.

The espionage threat goes beyond national borders. Nations bent on acquiring trade secrets and new technologies are also trying to break into corporate computer systems. According to a recent estimate, the governments of more than 125 countries are actively involved in industrial espionage. In 1997, the CIA identified France, Israel, China, Russia, Iran, and Cuba as the countries most likely to engage in illegal industrial espionage in the United States.

Swindlers

The Internet is the latest playground for con men, swindlers, and fraud artists, and it's a serious problem. Much of it is the same old garbage that telemarketing "boiler rooms" dished out in years past, such as bogus work-at-home opportunities, illegal pyramid schemes, chain letters, risky business opportunities, bogus franchises, phony goods that won't be delivered, over-priced scholarship searches, and get-rich-quick scams. Today, the distribution medium of choice includes email, Internet chat rooms, and Web sites.

Estimates of the scope of the problem vary, but the U.S. National Consumer's League believes that consumers are losing millions of dollars on a variety of Internet scams—and the figure is growing by leaps and bounds. Here's a sampler:

- **Rip and tear**   A Seattle man posted ads for Barbie dolls and other goods on the leading Internet auction site eBay.com, collected more than $32,000 in orders, and never delivered any goods—a type of swindle known to law enforcement as **rip and tear,** because the swindlers move to a new state once their activities are uncovered. The perpetrators believe that law enforcement would not be concerned with the relatively-small amounts involved in each transaction. In another of a growing number of rip and tear scams on Internet auction sites, a San Diego man was charged with duping Internet users out of more than $60,000 for Beanie Babies that were never delivered.

- **Pumping and dumping**   Crooks with alleged Mafia connections used Internet stock trading sites, chat rooms, Usenet discussions, and email to sing the praises of worthless companies in which they held stock—and after the share prices went up, they dumped the stocks and took some $50 million in profits. Called **pumping and dumping,** this activity is illegal under U.S. security laws.

- **Bogus goods**   Two Miami residents were indicted on charges of mail and wire fraud after selling hundreds of "Go-boxes," which purported to turn red traffic lights to green. The boxes, which were actually nothing more than strobe lights, were sold for between $69 and $150.

Shills

Internet auction sites such as eBay (**http://www.ebay.com**) are among the hottest on the Web, but they're attracting cybernetic versions of the same scams long perpetrated at live auctions. A **shill** is a secret operative who bids on another seller's item in order to drive up the price. The practice made headlines when an abstract painting's price shot from 25 cents to $135,805 after speculation that the work was a long-lost canvas by the renowned artist Richard Diekenborn. In this case, the shill was the seller, who used a different email address to bid up his own offering. In response, the auction site cancelled the sale and suspended the seller's account.

The practice may be more common than Internet auction sites are willing to admit. A group of sellers can band together, drive up each other's prices, and post glowing reviews of each others' selling and delivery practices. There's actually nothing illegal about any of this, as long as each member of the ring actually purchases the items if they should, by chance, win the auction. Shill bidding may also be close to impossible to detect. The telltale patterns can be detected only by piecing through bidding records, but eBay retains them for only 30 days.

If shill bidding is indeed a widespread practice, it's big business. The largest auction site, eBay, receives more than 1,000 bids per minute on more than 5 million items listed for sale. Auction sales are expected to top $10 billion by 2002.

Cyberstalkers and Sexual Predators

One of the newest and fastest growing of all crimes is **cyberstalking,** defined as the use of the Internet, email, and other electronic communication media to repeatedly harass or threaten a person. For example, a San Diego university student terrorized five female classmates for more than a year, sending them hundreds of violent and threatening emails. In an Internet chat room, a 16-year-old boy was contacted by a woman who asked him to make a videotape of himself being tied up and tickled. When the boy refused, the woman bombarded him with emails—more than 30,000 of them—demanding the videotape and threatening to tell the boy's parents. A former security guard used the Internet to terrorize a woman who refused his sexual advances. He impersonated his 28-year-old victim in Internet chat rooms, posting messages that she fantasized about being raped. On at least six occasions, the women received visitors—sometimes at night—who said they were there to rape her.

Cyberstalking has one thing in common with traditional stalking: most perpetrators are men, and most victims are women, particularly women in college. One in every eight women attending college has repeatedly been followed, watched, phoned, written, or emailed in ways that they found obsessive and which frightened them.

Children are at risk from online sexual predators, who are much more numerous than most parents realize. According to a study conducted by the National Center for Missing and Exploited Children, about one in every five kids has received invitations to engage in sexual activities while participating in Internet discussions. Online predators may encourage children to run away from home or meet them while their parents are away.

Enemies and Terrorists

Imagine the next war as some experts portray it. Without a shot being fired, the United States is thrown into economic chaos and forced to make major concessions to a foreign adversary. How? By means of **information warfare,** the use of information technologies to corrupt or destroy an enemy's information and industrial infrastructure.

A concerted enemy attack would include **electronic warfare** (the use of electronic devices to destroy or damage computer systems), **network warfare** (hacker-like attacks on the nation's network infrastructure, including the electronic banking system), and **structural sabotage** (attacks on information systems that support major transportation, finance, energy, and telecommunications). However, don't leave out old-fashioned explosives directed at computer centers. According to one expert, a well-coordinated bombing of only 100 key computer installations in the United States could bring the country's economy to a grinding halt.

How big is the threat? According to experts, information warfare is inevitable, but defenses are sorely lacking. A recent U.S. Department of Defense study disclosed that military systems were attacked a quarter of a million times in 1995. As a test, a Defense Department tiger team conducted 38,000 attacks of their own that same year. They were successful 65 percent of the time, and 63 percent of those attacks escaped detection. Former U.S. Deputy Attorney General Jaime Gorelick warns of a "cyber equivalent of Pearl Harbor," if the United States does not take steps to prepare for electronic attack.

Even if no enemy nation mounts an all-out information war on the United States, **information terrorism** is still increasingly likely. Thanks to

Destinations

For more on information warfare, including news reports, links, and analysis, see infowar.com (**http://www.infowar.com**).

the worldwide distribution of powerful but inexpensive microprocessors, virtually anyone can construct electronic warfare weapons from widely-available materials. These weapons include high-energy radio frequency (HERF) guns and electromagnetic pulse transformer (EMPT) bombs, which can damage or destroy computer systems at ranges of a quarter of a mile. A van loaded with such devices could cruise down Wall Street and bring chaos to the stock market.

If this scenario sounds frightening, remember that information technology is a double-edged sword. Information technology gives despots a potent weapon of war but also undermines their power by giving citizens a way to organize democratic resistance. In Russia, for example, email and fax machines played a major role in the failure of the 1989 military coup.

WHAT'S AT STAKE?

Breaches of computer security can be costly, even when no harm has occurred. As our entire economy and infrastructure moves to networked information systems, the potential costs grow higher every day.

Consumption of Staff Time

Even if intruders do no damage, they still cost companies money. When an intrusion occurs, the computer staff must drop everything they're doing and focus on the problem. After they've secured the system against the intruder, they must consider how they'll stop the next attack. They may spend days on the problem. It's no wonder that security currently accounts for an estimated 3 to 5 percent of all corporate expenditures on information systems.

Downtime

Ostensibly-harmless security breaches also cost money when an intrusion occurs and system administrators shut down the system rather than risk data loss. Financial losses may also include the loss of customers angered by slow service.

When rogue programs propagate by means of the Internet and affect thousands of systems, staff time and downtime add up. In 1988, a Cornell University graduate student released a damaging, self-replicating program called the Internet Worm that nearly brought the Internet to a standstill. Damages due to staff time and downtime losses reached nearly $100 million, even though little data loss actually occurred.

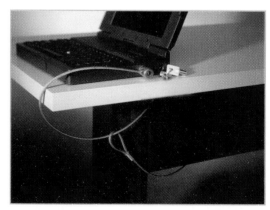

Fraud and Theft

Physical theft of computer equipment is a huge and growing problem, and it's particularly difficult to trace (see Figure 9B.2). An estimated 85 percent of computer thefts are inside jobs, leaving no signs of forced physical entry. In addition, it's difficult to trace components after they've been taken apart and reassembled. Universities are prime targets. For example, computer thieves hit the University of Michigan to the tune of $400,000 in losses annually. Particularly valuable are the microprocessor chips that drive computers. Employees at several large corporations have arrived at work only to find that their computers won't start. The problem? Overnight, somebody went through every computer in the building and pried out the processors. Memory shaving, in which knowledgeable thieves remove some of a computer's RAM chips but leave enough so that the computers are able to start is harder to detect. The crime might not be detected for days or weeks.

Figure 9B.2

For security measures, users should lock their doors and turn off their computers. In some cases, it may be wise to secure hardware to desks to prevent theft.

S P O T L I G H T

THE MP3 DEBATE

▶From the music industry's perspective, it's nothing short of an all-out war for survival. Thanks to a revolutionary new compression technology called MP3, it's possible to compress the huge amount of data stored on an audio CD down to a size small enough to transfer conveniently over the Internet. A track that consumes 40 MB of space on an audio CD, for example, can be compressed to 5 MB or less—and without any apparent loss in sound quality. The reason? MP3 uses a sophisticated lossy compression algorithm, which removes information that the human ear can't hear. Although it's illegal to make and distribute MP3 copies of copyrighted music, Internet users have been doing so for a number of years—and according to the music industry, its very survival is in doubt.

Even more alarming to the music industry is the arrival of music-sharing technologies such as Napster and Gnutella, which enable Internet users to make their MP3s available to others while online. After joining a Napster or Gnutella network, you can search for songs by a particular artist—and once you've found them, you can download the songs to your computer. Because Napster uses a central coordination point—the computers of Napster.com—to organize the network, it's an easy target for music industry lawsuits, but that's not true of Gnutella. With Gnutella, Internet users can form ad-hoc, fleeting networks of music exchangers that are virtually untraceable.

If MP3s are hurting the music industry so much, aren't music sales declining? According to a RIAA survey, CD sales are down in areas surrounding colleges and universities, where MP3 piracy is thought to be common. However, this survey omitted chain stores, such as Wal-Mart, even if they were located nearby. When this data is included, CD sales are up significantly (in the first quarter of 2000, they rose 8 percent). A new survey by the Digital Media Association explains a possible reason: 66 percent of those surveyed stated that they were prompted to purchase a CD after downloading an MP3 from the Internet.

Only 6 percent said they would be less likely to buy a CD after downloading music. The music industry's critics say that the stream of lawsuits targeted at illegal MP3s is reminiscent of the motion picture industry's panic over VCRs. After failing in their attempt to keep VCRs off the market due to fears of illegal duplication of copyrighted movies, the motion picture industry saw the public fall in love with movies—and movie attendance quadrupled.

Are college students the main culprits? Not according to another recent survey. The Pew Internet and American Life Project found that only 37 percent of those downloading music illegally are college students while 42 percent were between 30 and 49 years of age.

Internet users who download copyrighted music illegally say that the exorbitant price of CDs justifies their actions. And what's the reason for the high prices? The U.S. Federal Government found that five major music companies had illegally used marketing agreements to prevent price wars, inflate the price of CDs, and restrict the ability of retailers to offer discounts. According to the FTC, consumers were overcharged more than one-half billion dollars in a four-year period.

According to some recording artists, the industry hasn't just been gouging the public—the artists suffer, too. Courtney Love, the spouse of deceased rock legend Kurt Cobain, points out that even the few artists who sign what appear to be multi-million-dollar mega-deals often find themselves left with nothing while the music label walks away with huge profits. The artists don't even own the copyright to their own work. "They might as well be working in the 7-11," she says. Although the recording industry takes in $40 billion annually, the 273,000 working members of the Musician's Union in the United States make on average only $30,000 per year.

Not all MP3s are illegal. Artists are increasingly looking to MP3s as a way of getting around the music industry and reaching music consumers directly—and in some cases, this strategy is making the difference in their careers.

For music industry advocates, all the arguments in favor of illegal MP3 copying are just so much rationalization—a way of justifying an act that is both illegal and unfair to working musicians. But one thing's clear: in the coming years, more of the music we listen to will come from the Internet rather than music stores. Just how that transition is going to occur—and who's going to figure out how to make money from it—is far from clear at the moment.

Internet users who download copyrighted music illegally say that the high price of CDs justifies their actions.

Due to the high global demand for processor chips, shipments of such chips are often the target of holdups reminiscent of stagecoach robberies. A San Jose, California-based gang pulled off a series of armed heists totaling $10 million in computer chips, which were sold to firms in Taiwan. According to the Engineering and Safety Service of the American Insurance Service Group, losses from chip thefts totaled $8 billion in 1997 and will grow to $200 billion in the year 2000.

Notebook computers are a favorite target of airport thieves. Working in a team, they wait at the security belt until an unsuspecting passenger places a computer on the security system's conveyer belt. The two thieves then step in front of the passenger. The first one goes through easily, but the second one is loaded with metal jewelry and watches. Everyone must wait while the second thief slowly removes these items. When the passenger finally gets through, the notebook computer is gone.

Adverse Publicity

You may be surprised to learn that, according to one estimate, more than 40 percent of all computer crimes go unreported. Why? Suppose you're running a bank. You've lost $1 million due to computer theft. What's going to cost you more, covering the loss or telling the world that depositors' money isn't safe? Mum's the word.

According to news reports, computer attackers are taking advantage of adverse publicity fears by blackmailing financial institutions. In London, cyber gangs have reportedly extorted nearly $650 million from banks after demonstrating to senior executives that the gangs could completely wipe out the banks' information systems.

Vandalism

A surprising number of Web servers aren't properly secured, enabling any knowledgeable outsider to replace the existing content with prank material. This happens to people who ought to know better. In 1996, the CIA Web site was penetrated by a group of Swedish hackers, who altered the home page to say, "Welcome to the Central Stupidity Agency."

Character Assassination

Forged messages and Web pages can cause embarrassment and worse. A university professor in Texas was vilified by thousands of email messages and Usenet postings after someone forged a racist Usenet article in his name. In Beijing, a jealous fellow student forged an email message to the University of Michigan turning down an $18,000 scholarship. Fortunately, the forgery was discovered and the scholarship was reinstated, but only after a lengthy delay. Reportedly, a new Microsoft Word macro virus sends copies of a victim's Word documents to 23 different Usenet newsgroups under subject lines like "New Virus Alert!," "Important Princess Diana Info," and "How to find child pornography."

Loss of Privacy

If computer intruders make off with sensitive personal information, the potential for harm multiplies. In one Florida intrusion, a cracker made off with confidential medical records on 8,000 carriers of HIV, the virus that causes AIDS. Employees of the U.S. Social Security Administration used their computer access privileges to gather Social Security numbers and other information on 11,000 U.S. citizens, and sold this information to criminals specializing in credit card fraud.

Risks to Public Safety

Perhaps the greatest threat posed by security breaches is the threat to human life. And as computers are increasingly incorporated into safety-critical systems, such as air traffic control, the threat increases.

This threat nearly became a reality when a 14-year-old knocked out phone and radio service to a regional airport's communications tower. Although the hacker did not realize he had accessed an airport computer and meant no harm, his actions paralyzed the airport's computer system and forced air traffic controllers to rely on cellular phones and battery-powered radios to direct airplanes. Fortunately, the attack came when traffic was light. Had the airport's computers gone down in the midst of peak traffic, the outcome might have been tragic.

Should information terrorism or information warfare materialize, it could cause catastrophic harm. By paralyzing transportation and power infrastructures, attackers could completely disrupt the distribution of electricity, food, water, and medical supplies.

Denial of Service

By exploiting some of the most-troubling flaws in the Internet's basic structure, hackers have recently learned how to launch the latest type of assault: a **denial-of-service attack** (also called syn flooding, due to technical details concerning the attack method). In such an attack, hackers bog down an Internet server so that it becomes overloaded and cannot function. New York City service provider Panix, the victim of a two-week denial-of-service attack, nearly went out of business because the firm's customers could not log on during the entire ordeal.

PLAYING IT SAFE

What can we do to protect computer systems and users from attackers? This section discusses several measures that safeguard computer systems, but it's important to remember that none of them can make a computer system 100 percent secure. A tradeoff exists between security and usability: the more secure the system, the less useful it becomes due to the restrictions imposed by the security tools. The only totally-secure computer system is the one that's been junked and hauled to the landfill.

Figure 9B.3

A UPS is a battery-powered device that provides power to your computer for a limited time during a power outage.

Protecting Computers from Power-Related Problems

Some of a computer's enemies aren't human, as you'll learn to your dismay—if you haven't already. Consider this: you've just spent three hours typing a college paper on your PC. You hear a thunderstorm in the background, but you keep working anyway. Suddenly, it's dark—the power's gone. And so is your work, unless you saved it.

Power surges and **power outages** present serious threats to any computer system. Often caused by lightning storms, power surges can destroy sensitive electronic components, and outages carry the threat of data loss. To safeguard against data loss caused by surges and outages, some application programs offer an **autosave** feature, which backs up your work at a specified interval (such as every ten minutes). Should you experience a power outage, you'll lose no more than ten minutes of work. You can also equip your system with an **uninterruptible power supply (UPS),** a battery-powered device that goes to work instantly when it detects an outage or critical voltage drop (see Figure 9B.3). Large-scale computer systems have their own electrical generators that step in when the power fails.

Controlling Access

As you've learned, many security problems originate with purloined passwords. Passwords can be easy to guess or steal. If even one password has been guessed or stolen, system administrators cannot be certain whether the user currently logging on is an authorized user or an intruder bent on destroying data.

Callback systems can ensure that the person attempting to gain access to a computer is calling from a recognized telephone on specific days of the week and during certain hours. In a callback system, the user calls the computer and enters his or her account number and password, after which the computer terminates the connection. The computer verifies the user ID and password, the day, and the time of day. The computer then calls the user back at the telephone to which that user is assigned.

Callback systems help to reduce insider crime, but they're useless for public access systems, which still rely mainly on password authentication. New approaches require users to not only *know* something (such as a password or PIN number), but to *have* something as well. You're probably familiar with this approach because it's used in automated teller machines (ATMs): you must have your ATM card and your PIN number, or you can't get your money.

In "know + have" authentication, users can be required to use **tokens,** which are handheld electronic devices that generate a logon code. They can also be asked to provide **digital certificates,** which resemble computer ID cards. Increasingly popular are **smartcards,** credit card-sized electronic devices with their own internal memories (see Figure 9B.4). In tandem with a supplied PIN number, a smartcard can reliably establish that the person trying to gain access has authorization to do so, unless the owner carelessly writes the PIN number on the card itself (As many as one-fourth of all ATM card holders do this, according to banking security experts).

The most secure authentication approach is called **biometric authentication,** which uses a variety of techniques, including voice recognition, retinal scans, thumbprints, and facial recognition. If this sounds like something so futuristic that it belongs only in *Star Trek*, you may be surprised to learn that such systems are already in widespread use (see Figure 9B.5). In a Florida hospital, for example, doctors must supply a thumbprint to gain access to a database containing confidential patient information.

Using Firewalls

As you've learned, the Internet provides a new way for intruders to gain access to computer systems. Perhaps the best defense against such attacks is to pull the plug on the Internet connection, but few organizations want to do this. Instead, they try to insulate internal computers by means of a **firewall.** A firewall is a computer program that generally runs on its own dedicated computer. A properly-configured firewall permits an organization's internal computer users to access the external Internet, while placing severe limits on the ability of outsiders to access internal data. Firewalls are a necessity, but

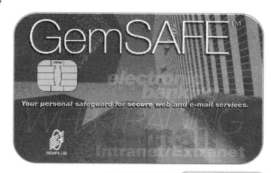

Figure   9B.4

Smartcards are credit card-sized devices with their own internal memories.

Figure   9B.5

Biometric authentication devices such as this retinal scanner are already in widespread use.

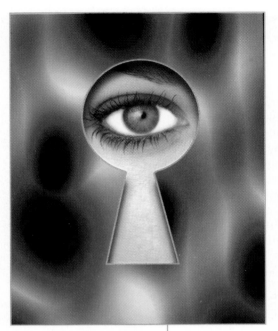

Information you want to keep away from unauthorized people must be either withheld from them or encrypted.

they have a major shortcoming. They provide no protection against insider pilferage.

Using Encryption

Because no foolproof means exist to protect all data from unauthorized access, it makes sense to make data unreadable to everyone except authorized eyes. This is precisely what **encryption** is for.

You can learn more about encryption (and the issues it raises) in Module 9A, but here's a definition: encryption is the science of scrambling messages so that nobody but the intended recipient can read them. It's said that encryption dates back to Roman times, when Julius Caesar dispatched military messages by scrambling the alphabet according to a set pattern (called a **key**). In the field, Caesar's generals used the key to unscramble (decrypt) the messages Caesar sent.

Many programs are available that enable computer users to encrypt computer data. By using encryption, companies can store sensitive data in scrambled form, so that even if an intruder were to steal the data, it wouldn't make any sense.

Consumers can use encryption, too. Web browsers are designed to use encryption automatically when users contact secure shopping sites on the Internet. However, many Web users do not realize that the default, **40-bit encryption** used by Web browsers is inadequate. The strength of an encryption technique is measured by the number of bits used in the key to encode the secret messages. 40 bits isn't enough—**128-bit encryption** is needed for a good level of protection. Due to U.S. restrictions on the export of strong encryption technology, however, 128-bit encryption is available only by downloading and installing an upgrade module. If you're using a Web browser for online shopping, be sure to do so.

Using Antivirus Programs

Antivirus programs, often called **vaccines** or virus checkers, are available for all types of computers. Most antivirus programs use a pattern-matching technique: they examine program and data files, looking for the telltale "signatures" of virus code. This technique has two major drawbacks: antivirus programs cannot find new viruses that aren't in their virus databases, and they can't deal with new types of viruses that alter themselves to evade detection. To cope with these shortcomings, the better antivirus programs offer frequent virus database updates and include programs that monitor system functions to detect virus activities.

Adhering strictly to a few guidelines can reduce the spread of a virus. Whenever a floppy disk has been used on another system or contains files from another system, that disk should always be checked for viruses. Any files that are downloaded from the Internet or bulletin board systems should also be carefully screened for viruses. If you're using Microsoft Word or other popular productivity programs, disable macros or upgrade to the latest program version, which offers protection against macro viruses.

Backing Up Data

Even if you take every precaution mentioned here, it's still possible to suffer a data loss. To minimize the effect of data loss, computer personnel and users should back up programs and data regularly. Backups should be stored

MOVERS & SHAKERS

Parry Aftab's Cyberangels

Are there angels in cyberspace? A couple in Fanwood, New Jersey has a ready answer to this question, and it's an emphatic yes! After their computer-addicted 13-year-old daughter ran away from home after a fight, the couple began to suspect that she had fled to the residence of an adult man who had been romancing the child online—so they contacted Cyberangels (**http://www.cyberangels.org**), a voluntary organization of some 1,650 Internet users worldwide. The group's purpose: to protect children in cyberspace.

Cyberangels has experienced a renaissance under the leadership of Parry Aftab, author of *The Parent's Guide to Protecting Your Children in Cyberspace* (McGraw-Hill). Aftab has worked with the UN's Internet safety effort and is an attorney specializing in technology and Internet law. Aftab took over Cyberangels "temporarily" after the group's founder quit. "Temporarily" became "permanent" after Aftab realized the scope of the problem. Under Aftab's leadership, Cyberangels has won respect from law enforcement agencies, Internet users, and the Internet industry for the group's many positive accomplishments.

Cyberangels' volunteers scour the Internet for online predators, cyberstalkers, and child pornographers, and they've been responsible for a number of arrests. One group of volunteers, called Cybermoms and Dads, monitors chat rooms, a favorite Internet hangout of adults who are hoping to entice kids into sexual liaisons. The group's elite unit, called Net Patrol, is a small group of highly-trained investigators who search for missing children, identify online sexual predators, locate and expose child pornography sites, and assist local police departments in prosecuting sexual predators. Each volunteer snares as many as four cyberstalkers a week.

Cyberangels receives nothing short of adulation from the thousands of families the organization has assisted, but it's often viewed with suspicion, Aftab concedes. Some people lump Cyberangels together with right-wing, moralistic groups that are intent on imposing censorship on the Internet, but that's not the case. Cyberangels' mission statement clearly affirms the group's belief that the Internet should be self-regulating and that further censorship isn't needed. What is needed, Aftab says, is more parents who are willing to supervise their children's online activities.

And what about the New Jersey couple? Their daughter's home, thanks to Cyberangels. The group successfully used its network of contacts to identify the child's online paramour.

---

away from the computer system so that, in the event of a fire or flood, they don't suffer the system's fate.

Full backups of everything stored on the computer should be made at least once each month. **Incremental backups,** which back up only those changes since the last incremental backup, should be made regularly, too—in a business environment, once or more per day.

Large organizations should also establish a written **disaster recovery plan.** The plan should have complete detailed instructions and include an alternate computing facility that can be used for emergency processing until a nonoperational computer can be repaired or replaced.

Avoiding Scams

To avoid getting scammed by Internet fraud, follow these tips:

- Do business with established companies that you know and trust.

- Read the fine print. If you're ordering something, make sure it's in stock and that the company promises to deliver within 30 days.

- Don't provide financial or other personal information or passwords to anyone, even if the request sounds legitimate.

- Be skeptical when somebody tells you about a great new company or great stock in an Internet chat room.

Preventing Cyberstalkers

While you're online, you can protect yourself against cyberstalkers. Follow these tips:

- Don't share any personal information such as your real name, in chat rooms. Use a name that is gender- and age-neutral. Do not post a user profile.

- Be extremely cautious about meeting anyone you've contacted online. If you do, meet in a public place and bring friends along.

- If a situation you've encountered online makes you afraid, contact the police immediately. Save all the communications you've received.

TAKEAWAY POINTS

- Most unauthorized computer access goes undetected and the perpetrators are never brought to justice.
- Financial losses due to computer attacks and intrusions are increasing rapidly.
- The Internet enables intruders to attack computer systems from almost anywhere in the world.
- Intruders have little difficulty obtaining passwords to computer systems, thanks to poor user practices in choosing passwords.
- Computer viruses are no longer limited to program files. They can infect the automated command sequences (called macros) within user documents, enabling them to spread rapidly.
- Although the press sensationalizes hacker and cracker attacks, most computer crime is accomplished by disgruntled employees.

- As crucial energy, transport, and financial infrastructures become increasingly dependent on networked information systems, the risk of electronic warfare rises.
- Even if crackers intend no harm, targeted companies can suffer huge losses due to downtime and consumption of staff time.
- Physical theft of computers and microprocessors is increasing rapidly, in part because it's difficult to trace stolen systems.
- Computer systems need tighter authentication using methods such as callback systems, smartcards, or biometric authentication.
- To protect your own data, you should back up your data regularly, disable macro features of productivity programs, and run an antivirus program regularly.

MODULE REVIEW

KEY TERMS AND CONCEPTS

antivirus program	encryption	salami shaving
authentication	file infectors	SATAN
autosave	firewall	shill
biometric authentication	full backups	shoulder surfing
boot sector virus	hacker ethic	smartcards
callback systems	hackers	social engineering
computer addiction	incremental backups	structural sabotage
computer virus	information terrorism	superuser status
computer virus authors	information warfare	time bombs
corporate espionage	key	tokens
crackers	logic bomb	trap doors
cyber gangs	macros	Trojan horse
cyberstalking	macro viruses	unauthorized access
data diddling	network warfare	undocumented features
denial-of-service attack	packet sniffers	uninterruptible power supply
digital certificates	password guessing	(UPS)
disaster recovery plan	power outages	vaccines
disgruntled employees	power surges	worm
dumpster diving	pumping and dumping	40-bit encryption
electronic warfare	rip and tear	128-bit encryption

TRUE/FALSE

Indicate whether the following statements are true or false.

1. The most-publicized computer security problems come from unauthorized access.

2. Most computer crime is an outside job.

3. In data diddling, a programmer alters a program so that it subtracts a small amount of money from each account.

4. Viruses are most typically spread when somebody inserts a floppy disk containing an infected program into a computer and starts the infected program.

5. Hackers are obsessed with gaining entry to highly-secure computer systems.

6. Physical theft of computer equipment is a growing problem.

7. Together with a supplied PIN number, a smartcard can reliably establish that a person trying to gain access to a computer system or a building has authorization to do so.

8. A callback system is one in which the computer calls the user back at the user's assigned telephone.

9. A firewall is designed to protect computer data from the heat generated during a fire and from the damage that can occur by smoke or firefighting measures.

10. A complete copy of the data and the files stored on a disk is referred to as an incremental backup.

MATCHING

Match each key term from the left column to the most accurate definition in the right column.

_____ 1. packet sniffer
_____ 2. social engineering
_____ 3. SATAN
_____ 4. shill
_____ 5. Trojan horse
_____ 6. time bomb
_____ 7. crackers
_____ 8. firewall
_____ 9. tokens
_____ 10. macro virus

a. a virus that sits on a system until a certain event or set of circumstances causes the program to be active

b. a computer program that generally runs on its own dedicated computer

c. a virus that takes advantage of the automatic command execution capabilities

d. a form of deception designed to get people to divulge sensitive information

e. a program that examines all the traffic on a section of the network

f. a security loophole analysis program designed for use by system administrators

g. handheld electronic devices that generate a logon code

h. a virus that contains hidden instructions to perform a malicious task

i. hackers obsessed with gaining entry to highly-secure computer systems

j. a secret operative who bids on another seller's auction item in order to drive up the price

MULTIPLE CHOICE

Circle the letter of the correct choice for each of the following.

1. Which of the following is not a technique used to obtain passwords?
a. guessing
b. dumpster diving
c. social engineering
d. encryption

2. Which of the following describes a programmer who alters a program so that it subtracts a very small amount of money from each account?
a. data diddling
b. salami shaving
c. unauthorized access
d. packet sniffing

3. Most viruses are:
a. file infectors.
b. boot sector viruses.
c. worms.
d. time bombs.

4. Computer hobbyists who enjoy pushing computer systems to their limits are known as:
a. crackers.
b. Trojan horses.
c. hackers.
d. cyber gang members.

5. The costs of computer security breaches include:
a. downtime.
b. adverse publicity.

c. an increased number of power surges.

d. a and b.

6. To protect against data loss caused by power surges and outages, some application programs offer what feature?

a. uninterruptible power supply

b. surge protection

c. autosave

d. denial of service

7. How often should you make full backups of your computer data?

a. hourly

b. daily

c. monthly

d. quarterly

8. The most-secure authentication approach is:

a. encryption.

b. biometric.

c. digital certification.

d. firewalls.

9. A firewall is usually used to protect a local area network from which of the following?

a. smoke damage

b. unauthorized access through the Internet

c. electronic funds transfer

d. buggy programs

10. Which of the following is not a type of access control?

a. callback systems

b. passwords

c. UPS system

d. locking door

FILL-IN

In the blank provided, write the correct answer for each of the following.

1. Typically, computer systems use some type of _____ technique for protection against unauthorized access.

2. Multiuser operating systems provide system administrators with _____ status.

3. In _____, insiders modify data so that it's difficult to tell that they've stolen funds or equipment.

4. A(n) _____ installs itself at the beginning of a hard drive where code is stored that automatically executes every time you start the computer.

5. In a computer network, a(n) _____ takes control of affected computers and uses their resources to attack other network-connected systems.

6. _____ bring crackers together by means of the Internet and physical meetings.

7. _____ is the use of information technologies to corrupt or destroy an enemy's informational and industrial infrastructures.

8. _____ uses one of a variety of techniques, including voice recognition, retinal scans, and thumbprints.

9. _____ can ensure that a person attempting to gain access to a computer is calling from a recognized telephone.

10. _____ is the science of scrambling messages so that nobody but the intended recipient can read them.

SHORT ANSWER

On a separate sheet of paper, answer the following questions.

1. What are some of the tricks intruders can use to obtain passwords?

2. Describe the differences between time bombs, worms, and Trojan horses.

3. Explain how macro viruses work.

4. Name several ways in which you can physically protect your computer and the data it contains.

5. How can disgruntled employees pose a risk to computer security?

6. What are some of the costs associated with computer security breaches?

7. What is the purpose of an uninterruptible power supply? When should it be used?

8. What is meant by backing up data? Develop a backup schedule for a microcomputer used in a small business.

9. Why do you think a daily incremental backup would be preferable to a full backup?

10. What are some of the items that should be addressed in a company's disaster recovery plan?

ETHICS: DOING THE RIGHT THING

WHAT YOU WILL LEARN . . .

When you have finished reading this module, you will be able to:

1. List the ways that people can get into serious legal or employment trouble by misusing computers.

2. Explain when copying software is legal and when it is not.

3. Define a moral dilemma and explain why ethical principles are helpful in resolving it.

4. Explain why respect is the basic principle of responsible computer use on a college or a university campus.

5. State why professional associations develop codes of ethics.

6. List the four basic areas of ethical behavior in a computing-related profession.

Can you imagine an electronic love triangle making headlines? That's just what happened after an incident on the WELL, a computer network based in northern California. A male user had been involved in electronic romances with at least two female users. Neither woman was aware of the other, and none of these people had ever met. The romances consisted solely of ardent electronic-mail exchanges. But when the two women discovered that they had the same "lover," they posted his name and urged other female subscribers to delete his mail. The resulting tumultuous debate made the cover of *Newsweek*.

This incident may seem amusing—unless you happen to be one of the people involved! But it does point out one of the challenges of new technologies: they push existing ethical and moral ideas into unpredicted areas, where it's far from certain just which rules apply. The two-timing man didn't feel that he was doing anything wrong because the romance existed only in cyberspace. But the women (not to mention many male and female observers) disagreed. They pointed out that electronic-mail friendships and romances can reach surprising emotional depth. Who's right?

Incidents such as this one highlight the moral uncertainties of new technologies, but computers haven't consigned all previous laws and morality to the dumpster. When you're using a computer, it's still wrong—not to mention illegal—to copy other people's intellectual work without first asking permission, or to break into a secured computer system without authorization. Still, computers raise new issues in which right and wrong aren't so easy to discern. Computer use can cause **moral dilemmas,** in which people run into difficulty when they try to figure out how the existing rules apply to a new situation.

A new branch of philosophy called **computer ethics** deals with computing-related moral dilemmas and also defines ethical principles for computer professionals. This module examines computer ethics, but it starts with issues in which right and wrong are easier to discern.

AVOIDING COMPUTER-RELATED LEGAL PROBLEMS

Every day, newspapers carry stories about people losing their jobs (and even going to jail) due to acts committed on computers while they're at work. In many cases, the offenders didn't realize they were doing anything wrong because the computer somehow made it okay.

Plagiarism

Let's start with a problem that gets many college students into serious trouble. It predates computers, but computers—and especially the Internet—make the temptation even greater.

Imagine this scenario: it's 4 A.M., and you have a paper due in your 9 o'clock class. While searching for sources on the Internet, you find a Web site with a nice little essay on your topic. There's no copyright notice. It seems as though the author *wants* people to copy it!

What's wrong with downloading the text, reworking it a bit, and handing it in? Plenty. It's called **plagiarism,** the presentation of somebody else's work as if it were your own.

Plagiarism is a serious offense. At some colleges, the first offense can get you thrown out of school. Even if your actions are not discovered now, an enemy or jealous coworker could find out later, and the evidence could destroy your career. The more famous you get, the more you're at risk.

At some colleges, plagiarism can get you thrown out of school on the first offense.

Destinations

Several sites make hundreds of thousands of public domain and shareware programs available for downloading from the Internet, including shareware.com (**http://www.shareware.com**) and Filez (**http://www.freewarefilez.com**).

Does this mean you can't use this Internet source you found? No, you just have to follow the rules. In college writing, it's fine to make use of someone else's effort as long as you use your own words and give credit. If you use a phrase or a few sentences from the source, enclose it in quotation marks. Attach a bibliography and list your sources.

Plagiarism may cause legal problems, too. Plagiarizing copyrighted material is called **copyright infringement,** and if you're caught red-handed you can be sued, and may have to pay damages in addition to compensating your victim for any proven financial losses due to your theft of the material. If you're tempted to copy anything from the Web, bear in mind that the United States is a signatory to international copyright regulations, which specify that an author does *not* need to include an explicit copyright notice to be protected under the law. Simply put, don't copy anything from a Web page without first asking permission.

Software Piracy

Imagine you've just copied a computer program. After all, it seems that everyone's doing it. Did you do something wrong?

Not necessarily. Some programmers place their products in the **public domain,** which means people are free to copy the program, or even modify it, if they want. Don't assume that a program is in the public domain, however, unless you see a note (often in the form of a "read me" text file) that explicitly says this.

Some software is made available under the provisions of the Free Software Foundation's **General Public License (GPL).** This license specifies that anyone may freely copy, use, and modify the software, but no one can sell the software for profit. For example, most Linux software is available under the provisions of GPL. Recently, Netscape Communications, Inc., decided to distribute the company's popular Netscape Communicator software under GPL terms.

Unlike public domain software, **shareware** programs are **copyrighted.** (When a work is copyrighted, you cannot copy or modify it without asking permission.) You can, however, freely copy trial versions of shareware programs. Shareware authors make evaluation versions of their programs available on a try-before-you-buy basis. When the evaluation period expires, you must pay the **registration fee** or delete the software from your disk. If you continue using the software past this date without paying the fee, you violate the author's copyright.

Most commercial software is copyrighted. To use it, you must purchase the program, although what you're really purchasing is a **software license,** which outlines what you can and can't do. Generally, software publishers grant you the right to make **archival backups** of the program disks.

Organizations with many computers can buy software for all their computers at a reduced price per unit. This agreement, called a **site license,** is a contract with the software publisher. The contract allows multiple copies of software to be made for use in the organization. Taking copies outside the organization violates the contract.

Now that you understand the various ways in which software publishers make programs available, you can tell whether you're guilty of **software piracy.** All of the following actions are illegal:

- Incorporating all or part of a GPL-licensed program in a commercial program that you offer for sale.

- Continuing to use a shareware program past the evaluation program's expiration date, even though you didn't pay the registration fee.

- Violating the terms of a software license, even if you've paid for the program. For example, many licenses forbid you to install and use more than one copy of a program at a time, so you're guilty of an infringement if you have copies of the same program on your desktop and notebook computers.

■ Making copies of site-licensed programs for your personal use at home.

■ Giving or selling copies of commercial programs to others.

How serious is software piracy? It's common—especially on college campuses—but that doesn't make it right. What's more, software piracy is a felony (see Figure 9C.1). If you're convicted of a felony, you lose the right to vote and have probably ruined your chances for a successful career.

Do you have pirated programs on your computer? The police aren't likely to storm into your dorm room and haul you away, kicking and screaming. Most software piracy prosecutions target individuals who are trying to distribute or sell infringing copies or companies that have illegally made multiple copies for their employees. At Bates College, students were arrested after investigators discovered that they were distributing copies of Microsoft Office 2000 from a Web site based on the College's server. They were charged with aggravated invasion of computer privacy, a crime that carries a maximum sentence of five years in prison, a $5,000 fine, or both. Even though the risk of prosecution is small, you should delete these programs right away for one simple reason: it's illegal. (It's also unethical, as you'll learn in a subsequent section.)

If you still don't see the need to delete pirated software from your computer, consider this: it's very, very wise to become accustomed to a zero-tolerance approach to pirated software. If you're caught with an infringing program at work, you could lose your job. A company can't risk retaining employees who expose the firm to prosecution.

Figure 9C.1

The Software Publisher's Association (SPA) is trying to raise consciousness about software piracy.

Copyright Infringement

Increasing numbers of Internet users seem to believe that sharing illegally-made copies of copyrighted music is permissible because so many people are doing it. But it's not. At the University of Oregon, a student was charged with criminal copyright infringement—a Federal crime—after making thousands of MP3s available on his Web site. He faced potential penalties of up to three years in prison and $250,000 in fines. At Carnegie-Mellon University, 71 students were disciplined for posting illegally-duplicated music files on their sites.

Copyright violators are endlessly creative when it comes to developing rationalizations for their illegal behavior. You may hear that it's OK to download a copyrighted MP3 file as long as you keep it no longer than 24 hours, but that's false. If you upload music copied from a CD you've paid for, you're still violating the law. Spreading a band's copyrighted music around isn't justified by saying it's "free advertising." If the group wants advertising, they'll arrange for it themselves. And don't fall into the trap of thinking that sharing MP3s is legal as long as you don't charge any money from them. You're still taking royalties away from copyright holders, and it's still illegal.

You'll often hear people use the term **fair use** to justify illegal copying. The fair use doctrine does justify *limited* uses of copyrighted material without payment to, or permission from, the copyright holder, but it is sharply limited. The fair use doctrine holds that a *brief* selection from a copyrighted work may be excerpted for the purposes of commentary, parody, news reporting, research, and education. Such excerpts are short—generally, no

To learn what's legal—
and what's not—about
music copying, visit
**http://www.sound
byting.com.**

**Ethics is the branch of
philosophy concerned
with determining what's
right and wrong, espe-
cially in the context of
moral dilemmas.**

more than 5 percent of the original work—and they should not harm the commercial value of the work. In general, the reproduction of an entire work is almost never justifiable by means of the fair use doctrine.

INTRODUCING ETHICS

In *Star Trek II: The Wrath of Khan*, Spock saves the ship by entering a contaminated propulsion chamber and performing a needed repair, but in the process exposes himself to lethal radiation. As he dies, he tells Kirk, "The needs of the many outweigh the needs of the few—or the one." Here, Spock is voicing an **ethical principle,** a principle that helps people find their way through moral dilemmas. (Although supposedly from the planet Vulcan, Spock's philosophy is of terrestrial origin: it's called utilitarianism, and it was invented by an eighteenth-century British philosopher named Jeremy Bentham.) **Ethics** is the branch of philosophy concerned with determining what's right and wrong, especially in the context of moral dilemmas.

As this chapter's opening suggests, computers cause new moral dilemmas by pushing people into unprecedented situations. Computer ethics explores the ways that ethical principles can be used to think through the moral dilemmas caused by computer use.

Moral Dilemmas

It's easy to say that you don't need to worry about ethics—you'll just do the right thing. But that's the trouble with moral dilemmas: when you're in one, it's difficult to tell what's right and what's wrong, even if you're the most moral person around.

Moral dilemmas arise in two situations:

- **When it's not clear which, if any, moral rule applies**   In the Internet two-timing incident discussed at the beginning of this module, do real-life courtship rules really apply to an online chat group? Are these relationships real?

- **When two or more rules apply, and they conflict**   You've just discovered that your friend is making and selling CD-ROM discs containing pirated copies of your school's site-licensed software. You've told your friend that it's wrong and he should stop, but he persists. The copies could get your school in a lot of trouble. What's more important: your loyalty to your friend or your obligations to your school?

Moral dilemmas aren't fun. When you find yourself in the middle of one, it's a lonely feeling, and people often disagree about what you should do. Ethical principles come in handy because they help you think through your options.

Ethical Principles

Over the centuries, philosophers have come up with many ethical principles. To some, it's disconcerting to find that these principles sometimes conflict. In the end, though, an ethical principle is only a tool you can use to think through a difficult situation. You must make your own choice and live with the consequences.

The following lists three of the most-useful ethical principles:

- **An act is ethical if, were everyone to act the same way, society as a whole would benefit**   Here's a good argument against software piracy. If everyone stole software, programmers would have little incentive to develop innovative programs. When we refuse to tolerate software piracy, everyone wins.

- **An act is ethical if it treats people as an end in themselves, rather than as a means to an end**   If the cybernetic two-timer had spent more time thinking about the fact that people with feelings were on the other end of the chat line, he might not have been so eager to play his little game. In this view, the fact that the relationships took place by means of the computer becomes irrelevant. He was using the relationships as a means to an end (his own ego gratification, perhaps). From this perspective, what he did is unethical.

- **An act is ethical if impartial observers would judge that it is fair to all parties concerned**   A few years ago, software publishers were so concerned about software piracy that they implemented **copyright protection schemes** in their programs. Although these schemes prevented unauthorized duplication of the programs, they slowed down users' computers and left them without any convenient recourse if the software was lost due to a hard disk crash. Is it fair to punish legitimate users to prevent others from engaging in criminal activity?

When you find yourself in the middle of a moral dilemma, it's difficult to tell what's right and what's wrong, even if you're the most moral person around.

Thinking Through Moral Dilemmas

If you find yourself in a moral dilemma related to computer use, be sure to get help. Talk to people you trust. Make sure you have all the facts. Think through alternative courses of action, based on differing principles. Find a solution that you can be proud of. If you're not sure what that means, here's a handy, practical guide:

- You'd be proud to tell your mom or dad.

- If you were in the other person's shoes, you'd have to admit that your action was fair.

- If you did it at work, your company's customers would agree that you did the right thing and they'd be even more eager to buy your company's products.

- You wouldn't mind reading about your action on the front page of your hometown newspaper.

COMPUTER ETHICS FOR COMPUTER USERS

How do these ethics concepts apply to you, the college computer user? It all boils down to one word: respect. Use campus computers in a way that shows respect for yourself, for others, and for academic integrity. The following identifies some respectful methods:

- **Respecting yourself**   If you obtain an account and password to use the campus computer system, do not give your password to others. They could do something that gets you in trouble! In addition, don't say or do anything on the Internet that could reflect poorly on you, even if you think no one will ever find out.

- **Respecting others**   Don't use a computer to threaten or harass anyone. Avoid using more than your share of computing resources, such as disk space. If you publish a Web page, remember that you're doing so on your college's computers, and your page's contents affect the college's public image.

DoS attack

One of the newest ways hackers are wreaking havoc is through "denial of service" (DoS) attacks on networks. A DoS attack is designed to cripple a network by flooding it with useless traffic. This keeps legitimate users of the network from using its resources, and can be costly in terms of downtime and lost productivity.

■ **Respecting academic integrity**   Always give credit for text you've copied from the Internet. Ask permission before you copy pictures. Don't copy or distribute software unless the license specifically says you can.

Your college probably has its own code of conduct for computer users. Read it carefully and follow the rules.

Ten Commandments for Computer Ethics

The Computer Ethics Institute of the Brookings Institution, located in Washington, D.C., has developed the following "Ten Commandments" for computer users, programmers, and system designers:

1. Thou shalt not use a computer to harm other people.
2. Thou shalt not interfere with other people's computer work.
3. Thou shalt not snoop around in other people's files.
4. Thou shalt not use a computer to steal.
5. Thou shalt not use a computer to bear false witness.
6. Thou shalt not copy or use proprietary software for which you have not paid.
7. Thou shalt not use other people's computer resources without authorization or proper compensation.
8. Thou shalt not appropriate other people's intellectual output.
9. Thou shalt think about the social consequences of the program you write or the system you design.
10. Thou shalt use a computer in ways that show consideration and respect for your fellow humans.

Netiquette

General principles such as the "Ten Commandments for Computer Ethics" are useful for overall guidance, but they don't provide specific help for the special situations you'll run into online—such as an unwanted sexual advance in a MUD (multi-user Dungeons and Dragons game). As a result, computer and Internet users have developed a lengthy series of specific behavior guidelines for the various Internet services available, such as email, mailing lists, Usenet, Internet Relay Chat (IRC), MUDs, and MOOs. Called **netiquette,** these guidelines provide specific pointers on how to show respect for others—and for yourself—while you're online.

Here's a sample, based on Arlene Rinaldi's "Netiquette Home Page" (**http://www.fau.edu/netiquette/net/netiquette.html**) and other Internet sources:

■ **Mailing lists**   After you join a mailing list, read the discussion for a few days to see what kinds of questions are welcomed and how to meaningfully participate. If the list has a FAQ ("Frequently Asked Questions") document posted on the Web, be sure to read it before posting a question to the list, as it may already have been answered in the FAQ. Bear in mind that some people using the list may not speak English as their native tongue, so don't belittle people for spelling lists. Don't post inflammatory messages, and never post in anger. If you agree with something, don't post a message that says "Me too"—you're just wasting everyone's time. If you need to unsubscribe from the list, don't post messages requesting that somebody do this for you; find out how to send the correct command to the list server.

■ **Email**   Check your email daily and promptly respond to the messages you've been sent. Download or delete messages once you've read them so that you don't exceed your disk usage quota. Remember that email isn't private. You should never send a message that contains anything you wouldn't want others to read. Always speak of others professionally and courteously. Since email is easily forwarded, the person you're describing may eventually see the message. Check your computer frequently for viruses that can propagate by means of email messages. Keep your messages short and to the point—focus on one subject per message. Don't type in all capital letters, since this comes across as SHOUTING. Watch out for sarcasm and humor in email; often, it fails to come across as a joke. Don't request a return receipt, as some people consider this to be an invasion of privacy.

- **Internet Relay Chat (IRC)**   Learn what commonly-used IRC abbreviations such as BRB ("Be Right Back") mean so that you don't pester others to explain them. In a new channel, listen to the discussion for a while so you can figure out how to join in meaningfully. Don't flood the channel with text so that others can't communicate, and lay off the colors, beeps, and scripts that interfere with the flow of dialogue. Don't harass other users with unwanted invitations. If somebody tells you to type in a command, don't do it—it may be a trick. Learn how to use the ignore command if someone is bothering you.

COMPUTER ETHICS FOR COMPUTER PROFESSIONALS

Suppose you hire an engineer to build a bridge. Within months, it falls down, injuring several people. It turns out that your so-called engineer never took any courses in bridge construction. As you investigate further, you learn that the engineer received a 15 percent kickback from a heartily-recommended contractor who sold you substandard materials. You probably would not have very much confidence in the next engineer you hire! As this example suggests, no profession can stay in business for long without a rigorous (and enforced) code of professional ethics. That's why professional engineers subscribe to ethical **codes of conduct.** Many such codes exist: they're developed by professional associations, such as the Association for Computing Machinery (ACM). These codes would expressly forbid the actions undertaken by this engineer. Figure 9C.2 is an excerpt from the Code of Ethics of the Institute for Certification of Computing Professionals.

Safety First

The field of computer ethics tries to specify ethical codes for computing professionals. Most of these codes closely resemble engineering ethical codes, and for good reason: like engineers, computer professionals create products that affect many people and may expose them to the risk of personal injury or even death. Increasingly, computer systems and computer programs figure prominently in safety-critical systems, including transportation monitoring systems (such as air traffic control) and critical patient monitoring.

Codes of Conduct and Good Practice for Certified Computing Professionals

The essential elements relating to conduct that identify a professional activity are:
- A high standard of skill and knowledge
- A confidential relationship with people served
- Public reliance upon the standards of conduct in established practice
- The observance of an ethical code

Therefore, these Codes have been formulated to strengthen the professional status of certified computing professionals.

Figure   9C.2

Excerpt from the Code of Ethics of the Institute for Certification of Computing Professionals.

At the core of every engineering or computer code of ethics is a professional person's highest and most indispensible aim: to preserve and protect human life and to avoid harm or injury. If we, the public, are to trust professional people, we must be able to believe that they have the inner virtue needed to protect our safety and welfare, even if doing so means that the professional person suffers financially.

Additional Ethical Responsibilities

Safety is important to everyone, but the public has a right to expect additional ethical responsibilities in a professional person. Professionals in any branch of computing should also have the following qualities:

- **Competence**   Professionals keep up with the latest knowledge in their fields by reading professional journals, attending conferences, and taking refresher courses as needed. In addition, professionals perform services only in their areas of competence. They make sure all their work meets the highest possible standards of quality.

- **Responsibility**   Professionals are loyal to their clients or employers. They do not disclose confidential information concerning a project, even if they leave a client or firm's employment. Professionals are also honest: if a project seems likely to fail, they say so. They turn down work if accepting it would place them in a conflict of interest.

- **Integrity**   Professionals express opinions only when they are based on fact. They are impartial in their judgment and do not change their judgment in response to external pressure.

The ACM Code of Conduct

Of all the computing associations' codes of conduct, the one developed by the Association for Computing Machinery (ACM) is considered the most innovative and far-reaching. According to the ACM code, a computing professional:

- Contributes to society and human well-being.

- Avoids harm to others.

- Is honest and trustworthy.

- Is fair and takes action not to discriminate on the basis of race, sex, religion, age, disability, or national origin.

- Honors property rights, including copyrights and patents.

- Gives proper credit when using the intellectual property of others.

- Respects the right of other individuals to privacy.

- Honors confidentiality.

Like previous engineering codes of conduct, the ACM code places public safety and well-being at the top of the list. Unlike previous codes, it adds a new and important dimension of professionalism: active intervention to prevent sexual, racial, and other forms of discrimination.

Programmer Liability

Even the most ethical programmer can produce a program with errors. Most complex programs have so many possible combinations of conditions that to test for every combination is not feasible. In some cases, the tests would take years. In other cases, no one could think of a test for all the possibilities. All experienced programmers know that any programs of any size can have bugs. If the program results in injury or death, who's at fault?

Destinations

Dozens of associations govern professionals within computing fields. For links to their codes of ethics, see the Illinois Institute of Technology's Codes of Ethics Online: Computing and Information Systems page (**http://csep.iit.edu/ codes/computer.html**).

SPOTLIGHT

NOT WHAT THE DOCTOR ORDERED

The 33-year-old oil worker was undergoing radiation treatment following the surgical removal of a cancerous tumor on his shoulder. The technician told him that the treatment was safe and he wouldn't feel a thing. After adjusting the computerized radiation device, called a Therac-25, the technician stepped behind a screen and began the treatment. Moments later, the patient screamed in agony. He demanded to know whether he had received a radiation overdose. The technician assured him he had not because, according to the Therac-25's display, the patient had not received even the prescribed dose. However, the patient grew increasingly ill in the days following the exposure. He vomited blood and needed morphine to blunt the wracking pain. Soon, he fell into a coma and died. In the following months, five more patients were to die or suffer severe, irreversible injuries after treatment with the Therac-25.

What went wrong with the Therac-25? Just about everything, it seems. Unable to reproduce the problem, the manufacturer at first attempted to blame the hardware, and implemented "fixes" that didn't address the underlying problems: overconfidence in software and poor software design. The Therac-25's designers placed too much confidence in the computer software. For this reason, they removed hardware interlocking safety systems that had been standard on previous models. The software itself was very-poorly designed, and several bugs existed that could result in a patient overdose. However, the machine's poor user interface and lack of overdose detection left operators in the dark.

Who's liable for the death and suffering caused by the Therac-25? It's not so easy to decide as you might think. Should the physician have understood the machine's risks and explained these to the patient before prescribing the treatment? Is the technician at fault? Are the programmers to blame—or the managers who failed to devote sufficient funds for thorough product safety testing? Because litigation over the Therac-25 incident was settled out of court, these questions were never answered in a court of law.

In the United States, it's still far from clear who's responsible for deaths or injuries attributable to poorly-designed computer software or systems. A patchwork of conflicting state laws and court decisions leaves this question unclear. In an attempt to clarify the law, the National Conference of Commissioners on Uniform State Laws (NCCUSL), which is responsible for drafting changes to the U.S. Uniform Commercial Code (UCC), proposed changes to U.S. state laws concerning the liability of software publishers. The proposed revision to the commercial code, called UCITA (short for Uniform Computer Information Transactions Act), was approved by the NCCUSL and put forward for adoption by the fifty U.S. states.

How does UCITA resolve the liability issue? Usually, by absolving the software industry for any liability beyond the cost of replacing defective software. According to its critics, UCITA is a giveaway for the software industry, whose lobbyists strongly shaped its development. (The chair of the UCITA committee is a senior attorney for Microsoft Corporation.) And they're not alone. Also opposed to UCITA are 24 U.S. state Attorneys General, senior staff on the U.S. Federal Trade Commission, and a host of legal scholars. UCITA's defenders claim that it's impossible to market software when consumers mount so many frivolous liability lawsuits.

At this writing, the proposed legislation is under consideration at the state level, and has already been adopted by two states (Virginia and Maryland).

Consider the following situation. An airplane flying in poor visibility uses a computer to guide the plane, which is a common occurrence. The air traffic control system is also computer-based. The plane crashes. The investigation discloses minor bugs in both computer programs. If the plane's computer had been dealing with a person in the tower rather than a computer, or if the air traffic control program had been interacting with a human pilot, the crash would not have occurred. Where does the liability lie for the loss of life and property?

Because bugs are inevitable and programmers cannot predict all the different ways programs interact with their environment, most computer experts believe that it's wrong to single out programmers for blame. Software companies are at fault, too, if they fail to test and document their products. And the organization that buys the software may share part of the blame, too, if they fail to train their personnel to use the system and understand its possible shortcomings.

Recognizing these facts, a new field called **software engineering** attempts to apply the principles of mainstream engineering to software production. Among other things, these principles call for an external, impartial review of a project at various stages before completion. Computer scientists are also working on **fault-tolerant systems,** which can keep working even if they encounter a glitch.

Computer Ethics in Business

A business or organization must protect its data from loss and damage, from misuse and error, and from unauthorized access. Otherwise, the organization is not serving its clients effectively.

To protect data from loss, an organization must have proper backup procedures. Backup procedures involve making copies of data files for protection against data loss.

Protecting data from misuse or error is difficult for any organization. Misuse can arise, for example, from not using the appropriate software or not using the software properly.

Data that has not been properly maintained can have serious effects on the individual or organization it relates to. Errors in data can and do occur. It is the ethical responsibility of the organization dealing with the data to ensure that its data is as correct as possible.

Another type of data misuse occurs when an employee or company fails to keep data confidential. A breach of confidentiality occurs when an employee looks up data about a person in the database and uses that information outside the specific job. For example, according to a recent press report, some IRS employees routinely looked up the tax returns of neighbors and celebrities. Thanks to a public outcry, such actions are now grounds for termination.

Companies may punish employees for looking up customer data, but many of them think nothing of selling it to third parties. A mail-order company, for example, can gain needed revenue by selling customer lists to firms trying to market related products. Privacy advocates believe that it's unethical to divulge customer data without first asking the customer's permission.

Whistle-Blowing

What happens when a company's profit-seeking goals conflict with a computer professional's code of conduct? For example, the ACM Code of Ethics tells computing professionals to respect people's privacy. What if you're hired to write software that gathers information about customers without their knowledge?

People who have lived through situations like this agree that none of the options available are attractive. You can quit and look for another job, or you can refuse to perform the requested task, although you will probably be fired. If the requested task poses a danger to the public or appears to be illegal, you can report the company's intentions to regulatory agencies or the press, an action called **whistle-blowing.** Although there are some laws protecting whistle-blowers, most wind up unemployed—and permanently blacklisted. And if your whistle-blowing actions cause the government to shut down your company, harming not only you but all your coworkers as well, there's a great social risk involved. Often, there's no clear-cut solution.

As this discussion illustrates, codes of ethics don't solve every ethical problem. They provide the needed guidance, but they can't save everyone from moral dilemmas.

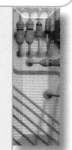

IMPACTS

Copyright vs. Free Speech: Where's the Balance?

Which matters more, protecting the rights of copyright holders or protecting free speech rights? Soon, the courts will have to choose, because the two are headed for direct conflict.

Changes in U.S. copyright law are responsible for the coming confrontation between copyright and free speech. At the behest of lobbyists working for Hollywood and the music industry, the U.S. Congress passed the Digital Millennium Copyright Act (DMCA) in 1998. Thanks to the DMCA, it's now a Federal crime to circumvent any copyright-protection scheme that is used to protect digitized works from unauthorized duplication. In addition, any copyright holder who believes that a Web site contains an infringing work can bring the site down without going to a judge. The copyright holder need only send a certified letter to the Internet service provider (ISP) that houses the site. If the ISP refuses to remove the allegedly-infringing material, the ISP automatically becomes a co-defendant in the event of a lawsuit. Prior to the DMCA, copyright holders had to go to a judge and obtain an injunction before they could shut down a Web site containing infringing material—and that's an expensive process. Thanks to the DMCA, it's easier for copyright holders to get infringing material off the Internet. What's more, the DMCA pits Web publishers against their Internet service providers. After all, how many ISPs would refuse to remove an allegedly-infringing Web page that is housed on their computers, and in the process implicate themselves in a lawsuit?

The DMCA's defenders say that strong measures are needed to stop the rampant duplication of copyrighted works on the Internet. On the other hand, free speech advocates warned Congress that the DMCA would be used to stifle legitimate expression under the fair use provisions of copyright law. Under these guidelines, it's sometimes permissible to reproduce brief portions of a work without asking for permission or paying royalties.

To qualify as fair use, the copying must be done for the purposes of commentary, parody, education, or scholarly analysis. In addition, copying the work shouldn't interfere with the work's commercial value. Normally, one may copy only a small portion of a copyrighted work for such purposes (5 percent or less). However, under **very** rare circumstances, it's defensible to reproduce a copyrighted work in its entirety, but such copying can be justified only when the reproduction of the entire work is clearly in the public's interest. In the late-1960s, anti-war activist Daniel Ellsberg published the **Pentagon Papers,** a secret U.S. Defense Department report that portrayed the Vietnam War as unwinnable. Nixon administration officials contemplated an attempt to suppress the **Papers'** publication on the grounds of copyright violation, but Justice Department attorneys advised the administration that the courts wouldn't agree. In a democracy, the public's right to know sometimes outweighs a copyright holder's interests.

Since the DMCA's passage, copyright holders have successfully used the DMCA's provisions to suppress Web sites containing allegedly-infringing material—and in several cases, the motivation seems to include a desire to keep the material away from the public's eye. For example, Big Three automaker Ford threatened to use the DMCA to shut down a Mustang enthusiasts' Web site, called FordUnleashed, after the site published a leaked internal document admitting quality problems with Ford's 1999 CobraSVT.

There's nothing new about copyright holders threatening alleged infringers with lawsuits, but the DMCA makes it easy, since you don't have to go to a judge to get the infringing site shut down. According to free speech advocates, that's too easy—and the result could be a "chilling effect" on the freedom of U.S. citizens to criticize corporations, religious groups, and their own government.

In the late-1960s, anti-war activist Daniel Ellsberg published the **Pentagon Papers,** a secret U.S. Defense Department report that portrayed the Vietnam War as unwinnable.

TAKEAWAY POINTS

- A new branch of philosophy called computer ethics deals with computing-related moral dilemmas and also defines ethical principles for computer professionals.

- Plagiarism, the presentation of somebody else's work as if it were your own, is a serious offense that can get you thrown out of some colleges. Don't copy anything from a Web page without first asking permission.

- Some programmers place their products in the public domain, which means anyone is free to copy or modify the program. Shareware programs are copyrighted. Software piracy is the unauthorized duplication of copyrighted software. It's a felony.

- Internet service providers are not liable for content transmitted by means of their systems. Consequently, they make no attempt to censor it.

- Moral dilemmas arise when (1) it's not clear which, if any, moral rule applies, and (2) two or more rules apply, but they conflict.

- The field of computer ethics tries to specify ethical codes for computing professionals. Of all the computing association's codes of conduct, the one developed by the Association for Computing Machinery (ACM) is considered to be the most innovative and far-reaching.

MODULE REVIEW

KEY TERMS AND CONCEPTS

archival backups
codes of conduct
computer ethics
copyright
copyright infringement
copyright protection schemes
ethical principle
ethics

fair use
fault-tolerant systems
General Public License (GPL)
moral dilemmas
netiquette
plagiarism
public domain

registration fee
shareware
site license
software engineering
software license
software piracy
whistle-blowing

TRUE/FALSE

Indicate whether the following statements are true or false.

1. Computer ethics is a new branch of philosophy that deals with computing-related moral dilemmas.

2. You do not need permission to copy something off the Web.

3. Software in the public domain can be freely copied without violating any laws.

4. Shareware is a software distribution scheme that allows you to make copies of the software and try it before you buy.

5. Software piracy refers to the unauthorized distribution of software.

6. Although it's a serious problem, software piracy is only a misdemeanor.

7. Computers are causing new moral dilemmas by pushing people into unprecedented scenarios.

8. The products created by computer professionals affect many people and potentially expose them to personal injury and, in some cases, death.

9. Of all the computing associations' codes of conduct, the one developed by the Data Processing Management Association (DPMA) is considered the most innovative.

10. If a requested task poses a danger to the public or appears to be illegal, you can report the company's intentions to regulatory agencies or the press.

MATCHING

Match each key term from the left column to the most accurate definition in the right column.

_____   1. computer ethics

_____   2. copyright infringement

_____   3. shareware

_____   4. copyrighted

_____   5. software license

_____   6. site license

_____   7. ethics

_____   8. software engineering

_____   9. fault-tolerant systems

_____ 10. whistle-blowing

a. a branch of philosophy concerned with determining what's right and wrong

b. copyrighted programs you can evaluate on a try-before-you-buy basis

c. accompanies software and describes what you can and cannot do to it

d. the act of reporting a company's actions to a regulatory agency or the press

e. deals with computing-related moral dilemmas

f. plagiarizing copyrighted material

g. computer systems that continue to work even when they encounter glitches

h. a contract with a software publisher that allows multiple copies of software for an organization

i. characterizes something you can't copy or modify without permission

j. attempts to apply the principles of mainstream engineering to software production

MULTIPLE CHOICE

Circle the letter of the correct choice for each of the following.

1. Which new branch of philosophy deals with computing-related moral dilemmas?
   a. computer standards
   b. computer ethics
   c. technology principles
   d. none of the above

2. Which of the following is unethical computer use?
   a. avoiding harming others
   b. honoring confidentiality
   c. speaking the truth
   d. borrowing software so you can make a copy

3. Which of the following is software that you can copy and modify legally?
   a. public domain software
   b. shareware
   c. a and b
   d. It is illegal to copy and modify any type of software.

4. What kind of crime is software piracy?
   a. a misdemeanor
   b. a felony
   c. a capital crime
   d. legal

5. In what circumstance is it usually justifiable to make a copy of software?
   a. when you want to make additional copies to sell
   b. when you want to distribute the software to your friends
   c. when you need an archival back-up of the program disks
   d. never

6. Which of the following is characteristic of an ethical act?
   a. when everyone acts the same way and society as a whole would benefit
   b. when it treats people as an end in themselves rather than a means to an end
   c. when impartial observers would judge that it is fair to all parties concerned
   d. all of the above

7. In the field of computer ethics, computing professionals abide by which of the following?
   a. principles
   b. regulations
   c. codes
   d. standards

8. Which of the following is untrue regarding safety?
   a. Computer programs do not figure prominently in safety-critical systems, but computer systems do.
   b. Both computer systems and computer programs are important to consider in safety-critical systems.
   c. Computer professionals create products that affect many people and may expose them to the risk of personal injury or even death.
   d. none of the above

9. Which of the following terms describes when an employee reports a company's intentions to the press or a regulatory agency?
   a. a code of conduct
   b. hacking
   c. a moral dilemma
   d. Whistle-blowing

10. To protect data from loss, an organization must have which of the following?
   a. academic integrity
   b. computer ethics
   c. proper backup procedures
   d. codes of conduct

FILL-IN

In the blank provided, write the correct answer for each of the following.

1. The new branch of philosophy that deals with computing-related moral dilemmas is _____ .

2. _____ is presenting someone else's work as if it were your own.

3. Some programmers place their products in the _____, which means anyone is free to copy or modify their programs.

4. _____ is copyrighted software that you can try for free, but you must pay a registration fee if you are going to keep it.

5. Making illegal copies of copyrighted software is called _____.

6. A contract to buy software to make several copies to use in an organization, at a reduced per-copy price, is called a(n) _____.

7. A(n) _____ specifies that anyone may freely copy, use, and modify software, but no one can sell the software for a profit.

8. _____ is the branch of philosophy concerned with determining what's right and wrong, especially in the context of moral dilemmas.

9. Professional engineers subscribe to ethical codes of _____.

10. _____ attempts to apply the principles of mainstream engineering to software production.

SHORT ANSWER

On a separate sheet of paper, answer the following questions.

1. Under what circumstances can software be legally copied?

2. Why is software piracy considered a crime?

3. What is a site license? How does a site license affect the copying of software?

4. If you're writing a college paper and want to reference someone else's work, what do you need to do?

5. Identify three qualities computing professionals should exhibit.

6. List the eight general moral imperatives the ACM developed for computer professionals and users to follow.

7. What is programmer liability? How could the issue of programmer liability arise?

8. What are the goals of software engineering?

9. Why is it important for a company to practice proper backup procedures?

10. What is whistle-blowing and in what circumstances would you find yourself in such a position?

PFSweb, Inc.

Think about the last time you purchased something from the Web. Maybe it was a CD, a book, or clothing. Maybe something even bigger. When the Web site asked for your credit card payment information, did you hesitate or jump right in? Not too long ago, making the leap from "browser" to "buyer" on a Web site was a big one for many people. There was fear that the personal data and financial information entered and transformed into bits to travel along communications channels would be intercepted and somehow used fraudulently. After all, we've heard the horror stories about how someone's credit card number ended up in the wrong hands, and now that person's credit history is ruined. Or how personal information was sold without consent, and now

```
1: 94087
10:01:52  File:C:\ICVERIFY\data0000\BATCHIN.D
10:01:52  PGMS$TnIS 10945ICVERIFY VERSION: 6.
10:01:52  Save:BT|C6| 0 0 0 10 10
10:01:52  PROCESSING 0: PRE AUTH 2: 000000003
1: 94087
10:01:52  C6|6011000660105564|DS|T 2-1 16 0|N
10:01:52  PGMS$A TAIS 10948ICVERIFY VERSION:
10:01:52  File:C:\ICVERIFY\data0006\ICVERIFC.
10:01:52  File:C:\ICVERIFY\data0006\ICVERIFC.
10:01:52  File:C:\ICVERIFY\data0006\ICVERIFC.
10:01:52  ps2000:|        |-1 2
10:01:52  PGMS$C ACTAIS 11002ICVERIFY VERSIO
10:01:53  SEND MESSAGE:(STX)V.335110011000992
FS)1001(FS)00006671(FS)A
```

junk mail for all kinds of bizarre merchandise fills the mailbox. These concerns are not without merit for today's Web-based organizations.

Fortunately, companies wanting to do business online are addressing these concerns. Encryption techniques, codes of conduct, and specialized software all are employed in an effort to win consumer confidence and increase sales. PFSweb uses special software to detect the possibility of fraudulent orders via its clients' Web sites. The software is called CyberSource, and can not only perform credit card authorizations, but can also examine the buying trend for a particular credit card number. So, if a very large order for electronics equipment comes in, the credit card number is checked to see if any other large purchases were made recently with that card. The software can also prevent delivery of expensive items to neighborhoods known to have problems with theft and fraud.

What do you think? What concerns do you have about purchasing over the Internet? How has PFSweb addressed those concerns? Can you think of other ways e-commerce companies can reduce buyers' concerns, or make transactions even more secure?

WebLink Go to **www.prenhall.com/ pfaffenberger** to see video from PFSweb about their handling of privacy, security and fraud.

E-COMMERCE IN ACTION

10

CHAPTER

Computers and You

With this chapter, you're reaching the end of your journey towards computer fluency, and you've learned a great deal. Now it's time to make this knowledge work for you. This chapter is designed to help you empower yourself to take full advantage of the information technology boom, whether you do so by purchasing your own system, safeguarding your health in the Cyber Age, planning a career in the IT industry, or figuring out where this technology's headed.

For openers, Module 10A provides useful guidance for an important purchase you're likely to make: your own computer. Assuming you're familiar with the essential terminology introduced in Chapter 2, Module 10A cuts right to the chase and tells you what to look for—and what to avoid.

Module 10B examines the health concerns you should have after you've purchased your system, including threats to your vision and dexterity. If you take to computing in a big way, you might consider a career in information technology, the subject of Module 10C. As you'll see, there's plenty of opportunity—but it's not the right career for everyone. Module 10D pulls out the crystal ball and considers just where this technology is headed, both in the short run and in the long run, when the achievement of artificial intelligence (AI) seems likely. According to some AI critics, we might be creating machines that will one day wipe us out—but fortunately, that's a worry for the long run. For now, your main concern is to keep your PC from wiping out your bank account. For some great tips, dive in.

M O D U L E S

BUYING AND UPGRADING YOUR COMPUTER SYSTEM

10A

MODULE

WHAT YOU WILL LEARN . . .

When you have finished reading this module, you will be able to:

1. Explain why it's a bad idea to choose hardware without considering your software needs.

2. Discuss the differences between Macintosh and Windows PC systems.

3. Explain why a notebook computer isn't the best choice for college students.

4. Choose the right computer hardware and printer for your needs.

5. Explain how to take care of and upgrade your computer system.

If you've decided to purchase a computer, you're not alone. Many college students already own a computer. At some schools, it's unusual *not* to own one. At a typical state university, as many as 80 percent of students own a computer and make full use of the high-speed network connections available in their dorm rooms. Increasing numbers of colleges are even expecting students to purchase a computer upon entering the university.

Savvy college students know that computer ownership is a wise move. At America's "Most Wired" schools, according to *Yahoo! Internet Life,* between 80 and 100 percent of the courses require students to access online materials or submit work using the campus network. Elsewhere, the percentage of courses requiring online work is growing quickly. Owning your own system can mean avoiding lengthy waits in a crowded computer lab.

What's more, owning a computer is the best way to ensure computer literacy. Employers are demanding higher levels of computer literacy than ever before. According to a recent study, more than 83 percent of surveyed employers described computer literacy as "important" or "very important" in a hiring decision. Particularly attractive to employers were the following skills: word processing (96 percent), email (93 percent), spreadsheet analysis (86 percent), database entry and editing (83 percent), use of presentation software (75 percent), and Internet searching (63 percent). You'll be wise to buy a system that can run all this software, and try to use as much of it as you can while you're still in school.

GET STARTED THE RIGHT WAY

There's a right way and a wrong way to select a computer. The right way involves determining your software needs and then choosing the computer that runs this software. What's the wrong way? Getting excited about some cool new computer and then finding out that it's the wrong system for your needs.

For this reason, this section begins by alerting you to the pitfalls of the hardware-first approach. Then we can start talking about doing things the right way.

Notebook or Desktop?

Notebook computers rival desktop machines these days, and perhaps you're dreaming about carrying a high-powered notebook computer around campus. The best of them are truly awesome machines, with big (14.1 inch) displays and fast processors. You could even take one to class and take notes on your computer.

Time for a reality check. For college use, a notebook computer isn't the best idea in the world. Let's start with note-taking. Do you think your classmates—let alone your professor—will like the constant clickity-clack? Another good reason to avoid using a computer to take notes is that the best students take notes that combine text with all sorts of graphics (circles, arrows, flow diagrams, and more). A computer forces you to restrict your note-taking to text only, unless you're willing to spend a lot of time trying to draw pictures with a mouse (You'll miss half the lecture if you do).

You should also consider that notebooks are easy to lose or steal, and if your notebook is missing, it could be a catastrophe. Imagine losing your computer the night before a major project is due. Some professors won't accept its loss as a reason for an extension: they'll say you should have made a backup. More than 250,000 notebook computers are stolen each year, mostly at airports and hotels, but thieves are also targeting college campuses now. At the

Although notebook computers are useful for course work, don't be seduced by the power of notebook computers for your use in class. During a lecture, a notebook forces you to restrict your note-taking to text only, and notebooks are easy to lose or steal.

University of California, Berkeley, for example, campus security officials recently reported a steep increase in notebook thefts, and similar reports are coming in from other colleges and universities.

A final point is that notebook computers aren't designed for prolonged use. To safeguard your health while using the computer (see Module 10B), you're best off with a desktop computer.

Still, you might decide that the notebook route is best for you or you may have no choice. Some colleges require students to purchase notebook computers. If you buy one, keep your eye on it!

Mac or PC?

Explore IT Lab

Buying a Computer

You've decided to buy a computer, and start talking to computer users to get their suggestions. This leads to a startling discovery: computer users are similar to two warring groups of intolerant ideologues, each convinced that it has truth on its side. One prefers the Macintosh, and the other prefers Windows. Each thinks the other platform is terrible—horrible—and wouldn't be caught dead using it! Worse, they'll try to pressure you to go one way or the other.

Don't give in to this pressure. Here's the truth: *today's top-of-the-line Macintoshes and PCs are virtually indistinguishable in terms of features and performance.* What's more, excellent software for all the important applications you'll need to learn (word processing, email, spreadsheets, database software, presentation graphics, and Web browsers) is available for both platforms. Macs used to be easier to set up and use, but that's no longer true, thanks to improvements in Microsoft Windows.

So is it a toss-up? Not quite. Some minor differences between Macs and PCs can become major issues for some people. For example, Macs and Mac software generally rely more heavily on the mouse for program control and provide fewer keyboard shortcuts. For somebody with a serious repetitive stress injury (RSI) involving tennis elbow, which restricts mouse usage, the Mac's reliance on the mouse is an important consideration. For more information on RSI, see Module 10B.

Career interests enter into the Mac vs. PC picture, too. In general, Macs have a strong niche market in artistic fields, such as publishing, music, graphics, illustration, and Web site design. PCs figure prominently on the desktops of engineers and business people. The classic stereotype is that the successful artist has a Mac, but her accountant uses a PC. Watch out for these stereotypes, though. Using that stereotype, you might think that scientists would go for PCs, but that's not necessarily the case. In the "wet" sciences (chemistry and biology), Macs have many advantages and for good reason. These sciences involve visual representation, an area in which Macs excel.

If you're on a budget, consider the cost angle, too. On average, Macs and Mac peripherals are somewhat more expensive than comparably-equipped PCs, although the price gap has narrowed recently.

What distinguishes Macs from PCs is software availability. For economic reasons, far more programs are available for Windows PCs than for Macintoshes. Only one Macintosh is sold for every twenty Windows PCs. Many software companies that formerly focused on the Macintosh are de-emphasizing Macintosh software and bringing out more Windows products. Other software publishers are also dropping Mac products. For example, Autodesk, publishers of the top-selling CAD program, (AutoCAD) has dropped its sluggish-selling Mac version to focus on its Windows products. This fact alone pretty much rules out the Mac if you're interested in architecture or engineering. Even software publishers that continue to support the Mac typically bring out the Mac versions later, and don't include as many features.

Does software availability make a difference? If you're planning to use your computer only for basic applications, such as word processing, email, Web browsing, and spreadsheets, the Mac vs. PC issue simply isn't important. But what if you declare a major a couple of years from now, only to find that your professors want you to use special-purpose programs designed to run on some other computer? This point doesn't rule out a Macintosh, especially if you're going into an arts-related field, but it does bring us back to our first point. Consider your software needs first, and then select the hardware.

One other point in favor of the PC is the advantage of Linux (see Module 3A). Although a version of Linux is available for the Macintosh, the PC version is where you'll find all the action. As you learned in Module 3A, you can run Linux on the same hard drive as Windows, giving you the best of both worlds.

Top-of-the-Line or Bargain Bin Special?

Should you buy a top-of-the-line system, or try to save some money by getting a slower, older model? A good argument for getting the best system you can afford is that you don't want it to become obsolete before graduation. In your senior year, do you want to spend time upgrading your hard drive, running the risk of damaging one of the internal components, when you should be focusing on your studies?

The most important consideration here is the type of software you're planning to run. If you will be using your computer for the basic applications such as word processing, you don't need the most-powerful computer available. For $1,000, you can buy an excellent computer for general-purpose computing. But what if you decide to declare a major in mechanical engineering? You might want to run a CAD package, and CAD programs demand a fast system with lots of memory. The same goes for any graphics-intensive software, such as illustration programs, and for advanced financial modeling programs.

Macs have a strong niche market in artistic fields, such as publishing, music, graphics, illustration, and Web site design. PCs figure prominently on the desktops of engineers and business people.

ANTICIPATE YOUR SOFTWARE NEEDS

Now it's time for some research: you want to find out which programs students in your major field of study are using, and which programs are used by graduates working in the career you're planning to pursue.

The best way to find out the answer to the first question is to visit the department and ask around. Find the computer lab where upper-division students hang out, watch what they're doing, and ask their advice. You'll get some great tips. It might turn out that one of your major's required courses uses analytical software that only runs on a PC capable of crunching numbers at 300 MHz, or uses a design program that only runs on a Mac loaded with memory.

To find out what type of computer is preferred by people working in your chosen career, interview. If someone in your family works in that career, you already have one person to talk to. From there, you can get additional leads.

CHOOSE THE RIGHT HARDWARE

You've decided what software you need, and you've settled the Mac vs. Windows PC issue. Now you have to make some crucial decisions regarding processor speed and type, memory amounts, CD-ROM drive speed, and

Destinations

As you're checking out systems that offer specific components, such as a particular hard disk brand and model, check the Web for product reviews. For reviews of Windows PC hardware, try **PC Magazine (http://www. pcmag.com)**. For Macs, try **MacWorld (http:// www.macworld.com)**. Follow the links to the search page.

much more. It's a frustrating process. What's worse, improved products come along so quickly that even the experts get confused. In the following sections, you'll find some tips that should help.

Processors

Of all the choices you make when you buy a computer, the microprocessor is the most important. Strictly speaking, the microprocessor (called a processor or a CPU for short) *is* the computer, which is why it's the most-important component in terms of shaping the system's overall performance.

In general, the higher the processor's **clock speed** (see Module 2A), the faster the computer. Remember though, that clock speed comparisons make sense only when you're looking at one brand and model of processor. For example, a Pentium III running at 600 MHz is faster than a Celeron running at 650 MHz.

Memory

The next item to consider when buying a computer is the amount of memory you need. Two important issues to determine are how much random-access memory (RAM) you need and whether your system is equipped with cache memory.

RAM

The more memory you can get, the better. Windows 98 and Mac OS theoretically require only 16MB, but it isn't fun to run either of these operating systems with so little RAM. When you try to run two or more programs, there's no more room in the memory, so the operating system has to store portions of the program on your hard disk. The result is sluggish performance. You should get at least 32MB of RAM. If you're planning to run a Web browser, go for 64MB. Other operating systems require more memory. Windows 2000 and Mac OS X require 64MB of RAM—and once again, that's a bare minimum. You'll be wise to equip these operating systems with at least 128MB of RAM.

You'll encounter several memory technologies in your search. Currently, the fastest is called Synchronous DRAM (SDRAM). For PCs with Pentium III processors, you need SDRAM capable of running at a bus speed of 100 MHz. This type of RAM is often called PC100 SDRAM.

Secondary Cache

Be aware that processors that omit an on-board secondary cache (also called L2 cache) will run more slowly than processors including this feature. For example, the AMD Athlon 1000 processor runs at a very high clock speed— 1,000 MHz—but it's slower than a Pentium III 850. The reason: the Pentium has an on-board secondary cache (also called a *backside cache*), but the Athlon 1000 doesn't.

Hard Disks

A common mistake made by first-time buyers is to underestimate the amount of disk storage they will need. Today, 6GB (gigabytes) sounds like a lot, but you won't believe how quickly you will fill it up. A good rule of thumb is to use no more than 25 percent of your hard disk space for the operating system and applications. Because Windows 98 or Windows 2000 and Microsoft Office will consume up to 2GB of your disk space, a 6GB drive will exceed the 25 percent guideline if you install additional applications. It's not that expensive to get a larger hard disk. Be wise, and get the largest drive you can afford. A capacity such as 8GB may sound absurdly large, but you'll fill it up eventually. If you're thinking of installing Linux as well as Windows, you'll need at least 8MB, and 12MB would be better. Increasingly common are reasonably inexpensive hard drives with 26GB of capacity or more.

Among computer systems that have the same processor, hard disk speed makes the biggest contribution to overall system speed. Suppose you're looking at two Pentium III systems with 850 MHz processors. The less-expensive one might use a slow hard drive, which can slow the system down so much that it isn't much faster than a well-designed 600 MHz system (see Module 2B for a discussion of hard disk speed). In particular, pay attention to rotation speed: drives that spin at 5,400 RPM are bottom-line products. The better drives spin at 7,200 or 10,000 RPM.

Figure   10A.1

DVD discs can store more data than CD-ROM discs and a DVD drive also will read ordinary CD-ROM discs.

To install new software, most of which is distributed on CD-ROM discs, you'll want a CD-ROM drive. If you plan to use the drive only for installing new software, speed isn't vitally important, so here's a place to save money. You can get CD-ROM drives with speeds up to 70× (seventy times the original CD-ROM standard of 150 Kbps), but you might be perfectly happy with a bargain-basement 24× drive. If you're looking to buy the best, consider a DVD drive instead of a CD-ROM. You'll be able to read DVD discs, which can store more data than CD-ROM discs (up to 4.7GB). As an added bonus, DVD drives can read ordinary CD-ROM discs, too (see Figure 10A.1 on previous page).

Increasingly popular are internal Zip drives for backup and supplemental storage. You can add a Zip drive with 100MB-removable disks for about $100. Another option is Sony's HiFD, a removable storage drive that uses 200MB cartridges. HiFD has a big advantage: it's backward-compatible with 3.5-inch floppy disks.

Video Cards and Monitors

The computer's **video card** determines the quality and resolution of the display you see on your monitor. The current standard display for a Windows PC is a **Super Video Graphics Array (SVGA)** monitor with a resolution of either 1024 × 768 or 1280 × 1024. High-end video cards can display resolutions of 1600 × 1200. The higher the resolution, the more memory is required. To display 1600 × 1200 resolution with a color palette of 16.7 million colors, for example, you need to equip your video card with 8MB of **video RAM (VRAM),** memory that's set aside for video processing purposes.

Advanced systems offer a special bus design that directly connects the video circuits with the microprocessor, increasing performance speed considerably. In Windows PCs, the best systems currently offer an **Accelerated Graphics Port (AGP),** which transfers video data much more quickly than the standard PCI interface.

If you plan to run Microsoft Windows, look for a system that has a **graphics accelerator.** Built into the video card, this accessory can double or triple the performance of Windows.

On Macintosh systems, watch out for undersized video memory. If the Macintosh you are planning to buy has 512KB of VRAM, you will be wise to have more installed when you buy your system.

Monitors are available in different sizes. You can purchase anything from a 14-inch to a 21-inch monitor, although large monitors are more expensive. Increasingly, a 17-inch monitor is considered the industry standard. If you

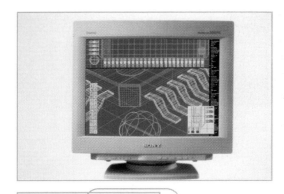

plan to get into desktop publishing or CAD, you may want to upgrade to a 21-inch monitor (see Figure 10A.2).

The monitor's **dot pitch** (also called aperture grill) is also important. This is a physical characteristic that affects the smallest dot the screen can display. Don't buy a monitor with a dot pitch larger than .28mm—the smaller, the better.

Modems

If you plan to log on to the campus network by means of a telephone connection, you need a modem. Today's standard is the 56 Kbps V.90 protocol, the officially-sanctioned standard. Avoid inexpensive modems that use the X.2 or K56flex protocols, which were marketed before the V.90 protocol's publication. Although many service providers continue to support X.2 and K56flex, this support is being phased out now that the V.90 protocol has been approved. Check with your campus computer center to find out which modem protocols they support.

Figure **10A.2**

A 17-inch monitor is considered to be the industry standard. If you plan to get into desktop publishing or CAD, however, you may want to upgrade to a 21-inch monitor.

Network Cards

If you're planning to connect your computer to the campus network, you need a network interface card (NIC). Check with your college's computer center to find out what kind of network card you need. Most colleges run 10 Mbps (10baseT) Ethernets, but a few require you to get a 100 Mbps (100baseT) network card.

On Macintoshes, support for Ethernet networks is built in, but you will need a **transceiver,** a device that handles the electrical connection between the cable and the Mac's Ethernet port. On Windows PCs, you need an Ethernet card, which includes the transceiver (see Figure 10A.3). Look for a card that plugs into your computer's PCI bus.

Sound

To take full advantage of the Internet's multimedia capabilities, you will need a sound card and speakers.

On Macs, the sound is built in. You will need external speakers, though, to hear sounds in stereo.

Figure **10A.3**

An Ethernet card.

On Windows PCs, you'll need to equip your system with a sound card. Look for a sound card that offers **wavetable synthesis,** which uses stored samples of real musical instrument sounds, as well as a **Peripheral Computer Interconnect (PCI)** interface, which reduces demands on your processor.

For the richest sound, equip your system with a subwoofer, which reproduces bass notes more realistically.

Be aware that many computer makers give you throwaway speakers, especially with the lowest-priced systems. If sound matters a lot to you—and it does to most college students—consider upgrading to a higher-quality, name-brand speaker system.

Keyboard and Mouse

Most computers come with standard keyboards. If you're worried about repetitive stress injury (RSI)—and you should be—consider upgrading to an ergonomic keyboard, such as the Microsoft Natural Keyboard. For more information on RSI, see Module 10B.

S P O T L I G H T

A COMPUTER IN EVERY HOME

▶ We live in a computerized society. Two decades ago, it would have been unthinkable to make the assertion "A computer in every home." Today, however, you need to look no further than your kitchen or living room to prove the point. Most homes have many computers, and the occupants may not even know it.

Embedded systems are computers built into a piece of equipment to make it run better or more conveniently. These systems may be as small as your fingernail or as large as a package of hot dogs. When someone mentions embedded systems, people typically think of automobiles. Computers have been used in automobiles for years to help control their complex operations.

Our homes contain many everyday devices that rely on embedded systems as well. For instance, your microwave oven uses a computer to know when your bag of popcorn is popped just right. Your new dishwasher probably uses one or more computers to get the water temperature right and spray it on the

dishes at the proper pressure. You can also find computers in toasters, blenders, espresso machines, and coffee pots.

The living room has even more computers. Your music comes through a digital tuner that uses a computer to control the station to which you are tuned, as well as the sound produced. When you pop in a compact disc, computers control the positioning of the laser beam and the decoding of the signal it picks up. If you watch a television show, the picture is probably controlled by a computer in the set. If you have one of those fancy picture-in-a-picture models, it's a sure bet that a computer is involved.

Many homes now have satellite dishes or digital cable television. The boxes that sit on top of your television are nothing more than computers that decode the signal and process it so your television can use it. Your VCR uses computers to help process the signals on the tape. Newer models can even analyze the video tape to give you the highest quality recording possible.

These uses of computers do not include the obvious ones. Your children may have a video game that allows them to blow away the latest alien invasion or play on the dream team of their choice. These systems are nothing but specialized computers. Over in your study or on that spare table in the corner, you may have your own computer for doing the family finances or connecting to the Internet.

This home tour describes not a home of the future, but the average home of today. As computers make more and more inroads, they will become even more omnipresent. They will control our refrigerators, our interior lighting, and the security lights outside the house. They will even turn on the sprinklers based on the dryness of the soil.

Eventually, the computers in each of these home devices will be connected so they can work in harmony. For instance, you might want to wake up to a fresh pot of coffee in a 73-degree home with an 84-degree bath waiting while listening to the works of Bach. You could do this if all the computer-controlled devices were hooked to a central computer that allowed you to make your choices the night before.

Is it science fiction? No. It's coming our way faster than any of us are even aware.

Given the increasing number of home devices that rely on embedded systems, someday our homes will become virtual computers.

Most systems also come with a basic mouse, but you can ask for an upgrade. With Windows PCs, there's good reason to do so, thanks to the improved mouse support built into Windows 98. Any mouse that supports Microsoft's IntelliMouse standard includes a wheel, which enables you to scroll through documents with ease.

Uninterruptible Power Supply (UPS)

Many professors don't accept the excuse of, "I'm sorry I don't have my paper. I finished it, and then a power outage wiped out my work," which means using a computer for college work can be risky. Considering the comparatively low price of today's uninterruptible power supply (UPS)—you can get one for less than $200—it's wise to consider buying one for your campus computer. That's especially true if you notice frequent power outages.

GET THE RIGHT PRINTER

As you've learned, printers fall into four basic categories: color ink-jet printers, monochrome laser printers, color laser printers, and multifunction printers that include faxing and scanning as well as printing. For college use, cost considerations will probably rule out color laser and multifunction printers, so you'll most likely choose between color ink-jet and monochrome laser printers.

Destinations

To compare prices from several vendors, take a look at NetBuyer (**http://www.netbuyer.com**) or PC-Today (**http://www.pc-today.com**).

Which is best depends on your budget. Although monochrome laser printers are more expensive than color ink-jet printers, laser printers are cheaper to use in the long run because laser toner cartridges, priced on a cost-per-page basis, are cheaper than ink-jet cartridges. The difference really goes up when you're printing in color. Printing a full-page color photograph could cost as much as $1 to $2 per page. You can hold costs down if you use color printing only when it really matters (for example, when you're preparing transparencies for a class presentation).

Speed matters, too. The slowest laser printers are faster than the fastest ink-jet printers, and the slowest ink-jet printers operate at a glacial pace. High-end laser printers can print as many as 17 ppm (pages per minute). Still, the best ink-jet printers churn out black-and-white pages at a peppy pace of 9 ppm. If you go the ink-jet route, look for a printer that can print at least 4 ppm.

SHOP WISELY

Whether you're looking for a Windows PC or a Macintosh, you need to consider whether you want to purchase your system locally or from a mail-order company (see Figure 10A.4). If you buy locally, you can resolve problems quickly by going back to the store. (With a telephone-ordered system, you have to call the company's technical support line.)

Figure 10A.4

If you buy a computer locally, you can resolve problems quickly by going back to the store.

But don't rule out mail or online ordering. Look for mail-order companies that have been in business a long time—and particularly those that offer a no-questions-asked return policy for the first 30 days. Without such a policy, you could get stuck with a "lemon" system that even the manufacturer won't be able to repair. Avoid new companies that offer the lowest prices, as they may have tried to cut their margins too thin. The worst-case scenario is that the company goes out of business after they get your money but before they ship your computer. You'll be paying for somebody's trip to the Bahamas! Be aware, though, that the lowest price isn't always the best deal—particularly if the item isn't in stock and will take

Shopping Comparison Worksheet

Vendor _____   Date _____

   Brand Name _____

   Model _____

   Real Price _____ (including selected components)

Microprocessor

   Brand _____

   Model _____

   Speed _____ MHz

RAM

   Type _____

   Amount _____ MB

Hard drive

   Capacity _____ MB   Seek time _____ ns

   Speed _____ rpm   Interface _____

Monitor

   Size _____ x_____ pixels   Dot pitch _____ mm

Video card

   Memory _____ MB   Max. resolution _____ x _____ pixels

   Accelerated? . . . . yes   no

Floppy drive(s)

   Capacity _____ KB   Number _____

Removable drive

   Type _____

   Location . . . . internal   external

CD-ROM drive

   Speed _____

Speakers

   Included? . . . . yes   no   Upgraded? . . . . yes   no

Subwoofer

   Included? . . . . yes   no

Modem

   Included? . . . . yes   no   Protocol _____

   Speed . . . . 28.8Kbps   56 Kbps

Network card

   Included? . . . . yes   no   Speed (10/100) _____

Keyboard

   Upgraded? . . . . yes   no   Model _____

Mouse

   Included? . . . . yes   no   Upgraded? _____

UPS

   Included? . . . . yes   no

Warranty _____

Service location _____

Typical service turnaround time _____

Figure 10A.5

Shopping Comparison
Worksheet.

Destinations

Looking for low prices on
the Internet?
Pricewatch.com (**http://
www.pricewatch.com**)
compares computer
equipment prices from
dozens of online vendors,
enabling you to find the
lowest price quickly.

months to reach you. Don't forget about shipping and "handling" charges,
too, which could add considerably to the price of a system.

Make sure you're not comparing apples and oranges. Some quoted prices
include accessories such as modems and monitors; others do not. To establish
a level playing field for comparison, use the Shopping Comparison Worksheet
(Figure 10A.5). For the system's actual price, get a quote that includes all the
accessories you want, such as a modem, a monitor, and a UPS.

Buying Used

What about buying a used system? It's risky. If you're buying from an individual, chances are the system is priced too high. People just can't believe how quickly computers lose their value. They think their systems are worth a lot more than they actually are. Try this for yourself: find some used computer ads in your local newspaper and then find out how much it would cost to buy the same system new, if it's still on the market. Chances are the new system is cheaper than the used one!

Name-Brand Windows PCs

The name-brand PC manufacturers, such as Compaq, Dell, and Gateway 2000, offer high-quality systems at competitive prices. You can buy some of these systems from retail or mail-order stores, but many are available only by contacting the vendor directly.

For your money, you can get a system that's been extensively checked out before it's shipped and has a good warranty. If you're buying extended warranty protection that includes on-site service, make sure the on-site service is really available where you live. You may find out that the service is available only in major metropolitan areas. Make sure you get 24-hour technical support—you'll need it if something goes wrong at 2 A.M., the night before a paper is due. (Computers seem to break down at the worst times.)

One disadvantage of name-brand systems is their use of proprietary components. If something breaks down, you have only one repair option: go back to the manufacturer. And after the warranty has expired, you may find that you'll pay a premium price for parts and repairs.

Generic Windows PCs

In most cities, you'll find local computer stores that assemble their own systems using off-the-shelf components. Often, these systems are just as fast (and just as reliable) as the name-brand systems just discussed because they use the same components. You save because you don't pay for the name-brand company's marketing and distribution costs.

What you may not get from such stores is adequate technical support, and the warranty may not mean much if the company goes bankrupt. (Many do; the industry's profit margin is razor-thin.)

Buying a no-name system is risky, but it has a big payoff if you buy a good system. Since it's made with off-the-shelf components, you can fix it yourself by simply replacing the damaged component.

Building Your Own Windows PC

In the past, building your own PC was a great way to save money. You buy the components separately—the case and power supply, motherboard, memory, drives, and cards—and put it all together. The motherboard's manual tells you what to do, and some motherboards come with an instructional video you can watch. It's a great feeling to build a PC, press the "On" button, and see the computer's initial display appear on the screen.

Today, building your own PC is not worthwhile. At best, you'll save $100 to $200. At worst, you'll damage some components and spend days trying to fix the problem.

CARING FOR YOUR COMPUTER SYSTEM

After your computer is running smoothly, it will probably keep running. Chances are it will run flawlessly for years if you follow a few precautions:

- Equip your system with a **surge protector** to protect all your system components from power surges caused by lightning or other power irregularities (see Figure 10A.6).

- Don't plug your dorm refrigerator into the same outlet as the one the computer's using.

- Make sure there's sufficient air circulation around the components. Don't block the air intake grills.

- If you add or remove any cables, make sure you switch off the power first.

- Make sure the cables aren't stretched or mashed by furniture.

- Avoid eating or drinking while you're using your computer. Crumbs can gum up your keyboard. Spilled liquids can ruin the keyboard, or an entire system, if you're especially klutzy. If you are hungry or thirsty, take a break!

- Don't switch off the power without following the proper shut-down procedure.

- To keep your hard disk running smoothly, run a disk defragmentation program regularly. This program ensures that related data is stored as a unit, thus increasing retrieval speed.

- Get a virus checker and run it frequently. Don't install and run any software someone gives you on a floppy disk until you run a virus checker on the disk and its contents. If someone gives you a document file on a floppy disk, be sure to check for macro viruses.

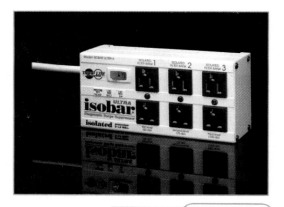

Figure 10A.6

You should use a surge protector to protect all your system components from power surges caused by lightning or other power irregularities.

Be sure to keep your computer clean, too by following these steps:

- Clean your computer and printer with a damp, soft, lint-free cloth.

- To clean your monitor, spray some window cleaner on a soft, lint-free cloth—*not* directly on the monitor—and then wipe the surface clean.

- If your mouse gets gummed up, twist off the ring on the bottom of the mouse, remove the ball, and clean the ball with warm, soapy water. Rinse and dry thoroughly with a clean, lint-free cloth. Clean the rollers with a cotton swab, and remove any lint that may have accumulated.

UPGRADING YOUR SYSTEM

Many computer owners improve their system's performance by adding new hardware to their systems, such as modems, sound cards, and additional memory. This section discusses the two most common hardware upgrades: adding expansion boards and memory.

Before you decide to upgrade your computer, be aware that doing so may violate your computer's warranty (read the warranty to find out). You may need to take your computer to an authorized service center to get an upgrade without violating the warranty.

Removing the Cover

To upgrade your system, begin by unplugging the power cord and removing all the cables attached to the back of the unit. Make a note of which cable went where so you can correctly plug the cables back in later. With most systems, you can remove the cover by removing the screws on the back of the case. If you don't know how to remove the cover, consult your computer manual. Keep the screws in a cup or bowl so they will be handy when you reassemble the computer.

Adding Expansion Boards

To add an expansion board to your system, identify the correct type of expansion slot (ISA, PCI, or AGP) and unscrew the metal insert that blocks the slot's access hole. Save the screw, but discard the insert. Gently but firmly press the board into the slot. Don't try to force it, though, and stop pressing if the motherboard flexes. (If the motherboard flexes, it is not properly supported, and you should take your computer to the dealer to have this repaired.) When you've pressed the board fully into place, screw it down, using the screw you removed from the metal insert. Before replacing the cover, carefully check to make sure the board is fully inserted.

Upgrading Memory

Many users find that their systems perform faster when they add more memory. With additional memory, it's less likely that the operating system will need to use virtual memory, which slows the computer down. In order to upgrade your computer's memory, you'll find it helpful to learn a few terms and concepts.

Older computers use memory chips supplied on 72-pin **Single Inline Memory Modules (SIMMs);** while most newer computers use 168-pin **Dual Inline Memory Modules (DIMMs).** SIMMs and DIMMs are printed circuit boards (with affixed memory chips) that are designed to snap into specially-designed sockets on the computer's motherboard. Most motherboards have either four SIMM sockets or two to three DIMM sockets (see Figure 10A.7). Since SIMMs must be installed in pairs, this limits their flexibility.

SIMMs and DIMMS are available in various capacities, ranging from 8MB to 128MB each. You need to consult your computer's manual to determine whether your computer uses SIMMs or DIMMs, and where you can add them. For example, suppose your computer has two 8MB SIMMs in the first two sockets, leaving two sockets empty. Because you must install SIMMs in pairs, you can add two 8MB SIMMs (for a total of 32MB of memory), two 16MB SIMMs (for a total of 48MB of memory), or two 32MB SIMMs (for a total of 80MB of memory). You may be able to add even more memory, but some motherboards place a limit on the amount of memory you can install. You don't need to install DIMMs in pairs, so they're easier to work with.

Consult your computer's manual to determine which type of memory technology your computer uses. Older computers use the slowest of these technologies, **fast-page mode (FPM) DRAM,** which is available only in SIMMs. Newer computers use the faster **extended data out (EDO) DRAM,** which is available in both SIMMs and DIMMs. Still newer computers use the fastest-available memory technology, called **synchronous dynamic RAM (SDRAM),** which is available only in DIMMs.

You also need to consider the memory chips' speed. FPM and EDO DRAM chips are rated in *nanoseconds (ns)* (billionths of a second). The smaller the number, the faster the chip. Pentiums require 60ns chips, while older systems can work with 70ns or 80ns chips. For SDRAM chips, the speed is rated in *megahertz (MHz)* (millions of cycles per second), and this speed must match the speed of the motherboard's data bus (66 MHz, or 100 MHz, or 133 MHz).

Figure 10A.7

A 100 MHz motherboard. Most motherboards have four SIMM sockets, or two to three DIMM sockets.

IMPACTS

The Latest Landfill Crisis?
Obsolete Computers

Imagine a pile of junk that's one square acre at the base and nearly one mile high. That's how much space 315 million computers takes up—and according to projections, that's the number of PCs that will have been sent to landfills by the year 2005. Currently, more than two million tons of scrap electronics wind up in landfills each year, but that's just the tip of the iceberg. Although U.S. environmental protection laws forbid businesses from placing obsolete computers in landfills, there's nothing to stop individuals from doing so—and increasingly, they've got lots of disused computer equipment sitting around. Experts believe that most obsolete computers are tucked away in closets and basements, largely because nobody can figure out what to do with them. As more systems are replaced, today's relative trickle—if two million tons can be considered a "trickle"—will turn into a deluge, one that could develop into a genuine environmental disaster.

What's wrong with sending computers to the landfill? For starters, they contain toxic substances. What's more, these substances are heavy metals that are likely to escape the confines of poorly-designed landfills. Lead—as much as five to eight pounds of it—is commonly found in a computer monitors' cathode ray tube (CRT). That pile of computers headed for the landfill contains 1.2 million pounds of lead, as well as two million pounds of cadmium (so poisonous that it can kill), 400,000 pounds of highly-toxic mercury, and scores of additional hazardous substances, not to mention some 4 billion pounds of environmentally-unfriendly plastic.

Obsolete computers aren't without value, particularly to low-income users who can't afford the latest and greatest. Charitable organizations such as the Salvation Army are adding older computers to their thrift shop lines, but they aren't hot sellers. Most would-be buyers are scared off by the possibility that an older computer isn't Y2K-compliant, for example, or won't let them connect to the Internet.

There's one bright spot in this picture: the typical computer contains some valuable materials, including steel, copper, aluminum and silver. Circuit boards also contain small amounts of gold and silver, but don't start nursing a get-rich fantasy. You'd be lucky to get ten ounces of gold out of 2,000 pounds of discarded circuit boards, which is only worth the expense of extracting it. Still, according to one projection, the value of all these recyclable materials will lead to the recycling of more than two million computers per year by 2005—but that's not enough.

Computer recycling isn't growing fast enough to hold back the wave of toxic materials headed for the landfills. That's why it's important for cities and counties to start developing computer recycling programs right now, before the deluge hits. In Cuyahoga County, Ohio, for example, unwanted computers are collected. If they're still usable, they're refurbished for county schoolchildren. If not, they're recycled.

It's a public service to recycle an older computer rather than tossing it into the landfill, but people should remember that a functional computer might wind up in a thrift shop or a schoolchild's desk, experts say. Be sure to reformat the hard drive so that personal information, such as tax records, contact information, email, and other private data isn't part of the thrift-shop package.

When you purchase memory modules, the salesperson will help you determine which type of module you need and how much memory you can install.

Before you install memory modules, you also need to be aware that memory chips are easily destroyed by static electricity. Do not attempt to install memory chips without wearing a **grounding strap,** a wrist-attached device that grounds your body so that you can't zap the chips. Also, don't try to force the memory modules into their receptacles, as they're supposed to snap in gently. If they won't go in, you don't have the module aligned correctly, or you may have the wrong type of module.

To install the module, identify the correct socket (check your computer's manual to make sure) and then make sure you have oriented the module correctly. (You can insert it only one way.) For SIMM modules, hold the socket at a steep angle to the motherboard and insert it into the socket until it goes all the way in. For DIMM modules, push the module straight down into the socket. When you are sure that the module is properly seated in the slot, lock

Destinations

Kingston, a leading marketer of memory chips, provides detailed information on memory upgrades for specific brands and models of computers. Learn more about upgrading your computer's memory at **http://www. kingston.com/catalog/ memory/mem-idx.com.**

it in place. For SIMM modules, you do this by tilting the module up so that it is perpendicular to the motherboard (you'll hear it snap into place). For DIMM modules, pull the levers on both sides of the receptacle.

Replacing the Cover

When you have checked your work and you're satisfied that the new hardware is correctly installed, replace the cover and screw it down firmly. Replace the cables and then restart your system. If you added Plug and Play devices, you'll see on-screen instructions that help you configure your computer to use your new hardware.

TAKEAWAY POINTS

- Don't buy a computer without first determining which programs you need to run.
- For college use, avoid notebook computers unless you're certain you can live with the risk of losing your computer or having it stolen.
- If you can afford to do so, try to buy a higher-end system that won't become obsolete before you graduate.
- The processor isn't the only component that determines total system performance. The sharpest systems have fast processors, but they also have fast hard drives, fast memory, and graphics accelerator cards.
- For both Windows and Macs, you'll be happiest with a system that has at least 32MB of SDRAM (preferably 64MB), 512KB of secondary cache, the largest hard disk you can afford, a graphics accelerator card with at least 2MB of VRAM, a 17-inch monitor, and

upgrades in the mouse, keyboard, and speaker departments.
- Equip your computer with an uninterruptible power supply (UPS).
- Consider a color ink-jet printer over a monochrome laser printer only if you can live with slower printing speeds and costlier per-page operation.
- Buy your system from an established company that offers a no-questions-asked 30-day refund.
- Take good care of your system by protecting it from electrical surges, overheating, smashed cables, and food and drinks.
- Many computer owners improve their system's performance by adding new hardware to their systems, such as modems, sound cards, and additional memory. The two most common hardware upgrades are adding expansion boards and adding memory.

MODULE REVIEW

KEY TERMS AND CONCEPTS

Accelerated Graphics Port (AGP)
clock speed
dot pitch
Dual Inline Memory Modules
   (DIMMs)
extended data out (EDO)
   DRAM
fast-page mode (FPM) DRAM

graphics accelerator
grounding strap
Peripheral Computer
   Interconnect (PCI)
Single Inline Memory Modules
   (SIMMs)
Super Video Graphics Array
   (SVGA)

surge protector
synchronous dynamic RAM
   (SDRAM)
transceiver
video card
video RAM (VRAM)
wavetable synthesis

TRUE/FALSE

Indicate whether the following statements are true or false.

1. Before you consider buying a computer, you should first determine your software needs.

2. To safeguard your health while using a computer, you're better off using a notebook computer.

3. Today's top-of-the line PCs and Macintoshes are virtually identical in terms of features and performance.

4. PCs have a strong niche market in artistic fields such as publishing, graphics, and music.

5. Clock speed comparisons make sense only when you're looking at one brand and model of microprocessor.

6. Without secondary cache, a computer system will run slower.

7. CD-ROM drives can read DVD disks.

8. A 21-inch monitor is the industry standard.

9. Support for Ethernet cards is built into Macintoshes.

10. Although buying a generic computer system is risky, you may be able to fix the system yourself by removing the damaged component and replacing it with a new one.

MATCHING

Match each key term from the left column to the most accurate definition in the right column.

_____ 1. accelerated graphics port

_____ 2. video card

_____ 3. graphics accelerator

_____ 4. dot pitch

_____ 5. transceiver

_____ 6. wavetable synthesis

_____ 7. grounding strap

_____ 8. surge protector

_____ 9. synchronous dynamic RAM

_____ 10. dual inline memory module (DIMM)

a. an accessory built into a video card that improves Windows' performance

b. the fastest available computer technology

c. a device that handles the electrical connection between the cable and the Mac's Ethernet port

d. this determines the quality and resolution of the display you see on your monitor

e. a physical characteristic that affects the smallest dot the screen can display

f. a device which transfers video data more quickly than the standard PCI interface

g. a printed circuit board that snaps into a computer's motherboard

h. a device that protects all system components from power surges caused by power irregularities

i. this uses stored samples of real musical instrument sounds

j. a wrist-attached device that grounds your body so you can't zap the chips

MULTIPLE CHOICE

Circle the letter of the correct choice for each of the following.

1. Before you buy a computer, which of the following tasks should you perform first?
   a. select the computer hardware
   b. analyze your software needs
   c. buy the best software on the market
   d. learn about the kinds of computers available

2. Which of the following is not true about using notebook computers in class?
   a. The keyboarding may be disruptive to other class members.
   b. Their size makes them vulnerable to theft or loss.
   c. They are great for typing lecture notes and drawing diagrams.
   d. They are not designed for prolonged use.

3. Which of the following truly distinguishes Macs from PCs?
   a. performance
   b. features
   c. ease of use
   d. software availability

4. When analyzing your software needs, which of the following is important?
   a. Discover what software students in your major field of study are using.
   b. Discover what software graduates working in your chosen career are using.
   c. Talk to computer vendors and seek their advice.
   d. a and b

5. When it's time to select the hardware, which of the following is the most important consideration?
   a. the microprocessor
   b. the brand name
   c. memory
   d. the clock speed

6. Clock speed comparisons make sense only when you're in which of the following circumstances?
   a. determining whether to buy a Mac or PC
   b. selecting a CD-ROM drive
   c. looking at one brand and model of processor
   d. considering several different memory technologies

7. Which of the following is a common mistake many first time buyers make?
   a. selecting the wrong software for their hardware needs
   b. choosing a Mac over a PC
   c. installing software themselves
   d. underestimating the amount of disk storage they'll need

8. Which of the following is the current standard video display for a Windows PC?
   a. Video RAM (VRAM)
   b. Super Video Graphics Array (SVGA)
   c. Advanced Graphics Port (AGP)
   d. 17-inch

9. Which of the following will protect your computer from unexpected power surges?
   a. making sure there's sufficient air circulation
   b. surge protector
   c. practicing proper shut-down procedures
   d. surge checker program

10. Which of the following is not a sound computer care tip?
    a. Ensure that sufficient air circulation exists around the components.
    b. Run a disk defragmentation program regularly to maintain the hard disk.
    c. Spray window cleaner directly on your monitor and wipe it clean.
    d. Purchase a virus checker and run it frequently.

FILL-IN

In the blank provided, write the correct answer for each of the following.

1. Generally, the higher the processor's _____, the faster the computer.

2. The computer's _____ determines the quality and resolution of the display you see on your monitor.

3. The current standard display for a Windows PC is a(n) _____.

4. Memory that's set aside for video processing purposes is called _____.

5. The monitor's _____ is a physical characteristic that affects the smallest dot the screen can display.

6. The slowest memory technology for older computers is called _____.

7. Although support for Ethernet networks is built into Macintoshes, you need to get a(n) _____, a device that handles the electrical connection between the cable and the Mac's Ethernet port.

8. Look for a sound card that offers _____, which uses stored samples of real musical instrument sounds.

9. Equip your system with a(n) _____ to protect all your system components from power surges.

10. Older computers use memory chips supplied on 72-pin _____ modules.

SHORT ANSWER

On a separate sheet of paper, answer the following questions.

1. Why is it important to consider software needs before purchasing hardware?

2. What items might you include in a software needs assessment?

3. Explain the pros and cons of purchasing a PC over a Mac.

4. What are some things you need to consider before purchasing a printer?

5. How much RAM would you need if you were purchasing a computer? Justify that amount.

6. What considerations do you need to think about before purchasing a computer through a mail-order company?

7. What things should you consider when selecting a video card and a monitor?

8. What are the problems inherent in purchasing a used computer system?

9. What are the advantages and disadvantages of purchasing a generic PC?

10. What precautions can you take to protect your computer system?

10B

MODULE

WHAT YOU WILL LEARN . . .

When you have finished reading this module, you will be able to:

1. Understand the health risks associated with prolonged computer use.
2. Discuss how to avoid eyestrain when using a computer.
3. Explain how to avoid cumulative trauma disorder.
4. List at least three computer accessories that can reduce the risk of eyestrain or cumulative trauma disorder.
5. Distinguish between accessible and assistive computer technologies for computers with disabilities.

Will you glow in the dark after using your computer? Some people still worry about the health effects from the minute amounts of radiation generated by computer displays, but there's good news. Recent research has dispelled the long-standing fears about the adverse health effects of monitor use.

However, computer users aren't free from other health risks. Prolonged computer usage can cause a number of health problems, ranging from relatively minor (and reversible) eyestrain to debilitating, chronic nerve and tendon disorders that can destroy a successful career. In this module, you'll learn how to protect yourself from the two leading types of computer-related health risk: computer vision syndrome (CVS) and cumulative trauma disorder (CTD), also called repetitive strain injury (RSI).

Should these risks concern you while you're in college, or is this only a workplace issue? Here are the facts: increasingly, college students are falling victim to computer-induced injuries. At MIT, for example, the student health service noted a 44 percent increase in diagnosed computer-related injuries in the three years from 1995 to 1998. Some of these were so serious that the affected students needed almost constant assistance to perform their schoolwork. You'll be wise to learn how to prevent these injuries now, while you're still healthy.

EYESIGHT PROBLEMS

Here's a troubling statistic: in 1997, 15 million people in the United States alone sought professional help for eye problems that were later attributed to prolonged computer use. According to the U.S. National Institute for Occupational Safety and Health (NIOSH), that's just the tip of the iceberg. NIOSH estimates that at least 60 million people are experiencing eye problems as a result of prolonged computer use. If you work with a computer more than three hours per day, there's a 90 percent chance that you'll have eye problems. The cost of these problems to the U.S. economy is an estimated $1 billion annually.

Computer Vision Syndrome (CVS)

There's a name for these problems: **computer vision syndrome (CVS).** Its symptoms include temporary nearsightedness, blurred vision or difficulty focusing, fatigue, headaches, backaches, and dry or watery eyes. The good news is that CVS symptoms typically do not become permanent if treated correctly.

What's the cause of CVS? It's a combination of two adverse factors: infrequent blinking, and the inherent difficulty of focusing the eye on an image made up of little dots. When staring at a computer screen, people blink less—only one-third as much as somebody who's not using a computer. As a result, their eyes get dry, and that makes it harder to focus. Unfortunately, it's particularly difficult and tiring to focus on a computer display because the image consists of thousands of tiny dots. The eye strains to resolve the dots into a sharp, focused image, and tires quickly. To understand why, think of focusing a camera on something. You move the lens in and out until you get the focus right. With a computer, that's what your eyes must do, over and over.

Preventing CVS

To safeguard your eyes while you're working with the computer, do the following:

- **Blink often**   Tape a note on your monitor until you get in the habit of reminding yourself.

- **Reduce glare**   Draw the blinds, if you can, or orient your monitor so that it's not facing an open window.

■ **Eliminate screen flicker** Make sure you're using the maximum **refresh rate** that's supported by your video card and monitor. The refresh rate refers to the number of times per second that the video adapter refreshes the screen display. Low refresh rates cause the screen to flicker, increasing the strain on your eyes.

■ **Balance the illumination** Ambient light should have the same perceived luminance as the monitor. If needed, turn off some lights, but don't work in the dark.

■ **Adjust your monitor's position** Arrange the monitor so that the top line of on-screen text is at eye level. Placing a monitor too high exposes more of the eye, causing it to dry out. Keep the monitor within 18 to 24 inches of your eyes.

■ **Clean your screen** Staring through all that yuck places extra stress on your eyes.

■ **Take a break** At least once every two hours, get up, walk to a window, and look at a distant object.

Accessories for Eye Protection

If you're still having eye problems after taking the preceding eye protection steps, consider using an eye protection accessory.

■ **Special computer glasses** Visit your eye doctor and ask for a PRIO VDT vision test, which simulates the conditions of using a computer display. You may need special prescription glasses to use your computer comfortably.

■ **Try a computer eye wash** Your pharmacy should have a new product: specially-formulated eye washes for computer users. The product's medication helps your eyes stay wet, even if you forget to blink.

■ **Consider a magnification system** New computer display magnifiers enable you to maintain focus from farther away, which results in less eyestrain (see Figure 10B.1). Why? It's much less work to focus on an object that's farther away as long as it's magnified so that you don't trade one type of eye strain for another.

■ **Get a glare shield** You may need this accessory if you can't adjust your monitor's orientation to avoid reflections.

Figure 10B.1

Bausch and Lomb's MagniViewer enables users to maintain focus on the computer screen from a greater distance.

Techtalk

ergonomics
Ergonomics is the science of designing machines and work furniture so that people can more easily and safely perform their tasks.

CUMULATIVE TRAUMA DISORDERS

Musicians have complained about it for years, and now it's a growing problem for computer users: **cumulative trauma disorder (CTD),** also called **repetitive strain injury (RSI).** CTD is caused by constantly-repeated motions and exertions that eventually cause pain and may lead to physical impairment. CTD diagnoses have increased by nearly 800 percent in the last decade. According to an estimate by the U.S. Department of Labor, about half the nation's workforce will have experienced some kind of repetitive stress injury by 2000, resulting in a $100 billion cost to the U.S. economy. The U.S. Secretary of Labor claims that cumulative trauma disorders are the chief cause of workplace-related illness today, figuring in 62 percent of illness reports.

But there's good news, too: CTD can be prevented or greatly reduced. At Sun Microsystems, for example, worker training and new, ergonomically-

SPOTLIGHT

THE WORLD AT YOUR·FINGERTIPS

We are all familiar with keyboards and mice as traditional input devices. The world is full of all sorts of other input devices as well. One popular type of input device uses touch technology. Touching is an intuitive way to get input from a user, and an entire industry segment has grown up around this technology.

Technically, touch technology is divided into two general areas. Touch screens are typically devices that fit over the front of existing monitors. Touch monitors, on the other hand, are monitors designed from the ground up to use touch technology. Touch screens and touch monitors often use similar or identical technology, and thus the terms are viewed as interchangeable in casual usage.

Touch technology allows you to touch the computer screen directly to make your selections. For instance, if you were looking at a Web page, you would touch the links that lead to additional information, rather than clicking with a mouse.

The technology behind touch screens is not new. It was developed approximately three decades ago, and has since grown into a $200 million market. In traditional touch screen technology, a series of small sensors surround the front of a regular monitor screen.

The sensors are used to invisibly divide the screen into a grid. When you touch the screen, the sensors pick up the location of where you touched. This information is transmitted to your software, in much the same way the click of a mouse button is transmitted.

More recent technology, known as resistive touch technology, allows the screen to respond to how hard you touch it. With this technology, the monitor face has two layers of Mylar coated with a special transparent conducting material. When the user touches the screen, the two layers are pressed together. The harder the pressure exerted by the touch, the more electrical current is generated. The advantages of the newer resistive touch screens is that they can be used by people wearing gloves or pointing with sharp objects, such as a pencil or a pen.

For many users, touch screens are superior to other input devices. Whereas repetitive movements using keyboards or mice can cause RSI problems, touch pads rely on people to simply touch things. This natural motion reduces the risk of many types of RSI. Touch screens are used frequently in industrial, retail, financial, and information service environments. Many ATM machines use touch screens, and many tourist areas include information kiosks that use touch screen technology.

In some environments, touch screens may be the only realistic way to generate input. For instance, when working with children who have attention deficit disorder, it's often a challenge to teach keyboarding skills. The same children may react positively to simply touching pictures, words, or icons on the screen. Likewise, people with disabilities who might not be able to effectively type can often point to a screen to control a computer.

Touch screens not only are easy to use but can often be used anywhere you would normally use a mouse. Simply attach the touch screen to the same computer connection you use for the mouse, and you are ready to take advantage of touch technology. Press on the screen and it is the same as holding down the mouse button. Tap twice, and it is the same as a double-click. Drag your finger around the screen and your program thinks you are dragging the mouse pointer.

As the computer continues to make headway into more areas of our lives, simple input devices—including those that use touch technology—will continue to grow as well. It may not be far in the future before we see computer control centers for our homes and cars, all controlled from a simple touch screen interface.

Touching is an intuitive way to get input from a user.

Computer-Related CTDs

When you use a computer, you perform many motions repeatedly, especially typing and moving the mouse (see Figure 10B.2). These motions can create cumulative trauma disorders, an umbrella term for a variety of injuries to the following:

- **Tendons** Tendons and their sheaths can become irritated from repeated exertion. For example, "tennis elbow" is a common, sports-related form of **tendinitis,** an inflammation of a tendon.

- **Nerves** Nerves can be damaged by repeated rubbing and squeezing. In **carpal tunnel syndrome (CTS),** the most frequent form of CTD, the nerves passing through the carpal bone—a bone in the wrist that forms a narrow tunnel for nerves to pass through—are damaged by prolonged typing with the improper wrist angle.

Figure 10B.2

Typing on a keyboard and moving a mouse can create cumulative trauma disorders such as tendinitis and carpal tunnel syndrome.

Symptoms

Cumulative trauma disorders can affect the neck, shoulders, upper back, upper arm, elbows, forearms, wrists, and fingers. Some of the early warning signs include:

- Weakness in the hands and forearms.

- Fatigue, lack of endurance, or feeling of heaviness.

- Numbness, tingling, diminished sensation, or tremors.

- Hyperawareness of hands or forearms.

- Frequent clumsiness, lack of control or coordination.

- Stiff, cramped, swollen, or cold hands.

- Difficulty opening, closing, and using hands (for example, trouble turning pages, holding a mug, or buttoning clothes).

- Tendency of the hands to fall asleep.

- Waking up with wrist pain or numb hands during early morning hours.

- Pain (achy, shooting, burning, deep) or soreness.

If you experience any of these symptoms, see a doctor immediately. Early recognition and treatment is known to reduce the severity of CTD injuries.

How Serious Are CTDs?

Cumulative trauma disorders are not life threatening, but they can lead to crippling pain and, at their worst, they can ruin careers. Programmers, writers, journalists, and other professionals who spend long hours at the keyboard have suddenly found themselves unable to continue working.

Destinations

To learn more about the anatomy, diagnosis, and surgical treatments associated with carpal tunnel syndrome, check out **http://www.sechrest. com/mmg/cts/ctsintro. html.**

Why? Although physicians can cure some CDT-related illnesses, the most serious forms lead to permanent disability. At the extreme, victims may not be able to perform common household tasks, such as cooking and cleaning.

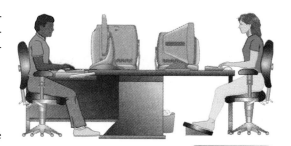

Preventing Cumulative Trauma Disorder

You can greatly reduce the risk of contracting a cumulative trauma disorder if you observe some precautions (see Figure 10B.3):

- Take frequent rest breaks and do some stretching exercises when you do.
- Maintain good posture.
- Keep your wrists in a neutral rather than twisted position, with your hands "floating" above the keyboard.
- Keep your arms and hands warm to promote good circulation.
- Don't lean on your elbows (this can irritate nerves).
- Make your elbow form a 90-degree angle. Adjust the chair and monitor height, if necessary.
- Don't let your shoulders shrug or round forward as you reach for the keyboard. Move the chair closer instead.
- Keep your back straight.
- Adjust your chair so that your thighs are parallel to the floor, and plant your feet firmly on the floor.
- When using a mouse, keep your wrist straight and avoid pressing the buttons too hard.

Accessories for CTD Prevention

To prevent CTD, consider equipping your computer system with some or all of the following:

- **Reminder software** You can install software that reminds you to take breaks. Stretch Break (*http://www. paratec.com*) pops up at an interval you specify, and an animation shows you how to perform exercises designed to reduce stress on the arms, back, legs, and waist.
- **Ergonomic keyboards** By splitting the keyboard into two panels and rotating each panel outward, ergonomic keyboards help you keep your wrists straight.
- **Speech recognition software** Advances in speech recognition make this technology a viable option, not only for people already suffering from RSI problems, but also for those who would like to avoid them.
- **Alternative pointing devices** If you believe you're experiencing discomfort due to mouse usage, consider using a trackball or a touchpad pointer.
- **Ergonomic chair** Specially-designed chairs can help you maintain proper posture (see Figure 10B.4).

Figure 10B.3

You can reduce the risk of contracting a cumulative trauma disorder if you observe some precautions such as maintaining good posture, keeping your wrists in a neutral position, and adjusting the monitor and chair height so that your elbow forms a 90-degree angle when typing at the keyboard.

Figure 10B.4

An ergonomic chair like the DuoBack by Grahl keeps pressure off the backbone by supporting each side of your back.

Destinations

Hunter Digital makes a foot-controlled mouse to prevent CTDs. To learn more about this product, check out **http://www. footmouse.com.**

Destinations

Grahl Industries **(http://www.grahl.com)** specializes in ergonomic chairs, keyboard armrests, and other aids designed to prevent RSIs.

Destinations

The Trace Center at the University of Michigan **(http://trace.wisc.edu/)** is one of the Web's leading sites concerning technology for people with disabilities.

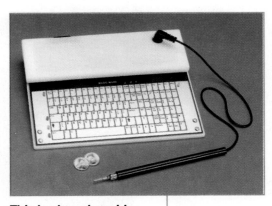

This keyboard enables people with limited dexterity to use the computer.

Improving Computer Access for People with Disabilities

For people with limited vision, hearing, or dexterity, computers are a double-edged sword. Thoughtfully-designed computer systems and software can open the door to a full participation in society, but poor designs can slam that same door shut. For people with limited or no vision, thoughtless software design can prevent such users from using the software at all. For example, one of the major online services required users to run a proprietary interface program that is installed on the subscriber's PC. The problem is, there's no way to initiate a connection without clicking an on-screen icon. All too often, programs signal important events by sounding a beep with the computer's speaker. However, people with limited or no hearing won't know that something's just happened. As blind computer programmer T.V. Raman points out, a poorly-designed feature that's inconvenient for non-disabled users can be a showstopper for people with disabilities.

As the above examples suggest, computer programs can quite often be made more accessible for people with disabilities by following a few simple design rules, which are not expensive to implement. The term **accessible software** refers to programs that are specifically designed and tested so that they can be used successfully by people with limited vision, hearing, and dexterity. For people with limited vision, it's important to enable high-contrast color options, avoid subtle visual cues, provide keyboard shortcuts for every program feature, and describe the meaning of information and cues that are presented by means of graphics. For people with limited or no hearing, it's vital to provide visual as well as auditory signals (the program should never provide information by means of sound alone). These features are quite easy to implement.

For users with severe disabilities, **assistive technologies** may be required. **Screenreaders** enable blind users to interact with GUI software to read the text in on-screen menus and dialog boxes. Special keyboards, such as In Touch System's Magic Wand keyboard, enable people with limited or no hand movement to access PCs or Macintosh computers. **Braille output devices** produced embossed Braille printouts. (Braille is a system of printing and writing for people who are blind. Characters are represented by points or dots that can be detected through the sense of touch.) Speech recognition software can be used both to control the computer and to input text. For people with severe dexterity or motion disabilities, **on-screen keyboard utilities** enable them to select keyboard characters by pointing with a wand. To relieve the tedium of picking out characters one-by-one, **word completion prediction programs,** such as Telepathic 2000 (Madentec, Inc.), use a sophisticated algorithm to try to predict the next word you will type.

MOVERS & SHAKERS

Zero-Cost Assistive Technology for the Blind

Sometimes, the latest and greatest technology isn't necessarily the best. For people who are blind or who have severely-limited vision, the graphical user interface (GUI) is nothing short of a disaster. It's very difficult to use a GUI-based interface without being able to see the visual cues, such as message boxes and alert boxes, that pop up who-knows-where on-screen. Although assistive technologies such as screenreading programs enable such users to navigate GUI environments such as Microsoft Windows, they're a pain to use. They can "read" what's on-screen by means of speech synthesis software, but all too often it's difficult to understand just what the spoken text means when it's divorced from its visual context. What's more, the better screenreaders are expensive. One of the leading programs lists for $795, which is beyond the means of many people with limited or no vision.

That's the reason T.V. Raman, an IBM programmer who has been blind since he was 14, decided to develop Emacspeak, a no-cost assistive software package that's based on some decidedly old-hat technology. Emacspeak is based on Emacs, a venerable text editing program that dates back to the 1970s. Widely used in the UNIX and Linux communities, Emacs evolved over the years into a very comprehensive utility that goes far beyond text-editing capabilities. With Emacs, you can read and send email, browse the Web with a text-only browser, and directly access thousands of text-mode programs and utilities. By means of a carefully-designed speech synthesis interface, Emacspeak enables a user to work with Emacs without having to see anything on-screen—and what's more, the context is always meaningful, thanks to Emacspeak's "auditory icons," sounds that alert the user to specific events (such as the arrival of a mail message).

Thanks to Raman's efforts and Emacspeak, thousands of people with limited or no vision are able to use the computer and participate in the emerging information economy. In addition, Emacspeak has evolved into the first no-cost assistive software platform. Coupled with the freely-distributed Linux operating system and ViaVoice speech synthesis software from IBM, which is also freely distributed, the only cost for setting up a capable assistive system is the price of an inexpensive PC—and since Emacspeak doesn't require a graphical user interface, it can run quite speedily on PCs that might otherwise wind up in landfills.

TAKEAWAY POINTS

- The symptoms of Computer Vision Syndrome (CVS) include temporary nearsightedness, blurred vision, difficulty in focusing, dry or watery eyes, headaches, and backaches.

- CVS is caused by reduced blinking frequency and the difficulty of focusing on the computer display.

- To prevent CVS, remember to blink often, reduce glare, eliminate screen flicker, balance the room's illumination, keep your screen clean, and take frequent breaks. If these measures don't work, you may need special prescription glasses.

- Cumulative trauma disorder (CTD) can be serious and pose a grave threat to public health. It involves injuries to tendons and nerves due to repetitive motions, such as typing.

- CTD symptoms include weakness in the hands and forearms, fatigue, numbness or tingling in the hands or wrist, difficulty using the hands, a tendency of the hands to fall asleep, waking up at night with numb or painful hands or wrists, and hand or wrist pain. See a doctor immediately if you have any of these symptoms.

- To prevent CTD, take breaks, watch your posture, keep your wrists straight, and adjust your chair so that your elbows form a right angle. Consider purchasing an ergonomic keyboard.

- Accessible software refers to programs that are specifically designed and tested so that they can be used successfully by people with limited vision, hearing, and dexterity. For users with severe disabilities, assistive technologies may be required. For example, screenreaders enable blind users to interact with GUI software by reading the text in on-screen menus and dialog boxes.

MODULE REVIEW

KEY TERMS AND CONCEPTS

accessible software
assistive technologies
Braille output devices
carpal tunnel syndrome (CTS)
computer vision syndrome (CVS)

cumulative trauma disorder (CTD)
on-screen keyboard utilities
refresh rate
repetitive strain injury (RSI)

screenreaders
tendinitis
word completion prediction programs

TRUE/FALSE

Indicate whether the following statements are true or false.

1. The two leading types of computer-related health risk are computer vision syndrome (CVS) and cumulative trauma disorder (CTD).

2. One of the causes of CVS is radiation emitted by monitors.

3. When people are staring at a computer screen, they blink only one-third as often as normal.

4. CTDs cannot be prevented.

5. Carpal tunnel syndrome (CTS) is the most common form of CTD.

6. Extreme cases of cumulative trauma disorders can result in permanent disabilities.

7. Ergonomic keyboards don't really help reduce CTDs.

8. An ergonomic chair can help you maintain proper posture.

9. Alternative pointing devices are available that can reduce CTDs related to mouse usage.

10. Computer programs can be made more accessible for people with disabilities by following a few simple design rules, but these are expensive to implement.

MATCHING

Match each key term from the left column to the most accurate definition in the right column.

_____ 1. computer vision syndrome

_____ 2. cumulative trauma disorder

_____ 3. refresh rate

_____ 4. carpal tunnel syndrome

_____ 5. accessible software

a. this refers to the number of times per second that the video adapter refreshes the screen display

b. an eyesight disorder that results from focusing on a computer screen for long periods of time

c. the most common type of repetitive strain injury

d. this refers to programs that are specifically designed and tested so that they can be used successfully by people with limited vision, hearing, and dexterity

e. an injury involving damage to sensitive nerve tissue due to motions repeated thousands of times daily

MULTIPLE CHOICE

Circle the letter of the correct choice for each of the following.

1. If you work with a computer more than three hours per day, what are your chances of having eye problems related to computer use?
   a. 30 percent
   b. 50 percent
   c. 73 percent
   d. 90 percent

2. Which of the following is not a safeguard against CVS?
   a. reduce screen glare
   b. blink more often
   c. remove your glasses
   d. clean your screen

3. Which of the following is not a potential treatment for computer vision syndrome?
   a. consider a magnification system
   b. get a glare shield
   c. reduce the size of your computer screen
   d. try a computer eye wash

4. What does the acronym RSI stand for?
   a. repetitive strain injury
   b. recent systematic injury
   c. random symbolic industry
   d. repetition straining injury

5. CTD disorders have increased what percentage in the past decade?
   a. 150 percent
   b. 400 percent
   c. 800 percent
   d. 900 percent

6. Which of the following is the leading cause of carpal tunnel syndrome?
   a. prolonged typing with an improper wrist angle
   b. not using mice and other pointing devices
   c. using too much pressure when typing
   d. typing with only two fingers

7. Cumulative trauma disorders are an umbrella term for injuries to which of the following?
   a. fingers and wrists
   b. nerves and joints
   c. tendons and soft tissues
   d. tendons and nerves

8. Which of the following is not an area normally affected by CTDs?
   a. ankles
   b. upper back
   c. wrists
   d. shoulders

9. What is a good way to reduce the risk of developing a CTD?
   a. Balance the illumination between the ambient light in the room and the monitor.
   b. Maintain good posture while working on the computer.
   c. Back up your computer data often.
   d. Reduce the number of colors used in computer displays.

10. Which piece of equipment helps keep your wrists straight?
    a. ergonomic chair
    b. trackball
    c. touchpad
    d. ergonomic keyboard

FILL-IN

In the blank provided, write the correct answer for each of the following.

1. Symptoms of _____ include temporary nearsightedness, blurred vision, headaches, and dry or watery eyes.

2. _____ is caused by constantly-repeated motions and exertions that eventually cause pain and may lead to physical impairment.

3. A(n) _____ is an accessory you place over your monitor to avoid reflections.

4. _____ is the most common CTD.

5. _____ are specially designed chairs that can help you maintain proper posture.

6. _____ is an inflammation of a tendon.

7. To eliminate screen flicker, make sure you use the maximum _____ that's supported by your video card and monitor.

8. _____ enable blind users to interact with GUI software by reading the text in on-screen menus and dialog boxes.

9. For people with severe dexterity or motion disabilities, _____ enable them to select keyboard characters by pointing with a wand.

10. _____ use a sophisticated algorithm to try to predict the next word you will type.

SHORT ANSWER

On a separate sheet of paper, answer the following questions.

1. Identify the two major categories of medical problems associated with computer use.

2. What are the symptoms associated with computer vision syndrome? Can they become permanent?

3. What self-remedies can be used to treat CVS?

4. If your efforts to reduce CVS do not work, what other remedies are available?

5. What areas of the body can be affected by cumulative trauma disorder?

6. What are the symptoms of cumulative trauma disorder? What should you do if you experience any of the symptoms?

7. What precautions can be taken to reduce the risk of developing a CTD?

8. In what ways can employers be active in addressing CTD-related issues?

9. How do ergonomic keyboards work? What benefits do they offer?

10. What types of accessories are available to help prevent CTDs?

10C

MODULE

OUTLINE

WHAT YOU WILL LEARN . . .

When you have finished reading this module, you will be able to:

1. Describe the traditional information technology (IT) career path.
2. Explain the differences among computer science (CS), systems engineering, and computer information science (CIS) curricula in colleges and universities.
3. List the two settings in which most IT workers find employment.
4. List at least three typical job titles in IS departments and vendor companies.
5. List at least three business skills IS managers want in new IT workers.
6. List at least three technical skills currently in high demand.
7. Discuss the positive and negative aspects of certification.

In the coming years, companies will need many more skilled information technology (IT) workers than they are likely to find. According to current United States government projections, by 2003 companies will have purchased 800 million computers, at a cost of $7.5 trillion, to create the information systems they need to remain competitive. These companies will create an estimated 95,000 new information technology jobs each year, creating a huge demand for new, skilled IT personnel. By 2005, the service sector will need 158 percent more systems analysts, 142 percent more computer scientists and engineers, and 37 percent more programmers. But United States colleges and universities are turning out only about 50,000 graduates with computer science, systems engineering, or computer information systems degrees.

What this means for you is opportunity. If you have the right background and skills, you can find a job in the IT industry. With the high demand for skilled personnel, salaries are rising off the charts. Students straight out of college computer science, systems engineering, and computer information systems programs are getting job offers in the $40,000 to $50,000 range. In Annapolis, MD, a high school student with UNIX network administration skills was offered—and accepted—a job with a $70,000 salary.

Of course, as with any career, computing-related jobs aren't for everyone. IT careers are a particularly poor choice for anyone who dislikes learning new knowledge and skills: change, not continuity, is the norm. And today's job market has no such thing as job security. In a computer-related field, you will probably work in as many as five or six different jobs before you retire.

Is a career in information technology for you? In this section, you'll take a closer look at the traditional path to the best IT careers, which normally require (at a minimum) a four-year college degree. Later in this module, you'll learn about new IT career paths that have been created by the strong demand for skilled IT workers as well as rapid technological change. As you'll see, more ways than ever are available to pursue a career in information technology.

TRADITIONAL INFORMATION TECHNOLOGY (IT) CAREER PATHS

Ten years ago, most people got into IT careers by obtaining a computer-related bachelor's degree and landing a job with a corporate **information systems (IS) department** (see Table 10C.1) or a software development firm (see Table 10C.2), also called a **vendor.** The four-year college degree was and is a prerequisite for the best jobs. In a recent survey, 83 percent of surveyed U.S. corporations stated that they required a four-year college degree for entry-level programming jobs.

Before the era of corporate downsizing and dramatic reductions in job security, IT workers could remain with a firm for many years, perhaps until retirement. They could climb the corporate ladder by earning advanced degrees in their fields or by moving into management.

To stay on top of current trends, IT employees also consulted trade and professional journals and attended professional conferences. Workers with business savvy and good communication skills could move into manage-

In traditional career paths, IT professionals could climb the corporate ladder by earning advanced degrees or by moving into management.

Typical Job Titles and Responsibilities in a Corporate IS Department			Table 10C.1

Job Title	Responsibilities	Salary Range
Chief Information Officer (CIO)	Senior-level management position which defines the IS department's mission, objectives, and budgets, and creates a strategic plan for the enterprise's information systems	$120,000 to $300,000
Director of Computer Operations	Middle management position which emphasizes the overall system reliability	$70,000 to $100,000
Director of Network Services	Middle management position which emphasizes the overall network reliability	$75,000 to $125,000
Network Engineer	Installs, maintains, and supports computer networks, interacts with users, and troubleshoots problems	$40,000 to $90,000
Systems Programmer/ Administrator	Installs, maintains, and supports the operating system	$40,000 to $90,000
Client/Server Manager	Installs, maintains, and supports client/server applications	$70,000 to $90,000
Systems Analyst	Interacts with users and application developers to design information systems	$50,000 to $90,000
Programmer/ Analyst	Designs, codes, and tests software according to specifications	$40,000 to $75,000
Programmer	Writes code according to specifications	$40,000 to $60,000

ment. If employees needed to acquire additional skills, the employer might arrange (and pay) for additional training. As you'll learn in this module, the traditional IT career path still exists, but it's changing. Let's look first at the components of a traditional IT career.

Training for Traditional IT Careers

Reflecting the long-standing split in computing between science and business, education for traditional IT careers has been divided between two very different academic departments: computer science and computer information systems. In recent years, systems engineering has offered a middle-ground approach, offering the rigor of an engineering approach combined with a real-world focus on the realities of information systems in contemporary business.

Computer Science

Computer science (CS) uses the principles of scientific and engineering research to improve computing. In general, computer science departments emphasize the theoretical rather than the practical aspects of computing,

Table 10C.2

Typical Job Titles and Responsibilities in a Software Development Firm		
Job Title	**Responsibilities**	**Salary Range**
Director of Research and Development	Senior-level management position in charge of all product development activities	$140,000 to $200,000
Software Architect	Computer scientists who are challenged to create new, cutting-edge technologies	$95,000 to $150,000
Software Engineer	Manages the details of software development projects	$75,000 to $125,000
System Engineer	Assists the sales staff by working current and prospective customers, and gives technical presentations and supports products on-site	$55,000 to $100,000
Software Developer	Develops new programs under the direction of the software architect	$50,000 to $75,000
Customer Support Technician	Provides assistance to customers who need help with products	$40,000 to $90,000

and they focus on cutting-edge technology and fundamental principles rather than teaching marketable skills. At most colleges and universities, computer science programs grew out of mathematics programs and are often housed in the engineering school.

Computer science training is highly technical and usually involves several semesters of higher mathematics (such as calculus), as well as training in several programming languages and theoretical topics such as programming language structure, advanced computer graphics, artificial intelligence, and relational database design. Qualified CS graduates find that their theoretical and analytical skills make them attractive for jobs in cutting-edge software development firms. The skills of these graduates may also be needed by IS departments that are working with advanced technology or developing software in-house.

Computer Information Systems

Figure 10C.1

With their business savvy and communication skills, CIS graduates are more likely to find jobs in corporate IS departments.

Generally located in business schools, **computer information systems (CIS)** departments are often the mirror image of the CS department. They're focused on the practical rather than the theoretical and emphasize the skills that businesses need right now. Apart from coursework in programming and systems analysis, skills such as business smarts (including coursework in finance and marketing), first-rate communication skills, and the interpersonal skills needed for effective teamwork and leadership are strongly emphasized. With their business savvy and communication skills, CIS graduates are more likely to find jobs in corporate IS departments, but software development firms also need IT personnel who have excellent communication skills as well as technical ability (see Figure 10C.1).

Systems Engineering

The engineering discipline called **systems engineering** applies the scientific method to creating and maintaining quality systems, whether in business or in industry. Unlike other engineering disciplines, systems engineering looks at the whole picture, including the people and the organization as well as the technologies. The principles of systems engineering are useful for software development, systems analysis, and program development. Systems engineering students typically learn strong project management skills and its graduates are in high demand.

Electrical Engineering

The engineering discipline called **electrical engineering (EE)** offers a strong focus on digital circuit design as well as cutting-edge communication technologies. It's the major choice if your interests lean more towards hardware than software.

Traditional Methods of Continuing Education

In traditional IT careers, professionals kept up with new technology by going to seminars, subscribing to computer periodicals, attending conferences and shows, and actively participating in a professional association.

Training Seminars

Computer-related seminars, usually lasting from one day to one week, are widely available. Typically, they are presented by the developer of a new hardware or software product or by a company specializing in training for a new technology (see Figure 10C.2).

Traditionally, companies view formal training as a wise investment and pay for training seminars. According to one study, a single hour of focused, professional instruction is worth six employee hours of ad hoc learning. In 1997, U.S. companies spent $5.4 billion on technology training.

Computer Magazines, Newspapers, and Journals

Computer-related trade journals are an indispensable resource for IT professionals. Some, such as *Computerworld*, cover the entire spectrum of computer issues. Others are aimed at a specific part of the computer industry, such as technology management (*Information Week*), networking (*LAN Times*), or office automation (*InfoSystems*). Over a hundred of these types of periodicals are in print. If you have a particular area of interest, you can probably find a periodical that reports fast-breaking developments in your field.

Conferences and Shows

One way to keep in touch with your profession is to attend conferences and trade shows. **Trade shows** are annual meetings in which computer product manufacturers, designers, and dealers showcase their products. Job fairs and on-the-spot interviews provide many incentives for job seekers. Additionally, training seminars and product showcases provide many opportunities for skill and knowledge development.

The largest computer-related trade show is the annual COMDEX show in Las Vegas, Nevada. With 4,000 members of the press and nearly one-quarter

Destinations

Most computer industry trade journals are published on the Internet as well as in print media. At their Web site, you can read the current issue, and you can also search the publications' archives. Leading sites include CMPnet at **http://www. cmpnet.com** (which contains **Byte, EE Times, Information Week, LAN Times, UnixWorld,** and many more).

Figure 10C.2

Typically, computer seminars are presented by the developer of a new hardware or software product or by a company specializing in training for a new technology.

Destinations

Add TV to your list of bona fide ways to learn more about computers and technology. There's an entire channel devoted to the industry called TechTV. The channel features shows on the Internet, cybercrime, technology news, and new products, to name a few. A listing of shows, as well as useful, non-broadcast information, can be found at the channel's Web site, **http://www.techtv.com.**

COMDEX is an annual event held in various locations around the world. To learn more about it, visit their Web site at http://www.comdex.com.

million attendees present, COMDEX provides the perfect opportunity to roll out new products. COMDEX also sponsors regional events, which are also well attended. Growing in importance is NetWorld + InterOP, a spring Las Vegas show that focuses on Internet and networking technologies.

Professional Organizations

Joining one of the many professional associations can help you keep up with your area of interest, as well as provide valuable contacts for your career. Some associations have local chapters, and most offer publications, seminars, training, and conferences for its members. Here are some of the most important organizations:

- **Association for Computing Machinery (ACM)** Focusing on computer science, this organization features many special-interest groups (SIGs) in such areas as databases, artificial intelligence, microcomputers, and computer graphics. Visit ACM's Web site at **http://www.acm.org.**

- **Association for Women in Computing (AWC)** This professional organization is devoted to promoting women in computing (**http://www.awc-hq.org**).

- **Association of Internet Professionals (AIP)** This is the premier association for Internet professionals (**http://www.association.org**).

- **Data Processing Management Association (DPMA)** This is the premier organization for CIS personnel and managers.

- **Network Professional Association (NPA)** This organization focuses on the professional advancement of networking experts and offers a non-vendor-based skills certification program (**http://www.npa.org**).

Jobs for Nondegreed IT Workers

In the traditional IT job picture, workers who lack four-year college degrees generally find that they can't get the best IT jobs, such as programming and system analyst positions. Nondegreed candidates who possessed the needed qualifications, however, could find jobs as data entry clerks, help desk technicians, and technical writers. As you'll learn in the next section, this picture is changing.

NEW INFORMATION TECHNOLOGY (IT) CAREER PATHS

IT careers are changing, driven by both rapid technological change and shifts in the nature of today's businesses. Increasingly, a four-year college degree isn't sufficient to convince prospective employers that would-be employees possess their needed skills, since many of these skills aren't yet widely taught in colleges and universities.

As you'll see in this section, these skills include communication skills, business savvy, and technical skills in fast-breaking areas such as the Internet and Microsoft Windows NT. Some companies are hiring skilled applicants who don't have a four-year college degree, if they can demonstrate that they possess the needed skills. In especially tight job markets, companies have even hired students who are still in high school. But by lacking degrees, these employees are at risk of losing their jobs should their technological skills become obsolete. Nonetheless, most IT jobs still require a four-year college degree.

The changing patterns of employment have also affected IT careers. Today, IT workers can't rely on a company's paternalism to guide their career development, and they can't even count on keeping their jobs. Corporate downsizing, mergers, and acquisitions may suddenly put you out of work. For this reason, IT workers must become savvy managers of their own careers. If you choose an IT career, you may have as many as five or more jobs before you retire. And you may forsake the job market altogether, preferring—as increasing numbers of IT professionals do—to work as an independent contractor or consultant. Whichever path you choose, it's increasingly the worker's responsibility to obtain the training needed to keep up with fast-breaking technological change.

Sought-After Business Skills

Ten years ago, most IT jobs were internally focused. IT professionals worked inside companies, where they created and supported computer services such as payroll and inventory systems. But this picture is changing—and it's changing radically.

Today, driven by new network-based information systems, jobs increasingly combine an internal and an external focus. IT professionals are expected to work with a company's external partners and often with customers, or partnering in teams made up of people from different divisions of the enterprise (see Figure 10C.3). Rather than performing a specific function, like the proverbial cog in the corporate wheel, they're much more likely to work on a series of projects in which they'll use differing skills. For all these reasons, today's businesses are looking for workers with the following "soft" skills in addition to "hard" technical knowledge:

Figure   10C.3

IT professionals work in teams with other professionals from finance, marketing, and other corporate divisions.

- **Teamwork**   Increasingly, IT personnel are working in teams with workers from the finance, marketing, and other corporate divisions. IT workers need to appreciate the varying intellectual styles, work effectively in a team environment, and understand business perspectives.

- **Project management**   The ability to plan and budget a project—especially using project management software—is an advantage in hiring decisions.

- **Communication**   Every employee needs communication skills now, even those who formerly worked internally and seldom had contact with people outside their departments. You'll need excellent writing and interpersonal skills, including the ability to give presentations by using presentation graphics software.

- **Business savvy**   Information technology is now part of most companies' strategic planning, and IT employees are expected to possess some knowledge of business. The wise student also takes courses in general business subjects, including finance and marketing.

Older, experienced IT workers who suffer job losses due to downsizing may have difficulty finding employment if they do not possess these skills. In the past, you could focus on technology and ignore business and communication skills, but that's no longer true.

SPOTLIGHT

JOB SEARCHING ON THE INTERNET

▶How would you like to send your résumé to more than 52 million potential readers? Afraid you can't afford the postage? Don't despair: you can accomplish this very feat by using any number of online services that post your résumé on the Internet for potential employers to view.

One such company is Online Career Center, Inc. (OCC) of Indianapolis, Indiana. OCC is the Internet's leading employment Web site: more than 1.6 million visitors access OCC's job listing and résumé databases every month. The database is searchable by keyword, industry, company, or geographic location to assist both employers and applicants in using the Internet effectively. More than 115,000 current job listings are available, as well as company information and profiles with hyperlinks back to the corporate Web sites.

Corporate recruiters launched OCC in 1992 to reduce recruitment costs, thus allowing them to play an active role in the design, development, and direction of online services for recruitment and human resource management. In the years since it was launched, thousands of companies have joined OCC.

Companies that have joined OCC can run recruitment advertising, place their company profiles, and also gain access to a database of over 150,000 current résumés. Employers can submit ads or post information in any number of ways. The easiest method is to directly access the OCC Web site, but employers can also contact OCC by email, phone, fax, or regular mail. Like most newspaper classified services, OCC also handles blind ads on behalf of member companies that would rather remain anonymous initially.

Company recruiters access the center's database to post job openings or sort through résumés by region, profession, or other criteria. Not limited to computer industry jobs, the career service is used by more than 12,000 leading companies.

The services offered by OCC are free for a job seeker with a computer. All that's necessary is to visit the OCC Web site at **http://www.occ.com/.** Job seekers who do not have access to a computer can mail a typed résumé to Online Résumé Service, 1713 Hemlock Lane, Plainfield, IN 46168. For a small fee, a résumé of up to three pages (including a cover letter) will be posted on the Internet for a full year.

OCC also offers job seekers a powerful feature: if you are looking for a specific type of job, you can set up personalized search agents. You simply select the criteria you are looking for in a job, and then your search agent will keep you informed of any new openings that are posted. The agent constantly searches OCC's job listing database and will send out notices on a daily basis.

Because the Internet is worldwide, OCC's services are also available worldwide, with a strong presence in Canada, Europe, Asia, Australia, and Pacific Rim countries. OCC is also available at virtually every college in America, as well as at colleges and universities in many foreign countries.

Popular job search wisdom claims that networking is everything. With the Internet and companies such as OCC, this advice takes on a whole new meaning.

Sought-After Technology Skills

Businesses are also demanding new types of skills from their employees. Here's what's emerging as of this writing:

- **Networking** Skills related to networking include familiarity with Ethernet, TCP/IP (Internet protocols), and LAN administration.

- **Microsoft Windows NT** Projected sales of NT Workstation show steep increases, rising from 7 million units sold in 1997 to a projected 44.6 million in 2000.

- **UNIX** Despite the success of Windows NT, UNIX isn't going away. A strong demand exists for IT workers skilled in UNIX operating system configuration, maintenance, UNIX networking, and UNIX system programming.

- **TCP/IP** Knowledge of the protocols underlying the Internet are in strong demand, both for external Web servers and for internal intranets.

New Jobs in Information Technology		Table 10C.3
Job Title	**Responsibilities**	
Interactive digital media specialist	Uses multimedia software to create engaging presentations, including animation and video	
Webmaster	Designs and maintains a Web server and related database servers	
Web application engineer	Designs, develops, tests, and documents new Web-based services for Web sites	
Web specialist	Works with internal and external customers to create high-quality content pages for Web sites	

- **Oracle**   Companies are looking for workers who have experience working with this company's products, including the Oracle relational database and client/server application tools.

- **C++**   This object-oriented programming language is the language of choice for cutting-edge software development, both among vendors (software publishers) and corporate development shops.

- **Microsoft Visual BASIC**   Rapid application development and code reusability make this language a winner for quick solutions.

Although a four-year degree in CS or CIS may fail to give you some of these desirable skills, the best preparation for a successful IT career still involves the invaluable theoretical background you will get from a four-year college degree.

NEW TECHNOLOGIES, NEW JOBS

New technology brings not just more jobs, but new *types* of jobs (see Table 10C.3). For example, Web page design involves technical skills and knowledge in areas such as HTTP, HTML, CGI programming, and server configuration. But that's not enough. Increasingly, companies are looking for **Webmasters** (Web server managers and content developers) who understand marketing, advertising, and graphic design. What's required is not only technical skills and business smarts but artistic sensitivity, including some background in the aesthetics of design and color, coupled with a good deal of creativity (see Figure 10C.4).

Although a bachelor's degree is still a prerequisite for IT careers in most companies, employers are increasingly recognizing that a degree alone may not guarantee that a new employee possesses the needed skills. One reason: many of these new jobs are inherently cross-disciplinary, involving artistic or communication skills as well as top-notch technical ability. Existing CS and CIS programs may produce graduates who lack creativity, marketing savvy, graphics design experience, or communication abilities. For this reason, many companies are hiring students who have taken many computer courses but possess degrees in other fields, such as design, marketing, or English.

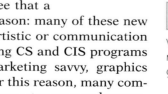

Figure   10C.4

Webmasters must understand marketing, advertising, and graphic design.

Certification

The rapid change in information technology is creating a demand for new ways to ensure that employment applicants possess their claimed skills. In

Table 10C.4

Selected Certification Programs

Certification Program	Description
Microsoft Certified Systems and Engineer (MCSE)	Microsoft Windows NT Server, BackOffice applications, operating system and network configuration and maintenance as well as LAN-based client/server development (Microsoft Corporation)
Microsoft Certified Systems Engineer (MCSE) + Internet	Microsoft Windows NT Server configuration and maintenance for Internet and intranet sites (Microsoft Corporation)
Microsoft Certified Solution Developer (MCSD)	Programming and application development with Microsoft development tools, such as Visual BASIC (Microsoft Corporation)
Certified NetWare Engineer (CNE)	Novell networking and NetWare network operating systems (Novell Corporation)
Certified Java Programmer	Programming in Java (Sun Microsystems)
Certified Java Developer	Programming and application development in Java (Sun Microsystems)

traditional IT careers, the four-year college degree assured a certain level of competence, but that's no longer entirely true. Many of the skills today's companies need are so new that they are not yet widely taught in colleges and universities (which often need one or two years to alter their curricula). Certification is increasingly seen as a way that employers can assure themselves that newly-hired workers can do the necessary tasks.

In brief, **certification** is a skills-and-knowledge assessment process organized by computer industry vendors (and sometimes by professional associations). To obtain a certificate, choose your preferred method of training. You can either take courses at a college or a private training center, or study on your own using vendor-approved books and CD-ROM materials (see Table 10C.4). When you're ready, you will take a tough, comprehensive examination. If you pass, you get the certificate. Unlike a college degree, the certificate isn't good for life. To retain certification, you may need to take brush-up courses and exams periodically, sometimes as often as every six months.

Benefits of Certification

What's the payoff for job applications? A certificate won't guarantee a job or even higher pay, but it does provide a benchmark that enables prospective employers to assess your skills in an applicant pool. In areas of high demand, certification can translate into an increase of 10 to 15 percent in initial salary offers. Applicants who possess the Microsoft Certified Systems Engineer (MCSE) certificate may gain as much as $10,000 in starting salary.

What's the payoff for employers? Although the effect of certification hasn't been rigorously studied by independent investigators, vendors and trainers claim that employers who hire certified employees have less downtime and lower IT costs.

Risks of Certification

Certification entails some risks for employees and employers alike. The reason lies in the nature of the certification process, which emphasizes a form of learning that is both narrow (focused on a specific technology) and deep (rigorous and thorough).

For employees, certification requires that you devote a great deal of time and effort on a specific vendor's technology. But changing technology may make vendor-specific skills less marketable. If you're certified as a Novell NetWare technician, for example, you won't impress a prospective employer who's running a Windows NT network. (Windows NT has gained considerable market share at the expense of Novell's NetWare systems.) If you make a bad bet on which certificate to pursue, you could wind up with excellent skills in a technology that's considered to be obsolete.

For employers, hiring people with narrow training is a risk. Specifically, narrowly-trained people may not be able to adjust to rapidly-changing technology. That's why it's a good idea to take as many CS and CIS courses as you can. With a solid theoretical foundation, you can learn new skills throughout your career. In itself, certification isn't a ticket to a high-paying job or a satisfying career. You'll prove most attractive to employers if you combine certification with a good college record, communication skills, and business courses. In addition, just having one skill isn't enough. Some companies expect employees to possess strong skills in as many as four or five areas.

THE EFFECT OF COMPUTERS ON OVERALL EMPLOYMENT

Although computers are creating new job opportunities, they're also shifting the labor demand toward skilled workers, particularly those with computer skills. As a result, skilled workers earn more, while the wages paid to unskilled workers have stagnated over the past twenty years. Partly as a consequence, the gap between the rich and the poor has widened as educated, skilled workers have taken advantage of new, technology-based opportunities. Technology isn't the only cause of this trend; it's also fueled by the exodus of low-paying, unskilled jobs to foreign countries, where labor is cheaper. But the fact remains that computer and information literacy have never been more important to a person's future.

Technology is also eliminating some jobs by automating them out of existence. One purpose of advanced technology is to free humans from drudgery and make work more efficient, but as a result, fewer workers may be required. For instance, computer-guided robots are taking over many manufacturing jobs that people once held (see Figure 10C.5). This process is called **automation** (the replacement of human workers by machines).

The jobs most likely to be eliminated by computers involve repetitive, semiskilled tasks. For example, the U.S. Postal Service eliminated nearly 100,000 jobs formerly held by workers who read and sorted envelopes. Today, automated equipment does most of the work without human intervention.

When advancing technology makes an entire job category obsolete, **structural unemployment** has occurred. Structural unemployment differs from the normal up-and-down cycles of layoffs and rehires. People who lose jobs because of structural unemployment are not going to get them back. Their only option is to retrain themselves to work in other careers.

Who will survive (and flourish) in a computer-driven economy? The answer is simple: the survivors will be people who are highly-educated, who know that education is a lifelong process, and who adapt quickly to change. Just consider this: according to the author of a recent book on career survival, half of all the jobs that will be available in ten years do not even exist today.

Figure 10C.5

Computer-guided robots are handling many manufacturing jobs that people once held.

CURRENTS

Is There an Acute Shortage of IT Workers—or Just Rampant Age Discrimination?

It's a story you'll hear quite often in Silicon Valley. A 45-year-old computer programmer lost his job at a major software firm, but before he was let go, he was asked to train his successor: a 22-year-old programmer from India, who was residing in the United States temporarily on an H1-B visa. Created by the U.S. Congress in response to the software industry's concerns about severe shortages of IT workers, the H1-B program enables qualified technical professionals from other countries to work in the United States temporarily.

Critics of the program charge that the worker shortage wouldn't exist if companies were willing to retrain older workers, and that the H1-B program facilitates what amounts to widespread age discrimination in the software industry. Countering this charge, industry spokespersons insist that it's far too expensive and time-consuming to retrain older programmers who know nothing about today's cutting-edge technologies, such as C++, Java, and Web database interfaces. If they prefer younger programmers, these spokespeople insist, it's simply because younger programmers are far more likely to have the skills they need.

Who's right? In the absence of reliable statistics, it's difficult to know for sure. According to one study, the unemployment rate for IT workers aged 50 and over is an appalling 17 percent. However, another study came up with conflicting findings, and suggested that the unemployment rate for older IT workers is in line with the overall U.S. workforce figures. Another study found that, after twenty years, fewer than one out of every five programmers were still working in the profession—but this doesn't necessarily mean that these workers were let go. They may have moved into management, changed careers, or opened consulting businesses. Software industry spokeswoman Susan Marshall scoffs at the age discrimination allegation, noting that she isn't aware of a single successful age discrimination lawsuit brought against the software industry. But this claim isn't convincing. Many older workers find to their dismay that it is very difficult (indeed, nearly impossible) to win an age discrimination lawsuit.

The statistics don't tell the full story, but there's plenty of anecdotal evidence highlighting the difficulties older workers face. High-flying software and e-commerce companies tend to prefer younger, unmarried workers who have the enthusiasm and stamina to put in 80-hour work weeks. In such companies, workers with homes and families may be perceived to be something other than completely dedicated. In addition, some of these companies are run by twenty-something millionaires who don't feel comfortable interviewing job candidates twice their age. After all, why hire older workers when talented, young H1-B workers are available—and will accept wages that are 30 percent lower than those received by U.S. workers? In addition, H1-B workers aren't very likely to protest poor working conditions or cause problems for management. Otherwise, if they lose their jobs, they will very likely be required to leave the United States.

The debate concerning the H1-B program will continue, but there's one conclusion that you'll be wise to draw from this discussion: if you're interested in a career in the IT industry, you should be aware that today's hot skill set could be tomorrow's prescription for unemployment. You won't be able to rest on your achievements in college. Instead, you'll need to dedicate yourself to lifelong learning—and your career survival may depend on your ability to sense where technology's headed and what you should learn to make yourself indispensable.

TAKEAWAY POINTS

- Traditionally, information technology (IT) careers required a four-year college degree in computer science (CS) or computer information systems (CIS). Employment was long-term and employers provided training if additional skills were needed.

- Training in computer science emphasizes the theoretical and cutting-edge aspects of computing. Training in computer information systems emphasizes the more practical aspects of computing in business settings.

- IT workers typically find employment in corporate information systems (IS) departments and vendor companies.

- Today, recruiters are looking for teamwork, project management skills, communication skills, and business savvy as well as technical skills.

- Recruiters are looking for workers with knowledge and experience of networking, Microsoft Windows NT, UNIX, C++, and the Internet.

- Certification provides one means of demonstrating your skills to an employer, but it shouldn't take the place of a sound background in computer science or computer information systems.

MODULE REVIEW

KEY TERMS AND CONCEPTS

automation	electrical engineering (EE)	systems engineering
certification	information systems (IS)	trade shows
computer information systems	department	vendor
(CIS)	structural unemployment	Webmasters
computer science (CS)		

TRUE/FALSE

Indicate whether the following statements are true or false.

1. Ten years ago, most people in IT careers had a bachelor's degree in a computer-related field and got a job in a corporate information systems department.

2. Today, IT professionals are guaranteed to climb the corporate ladder if they earn advanced degrees in their field.

3. Traditionally, IT careers have been divided between two academic departments: computer engineering and business technology.

4. Most companies today do not recognize the value of sending their employees to training seminars.

5. One of the ways IT professionals keep up with new technology is through reading computer magazines and journals.

6. Changes in IT careers are being driven by rapid technological change and changes in the way organizations conduct business.

7. In today's business environment, you can still rely on the company you work for to guide your career development.

8. Today, a college degree is no longer a prerequisite for IT careers in most companies.

9. Hot skills related to networking include Ethernet, TCP/IP, and LAN administration.

10. Certification is viewed by many as a way that employers can assure themselves that new employees can perform all necessary tasks.

MATCHING

Match each key term from the left column to the most accurate definition in the right column.

_____ 1. computer science

_____ 2. project management

_____ 3. vendor

_____ 4. systems engineering

_____ 5. electrical engineering

_____ 6. Association for Computing Machinery

_____ 7. Webmasters

_____ 8. certification

_____ 9. automation

_____ 10. structural unemployment

a. an organization featuring special interest groups in areas such as databases, microcomputers, and computer graphics

b. this applies the scientific method to creating and maintaining quality systems

c. the replacement of human workers by machines

d. Web server managers and content developers

e. a software development firm, for one

f. this uses the principles of scientific and engineering research to improve computing

g. the ability to plan and budget a project

h. situation when advancing technology makes an entire job category obsolete

i. a skills and knowledge assessment process organized by computer industry vendors

j. this offers a strong focus on digital circuit design as well as cutting-edge communication technologies

MULTIPLE CHOICE

Circle the letter of the correct choice for each of the following.

1. Which of the following characteristics is not true of the traditional career path in information technology (IT)?
   a. A computer-related bachelor's degree was a must.
   b. IT employees who had business savvy and good communication skills could move into management.
   c. If one wanted a successful career in IT, it was important not to stay with any one company for very long.
   d. To keep up with trends, IT professionals read professional journals and attended conferences.

2. Which of the following is not a typical job title in a corporate IS department?
   a. Director of Computer Operations
   b. Software Architect
   c. Network Engineer
   d. Programmer/Analyst

3. Which of the following is not a typical job title in a software development firm?
   a. Director of Research and Development
   b. Software Engineer
   c. Customer Support Technician
   d. Client/Server Manager

4. Which of the following is not associated with computer science departments?

a. CS departments are focused on the theoretical, rather than the practical, aspects of computing.
b. CS departments are focused on the practical, rather than the theoretical, aspects of computing.
c. CS graduates are more likely than CIS graduates to find jobs in cutting-edge software development firms.
d. CS uses the principles of scientific and engineering research to improve computing.

5. Which of the following is a traditional method of continuing education?
   a. conferences
   b. project management
   c. professional organizations
   d. a and c

6. Which of the following is not a professional organization designed to help IT professionals keep up with their areas of interest?
   a. Association for Computers and Machines (AC&M)
   b. Data Processing Management Association (DPMA)
   c. Association for Women in Computing (AWC)
   d. Association for Computing Machinery (ACM)

7. Today's businesses are looking for employees with which of the following "soft" skills?
   a. project management
   b. C++
   c. networking
   d. TCP/IP

8. Which of the following is one of the new, hot technological skills businesses are demanding of employees?
   a. certification
   b. Windows NT
   c. Visual Oracle
   d. Linux

9. Which of the following is not a new job in information technology?
   a. Webmaster
   b. Web specialist
   c. Systems analyst
   d. Interactive digital media specialist

10. Which of the following is a certification program?
    a. Association of Computer Machinery Certificate
    b. Certified NetWare Engineer
    c. Macintosh Certified Solution Developer
    d. Certified BASIC Programmer

FILL-IN

In the blank provided, write the correct answer for each of the following.

1. Many years ago, most people got into IT careers by obtaining a computer-related degree and getting a job with a corporate _____.

2. _____ departments emphasize the theoretical rather than the practical aspects of computing.

3. _____ departments emphasize business coursework, interpersonal skills, and communications skills.

4. The premier organization for CIS personnel and managers is the _____.

5. _____ are annual meetings in which computer product manufacturers, designers, and dealers showcase their products.

6. The engineering discipline called _____ applies the scientific method to creating and maintaining quality systems, whether in business or in industry.

7. When it comes to Web design, companies are increasingly looking for _____ who understand marketing, advertising, and graphic design.

8. _____ is a skills and knowledge assessment process that is organized by computer industry vendors.

9. The process in which computers replace human workers is called _____.

10. When advancing technology makes an entire job category obsolete, _____ has occurred.

SHORT ANSWER

On a separate sheet of paper, answer the following questions.

1. Describe the characteristics of the traditional IT career path? How does it differ from the IT career path today?

2. What are some of the typical job titles and responsibilities in a corporate IS department?

3. What are some of the typical job titles and responsibilities in a software development firm?

4. What are some of the basic differences between the computer science and computer information systems departments?

5. Describe in detail some of the traditional methods associated with continuing education.

6. What are some of the ways in which IT careers are changing? What are the factors behind the changes?

7. What kinds of business and technology skills are many of today's employers looking for?

8. Describe some of the typical job titles and responsibilities associated with the newest jobs in information technology.

9. What is certification? What are its benefits and risks?

10. What kind of effect are computers having on employment overall?

10D

MODULE

OUTLINE

WHAT YOU WILL LEARN . . .

After you have finished reading this module, you will be able to:

1. Describe the two trends currently driving the expansion of computers and networks throughout society.
2. Discuss how computers will change if these two trends remain in effect.
3. State the current status of efforts to endow computers with some or all attributes of human intelligence.
4. Summarize the achievements in artificial intelligence (AI) research.

What will computers be like in the future? It's easy to predict the future: the hard part is in getting it right, particularly where technology is concerned. Past predictions don't offer much comfort. In 1876, a Western Union official said, "The telephone has too many shortcomings to be seriously considered as a means of communication. The device is inherently of no value." A century later, the chairman of a minicomputer corporation stated that there was no reason anyone would want a computer in the home.

Predicting the future will never be an exact science, but it's possible to approach the task in an organized way. In the field called *future studies*, scholars rely on a variety of methods to develop more accurate predictions. One method, called *trend extrapolation*, identifies current trends and projects them. In this module, you'll look at the trends driving contemporary computing, and you'll explore what may happen if these trends continue operating for the next several decades. You'll also examine the potential impact of artificial intelligence (AI), if computer designers succeed in creating a truly-intelligent machine.

TOMORROW'S HARDWARE: FASTER, CHEAPER, CONNECTED

Could the history of the next fifty years be described simply by stating two laws of technology and economics? Consider these:

- **Moore's Law** Intel Corporation Chairman Gordon Moore predicted more than thirty years ago that microprocessors and other miniature circuits would double in circuit density (and therefore in processing power) every 18 to 24 months. Moore's Law still holds true, and experts believe that the trend should continue for at least another decade (and perhaps for twenty more years) until the process of miniaturization of silicon components runs into physical barriers. If Moore's Law continues until the middle of the next century, computers will be ten billion times more powerful than today's fastest machines. Storage technology shows a similar trend: steep rises in capacity and steep declines in cost.

- **Metcalfe's Law** Ethernet inventor Bob Metcalfe predicts that the value of a computer network grows in proportion to the square of the number of people connected to it. Consider that a telephone line that connects two people is of limited value, but a telephone system that connects an entire city becomes an indispensable resource for every aspect of life. Under Metcalfe's Law, for example, a network with two people connected has a value of 4, but a network with four people connected has a value of 16. According to some predictions, the Internet will ultimately connect one billion users worldwide.

If you put these two laws together, you get a potent mixture. The computer industry is now giving us *networked* machines that double in power every 18 to 24 months, even as the networks they're connected to are rapidly growing in size.

As computers become faster, cheaper, and more valuable, they'll encourage the trend toward the digitization of all the world's information and knowledge—the entire storehouse of accumulated human experience. And as digitization proceeds, the result will be increasing convergence among all media,

As computers become faster, cheaper, and more valuable, they'll encourage the trend toward the digitization of all the world's information and knowledge.

Table 10D.1	The Typical Personal Computer: 1999 and 2005		
	Component	1999	2005
	RAM	64MB	1GB
	Processor speed (instructions per second)	400 million	7 billion
	Circuit density (number of transistors)	7.5 million	125 million
	Hard disk capacity	8GB	135GB
	Average Internet connection speed	56,000 (bits per second)	1 million (bits per second)

communication, and networking technologies, and the boundaries between telephones, newspapers, radio, television, and computers will fade away.

The Short Term

In the next several years, you'll see Moore's and Metcalfe's Laws at work. Table 10D.1 lists the characteristics of a circa 2005 personal computer, based on the assumption that Moore's Law will remain in effect. Besides these performance improvements, you'll see some basic changes in the standard PC's hardware, such as the use of flat-panel LCD displays in place of the bulky cathode ray tube (CRT) monitors. High-capacity, read/write optical drives will be standard equipment, while new network technologies will bring megabit bandwidth to homes and offices.

The Long Term

What will computing be like several decades from now? By 2020, Moore's Law predicts that all the components of unbelievably-powerful computers will be accommodated on just one tiny silicon chip, which can be mass-produced at a cost of $500 or less. These chips will include super-fast processors (capable of performing a trillion instructions per second), huge amounts of RAM, video circuitry—the works. And they'll cost less than $500. In some scenarios, they could cost as little as $100.

Recognizing the trends toward lower cost and miniaturization, some computer scientists speak of **ubiquitous computing.** (The term *ubiquitous* means *everywhere.*) In ubiquitous computing, computers are everywhere, and they fade into the background, providing computer-based intelligence all around us. Your car will inform you when it needs maintenance. If you're short on coffee, your pantry will automatically initiate an electronic order to the virtual grocery store, and a courier will deliver the coffee within minutes. You'll jot down notes on what appears to be a piece of paper, but everything you write will be automatically copied to a computer and then sorted and organized for storage. If you're missing a phone number you jotted down in haste, don't worry: it will be in your computerized address book. You'll wear computers, too. Tiny computers in your eyeglasses, for example, will adjust the lenses to light variations and display maps to help you find your way if you get lost.

The Limits of Trend Extrapolation

Like any method of predicting the future, trend extrapolation is only as good as the assumptions that underlie it. Moore's Law may break down if engineers encounter physical barriers to the further miniaturization of electronic components. If so, future computers won't be as powerful or as inexpensive as trend extrapolation predicts. A second limitation of trend extrapolation lies in its failure to consider the impact of major technological breakthroughs, such as artificial intelligence (AI), the subject of the next section. If artificial intelligence is achieved, the future impact of computing will be far greater than trend extrapolation predicts.

ARTIFICIAL INTELLIGENCE: TOWARD THE SMART MACHINE?

In the classic sci-fi adventure *2001*, a glitch in an intelligent computer's programming brings ruin and death to a manned expedition to Jupiter. Concluding that the ship's human crew represented a danger to the mission, the computer (named Hal 9000) decides to eliminate them. As envisioned in the film, Hal 9000 exhibits many of the characteristics of human intelligence, such as the ability to reason, to converse in **natural language** (ordinary human speech), and to formulate a plan or strategy. But Hal 9000 currently exists only in the imagination of science fiction writers.

The field that attempts to endow computers with intelligence is known as **artificial intelligence (AI),** but it has met with only partial success due to the many formidable obstacles the field has encountered. As you'll see in this section, AI specialists have succeeded in creating special-purpose programs that exhibit some aspects of human intelligence, but these programs cannot function intelligently outside the context for which they were designed. What's in store for the future? Computer scientists are sharply divided among optimists who believe that these problems will be overcome and pessimists who believe that the underlying problems are so difficult that they are impossible to solve.

Let's start with the big question: just what is intelligence?

Defining Intelligence

Scientists and philosophers do not agree on the definition of *intelligence,* except for one point: intelligence has many components. An intelligent creature can do some or all of the following:

- Learn and retain the learned knowledge.
- Reason on the basis of this knowledge.
- Adapt to new circumstances.
- Plan (develop strategies).
- Communicate.
- Recognize patterns.

Scientists still know very little about the human brain, but it's already clear that the brain is far more complex and works differently than any computer. The average adult's brain contains approximately 100 billion neurons (nerve cells) linked in complex, interconnected pathways. For any given operation, thousands of neurons may come into play. Operations are both electrical and chemical. Various areas of the brain are known to govern specific functions, such as sensory input, vision, hearing, speech, emotions, reasoning, and memory.

How does the human brain compare to a computer? Some speculative estimates are shown in Table 10D.2. Compared to computers, the human brain accepts voluminous amounts of input and stores an unbelievable

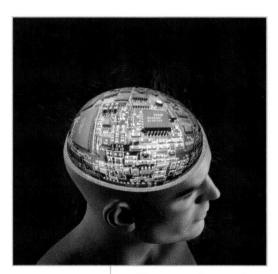

Artificial intelligence is the field that attempts to endow computers with intelligence. Although scientists know little about the human brain, it's clear that the brain is far more complex than any computer.

Table 10D.2	The Human Brain As a CPU (Speculative Estimates)	
Operation	**Estimated Speed or Capacity**	
Input	Fast (1 gigabit per second); the human retina can achieve a resolution of approximately 127 million "pixels"	
Processing	Fast for pattern recognition (10 billion instructions per second); slow for calculations (2-100 per second)	
Output	Slow (speech: 100 bits per second)	
Storage	Very large (10 terabytes) but retrieval can be uncertain	

Destinations

For information on artificial intelligence, an excellent starting point is AI on the Web (**http://www.cs.berkeley.edu/~russell/ai.html**). You can also try the Canadian Research Council's Artificial Intelligence Resources (**http://ai.iit.nrc.ca/ai_point.html**).

Destinations

To learn more about recent winners of the Loebner Prize, visit the Loebner Prize Home Page at **http://www.loebner.net/Prizef/loebner-prize.html**.

amount of data. In terms of processing, the human brain excels at pattern recognition (for example, recognizing faces and understanding speech), but it's a slow calculator. In contrast, computers accept much smaller amounts of input and do a poor job of recognizing patterns, but they can calculate rapidly and produce output much faster than humans can.

The Turing Test

As you've just learned, there's no scientific consensus on what constitutes intelligence. So how do we tell whether a computer is intelligent? For British computer scientist Alan Turing, the answer is easy: a computer is intelligent if a team of unbiased judges cannot tell the difference between computer-generated and human output.

Writing in the 1950s, Turing envisioned what AI specialists now call a **Turing Test.** In a Turing Test, a person sits at a computer and types questions. The computer is connected to two other hidden computers. At one, a human being reads the questions and types responses. At the other, a computer with no human assistance runs a program that also gives answers. If the person typing the question can't tell the difference between the human's answers and the computer's answers, Turing said, the computer is intelligent.

By Turing's standard, computers long ago passed the Turing Test. In the mid-1960s, Joseph Weizenbaum, a computer scientist at MIT, wrote a simple program called ELIZA, that mimics a human therapist. If you type, "I'm worried about my girlfriend," the program responds, "Tell me more about your girlfriend." The program is actually very simple: if the user types a word on the program's built-in list, such as girlfriend, father, guilt, or problem, the program copies this word and puts it into the response. Even so, some people were fooled into thinking they were conversing with a real therapist.

ELIZA didn't fool people for long, but today's programs are larger and more resourceful. In the First Annual Loebner Prize Competition, held at the Boston Computer Museum in 1991, ten human judges tried to determine which of eight display screens showed text produced by people and which ones displayed text produced by the computer. An advanced program called PC Therapist tricked half the judges into thinking that the program was a human being. The 1998 Loebner Prize winner, a program called Fred, is an even better chatter. Fred used a number of tricks to evade questions you might ask in an attempt to trip up the programming.

Does the Turing Test withstand scrutiny? According to most philosophers and psychologists, the Turing Test's type-and-response method is too simplistic. For example, many programmers have learned how to create a chat response program that can trick judges. The only intelligence that comes into play here is that of the human judges, who must use their immense pattern recognition and memory capabilities to make sense of these program's sometimes odd responses.

Brute Force

The human brain excels at recognizing patterns, while the computer excels at performing computations. Instead of trying to get a computer to work the way the human brain does, why not use the computer's calculation capabilities to simulate human intelligence? After all, what matters is the outcome, not the process.

That's exactly the reasoning behind an entire generation of chess-playing programs, which have long been pitted against human chess masters. These programs don't work the way human chess players do. They don't plan, strategize, or learn from experience. Instead, they examine each board position, calculate *all* the possible moves that can be made, and select the best one. This is called the **brute force** approach to artificial intelligence. A brute force technique relies on the computer's fast processing capabilities to repeat a simple operation until an answer is found.

British computer scientist Alan Turing. According to most psychologists, the Turing Test's type-and-response method is too simplistic to accurately prove intelligence.

Good chess-playing programs can easily defeat novice or intermediate players. Until 1997, no chess-playing program had ever defeated an international chess champion. But that changed forever on May 11, 1997, when an IBM-designed chess-playing system, called Deep Blue, defeated Russian chess master Garry Kasparov (see Figure 10D.1). Combining a supercomputer with specialized programming, Deep Blue can examine more than 200 million alternative plays per second. What's more, Deep Blue works without emotions, which may have hampered Kasparov. During the match, Kasparov was increasingly angered by what he saw as the IBM programmers' attempt to analyze Kasparov's game and to write a program specifically designed to defeat *him*.

Is Deep Blue intelligent? Deep Blue's programmers are the first to deny that Deep Blue possesses anything like human intelligence. It's simply a very fast program that examines a chess situation and calculates the optimum move. Furthermore, it can't drive to the chess match, converse with the match's organizers (or even recognize who they are), or reach out and move the chess pieces on the playing board. Still, Deep Blue's success suggests that computers don't have to work the way the human brain does to exhibit some of the characteristics associated with human intelligence.

Figure 10D.1

On May 11, 1997, Deep Blue defeated Russian chess master Garry Kasparov.

AI Achievements

In the early years of AI research, computer scientists sometimes made exuberant predictions. In 1967, Marvin Minsky, one of the founders of AI research, declared that by the 1990s computers intelligent enough to converse with humans and drive automobiles would be commonplace. Because today's typical computer lacks these capabilities, Minsky's prediction is often ridiculed. But Minsky might have the last laugh. Today's special-purpose AI systems may not combine all the attributes of human intelligence in a single system, but they can and do emulate human brain power in selected areas.

As long as you're not looking for a walking, talking computer that has all the attributes of human intelligence, Minsky's prediction rings surprisingly true. For example, PEGASUS, a spoken language interface connected to

SPOTLIGHT

I'D KNOW THAT FACE ANYWHERE

▶ One of the abilities we associate with human intelligence is pattern recognition, the ability to process a wealth of unbelievably complex visual data and recognize something—such as an old friend in a sea of faces. If you think we're alone in this ability, you'd better think again, because computers are catching up—and fast. Already in use in airports, banks, and even the streets of East London, face-recognition systems scan human faces for known regularities that are as distinctive as an individual's fingerprint. Often, the scanning occurs without your knowledge. At airports and banks, face recognition systems are looking for known terrorists and criminals, as are the systems in use on East London streets. Recently, the East London system identified several potential troublemakers at a big soccer match, and reportedly reduced crime in the area by 70 percent.

What's so distinctive about your face? It's not as complicated as you'd think. Although the human face has some sixty "landmarks," or features that can have distinctive patterns, it only takes a little more than a dozen of them to establish a positive facial identification—and it doesn't matter whether you wear glasses or grow a beard.

Face-recognition systems have already proven their value as crime-fighters. In Las Vegas, Nevada, casinos use them to watch for known cardsharks, who prey on other customers' naivete. In the future, face-recognition systems might replace PIN numbers at ATMs, passwords at computers, and passcards at security checkpoints.

Despite its crime- and fraud-fighting potential, face-recognition technology raises some disturbing implications for privacy. As corporations and governments share ever-growing databases of recognized faces, people will lose their anonymity. For example, a videotape shot at a political rally could be used to positively identify all or most of the people in attendance. At its worst, the technology could be used for the kind of intrusive, totalitarian regulation imagined in the most pessimistic science fiction novels, such as George Orwell's *1984*, in which every individual's words and deeds are exhaustively tracked and monitored for signs of disloyalty. With the right mix of regulation and ethical development, face recognition technology could continue to mature into an important deterrent to crime. But if Big Brother arrives, one thing's for certain: he'll know your face.

In the future, face-recognition systems might replace PIN numbers at ATMs, passwords at computers, and passcards at security checkpoints.

American Airlines' SABRE reservation system, enables subscribers to obtain flight information and make flight reservations by conversing with the computer through a telephone. In addition, an onboard computer equipped with a video monitoring system recently drove a van from Washington, D.C. to San Diego, California, averaging 63 mph, 24 hours per day. The progress has been piecemeal but is nevertheless impressive. This section summarizes AI's achievements thus far.

Natural Language

The term *natural language* refers to the speech people use every day. Computers would be much easier to use if they could understand natural language, whether by spoken or typed input. For example, instead of searching through folder after folder in search of a missing file, imagine asking the computer, "Where's that file I created a couple of days ago? You know, the one in which I wrote about those two paintings we saw in my art history class?"

Despite years of effort to create natural language interfaces, computers are still not good at understanding what they hear and acting on this understanding. Much of what passes for a natural language interface amounts to word matching. For example, you can navigate a Macintosh's folders by speaking their names and giving a few simple commands, such as "Open" or "Close." Combined with software that can parse (decode) a sentence's grammatical structure, word matching programs can work well in areas with highly-specialized vocabularies of a few thousand words.

Attempts to create natural language systems of more general capabilities have run into profound problems, such as the ambiguity of human language. The term *intelligence*, for instance, has at least four other senses, or meanings, besides the one we're talking about here. In the military, for example, *intelligence* means knowledge about the enemy. A program capable of understanding the various senses of a word would have to know a great deal about the world. For example, natural language software should be able to understand that "the day before Christmas" is December 24. The underlying problems are exceedingly complex and will require many more years of research to solve.

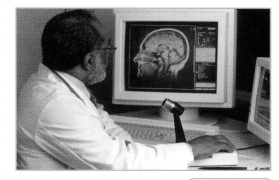

Natural language understanding may lie in computing's future, but major advances have been made in **speech recognition**, in which computers translate spoken speech into text (see Figure 10D.2). Previously, speech recognition software worked only if the speaker paused between words, and the software required a long period of training to become familiar with the speaker's vocalization patterns. New software is much better at continuous speech recognition (recognizing words spoken without a pause between them).

Continuous speech recognition is the first step toward a true natural language interface, because such an interface would require the computer to recognize anyone's natural speech. With reliable speech recognition technology, the day is closer when you'll be able to control a computer by talking to it in ordinary speech.

Figure 10D.2

Major advances have been made in speech recognition, in which computers translate spoken speech into text.

Machine Translation

In the 1960s, experts confidently predicted that **machine translation**—the use of computers to translate foreign language text automatically—could be achieved quite easily. But many problems emerged, including how to resolve ambiguity (for example, compare the word *pen* in the following two sentences: "My pen is in my pocket" and "Charlie is doing 25-to-life in the pen"). After many years of work, automatic translation software is coming closer to the dream of machine translation. The software is fast—one program can translate 300,000 words per hour—but the results are riddled with errors. Still, the results are good enough to provide a working draft for human translators. Some systems make only three to five errors for every hundred words translated.

Destinations

Try machine translation yourself by visiting Babelfish, an online Web translator created by AltaVista (Digital Equipment Corporation). Access Babelfish (**http:// babelfish.altavista. digital.com**), choose the translation language, and type some text in the text box. When you click "Translate," you'll see the translation right away.

Expert Systems

Will your next doctor be a computer? Research in **expert systems** attempts to formulate the knowledge of human experts according to if-then rules ("if you have a temperature, then you may have an infection"). These rules formally express the knowledge used by human experts as they reason their way to a conclusion. The process of eliciting these rules from human experts is called **knowledge representation.** Once elicited, the rules are captured in expert systems. Expert systems use these rules to make a conclusion, the same way a human expert does.

An expert system relies on a **knowledge base** (a database of represented knowledge). To use the expert system, you must supply information to the program. Based on the information you supply, the program consults its knowledge base and draws a conclusion, if possible.

Early proponents of expert systems thought that their programs would eventually replace human experts, but these predictions have not materialized. Expert systems work best where they're limited to sharply-defined subjects, such as jet engine maintenance, planning and scheduling, diagnosis and troubleshooting of a specific device, or financial decision-making. Expert system technology is making its appearance in application software, too. Microsoft Word uses rule-based reasoning to check documents for grammatical errors. MailJail, a junk email detection accessory for Outlook 98, screens out unwanted or unsolicited email, or *spam*. Created by Omron Advanced Systems, Inc., MailJail uses more than 600 rules to decide whether an incoming message is junk mail.

Intelligent Agents

Imagine having a helper inside your computer that can converse with you, understand your needs, and offer assistance. These helpers, called **agents,** can sample conversations in thousands of newsgroups and recommend items of interest, find human experts who can solve specific problems, negotiate the best price for something you're trying to buy, or understand your interests and scout ahead for Web pages you'll want to see.

If you're using Microsoft Office software, you're probably familiar with an agent called the Office Assistant, an agent that springs into action when the program deduces that you're performing a certain type of action.

Pattern Recognition

Imagine a computer that can see in a way that goes beyond recording a digitized image. By means of a digital camera, computers equipped with **pattern recognition** software can process what they're seeing and draw connections between the patterns they perceive and stored patterns in a database. Pattern-recognizing computers are already used for security. In fact, a new type of video surveillance camera can detect suspicious movement patterns among shoppers and alert security personnel. Pattern recognition software is playing an important role in data mining, discovering previously-unnoticed trends in massive amounts of transaction data.

Fuzzy Logic

The term **fuzzy logic** suggests inaccurate logic, but it refers to a type of logic that may ultimately prove *more* accurate than the type of yes-no, on-off logic that computers use. With fuzzy logic, it's possible to express a proposition with varying degrees of confidence about its truthfulness. You hear fuzzy logic all the time in weather reports: "A 40 percent chance of showers this afternoon." Such a prediction is usually more accurate than saying there's a zero percent chance of rain or a 100 percent chance of rain. Fuzzy logic helps make expert systems and other AI-based software work better by automating forms of reasoning that people use. An example of an application of fuzzy logic is the circuitry that enables a handheld video camera to adjust to jiggling and show a steady picture. The circuitry figures out what probably should and should not move and adjusts the image accordingly.

Robots

Late at night, Dottie cleans the floors in a Richmond, Virginia office building. The work is dull and repetitive, but she doesn't mind. She's never late to work, doesn't call in sick, and doesn't even receive a salary. Dottie is a **robot,** created by Cyberclean, a company that's going after a $50 billion industrial cleaning market. A robot is a computer-based device programmed to perform motions that can accomplish useful tasks. But can robots do so safely? Using video sensors, Dottie observes simple rules to avoid doing any damage, such as stopping and waiting if somebody walks in front of her. When her work is finished, she returns to her charging station.

Dottie is at the cutting edge of **robotics,** a field that has transformed industrial production. In 1997, the annual market for industrial robots passed the $1 billion mark. Increasingly, robots are performing tasks such as assembly, welding, material handling, and material transport (see Figure 10D.3). According to a recent estimate, more than one million industrial robots will be in use by 2001, with more than half of them in Japan. Robots are being used in medicine, too. Rock-steady surgical robots are saving lives where natural hand tremors could lead to fatal consequences. Robots are also used for exploring hazardous environments, such as the radioactive ruins of the Chernobyl Unit 4 nuclear power plant.

So where's the personal robot, which will someday mow the lawn, clean the house, and shampoo the carpets? Most experts agree that the personal robot is about a decade or two away. Robots are too expensive for consumers right now, but that will change as the market demand grows.

Strong AI

Although piecemeal advances in artificial intelligence are transforming the computers and software we use every day, the decades-old dream of creating a truly intelligent computer seems as far away as ever. What's been achieved so far is a semblance of intelligence within only highly-restricted areas of knowledge, such as routing parts through a factory or making airline reservations. Is the dream of true machine intelligence still alive? Proponents of **strong AI** believe that it is and that the achievement of artificial intelligence is only decades away.

What is needed to achieve true artificial intelligence? Everyone agrees that an intelligent computer would need a high proportion of the knowledge that people carry around in their heads every day, such as the fact that Philadelphia is a city on the East Coast, and that East Coast cities can be unbearably hot in the summer. This type of knowledge is used constantly. If someone tells you, "My friend went to work in Philadelphia for the summer," you can respond, "She must not mind the heat!" But there's considerable disagreement about how this knowledge can be provided to a computer. Should humans provide such knowledge, or should computers learn it on their own? Two AI projects, Cyc and Cog, illustrate these two different approaches to knowledge acquisition.

Figure 10D.3

Increasingly, robots are performing tasks such as assembly, welding, material handling, and material transport.

  Destinations

Would you like to build your own robot? Visit MondoTronics Robot Store (**http://www.robotstore.com**), where you'll find nearly 300 robot kits and accessories.

Cyc

In Austin, TX, computer scientist Douglas B. Lenat is programming a computer called Cyc (pronounced "sike," from "encyclopedia") with basic facts about the world that everyone knows, such as "mountain climbing is dangerous" and "birds have feathers." The goal is to create a computer that knows as much as a 12-year-old. The challenge is that 12-year-olds know a great deal. Lenat's staff has spent more than a decade feeding basic knowledge into Cyc (the computer now stores over one million rules) and they're still many years away from achieving their goal. At some point, though, Cyc's designers say that the computer will be able to learn on its own, reading material from the Internet and asking questions when it can't understand something.

Cog

A different approach to strong AI is taken by MIT professor Rodney A. Brooks, who believes that Lenat is approaching the problem the wrong way. In the natural world, intelligence arose as organisms tried to survive. The path to artificial intelligence, Brooks argues, lies in creating robots that, unlike Cyc, have minimal preprogrammed knowledge. What they do have is massive sensory input (sight, hearing, and touch) coupled with artificially-programmed "desires." For Brooks, intelligence isn't reasoning, but rather a set of behaviors acquired as organisms interact with their environment. To make his point, Brooks and his students have constructed a series of impressive insect-like robots that have learned how to crawl across fields strewn with boulders (and even steal soda cans from students' desks). Their latest project is Cog, a humanoid robot that's currently in its infancy.

Neural Networks

Yet another approach to strong AI involves creating computers that mimic the structure of the human brain. Called **neural networks** (or neural nets), these computers are composed of hundreds or thousands of tiny processors that are interconnected in multiple ways, just like neurons in the human brain.

Although little is known about how the human brain works, its physical structure has been explored. Anatomists know that the brain contains billions of brain cells, called neurons (see Figure 10D.4). These neurons are connected by current-conducting nerve fibers called ganglia. Often, a single neuron has many ganglia attached to it, forming a dense and complex network of interconnections. Scientists believe that when people learn things, some connections are reinforced and grow stronger.

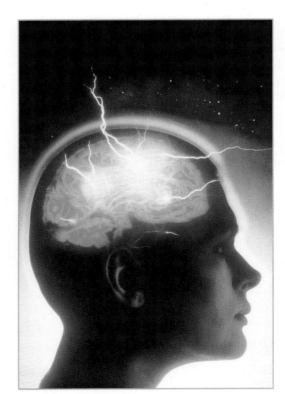

Figure 10D.4

The brain contains billions of neurons. In a neural net, thousands of computer processing units are connected in multiple ways, just as the neurons in the brain are connected.

In a neural net, thousands of computer processing units are connected in multiple ways, just as the neurons in a brain are connected. However, neural nets aren't programmed: they're trained. The net learns by trial and error, just the way humans do. An incorrect guess weakens a particular pattern of connections, while a correct guess reinforces the pattern. After the training is finished, the neural net knows how to do something, such as operate a robot. Neural nets behave much the way brains behave. In fact, neural nets exhibit electromagnetic waves that are surprisingly similar to the brain waves in humans. None of today's neural nets approaches the complexity of even an animal's brain, but more complex neural nets are planned.

Ordinary computers are good at solving problems that require linear thinking, logical rules, and step-by-step instructions. In contrast, neural nets are good at recognizing patterns, dealing with complexity, and learning from experience.

Neural nets are emerging from laboratories and finding their way into commercial applications. Right now, neural nets are comparing signatures made in banks with stored signatures, monitoring the state of aircraft engines, and predicting trends in the stock market.

Genetic Algorithms

Intelligence is a byproduct of evolution through the mechanism of natural selection. So why not try to create artificial intelligence by creating laboratory conditions in which the most intelligent programs survive? That's the object of research based on **genetic algorithms.**

According to the evolutionary theories of biology, organisms try to survive. Occasional errors in the genetic code introduce mutations (leading to change) and sometimes these changes are advantageous and give the organism a better chance of survival. Organisms with an advantageous genetic code dominate because they have more opportunities to reproduce.

Genetic algorithm research mimics nature in the following way: a number of algorithms are placed into a computer environment and are given the potential to mutate in random ways. All the algorithms compete to try to solve the problem. Over time, one algorithm emerges as the best at tackling the problem. Where's the AI connection here? AI requires the creation of algorithms that can mimic the behavior of intelligent beings, but such algorithms are difficult to discover. Genetic algorithm techniques offer a new way to discover these algorithms.

IMPACTS

Sharing the World with Machines Who Think

Fast-forward 50 or 100 years. Moore's Law still holds, scientists have achieved artificial intelligence, and we're surrounded by smart machines—"machines who think," as AI chronicler Pamela McCorduck describes in her book by the same name. A million times faster and smarter than the computers of the early 2000s, these machines converse with us, live with us, and become deeply involved in our lives, perhaps on an emotional level as well as a functional one. Will such machines possess consciousness (an awareness of their existence)? If so, will erasing their memories raise severe ethical and legal issues? Will a futuristic civil rights movement push for the acceptance of machine intelligences as full members of human society?

One thing's for sure: if artificial intelligence is achieved, the transition won't be easy—and that's especially true if artificial intelligences prove to be superior to human brainpower. (After his experience with Deep Blue, for example, chess champion Garry Kasparov experienced a wave of conflicting emotions, including awe at Deep Blue's apparent flashes of insight, anger at being defeated by a machine, and embarrassment for having let down humanity.) As you're leaving for a job interview, imagine the household neural net/fuzzy logic system saying, "You really shouldn't wear that outfit for this particular interview. You'll reduce your chance of getting the job by 19 percent." Perhaps the most frightening question is, will our own creations turn on us?

Just a few years ago, only crackpots and doomsayers found the prospect of artificial intelligence so frightening that they called for a halt to AI research. But their ranks have been joined by one of the most respected pioneers in the computer industry: Bill Joy, a co-founder of Sun Microsystems. According to Joy, several cutting-edge technologies—including not only artificial intelligence but also genetics and nanotechnology—could create a race of half-machine, half-living entities that could easily self-replicate and, like one of today's computer viruses, escape from our control—and that could mean curtains for humanity. "If you don't believe extinction could happen," Joy told a reporter, "check the fossil record." Joy insists that some types of scientific research need to be stopped—and AI is at the top of his list.

Other AI critics aren't sure that scientific progress can be stopped, even if there's broad agreement that it isn't desirable. After all, few scientists felt that developing the hydrogen bomb was a particularly good idea, but they were driven to do so by Cold War competition between the United States and Soviet Union. The key, they assert, lies in "raising" artificial intelligences so that they become an asset to human society instead of a threat.

As with all things having to do with computers, the key may lie in the programming. Isaac Asimov's classic novel, I, Robot (1950), introduces a world in which AI-based robots are commonplace. To prevent the robots from taking over, they're encoded with the Three Laws of Robotics:

- First Law: a robot may not injure a human being or, through inaction, allow a human being to come to harm.

- Second Law: a robot must obey the orders given to it by human beings except where such orders may conflict with the First Law.

- Third Law: a robot must protect its own existence as long as such protection does not conflict with the First or Second Law.

Hans Moravec, director of Carnegie-Mellon University's robotics research program, believes that Asimov's laws hold the key. "You'll learn to like robots," Moravec says. "They'll be nicer than human beings." But there might not be room left for people in a world run compassionately and efficiently by super-human intelligences. Self-replicating, super-intelligent robots will be our offspring, Moravec says, and "It behooves us to bow out when we can no longer contribute." However, Joy disagrees. "If I thought [robots'] long-term goal was to replace me . . . , I'd say, 'Bring out the sledgehammers.' "

TAKEAWAY POINTS

- Moore's Law predicts that microprocessors and other miniature circuits will double in density every 18 to 24 months. Moore's Law is expected to continue to operate for at least two more decades.
- Metcalfe's Law states that the value of a computer network grows in proportion to the square of the number of people connected to it. The more that people connect to the Internet, the more valuable it becomes.
- By 2020, computers will surround us (we'll even wear them) and they'll fade into the background, providing functionality and intelligence for all the tasks we perform.
- Artificial intelligence (AI) is the field that attempts to endow computers with some of the attributes of human intelligence, such as the capacity to learn, reason, plan, communicate, and recognize patterns.
- Brute force techniques can create systems that rival or beat human intelligence in highly-specialized areas, such as chess, but AI has yet to create a computer that possesses anything like the general intelligence of a human being.
- AI research has made progress in limited areas, such as speech recognition, machine translation, expert systems, and industrial robotics.
- Strong AI researchers try to create computers with true artificial intelligence, but little consensus exists on how this goal can be achieved.

MODULE REVIEW

KEY TERMS AND CONCEPTS

agents	knowledge base	robot
artificial intelligence (AI)	knowledge representation	robotics
brute force	machine translation	speech recognition
expert systems	natural language	strong AI
fuzzy logic	neural networks	Turing Test
genetic algorithms	pattern recognition	ubiquitous computing

TRUE/FALSE

Indicate whether the following statements are true or false.

1. Metcalfe's Law predicts that the value of a computer network grows in proportion to the square of the total number of people connected to it.

2. The field that attempts to bestow computers with intelligence is called artificial intelligence.

3. Scientists and philosophers typically agree on the definition of intelligence.

4. A computer is far more complex than a human brain.

5. According to most psychologists, the Turing Test's type-and-response method is too complex.

6. A brute force technique relies on a computer's fast processing capabilities to repeat a simple operation until an answer is found.

7. Natural language refers to the language only a computer understands.

8. Fuzzy logic may prove to be more accurate than the yes-no, on-off logic that computers use.

9. Neural networks are computers that mimic the structure of the human brain.

10. AI requires the creation of algorithms that can mimic human behavior.

MATCHING

Match each key term from the left column to the most accurate definition in the right column.

_____ 1. ubiquitous computing

_____ 2. natural language

_____ 3. artificial intelligence

_____ 4. knowledge base

_____ 5. knowledge representation

_____ 6. fuzzy logic

_____ 7. robotics

_____ 8. neural networks

_____ 9. strong AI

_____ 10. genetic algorithms

a. the process of eliciting if-then rules from human experts

b. a research focus based on the conviction that computers will achieve the ultimate goal of AI, namely the creation of machines rivaling human intelligence

c. a database of represented knowledge

d. a branch of logic concerned with propositions that have varying degrees of precision or confidence

e. an automated program development environment in which various alternative approaches to solving a problem are introduced

f. this describes computers being everywhere and fading into the background

g. computers that mimic the structure of the human brain

h. the field that attempts to endow computers with intelligence

i. a field that has transformed industrial production

j. ordinary human speech

MULTIPLE CHOICE

Circle the letter of the correct choice for each of the following.

1. Which of the following is not true of Moore's law?
   a. The value of a network grows steeply as more people connect.
   b. Microprocessors should double in circuit density every 18 to 24 months.
   c. By 2020, Moore's Law predicts that all components of a powerful PC will fit on one tiny silicon chip.
   d. If Moore's law continues until the middle of the next century, computers will exist that are 10 billion times faster than today's fastest computers.

2. Which of the following is a potential limit of trend extrapolation?
   a. The AI field may continue to meet further obstacles.
   b. Engineers may run into physical barriers to miniaturization.
   c. No one will ever be able to agree on a definition of intelligence.
   d. The computer will never be able to simulate human intelligence.

3. Which of the following is a not a component of intelligence?
   a. learning and retaining knowledge
   b. adapting to new circumstances
   c. communicating
   d. speech recognition

4. Which of the following is an AI achievement?
   a. machine language
   b. the Turing Test
   c. machine translation
   d. expert systems

5. Which of the following is untrue of natural languages?
   a. They refer to the speech people use every day.
   b. They enable computers to translate foreign language text with ease.
   c. Attempts to create these systems have run into profound problems.
   d. Major advances have been made in speech recognition.

6. An expert system relies on which of the following?
   a. a knowledge base
   b. an intelligent agent
   c. pattern recognition
   d. fuzzy logic

7. Which of the following is not a characteristic of fuzzy logic?
   a. The term suggests that the logic is inaccurate.
   b. Fuzzy logic is used in weather reports.
   c. Fuzzy logic enables computer programs to perform processing operations faster.
   d. Fuzzy logic helps make expert systems work better.

8. What field has transformed industrial production?
   a. neural networks
   b. fuzzy logic
   c. strong AI
   d. robotics

9. Which of the following is not a characteristic of neural networks?
   a. Neural nets are trained, not programmed.
   b. Neural nets resemble the connections in the human brain.
   c. Neural nets can recognize patterns and learn from experience.

   d. Neural nets create AI by creating laboratory conditions in which the most intelligent programs survive.

10. Genetic algorithm techniques offer a new way to discover what kind of algorithms?
    a. those that can mimic the inner workings of the brain
    b. those that can mimic the behavior of intelligent beings
    c. those than can mimic the behavior of neural networks
    d. none of the above

FILL-IN

In the blank provided, write the correct answer for each of the following.

1. In _____, computers are everywhere, providing computer-based intelligence all around us.

2. The field that attempts to bestow computers with intelligence is called _____.

3. According to most philosophers and psychologists, the type-and-response method of the _____ is too simplistic.

4. A(n) _____ technique relies on the computer's fast processing capabilities to repeat a simple operation until an answer is found.

5. The term _____ refers to the speech people use every day.

6. Major advances have been made in _____, in which computers translate speech into text.

7. The use of computers to translate foreign language text is called _____.

8. A(n) _____ is a database of represented knowledge.

9. Computers equipped with _____ software can process what they see and draw connections between the patterns they perceive and the stored patterns in a database.

10. In a(n) _____, thousands of computer processing units are connected in many ways, just as the neurons in the brain are connected.

SHORT ANSWER

On a separate sheet of paper, answer the following questions.

1. How do the predictions in Moore's Law directly affect those in Metcalfe's Law?

2. Assuming Moore's Law remains constant, describe the characteristics of a personal computer in the year 2005.

3. In what ways is the human brain more complex than a computer?

4. What are the components that, according to many philosophers and psychologists, make up an intelligent being?

5. How are the operations of the human brain like the operations of a CPU?

6. What are some of the roadblocks to creating natural language systems?

7. What is the difference between knowledge representation and a knowledge base?

8. How do intelligent agents assist computer users?

9. How does pattern recognition software work, and how is it used today?

10. Describe some of the ways neural networks are being used today.

PFSweb, Inc.

Steve Graham is an anthropologist. At least that's the way he sees his job as Chief Technology Officer (CTO) at PFSweb, Inc. What does anthropology have to do with computers and e-commerce, you say? More than you might think. Anthropologists study cultural change, and most of what Steve does involves change: corporate culture change. On a daily basis, Steve challenges both clients and colleagues to consider how technology is changing the very core of business relationships and transactions, and then requires them to act. The reality of e-commerce today is that it's filled with change—companies come

and go, new products flash onto the scene and are just as quickly replaced with newer ones, and so on.

Careers in the e-commerce field come in all shapes and sizes, large companies and small. For instance, there's the graphic artist who creates the logos and art programs we see on every web site. There's the marketing brand manager who used to sell products via traditional media, and now must add the Web to the list of channels to be managed to drive additional profit from the company's product lines. Or the small business owner that wants to grow beyond its existing four walls. These people have one thing in common: a need for skills to help them adapt and succeed.

What do you think? Do you want to work in the fast-paced world of e-commerce? What skills do you already possess that might signal your own potential for success? What additional skills do you need, and how might you gain those skills?

WebLink Go to **www.prenhall.com/ pfaffenberger** to see video of Steve Graham discussing the skills necessary for success in a wired world.

E-COMMERCE IN ACTION

MODULE 1A

True/False
1. T   3. F   5. F   7. T   9. F

Matching
1. E   3. B   5. H   7. C
9. A

Multiple Choice
1. D   3. B   5. C   7. B
9. D

Fill-In
1. computer; input; processing; output; storage
3. interactive
5. microprocessor
7. workstations
9. resource

MODULE 1B

True/False
1. F   3. T   5. F   7. T   9. T

Matching
1. d   3. b   5. a   7. f   9. e

Multiple Choice
1. c   3. a   5. d   7. c   9. c

Fill-In
1. semiconductor
3. general purpose computer
5. transistors
7. American Standard Code for Information Interchange or ASCII
9. very-large-scale integration or VLSI

MODULE 2A

True/False
1. T   3. F   5. F   7. T
9. F

Matching
1. g   3. f   5. a   7. c   9. b

Multiple Choice
1. d   3. d   5. b   7. c
9. a

Fill-In
1. data transfer rate
3. Plug and Play
5. microprocessor
7. superscalar; superscalar architecture
9. benchmark

MODULE 2B

True/False
1. T   3. F   5. T   7. F
9. F

Matching
1. d   3. i   5. g   7. j
9. e

Multiple Choice
1. c   3. b   5. b   7. a
9. b

Fill-In
1. sequential
3. Online
5. write-protect tab or write-protect notch
7. bad sectors
9. hard disk controller

MODULE 2C

True/False
1. T   3. F   5. T   7. F
9. T

Matching
1. e   3. g   5. h   7. j   9. b

Multiple Choice
1. b   3. a   5. c   7. a
9. a

Fill-In
1. diatrical
3. touch screen

5. digital camera
7. Video RAM or VRAM
9. noninterlaced

5. object
7. Justified
9. table

5. file management
7. warehouses
9. data marts

MODULE 3A

True/False
1. T   3. T   5. F   7. T   9. F

Matching
1. f   3. e   5. b   7. a   9. g

Multiple Choice
1. a   3. d   5. a   7. c   9. a

Fill-In
1. operating system
3. swap file
5. PARC
7. Linux
9. File compression utilities

MODULE 3B

True/False
1. F   3. T   5. T   7. T   9. F

Matching
1. d   3. a   5. g   7. j   9. e

Multiple Choice
1. b   3. a   5. a   7. b   9. a

Fill-In
1. application
3. vertical
5. Freeware
7. copy-protected
9. wizards

MODULE 4A

True/False
1. F   3. F   5. F   7. F   9. T

Matching
1. e   3. h.   5. b   7. i   9. f

Multiple Choice
1. d   3. c   5. d   7. c   9. c

Fill-In
1. word wrapping
3. autocorrect

MODULE 4B

True/False
1. T   3. T   5. F   7. T   9. T

Matching
1. f   3. i   5. j   7. c   9. b

Multiple Choice
1. a   3. b   5. a   7. a   9. b

Fill-In
1. simulations
3. value
5. Numeric formats
7. Replication
9. absolute

MODULE 4C

True/False
1. F   3. T   5. F   7. T   9. F

Matching
1. h   3. d   5. a   7. j   9. i

Multiple Choice
1. c   3. a   5. a   7. d   9. a

Fill-In
1. Visual aids
3. Transparencies
5. Normal
7. AutoContent Wizard
9. placeholder

MODULE 4D

True/False
1. T   3. T   5. F   7. T   9. T

Matching
1. e   3. g   5. i   7. f   9. j

Multiple Choice
1. c   3. a   5. c   7. b   9. d

Fill-In
1. database
3. integrity

MODULE 5A

True/False
1. T   3. T   5. T   7. F   9. T

Matching
1. e   3. d   5. h   7. b   9. f

Multiple Choice
1. c   3. a   5. a   7. b   9. b

Fill-In
1. bit-mapped
3. page description language
5. QuickTime
7. streaming audio
9. scripting language

MODULE 5B

True/False
1. T   3. T   5. F

Matching
1. c   3. e   5. b

Multiple Choice
1. c   3. a   5. c

Fill-In
1. Virtual reality
3. Virtual Reality Modeling Language
5. graphical MUDs or gMUD

MODULE 6A

True/False
1. T   3. T   5. F   7. T   9. T

Matching
1. d   3. a   5. c   7. b   9. g.

Multiple Choice
1. b   3. a   5. d   7. c   9. b

Fill-In
1. Telecommunications
3. private branch exchange or PBX

5. modulation
7. bits per second
9. Personal Communication Service or PCS

MODULE 6B

True/False
1. T   3. F   5. F   7. T   9. T

Matching
1. b   3. j   5. a   7. e   9. h

Multiple Choice
1. b   3. d   5. c   7. d   9. b

Fill-In
1. network
3. open protocol
5. workstation
7. bus
9. backbones

MODULE 7A

True/False
1. T   3. T   5. F   7. T   9. F

Matching
1. d   3. a   5. g   7. b   9. e

Multiple Choice
1. d   3. d   5. b   7. a   9. d

Fill-In
1. Internet
3. portal
5. Electronic mail
7. uniform resource locator or URL
9. newsgroups

MODULE 7B

True/False
1. T   3. F   5. F   7. T   9. F

Matching
1. i   3. g   5. a   7. d
9. b

Multiple Choice
1. b   3. c   5. b   7. b
9. b

Fill-In
1. Hypertext
3. markup language
5. search engine
7. proximity operator
9. secure mode

MODULE 7C

True/False
1. F   3. F   5. T   7. T   9. F

Matching
1. h   3. f   5. g   7. b   9. e

Multiple Choice
1. c   3. d   5. c   7. c   9. d

Fill-In
1. server; client
3. Post Office
5. Default
7. Filters
9. list servers or reflectors

MODULE 7D

True/False
1. F   3. T   5. T   7. F   9. T

Matching
1. f   3. a   5. b   7. j   9. d

Multiple Choice
1. d   3. c   5. c   7. b   9. b

Fill-In
1. acceptable use policies
3. Cascading Style Sheets
5. block
7. WYSIWYG editors
9. Relative

MODULE 8A

True/False
1. T   3. T   5. T   7. F   9. T

Matching
1. h   3. g   5. c   7. a   9. d

Multiple Choice
1. c   3. b   5. d   7. a   9. b

Fill-In
1. organization
3. Artificial
5. transaction processing
7. expert system
9. business process reengineering or reengineering

MODULE 8B

True/False
1. T   3. T   5. F   7. T   9. T

Matching
1. e   3. j   5. a   7. i   9. d

Multiple Choice
1. c   3. a   5. c   7. d   9. d

Fill-In
1. Systems analysis
3. waterfall model
5. Gantt chart
7. project dictionary
9. computer-based

MODULE 8C

True/False
1. T   3. F   5. F   7. T   9. F

Matching
1. i   3. j   5. f   7. c   9. g

Multiple Choice
1. c   3. d   5. a   7. a   9. d

Fill-In
1. Machine language
3. compiler
5. object
7. program specification
9. Pseudocode

MODULE 9A

True/False
1. T   3. T   5. F   7. T   9. T

Matching
1. e   3. c   5. i   7. b
9. f

Multiple Choice

1. a 3. b 5. c 7. b 9. b

Fill-In

1. database vendors
3. ad networks; cookies
5. banner ad
7. Rot-13
9. bits

MODULE 9B

True/False

1. T 3. F 5. F 7. T 9. F

Matching

1. e 3. f 5. h 7. i 9. g

Multiple Choice

1. d 3. a 5. d 7. c 9. b

Fill-In

1. authentication
3. data diddling
5. worm
7. information warfare
9. Callback systems

MODULE 9C

True/False

1. T 3. T 5. F 7. T 9. F

Matching

1. e 3. b 5. c 7. a 9. g

Multiple Choice

1. b 3. a 5. c 7. c 9. b

Fill-In

1. computer ethics
3. public domain

5. software piracy
7. General Public License
9. conduct

MODULE 10A

True/False

1. T 3. T 5. T 7. F 9. T

Matching

1. f 3. a 5. c 7. j 9. b

Multiple Choice

1. b 3. d 5. a 7. d 9. b

Fill-In

1. clock speed
3. Super Video Graphics Array, SVGA
5. dot pitch
7. transceiver
9. surge protector

MODULE 10B

True/False

1. T 3. T 5. T 7. F 9. T

Matching

1. b 3. a 5. d

Multiple Choice

1. d 3. c 5. c 7. d 9. c

Fill-In

1. computer vision syndrome
3. glare shield
5. Ergonomic chairs
7. refresh rate
9. on-screen keyboard utilities

MODULE 10C

True/False

1. T 3. F 5. T 7. F 9. T

Matching

1. f 3. e 5. j 7. d 9. c

Multiple Choice

1. c 3. d 5. d 7. a 9. c

Fill-In

1. information systems department
3. Computer information systems
5. Trade shows
7. Webmasters
9. automation

MODULE 10D

True/False

1. T 3. F 5. F 7. F 9. T

Matching

1. f 3. h 5. a 7. i 9. b

Multiple Choice

1. a 3. d 5. b 7. a 9. d

Fill-In

1. ubiquitous computing
3. Turing Test
5. natural language
7. machine translation
9. pattern recognition

Note: See Glossary for definitions.

3GL See third-generation language.

4GL See fourth-generation language.

ADSL See Asymmetric Digital Subscriber Line.

AGP See Accelerated Graphics Port.

AGV See automatic guided vehicle.

AI See artificial intelligence.

ALU See arithmetic-logic unit.

ASCII See American Standard Code for Information Interchange.

ATA See Advanced Technology Attachment.

AUP See acceptable use policy.

BIOS See Basic Input/Output System.

BMP See Windows bitmap.

BPR See business process reengineering.

bps See bits per second.

BRI See Basic Rate Interface.

CA See certificate authority.

CAD See computer-aided design.

CAI See computer-assisted instruction.

CAM See computer-aided manufacturing.

CAPE See computer-aided production engineering.

CASE See computer-aided software engineering.

cat-5 See category 5.

CAVE See Cave Automated Virtual Environment.

CBE See computer-based education.

CBT See computer-based training.

CCD See charge-coupled device.

CD-R See Compact Disc-Recordable.

CD-ROM See Compact Disc Read-Only Memory or CD-ROM drive.

CD-RW See Compact Disc-Rewritable.

CIM See computer-integrated manufacturing.

CIS See computer information system.

CIS See computerized information system.

CISC See complex instruction set computer.

CMI See computer-managed instruction.

CMOS See complementary metal-oxide semiconductor.

COM See Component Object Model.

CORBA See Common Object Request Broker Architecture.

CPU See central processing unit.

CRT See cathode ray tube.

CS See computer science.

CSCW See computer-supported cooperative work.

CSS See cascading style sheet.

CTD See cumulative trauma disorder.

CTS See carpal tunnel syndrome.

CVS See computer vision syndrome.

DBS See Direct Broadcast Satellite.

DIMM See Dual In-Line Memory Module (DIMM).

DMA See Direct Memory Access.

DoS See denial-of-service.

DRAM See dynamic random-access memory.

DSL See Digital Subscriber Line.

DSS See decision support system.

DTP See desktop publishing.

DTV See digital television.

DVD See digital video disc.

DVD-RAM See digital video disc-RAM.

DVD-ROM See digital video disc-ROM.

EBCDIC See Extended Binary Coded Decimal Interchange Code.

EDI See electronic data interchange.

EE See electrical engineering.

EIDE See Enhanced IDE.

EIS See executive information system.

EPIRB See Emergency Position Indicating Radio Beacons.

EPS See Encapsulated PostScript.

ERD See entity-relationship diagram.

ERMA See Electronic Recording Machine—Accounting.

ESS See executive support system.

FAT See file allocation table.

FED See field emission display.

FPU See floating-point unit.

GIF See Graphics Interchange Format.

GPL See General Public License.

GPS See Global Positioning System.

GUI See graphical user interface.

HGP See Human Genome Project.

HMD See head-mounted display.

HTML See Hypertext Markup Language.

HTTP   See Hypertext Transfer Protocol.

IC   See integrated circuit.

IDE   See Integrated Drive Electronics.

IIOP   See Internet Inter-Orb Protocol.

ILS   See integrated learning system.

IMAP   See Internet Message Access Protocol.

IP   See Internet Protocol.

IS   See information systems.

ISA   See Industry Standard Architecture.

ISDN   See Integrated Services Digital Network.

ITS   See Intelligent Transportation System.

ITU   See International Telecommunications Union.

IXC   See interexchange carrier.

JAD   See joint application development.

JIT   See job instruction training.

JIT   See just-in-time.

JPEG   See Joint Photographic Experts Group.

K   See kilobyte.

KB   See kilobyte.

L2   See level 2.

LAN   See local area network.

LATA   See local access and transport area.

LCD   See liquid crystal display.

LEC   See local exchange carrier.

LSI   See large-scale integration.

M   See megabyte.

MAN   See metropolitan area network.

MB   See megabyte.

MICR   See magnetic-ink character recognition.

MIDI   See Musical Instrument Digital Interface.

MIME   See Multipurpose Internet Mail Extensions.

MIS   See management information system.

MO   See magneto-optic.

MP3   See MPEG Audio Layer 3.

MPEG   See Moving Picture Experts Group.

MRI   See magnetic resonance imaging.

MSI   See medium-scale integration.

MUD   See multiuser dungeon.

NC   See network computer.

NIC   See network interface card.

OCR   See optical character recognition.

OLAP   See online analytical processing.

OLE   See object linking and embedding.

OMR   See optical mark reader.

OO   See object-oriented.

OOP   See object-oriented programming.

OS   See operating system.

P3P   See Platform for Privacy Preferences.

PBX   See private branch exchanges.

PC   See personal computer.

PCI   See Peripheral Component Interconnect.

PCS   See Personal Communication Service.

PDA   See personal digital assistant.

PDL   See page description language.

PDLC   See program development life cycle.

PDN   See public data network.

PICS   See Platform for Internet Content Selection.

PIM   See personal information manager.

PNG   See Portable Network Graphics.

PNP   See Plug and Play.

POP   See point of presence.

POP   See Post Office Protocol.

POS   See point-of-sale.

PSTN   See public switched telephone network.

PVC   See permanent virtual circuit.

QBE   See query by example.

QIC   See quarter-inch cartridge.

QoS   See quality of service.

RAD   See rapid application development.

RAM   See random-access memory.

RBOCs   See Regional Bell Operating Companies.

RFP   See request for proposal.

RFQ   See request for quotation.

RISC   See reduced instruction set computer.

ROI   See return on investment.

ROM   See read-only memory.

RSI   See repetitive strain injury.

SCSI   See Small Computer System Interface.

SDLC   See systems development life cycle.

SDRAM   See Synchronous DRAM.

SMIL   See Synchronized Multimedia Integration Language.

SMTP   See Simple Mail Transport Protocol.

SOHO   See small office/home office.

SONET   See Synchronous Optical Network.

SQL   See Structured Query Language.

SSI   See small-scale integration.

SVGA   See Super Video Graphics Array.

TFT   See thin film transistor.

TPS   See transaction processing system.

UPC   See universal product code.

UPS   See uninterruptible power supply.

URL   See Uniform Resource Locator.

USB   See Universal Serial Bus.

VAN   See value-added network.

VAR   See value-added reseller.

VB   See Visual BASIC.

VLSI   See very-large-scale integration.

VPN   See virtual private network.

VR   See virtual reality.

W3C   See World Wide Web Consortium.

WAN   See wide area network.

WORM   See write once, read many.

WWW   See World Wide Web.

XML   See Extensible Markup Language.

Y2K   See Year 2000.

Definitions

@ In an email address, a symbol used to separate the user name from the name of the computer on which the user's mailbox is stored (for example, **frodo@bagend.org**). Pronounced "at."

3-D rendering Transforming graphics images by adding shading and light sources so that they appear to be three-dimensional.

10baseT An Ethernet local area network capable of transmitting 10 megabits of data per second through twisted-pair cabling.

128-bit domestic-level encryption A level of encryption used for secure Web sites and email that uses an encryption bit length of 128 bits. This bit length prevents the message from being intercepted and decoded, but current U.S. export regulations prevent U.S. companies from exporting software that incorporates this strong level of encryption.

1394 port An input-output port that combines high-speed performance (up to 400 Mbps) with the ability to guarantee data delivery at a specified speed, making the port ideal for use with real-time devices such as digital video cameras. Synonymous with FireWire, which is Apple Computers name for this technology.

40-bit encryption A minimal level of encryption supplied with most Web browsers. Although this encryption level is insufficient to guarantee confidentiality during Internet information transfers, it is weak enough to escape U.S. export regulations.

A

abacus A digital computer that originated thousands of years ago. Calculations are performed by using sliding beads to represent figures and by following rules to perform mathematical operations.

absolute cell reference A spreadsheet cell reference that doesn't adjust when you copy or move a formula.

absolute hyperlink In an HTML document, a hyperlink that fully and precisely specifies the file location of the referenced remote document. An absolute link specifies the protocol (such as http:// or ftp://), as well as the name of the computer and the location of the referenced file in the computer's directory structure.

Accelerated Graphics Port (AGP) A port specification developed by Intel Corporation to support high-speed, high-resolution graphics, including 3-D graphics.

accelerator A circuit board that speeds up some function of your computer.

acceptable use policy (AUP) An Internet service provider (ISP) policy that indicates which types of uses are permissible.

acceptance testing In information systems development, the examination of programs by users. See also *application testing*.

access speed The amount of time that lapses between a request for information from memory and the delivery of the information. Also called *access time*.

access time See *access speed*.

accessible software Software that is designed to be easily and conveniently used by people with limited vision, hearing, or dexterity.

account On a multiuser computer system, a user information profile that includes the user's name, password, and home directory location. Unlike a *profile* on a consumer-oriented operating system, an account provides basic security features that prevent users from accessing or overwriting each others' files.

active cell In a spreadsheet program, the cell in which the cell pointer is located. The contents of the active cell is displayed in the formula bar.

active monitoring In online banking, a security measure in which a security team constantly monitors the system that holds account information for the telltale signs of unauthorized access.

active-matrix LCD A full-color liquid-crystal display (LCD) in which each of the screen's pixels is controlled by its own transistor. Active-matrix displays offer higher resolution, contrast, and vertical refresh rate than less expensive passive-matrix displays. Also called thin film transistor (TFT).

ActiveX control A small program that can be downloaded from a Web page and used to add functionality to a Web browser. ActiveX controls require Microsoft Windows and Microsoft Internet Explorer and are usually written in Visual BASIC (VB).

activity light A light-emitting diode (LED) that illuminates when a disk drive is sending or receiving data.

ad network On the World Wide Web, a commercial service that uses cookies to track user's movements and browsing preferences through all of the network's participating sites. This information is used to present the user with advertisements tailored to the user's interest.

adapter 1. A circuit board that plugs into an expansion slot in a computer, giving the computer additional capabilities. Synonymous with card. Popular adapters for personal computers include video adapters that produce video output, memory expansion boards, internal modems, and sound boards. 2. A transformer that enables a computer or peripheral to work with line voltage that differs from its electrical requirements.

advanced intelligent tape (AIT) An advanced, high-end tape backup standard that is used by organizations to back up the entire contents of a file server or other mission critical systems.

Advanced Technology Attachment (ATA) See *Integrated Drive Electronics (IDE)*.

agent An automatic program that is designed to operate on the user's behalf, performing a specific function in the background. When the agent has achieved its goal, it reports to the user.

aggregate query In a database management program, a *query* that instructs the program to sum the specified data and display the result.

alert box In a graphical user interface (GUI), a dialog box that appears on-screen to either warn you that the command you've given may result in lost work or other errors, or that explains why an action can't be completed.

algorithm A mathematical or logical procedure for solving a problem.

algorithmic art In computer art, the use of an unfolding mathematical procedure as a means of artistic expression.

alias A secondary or symbolic name for a computer user or group of users. Group aliases provide a handy way to send email to two or more people simultaneously.

alt newsgroups In Usenet, a category of newsgroups in which anyone with the requisite technical knowledge can originate a group. However, Usenet administrators are not obligated to carry these newsgroups.

American Standard Code for Information Interchange (ASCII) A standard computer character set consisting of 96 uppercase and lowercase letters along with 32 nonprinting control characters. Developed in 1963, ASCII was the first computer industry standard.

analog Based on continuously varying values or voltages. Analog techniques are used for the reproduction of music in standard LP records and audio cassettes. See *digital*.

Analytical Engine A device planned by Charles Babbage in the nineteenth century. Never completed, this device would have been a full modern computer with an IPOS cycle and punched cards for data input.

analytical graphics As opposed to *presentation graphics*, a type of graphics application in which the user attempts to display all or most of the data so that the underlying patterns become visible.

anchor text In the World Wide Web, the on-screen text of a hyperlink.

animation A method of creating the illusion of movement by saving a series of images that show slight changes in the position of the displayed objects, and then displaying these images fast enough that the eye perceives smooth movement.

anonymity On the Internet, the ability to post a message or display Web sites without divulging one's identity. Anonymity is much more difficult to obtain than most Internet users realize.

anonymous FTP An Internet service that enables you to contact a distant computer system to which you have no access rights, log on to its public directories, and transfer files from that computer to your own.

antivirus program A utility that checks for and removes computer viruses from memory and disks.

applet 1. A small- to medium-sized computer program that provides a specific function, such as emulating a calculator. 2. In Java, a miniprogram embedded in a Web document that, when downloaded, is executed by the browser. Both leading browsers (Netscape Communicator and Microsoft Internet Explorer) can execute Java applets.

AppleTalk A networking protocol developed by Apple Computer that enables Apple Macintosh computers to connect by LocalTalk, EtherTalk, and token ring networks.

application software Programs that enable you to do something useful with the computer, such as writing or accounting (as opposed to utilities, which are programs that help you maintain the computer).

application testing In information systems development, the examination of

programs individually, and then further examination of the programs as they function together.

application workspace The area within an application window that displays the document.

archival backup A procedure in which a backup utility backs up all files on the hard disk by copying them to floppy disks, tape, or some other backup medium. See incremental backup.

archive A file that contains two or more files that have been stored together for convenient archiving or network transmission.

arithmetic operations One of the two groups of operations performed by the arithmetic-logic unit (ALU). The arithmetic operations are addition, subtraction, multiplication, and division.

arithmetic-logic unit (ALU) The portion of the central processing unit (CPU) that makes all the decisions for the microprocessor, based on the mathematical computations and logic functions that it performs.

arithmetic operators A set of symbols corresponding to the standard operations of grade-school arithmetic (addition, subtraction, multiplication, and division).

arrow keys See *cursor-movement keys*.

article In Usenet, a message that begins discussion on a new subject. Compare *follow-up article*.

artificial intelligence (AI) A computer science field that tries to improve computers by endowing them with some of the characteristics associated with human intelligence, such as the capability to understand natural language and to reason under conditions of uncertainty.

artificial system A collection of components constructed by people and organized into a functioning whole to accomplish a goal.

aspect ratio In computer graphics, the ratio between an image's horizontal and vertical dimensions.

assembler A program that transforms source code in assembly language into machine language readable by a computer.

assembly language A low-level programming language in which each program statement corresponds to an instruction that the microprocessor can carry out.

assistive technology A technology that helps people with limited vision, hearing, or dexterity to use the computer comfortably and productively.

Asymmetric Digital Subscriber Line (ADSL) A type of Digital Subscriber Line (DSL) service for Internet access. ADSL enables download speeds of up to 1.5 Mbps.

asynchronous Not kept in time (synchrony) by the pulses of a system clock or some other timing device.

asynchronous communication A method of data communication in which the transmission of bits of data isn't synchronized by a clock signal, but instead is accomplished by sending bits one after another, with a start bit and a stop bit to mark the beginning and end, respectively, of each data unit.

ATA (AT Attachment) A hard disk interface originally designed by IBM for its 1984 Personal Computer AT. More recent versions, such as ATA/66 and Ultra ATA (also called Ultra DMA) offer performance approaching that of *SCSI* hard drives.

ATA-2 See *Enhanced IDE (EIDE)*.

attachment A binary file, such as a program or a compressed word processing document, that has been attached to an email message.

attribute In HTML, an optional or required setting that controls specific characteristics of an element and enables authors to specify values for these characteristics.

authentication In computer security, a method of preventing unauthorized users from accessing a computer system, usually by requesting a password.

authoring tools In multimedia, application programs that enable the user to blend audio files, video, and animation with text and traditional graphics.

autocorrect In a word processing program, a feature that automatically corrects common typographical errors as you type.

automated teller machine (ATM) A computer-based kiosk that provides bank customers with 24-hour access to their funds.

automatic Able to run without human intervention.

automatic guided vehicle (AGV) In computer-integrated manufacturing, a small automated machine that provides supplies where they are needed.

automation The replacement of human workers by machines.

autorepeat A keyboard function that causes a character to repeat if you hold down the key.

autosave A software feature that backs up open documents at a user-specified interval.

avatar In a graphical MUD, a character that represents the person who is controlling the avatar's appearance, movement, and interaction with other characters.

B

backbone In a wide area network (WAN), such as the Internet, a high-speed, high-capacity medium that transfers data over hundreds or thousands of miles. A variety of physical media are used for backbone services, including microwave relay, satellites, and dedicated telephone lines.

background application In a multitasking operating system, any inactive application. Compare foreground application.

background color In HTML, the color assigned to the background of a Web page.

background graphic In HTML, a graphic displayed as a Web page's background. Most browsers automatically repeat (tile) a background graphic so that the image fills the entire page, even if the browser window is enlarged.

backup A file (or group of files) containing copies of important data. These files may be specially formatted so that, should the need arise, they can be used to restore the contents of the hard disk in the event of a hard disk failure.

backup file A copy of a file created as a precaution in case anything happens to the original.

backup utility A program that copies data from a secondary storage device (most commonly a hard disk) to a backup medium, such as a tape cartridge.

bad sector In magnetic storage media such as hard drives, a *sector* of the disk's surface that is physically damaged to the point that it can no longer store data safely.

bandwidth The amount of data that can be transmitted through a given communications channel, such as a computer network.

banner ad On the World Wide Web, a paid advertisement—often rectangular in shape, like a banner—that contains a hyperlink to the advertiser's page.

bar chart In presentation graphics, a graph with horizontal bars (rectangles) commonly used to show the values of the items being compared.

bar code A binary coding system using bars of varying thickness or position that provide information that can be scanned into a computer

bar code reader An input device that scans bar codes and, with special software, converts the bar code into readable data.

baseline The line on which the base (but not the extender, if any) of each character is positioned. An extender is the portion of certain letters (such as *p* and *y*) that extend below the baseline.

BASIC Acronym for Beginner's All-Purpose Symbolic Instruction Code. An easy-to-use high-level programming language developed in 1964 for instruction.

Basic Input/Output System (BIOS) Read-only memory (ROM) built into the computer's memory that contains the instructions needed to start the computer and work with input and output devices.

Basic Rate Interface (BRI) In ISDN, the basic digital telephone and data service that is designed for residences. BRI offers two 56 Kbps or 64 Kbps channels for voice, graphics, and data, plus one 16,000 bps channel for signaling purposes.

batch processing A mode of computer operation in which program instructions are executed one after the other without user intervention. Batch processing uses computer resources efficiently but is less convenient than interactive processing, in which you see the results of your commands on-screen so that you can correct errors and make necessary adjustments before completing the operation.

benchmark A standard measurement used to test the performance of different brands of equipment.

beta version In software testing, a preliminary version of a program that is widely distributed before commercial release to users who test the program by operating it under realistic conditions.

binary file A file containing data or program instructions in a computer-readable format that is unreadable to humans. The opposite of a binary file is an ASCII file.

binary numbers A number system with a base (radix) of 2, unlike the number systems most of us use, which have bases of 10 (decimal numbers), 12 (feet and inches), and 60 (time). Binary numbers are preferred for computers for precision and economy. Building an electronic circuit that can detect the difference between two states (high current and low current, or 0 and 1) is easy and inexpensive; building a circuit that detects the difference among 10 states (0 through 9) is much more difficult and expensive. The word bit derives from the phrase binary digit.

bioinformatics A field that develops database software for storing genetic information and making it available for widespread use.

biological feedback device A device that translates eye movements, body movements, and brain waves into computer input.

biometric authentication A method of authentication that requires a biological scan of some sort, such as a retinal scan or voice recognition.

bit The basic unit of information in a binary numbering system.

bit depth In a scanner, the length (expressed in bits) of the storage unit used to store information about the scanned image. The greater the bit depth, the better the scanner's resolution.

bit length In encryption, the length (expressed in bits) of the key used to encode and decode plaintext data. The greater the bit length, the stronger (less breakable) the encryption.

bitmapped graphics Images formed by a pattern of tiny dots, each of which corresponds to a pixel on the computer's display. Also called raster graphics.

bits per second (bps) In asynchronous communications, a measurement of data transmission speed. In personal computing, bps rates frequently are used to measure the performance of modems and serial ports.

biz newsgroups In Usenet, a category of newsgroups devoted to commercial concerns.

block element In HTML, one of two basic types of elements (the other is inline element). A block element starts on a new line and comprises a separate paragraph, or block. Block elements include P (text paragraph), BLOCKQUOTE (indented quotation), and UL (bulleted list).

body In HTML, one of two elements that make up an HTML document's global structure. The body contains the text and markup that is visible in a browser window.

body type The font (usually 8- to 12-point) used to set paragraphs of text. The body font is different than the font used to set headings, captions, and other typographical elements.

bold In character formatting, a character style in which the letters of a font appear thicker and darker than normal.

Boolean search A database or Web search that uses the logical operators AND, OR, and NOT to specify the logical relationship between search concepts.

boot To start the computer. See *cold boot* and *warm boot.*

boot sector A portion of the computers hard disk that is reserved for essential programs used when the computer is switched on.

boot sector virus A computer virus that copies itself to the beginning of a hard drive, where it is automatically executed when the computer is turned on.

boot sequence The series of operations that the computer runs through every time the power is switched on. The same sequence occurs when the computer is restarted. See *cold boot* and *warm boot.*

bootstrap loader A program stored in the computer's read-only memory (ROM) that enables the computer to begin operating when the power is first switched on.

bounce message An email message informing the user that another email message could not be delivered to its intended recipient. The failure may be due to an incorrectly typed email address or to a network problem.

Braille output devices An output device that prints computer output in raised Braille letters, which can be read by people with severely limited or no vision.

branch control structure See selection control structure.

broadband A type of data communication in which a technique called multiplexing is used to enable a single transmission line to carry more than one signal.

Broadband ISDN (B-ISDN) A high-bandwidth digital telephone standard for transmitting up to 1.5 Mbps over fiber optic cables. See *Basic Rate Interface* and *Integrated Services Digital Network.*

broken link On the World Wide Web, a hyperlink that refers to a resource (such as a sound or a Web page) that has been moved or deleted. Synonymous with stale link.

browse view In a database, a way of viewing records one by one.

browser A program that enables the user to navigate the Web. The two leading browsers are Netscape Navigator, part of Netscape Communication's Netscape Communicator package, and Microsoft Internet Explorer. A browser serves as the client for Web and other types of Internet servers.

brute force In programming, a crude technique for solving a difficult problem by repeating a simple procedure many times. Computer spell-checkers use a brute-force technique. They don't really "check spelling"; they merely compare all the words in a document to a dictionary of correctly spelled words.

bug A programming error that causes a program or a computer system to perform erratically, produce incorrect results, or crash. The term bug was coined when a real insect was discovered to have fouled up one of the circuits of the first electronic digital computer, the ENIAC. A hardware problem is called a glitch.

build In a presentation graphics program, a type of bulleted list in which the bullet items appear one by one. Animation effects enable the new items to slide in from the side.

build-or-buy decision In the development of information systems, the choice of building a new system within the organization or purchasing it from an outside vendor.

built-in function In a spreadsheet program, a complex formula that is automated with a simple command. To add a large column of numbers, for example, you can use the sum function instead of typing each cell address.

bus mouse A type of mouse that connects to an expansion board mounted on the computer's expansion bus.

bus topology The physical layout of a local area network that does not use a central or host computer. Instead, each node manages part of the network, and information is transmitted directly from one computer to another.

business process reengineering (BPR) The use of information technology to bring about major changes and cost savings in an organization's structure. Also called reengineering.

byte Eight bits grouped to represent a character (a letter, a number, or a symbol).

C

C A high-level programming language developed by Bell Labs in the 1970s. C combines the virtues of high-level programming with the efficiency of assembly language but is somewhat difficult to learn.

C++ A flexible high-level programming language derived from C that supports object-oriented programming but does not require programmers to adhere to the object-oriented model.

cable modem A device that enables a computer to access the Internet by means of a cable TV connection. Some cable modems enable downloading only; you need an analog (POTS) phone line and an analog modem to upload data. The best cable modems enable two-way communications through the cable TV system and do not require a phone line. Cable modems enable Internet access speeds of up to 1.5 Mbps, although most users typically experience slower speeds due to network congestion.

cache memory A small unit of ultra-fast memory used to store recently accessed or frequently accessed data, increasing a computer system's overall performance.

calculated field In a database management program, a *query* that instructs the program to perform an arithmetic operation on the specified data and display the result.

calculator A device designed to help people solve mathematical problems.

call center A computer-based telephone routing system that automatically connects credit card authorization systems to authorization services.

callback system A method of network control that serves as a deterrent to system sabotage by verifying the user ID, password, and telephone number of the individual trying to access the system.

cancel button In a spreadsheet program, a button positioned near the entry bar that cancels the text inserted in the entry bar area.

Caps Lock A toggle key that switches the keyboard into a mode in which uppercase letters are produced without depressing the Shift key.

car navigation system A computer-based driving accessory that displays digitized maps and tracks the car's location using a satellite-based positioning system.

card reader A device capable of reading information on flash memory cards and transferring it to a computer.

carpal tunnel syndrome (CTS) A painful swelling of the tendons and the sheaths around them in the wrist.

cascading style sheet (CSS) In Web publishing, a way to specify document formats in which specific formatting attributes (such as alignment, text style, font, and font size) are assigned to specific HTML tags, so that all subsequent uses of the tag in the same page take on the same formats. Like a style sheet in a word processing document, CSS enables a Web designer to make a single change that affects all the text marked with the same tag.

case control structure In structured programming, a logical construction of programming commands that contains a set of possible conditions and instructions that are executed if those conditions are true.

CAT (computerized axial tomography) scanner In health care, a computer-controlled imaging device used to diagnose patients.

category 5 (cat-5) A type of twisted-pair cable used for high-performance digital telephone and computer network wiring.

cathode ray tube (CRT) A vacuum tube that uses an electron gun to emit a beam of electrons that illuminates phosphorus on-screen as the beam sweeps across the screen repeatedly.

Cave Automated Virtual Environment (CAVE) A virtual reality environment that replaces headsets with 3-D glasses and uses the walls, ceiling, and floor to display projected three-dimensional images.

CD-ROM drive A read-only disk drive that reads data encoded on compact disks and transfers this data to a computer.

cell In a spreadsheet, a rectangle formed by the intersection of a row and a column in which you enter information in the form of text (a label) or numbers (a value).

cell address In a spreadsheet, a unique identifier associated with each cell.

cell reference In a spreadsheet, a way of specifying the value in another cell by entering its cell address.

cell site In a cellular telephone network, an area in which a transmitting station repeats the system's broadcast signals so that the signal remains strong even though the user may move from one cell site to another.

cellular telephone A radio-based telephone system that provides widespread coverage through the use of repeating transmitters placed in zones (called cells). The zones are close enough so that signal strength is maintained throughout the calling area.

centered alignment In word processing, a way of formatting a block of text so that it is centered on the page, leaving both ends unaligned.

central processing unit (CPU) The computer's processing and control circuitry, including the arithmetic-logic unit (ALU) and the control unit.

certificate authority (CA) In computer security, a company that verifies the identity of individuals and issues digital certificates attesting to the veracity of this identity.

certification An endorsement of professional competence that is awarded on successful completion of a rigorous test.

channel In Internet Relay Chat (IRC), a chat group in which as many as several dozen people carry on a text-based conversation on a specific topic.

character Any letter, number, punctuation mark, or symbol produced on-screen by the press of a key or a key combination.

character code An algorithm used to translate between the numerical language of the computer and characters readable by humans.

character formatting The appearance of text, including character size, typeface, and emphasis.

character set The collection of characters that a given computer is able to process and display on-screen.

charge-coupled device (CCD) A small matrix of light-sensitive elements used in digital cameras and scanners.

chart type In a spreadsheet program, a style of chart, such as column chart, bar chart, line chart, and pie chart.

check-screening system A computer system used in point-of-sale (POS) terminals that reads a check's account number and accesses a database of delinquent accounts.

child directory A directory inside another directory.

chip A small wafer of silicon containing very complex electrical circuits.

chipset A collection of supporting components that are all designed to work together smoothly on a computer motherboard.

circuit switching A type of telecommunications network in which high-speed electronic switches create a direct connection between two communicating devices. The telephone system is a circuit-switching network.

citation In a word processing document, a reference to a bibliographic item that is referenced within the text. Citation options include footnotes and endnotes.

citation format A set of guidelines for typing footnote or bibliographic information. When you write a paper for a college class, you will be asked to follow a certain citation format.

citing sources Providing enough information about the source of information you are using so that an interested or critical reader can locate this source without difficulty.

class In object-oriented (OO) programming, a category of objects that performs a certain function. The class defines the properties of an object, including definitions of the object's variables and the procedures that need to be followed to get the object to do something.

click To quickly press and release a mouse button.

click and mortar In electronic commerce, a retail strategy in which a Web retail site is paired with a chain of local retail stores. Customers prefer this strategy because they can return or exchange unwanted goods more easily.

client 1. In a client/server network, a program that runs on users' computers and enables them to access a certain type of data. 2. On a computer network, a program capable of contacting the server and obtaining needed information.

client/server A method of organizing software use on a computer network that divides programs into servers (programs that make information available) and clients (programs that enable users to access a certain type of data).

client/server computing A software application design framework for computer networks in which software services are divided into two parts, a client part and a server part.

client/server network A computer network in which some computers are dedicated to function as servers, making information available to client programs running on users' computers.

clip art A collection of graphical images stored on disk and available for use in a page layout or presentation graphics program.

clipboard A temporary storage location used to hold information after it has been copied or cut. See cut and paste.

clock speed The speed of the internal clock of a microprocessor that sets the pace at which operations proceed in the computer's internal processing circuitry.

clock tick   One "beat" of the computer's internal clock.

clone   A functional copy of a hardware device, such as a personal computer. Although clones of Apple Macintosh computers exist, this term almost always refers to clones of IBM computers and their microprocessors. Compare IBM compatible.

close   To remove a window from the desktop. With most applications, closing the last window terminates the application.

closed architecture   See *proprietary architecture.*

cluster   On a magnetic disk, a storage unit that consists of two or more sectors.

coaxial cable   A high-bandwidth connecting cable in which an insulated wire runs through the middle of the cable.

COBOL (Common Business-Oriented Language)   An early, high-level programming language for business applications.

code of conduct   A set of ethical principles developed by a professional association, such as the Association for Computing Machinery (ACM).

code-and-fix   In programming, an early method of program development in which the programmer first created a program, and then tried to correct its shortcomings.

codec   A standard for compressing and decompressing video information to reduce the size of digitized multimedia files.

cold boot   A system start that involves powering up the computer. Compare *warm boot.*

collaboratory   A laboratory that is made accessible to distant researchers by means of the Internet.

collision   In local area networks (LANs), a garbled transmission that results when two or more workstations transmit to the same network cable at exactly the same time. Networks have means of preventing collisions.

color depth   The number of colors that can be displayed on a monitor at one time.

color laser printer   A nonimpact high-resolution printer capable of printing in color.

column   In a spreadsheet, a block of cells going down the screen.

column chart   In presentation graphics, a graph with vertical columns. Column graphs are commonly used to show the values of items as they vary at precise intervals over a period of time.

columnar report   In a database management program, a *report* that groups the requested data in a printout organized by columns. Each line of the report corresponds to one record in the database.

command   A user-initiated instruction that tells a program which task to peform.

command line   An area where commands are typed in a command-line user interface.

command-line user interface   In an operating system, a variety of user interface that requires users to type commands one line at a time.

commercial software   Copyrighted software that must be paid for before it can be used.

common carrier   A public telephone or data communications utility.

common carrier immunity   A basic principle of telecommunications law that absolves telecommunications carriers of responsibility for any legal or criminal liability resulting from messages transmitted by their networks.

Common Object Request Broker Architecture (CORBA)   In object-oriented (OO) programming, a leading standard that defines how objects can communicate with each other across a network.

communication device   Any hardware device that is capable of moving data into or out of the computer.

Compact Disc Read-Only Memory (CD-ROM)   A standard for storing read-only computer data on optical compact disks (CDs), which can be read by CD-ROM drives.

Compact Disc-Recordable (CD-R)   A "write-once" optical storage technology that uses a CD-R drive to record data on CD-R discs. Once you've recorded on the disc, you can't erase the stored data or write over the disc again. You can play the recorded CD on most CD-ROM drives.

Compact Disc-Rewritable (CD-RW)   A read/write optical storage technology that uses a CD-R drive to record data on CD-RW discs. You can erase the recorded data and write new data as you please. Most CD-ROM drives can read the recorded data. CD-RW drives can also write to CD-R discs, but you can only write to CD-R discs once.

CompactFlash   A popular flash memory storage device that can store up to 128 MB of digital camera images.

compatibility   The ability of a computer, device, or program to function with or as a substitute for a given make and model of computer, device, or program.

compatible   The capability to function with or substitute for a given make and model of computer, device, or program.

compatible computers   Computer systems capable of using the same programs and peripherals.

compiler   A program that translates source code in a third-generation programming language into machine code readable by a computer.

complementary metal-oxide semiconductor (CMOS)   A type of semiconductor often used in computers for battery-powered circuits that store the date, time, and system configuration information.

complex instruction set computer (CISC)   A type of central processing unit that can recognize as many as 100 or more instructions and carry out most computations directly.

Component Object Model (COM)   In object-oriented (OO) programming, a standard developed by Microsoft Corporation used to define how objects communicate with each other over networks.

component reusability   In programming, the capability to create a program module that can perform a specific task and be used in another program with little or no modification.

computer   A machine that can physically represent data, process this data by following a set of instructions, store the results of the processing, and display the results so that people can use them.

computer addiction   A psychological disorder characterized by compulsive and prolonged computer usage.

computer ethics   A new branch of philosophy dealing with computing-related moral dilemmas.

computer fluency   A high level of computer conceptual knowledge and skills sufficient to enable a user to apply the computer creatively in novel situations

computer information system (CIS)   A computer system in which all components are designed to work together.

computer literacy   A standard of knowledge and skills regarding computers that is sufficient to prepare an individual for working and living in a computerized society.

computer network   A collection of computers that have been connected together so they can exchange data.

computer science (CS)   A scientific discipline that focuses on the theoretical aspects of improving computers and computer software.

computer system   A collection of related computer components that have all been designed to work smoothly together.

computer virus   A program, designed as a prank or as sabotage, that replicates itself by attaching to other programs and carrying out unwanted and sometimes dangerous operations.

computer virus author   A programmer who creates computer viruses to vandalize computer systems.

computer vision syndrome (CVS)   An eyesight disorder, such as temporary nearsightedness and blurred vision, that results from focusing closely on a computer screen for long periods of time.

computer-aided design (CAD)   An application that enables engineers and architects to design parts and structures. The user can rotate the design in three dimensions and zoom in for a more detailed look. Also see *computer-aided manufacturing (CAM).*

computer-aided manufacturing (CAM)   Software used to drive computer-controlled manufacturing equipment. CAM systems often use output from computer-aided design applications (CAD).

computer-aided production engineering (CAPE)   See *virtual manufacturing.*

computer-aided software engineering (CASE)   Software that provides tools to help with every phase in systems development and enables developers to create data flow diagrams, data dictionary entries, and structure charts.

computer-assisted instruction (CAI)   The use of computers to implement programmed instruction. More broadly, CAI describes any use of computers in education.

computer-based education (CBE)   A generic term that describes any use of computers for educational purposes.

computer-based training (CBT)   The use of computer-assisted instruction (CAI) programs to educate adults.

computer-integrated manufacturing (CIM)   The integration of computer technology with manufacturing processes.

computerized information system (CIS)   A computer-based information system, composed of data, hardware, software, trained personnel, and procedures, that provides essential services to organizations; collects mission-critical data, processes this data, stores the data and the results of processing, and disseminates information throughout the organization.

computer-managed instruction (CMI) The use of computers to help instructors manage administrative teaching tasks, such as tracking grades.

computer-supported cooperative work (CSCW) A collection of applications that supports the information needs of workgroups. These applications include email, videoconferencing, and group scheduling systems.

condensed spacing In character formatting, a character style in which characters are squeezed together more tightly than normal.

conditional control structure See *selection control structure*.

configuration file A file that stores the choices you make when you install a program so that these choices are available each time the program starts.

confirmation A message originated by a program that verifies that a user command has been completed successfully.

congestion In a packet switching network, a performance interruption that occurs when a segment of the network experiences overload.

congestion management system In transportation engineering, a computer-based system that reduces traffic congestion by means of traffic light synchronization and other techniques.

connectionless Not directly connected to another computer on the network. A connectionless network protocol enables two networked computers to exchange data without requiring an active connection to exist between them.

connector A component that enables users or technicians to connect a cable securely to the computers case. A male connector contains pins or plugs that fit into the corresponding female connector.

constructivism A school reform movement that places emphasis on students constructing knowledge for themselves rather than learning it by rote.

contact manager A program that helps you keep track of contacts by maintaining a list of addresses, phone numbers, and fax numbers. Information is also maintained through the use of a notepad, automatic telephone dialing with a modem, and search and sort capabilities.

content model In HTML, a specification of the type of information that can be placed between the start and end tags of an element.

contention In a computer network, a problem that arises when two or more computers try to access the network at the same time. Contention can result in collisions, which can destroy data.

contention management In a computer network, the use of one of several techniques for managing contention and preventing collisions.

context menu See *popup menu*.

continuous speech recognition The decoding of continuous human speech (without artificial pauses) into transcribed text by means of a computer program.

control In a graphical user interface, an area of a window that enables the user to choose or specify options. Available controls include radio buttons (also called option buttons), checkboxes, drop-down list boxes, and text boxes.

control method In an information system, a technique used to reduce the flow of information to people who do not need it (such as routing information so

that it goes to only those people who really need to see the information).

control structure In structured programming, a logical element that governs program instruction execution.

control unit A component of the central processing unit (CPU) that obtains program instructions and sends signals to carry out those instructions.

conversion utility A special translation program that enables a program to read and create files in formats other than those the program normally creates.

cookie A text file that is deposited on a Web user's computer system, without the user's knowledge or consent, that may contain identifying information. This information is used for a variety of purposes, such as retaining the user's preferences or compiling information about the user's Web browsing behavior.

cooperative multitasking In operating systems, a method of running more than one application at a time. If the active application crashes, however, the whole system must be restarted.

copper wire In telecommunications, a type of network cabling that uses strands of copper coated with insulation.

copy In the editing process, a command that enables the user to duplicate selected text, store this text in a temporary storage location called the clipboard, and insert (*paste*) the text in a new location.

copy protected Secured against unauthorized copying by some means, such as the inclusion of a necessary piece of hardware.

copyright infringement The act of using material from a copyrighted source without getting permission to do so.

copyright protection scheme A method used by software manufacturers to ensure that users cannot produce unauthorized copies of copyrighted software.

copyrighted Protected legally against copying or modification without first obtaining permission.

cordless mouse A type of mouse that connects to the computer by means of an infrared port.

corporate espionage The unauthorized access of corporate information, usually to the benefit of one of the corporation's competitors.

cost/benefit analysis An examination of the losses and gains, both tangible and intangible, related to a project.

cracker A computer user obsessed with gaining entry into highly secure computer systems.

crash An abnormal termination of program execution.

credit card authorization A system used in point-of-sale (POS) terminals that connects to an authorization service through a call center each time a credit card purchase is made.

critical thinking The capacity to evaluate the quality of information.

cross-functional team A method of designing products in which people who were formerly separated, such as engineering and finance professionals, work together in a team from the beginning of a project.

cross-platform network A computer network that includes more than one type or brand of hardware and operating system. In many colleges and universities, for example, the campus local area

network includes Macintoshes, UNIX computers, and Windows PCs.

cross-platform programming language A programming language that can create programs capable of running on many different types of computers.

cross platform standard A standard that assures interoperability on two or more brands or types of computers or computer operating systems.

crosstab In a database management program, a type of query that produces sums, averages, and other statistics for grouped data.

cumulative trauma disorder (CTD) An injury involving damage to sensitive nerve tissue due to motions repeated thousands of times daily (such as mouse movements or keystrokes). Also called repetitive stress injury (RSI).

cursor A flashing bar, an underline character, or a box that indicates where keystrokes will appear when typed. Also called insertion point.

cursor-movement keys A set of keys on the keyboard that move the location of the cursor on the screen. The numeric keypad can also move the cursor when in the appropriate mode. Also called arrow keys.

custom software Application software designed for a company by a professional programmer or programming team. Custom software is usually very expensive.

cut and paste An editing operation in which characters or graphics are copied into a temporary storage location (called the clipboard) and then inserted somewhere else.

cyber gang A group of computer users obsessed with gaining entry into highly secure computer systems.

cyberstalking A form of harrassment in which an individual is repeatedly subject to unwanted electronic mail or advances in chat rooms.

cylinder A single track location on all the platters of a hard disk. See *track* and *platter*.

D

data The raw material of computing: unorganized information represented for computer processing.

data archiving The process of transferring infrequently used data to backup devices, where the data will be accessible should the need arise.

data backup The process of making copies of frequently used, important data so that it can be restored in the event of a catastrophic system failure, such as the loss of a hard disk drive.

data bus A high-speed freeway of parallel connections that enables the CPU to communicate at high speeds with memory.

data compression The reduction of a file's size so that the file can be stored without taking up as much storage space and can be transferred more quickly over a computer network. Two types of compression are lossless compression (the compressed file can be decompressed without losing any original information) and lossy compression (some of the original information is permanently removed).

data dictionary In information systems development, a collection of definitions of all data types that may be input into the system.

data diddling A computer crime in which data is modified to conceal the theft or embezzlement.

data file A named unit of information storage that contains data rather than program instructions.

data flow diagram A graphical representation of the flow of data through an information system.

data glove A device that translates hand and arm movements into computer input.

data independence In a database, the storage of data in such a way that it is not locked into use by a particular application.

data integrity In a database, the validity of the stored data; specifically, its freedom from error due to improper data entry, hardware malfunctions, or transmission errors.

data mart A large database that contains all the data used by one of the divisions of an organization.

data mining The analysis of data stored in data warehouses to search for previously unknown patterns.

data processing A professional field that focuses on the use of computers to create transaction processing systems for businesses.

data projector An output device that projects a computer's video output onto a large screen so that an audience can see it.

data redundancy In a database, a design error in which the same data appears more than once, creating opportunities for discrepant data entry and increasing the chance that the data will be processed incorrectly.

data storage hierarchy In data processing, a means of conceptualizing storage that envisions a scale ranging from the smallest unit of data (the bit) to the largest (the file).

data transfer rate 1. In secondary storage devices, the maximum number of bits per second that can be sent from the hard disk to the computer. The rate is determined by the drive interface. 2. The speed, expressed in bits per second (bps), at which a modem can transfer, or is transferring, data over a telephone line.

data type In a database or spreadsheet program, a particular type of information, such as a date, a time, or a name.

data validation In a database, a method of increasing the validity of data by defining acceptable input ranges for each field in the record.

data warehouse A very large database, containing as many as a trillion data records, that stores all of a firm's data and makes this data available for exploratory analysis (called data mining).

database A collection of information stored in an organized way.

database file A file containing data that has been stored in the proprietary file format of a database program.

database management system (DBMS) An application that enables users to create databases that contain links from several files. Database management systems are usually more expensive than file management programs.

database object In Microsoft Access, a tool for designing and using database components (including tables, forms, and queries).

database program An application that stores information so that needed information can be quickly located, organized, and displayed.

database server In a client/server computing network, a program that makes the information stored in databases available to two or more authorized users.

database vendor 1. A company that compiles information into large databases. 2. A company that creates and sells database software.

Datasheet View In Microsoft Access and Microsoft Excel, a data viewing option that enables the user to view the numerical data underlying a chart or a table.

date field In a database, a space that accepts only date information.

daughterboard An auxiliary circuit board that is designed to mount on the surface of a motherboard.

dead key A keyboard shortcut that adds a diacritical mark to the next letter you type.

debugging In programming, the process of finding and correcting errors, or bugs, in the source code of a computer program.

decision support system (DSS) A program that helps management analyze data to make decisions on semistructured problems.

declarative language A language that can be used to identify the components of a text. Synonymous with markup language.

decode One of four basic operations carried out by the control unit of a microprocessor. The decode operation figures out what a program instruction is telling the computer to do.

decrement To decrease (v.). A specified unit by which a quantity should be decreased (n.).

defamation An unfounded attack on the character or reputation of an individual or company.

default In a computer program, a fallback setting or configuration value that is used unless the user specifically chooses a different one.

default folder In email, a folder that appears automatically when you set up your email account and cannot be deleted. The inbox folder, sent mail folder, and deleted mail folder are all default folders.

default start page The Web document that appears when you start your Web browser or click the Home button. Most Web browsers are set up to display the browser company's home page, but you can easily change this setting so that the browser displays a more useful default home page.

default user interface In an operating system, the user interface (the means of interacting with the user) that appears automatically, based on preset options in the program. Some operating systems enable users to choose more than one user interface.

delete query In a database management program, a type of query that deletes records throughout the database that conform to the specified criteria.

deliverable In the development of an information system, the outcome of a particular phase of the system's development life cycle (SDLC).

Delphi An object-oriented programming compiler based on Pascal. Although Delphi is similar to Microsoft's Visual Basic (VB), it has not been able to match Visual Basic's success.

demodulation In telecommunications, the process of receiving and transforming an analog signal into its digital equivalent so that a computer can use the information.

demote In an outlining utility, to lower the status of a heading (for example, by moving it from II to B).

denial-of-service (DoS) attack A form of network vandalism that attempts to make a service unavailable to other users, generally by flooding the service with meaningless data. Also called syn flooding.

deregulation A type of legislative reform in which government protections or regulations are removed in an effort to spur competition.

Design view In Microsoft Access, a view of the database that enables the user to create or alter the structure of tables, forms, or queries.

desktop computer A personal computer designed for an individual's use. Desktop computers are increasingly used to gain access to the resources of computer networks.

desktop environment A user interface that simulates a knowledge worker's desktop by depicting computer resources as if they were files and folders.

desktop publishing (DTP) The combination of text, graphics, and advanced formatting to create a visually appealing document.

device driver A program file that contains specific information needed by the operating system to function with a specific brand of model of device.

diacritical mark A mark added to a character in a language other than English, such as an accent, tilde, or umlaut.

dialog box In a graphical user interface (GUI), an on-screen message box used to request information from the user.

Difference Engine A clockwork calculating machine created by Charles Babbage in the nineteenth century and capable of solving equations and printing tables. Technology at the time had not advanced enough to produce this invention.

digital A form of representation in which distinct objects, or digits, are used to stand for something in the real world, such as temperature or time, so that counting can be performed precisely.

digital audio tape (DAT) A magnetic tape backup medium that offers data backup capabilities at relatively low cost.

digital camera A camera that records an image by means of a digital imaging system, such as a charged-coupled device (CCD), and stores the image in memory or on a disk.

digital certificate A form of digital ID used to obtain access to a computer system or prove one's identity while shopping on the Web. Certificates are issued by independent, third-party organizations called certificate authorities (CA).

digital data storage (DDS) A *digital audio tape (DAT)* storage medium that stores up to 40 GB of backup data on a single cartridge.

digital light processing (DLP) projector A computer projection device that employs millions of microscopic mirrors, embedded in a microchip, to produce a brilliant, sharp image.

digital linear tape (DLT) A tape backup medium that offers faster data transfer rates and more storage capacity than *quarter-inch cartridge (QIC)* or *digital audio* *tape (DAT)* drives, at a significantly higher cost.

digital rights   A type of intellectual property right that gives the holder the lawful ability to sell digital reproductions of a work.

Digital Subscriber Line (DSL)   A general term for several technologies that enable high-speed Internet access through twisted-pair telephone lines. Also called xDSL. See *Asymmetric Digital Subscriber Line (ADSL)*.

Digital Video Disk (DVD)   A digital optical disc format capable of storing up to 17 GB on a single disc, enough for a feature-length movie. DVD is designed to be used with a video player and a television. DVD discs can be read also by DVD-ROM drives.

Digital Video Disk-RAM (DVD-RAM)   A digital video disk (DVD) format that enables users to record up to 2.6GB of data.

Digital Video Disk-ROM (DVD-ROM)   A digital video disk (DVD) format capable of storing up to 4.7GB of data, transferring data at higher speeds, and reading digital video disk and existing CD-ROM discs. Future DVD-ROM drives will offer capacities up to 17GB.

digitizing tablet   In computer-aided graphics, a peripheral device used with a pointing device to convert handdrawn graphics into data that a computer can process.

direct access file   In business data processing, a type of data file in which the computer can gain direct and immediate access to a particular unit of storage, without having to go through a sequence of data.

Direct Broadcast Satellite (DBS)   A consumer satellite technology that offers cable channels and one-way Internet access. To use DBS for an Internet connection, a modem and phone line are required to upload data.

direct conversion   In the development of an information system, the termination of the current system and the immediate institution of the new system in the whole organization.

directory   A logical storage unit, often represented as a folder, that enables computer users to group files in named, hierarchically organized folders and subfolders. In magnetic and optical disks, a file that contains a list of all the files contained on the disk and information about each file.

disaster recovery plan   A written plan, with detailed instructions, specifying an alternative computing facility to use for emergency processing until a destroyed computer can be replaced.

discrete speech recognition   A speech recognition technology that is able to recognize human speech only when the speaker stops speaking between words.

disgruntled employee   A current or former employee who has real or imagined grievances. Most computer crime and sabotage stems from disgruntled employers and embezzlers rather than external intruders.

disintermediation   The process of removing an intermediary, such as a car salesperson, by providing a customer with direct access to rich information and warehouse-size selection and stock.

disk cache   A small amount of memory (up to 512KB), usually built into the electronics of a disk drive, used to store frequently accessed data. Disk caches can significantly improve the performance of a disk drive.

disk cartridge   A removable cartridge containing one or more rigid disks similar to those found in hard disks.

disk cleanup utility   A utility program that removes unneeded temporary files.

disk drive   A secondary storage mechanism that stores and retrieves information on a disk by using a read/write head. Disk drives are random access devices.

disk scanner   A utility program that can detect and resolve a variety of physical and logical problems related to file storage.

display   The visual output of a computer, usually portrayed by a monitor or a liquid crystal display (LCD).

display adapter   See *video adapter*.

display type   In word processing or desktop publishing, the typeface or font used for titles and heading text. Sans serif fonts are usually chosen for display type.

distance learning   The use of telecommunications (and increasingly the Internet) to provide educational outreach programs for students at remote locations.

distributed hypermedia system   A network-based content development system in which individuals connected to the network can each make a small contribution by developing content related to their area of expertise. The Web is a distributed hypermedia system.

document   A file created with an application program, such as a word processing or spreadsheet program.

document formatting   In a word processing document, options that alter the appearance of the entire document, such as orientation and paper size.

documentation   In information systems development, the recording of all information pertinent to the development of an information system, usually in a project notebook.

document-centric   In a software suite, a user interface concept in which what counts is the document the user is creating rather than the software being used to create a portion of the document. Menus and toolbars dynamically and automatically change to those relevant to the type of data being edited.

document map   In a word processing program, an on-screen window that provides a visual guide to the document's overall organization.

domain   In a computer network, a group of computers that are administered as a unit. Network administrators are responsible for all the computers in their domains. On the Internet, this term refers to all the computers that are collectively addressable within one of the four parts of an IP address. For example, the first part of an IP address specifies the number of a computer network. All the computers within this network are part of the same domain.

domain name   On the Internet, a readable computer address (such as www.microsoft.com) that identifies the location of a computer on the network.

domain name registration   In the Internet, a process by which individuals and companies can obtain a domain name (such as www.c34.org) and link this name to a specific Internet address (IP address).

domain name server   An Internet server program that maintains a table showing the current IP addresses assigned to domain names. Also called DNS server or name server.

Domain Name System (DNS)   The conceptual system, standards, and names that make up the hierarchical organization of the Internet into named domains.

dongle   A small peripheral that must be connected to a user's computer for the particular copy-protected program to function.

dot pitch   On a monitor, the space (measured in millimeters) between each physical dot on the screen.

dot-matrix printer   An impact printer that forms text and graphic images by hammering the ends of pins against a ribbon in a pattern (matrix) of dots. Dot-matrix printers produce near-letter quality printouts.

double-click   To quickly press and release a mouse button twice.

double-density (DD)   A floppy disk format that offers up to 800 KB of storage.

download   To transfer a file from another computer to your computer by means of a modem and a telephone line. See *upload*.

downsizing   In corporate management, a cost-reduction strategy involving layoffs to make a firm leaner and more competitive. Downsizing often accompanies technology-driven restructuring that theoretically enables fewer employees to do the same or more work.

downwardly compatible   Capable of running without modification when using earlier computer components or files created with earlier software versions.

drag   To move the mouse while holding down a mouse button.

drag handle   In a graphics program, a small rectangular mark that appears on an image's border that enables the user to drag, scale, or size the graphic image.

drawing program   An application program used to create, edit, and display vector graphics.

drill-and-repeat test   In programmed instruction, a method of testing students and ensuring that they learn the material. If students miss questions on a drill-and-repeat test, they are guided back to the material that explains the missed questions.

drill-down   A technique used by managers to view information in a data warehouse. By drilling down to lower levels of the database, the manager can focus on sales regions, offices, and then individual salespeople, and view summaries at each level.

drive bay   A receptacle or opening into which you can install a floppy drive, a CD-ROM or DVD-ROM drive, or a removable drive.

drive interface   The electrical pathway between a secondary storage device, such a hard disk, and the computer. The drive interface is a leading factor in determining the speed of a storage device.

Dual Inline Memory Module (DIMM)   A plug-in memory module that contains RAM chips. DIMMs use a 64-bit bus to transfer data between the memory and the processor, which is required for many new computers.

dual scan LCD   See *passive matrix LCD*.

dumpster diving   A technique used to gain unauthorized access to computer systems by retrieving user IDs and passwords from an organization's trash.

DVD-RAM   See *digital video disk-RAM.*

DVD-ROM   See *digital video disk-ROM.*

DVD-ROM drive   A read-only disk drive that reads the data encoded on DVD-ROM disks and transfers this data to a computer.

dye sublimation printer   A thermal transfer printer that produces results that rival high-quality color photographs. Dye sublimation printers are slow and extremely expensive.

dynamic random-access memory (DRAM)   A random access memory chip that must be refreshed periodically; otherwise, the data in the memory will be lost.

E

e-commerce   See *electronic commerce.*

economically feasible   Capable of being accomplished with available fiscal resources. This is usually determined by a cost/benefit analysis.

edit menu   In a graphical user interface (GUI), a pull-down menu that contains standard editing commands, such as Copy, Cut, and Paste.

edutainment   Software combining education and entertainment that provides educational material in the form of a game so that the education becomes entertainment.

effect   In a graphics program, a processing option that changes the appearance of an image. For example, some graphic programs can manipulate a photograph so that it looks like a watercolor painted on textured paper.

electrical engineering (EE)   An engineering discipline that is concerned with the design and improvement of electrical and electronic circuits.

electronic commerce   The use of the Internet and other wide area networks (WANs) for business-to-business and business-to-consumer transactions. Also called e-commerce.

electronic data interchange (EDI)   A communications standard for the electronic exchange of financial information through information services.

electronic mail (email)   The use of a computer network to send and receive messages.

Electronic Recording Machine—Accounting (ERMA)   A computer system developed in 1959 by General Electric that could read special characters. ERMA had a major effect on the banking business, where it was used to digitize checking account information.

electronic vault   In online banking, a mainframe computer that stores account holder's information.

electronic warfare   In information warfare, the use of electronic devices to destroy or damage computer systems.

electronics   A field within electric engineering that is concerned with the use of transistors to amplify or switch the direction of electrical current.

element   In HTML, a distinctive component of a document's structure, such as a title, heading, or list. HTML divides elements into two categories: head elements (such as the document's title) and body elements (headings, paragraphs, links, and text).

element name   In HTML, the code name used to differentiate an element, such as a level-one heading (H1) or a paragraph (P).

email address   A series of characters that precisely identifies the location of a person's electronic mailbox. On the Internet, email addresses consist of a mailbox name (such as **jsmith**) followed by an at sign (**@**) and the computer's domain name (as in **jsmith@hummer. virginia.edu**).

email client   A program or a program module that provides email services for computer users, including receiving mail into a locally stored inbox, sending email to other network users, replying to received messages, and storing received messages. The better programs include address books, mail filters, and the capability to compose and read messages coded in HTML. Also called user agent.

email server   An application that stores incoming mail until it is downloaded by an email client and sends mail across the Internet.

emergency disk   A disk that can be used to start the computer in case the operating system becomes unusable for some reason.

Emergency Position Indicating Radio Beacons (EPIRB)   A yachting safety device that emits a radio signal indicating the device's precise position, which the device determines by using signals from geographical positioning system (GPS) satellites.

emoticon   See *smiley.*

empty element   In HTML, an element that does not permit the inclusion of any content. The <BR> element is an example of an empty element.

Encapsulated PostScript (EPS)   A graphics format used to print images on PostScript printers.

encapsulation   In object-oriented programming, the hiding of all internal information of objects from other objects.

encryption   The process of converting a message into a ciphertext (an encrypted message) by using a key, so that the message appears to be nothing but gibberish. The intended recipient, however, can apply the key to decrypt and read the message. See also *public key cryptography* and *rot-13.*

end tag   In HTML, the closing component of an element, such as </A>. All elements begin with a start tag; most require an end tag.

endnote   In a word processing program, a feature that automatically positions and prints footnotes at the end of a document, rather than the bottom of the page.

Enhanced IDE (EIDE)   An improved version of the IDE drive interface offering faster data transfer rates, access to drives larger than 528 MB, and access to four secondary storage devices instead of two. Also called ATA-2.

enhanced keyboard   A keyboard with 101 keys that is typically supplied with desktop computers in the United States.

enhanced parallel port (EPP)   A type of parallel port that, unlike the older Centronics parallel port standard, supports bi-directional communication between the computer and printer and offers significantly faster transmission speeds (up to 2 Mbps). EPP is a standard defined by an international standards body. Compare *extended capabilities port (EPP).*

ENIAC (Electronic Numerical Integrator and Computer)   Considered the first large-scale electronic digital computer ever assembled, created in 1946 by Dr. John Mauchly and J. Presper Eckert.

enter button   In a spreadsheet program, a button that confirms the text typed in the entry bar area and inserts this text into the active cell.

enterprise-wide system   An information system available throughout an organization, including its branch offices.

entity-relationship diagram (ERD)   In the design of information systems, a diagram that shows all the entities (organizations, departments, users, programs, and data) that play roles in the system, as well as the relationships between those entities.

entry-level drive   A storage device typically found on the least expensive computers marketed at a given time.

ergonomic keyboard   A keyboard designed to reduce (but not eliminate) the chance of a cumulative trauma disorder (CTD), an injury involving damage to sensitive nerve tissue caused by motions repeated thousands of times daily.

error message   A message originated by a program that warns the user concerning a problem of some kind. The users intervention may be required to solve the problem.

Esc   A key that is often used to interrupt or cancel an operation.

Ethernet   A set of standards that defines local area networks (LANs) capable of operating at data transfer rates of 10 Mbps to 1 Gbps. About 80 percent of all LANs use one of several Ethernet standards.

Ethernet card   A network interface card (NIC) designed to work with Ethernet local area networks (LANs).

ethical principle   A principle that defines the justification for considering an act or a rule to be morally right or wrong. Ethical principles can help people find their way through moral dilemmas.

ethics   The branch of philosophy dealing with the determination of what is right or wrong, usually in the context of moral dilemmas.

e-trading site   On the Internet, an online brokerage that enables investors to buy and sell stocks without a human broker's intervention.

even parity   An error-checking technique that sets an extra bit to 1 if the number of 1 bits in a byte adds up to an odd number.

event-driven   In programming, a program design method that structures the program around a continuous loop, which cycles until an event occurs (such as the user clicking the mouse).

exception report   In a transaction processing system (TPS), a document that alerts someone of unexpected developments, such as high demand for a product.

exclusion operator   In database and Internet searching, a symbol or a word that tells the software to exclude records or documents containing a certain word or phrase.

executable file   A file containing a script or program that can execute instructions on the computer.

executable program   A program that will run on a certain type of computer.

execute   One of four basic operations carried out by the control unit of a microprocessor. The execute operation involves performing a requested action, such as adding or comparing two numbers.

execution cycle In a machine cycle, a phase consisting of the execute and write-back operations.

executive information system (EIS) A system that supports management's strategic planning function.

executive support system (ESS) A type of decision support system designed to provide high-level executives with information summarizing the overall performance of their organization on the most general level.

expanded spacing In character formatting, the provision of extra space between each character.

expansion board A circuit board that provides additional capabilities for a computer.

expansion card See *expansion board*.

expansion bus An electrical pathway that connects the microprocessor to the expansion slots. Also called I/O bus.

expansion slot A receptacle connected to the computer's expansion bus that accepts an expansion board.

expert system In artificial intelligence (AI), a program that relies on a database of if-then rules to draw inferences, in much the way a human expert does.

Extended Binary Coded Decimal Interchange Code (EBCDIC) A character encoding scheme developed by IBM and used on its mainframe computer systems.

extended character set A set of characters that can be accessed only by increasing the number of bits per character from the standard seven bits to eight bits (one byte). The extended character set was never standardized, so the PC and Macintosh versions are not compatible.

extended capabilities port (ECP) A parallel port standard that is virtually identical to the enhanced parallel port (EPP) standard, except that it was defined by two companies in advance of the issuance of the EPP standard.

extended data out (EDO) DRAM A type of dynamic RAM (DRAM) that provides faster speeds because it can begin fetching the next item to be stored in memory at the same time that it is sending an item to the CPU.

extended keyboard A Macintosh keyboard that closely resembles the enhanced keyboard sold with most desktop PCs.

Extensible Markup Language (XML) A set of rules for creating markup languages that enables Web authors to capture specific types of data by creating their own elements. XML can be used in HTML documents.

extension A three-letter suffix added to a DOS filename. The extension is often supplied by the application and indicates the type of application.

external drive bay In a computer case, a receptacle designed for mounting storage devices that is accessible from the outside of the case.

external modem A modem with its own case, cables, and power supply that plugs into the serial port of a computer.

extranet A corporate intranet that has been opened to external access to selected outside partners, including customers, research labs, and suppliers.

eye-gaze response system A biological feedback device that enables quadriplegics to control computers by moving their eyes around the screen.

F

facsimile machine A device that transmits scanned images via the telephone system (also known as fax machine).

facsimile transmission (fax) The sending and receiving of printed pages between two locations, using a telephone line and fax devices that digitize the page's image.

fair use An exception to copyright laws made to facilitate education, commentary, analysis, and scholarly research.

fall back In modems, to decrease the data transfer rate to accommodate communications with an older modem or across a dirty line. Some modems also fall forward if line noise conditions improve.

Fast ATA An *entry-level* hard drive interface standard that offers data transfer rates of up to 16 Mbps. Synonymous with Fast IDE and ATA-2.

Fast Ethernet An Ethernet standard for local area networks (LANs) that enables data transfer rates of 100 Mbps using twisted-pair cable.

Fast IDE See *Fast ATA*.

fast-page mode (FPM) DRAM A type of dynamic RAM (DRAM) that provides faster speeds because it can replace data stored within a row of a data page without having to replace the entire page.

fault-tolerant system A computer system under development by computer scientists that can keep running even if it encounters a glitch in programming.

fax modem A modem that also functions as a fax machine, giving the computer user the capability of sending word processing documents and other files as faxes.

fax-on-demand An information service in which faxes can be requested by means of a telephone call, and then automatically sent to the caller.

fax software A utility program that transforms a modem-equipped PC into a device capable of sending and receiving faxes.

fetch One of four basic operations carried out by the control unit of a microprocessor. The fetch operation retrieves the next program instruction from the computer's memory.

fiber-optic cable A network cable made from tiny strands of glasslike material that transmit light pulses with very high efficiency and can carry massive amounts of data.

field In a database, an area for storing a certain type of information.

field code In a word processing program, a code that, when inserted in the text, tells the program to perform an operation specified by the code, such as inserting the time and date when the document is printed.

field emission display (FED) A flat-panel display technology that uses tiny CRTs to produce each on-screen pixel.

file A document or other collection of information stored on a disk and identified as a unit by a unique name.

file allocation table (FAT) A hidden on-disk table that keeps vital records concerning exactly where the various components of a given file are stored. The file allocation table is created at the conclusion of the formatting process.

file compression utility A program to reduce the size of files without harming the data.

file defragmentation utility A program used to read all the files on a disk and rewrite them so that files are all stored in a contiguous manner. This process almost always improves disk performance by some degree.

file format See *format* (definition 1).

file infector A computer virus that attaches to a program file and, when that program is executed, spreads to other program files.

file management program An application that enables users to create customized databases and store and retrieve data from those databases.

file menu In a graphical user interface (GUI), a pull-down menu that contains standard file-management commands, such as Save and Save As.

file name A unique name given to a stored file.

file server In client/server computing, a computer that has been set aside (dedicated) to make program and data files available to client programs on the network.

file sharing In a local area network (LAN), the modification of a file's properties so that other users may read or even modify the file.

File Transfer Protocol (FTP) An Internet standard for the exchange of files between two computers connected to the Internet. With an FTP client, you can upload or download files from a computer that is running an FTP server. Normally, you need a user name and password to upload or download files from an FTP server, but some FTP servers provide a service called anonymous FTP, which enables anyone to download the files made available for public use.

file viewer A utility program that can display the contents of a certain type of file.

fill In a spreadsheet program, a copying operation that copies the contents of the current cell to the specified range.

filter In email, a rule that specifies the destination folder of messages conforming to certain criteria.

filtering software A program that attempts to prevent minors from accessing adult material on the Internet.

firewall A program that permits an organization's internal computer users to access the Internet but places severe limits on the ability of outsiders to access internal data.

FireWire port Synonymous with 1394 port. FireWire is Apple Computers name for 1394 port technology.

first sale doctrine A principle of copyright law stipulating that a person who legally obtains a copyrighted work may give or sell the work to another person without the author's permission.

fixed disk A hard drive that uses nonremovable platters.

flame In Usenet and email, a message that contains abusive, threatening, obscene, or inflammatory language.

flash BIOS See *flash memory*.

flash memory A special type of read-only memory (ROM) that enables users to upgrade information contained in memory chips. Also called flash BIOS.

flash memory card A credit card-sized memory module used with some digital cameras. The card stores digitized photographs without requiring electrical power to maintain the data.

flat file A type of file generated by a file management program. Flat files can be access in many different ways but cannot be linked to data in other files.

flatbed scanner A device that copies an image (text or graphics) from one side of a sheet of paper and translates it into a digital image.

flat-panel display A low-power, lightweight display used with notebook computers (and increasingly with desktop computers).

flicker An eye-straining visible distortion that occurs when the refresh rate of a display is below 60 Hz.

flight simulator A program that acts like the aircraft on which the pilot is training.

floating-point notation A method for storing and calculating numbers so that the location of the decimal point isn't fixed but floating. This allows the computer to work with very small and very large numbers.

floating-point unit (FPU) A portion of the microprocessor that handles operations in which the numbers are specified in floating-point notation.

floppy disk A removable and widely used data storage medium that uses a magnetically coated flexible disk of Mylar enclosed in a plastic envelope or case. Although 5.25-inch floppy disks were standard, they became obsolete due to the development of the smaller, more durable 3.5-inch disk.

floppy disk drive A mechanism that enables a computer to read and write information on

flowchart In structured programming, a diagram that shows the logic of a program.

flush left alignment In word processing, a way of formatting a block of text so that the left side is aligned but the right side is not.

flush right alignment In word processing, a way of formatting a block of text so that the right side is aligned but the left side is not.

fly-by-wire system In an aircraft, a computer-based control system that eliminates the pilot's direct physical control over the aircraft's control surfaces (such as flaps and rudders) in favor of computer-controlled mechanisms.

FM synthesis A method of generating and reproducing music in a sound card. FM synthesis produces sound similar to an inexpensive electronic keyboard.

folder A graphical representation of a directory. Most major operating systems display directories as though they were file folders.

folder list In an email program, a panel that shows the default and personal mail folders, including the inbox.

follow-up article In Usenet, a message posted in reply to another message.

font A set of characters that has a name (such as Times Roman) and a distinctive design that falls into one of two broad categories, serif (characters that have small finishing strokes) and sans serif (characters that lack finishing strokes).

footer An area at the bottom of the page, but above the bottom margin, that can be used for page numbers or for text that appears on each page of the document.

foot mouse A type of mouse that is controlled by motions of the feet rather than the hands.

footnote A type of citation that pairs an in-text (and usually numbered) reference

to a source citation that appears at the bottom of the page.

foreground application In a multitasking operating system, the active application.

form 1. In a database, an on-screen display of the fields in a record. 2. In HTML, a Web page that contains user input fields that can be used to create interactive services.

form letter A generic message sent to many people that uses database output to create the illusion that the message is individually written and addressed. Business word processing programs can generate form letters using a feature called mail merging.

format 1. A file storage standard used to write a certain type of data to a magnetic disk (also called file format). 2. To prepare a magnetic disk for first use. 3. In word processing, to choose the alignment, emphasis, or other presentation option so that the document will print with an attractive appearance.

formatting The process of modifying a document's appearance so that it looks good when printed.

formula In a spreadsheet program, a mathematical expression embedded in a cell that can include cell references. The cell displays the formula's result.

formula bar In a spreadsheet program, an area above the worksheet that displays the contents of the active cell. The formula bar enables the user to work with formulas, which normally do not appear in the cell.

Form Wizard In Microsoft Access, a *wizard* that guides the user through the process of creating a form.

FORTRAN An early third-generation language that enables scientists and engineers to write simple programs for solving mathematical equations.

fourth-generation language (4GL) A programming language that does not force the programmer to consider the procedure that must be followed to obtain the desired result.

fractal geometry The study of a certain type of irregular geometric shapes, in which the shape of internal components is similar to the overall shape. Fractal shapes are common in nature.

fragmentation A process in which the various components of a file are separated by normal reading and writing operations so that these components are not stored close together. The result is slower disk operation. A defragmentation utility can improve a disk's performance by placing these file components closer together.

frame In a word processing program, a unit of text or a graphic image that has been formatted so that it will appear and print in a precise location on the page. Material placed within frames does not "float" when text is inserted or deleted above the frame.

frame rate In a video or animation, a measurement of the number of still images shown per second.

frame relay A type of packet-switching network that enables an organization to connect to an external network's point of presence for a lower cost than a permanent leased line.

free email service A Web-based service that provides email accounts free of charge. The service is supported by advertising.

freeware Copyrighted software that can be freely copied but not sold.

frequently asked questions (FAQ) A document that contains topical information organized by the questions that are commonly asked concerning the topic.

front panel An area on the front of most computers containing various indicator lights and controls.

FTP client A program that is able to assist the user to upload or download files from an FTP site. There are many standalone FTP clients, and FTP downloading capabilities are built into Web browsers such as Netscape Navigator. Microsoft Internet Explorer 5.0 can upload files to FTP servers as well as download files.

FTP server In the Internet, a server program that enables external users to download or upload files from a specified directory or group of directories.

FTP site An Internet-accessible computer that is running an FTP server.

full backup The process of copying all files from a secondary storage device (most commonly a hard disk) to a backup media, such as a tape cartridge.

full-motion video A video presentation that gives the illusion of smooth, continuous action, even though it consists of a series of still pictures. The key to full-motion video is a frame rate fast enough to create the illusion of continuous movement.

function keys A row of keys positioned along the top of the keyboard, labeled F1 through F12, to which programs can assign various commands.

fuzzy logic A branch of logic concerned with propositions that have varying degrees of precision or confidence.

G

G or GB Abbreviation for gigabyte, approximately one billion (one thousand million) bytes or characters.

Gbps A data transfer rate of approximately one billion bits per second.

Gantt chart A bar chart that summarizes a project's schedule by showing how various activities proceed over time.

gas plasma display A flat-panel display technology. Although gas plasma displays have excellent image quality, they are very expensive and consume too much power to be used on portable computers.

genealogy program A special-purpose application program to assist in tracing and compiling family trees.

General Public License (GPL) A freeware software license, devised by the Open Software Foundation (OSF), stipulating that a given program can be obtained, used, and even modified, as long as the user agrees to not sell the software and to make the source code for any modifications available.

general-purpose computer A computer that can run a variety of programs, in contrast to an embedded or dedicated computer, which is locked to a single function or set of functions.

genetic algorithm An automated program development environment in which various alternative approaches to solving a problem are introduced; each is allowed to mutate periodically through the introduction of random changes. The various approaches compete in an effort to solve a specific problem. After a period of time, one approach may prove to be clearly superior than the others.

GIF animation A graphics file that contains more than one image stored using the GIF graphics file format. Also stored in the file is a brief script that indicates the sequence of images, and how long to display each image.

gigabit A unit of measurement approximately equal to 1 billion bits.

Gigabit Ethernet An Ethernet local area network (LAN) that is capable of achieving data transfer rates of 1 Gbps (one billion bits per second) using fiber-optic cable.

gigabit per second (Gbps) A data transfer measurement equivalent to one billion bits per second.

Gigabit per second Points of Presence (gigaPoPs) In Internet II, a high-speed testbed for the development of next-generation Internet protocols, a point of presence (POP) that provides access to a backbone service capable of data transfer rates in excess of 1 Gbps (one billion bits per second).

gigabyte (G or GB) A unit of measurement commonly used to state the capacity of memory or storage devices; equal to 1,024 megabytes, or approximately 1 billion bytes or characters.

glass cockpit In aviation, a cockpit characterized by a profusion of data displays.

Global Positioning System (GPS) A satellite-based system that enables portable GPS receivers to determine their location with an accuracy of 100 meters or less.

global structure In an HTML document, the top-level document structure created by using the HEAD and BODY tags.

global unique identifier (GUID) A uniquely identifying serial number assigned to Pentium III processor chips that can be used by Web servers to detect which computer is accessing a Web site.

graphical browser On the World Wide Web, a browser capable of displaying graphics images as well as text. Early browsers could display only text.

graphical user interface (GUI) An interface between the operating system and the user. Graphical user interfaces are the most popular of all user interfaces but also require the most system resources.

Graphical MUD A *multiuser dungeon (MUD)* that uses graphics instead of text to represent the interaction of characters in a virtual environment.

graphics accelerator A display adapter (video card) that contains its own dedicated processing circuitry and video memory (VRAM), enabling faster display of complex graphics images.

graphics file A file that stores the information needed to display a graphic. Popular graphics file formats include BMP (Windows bitmap), JPEG, and GIF.

Graphics Interchange Format (GIF) A bit-mapped color graphics file format capable of storing images with 256 colors. GIF incorporates a compression technique that reduces file size, making it ideal for use on a network. GIF is best used for images that have areas of solid color.

graphics output A type of output that consists of visual images, including charts and picture.

graphics tablet A graphics input device used with CAD applications to enter graphically data precisely.

grayscale monitor A monitor that displays black, white, and dozens or hundreds of shades of gray. Grayscale monitors are often used to prepare copy for noncolor printing.

grounding strap A wrist strap worn when repairing or upgrading computer components. The strap can be connected to an electrical ground to prevent the discharge of static electricity, which can ruin computer components that contain semiconductor chips.

group email address An email address that directs an email message to more than one person.

grouped query In a database management program, a type of query that organizes the results by groups.

groupware A type of software that facilitates computer-based cooperative work.

gutter In document formatting, an extra space on the side of each page that allows for binding.

H

hacker Traditionally, a computer user who enjoys pushing his or her computer capabilities to the limit, especially by using clever or novel approaches to solving problems. In the press, the term hacker has become synonymous with criminals who attempt unauthorized access to computer systems for criminal purposes, such as sabotage or theft. The computing community considers this usage inaccurate.

hacker ethic A set of moral principles common to the first-generation hacker community (roughly 1965–1982), described by Steven Levy in *Hackers* (1984). According to the hacker ethic, all technical information should, in principle, be freely available to all. Therefore, gaining entry to a system to explore data and increase knowledge is never unethical. Destroying, altering, or moving data in such a way that could cause injury or expense to others, however, is always unethical. In increasingly more states, unauthorized computer access is against the law. See also *cracker.*

handle In a spreadsheet program, a rectangular box on a cell corner that can be used to specify the size of a fill area.

handheld computer See *personal digital assistant.*

handheld scanner A scanner used to digitize images of small originals, such as photographs or small amounts of text.

handwriting recognition software A program that accepts handwriting as input and converts it into editable computer text.

hanging indent A type of indentation that does not indent the first line but does indent the following lines.

haptics A field of research in developing output devices that stimulate the sense of touch.

hard copy Printed computer output, differing from the data stored on disk or in memory.

hard disk A secondary storage medium that uses several rigid disks (platters) coated with a magnetically sensitive material and housed in a hermetically sealed mechanism. In almost all modern computers, the hard disk is by far the most important storage medium. Also called hard disk drive.

hard disk controller An electronic circuit that provides an interface between a hard disk and the computer's CPU.

hard disk drive See *hard disk.*

hardware The physical components, such as circuit boards, disk drives, displays, and printers, that make up a computer system.

hardware MPEG support Circuitry built into a computer to improve MPEG video playback speed and quality.

hashing In data processing, the process in which the position of a record is determined through the use of a mathematical computation to produce an address where the unique key field is stored.

hashing algorithm A mathematical formula used to determine the address of a record in a direct access file.

head In HTML, one of two main portions of the document (the other is the body). The head contains elements that do not appear in browser's display window.

head crash In a hard disk, the collision of a read/write head with the surface of the disk, generally caused by a sharp jolt to the computer's case. Head crashes can damage the read/write head, as well as create bad sectors.

header In email or a Usenet news article, the beginning of a message. The header contains important information about the sender's address, the subject of the message, and other information.

head-mounted display (HMD) A helmet equipped with stereo LCD displays used to experience virtual reality.

heat sink A heat-dissipating component that drains heat away from semiconductor devices, which can generate enough heat in the course of their operation to destroy themselves. Heat sinks are often used in combination with fans to cool semiconductor components.

help menu In a graphical user interface (GUI), a pull-down menu that provides access to interactive help utilities.

help screen In commercial software, information that appears on-screen that can provide assistance with using a particular program.

hexadecimal number A number that uses a base 16 number system rather than a decimal (or base 10) number system.

hierarchy In Usenet, a category that includes a variety of newsgroups devoted to a shared, general topic.

hierarchy chart In structured programming, a program planning chart that shows the top-down design of the program and the relationship between program modules. Also called structure chart.

high-density (HD) A floppy disk storage format that can store up to 1.44 MB of data.

high FD (HiFD) A Sony removable disk storage format that can store up to 200 MB using a drive that is also capable of reading 3.5-inch floppy disks.

high-level programming language A programming language that eliminates the need for programmers to understand the intimate details of how the computer processes data.

history list In a Web browser, a window that shows all the Web sites that the browser has accessed during a given period, such as the last 30 days.

home directory In a multiuser computer system, a directory that is set aside for an individual user.

home page 1. In any hypertext system, including the Web, a document intended to serve as an initial point of entry to a Web of related documents. Also called a welcome page, a home page contains general introductory information, as well as hyperlinks to related resources. A well-designed home page contains internal navigation buttons that help users find their way among the various documents that the home page makes available. 2. The start page that is automatically displayed when you start a Web browser or click the program's Home button. 3. A personal page listing an individual's contact information, and favorite links, and (generally) some information—ranging from cryptic to voluminous—about the individual's perspective on life.

horizontal application A general-purpose program widely used across an organization's functional divisions (such as marketing and finance). Horizontal applications are also popular in the consumer market.

horizontal scroll bar A scroll bar that enables the user to bring areas of a document into view that are hidden to the left or right.

host In a computer network, a computer that is fully connected to the network and is able to be addressed by other hosts.

hostile environment In laws concerning sexual harassment in the workplace, a working environment characterized by practices (such as sexually explicit jokes or calendars) that make some women feel as though the workplace is intended for males only.

HTML editor A program that provides assistance in preparing documents for the Web using HTML. The simplest HTML editor is a word processing program that enables you to type text and add HTML tags manually. Stand-alone HTML editors provide automated assistance with HTML coding and display some formats on-screen.

hub In a local area network (LAN), a device that connects several workstations and enables them to exchange data.

Human Genome Project (HGP) A research project seeking to identify the full set of genetic instructions inside human cells and find out what those instructions do.

hyperlink In a hypertext system, an underlined or otherwise emphasized word or phrase that, when clicked, displays another document.

hypermedia A hypertext system that uses various multimedia resources, such as sounds, animations, and videos, as a means of navigation as well as decoration.

hypertext A method of preparing and publishing text, ideally suited to the computer, in which readers can choose their own paths through the material. To prepare hypertext, you first "chunk" the information into small, manageable units, such as single pages of text. These units are called nodes. You then embed hyperlinks in the text. When the reader clicks a hyperlink, the hypertext software displays a different node. The process of navigating among the nodes linked in this way is called browsing. A collection of nodes interconnected by hyperlinks is called a web. The Web is a hypertext system on a global scale.

Hypertext Markup Language (HTML) A language for marking the portions of a document (called elements) so that, when accessed by a program called a Web browser, each portion appears with a distinctive format. HTML is the markup language behind the appearance of

documents on the Web. HTML is standardized by means of a document type definition in the Standard Generalized Markup Language (SGML). HTML includes capabilities that enable authors to insert hyperlinks, which when clicked display another HTML document. The agency responsible for standardizing HTML is the World Wide Web Consortium (W3C).

Hypertext Transfer Protocol (HTTP) The Internet standard that supports the exchange of information on the Web. By defining Universal Resource Locators (URLs) and how they can be used to retrieve resources anywhere on the Internet, HTTP enables Web authors to embed hyperlinks in Web documents. HTTP defines the process by which a Web client, called a browser, originates a request for information and sends it to a Web server, a program that responds to HTTP requests and provides the desired information.

I/O bus See *expansion bus*.

I/O device Generic term for any input or output device.

IBM compatible A computer that can use all or almost all software developed for the IBM Personal Computer and accepts the IBM computer's cards, adapters, and peripheral devices. Compare *clone*.

icon In a graphical user interface (GUI), a small picture that represents a program, a data file, or some other computer entity or function.

IDE/ATA See *Integrated Drive Electronics (IDE)*.

identify theft A form of fraud in which a thief obtains someone's Social Security number and other personal information, and then uses this information to obtain credit cards fraudulently.

image editor A sophisticated paint program for editing and transforming complex bitmapped images, such as photographs.

image processing system A filing system in which incoming documents are scanned and stored digitally.

impact printer A printer that generates output by striking the page with something solid.

inbox In email, a default folder that contains any new mail messages, as well as older messages that have not been moved or deleted.

inclusion operator In database or Web searching, a symbol or keyword that instructs the search software to make sure that any retrieved records or documents contain a certain word or phrase.

increment To increase (v.). A specified unit by which a quantity should be increased (n.).

incremental backup The process of copying files that have changed since the last full backup to a backup media, such as a tape cartridge.

indecency In U.S. law, the use of four-letter words or any other explicit reference to sexual or excretory acts that violates community decency standards.

index page In Web publishing, the page that the Web server displays by default (usually called index.html or default.html).

indexed file See *indexed sequential file*.

indexed sequential file A file with records that can be accessed either directly

(randomly) or sequentially. Also called indexed file.

Industry Standard Architecture (ISA) bus A bus architecture used for expansion slots introduced in the IBM PC/AT. Although they are slower than the PCI bus architecture, ISA expansion slots continue to appear in new computers for compatibility.

information hiding A modular programming technique in which information inside a module remains hidden with respect to other modules.

information kiosk An automated presentation system used for public information or employee training.

information literacy The capability to gather information, evaluate the information, and make an informed decision.

information overload A condition of confusion, stress, and indecision brought about by being inundated with information of variable value.

information processing cycle A complete sequence of operations involving data input, processing, storage, and output.

information reduction In an information system, a method of controlling information to prevent it from overwhelming people in an organization.

information system A purposefully designed system that brings data, computers, procedures, and people together to manage information important to an organization's mission.

information systems (IS) department In a complex organization, the division responsible for designing, installing, and maintaining the organization's information systems.

information terrorism The intimidation of a person, an organization, or a country by means of sabotage directed at information systems.

information warfare A military strategy that targets an opponent's information systems.

information-literate person Someone who knows how to gather information, evaluate the information, and make an informed decision.

infrared A data transmission medium that uses the same signaling technology used in TV remote controls.

inheritance In object-oriented (OO) programming, the capacity of an object to pass its characteristics to sub-classes.

inkjet printer A nonimpact printer that forms an image by spraying ink from a matrix of tiny jets.

inline element In HTML, an element that can be included in a block element. Some inline elements enable Web authors to choose presentation formats such as bold or italic.

input The information entered into a computer for processing.

input device Any device that is capable of accepting data so that it is properly represented for processing within the computer.

input/output (I/O) bus A collection of wires through which data travels from input/output devices to the computers main processing unit.

insert mode In word processing, a text insertion mode in which the inserted text pushes existing text to the right and down.

insertion point See *cursor*.

install To set up a program so that it is ready to function on a given computer system. The installation process may involve creating additional directories, making changes to system files, and other technical tasks. For this reason, most programs come with *setup programs* that handle the installation process automatically.

instruction A unique number assigned to an operation performed by a processor.

instruction cycle In a machine cycle, a phase consisting of the fetch and decode operations.

instruction set A list of specific instructions that a given brand and model of processor can perform.

intangible benefits Gains that have no fixed dollar value, such as access to improved information or increased sales due to improved customer services.

integer A whole number.

integrated circuit (IC) A semiconductor circuit containing more than one transistor and other electronic components; often referred to as a chip.

Integrated Drive Electronics (IDE) A popular secondary storage interface standard commonly found in PCs that offers relatively good performance at a low cost. Although IDE is a commonly used interface, newer computers use either Enhanced IDE (EIDE) or Ultra ATA. Also called Advanced Technology Attachment (ATA).

integrated learning system (ILS) A mainframe-based system used to bring computer-assisted instruction (CAI) to schools.

integrated program A program that combines three or more productivity software functions, including word processing, database management, and a spreadsheet.

Integrated Services Digital Network (ISDN) A worldwide standard for the delivery of digital telephone and data services to homes, schools, and offices using existing twisted-pair wiring. The three categories of ISDN services are Basic Rate Interface (BRI), Primary Rate Interface (PRI), and Broadband ISDN (B-ISDN).

Intelligent Transportation System (ITS) A system, partly funded by the U.S. government, to develop smart streets and smart cars. Such a system can warn travelers of congestion and suggest alternative routes.

interactive multimedia A presentation involving two or more media, such as text, graphics, or sound, and providing users with the ability to choose their own path through the information.

interactive processing A type of processing in which the various stages of the information processing cycle (input, processing, storage, and output) can be initiated and controlled by the user.

interexchange carrier (IXC) In the public switched telephone network (PSTN), a company that provides long-distance or regional trunk services between local telephone exchanges.

interface A means of connecting two dissimilar computer devices. An interface has two components, a physical component and a communications standard, called a protocol. The physical component provides the physical means for making a connection, while the protocol enables designers to design the devices so that they can exchange data with each other. The

computers standard parallel port is an example of an interface that has both a distinctive physical connector and a defining, standard protocol.

interlaced monitor A monitor that refreshes every other line of pixels with each pass of the cathode gun. This often results in screen flicker, and almost all monitors now are noninterlaced.

internal drive bay In a computer's case, a receptacle for mounting a storage device that is not easily accessible from outside the computer's case. Internal drive bays are typically used to mount nonremovable hard drives.

internal modem A modem that fits into the expansion bus of a personal computer. See also *external modem*.

International Telecommunications Union (ITU) A branch organization of the United Nations that sets international telecommunications standards.

Internet An enormous and rapidly growing system of linked computer networks, worldwide in scope, that facilitates data communication services such as remote logon, file transfer, electronic mail, the World Wide Web, and newsgroups. Relying on TCP/IP, the Internet assigns every connected computer a unique Internet address (called an IP address) so that any two connected computers can locate each other on the network and exchange data.

Internet 2 The next-generation Internet, still under development.

Internet address The unique, 32-bit address assigned to a computer that is connected to the Internet, represented in dotted decimal notation (for example, 128.117.38.5). Synonymous with IP address.

Internet client A user program for accessing information on the Internet, such as email or a Web site.

Internet Inter-Orb Protocol (IIOP) In object-oriented (OO) programming, a standard that allows Web browsers to request information from objects by using the Common Object Request Broker Architecture (CORBA).

Internet Message Access Protocol (IMAP) In Internet email, one of two fundamental protocols (the other is POP3) that governs how and where users store their incoming mail messages. IMAP4, the current version, stores messages on the mail server rather than facilitating downloading to the user's computer, as does the POP3 standard. For many users, this standard may prove more convenient than POP3 because all of one's mail is kept in one central location, where it can be organized, archived, and made available from remote locations. IMAP4 is supported by Netscape Messenger, the mail package in Netscape Communicator, Microsoft Outlook Express, and by other leading email programs.

Internet Protocol (IP) One of the two core Internet standards (the other is the Transmission Control Protocol, TCP). IP defines the standard that describes how an Internet-connected computer should break data down into packets for transmission across the network, and how those packets should be addressed so that they arrive at their destination. IP is the connectionless part of the TCP/IP protocols.

Internet protocols The standards that enable computer users to exchange data through the Internet. Also called TCP/IP.

Internet Relay Chat (IRC) A real-time, Internet-based chat service, in which one

can find "live" participants from the world over. IRC requires the use of an IRC client program, which displays a list of the current IRC channels. After joining a channel, you can see what other participants are typing on-screen, and you can type your own repartee.

Internet service A set of communication standards (protocols) and software (clients and servers) that defines how to access and exchange a certain type of information on the Internet. Examples of Internet services are email, FTP, Gopher, IRC, and Web.

Internet Service Provider (ISP) A company that provides Internet accounts and connections to individuals and businesses. Most ISPs offer a range of connection options, ranging from dial-up modem connections to high-speed ISDN and ADSL. Also provided is email, Usenet, and Web hosting.

Internet telephony The use of the Internet (or of nonpublic networks based on Internet technology) for the transmission of real-time voice data.

Internet telephony service providers A long-distance voice messaging service that provides telephone service by means of the Internet or private data networks using Internet technology.

InterNIC A consortium of two organizations that provide networking information services to the Internet community, under contract to the National Science Foundation (NSF). Currently, AT&T provides directory and database services, while Network Solutions, Inc., provides registration services for new domain names and IP addresses.

interoperability The ability to work with computers and operating systems of differing type and brand.

interpreter In programming, a translator that converts each instruction into machine-readable code and executes it one line at a time. Interpreters are often used for learning and debugging, due to their slow speed.

intranet A computer network based on Internet technology (TCP/IP) that meets the internal needs of a single organization or company. Not necessarily open to the external Internet and almost certainly not accessible from the outside, an intranet enables organizations to make internal resources available using familiar Internet. See also *extranet*.

IP address A 32-bit binary number that uniquely and precisely identifies the location of a particular computer on the Internet. Every computer that is directly connected to the Internet must have an IP address. Because binary numbers are so hard to read, IP addresses are given in four-part decimal numbers, each part representing 8 bits of the 32-bit address (for example, 128.143.7.226).

IPOS cycle A sequence of four basic types of computer operations that characterize everything computers do. These operations are input, processing, output, and storage.

IPv6 The Next Generation Internet Protocol, also known as IPng, is an evolutionary extension of the current Internet protocol suite that is under development by the Internet Engineering Task Force (IETF). IPv6 was originally intended to deal with the coming exhaustion of IP addresses, a serious problem caused by the Internet's rapid growth. However, the development effort has broadened to address a number of deficiencies in the current versions of the fundamental Internet protocols, including security, the lack of support for mobile computing, the need for automatic configuration of network devices, the lack of support for allocating bandwidth to high-priority data transfers, and other shortcomings of the current protocols. An unresolved question is whether the working committee will be able to persuade network equipment suppliers to upgrade to the new protocols.

IPX/SPX In local area networks (LANs), a protocol suite developed by Novell for use with the NetWare network operating system.

IrDA port A port housed on the exterior of a computer's case that is capable of sending and receiving computer data by means of infrared signals. The standards that define these signals are maintained by the Infrared Data Association (IrDA). IrDA ports are commonly found on notebook computers and personal digital assistants (PDAs).

ISDN adapter An internal or external accessory that enables a computer to connect to remote computer networks or the Internet by means of ISDN. (Inaccurately called an ISDN modem.)

italic A character format in which characters are slanted to the right.

iteration control structure See *repetition control structure.*

J

Java A cross-platform programming language created by Sun Microsystems that enables programmers to write a program that will execute on any computer capable of running a Java interpreter (which is built into today's leading Web browsers). Java is an object-oriented programming (OOP) language similar to C++, except that it eliminates some features of C++ that programmers find tedious and time-consuming. Java programs are compiled into applets (small programs executed by a browser) or applications (larger, stand-alone programs that require a Java interpreter to be present on the user's computer), but the compiled code contains no machine code. Instead, the output of the compiler is bytecode, an intermediary between source code and machine code that can be transmitted by computer networks, including the Internet.

Java Virtual Machine (VM) A Java interpreter and runtime environment for Java applets and Java applications. This environment is called a virtual machine because, no matter what kind of computer it is running on, it creates a simulated computer that provides the correct platform for executing Java programs. In addition, this approach insulates the computer's file system from rogue applications. Java VMs are available for most computers.

JavaScript A scripting language for Web publishing, developed by Netscape Communications, that enables Web authors to embed simple Java-like programming instructions in the HTML text of their Web pages.

job instruction training (JIT) A method of on-the-job training where decision-making is eliminated as much as possible.

joint application development (JAD) In information systems development, a method of system design that involves users at all stages of system development. See also *prototyping.*

Joint Photographic Experts Group (JPEG) A graphics file format, named after the group that designed it. JPEG graphics can display up to 16.7 million colors and use lossy compression to reduce file size. JPEG is best used for complex graphics such as photographs.

joystick An input device commonly used for games.

justification The alignment of text at the beginning and end of lines. Text can either be flush left, flush right, centered, or justified.

justified alignment In word processing, a way of formatting a block of text so that both the left and right sides are aligned.

just-in-time (JIT) manufacturing A method of monitoring inventory that triggers the manufacturing process only when inventory levels are low.

K

K or KB Abbreviation for kilobyte, approximately one thousand bytes or characters.

Kbps A data transfer rate of approximately one thousand bits per second.

kernel The essential, core portion of the operating system that is loaded into random access memory (RAM) when the computer is turned on and stays in RAM for the duration of the operating session. Also called supervisor program.

kerning The process of adjusting the space between wide and narrow characters so that the results are pleasing to the eye.

key In cryptography, the procedure used to encipher the message so that it appears to be just so much nonsense. The key also is required for decryption. Public key cryptography has two keys: a private key and a public key. A user makes the public key known to others, who use it to encrypt messages; these messages can be decrypted only by the intended recipient of a message, who uses the private key to do so.

key escrow The storage of users' encryption keys by an independent agency, which would divulge the keys to law enforcement investigators only on the production of a valid warrant. Key escrow is proposed by law enforcement officials concerned that encryption would prevent surveillance of criminal activities.

key recovery A method of unlocking the key used to encrypt messages so that the message could be read by law enforcement officials conducting a lawful investigation. Key recovery is proposed by law enforcement officials concerned that encryption would prevent surveillance of criminal activities.

keyboard An input device providing a set of alphabetic, numeric, punctuation, symbolic, and control keys.

keyword In a spreadsheet program, a command that executes a built-in function, such as adding a large number of cells.

kilobyte (K or KB) The basic unit of measurement for computer memory and disk capacity, equal to 1,024 bytes or characters.

kilobits per second (Kbps) A data transfer rate of approximately one thousand bits of computer data per second.

knowledge management system An information system that captures knowledge created by employees and makes it available to an organization.

L

label In a spreadsheet, a text entry that explains one or more numerical entries.

landscape In document formatting, a page layout in which the text runs across the wide orientation of the page.

laptop computer A portable computer larger than a notebook computer but small enough to be transported easily. Few are being made now that notebook computers have become so powerful.

large-scale integration (LSI) A technology used to assemble integrated circuits (IC). LSI was achieved in the early 1970s, and could fit up to 5,000 transistors on a single IC.

laser printer A popular nonimpact, high-resolution printer that uses a version of the electrostatic reproduction technology of copying machines.

last mile problem The lack of local network systems for high-bandwidth multimedia communications that can accommodate the Information Superhighway.

latency In a packet-switching network, a signal delay that is introduced by the time network routers consume as they route packets to their destination.

launch To start an application program.

layer In a computer network, a level of network functionality governed by specific network protocols. For example, the physical layer has protocols concerned with the transmission of signals over a specific type of cable.

LCD projector An output device that projects a computer's screen display on a screen similar to those used with slide projectors.

leader In word processing, a character that is automatically inserted before a tab stop.

leading The space between the lines of text. Pronounced "ledding."

leased line A permanently connected and conditioned telephone line that provides wide area network (WAN) connectivity to an organization or a business.

legacy Obsolete; most often used to describe old mainframe systems.

legacy system A technically obsolete information system that remains in use, often because it performs its job adequately or is too expensive to replace.

legend In a chart, an area that provides a key to the meaning of the symbols or colors used on the chart.

letter-quality printer A dot-matrix printer that can produce characters that appear to be fully formed, like those printed by a laser printer.

level 2 (L2) cache See *secondary cache.*

libel A form of *defamation* that occurs in writing.

life cycle In information systems, the birth, development, use, and eventual abandonment of the system.

light pen An input device that uses a light-sensitive stylus to draw on-screen or on a graphics tablet or to select items from a menu.

line chart A graph that uses lines to show the variations of data over time or to show the relationship between two numeric variables.

line printer In business data processing, a high-speed printer that prints an entire line of text at a time.

linker See *assembler.*

Linux A freeware operating system closely resembling UNIX developed for IBM-compatible PCs but also available for other platforms, including Macintosh.

Linux distribution A CD-ROM containing the Linux operating system and a collection of drivers, GUI interfaces, and application programs.

liquid crystal display (LCD) A small, flat-screen monitor that uses electrical current to control tiny crystals and form an image.

list server In email, a program that automatically sends a copy of every message submitted to the mailing list to the address of each of the mailing list's subscribers. Also called reflector.

list server address In a mailing list, the email address of the list server rather than the mailing list. To subscribe or unsubscribe to a mailing list, you send requests to the list server address.

list view In a database, a way of viewing database records as a list.

load To transfer program instructions from storage to memory.

loading The process of transferring data from an input or storage device into the computer's memory.

local access and transport area (LATA) In the public switched telephone network (PSTN), the area served by a local exchange carrier (LEC).

local area network (LAN) A computer network that connects computers in a limited geographical area (typically less than one mile) so that users can exchange information and share hardware, software, and data resources.

local exchange carrier (LEC) A telecommunications company that serves a local access and transport area (LATA).

local loop In the public switched telephone system (PSTN), the last segment of service delivery, typically consisting of analog connections from neighborhood distribution points.

local newsgroup In Usenet, a category of newsgroups that are devoted to the concerns of the organization (such as a university or company) running the local server.

LocalTalk A protocol developed by Apple Computer that provides peer-to-peer networking among Apple Macintosh computers and Macintosh-compatible peripherals such as laser printers. LocalTalk is a lower-level protocol that works with twisted-pair phone cables.

log in To authenticate yourself as a user with a valid account and usage privileges on a multiuser computer system or a computer network. To log in, you supply your user name and password.

log on To gain access to a computer system or network, generally by providing a user ID and password.

logic bomb A flaw concealed in an otherwise usable computer program that can be triggered to destroy or corrupt data.

logic error In programming, a mistake made by the programmer in designing the program. Logic errors will not surface by themselves during program execution because they are not errors in the structure of the statements and commands.

logical field In a database, a space that accepts only yes and no values.

logical operation One of the two groups of operations performed by the arithmetic-logic unit. Logical operations involve comparing two data items to see which one is larger or smaller.

looping See *repetition control structure.*

lossless compression In data compression, a method used to reduce the size of a file that enables the file to be restored to its original size without introducing errors. Most lossless compression techniques reduce file size by replacing lengthy but frequently occurring data sequences with short codes; to decompress the file, the compression software reverses this process and restores the lengthy data sequences to their original form.

lossy compression In data compression, a method of reducing the size of multimedia files by eliminating information that is not normally perceived by human beings.

low-level language A language that describes exactly the procedures to be carried out by a computer's central processing unit, such as machine or programming language.

M

M or MB Abbreviation for megabyte, approximately one million bytes or characters of information.

machine cycle A four-step process followed by the control unit that involves the fetch, decode, execute, and write-back operations. Also called processing cycle.

machine language The native binary language recognized consisting of 0s and 1s that is executed by a computer's central processing unit.

machine-dependent The dependence of a given computer program or component on a specific brand or type of computer equipment.

machine translation Language translation performed by the computer without human aid.

macro In application software, a user-defined command sequence that can be saved and executed to perform a complex action.

macro virus A computer virus that uses the automatic command execution capabilities of productivity software to spread itself and often to cause harm to computer data.

maglev (magnetic levitation) A railway technology in which magnetic fields are used to raise the train off the railway surface, thus eliminating friction and enabling speeds rivaling those of aircraft.

magnetic resonance imaging (MRI) In health care, a computer controlled imaging device used to diagnose patients.

magnetic-ink character recognition (MICR) system A scanning system developed by the banking industry in the 1950s. Check information is encoded onto each check before it is used to reduce processing time when the check comes back to the bank.

magnetic storage media In computer storage systems, any storage device that retains data using a magnetically sensitive material, such as the magnetic coating found on floppy disks or backup tapes.

magnetic storage medium A storage system that uses magnetically encoded disks or tapes to store data.

magneto-optic (MO) disc An erasable disk that combines magnetic particles used on tape and disk with new optical technology.

magneto-optical (MO) drive A data storage device that uses laser technology to heat an extremely small spot on a magneto-optical (MO) cartridge so that the magnetic medium used in the MO disk becomes capable of having its magnetic orientation changed by the read/write head.

mailbox name One of the two basic parts of a person's email address: the part to the left of the at sign (@), which specifies the name of the person's mailbox. To the right of the @ sign is the domain name of the computer that houses the mailbox. A person's mailbox name often is the same as his or her login name.

mailing list An email application that enables participants to send a message that will be mailed to all of the lists participants. Similarly, replies to this message (if not addressed only to the sender of the original message) will be seen by all participants.

mailing list address An email address that identifies the mailbox to which mailing list messages are sent.

mailto URL In HTML, a type of URL that enables Web authors to create a link to a person's email address. When the user clicks the mailto link, the browser displays a window for composing an email message to this address.

main board See *motherboard.*

mainframe A multiuser computer system that meets the computing needs of a large organization.

maintenance release In commercial software, a minor revision to software that corrects bugs or adds minor features.

management information system (MIS) A computer-based system that supports the information needs of management.

margin The space around the edge of the paper that is left blank when the document is printed.

margin loan In stock investing, a risky strategy in which investors borrow money to purchase stocks. The strategy pays off when share prices rise. In a bear (declining) market, however, investors who purchased stocks on margin loans may accumulate more debt than their finances can handle.

Mark Sense Character Recognition A data input system that can recognize pencil marks on printed forms.

markup language In text processing, a system of codes for marking the format of a unit of text that indicates only that a particular unit of text is a certain part of the document, such as an abstract, a title, or an author's name and affiliation. The actual formatting of the document part is left to another program, called a viewer, which displays the marked document and gives each document part a distinctive format (fonts, spacing, and so on). HTML is a markup language.

mass storage system A backup storage device used in a mainframe system. Mass storage systems can store hundreds or even thousands of high-capacity tape backup cartridges in a carousel-like system.

master In a graphics program, a template that contains the formatting and graphics that will appear on every page.

master file A file containing all the current data relevant to an application.

master page In desktop publishing (DTP), a page that acts as a template for how all other pages will appear.

master slide In presentation graphics, a template slide that contains a presentation's background and any additional information that will appear on every page of the finished presentation.

master view In a desktop publishing or presentation graphics program, a view that shows the underlying template that is used to display each page.

math coprocessor A separate chip that frees the main processor from performing mathematical operations, usually operations involving floating-point notation.

Mbps In networking, a data transfer rate of approximately 1 million bits per second.

medium-scale integration (MSI) A technology used to assemble integrated circuits (ICs). MSI was achieved in the late 1960s and could fit between 20 and 200 transistors on a single IC.

megabyte (M or MB) A measurement of storage capacity equal to 1,024 kilobytes, or approximately 1 million bytes or characters.

memory Circuitry that stores information temporarily so that it is readily available to the central processing unit (CPU).

memory address A code number that specifies a specific location in memory.

memory bus See *system bus*.

memory resident A program, such as an operating system's kernel, that resides in random access memory whenever the computer is turned on.

menu bar In a graphical user interface (GUI), a rectangular bar (generally positioned near the top of the application window) that provides access to pull-down menus. On the Macintosh, an active application's menu bar is always positioned at the top of the screen.

menu-driven user interface An interface between the operating system and the user in which text-based menus show options, rather than requiring the user to memorize the commands and type them in.

message list In an email program, a list of all current email messages.

message window In an email program, an on-screen panel that displays the contents of the message currently highlighted in the message list.

Metcalfe's Law A prediction formulated by Bob Metcalfe, creator of Ethernet, that the value of a network increases in proportion to the square of the number of people connected to the network.

method In object-oriented programming, a procedure or operation that processes or manipulates data.

metropolitan area network (MAN) A high-speed regional network typically used to connect universities with other research facilities in a large metropolitan area.

microcomputer A computer that uses a microprocessor as its CPU.

micron One thousandth of a millimeter.

microphone An input device that converts sound into electrical signals that can be processed by a computer.

microprocessor An integrated circuit containing the arithmetic-logic unit (ALU) and control unit of a computer's central processing unit (CPU).

Microsoft Windows Generic name for the various operating systems in the Microsoft Windows family, including Microsoft Windows CE, Microsoft Windows 3.1, Microsoft Windows 95,

Microsoft Windows 98, and Microsoft Windows NT.

Microsoft Windows 2000 Professional A high-performance operating system for corporate computer users that combines the features of Windows NT Workstation with the easy-to-use interface of Windows 98.

Microsoft Windows 2000 Server A high-performance operating system designed for use on client/server networks in corporations and other large organizations. Windows 2000 Server is the successor to Windows NT Server.

Microsoft Windows 3.x A family of programs developed by Microsoft Corporation, including Windows 3.1, Windows 3.11, and Windows for Workgroups 3.1. Although they are often treated like operating systems, these programs are actually MS-DOS applications.

Microsoft Windows 95 An operating system developed for IBM-compatible PCs by Microsoft Corporation. Unlike Windows 3.x, Microsoft Windows 95 is a true operating system that introduced numerous improvements over its predecessors. Microsoft Windows is a 32-bit operating system that is downwardly compatible with 16-bit programs developed for Windows 3.x. Also called Win 95.

Microsoft Windows 98 A 32-bit operating system developed for IBM-compatible PCs by Microsoft Windows as the successor to Windows 95. Windows 98 offers easier Internet connectivity and the availability to work with peripherals that require Universal Serial Bus (USB) or Accelerated Graphics Port (AGP) slots. Like Windows 95, Windows 98 is downwardly compatible with applications developed for Windows 3.x. Also called Win 98.

Microsoft Windows CE An operating system for palmtop and personal digital assistant computers developed by Microsoft Corporation.

Microsoft Windows NT A 32-bit operating system developed by Microsoft Corporation for use in corporate client/server networks. The operating system consists of two components, Microsoft Windows NT Workstation (for users' systems) and Microsoft Windows NT Server (for file servers).

Microsoft Windows NT Server A network operating system for file servers. When used with Microsoft's BackOffice suite of server software, Windows NT Server provides a suite of software for enterprise information system development, including messaging and database access.

Microsoft Windows NT Workstation A 32-bit operating system for networked client computers, developed by Microsoft Corporation.

microwave An electromagnetic radio wave with a very short frequency.

middleware In object-oriented programming, standards that define how programs find objects and determine what kind of information they contain.

millisecond (ms) A unit of measurement, equal to one-thousandth of a second, commonly used to specify the access time of hard disk drives.

minicomputer A multiuser computer that meets the needs of a small organization or a department in a large organization.

minimize To reduce the size of a window so that it appears only as an icon or an item on the taskbar.

mirroring/duplexing The technique used by *Level 1 RAID* devices to assure that each hard disk is paired with at least one additional disk that contains an exact copy of its data.

mirror site On the Internet, a duplicate version of a popular site that is created to ensure that users will be able to access the site without encountering errors or delays.

mission critical system An information system that is of decisive importance to an organization's primary mission. In a university, the information systems that handle student registration are mission critical systems. Compare safety critical system.

Mac OS The operating system and user interface developed by Apple Computer for Macintosh computers.

mnemonic In programming, an abbreviation or a word that makes it easier to remember a complex instruction.

modem A device that converts the digital signals generated by the serial port to the modulated analog signals required for transmission over a telephone line and, likewise, transforms incoming analog signals to their digital equivalents. The speed at which a modem (short for modulator/demodulator) transmits data is measured in units called bits per second, or bps. (Although bps is not technically the same as baud, the terms are often and erroneously used interchangeably.)

modulation The conversion of a digital signal to its analog equivalent, especially for the purposes of transmitting signals using telephone lines.

modular programming A programming style that breaks down program functions into modules, each of which accomplishes one function and contains all the source code and variables needed to accomplish that function.

modulation protocol In modems, the communications standard that governs how the modem translates between the computer's digital signals and the analog tones used to convey computer data over the Internet. Modulation protocols are defined by ITU standards. The V.90 protocol defines communication at 56 Kbps.

monitor A television-like device that produces an on-screen image.

monochrome monitor A monitor display that shows one color against a black or white background.

monospace font A typeface in which the width of every character is the same; produces output similar to a typewriter.

Moore's Law A prediction by Intel Corp. co-founder Gordon Moore that integrated circuit technology advancements would enable the semiconductor industry to double the number of components on a chip every 18 to 24 months.

moral dilemma A situation in which people run into difficulty trying to figure out how existing rules apply to a new situation.

morphing An animated special effect in which one image transforms into a second image.

motherboard A large circuit board containing the computer's central processing unit, support chips, random access memory, and expansion slots. Also called a main board.

motion capture An animation technique that involves filming actors dressed in costumes containing sensors, which record the actors' movements. The resulting action sequences provide a life-like basis for animation.

mouse A palm-size input device, with a ball built into the bottom, that is used to move a pointer on-screen to draw, select options from a menu, modify or move text, and issue commands.

Moving Picture Experts Group (MPEG) A set of standards for audio and video file formats and lossless compression, named after the group that created it.

MPEG Audio Layer 3 (MP3) A sound compression standard that can store a single song from an audio CD in a 3M file. MP3 files are easily shared over the Internet and are costing recording companies billions of dollars in lost royalties due to piracy.

MS-DOS An operating system for IBM-compatible PCs that uses a command-line user interface.

multifunction printer An inkjet or laser printer that also functions as a scanner, a fax machine, and a copier.

multimedia The presentation of information using graphics, video, sound, animation, and text.

multimedia CAI A version of computer-assisted instruction that makes use of the personal computer's multimedia capabilities, including high-quality sound, rich graphics, and video.

multiplayer online gaming The use of the Internet to enable two or more users to play against one another in popular computer games.

multiple series In a chart such as a bar chart or line chart, the use of more than one data series to compare two or more items.

multiple undo A feature of many of today's application programs that enables the user to undo more than one editing change. Some programs offer unlimited undo.

multiplexing A technique that enables more than one signal to be conveyed on a physical transmission medium.

multiprocessing The use of two or more processors in the same computer system at the same time.

Multipurpose Internet Mail Extensions (MIME) An Internet standard that specifies how Internet programs, such as email programs and Web browsers, can transfer multimedia files (including sounds, graphics, and video) through the Internet. Before the development of MIME, all data transferred through the Internet had to be coded in ASCII text.

multiscan monitor A monitor that automatically adjusts its refresh rate to the output of the video adapter.

multisession PhotoCD A standard for recording PhotoCD information onto a CD-ROM during several different recording sessions. Unlike standard CD-ROM drives, drives that are Multisession PhotoCD-compatible can read information recorded on a disk during several different pressings.

multitasking In operating systems, the capability to execute more than one application at a time. Multitasking shouldn't be confused with multiple program loading, in which two or more applications are present in random access memory (RAM) but only one executes at a time.

multithreading In multitasking, the capability of a computer to execute more than one task, called a thread, within a single program.

multiuser Designed to be used by more than one person at a time.

multiuser dungeon (MUD) A text-based environment in which multiple players can assume online personas and interact with each other by means of text chatting.

Musical Instrument Digital Interface (MIDI) A standard that specifies how musical sounds can be described in text files so that a MIDI-compatible synthesizer can reproduce the sounds. MIDI files are small, so they're often used to provide music that starts playing automatically when a Web page is accessed. To hear MIDI sounds, your computer needs a sound card. MIDI sounds best with wavetable synthesis sound cards, which include sound samples from real musical instruments.

N

name box In a spreadsheet program, an area that displays the name of the active cell.

native application A program that runs on a particular brand and model of processor or in a particular operating system.

natural language A human language, such as English or Japanese.

near-letter-quality printout Print quality that is almost as good as printed text.

near-online storage A type of storage that is not directly available, but can be made available by a simple action such as inserting a disk.

nest In structured programming, to embed one control structure inside another.

Netiquette Network etiquette A set of rules that reflect long-standing experience about getting along harmoniously in the electronic environment (email and newsgroups).

Netscape extensions Additions to standard HTML added in the mid-1990s by Netscape Communications, Inc., in an effort to provide Web designers with more presentation options.

network access point (NAP) In a wide area network (WAN), a location where local and regional service providers can connect to transcontinental backbone networks.

network architecture The overall design of a computer network that specifies its functionality at every level by means of protocols.

network computer (NC) A computer that provides much of a PC's functionality at a lower price. Network computers don't have disk drives because they get their software from the computer network.

network interface card (NIC) An adapter that enables a user to connect a network cable to a computer.

network laser printer A nonimpact, high-resolution printer capable of serving the printing needs of an entire department.

network operating system The software needed to enable data transfer and application usage over a local area network (LAN).

network version A version of an application program for use by more than one person at a time on a local area network (LAN).

network warfare A form of information warfare characterized by attacks on a society's information infrastructure, such as its banking and telecommunications networks.

neural network In artificial intelligence, a computer architecture that attempts to mimic the structure of the human brain. Neural nets "learn" by trial and error and are good at recognizing patterns and dealing with complexity.

Newsgroup In Usenet, a discussion group devoted to a single topic. Users post messages to the group, and those reading the discussion send reply messages to the author individually or post replies that can be read by the group as a whole.

node In a LAN, a connection point that can create, receive, or repeat a message.

nonimpact printer A printer that forms a text or graphics image by spraying or fusing ink to the page.

noninterlaced monitor A monitor that refreshes the entire screen with each pass of the cathode gun. Because this reduces flicker and eye strain, almost all monitors today are noninterlaced.

nonprocedural Not tied down to step-by-step procedures. In programming, a nonprocedural programming language does not force the programmer to consider the procedure that must be followed to obtain the desired result.

nonresident Not present in memory. A nonresident program must be loaded from secondary storage when it is needed.

nonvolatile Not susceptible to loss. If power is lost, the data is preserved.

normal layout In an application program, an onscreen rendition of the document's appearance that does not attempt to show all of the features that will appear in the printout.

normalization In database management, a formal process of database design that assures the elimination of duplicate data entry (data redundancy).

nanosecond (ns) A unit of time equal to one billionth of a second.

notebook computer A portable computer that is small enough to fit into an average-size briefcase but includes nearly all peripherals commonly found on desktop computers.

notes view In a presentation graphics program, a view of the presentation that enables you to see your speaker's notes.

NuBus A 32-bit wide expansion bus used by older Macintosh computers. Newer Macintoshes use the Peripheral Component Interconnect (PCI) bus.

Num Lock A toggle key that determines whether the numeric keypad functions in cursor movement mode or number entry mode.

numeric field In a database, a space that accepts only numbers.

numeric format In a spreadsheet program, the way values appear in cells. Examples of numeric formats are currency and date.

numeric keypad A set of keys, usually on the right side of the keyboard, for entering numerical data quickly. The numeric keypad can also move the cursor.

O

object In object-oriented programming (OOP), a unit of computer information that contains data and all the procedures or operations that can process or manipulate the data.

object code In programming, the machine-readable instructions created by a compiler from source code.

object linking and embedding (OLE) A Microsoft Windows standard that enables applications to exchange data and work with one another dynamically.

object-oriented database The newest type of database structure, well suited for multimedia applications, in which the result of a retrieval operation is an object of some kind, such as a document. Within this object are miniprograms that enable the object to perform tasks, such as displaying graphics. Object-oriented databases can incorporate sound, video, text, and graphics into a single database record.

object-oriented (OO) programming A programming technique that creates generic building blocks of a program (the objects). The user then assembles different sets of objects as needed to solve specific problems. Also called OOP, for object-oriented programming.

obscenity In U.S. law, a literary artistic work that is obviously designed to produce sexual arousal, violates established community standards, and has no literary, artistic, or scientific value.

odd parity An error-checking protocol in which the parity bit is set to 1 if the number of 1 digits in a byte equals an even number.

off-the-shelf software Ready-to-use software that is sold through mass-market channels and contains features usable by the largest possible user base. Synonymous with shrink-wrapped software.

office application An application program that is useful for anyone working with words, numbers, graphic images, and databases in a contemporary office setting. This category includes word processing, spreadsheet, and presentation graphics software, as well as database management programs designed for use by untrained users.

office suite A collection of separate office applications that have been designed to resemble each other as closely as possible and to exchange data smoothly. The leading office suite package is Microsoft Office. Compare integrated program.

offline storage A type of storage that is not readily available and is used to store infrequently accessed or backup data.

online Directly connected to the network.

online analytical processing (OLAP) In a decision support system (DSS), a method of providing rich, up-to-the-minute data from transaction databases.

online banking The use of a Web browser to access bank accounts, balance checkbooks, transfer funds, and pay bills.

online processing The processing of data immediately after it has been input by a user, as opposed to waiting until a predetermined time, as in batch processing.

online service A for-profit firm that makes current news, stock quotes, and other information available to its subscribers over standard telephone lines. Popular services include supervised chat rooms for text chatting and forums for topical discussion. Online services also provide Internet access.

online stock trading The purchase or sale of stock through the Internet.

online storage A type of storage that is directly available, such as a hard disk, and requires no special action on the user's part to enable.

on-screen keyboard utility An accessibility feature that displays a graphic image of a computer keyboard on-screen so that people with limited dexterity can type conveniently.

open To transfer an existing document from storage to memory.

open architecture A system in which all the system specifications are made public so that other companies may develop add-on products, such as adapters.

open protocol A network standard placed in the public domain and regulated by an independent standards organization.

operating system (OS) A program that integrates and controls the computer's internal functions and provides a user interface.

operationally feasible Capable of being accomplished with an organization's available resources.

optical character recognition (OCR) Software that automatically decodes imaged text into a text file. Most scanners come with OCR software.

optical mark reader (OMR) A reader that senses magnetized marks made by the magnetic particles in lead from a pencil.

optical resolution A measure of the sharpness with which a scanner can digitize an image.

optical storage media In computer storage systems, any storage device that retains data using surface patterns that can be detected by a laser beam.

optical storage medium A storage medium that uses a laser to read (and in some devices, to write) data that are physically encoded on the surface of plastic disks.

order of evaluation In any program that evaluates formulas, the order in which the various operations are performed. Some programs evaluate formula expressions from left to right, while others perform operations in a given order.

organization A collection of resources (personnel and equipment) arranged so that they can provide some kind of product or service.

orientation In document formatting, the layout of the page (either portrait or landscape).

outline view In a word processing or presentation graphics program, a document display mode that enables you to see an outline of the document or presentation.

outlining A word processing program feature that enables the user to display the document's headings and subheadings as entries in an outline.

output The results of processing information, typically shown on a monitor or a printer.

outsourcing The transfer of a project to an external contractor.

P

package A collection of programs. A common example of a package is Microsoft Office, which bundles a word processing program and a spreadsheet program with other applications.

packet In a packet-switching unit, a unit of data of a fixed size—not exceeding the network's maximum transmission unit (MTU) size—that has been prepared for network transmission. Each packet contains a header that indicates its origin and its destination. See also *packet switching*.

packet sniffer In computer security, a device that examines all traffic on a network and retrieves valuable information such as passwords and credit card numbers.

packet switching One of two fundamental architectures for a wide area network (WAN); the other is a circuit-switching network. In a packet-switching network such as the Internet, no effort is made to establish a single electrical circuit between two computing devices; for this reason, packet-switching networks are often called connectionless. Instead, the sending computer divides a message into packets, each of which contains the address of the destination computer, and dumps them onto the network. They are intercepted by devices called routers, which send the packets in the appropriate direction. The receiving computer assembles the packets, puts them in order, and delivers the received message to the appropriate application. Packet-switching networks are highly reliable and efficient, but they are not suited to the delivery of real-time voice and video.

page In virtual memory, a fixed size of program instructions and data that can be stored on the hard disk to free up random access memory.

page description language (PDL) A programming language capable of precisely describing the appearance of a printed page, including fonts and graphics.

page layout In an application program, an onscreen rendition of the document's appearance that shows all or almost all of the features that will appear in the printout.

paint program A program that enables the user to paint the screen by specifying the color of the individual pixels that make up the screen display.

paper size The size of the paper that is available for use in the printer. Most programs can work with a variety of paper sizes, but you must configure the program to work with nonstandard sizes.

paragraph In word processing, a unit of text that begins and ends with the Enter keystroke.

paragraph formatting In a word processing document, presentation options that can be applied to a block of text, such as justification and indentation.

parallel conversion In the development of an information system, the operation of both the new and old information systems at the same time to ensure the compatibility and reliability of the new system.

parallel port An interface that uses several side-by-side wires so that one or more bytes of computer data can travel in unison and arrive simultaneously. Parallel ports offer faster performance than serial ports, in which each bit of data must travel in a line, one after the other.

parallel processing The use of more than one processor to run two or more portions of a problem simultaneously.

parent directory In the relationship between a directory and a subdirectory, the directory that contains the subdirectory.

parity bit An extra bit added to a data word for *parity checking*.

parity checking A technique used to detect memory or data communication errors. The computer adds the number of bits in a one-byte data item, and if the parity bit setting disagrees with the sum of the other bits, the computer reports an error.

parity error An error that a computer reports when parity checking reveals that one or more parity bits are incorrect, indicating a probable error in data processing or data transmission.

partition A section of a storage device, such as a hard disk, that is prepared so that it can be treated as if it were a completely separate device for data storage and maintenance.

passive matrix LCD An inexpensive liquid crystal display (LCD) that sometimes generates image flaws and is too slow for full-motion video. Also called dual scan LCD.

password A unique word that a user types to log on to a system. Passwords should not be obvious and should be changed frequently.

password guessing In computer security, a method of defeating password authentication by guessing common passwords, such as personal names, obscene words, and the word password.

paste In the editing process, a command that inserts text stored in the clipboard at the cursor's location.

path The sequence of directories that the computer must follow to locate a file.

pattern recognition In artificial intelligence, the use of a computer system to recognize patterns, such as thumbprints, and associate this pattern with stored data or instructions.

PC card Synonymous with PCMCIA card. A computer accessory (such as a modem or network interface card) that is designed to fit into a compatible PC card slot mounted on the computers case. PC cards and slots are commonly used on notebook computers because they offer system expandability while consuming a small fraction of the space required for expansion cards.

peer-to-peer network A computer network design in which all the computers can access the public files located on other computers in a network.

pen computer A computer operated with a stylus, such as a personal digital assistant (PDA).

Pentium A 64-bit microprocessor manufactured by Intel, introduced in 1993. The Pentium introduced many improvements over the 80486, including a superscalar architecture and clock speeds up to 200 MHz. Also called Pentium Classic.

Pentium II A 64-bit microprocessor manufactured by Intel, introduced in 1998. The Pentium II includes the MMX instruction set, contains 7.5 million transistors, and runs at clock speeds of 233 MHz and higher.

Pentium MMX A 64-bit microprocessor manufactured by Intel and introduced in 1997. The Pentium MMX includes a set of multimedia extensions, 57 processor instructions that run multimedia applications faster. It contains 4.5 million transistors and runs at clock speeds up to 233 MHz.

Pentium Pro A 64-bit microprocessor manufactured by Intel, introduced in 1995. The Pentium Pro introduced many new features, such as enhanced pipelining and a large on-board cache. Because it is optimized to run only 32-bit software, however, the Pentium Pro is found mainly in servers and engineering workstations.

performance animation See *motion capture*.

peripheral A device connected to and controlled by a computer, but external to the computer's central processing unit.

Peripheral Component Interconnect (PCI) bus A bus architecture used for expansion slots and introduced by Intel Corporation in 1992. It has displaced the VESA local bus and has almost displaced the ISA bus.

permanent virtual circuit (PVC) A high-speed network connection that enables organizations to connect to external data networks at a lower cost than that of a leased line.

personal certificate A digital certificate attesting that a given individual who is trying to log on to an authenticated server really is the individual he or she claims to be. Personal certificates are issued by certificate authorities (CA).

Personal Communication Service (PCS) A digital cellular phone service that is rapidly replacing analog cellular phones.

personal computer (PC) A computer system that meets the computing needs of an individual. The term PC usually refers to an IBM-compatible personal computer.

personal digital assistant (PDA) A small, handheld computer that accepts input written on-screen with a stylus. Most include built-in software for appointments, scheduling, and email. Also called palmtop.

personal finance program A special-purpose application program that manages financial information. The best personal finance programs manage many types of information, including checking accounts, savings and investment plans, and credit card debt.

personal identification number (PIN) A number used by a bank customer to verify identity when a customer uses an ATM.

personal information manager (PIM) A program that stores and retrieves a variety of personal information, such as appointments. PIMs have been slow to gain acceptance due to their lack of convenience and portability.

personal laser printer A nonimpact high-resolution printer for use by individuals.

personal productivity program Application software, such as word processing software or a spreadsheet program, that assists individuals in doing their work more effectively and efficiently.

phased conversion In the development of an information system, the implementation of the new system in different time periods, one part at a time.

PhotoCD See *Multisession PhotoCD*.

photo checkout system A computer system that accesses a database of customer photos and displays the customer's picture when their credit card is used.

photo printer See *snapshot printer*.

phrase searching In database and Web searching, a search that retrieves only documents that contain the entire phrase.

physical modeling A technique used to simulate what occurs when a real musical instrument produces a sound, such as a plucked guitar string.

pie chart A graph that displays a data series as a circle to emphasize the relative contribution of each data item to the whole.

pilot conversion In the development of an information system, the institution of the new system in only one part of an organization. When that portion of the organization is satisfied with the system, the rest of the organization then starts using it.

pipelining A design that provides two or more processing pathways that can be used simultaneously.

pit A microscopic indentation in the surface of an optical disk that absorbs the light of the optical drive's laser, corresponding to a 0 in the computer's binary number system.

pixel The smallest picture element that a device can display and out of which the displayed image is constructed.

placeholder An area that is set aside to receive data of a certain type when this data becomes available.

plagiarism The presentation of somebody else's work as if it were one's own.

Plain Old Telephone Service (POTS) A term used to describe the standard analog telephone service.

Platform for Internet Content Selection (PICS) A voluntary rating system, widely endorsed by companies contributing to the Internet, used to inform users of cyberporn on the Internet.

Platform for Privacy Preferences (P3P) A set of standards developed by the World Wide Web Consortium (W3C) for informing Web users of a site's use of personal data.

platter In a hard drive, a fixed, rapidly rotating disk that is coated with a magnetically sensitive material. High-capacity hard drives typically have two or more platters.

plotter A printer that produces high-quality output by moving ink pens over the surface of the paper.

Plug and Play (PNP) A set of standards jointly developed by Intel Corporation and Microsoft that enables users of Microsoft Windows-based PCs to configure new hardware devices automatically.

plug-in program Software that directly interfaces with a particular program and gives it additional capabilities.

point A standard unit of measurement in character formatting and computer graphics that is equal to 1/72 inch.

point of presence (POP) A locality in which it is possible to obtain dialup access to the network by means of a local telephone call. Internet service providers (ISPs) provide POPs in towns and cities, but many rural areas are without local POPs.

point-of-sale (POS) terminal A computer-based cash register that enables transaction data to be captured at the checkout stand. Such terminals can automatically adjust inventory databases and enable managers to analyze sales patterns.

pointer An on-screen symbol, usually an arrow, that shows the current position of the mouse.

pointing device Any input device that is capable of moving the on-screen pointer in a graphical user interface (GUI), such as a mouse or trackball.

pointing stick A pointing device introduced by IBM that enables users to move the pointer around the screen by manipulating a small, stubby stick that protrudes slightly from the surface of the keyboard.

POP3 Also spelled POP-3. The current version of the Post Office Protocol (POP), an Internet standard for storing email on a mail server until you can access it and download it to your computer.

popup menu A menu that appears at the mouse pointer's position when you click the right mouse button.

port An interface that controls the flow of data between the central processing unit and external devices such as printers and monitors.

port conflict A hardware error that occurs when two peripherals try to use the same port on a computer system.

portable Able to be easily removed or inserted or transferred to a different type of computer system.

Portable Network Graphics (PNG) A graphics file format closely resembling the GIF format but lacking GIF's proprietary compression technique (which forces publishers of GIF-enabled graphics software to pay a licensing fee).

portal On the Web, a page that attempts to provide an attractive starting point for Web sessions. Typically included are links to breaking news, weather forecasts, stock quotes, free email service, sports scores, and a subject guide to information available on the Web. Leading portals include Netscape's NetCenter (www.netcenter.com), Yahoo (www.yahoo.com), and Snap! (www.snap.com).

portrait mode In document formatting, a page layout in which text runs down the narrow orientation of the page.

positioning performance A measure of how much time elapses from the initiation of drive activity until the hard disk has positioned the read/write head so that it can begin transferring data.

Post Office Protocol (POP) An Internet email standard that specifies how an Internet-connected computer can function as a mail-handling agent; the current version is POP3. Messages arrive at a user's electronic mailbox, which is housed on the service provider's computer. You can then download the mail to the workstation or computer and reply, print, or store it.

post-implementation system review In the development of an information system, the ongoing evaluation of the information system to determine whether it has met its goals.

PostScript A sophisticated page description language (PDL) widely used in desktop publishing.

Power Macintosh A line of Macintosh computers based on the Motorola Power PC processors, which use RISC design principles.

power-on self test (POST) The series of system integrity tests that a computer goes through every time it is started (cold boot) or restarted (warm boot). These tests verify that vital system components, such as the memory, are functioning properly.

power outage A sudden loss of electrical power, causing the loss of all unsaved information on a computer.

Power PC A series of processors developed by Motorola that utilize RISC design principles. Apple Computers Power Macintosh systems use Power PC processors.

processor socket In contemporary motherboard designs, a socket so that a knowledgeable user can mount a microprocessor chip without damaging the chip or the motherboard.

power supply A device that supplies power to a computer system by converting AC current to DC current and lowering the voltage.

power surge A sudden and sometimes destructive increase in the amount of voltage delivered through a power line.

power switch A switch that turns the computer on and off. Often located in the rear of a computer.

precedence The position of a given operation, such as addition or multiplication, within a program's default *order of evaluation.*

preemptive multitasking In operating systems, a method of running more than one application at a time. Unlike cooperative multitasking, preemptive multitasking allows other applications to continue running if one application crashes.

preferences A list of the user's preferences for an application program's configuration. Preferences are stored so that they remain in place the next time the program is opened.

preformatted A floppy disk that has been formatted before it is packaged and sold.

presentation graphics A software package used to make presentations visually attractive and easy to understand.

primary cache A small unit (8 KB to 32 KB) of ultra-fast memory included with a microprocessor and used to store frequently accessed data and improve overall system performance.

primary key In a sorting operation, the field or column that is used as the basis for sorting the data.

Primary Rate ISDN (PRI) An ISDN connection designed for medium-sized organizations that offers 23 64-Kbps data/voice channels.

print area In a spreadsheet program, a user-defined area that tells the program how much of the spreadsheet to print.

printed circuit board A flat piece of plastic or fiberglass to which complex patterns of copper pathways have been created by means of etching. These paths link integrated circuits and other electrical components.

printer An output device that prints computer-generated text or graphics onto paper or another physical medium.

print layout view In a word processing program, an on-screen view of the document in which all or most printed features are visible. The print layout view is fully editable.

print preview In a word processing program, an on-screen view of the document in which all printed features are visible. However, the document is not editable in this view.

privacy The right to live your life without undue intrusions into your personal affairs by government agencies or corporate marketers.

private branch exchanges (PBX) An organization's internal telephone system, which is usually digital.

procedural language A programming language that tells the computer what to do and how to do it.

procedure The steps that must be followed to accomplish a specific computer-related task.

processing The execution of arithmetic or comparison operations on data.

processing cycle See *machine cycle.*

productivity software Programs that help people perform general tasks such as word processing.

professional workstation A very powerful computer system for engineers, financial analysts, and other professionals who need exceptionally powerful processing and output capabilities. Professional workstations are very expensive.

profile In a consumer-oriented operating system such as Windows 98, a record of a user's preferences that is associated with a user name and password. If you set up two or more profiles, users see their own preferences. However, profiles do not prevent users from accessing and overwriting each others' files. Compare *account.*

program A list of instructions telling the computer what to do.

program development life cycle (PDLC) A step-by-step procedure used to develop software for information systems.

program file A file containing instructions written in a programming language to tell the computer what to do.

program listing In programming, a printout of the source code of a program.

program specification In software development, a technical description of the software needed by the information system. The program specification precisely defines input data, the processing that occurs, the output format, and the user interface.

programmable Capable of being controlled through instructions that can be varied to suit the needs of an individual.

programmer A person skilled in the use of one or more programming languages. Although most programmers have college degrees in computer science, certification is an increasingly popular way to demonstrate one's programming expertise.

programmed instruction A method of introducing new material by means of controlled steps in a workbook.

programming language An artificial language composed of a fixed vocabulary and a set of rules used to create instructions for a computer to follow.

project dictionary In the development of information systems, a compilation of all terminology relevant to the project.

project management program Software that tracks individual tasks that make up an entire job.

project notebook In the development of an information system, a place where information regarding system development is stored.

project plan A specification of the goals, scope, and individual activities that make up a project.

promote In an outlining utility, to increase the importance of a heading by moving it up in the hierarchy of outline categories (for example, by moving it from B to II).

proportional font A font that places more characters on a line and requires a different amount of space based on the shape of each character; a proportional font closely resembles printed text.

proprietary architecture A design developed by a company and treated as a trade secret; the design can be copied only on payment of a licensing fee. Also called closed architecture.

proprietary file format A data-storage format used by only the company that makes a specific program.

proprietary protocol In a network, a communications protocol developed by a company and not available for public use without payment of a licensing fee.

Protocol In data communications and networking, a standard specifying the format of data and the rules to be followed. Networks could not be easily or efficiently designed or maintained without protocols; a protocol specifies how a program should prepare data so that it can be sent to the next stage in the communication process. For example, email programs prepare messages so that they conform to prevailing Internet mail standards, which are recognized by every program involved in the transmission of mail over the network.

protocol stack In a computer network, a means of conceptualizing network architecture in which the various layers of network functionality are viewed as a vertical stack, like the layers of a layer cake, in computers linked to the network. When one computer sends a message to the network, the message goes down the stack and then traverses the network; on the receiving computer, the message goes up the stack.

protocol suite In a computer network, the total collection of network protocols that defines the network's functionality.

prototyping In information systems development, the creation of a working system model that is functional enough to draw feedback from users. Also called joint application development (JAD).

proximity operator In database and Web searching, a symbol or keyword that tells the search software to retrieve records or documents only if two specified search words occur within a certain number of words of each other.

PS/2 mouse A type of mouse that connects to the computer by means of the PS/2 port.

PS/2 port An input/output port that enables users to attach a specially designed mouse (called a PS/2 mouse) without requiring the use of the computers built-in serial ports.

pseudocode In structured programming, a stylized form of writing used as an alternative to flowcharts to describe the logic of a program.

public data network (PDN) A network that builds its own high-speed data communications network using microwaves, satellites, and optical fiber, and sells network bandwidth to companies and government agencies.

public domain software Noncopyrighted software that anyone may copy and use without charge or acknowledging the source.

public key In public key cryptography, the encoding key, which you make public so that others can send you encrypted messages. The message can be encoded with the public key, but it cannot be decoded without the private key, which you alone possess.

public key cryptography In cryptography, a revolutionary new method of encryption that does not require the message's receiver to have received the decoding key in a separate transmission.

The need to send the key, required to decode the message, is the chief vulnerability of previous encryption techniques. Public key cryptography has two keys: a public one and a private one. The public key is used for encryption, and the private key is used for decryption.

public switched telephone network (PSTN) The world telephone system, a massive network used for data communication as well as voice.

pull-down menu In a graphical user interface (GUI), a named item on the menu bar that, when clicked, displays an on-screen menu of commands and options.

pumping and dumping An illegal stock price manipulation tactic that involves purchasing shares of a worthless corporation and then driving the price up by making unsubstantiated claims about the company's value in Internet newsgroups and chat rooms. The perpetrator sells the shares after the stock price goes up but before other investors wise up to the ploy.

Q

quality of service (QoS) In a network, the guaranteed data transfer rate. A major drawback of the Internet for real-time voice and video, as well as for time-sensitive data communication, is that it cannot assure quality of service. Network congestion can delay the arrival of data.

quarter-inch cartridge (QIC) A tape cartridge using quarter-inch wide magnetic tape widely used for backup operations. QICs can hold up to 5 GB on a single cartridge.

query In database and Web searching, a search question phrased by typing keywords (and, optionally, search operators).

query by example (QBE) In a database, a method of requesting information by using a blank form that corresponds to the record form. You fill out one or more fields in the form, and the search software uses your response to try to match any records in the database that contain the data you supplied.

query language A retrieval and data-editing language for composing simple or complex requests for data.

query operator In a database management program, an operator that specifies the type of selection operator that the user wishes to perform.

QuickTime An Apple Computer-developed file and compression format for digital video.

quote In email, text from a previous message that is copied into a reply message.

QWERTY keyboard A keyboard that uses the standard keyboard layout in which the first five letters on the left of the top row spell "QWERTY."

R

RAID (Redundant Array of Inexpensive Disks) A storage device that groups two or more hard disks containing exactly the same data.

random access An information storage and retrieval technique in which the computer can access information directly, without having to go through a sequence of locations.

random access file See *direct access file*.

random-access memory (RAM) Another name for the computer's main working memory, where program instructions and data are stored to be easily accessed by the central processing unit through the processor's high-speed data bus. When a computer is turned off, all data in RAM is lost.

random access storage device A storage device that can begin reading data directly without having to go through a lengthy sequence of data.

range In a spreadsheet, a rectangular group of cells treated as a unit for a given operation.

range expression In a spreadsheet program, a statement that indicates a group of cells to be treated as a unit for an operation.

rapid application development (RAD) In object-oriented programming, a method of program development in which programmers work with a library of prebuilt objects, allowing them to build programs more quickly.

raster graphics See *bit-mapped graphics*.

ray tracing A 3-D rendering technique in which color intensity on a graphic object is varied to simulate light falling on the object from multiple directions.

read To retrieve data or program instructions from a storage device such as a hard or floppy disk.

read/write The capability of a primary or secondary storage device to record (write) data and to play back (read) data previously recorded or saved.

read/write head In a hard or floppy disk, the magnetic recording and playback device that travels back and forth across the surface of the disk, storing and retrieving data.

read/write medium A storage medium that enables users to write as well as read data. Compare *read-only*.

read-only Capable of being displayed or used but not altered or deleted.

read-only memory (ROM) The part of a computer's primary storage that contains essential computer instructions and doesn't lose its contents when the power is turned off. Information in read-only memory cannot be erased by the computer.

real-time processing A type of processing that deals with data as it is generated by an ongoing process, such as a live video feed or text chatting.

record In a database, a group of one or more fields that contains information about something.

redo In the editing process, a command that reverses the effect of the last undo command or repeats the last editing action.

reduced instruction set computer (RISC) A type of central processing unit in which the number of instructions the processor can execute is reduced to a minimum to increase processing speed.

reengineering See *business process reengineering (BPR)*.

reflector See *list server*.

refresh rate The frequency with which the screen is updated. The refresh rate determines whether the display appears to flicker.

Regional Bell Operating Companies (RBOCs) The local and regional telephone companies created after the divestiture of telephone monopoly AT&T.

register 1. In a microprocessor, a memory location used to store values and external memory addresses while the microprocessor performs logical and arithmetic operations on them. 2. In commercial software and shareware, contacting the software vendor and submitting a form that includes personal information such as the user's name and address. Registering allows the software vendor to inform the user of important information and software updates.

registration fee An amount of money that must be paid to the author of a piece of shareware to continue using it beyond the duration of the evaluation period.

registry In Microsoft Windows, an important system file that contains configuration settings that Windows requires in order to operate.

regular weight In character formatting, a darkness level that is normal for a given font.

relational database A type of database that uses the contents of a particular field as an index to reference particular records.

relative cell reference In a spreadsheet program, a cell reference that is automatically adjusted when it is relocated.

relative file A special type of direct access file that does not use a mathematical formula (hashing algorithm) to determine the address of records, but bases the address on the key field, which is numbered with an integer.

relative URL In HTML, a URL that refers to a file located in the same directory as the referring file or in a nearby directory.

removable drive A hard disk that uses a data cartridge that can be removed for storage and replaced with another.

removable hard disk A hard disk that uses a removable cartridge instead of a sealed unit with a fixed, nonremovable platter.

repetition control structure In structured programming, a logical construction of commands repeated over and over. Also called looping or iteration control structure.

repetitive strain injury (RSI) See *cumulative trauma disorder (CTD)*.

replication In a spreadsheet program, the duplication of a group of cells into another group of cells. Formulas are automatically adjusted to account for the new cell addresses.

report Output produced by a database program.

report file A file that holds a copy of a report in computer-accessible form until it is convenient to print it.

report generator In programming, a programming language for printing database reports. One of four parts of a database management system (DBMS) that helps the user design and generate reports and graphs in hard copy form.

report language In database management, a computer language that enables the user to specify which information to display or print.

request for proposal (RFP) In the development of information systems, a request to an outside vendor to write a proposal for the design, installation, and configuration of an information system.

request for quotation (RFQ) In the development of information systems, a request to an outside vender or value-added reseller (VAR) to quote a price for specific information components.

resolution A measurement, usually expressed in linear dots per inch (dpi) both horizontally and vertically, of the sharpness of an image generated by an output device such as a monitor or a printer.

resource In a network, any useful device or program that can be shared by the networks users. An example of a resource is a network-capable printer.

restore To return a window to its size and position before it was maximized.

résumé manager A program that provides expert assistance in the preparation of resumes.

return on investment (ROI) The overall financial yield of a project at the end of its lifetime. ROI is often used by managers to decide whether or not a project is a good investment.

ring topology The physical layout of a local network in which all nodes are attached in a circle, without a central host computer.

rip and tear A confidence scam that involves convincing people that they have won a large sweepstakes prize but they cannot obtain the needed information unless they pay a fee. The prize never materializes and the perpetrators disappear.

robot A computer-based device that is programmed to perform useful motions.

robotics A division of computer science that is devoted to improving the performance and capabilities of robots.

ROM BIOS (Basic Input/Output System) See *Basic Input/Output System (BIOS)*.

root directory The top-level directory in a secondary storage device.

rot-13 In Usenet newsgroups, a simple encryption technique that offsets each character by 13 places (so that an e becomes an r, for example).

rotational speed In hard disks, the number of revolutions the disks make in one minute (RPM). Rotational speed is the largest single factor in determining drive speed. Currently, hard disks have rotational speeds as high as 10,000 rpm.

router In a packet-switching network such as the Internet, one of two basic devices (the other is a host). A router is an electronic device that examines each packet of data it receives, and then decides which way to send it toward its destination.

row In a spreadsheet, a block of cells going across the screen.

RS-232 standard A standard maintained by an international standards organization that defines the operation of the serial ports commonly found on todays computers. Synonymous with RS-232C.

RS-422 standard A standard maintained by an international standards organization that defines the operation of the serial ports found on Apples Macintosh and some other computers. The RS-422 is a more recent version of the earlier RS-232 standard. It offers higher data transfer rates than its predecessor.

rule A straight line.

ruler A bar that measures the document horizontally or vertically with reference to the printed page's edges or margins. Typically, the ruler shows the cursor's current position, margin settings, indentations, and tab stops.

runtime Able to run without having the original installed application. A runtime version of a PowerPoint presentation, for example, can run on a computer that does not have Microsoft PowerPoint installed.

S

safety critical system Any computer system that could subject human beings to death or injury if it fails to operate correctly. The Federal Aviation Administrations air traffic control (ATC) system is an example of a safety critical system.

salami shaving A computer crime in which a program is altered so that it transfers a small amount of money from a large number of accounts to make a large profit.

sampling In sound cards, a sound synthesis technique that modifies sound samples of musical instruments.

sans serif font A typeface style for letters that does not include finishing strokes.

SATAN A network security diagnostic tool that exhaustively examines a network and reveals security holes. SATAN is a double-edged sword: In the hands of network administrators, it is a valuable tool for detecting and closing security loopholes. In the hands of intruders, it is an equally valuable tool for exposing remaining loopholes and gaining unauthorized access to a network.

satellite In data communications, a communications reflector placed in a geosynchronous (stationary) orbit.

save To transfer data from the computer's memory to a storage device for safekeeping.

save as A command that enables the user to store a document with a new name.

storage device A hardware component that is capable of retaining data even when electrical power is switched off. An example of a storage device is a hard disk. Compare *memory*.

scale To increase or decrease the size of an image without affecting the image's *aspect ratio*.

scaling In graphics, to adjust the scale of a chart to make sure that it conveys information effectively.

scanner A device that copies the image (text or graphic) on a sheet of paper and translates it into a digital image. Scanners use charge-coupled devices to digitize the image.

scientific visualization The use of computer systems to discover hidden patterns in large amounts of data.

screenreader An accessibility program that reads text appearing on various parts of the computer screen for people with limited or no vision.

script A short program written in a simple programming language, called a scripting language.

scroll To bring hidden parts of a document into view within the application workspace.

scroll arrow An arrow appearing within the scroll bar that enables the user to scroll up or down (or, in a horizontal scroll bar, left and right) by small increments.

scroll bar A vertical or horizontal bar that contains scroll arrows and a scroll box. The scroll bar enables the user to bring hidden portions of a document into view within the application workspace.

scroll box A rectangular control positioned within the scroll bar that enables the user to bring hidden portions of a document into view. Unlike *scroll arrows*, the scroll box is used to scroll by large increments.

scripting language A simple programming language that enables users to create useful programs (scripts) quickly. VBScript is one example of a scripting language.

search engine Any program that locates needed information in a database, but especially an Internet-accessible search service (such as AltaVista or HotBot) that enables you to search for information on the Internet.

search operator In a database or a Web search engine, a word or a symbol that enables to you specify your search with greater precision.

secondary cache A small unit (256K to 1 MB) of ultra-fast memory used to store frequently accessed data and improve overall system performance. The secondary cache is usually located on a separate circuit board from the microprocessor, although backside cache memory is located on the processor. Also called level 2 (L2) cache.

section In a word processing document, a portion of a document that is separated from the others so that it can contain unique formats, such as column layout or footnote numbering.

section break A nonprinting symbol that can be placed within a word processing document to create sections with the document.

sector A pie-shaped wedge of the concentric tracks encoded on a disk during formatting. Two or more sectors combine to form a cluster.

secure mode In a Web browser, a mode of operation in which all communication to and from the server is encrypted.

security The protection of valuable assets stored on computer systems or transmitted via computer networks.

seek time In a secondary storage device, the time it takes for the read/write head to reach the correct location on the disk. Seek times are often used with rotational speed to compare the performance of hard drives.

select To highlight something on-screen, usually with the mouse and other times with the keyboard.

selection control structure In structured programming, a method of handling a program branch by using an IF-THEN-ELSE structure. This is more efficient than using a GOTO statement. Also called conditional or branch control structure.

selective availability In the U.S. Geographical Positioning System (GPS), a Defense Department imposed signal degradation intended to make GPS signals useless for enemy missile guidance systems.

semiconductor A material that can selectively conduct or impede the flow of electrical current. By fabricating devices made of differing semiconductor materials arranged in layers, electronics manufacturers can mass-produce highly complex electronic devices at very low cost per unit.

sequence control structure In structured programming, a logical construction of programming commands executed in the order in which they appear.

sequencer A program that enables composers to write, record, edit, and play back musical notation on a computer.

sequential access An information storage and retrieval technique in which the computer must move through a sequence of stored data items to reach the item to be retrieved.

sequential file A file in which the entries are processed in the order in which they were encoded.

sequential storage device A storage device that cannot begin reading data until the device has moved through a sequence of data in order to locate the desired beginning point.

serial mouse A type of mouse that connects to the computer by means of a serial port.

serial port An input/output (I/O) interface that is designed to convey data in a bit-by-bit stream. Compare *parallel port.*

series In a spreadsheet program, a range of values used to generate a chart.

serif font A typeface style for letters that includes finishing strokes.

server A computer dedicated to providing information in response to external requests.

server address In a mailing list, the email address of the list server, rather than the address of the list itself. For subscribing and unsubscribing to a mailing list, send messages to the server, not the list.

set-top appliance A computer-based unit that works with cable TV data and enhances the television viewing experience (in some cases, by enabling Internet access).

setup program A utility program provided by a computers manufacturer that enables users to specify basic system configuration settings, such as the correct time and date and the type of hard disk that is installed in the system. Setup programs are accessible by pressing a special key (such as Delete) during the computers power-on self test (POST).

shading A formatting option in which a color or pattern appears in the background of a paragraph, table cell, or some other formatting unit.

shadow A type of character formatting in which characters appear with a simulated shadow.

shareware Copyrighted software that may be tried without expense but requires the payment of a registration fee if you decide to use it after a specified trial period.

sheetfed scanner A device that draws in single sheets of paper, copies an image (text or graphics), and translates the image into a digital image.

shell In an operating system, the portion of the program that provides the user interface.

shill In an auction, an accomplice of the seller who drives up prices by bidding for an item that the shill has no intention of buying.

shoulder surfing In computer security, a method of defeating password authentication by peeking over a user's shoulder and watching the keyboard as the user inputs his or her password.

shrink-wrapped software See *off-the-shelf software.*

signature In email and Usenet newsgroups, a brief file (of approximately three or four lines) that contains the message sender's name, organization, address, email address, and (optionally) telephone numbers. You can configure most systems to add this file automatically at the end of each message you send. Netiquette advises against long, complicated signatures, especially when posting to Usenet.

signature capture A computer system that captures a customer's signature digitally, so that the store can prove that a purchase was made.

Simple Mail Transport Protocol (SMTP) An email communication standard specifying how servers should send plaintext messages across the Internet.

simulation A method used to discover something about the real world by creating a working model of it, which can then be explored by varying its characteristics to see what happens.

Single In-Line Memory Module (SIMM) A plug-in memory module that contains RAM chips. SIMMs use a 32-bit bus to transfer data between the memory and the processor. Many newer computers have 64-bit busses that require DIMMs.

single-session CD A CD that can accept only one "burn" (recording) session.

single-tasking Capable of running only one application at a time.

site license An agreement with a software publisher that allows multiple copies of the software to be made for use within an organization.

site registration On the World Wide Web, a process used to gain entry to a Web site that requires you to provide your name, email address, and other personal information, which may be disclosed to marketing firms.

size To increase or decrease the size of one of the dimensions of an image. Compare *scale.*

slide In a presentation graphics program, an on-screen image sized in proportion to a 35mm slide.

slide layout In a presentation graphics program, a view of the document that shows each slide individually.

slide show view In a presentation graphics program, a view of the document that displays the slides in a sequence.

slide sorter view In a presentation graphics program, a view of your presentation in which all your slides are represented by small thumbnail graphics. You can restructure your presentation by dragging a slide to a new location.

slide view In a presentation graphics program, a view of your presentation that enables you to see your slides, just as they will appear when displayed for presentation purposes.

small caps In character formatting, a formatting option in which the lowercase letters appear as small capital letters.

Small Computer System Interface (SCSI) A bus standard for connecting peripheral devices to personal computers, including hard disks, CD-ROM disks, and scanners.

small office/home office (SOHO) Small businesses run out of homes or small offices—a rapidly growing market segment.

small-scale integration (SSI) A technology used to assemble integrated circuits (IC). SSI was the first integration technology used to build ICs and could fit only 10 or 20 transistors to a chip.

Smalltalk An early object-oriented programming language that many OO promoters believe is still the only pure OO language.

smart car A car with microprocessors that provide more control and interaction with the environment. A smart car can diagnose internal problems, operate safely, warn the driver of potential problems, and help with navigation.

smartcard A card that resembles a credit card but has a microprocessor and memory chip. Smart cards are used to access information ranging from a medical history to the purchase of goods, where the dollar amount is automatically debited.

SmartMedia A flash memory storage device designed for digital cameras that is capable of storing up to 128 MB of digital image data.

smiley In email and newsgroups, a sideways face made of ASCII characters that puts a message into context and compensates for the lack of verbal inflections and body language that plagues electronic communication. Also called emoticon.

snapshot printer A thermal transfer printer that prints the output of digital cameras at a maximum size of 4 by 6 inches. Snapshot printers are less expensive than other thermal transfer printers.

social engineering A method of defeating password authentication by impersonating a network administrator and asking users for their passwords.

socket In Internet and UNIX, a virtual port that enables client applications to connect to the appropriate server. To achieve a connection, a client needs to specify both the IP address and the port address of the server application.

soft copy A temporary form of output, as in a monitor display.

software One of two basic components of a computer system (the other is hardware). Software includes all the instructions that tell the computer what to do.

software crisis A period of time in the 1960s when programming was extremely inefficient due to poor programming practices.

software engineering A new field that applies the principles of mainstream engineering to software production.

software license An agreement included with most commercial software that stipulates what the user may and may not do with the software.

software piracy Unauthorized duplication of copyrighted software.

software suite A collection of full-featured, stand-alone programs that usually share a common command structure and have similar interfaces.

sole proprietorship A business run and owned by only one person.

solid-state device An electronic device that relies solely on semiconductors (rather than vacuum tubes) to switch or amplify electrical current.

solid-state disk (SDD) A storage device that is composed of high-speed RAM chips.

sort In a database, to rearrange records according to a predetermined order, such as alphabetical or chronological order.

sound board See *sound card.*

sound card An adapter that adds digital sound reproduction capabilities to an IBM-compatible PC. Also called a sound board.

sound file A file containing digitized sound that can be played back if a computer is equipped with multimedia.

sound format A specification of how a sound should be digitally represented. Sound formats usually include some type of data compression to reduce the size of sound files.

source code The typed program instructions that people write before the program has been translated into machine instructions that the computer can execute.

source data automation The process of capturing data at its source, eliminating the need to file paper documents or record data by keying it manually.

spaghetti code In programming, source code that contains numerous GOTO statements and is, in consequence, difficult to understand and prone to error.

spam Unsolicited email or newsgroup advertising.

spammer A person who sends unsolicited email messages containing advertisements.

speaker A device that plays the computer's audio output.

special-purpose program A program that performs a specific task, usually for a specific profession. Examples include printing greeting cards and calculating stresses in an engineering project.

speech recognition The use of a computer system to detect the words spoken by a human being into a microphone, and translate these words into text that appears on-screen. Compare *speech synthesis.*

speech recognition software A computer program that decodes human speech into transcribed text.

speech synthesis The capability of a computer to speak through synthesized computer-generated voices.

spindle speed The rotational speed of a hard disk, measured in revolutions per minute (RPM).

spinoff technology Devices based on discoveries originally made in military or space research.

spreadsheet A program that processes information in the form of tables. Table cells can hold values or mathematical formulas.

stale link On the Web, a hyperlink that refers to a document that has been moved or deleted.

standalone email client A program sold commercially that provides email services for computer users. Most people use email capabilities built into Web browsers rather than buying commercial programs.

standalone program An application sold individually.

standard newsgroups In Usenet, a collection of newsgroups that every Usenet site is expected to carry, if sufficient storage room exists. The standard newsgroup hierarchy includes the following newsgroup categories: comp.*, misc.*, news.*, rec.*, sci.*, soc.*, and talk.*. A voting process creates new newsgroups within the standard newsgroup hierarchies.

star topology The physical layout of a local network in which a host computer manages the network.

start tag In HTML, the first component of an element. The start tag contains the element's name, such as <H1> or <P>.

statistical function In a spreadsheet program, a built-in function that performs a useful task such as determining an average.

status bar An area within a typical application's window that is reserved for the program's messages to the user.

status indicator A small indicator light on a keyboard that shows when a toggle key keyboard function is turned on.

storage A general term for computer components that offer nonvolatile retention of computer data and program instructions.

storage device A hardware component that is capable of retaining data even when electrical power is switched off. An example of a storage device is a hard disk. Compare memory.

storage hierarchy A classification scheme that divides storage devices into three categories: online (directly available), near-online (easily available), offline (not easily available).

stored-program concept The idea underlying the architecture of all modern computers that the program should be stored in memory with the data.

streaming audio An Internet sound delivery technology that sends audio data as a continuous, compressed stream that is played back on-the-fly.

streaming video An Internet video delivery technology that sends video data as a continuous, compressed stream that is played back on-the-fly. Like streaming audio, streaming video begins playing almost immediately. A high-speed modem is required. Quality is marginal; the video appears in a small, on-screen window, and motion is jerky.

striping In RAID drives, a method of duplicating the data in which each disk contains a portion of each other disk's data.

strong AI In artificial intelligence, a research focus based on the conviction that computers will achieve the ultimate goal of artificial intelligence, namely, the creation of machines rivaling the intelligence of humans.

structural analysis and design tools Methods of graphical analysis that system analysts can use to convey a description of an information system to managers, programmers, and users.

structural sabotage In information warfare, attacks on the information systems that support transportation, finance, energy, and telecommunications.

structural unemployment Unemployment caused by advancing technology that makes an entire job obsolete.

structure In HTML, the overall pattern of a document's organization into units containing information of a certain type, such as titles, headings, or an abstract.

structure chart See *hierarchy chart.*

structured programming A set of quality standards that make programs more verbose but more readable, reliable, and easily maintained. The program is broken up into manageable components, each of which contributes to the overall goal of the program. Also called top-down program design.

Structured Query Language (SQL) In database management, a popular set of commands developed by IBM used to request information from databases.

style In word processing programs, a collection of formatting options that have been grouped and saved under a distinctive name so that they can be easily applied subsequently.

style sheet In word processing, desktop publishing, and Web publishing, a formatting method in which named styles are defined in a separate document. When changes are made to the style sheet, these changes are reflected in all the documents linked to the style sheet for formatting.

stylus A pen-shaped instrument used to draw on a graphics tablet or to input commands and handwriting to a personal digital assistant (PDA).

subdirectory A directory created in another directory. A subdirectory can contain files and additional subdirectories.

subject guide On the World Wide Web, an information discovery service that contains hyperlinks classified by subjects in broad categories and multiple levels of subcategories.

subnotebook A portable computer that omits some components (such as a CD-ROM drive) to cut down on weight and size.

subscript A character formatting option that places characters below the line.

summary report In a transaction processing system (TPS), a document that provides a quick overview of an organization's performance.

Super Video Graphics Array (SVGA) An enhancement of the VGA display standard that can display as much as 1,280 pixels by 1,024,768 lines with as many as 16.7 million colors.

supercomputer A sophisticated, expensive computer that executes complex calculations at the maximum speed permitted by state-of-the-art technology. Supercomputers are used mostly by the government and for scientific research.

SuperDisk A removable hard disk made by Imaton that can store up to 120 MB of data per disk. The drive can also work with 3.5-inch floppy disks.

superscalar architecture A design that lets the microprocessor take a sequential instruction and send several instructions at a time to separate execution units so that the processor can execute multiple instructions per cycle.

superscript A character formatting option that places text above the line.

superuser status In multiuser operating systems, a classification normally given only to network administrators, enabling them to access and modify virtually any file on the network. If intruders obtain superuser status, they can obtain the passwords of everyone on the network.

supervisor program See *kernel*.

surge A momentary and sometimes destructive increase in the amount of voltage delivered through a power line.

surge protector An inexpensive electrical device that prevents high-voltage surges from reaching a computer and damaging its circuitry.

swap file In virtual memory, a file on the hard disk used to store pages of virtual memory information.

swapping In virtual memory, the operation of exchanging program instructions and data between the swap file (located on the hard disk) and random access memory (RAM).

syn flooding See *denial-of-service (DoS) attack*.

Synchronized Multimedia Integration Language (SMIL) A scripting language that enhances Web browsers with multimedia capabilities without the use of plug-in programs.

synchronous communication In a computer network, the use of a timing device to demarcate units of data.

Synchronous DRAM (SDRAM) The fastest available memory chip technology.

Synchronous Optical Network (SONET) A standard for high-performance networks using optical fiber.

syntax The rules governing the structure of commands, statements, or instructions given to a computer.

syntax error In programming, a flaw in the structure of commands, statements, or instructions.

synthesizer An audio component that uses FM (frequency modulation), wavetable, or waveguide technology to create sounds imitative of actual musical instruments.

system A collection of components purposefully organized into a functioning whole to accomplish a goal.

system administrator In a multiuser computer system, the individual who is responsible for keeping the system running smoothly, performing backup and archiving operations, supervising user accounts, and securing the system against unauthorized intrusions.

system analyst A computer professional who helps plan, develop, and implement information systems.

system bus Also called memory bus.

system clock An electronic circuit in the computer that emits pulses at regular intervals, enabling the computer's internal components to operate in synchrony.

system requirements The stated minimum system performance capabilities required to run an application program, including the minimum amount of disk space, memory, and processor capacity.

system software All the software used to operate and maintain a computer system, including the operating system and utility programs.

system unit The case that houses the computer's internal processing circuitry, including the power supply, motherboard, modem, disk drives, expansion cards, and a speaker.

systems analysis A discipline devoted to the rational and organized planning, development, and implementation of artificial systems, including information systems.

systems development life cycle (SDLC) An organized way of planning and building information systems.

systems engineering A field of engineering devoted to the scientific study of artificial systems and the training of system analysts.

T

T1 A high-bandwidth telephone trunk line capable of transferring 1.544 megabits per second (Mbps) of data.

tab stop In a word processing program, a position within the current paragraph to which the cursor will move when the Tab key is depressed.

table In HTML, a matrix of rows and columns that appears on a Web page, if the user is browsing with a table-capable browser (such as Netscape Navigator).

tabular report In a database management program, a report format in which the data are displayed in a list format.

tactile display A display that stimulates the sense of touch using vibration, pressure, and temperature changes.

tag In HTML, a code that identifies an element (a certain part of a document, such as a heading or list) so that a Web browser can tell how to display it. Tags are enclosed by beginning and ending delimiters (angle brackets). Most tags begin with a start tag (delimited with <>), followed by the content and an end tag (delimited with </>).

tangible savings Reduced labor, service, and material costs due to the replacement of a system.

tax software An application capable of preparing tax payments using on-screen simulations of tax forms. Some tax programs include specialized tax forms and content-based advice to assist the user.

TCP/IP See *Internet protocols*.

technically feasible Able to be accomplished with respect to existing, proven technology.

telecommunication The use of the public switched telephone network (PSTN) and public data networks (PDN) for data communication.

telecommuting Performing work at home while linked to the office by means of a telecommunications-equipped computer system.

telemedicine The use of computers and the Internet to make high-quality health care available to underserved populations.

template A standard format used to create standardized documents.

tendonitis A physical disorder in which tendons and their sheaths become irritated from repeated exertion.

terminal An input/output device consisting of a keyboard and a video display that is commonly used with mainframe and minicomputer systems.

text box An area capable of containing text that can be inserted into a graphic image.

text field In a database, a space that accepts only characters.

text file A file containing nothing but standard characters, that is, letters, punctuation marks, and numbers.

text-only browser A Web browser that cannot display graphics.

text output A type of computer output that consists strictly of characters (letters, numbers, and punctuation marks).

text slide In a presentation, a slide that contains nothing but text.

thermal transfer printer A printer that uses a heat process to transfer colored dyes or inks to the paper's surface. Although thermal transfer printers are the best color printers currently available, they are very expensive.

thin film transistor (TFT) See *active-matrix LCD*.

third-generation language (3GL) A programming language that tells the computer what to do and how to do it, but also eliminates the need for understanding the intimate details of how the computer works.

thread 1. In multithreading, a single type of task that can be executed simultaneously with other tasks. 2. In Usenet, a series of articles on the same specific subject.

thumbnail A small version of a graphic image that enables you to see what it looks like before you spend time opening the much larger file containing the full version of the graphic image.

tile To size graphics or windows so that they are all the same size and take up all the available screen space.

time bomb A destructive program that sits harmlessly until a certain event or set of circumstances makes the program active.

time field In a database, a space that accepts only time information.

time series A type of column chart that shows changes over a period of time.

time-limited Capable of being used as a trial for a period of time, after which the software is unusable.

timesharing A technique for sharing the resources of a multiuser computer in which each user has the illusion that he or she is the only person using the system.

title bar In a graphical user interface (GUI), the top bar of an application window. The title bar typically contains the name of the application, the name of the document, and *window controls.*

toggle key A key on a keyboard that functions like a switch. When pressed, the function is turned on, and when pressed again, the function is turned off.

token A handheld electronic device used to gain access to a computer system, such as an automated teller machine (ATM).

toolbar In a graphical user interface (GUI), a bar near the top of the window that contains a row of graphical buttons. These buttons provide quick access to the most frequently used program commands.

tools menu In a graphical user interface (GUI), a menu that provides access to special program features and utilities, such as spell-checking.

top-down program design See *structured programming.*

topology The physical layout of a local area network.

touch screen A touch-sensitive display that enables users to input choices by touching a region of the screen.

touchpad An input device for portable computers that moves the pointer. The trackpad is a small pad in front of the keyboard that moves the pointer when the user moves a finger on the pad.

track One of several concentric circular bands on computer disks where data is recorded, similar to the grooves on a phonographic record. Tracks are created during formatting and are divided into sectors.

trackball An input device, similar to the mouse, that moves the pointer. The trackball looks something like an inverted mouse and does not require the desk space that a mouse does.

trackpoint An input device on some notebook computers that resembles a tiny pencil eraser; you move the cursor by pushing the tip of the trackpoint.

trade show An annual meeting in which computer product manufacturers, designers, and dealers display their products.

traditional organizational structure In an organization, a method used to distribute the core functions of the organization into divisions such as finance, human resources, and operations.

transaction An exchange of goods, services, or funds.

transaction file A file used to store input data until it can be processed.

transaction processing system (TPS) A system that handles the day-to-day operations of a company; examples include sales, purchases, orders, and returns.

transceiver A device used to regulate the electrical connection between a computer and a local area network (LAN).

transistor A device invented in 1947 by Bell Laboratories that controls the flow of electricity. Due to their small size, reduced power consumption, and lower heat output, transistors replaced vacuum tubes in the second generation of computers.

Transmission Control Protocol (TCP) One of two basic Internet protocols. TCP is the protocol (standard) that permits two Internet-connected computers to establish a reliable connection. TCP ensures reliable data delivery with a method known as Positive Acknowledgment with Re-Transmission (PAR). The computer that sends the data continues to do so until it receives a confirmation from the receiving computer that the data has been received intact.

transparency A clear acetate sheet used for presentations with an overhead projector.

trap door In computer security, a security hole created on purpose that can be exploited at a later time.

Trojan horse An application disguised as a useful program but containing instructions to perform a malicious task.

Turing Test A test developed by Alan Turing and used to determine whether a computer could be called intelligent. In a Turing Test, judges are asked to determine whether the output they see on computer displays is produced by a computer or a human being. If a computer program succeeds in tricking the judges into believing that only a human could have generated that output, the program is said to have passed the Turing Test.

turnover line In an indentation, the second and subsequent lines.

twisted pair An inexpensive copper cable used for telephone and data communications. The term twisted pair refers to the braiding of the paired wires, a practice that reduces interference from electrical fields.

typeface A complete collection of letters, punctuation marks, numbers, and special characters with a consistent and identifiable style. Also called font.

typeover mode In word processing, a text insertion mode in which new material replaces (types over) existing text.

U

ubiquitous computing A scenario for future computing in which computers are so numerous that they fade into the background, providing intelligence for virtually every aspect of daily life.

Ultra ATA A drive interface that offers data transfer rates twice as fast as its predecessor, Enhanced IDE (EDIE). Also called Ultra DMA (Direct Memory Access).

Ultra DMA (Direct Memory Access) See *Ultra ATA.*

Ultra DMA/66 An IDE hard disk standard capable of transferring data at speeds of up to 66 Mbps.

Ultra Wide SCSI A SCSI (Small Computer Systems Interface) standard that enables hard disk data transfer rates of 40 Mbps.

Ultra3 SCSI A SCSI standard that can transfer data at speeds of up to 160 Mbps. Synonymous with Ultra160 SCSI.

unauthorized access In computer security, the entry of an unauthorized intruder into a computer system.

undo In the editing process, a command that reverses the action of the last editing change.

undocumented feature A program capability not mentioned in the program's documentation.

Unicode A 16-bit character set capable of representing almost all of the world's languages, including non-Roman characters such as those in Chinese, Japanese, and Hindi.

Uniform Resource Locator (URL) In the World Wide Web, one of two basic kinds of Universal Resource Identifiers (URI), a string of characters that precisely identifies an Internet resource's type and location. For example, the following fictitious URL identifies a World Wide Web document **(http://),** indicates the domain name of the computer on which it is stored **(www.wolverine.virginia.edu),** fully describes the document's location in the directory structure **(~toros/winerefs/),** and includes the document's name and extension **(merlot.html).**

uninstall To remove a program from a computer system by using a special utility.

uninterruptible power supply (UPS) A device that provides power to a computer system for a short period of time if electrical power is lost.

universal product code (UPC) A label with a series of bars that can be either keyed in or read by a scanner to identify an item and determine its cost. UPC scanners are often found in point-of sale (POS) terminals.

Universal Serial Bus (USB) An external bus architecture that connects peripherals such as keyboards, mice, and digital cameras. USB offers many benefits over older serial architectures, such as support for 127 devices on a single port, Plug and Play, and higher transfer rates.

universal service A basic principle of U.S. telecommunications law, which holds that service providers have an obligation to provide service in areas where it is not economically attractive to do so, such as remote rural regions. Taxes are used to subsidize the extension of service to such areas.

UNIX A 32-bit operating system that features multiuser access, preemptive multitasking, multiprocessing, and other sophisticated features. UNIX is widely used for file servers in client/server networks.

update query In a database management program, a type of query in which the program makes changes to all records that conform to the specified criteria.

upgrade processor A microprocessor that upgrades older systems.

upgrade socket A receptacle on a motherboard for an upgrade processor.

upload To send a file to another computer by means of a computer network.

Usenet A worldwide computer-based discussion system that uses the Internet and other networks for transmission media. Discussion is channeled into more than 50,000 topically named newsgroups, which contain original contributions called articles, as well as commentaries on these articles called follow-up posts. As follow-up posts continue to appear on a given subject, a thread of discussion emerges; a threaded newsreader collates these articles together so readers can see the flow of the discussion.

Usenet server A computer running the software that enables users to read Usenet messages, post new messages, and reply to existing messages. The server software also ensures that new messages are shared with other messages so that all participating servers are able to make the same messages available.

user A person who uses a computer and its applications to perform tasks and produce results.

user agent See *email client.*

user ID A word or name that uniquely identifies a computer user. Synonymous with *user name.*

user interface The part of system software that interacts with the user.

user name A unique name that a system administrator assigns to you that you use as initial identification. You must type this name and also your password to gain access to the system.

utility program A program that is designed to assist the user with tasks related to computer system maintenance, such as defragmenting the hard drive.

V

V.34 An ITU modulation protocol for modems transmitting and receiving data at 28,800 bits per second (bps). An addition to the protocol enables transmission rates of up to 33.6 Kbps.

V.90 An ITU-regulated modulation protocol for modems transmitting and receiving data at 56 Kbps.

vaccine See *antivirus program.*

vacuum tube A device that controls the flow of electrons. Vacuum tubes were used extensively in first-generation computers, but failed often and were replaced shortly thereafter by transistors.

validation In a database, a method of increasing data integrity by ensuring that users enter the correct data type in each field.

valuable information Data that is timely, concise, helpful, and important.

value In a spreadsheet, a numeric entry.

value-added network (VAN) A public data network that provides value-added services for corporate customers, including end-to-end dedicated lines with guaranteed security. VANs, however, also charge an expensive per-byte fee.

value-added reseller (VAR) An independent company that selects system components and assembles them into a functioning system.

VBScript A scripting language used to write short programs (scripts) that can be embedded in Web pages.

vector graphic An image composed of distinct objects, such as lines or shapes,

that may be moved or edited independently. Each object is described by a complex mathematical formula.

vendor A company that sells goods or services.

vertical application A program for a particular line of business or for a division in a company.

very-large-scale integration (VLSI) A level of technological sophistication in the manufacturing of semiconductor chips that allows the equivalent of up to 1 million transistors to be placed on one chip.

VGA connector A physical connector that is designed to connect a VGA monitor to a video adapter.

video adapter Video circuitry that fits into an expansion bus and determines the quality of the display and resolution of your monitor. Also called display adapter.

video capture card An expansion board that accepts analog or digital video signals, which are then compressed and stored.

video card See *video adapter.*

video editor A program that enables you to view and edit a digitized video and to select special effects.

Video for Windows A Microsoft video and compression format for digital video.

video graphics adapter (VGA) A video adapter that conforms to the VGA specification, which is capable of displaying data at a resolution of 640 x 480.

Video Graphics Array (VGA) A display standard that can display 16 colors at a maximum resolution of 640 pixels by 480 pixels.

video output A type of computer output that consists of a series of still images that are played back at a fast enough rate to give the illusion of continuous motion.

video RAM (VRAM) A random access memory chip that maximizes the performance of video adapters.

viewable size The area of a monitor display used to display an image.

view menu In a graphical user interface (GUI), a menu that provides access to document viewing options, including *normal layout, print layout,* and document magnification (zoom) options.

virtual manufacturing A design process in which a powerful computer assembles digitally drawn parts to ensure that they fit well and function as planned. Also called computer-aided production engineering (CAPE).

virtual memory A means of increasing the size of a computer's random-access memory (RAM) by using part of the hard disk as an extension of RAM.

virtual private network (VPN) A method of connecting two physically separate local area networks (LAN) by using the Internet. Strong encryption is used to ensure privacy.

virtual reality (VR) A computer-generated illusion of three-dimensional space. On the Web, virtual reality sites enable Web users to explore three-dimensional virtual reality worlds by means of VR plug-in programs. These programs enable you to walk or "fly" through the three-dimensional space that these worlds offer.

Virtual Reality Modeling Language (VRML) A scripting language that enables programmers to specify the characteristics of a three-dimensional

world that is accessible on the Internet. VRML worlds can contain sounds, hyperlinks, videos, and animations as well as three-dimensional spaces, which can be explored by using a VRML plug-in.

visual aids Graphical supplements to a presentation, such as slides or transparencies.

Visual BASIC (VB) A programming language developed by Microsoft based on the BASIC programming language. Visual BASIC is one of the world's most widely used program development packages.

volatile Susceptible to loss; a way of saying that all the data disappears forever if the power fails.

W

warm boot To restart a computer that is already operating.

waterfall model A method in information systems development that returns the focus of the systems development project to a previous phase if an error is discovered in it.

waveform A type of digitized audio format used to record live sounds or music.

waveguide synthesis A method of generating and reproducing musical sounds in a sound card. Waveguide synthesis simulates what happens when a real musical instrument produces a sound; it is superior to wavetable and FM synthesis.

wavetable synthesis A method of generating and reproducing musical sounds in a sound card. Wavetable synthesis uses a prerecorded sample of dozens of orchestral instruments to determine how particular notes should sound. Wavetable synthesis is far superior to FM synthesis.

Web browser A program that runs on an Internet-connected computer and provides access to information on the World Wide Web (WWW).

Web layout In Microsoft Word, a document view that approximates the document's appearance if it were saved as a Web page and viewed by a Web browser.

Web integration A variety of techniques used to make information stored in databases available through Internet or intranet connections.

Web page A document you create to share with others on the Web. A Web page can include text, graphics, sound, animation, and video.

Web server On the Web, a program that accepts requests for information framed according to the Hypertext Transport Protocol (HTTP). The server processes these requests and sends the requested document.

Web site A computer that is accessible to the public Internet and is running a server program that makes Web pages available.

WebCam A low-cost video camera used for low-resolution videoconferencing on the Internet.

Webmaster A person responsible for the visual layout of a Web site, its written content, its links to other locations, and often the techniques to follow up on customers' inquiries.

what-if scenario In business, an experiment using make-believe data to see how it affects an outcome, such as sales volume.

weight   The darkness or thickness of a character.

wheel mouse   A type of mouse that has a dial that can be used to scroll through data on-screen.

whistleblowing   Reporting illegal or unethical actions of a company to a regulatory agency or the press.

wide area network (WAN)   A commercial data network that provides data communications services for businesses and government agencies. Most WANs use the X.25 protocols, which overcome problems related to noisy analog telephone lines.

wildcard   A symbol that stands for any character or any group of characters.

Win 95   See *Microsoft Windows 95.*

Win 98   See *Microsoft Windows 98.*

window controls   In a graphical user interface (GUI), a group of window management controls than enable the user to minimize, maximize, restore, or close the window.

Windows bitmap (BMP)   A bitmapped graphics format developed for Microsoft Windows.

wireless communication   A means of linking computers using infrared or radio signals.

wireless keyboard   A type of keyboard that connects to the computer by means of infrared signals.

wizard   In a graphical user interface (GUI), a series of dialog boxes that guide the user through a complex process, such as importing data into an application.

word completion prediction program   An accessibility feature designed for people with limited dexterity that presents a menu of possible word completions.

word processing program   An office application that enables the user to create, edit, format, and print textual documents.

word size   The number of bits a computer can work with at one time.

word wrapping   A word processing feature that automatically moves words down to the beginning of the next line if they extend beyond the right margin.

workbook   In a spreadsheet program, a file that can contain two more

spreadsheets, each of which has its own page in the workbook.

workflow automation   An information system in which documents are automatically sent to the people who need to see them.

workgroup   A team of two or more people working on the same project.

worksheet   The graphical accounting pad that appears in spreadsheet programs. Also called spreadsheet.

worksheet tab   In a spreadsheet program, a tab that enables the user to determine which worksheet to display within a workbook.

workstation   A powerful desktop computer that meets the computing needs of engineers, architects, and other professionals who require detailed graphic displays. In a LAN, a workstation runs application programs and serves as an access point to the network.

World Wide Web (WWW)   A global hypertext system that uses the Internet as its transport mechanism. In a hypertext system, you navigate by clicking hyperlinks, which display another document (which also contains hyperlinks). Most Web documents are created using HTML, a markup language that is easy to learn and will soon be supplanted by automated tools. Incorporating hypermedia (graphics, sounds, animations, and video), the Web has become the ideal medium for publishing information on the Internet. See also *Web browser.*

World Wide Web Consortium (W3C)   An independent standards body made up of university researchers and industry practitioners devoted to setting effective standards to promote the orderly growth of the World Wide Web. Housed at the Massachusetts Institute of Technology (MIT), W3C sets standards for HTML and many other aspects of Web usage.

worm   A program resembling a computer virus that can spread over networks.

write   To record data on a computer storage device.

write once, read many   An optical disk drive with storage capacities of up to 15G. After data is written, it becomes a read-only storage medium.

write-back   One of four basic operations carried out by the control unit of a microprocessor. The write-back operation involves writing the results of previous operations to an internal register.

write-protection tab   On a floppy disk, a tab that prevents the computer from overwriting or erasing the disk's contents.

WYSIWYG   A type of on-screen document view in which the user sees the results of formatting choices on-screen. WYSIWYG stands for "what-you-see-is-what-you-get."

X

X.25   A packet-switching network protocol optimized for use on noisy analog telephone lines.

X-10   A standard for computer-controlled home automation devices.

xDSL   See *Digital Subscriber Line (DSL).*

Xeon   A 64-bit microprocessor manufactured by Intel. Introduced in 1998, the Xeon uses a wider socket with more contacts to increase communication speed between the processor and components on the motherboard. Due to its high cost, the Xeon is used mostly in servers and high-end workstations.

Z

zero force insertion (ZIF) socket   A receptacle for microprocessors that makes it easy to remove and install them without the risk of bending pins.

Zip disk   A removable storage medium that combines the convenience of a floppy disk with the storage capacity of a small hard disk (100 to 200 MB).

Zip drive   A popular removable storage medium, created by Iomega Corporation, that provides 100 MB of storage on relatively inexpensive ($10 each) portable disks.

zoom   To increase or decrease the magnification level of a document as displayed in the application workspace.

zoom level   The degree of magnification of a document within the application workspace.

CHAPTER 1

Page 5
Chuck Savage/The Stock Market (*top left*)
Peter Vadnai/The Stock Market (*bottom left*)
Stephen Agricola/Stock Boston (*top right*)
Bill Bachmann/Stock Boston (*middle right*)
Jon Feingersh/The Stock Market (*bottom right*)

Page 9
Richard Gross/The Stock Market

Page 13
© Fourmy/REA/SABA

Page 25
The Stock Market

Page 44
© Bettmann/CORBIS

Figure 1A.1
The Stock Market

Figure 1A.5
Sun Microsystems (*top left*)

Figure 1A.5
NEC Computer Systems Division (*bottom left*)

Figure 1A.5
Courtesy of International Business Machines Corporation (*top right*)

Figure 1A.5
Hewlett-Packard Co. (*bottom right*)

Figure 1A.6
Silicon Graphics Inc. (*top left*)

Figure 1A.6
Hewlett-Packard Company (*bottom left*)

Figure 1A.6
Courtesy of International Business Machines Corporation (*top right*)

Figure 1A.6
Silicon Graphics, Inc. (*bottom right*)

Figure 1B.1
© Ed Young/CORBIS (*top, p. 32*)

Figure 1B.1
© Bettmann/CORBIS (*bottom, p. 32*)

Figure 1B.1
Courtesy of International Business Machines Corporation (*top, p. 33*)

Figure 1B.1
Jean-Loup Charmet/Photo Researchers, Inc. (*middle, p. 33*)

Figure 1B.1
IBM Corporation (*bottom, p. 33*)

Figure 1B.1
IBM Corporation (*top, p. 34*)

Figure 1B.1
Iowa State University Library/University Archives (*bottom, p. 34*)

Figure 1B.1
IBM Corporation (*bottom, p. 35*)

Figure 1B.1
© Bettmann/CORBIS (*top, p. 35*)

Figure 1B.2
Courtesy of International Business Machines Corporation

Figure 1B.3
Courtesy of the Charles Babbage Institute

Figures 1B.4, 1B.5, 1B.6, 1B.7, 1B.8
Copyright © 1999 by Courtesy of International Business Machines Corporation

Figure 1B.9
Courtesy of the Charles Baggage Institute

Figure 1B.10
Photo Courtesy of Intel Corporation

Figure 1B.11
Apple Computer, Inc.

Figure 1B.12
Courtesy of International Business Machines Corporation

Figure 1B.13
Apple Computer, Inc.

CHAPTER 2

Page 57
Bonnie Kamin/PhotoEdit

Page 58
Courtesy of International
    Business Machines
    Corporation (*top*)
Courtesy of Apple/Photographer
    Mark Laita (*bottom*)

Page 60
Toshiba America Information
    Systems, Inc. (*top left*)
AP/Wide World Photos (*top right*)
Courtesy of International
    Business Machines
    Corporation (*bottom left*)

Page 71
Bonnie Kamin

Page 90
The Stock Market

Page 138
Hironori Miyata/FDB/Liaison
    Agency Inc.

Page 143
PFSweb, Inc.

Figure 2A.2
Courtesy of Toshiba

Figure 2A.4
Copyright © 1999 by Photo
    Courtesy of Intel Corporation

Figures 2A.5, 2A.6
Courtesy of Giga-Byte
    Technology

Figures 2A.10, 2A.11
Courtesy of Intel Corporation

Figure 2A.12
Advanced Micro Devices

Figures 2B.1a, 2B.1b
Seagate Technology, Inc.

Figure 2B.3a
Courtesy of International
    Business Machines
    Corporation

Figure 2B.3b
Bonnie Kamin/PhotoEdit

Figures 2B.6a, 2B.6b
Courtesy of International
    Business Machines
    Corporation

Figure 2B.7
Shelly R. Harrison Photography

Figure 2B.11
Courtesy Iomega

Figure 2B.12
Seagate Technology, Inc.

Figures 2B.16, 2B.17, 2B.18, 2B.19
Courtesy of Advanced Computer
    & Network Corporation

Figure 2B.20
Courtesy Iomega

Figure 2B.21
Seagate Technology, Inc.

Figure 2B.22
Michael A. Keller Studios
    Ltd./The Stock Market

Figure 2B.23
Courtesy of Toshiba Amercia
    Electronic Components, Inc.

Figure 2C.1
Courtesy of International
    Business Machines
    Corporation

Figure 2C.3
Courtesy Microsoft Corporation

Figure 2C.4
Peter Beck/The Stock Market

Figure 2C.7a
Courtesy of Kensington
    Technology Group

Figure 2C.7b
Courtesy of CyberStuff

Figure 2C.7c
Courtesy of Kensington
    Technology Group

Figure 2C.7d
Apple Computer, Inc.

Figure 2C.7e
Courtesy of International
    Business Machines
    Corporation

Figure 2C.7f
MicroTouch Systems, Inc.

Figure 2C.7g
Courtesy of ALPS

Figure 2C.8
Microsoft Corporation

Figure 2C.9
Courtesy of Hunter Digital

Figure 2C.10
Courtesy of Interlink Electronics

Figure 2C.11
Bob Daemmrich/Stock Boston

Figure 2C.12
Courtesy Fastpoint Technology

Figure 2C.13
SuperStock, Inc.

Figure 2C.14
Photo courtesy of Intel
    Corporation

Figure 2C.15
Courtesy of Eastman Kodak
    Company

Figure 2C.16
Intermec Technologies
    Corporation

Figure 2C.17
© J. Greenberg/The Image Works

Figure 2C.19
Charles Gupton/Stock Boston

Figure 2C.21
Toshiba Corporation

Figure 2C.22
Sun Microsystems, Inc.

Figures 2C.25a, 2C.25b
Lexmark International, Inc.

Figure 2C.26
Fargo Electronics, Inc.

Figure 2C.27
Courtesy of Xerox Corporation

CHAPTER 3

Page 158
Charles Bennett/AP/Wide World
    Photos

Page 172
The Stock Market

Page 175
SuperStock, Inc.

Page 185
PFSweb, Inc.

Figure 3B.1
Peter Saloutos/The Stock Market

Figure 3B.4
Luno Bruno/AP/Wide World
    Photos

CHAPTER 4

Page 201
Peter Beck/The Stock Market

Page 203
Shelly R. Harrison Photography

Page 215
Used with permission of Etrade

Page 232
© 1996 Ryszard Horowitz/The
Stock Market

Page 239
© 1996 Jose Pelaez/The Stock
Market

Page 240
Table Mesa Production/West
Stock

Page 250
Used with the permission of
Data Mining Technology at
www.datamine.com

Page 259
Shelly R. Harrison Photography

Page 265
PFSweb, Inc.

CHAPTER 5

Page 273
© The Stock Market/Thom Lang,
1997

Page 275
© The Stock Market/Sanford/
Agliolo, 1997

Page 282
© The Stock Market/Firefly
Productions, 1997

Page 289
PFSweb, Inc.

Figure 5A.1
© The Stock Market/Lightscapes,
1997

Figure 5A.2
© The Stock Market/Mike
Venables, 1996

Figure 5A.3
Metacreations

CHAPTER 6

Page 300
© 1995 Gabe Palmer/The Stock
Market

Page 304
© 1997 William Whitehurst/The
Stock Market

Page 306
Courtesy of Net2Phone

Figure 6A.1
Judith A. Walters/West Stock

Figures 6A.2, 6A.3
Fotopic International/West Stock

Figure 6A.4
NASA/West Stock

Figure 6A.5
Bryan Peterson/West Stock

Figure 6A.9
© 1992 John Maher/The Stock
Market

Figure 6A.10
WebTV is a trademark of WebTV
Networks, Inc.

CHAPTER 7

Page 337
Mendola Ltd./The Stock Market

Page 340
AOL Welcome Screen screenshot
copyright 2000 America
Online, Inc. Used with
permission

Page 341
The Stock Market

Page 342
Netscape communicator browser
window © 1999 Netscape
Communications Corporation.
Used with permission.
Netscape Communications has
not authorized, sponsored,
endorsed, or approved this
publication and is not
responsible for its content.

Page 343
Dennis Novak/The Image Bank

Page 345
Kevin Atkinson

Page 347
Used with permission of
deja.com

Page 350
Used with permission of
Internet.com and
www.thelist.com

Page 353
Rick Bowmer/AP/Wide World
Photos

Page 362
Courtesy of Monster.com (*top*)

Page 363
Courtesy of Monster.com (*bottom*)

Page 364
Used with permission of Yahoo!
Inc. (*top*)

Page 364
© 2000 Lycos, Inc. Lycos © is a
registered trademark of
Carnegie Mellon University. All
rights reserved. (*bottom*)

Page 365
Used with permission of
careerbuilder.com

Page 368
Richard Drew/AP/Wide World
Photos

Page 369
Kevin Atkinson

Page 370
These materials have been
reproduced with the
permission of eBay, Inc.
Copyright © eBay, Inc. All
rights reserved. (*top*)

Page 370
Used with permission of
Autobytel.com (*bottom*)

Page 371
Used with permission of
Peapod.com

Page 372
Jon Feingersh/The Stock Market

Page 419
PFSweb, Inc.

Figure 7D.10
© Eddie Bauer, Inc. 2000

CHAPTER 8

Page 428
© 1995 Chris Collins/The Stock
Market

Page 432
Courtesy of DaimlerChrysler
Corporation

Page 433
© 1996 Tom Callicott/Weststock

Page 434
Courtesy of PSC Inc.

real-time voice and video, 347–348
satellite access, 294, 349
services, 342–348
shell access, 349
software, 341–342
TCP/IP, 45, 46, 350, 351
Telnet, 348
uploading, 343
Usenet, 344, 346–347
Veronica, 348
virtual reality and, 283
wide area networks (WANs), 339
World Wide Web. *See* World Wide Web
Internet addresses, 338, 352
Internet crime. *See generally* Crime and security
Internet faxing, 307
Internet Inter-Orb Protocol (IIOP), 459
Internet Message Access Protocol (IMAP), 380, 381
Internet Protocol (IP), 351
Internet Relay Chat (IRC), 347
netiquette, 521
Internet service providers (ISPs), 25, 337, 350
Internet services, 25
Internet telephony, 305–306
Internet telephony service providers (ITSPs), 305
InterNIC, 351
Interoperability [Internet], 338–339
Interpreters, 455
Intranets, 352
IP addresses, 338, 352
IPX/SPX, 323
IRC, 347
netiquette, 521
IrDA Port, 63
ISDN, 300–301
ISPs, 25, 337, 350
Italics, 198
ITSPs, 305

J

Jacquard's loom, 33
Java, 462
JavaScript, 464
Java Virtual Machine, 462
Jobs. *See* Careers and employment
Jobs, Steve, 41, 43
Job searching on the Internet, 568
Joint Photographic Experts Group (JPEG), 272
Joysticks, 124
JPEGs, 272
Justified alignment [paragraphs], 199

K

Kernel [OS], 147
Kerning [characters], 198
Keyboards, 16, 114–119
alternatives, 117
autorepeat function, 114
buying issues, 538
character representation, 114
cumulative trauma disorder (CTD), 118

cursor movement keys, 115
enhanced, 114, 115
ergonomic, 118–119
extended, 114
function keys, 116
health risks, 118–119
insertion point, 114
international character entry, 117–118
modifier keys, 116–117
numeric keypad, 116
on-screen keyboard utilities, 556
repetitive strain injury (RSI), 118
special keys, 114
toggle keys, 116
using, 114
windows keys, 117
wireless, 114
Key escrow plan, 487
Keylock, 64
Keys [encryption], 486–487, 508
Keyword [spreadsheet functions], 219
Kilobits per second (Kbps), 59
Kilobyte, 59
Kiosks, 124
multimedia, 270
Knowledge management system, 431

L

Labels [spreadsheet software], 212
Land, 91
Landfills of obsolete computers, 545
Landscape orientation, 200
Languages. *See* Programming languages
LANs. *See* Local area networks (LANs)
Laptop computers, 21
buying issues, 533–534
Large-scale integration (LSI), 40
Laser printers, 17, 136
Last mile problem [telecommunications], 297
Last mile technologies [digital telephony], 300
Latency [hard disks], 99
Launching applications, 152, 176
L2 cache, 77
buying issues, 536
LCD displays, 17
LCD projectors, 134
LCDs, 133
Leaders [paragraphs], 199
Leading, 199
Leased lines (WANs), 325–326
Leased telecommunication lines, 296
Legal problems, 515–518
copyright infringement, 517–518
copyright *vs.* Free Speech, 525
crimes. *See* Crime and security
defamation, 481
libel, 481
plagiarism, 515–516
programmer liability, 522–524
software piracy, 169, 170, 516–517
whistle-blowing, 524
Legends [spreadsheet charts], 224
Leibniz's calculator, 33

Letter-quality printers, 135
Level 2 (L2) cache, 77
buying issues, 536
Libel, 481
Licenses [software], 169–171
Light pens, 124
Line chart [spreadsheet software], 224
Line printers, 135
Linker [programming], 455
Linux, 156–157
GNOME, 151
Liquid crystal displays (LCD), 133
List servers, 387
"Loading" programs, 22
Loading the OS, 158
Local access and transport area (LATA), 293
Local area networks (LANs), 19, 314, 319
AppleTalk, 323
bus topology, 321–322
client/server network, 320
coaxial cable, 321
collisions, 321
contention, 321
contention management, 322
Ethernet, 322
Fast Ethernet, 322
fiber-optic cable, 321
file sharing, 320
Gigabit Ethernet, 319
gigabits per second, 319
history, 45
hubs, 322
infrared, 321
Internet connections, 339, 349
IPX/SPX, 323
LAN-to-LAN connections (WANs), 328
LocalTalk, 323
media, 320–321
NetBEUI, 323
network interface cards (NICs), 319–320
nodes, 319–320
operating system, 320
peer-to-peer networks, 320
protocols, 323
radio, 321
ring topology, 322
software, 320
star topology, 322
TCP/IP, 323
technologies, 322–323
10baseT, 322
tokens, 322
topologies, 321–322
twisted pair, 320
workstations, 319
Local exchange carriers (LECs), 293–294
Local newsgroups, 346, 347
LocalTalk, 323
Logic bombs, 500
Logic errors [PDLC], 468
Logic operations, 68
Login, 152, 159
"Look and feel," 42
Lookup Wizard [database software], 253